HISTORY AND HERITAGE

HISTORY AND HERITAGE

The Social Origins of the British Industrial Relations System

Alan Fox

London
GEORGE ALLEN & UNWIN
Boston   Sydney

George Allen & Unwin (Publishers) Ltd,
40 Museum Street, London WC1A 1LU, UK

George Allen & Unwin (Publishers) Ltd,
Park Lane, Hemel Hempstead, Herts HP2 4TE, UK

Allen & Unwin, Inc.,
Fifty Cross Street, Winchester, Mass. 01890, USA

George Allen & Unwin Australia Pty Ltd,
8 Napier Street, North Sydney, NSW 2060, Australia

First published in 1985

British Library Cataloguing in Publication Data

Fox, Alan
  History and heritage.
1. Industrial relations – Great Britain
– History
I. Title
331'.0941   HD 8388
ISBN 0–04–331099–0

Library of Congress Cataloging in Publication Data

Fox, Alan.
  History and heritage.
Bibliography: p.
Includes index.
1. Industrial relations – Great Britain – History.
2. Great Britain – Social conditions. I. Title.
HD8388.F68 1985   331'.0941   84–12370
ISBN 0–04–331099–0 (alk. paper)

Set in 10 on 11 point Bembo by Computape (Pickering) Ltd, N. Yorkshire
and printed in Great Britain by Mackays of Chatham

For Stephen and Andrew

Contents

No man can be a politician except he be first a historian or traveller, for except he can see what must be, or what may be, he is no politician . . . he that neither knows what has been, nor what is, can never tell what must be nor what may be. (James Harrington, 1656)

Men make their own history, but they do not make it just as they please; they do not make it under circumstances chosen by themselves, but under circumstances directly encountered, given, and transmitted from the past. (Karl Marx, 1852)

Meanwhile England . . . is changing. And like everything else it can change only in certain directions, which up to a point can be foreseen. That is not to say that the future is fixed, merely that certain alternatives are possible and others not. (George Orwell, 1941)

Social structures, types and attitudes are coins that do not readily melt. Once they are formed they persist, possibly for centuries . . . (J. A. Schumpeter, 1954)

Preface

The purpose of this book is to attempt an answer to the question: how did Britain's industrial relations system, its institutions, its characteristic texture and its place in the wider society, come to be what they are? 'System' in this context refers to the set of arrangements by which terms and conditions of employment are predominantly determined by competitive, sectional collective bargaining between 'voluntary' (that is, non-state) organisations representative of wage- and salary-earners, on the one hand, and employers or representative organisations of employers on the other. These relationships have been seen down the ages by domestic and foreign observers alike as strongly characterised by adversary, win–lose postures; characteristics which, taken together with what are regarded as unusually restrictionist policies among Britain's workforce, are often judged as having contributed to Britain's relative economic decline. What has baffled many observers is that neither on the workers' nor on the employers' side have these adversary postures at the workplace expressed themselves in policies of total war on the political level. Only to a very limited extent have they been translated into revolutionary political stances among employees or destructively aggressive stances among employers. Nor, for over one and a half centuries, has the British state attempted to put down these worker combinations, widely deemed responsible for so much industrial difficulty; indeed, its agencies began a hundred years ago to encourage employers to recognise them.

These and other features of the system are familiar enough and are not infrequently referred to as having their roots in history. Outside specialist monographs dealing with particular limited aspects, however, the extent, precise nature and significance of historical origins and continuities are more often asserted and assumed than demonstrated and explained. I have sought here to demonstrate and explain them. I have brought together all the principal strands which have contributed to the system and argued their relevance explicitly in a way which permits critical examination and appraisal. The result offers a broad picture of the economic, political, social and legal circumstances within which the system was shaped by participants and interested parties.

But I have also been concerned at some points to identify certain of what have been called the 'suppressed alternatives' of history where these have relevance and interest for the industrial relations system. I have tried, too, to indicate points at which events might conceivably have taken a somewhat different course; to indicate movements and forces which might have influenced industrial relations development had they been stronger; and to indicate some strategic accidents of personality that affected it.

This broad focus, concerned as it is, in certain key periods, with examining the social context within which industrial relations were being conducted, obviously involves dwelling at some length upon matters not normally discussed in industrial relations literature. Political theory, upper-class strategies of rule, the concept of the British state, the nature of English law, the Victorian middle-class concept of service, social imperialism, the personality and political convictions of Stanley Baldwin, the reasons for the failure of British fascism: these are among the themes I have found relevant for understanding why the industrial relations system grew as it did and not in some other way.

This interest in a wide and variegated perspective had three consequences. First, it led me to examine certain phases of industrial relations history in some detail but to hurry past others: it will soon become obvious that this is not intended as 'history' in the ordinary sense. Secondly, it led me to chance my arm in fields of inquiry of which I have no trained experience. No doubt I shall richly deserve some of the kicks and blows visited upon me by irritated specialists. Thirdly, I run the risk of irritating specialists in another way. Not all my hoped-for audiences will have covered all the ground touched on in this book. In enlarging on relevant themes from widely diverse fields of study I cannot avoid presenting, on any one theme, data and ideas that will be unfamiliar to some but perhaps boringly familiar to others. I can only ask for patience from the latter in the belief that on other themes the situations will be reversed. The problem is unavoidable in any effort at synthesis. I have considered these risks worth running, since in my view there is a need of attempts to bring together the findings of different fields of study in order to explain the wider historical context within which a particular set of institutions has developed. The need derives not only from intrinsic academic interest. History is still undervalued as a necessary contribution to social understanding. To a considerable extent, though far from entirely, we are the products of our history; a fact often forgotten or ignored by our masters. This becomes especially important when they aspire, consciously or otherwise, to change the behaviour patterns of large numbers of people. Industrial relations behaviour has seen many such attempts. Clemenceau observed that war was too important to be left to the generals; in the same spirit, governments, managers and men of affairs have usually considered that work was too important to be left to the workers. Great efforts have been made down the ages to change their attitude towards it and towards the managers who organise and direct it. More recently some of this anxiety has been directed upon the motivation and performance of managers themselves.

Whether these attempts to change behaviour come from the political right or the political left, they are more likely to be rationally informed if they rest on knowledge not only of the present structures of work and power – a subject in itself which could not be dealt with here – but also of the historical nature and origins of the behaviours concerned. This permits informed judgements about their persistence and deep-rootedness and – since every change has its price – about the social costs that would be involved if attempts were made to impose such changes against the historical grain. Massive and stubborn resistances are apt to be encountered by attempts to transform basic, long-standing responses of large numbers of people in their everyday behaviour; or by attempts to reverse institutional dispositions that have been shaped over a long period; or by attempts to repudiate expectations that have likewise been generated by persistent historical continuities. If the costs seem disproportionate they might be avoided by adapting the objective in ways which make possible its pursuit by methods that work *with* the historical grain.

In trying to get the feel of this historical grain so far as the industrial relations system is concerned we shall find ourselves ranging widely and far back. A few examples will illustrate the themes pursued in the following chapters. The artisan–craft tradition by which the British trade union movement more than any other was deeply marked is a pre-industrial and pre-capitalist tradition. The individualism that also shaped that movement and the society in which it was embedded goes equally far back. Some of the social and political links that affected its nature and fortunes in the nineteenth century are illuminated by the power struggles of the seventeenth and by the structure of organised religion. The governing class fashioned a certain strategy of rule, along with its legitimations and ideology, in the eighteenth century, and its success contributed to its retention much later when issues relevant to industrial relations had to be decided. The importance here of the institutions and ideologies of the rule of law and the myth of state 'even-handedness' between the classes can hardly be exaggerated. These and many other features will be seen to have contributed to the industrial relations element in – to use George Orwell's words – 'the strange mixture of reality and illusion, democracy and privilege, humbug and decency, the subtle network of compromises, by which the nation keeps itself in its familiar shape' (Orwell, 1982, p.46).

I decided that this complex tale would be easier to read if I was generous rather than niggardly in illustration – shorter books are not necessarily more comprehensible than longer books and I am, after all, trying to convey a whole texture of ruling style and subordinate response which manifests itself in a variety of ways. There will no doubt be points at which my interpretations can be challenged but I hope that the challengers will follow up the implications for the wider questions I have raised. In order to make critical appraisal easier and perhaps more precise I have supplied liberal referencing, so that the bricks from which the structure of the argument is built can be readily identified.

ALAN FOX

1

Pre-Industrial England

Central Features of the Heritage

In the south transept of Gloucester cathedral a memorial tablet raised in 1799 pays tribute to Josiah Tucker, long its dean and an acute observer of the clothmaking industry which was scattered widely throughout the south-western counties as well as East Anglia and Yorkshire. It records that he was 'eminently conspicuous for political discernment on the important subject of national commerce, for the free spirit of which, unrestrained by monopoly and colonial preference, he firmly contended against prepossessions long and generally entertained . . . he lived to see his opinions established on the sure basis of experience'.

Clothmaking had for centuries been England's largest manufacturing industry. In 1757, in one of his references to its labour relations in the south-west, Tucker had noted the figure of the wealthy capitalist clothier, living like a country gentleman, whom his large workforce, divided from him by a gulf at least as wide as that which separates the modern large-scale company director from his employees, 'are to look upon as their pay-master'. But, he continued,

will they not also sometimes look upon him as their tyrant? And as great numbers of them work together in the same shop, will they not have it the more in their power to vitiate and corrupt each other, to cabal and associate against their masters and to break out into mobs and riots upon every little occasion? . . . these conjectures are too frequently supported by facts . . . The master . . . however well disposed himself is continually tempted by his situation to be proud and overbearing, to consider his people as the scum of the earth, whom he has a right to squeeze whenever he can; because they ought to be kept low and not to rise up in competition with their superiors. The journeymen on the contrary are equally tempted by their situation to envy the high station and superior fortunes of their masters; and to envy them the more in proportion as they find themselves deprived of the hopes of advancing themselves to the same degree by any stretch of industry or superior skill. Hence their self-love takes a wrong turn, destructive to themselves and others. They think it no crime to get as much wages and do as little for it as they possible can, to lie and cheat and do any bad thing, provided it is only against their master and their common enemy, with whom no faith is to be kept. (George, 1953, 48–50)

Tucker describes here, in the industry where capitalist organisation had so far most fully established itself, many of those features of England's industrial relations which, though never universal, were often to be selected for special comment by domestic and foreign observers over the next two centuries. From his observations can be abstracted many of the variables we need to explore if we are to understand the historical roots of much present-day behaviour. The nature of industrial and social structures; the fact that the participants perceived and reacted to those structures in certain ways rather than others; the social and cultural reasons for these specific perceptions and reactions; the wider social context which shaped them but which, in turn, was modified by their responses to that shaping – these are among the factors that we shall find to be relevant. Thus is defined the first stage of our task. What were the social forces producing this pattern of relations, sketched in 1757 by Dean Tucker in a description which would be hailed by many today as identifying a significant contributory factor to the nation's economic difficulties down the years? Some of the most central among them can be identified in movements and ideologies of the sixteenth and seventeenth centuries, in certain cases even earlier. If we wish, for example, to grasp the full nature and persistence of the postures exhibited even today within many manual and professional occupations we must note their origins in the traditions and practices of pre-capitalist, medieval, corporate regulation. Even more fundamentally, when we take stock of the early trade unions and other ingredients of what was to become Britain's industrial relations system, we need to note that they emerged within the social context of a shifting balance between two coexistent but sharply differing methods of 'social control'. What was the nature of these methods, and what were their implications for employment relations, for wider relations between higher and lower orders and for conceptions of the state? In answering these questions we begin to get some sense of the social forces from which the industrial relations system was forged.

Systems of Control: Paternalism

All societies contain many diverse control systems which seek to regulate, in widely varying ways, the behaviour of their members. These include legal, economic, religious, social and administrative structures and ideologies, operated or supported with differing methods and emphases by governments, state agencies, voluntary institutions and a host of formal and informal organisations and groupings. These collectives have varying primary objectives, but most of them share a desire to uphold, among other things, all or some aspects of the status quo and this is included among the aims of their control system. This is certainly not true of all. An urban guerrilla group may be dedicated to total destruction of the existing social order, but it will still need a control system for disciplining the behaviour and for shaping the perceptions of its members. Of those many control systems which are so saliently committed to upholding the status quo that they are sometimes defined, vaguely but conveniently, as constituting the Establishment, some exist to enable members of equal rank, class, or status to keep each other up to the mark in terms of some desired standard or style of behaviour. The systems we shall be concerned with here, however, exist to facilitate control over those of lower rank, class, or status. Specially relevant for our present purpose are two systems which, as applied to the economic sphere, had by Tucker's time long coexisted in England but whose strength relative to each other had been changing since at least the fifteenth century. They are control through paternalism and control through an individualistic market order. Both were supplemented by direct coercion, but each had its own characteristic pattern of behaviours and responses.

Paternalism is too large and loose a term to be used without careful definition. It carries, for example, a weak sense which may imply no more than the benign if calculated practices of 'the good employer'. The strongest sense, which will be used here, implies a more complex situation which can be found in certain conceptions of the relationship not only between employer and employee, but also between parent and child, elder and younger siblings, officer and private, teacher and pupil, and, for that matter, the Victorian middle-class husband and wife. The key principle is that the junior, subordinate, or inferior participant is defined as having certain 'true' or 'real' interests which he or she is incapable of perceiving or pursuing. Responsibility for those interests is therefore vested in the senior or superior, who demands to receive in return the willing obedience of the person under his or her protection. Reciprocity is of the essence. To assert protection is very often to assert control.

In the economic sphere, the doctrine of paternalism in this strong sense implied that the employer, acting under religious, moral, or social obligations, conducted himself accordingly towards his employees and did not seek to maximise his more obvious short-term personal advantage. In its full historical application, paternalism implied that economic maximising along any dimension– towards customers, suppliers, fellow-producers, or employees – was unacceptable. Reciprocal obligations expressed the notion that economic behaviour must be regulated by ethical constraints. For employees this included the principle that, in return for the employer's acceptance of responsibility for them, he was entitled to demand and, if necessary, exact their obedience.

The whole doctrine, in its broad social as well as its economic application, rested upon assertions by the well-placed of a natural hierarchy of worth, wisdom and consciousness of 'station' and 'duty'. The legal imagery of 'master and servant' which expressed – but outlasted – the paternalist system was 'rooted in a society in which everyone was presumed to belong somewhere, and the great parameters of belonging were kinship, locality, religion, occupation, and social class. In all spheres of life, including spiritual communion, *subordination to legitimate authority* was thought to be a natural, inevitable, and even welcome accompaniment of moral grace and practical virtue' (Selznick, 1969, p. 123, italics in

original). From the bottom of the social pyramid upwards, all were vertically bonded by mutual obligations to some superior. The apex of such a
pyramid, represented historically by the monarchy and the highest organs
of the state, were venerated by those for whom the system was the
accepted method of maintaining social order and the status quo.

Apparent in all the examples given above is the possibility of exploitation by the dominant party, achieved by enforcing obedience to some
command or policy which, though presented as serving the real interests
of the subordinate, is designed to serve only those of the superior. There
may, as a result, be no such symmetry as the full paternalism concept
implies, but rather an asymmetrical relationship in which a paternalist
rhetoric or ideology seeks to mask the absence of care or concern on the
part of the superior. Within a social order professing paternalism,
however, situations displaying total and consistent absence of concern are
probably rare. Under certain conditions paternalism has proved so valuable a system of control as often to be thought worth a certain amount of
nurture and, in any case, paternalistic care may bring some additional
benefit to the superior as well as obedience, thereby enabling him to derive
the best of both worlds.

There are further implications of the paternalist equation which can
usefully be teased out. Those who wish to assert absolutist rule over others
may find it useful to declare a paternalist concern for the interests of the
subjected, since this can be used to deny legitimacy to disobedience and
revolt. Disaffected persons can be condemned as wickedly ungrateful,
presumptuous in claiming to know better than their natural superiors
where their own true interests lie, and subversive in seeking to disrupt the
natural hierarchy of leadership and responsibility. By the same token, for
the subordinate to throw off protection, whether nominal or real, and to
declare an intention of relying on self-help, threatens the superior's control
by destroying the reciprocity through which the subordinate trades his
obedience for the superior's care.

Conversely, for the superior to disclaim responsibility for the subordinate invites the latter to withhold his obedience. It does not follow,
however, that the subordinate's complaints of maltreatment will be
assumed to exempt him from the duty of obedience, since he is defined as
lacking insight into his own true interests. Long-run benefit may be held
to require short-term hardship and in the last resort there can be invoked
the process of being cruel only to be kind. Complaint may be considered as
merely compounding his sin with ingratitude. In any case, we find
ourselves with the possibility already contemplated – that the superior
may be able to enforce obedience even in the absence of any reciprocating
protection. The question might well be put as to the necessity in such a
case of the paternalist ideology or rhetoric. The subordinates themselves
are unlikely to be under any misapprehension as to what is happening.
Who, then, is being fooled? The answer may well be: a number of
important and influential groups, not least the controllers themselves.
Total cynicism is rare; most of us, including most rulers, feel a need to
believe in our own righteousness. And if a dominant group or class seeks
to convince a subordinate class of a given doctrine or ideology it will

certainly have to convince itself first. However cynical about means, it must suspend cynicism about ends. Some capacity for this is probably a functional necessity for most rulers. But, in any case, it may be important for them that other groups in the organisation or society are provided with the ideological means to convince themselves that subordinates and dependants are being treated appropriately and that this justifies them in their own comforts and privileges. There is no occasion for surprise, therefore, that even where ruling groups lean heavily on direct coercion they feel the need for a justifying ideology.

Systems of Control: Market Individualism

In contrast to all this, the creed of individualism takes as its starting point the principle that the individual himself is the best judge of his own interests and that to postulate his having 'real' interests which are perceivable only by certain other authoritative persons is – except under certain family and functional necessities – to invite tyranny. Historically, this principle became a logical necessity in England after the sixteenth century for those seeking to assert their political freedom against would-be absolutist rule, or their religious freedom against an authoritarian ecclesiastical hierarchy, or their economic freedom against statutory, religious, or moral impediments to economic enterprise. Freedom was claimed on the grounds that men were self-determining agents who must be allowed to make their own political or religious choices or conclude their own self-interested contracts with each other in the market. This claim was reinforced by the assertion that the rights and freedoms of the individual must take precedence over those of any wider grouping or the state. Those asserting individual freedoms had to argue against the notion that they owed allegiance to some superior authority or higher good whose claims overrode their own self-interest. From there it was a short step to the argument that the state was due no special veneration inasmuch as it had no reality, meaning, or purposes which transcended those of the individuals composing it.

Thrusts of this kind in the economic sphere, rendered increasingly pressing by prospects of unlimited gain as economic life quickened, were likely to make short work of the old medieval paternalist teaching that economic behaviour must be guided and contained by religious, moral, or social obligations. Moreover, those aiming to, and those who had already, become rich did not care for the implication that they were greedy usurers and could even find such a context marginally obstructive. They were likely to prefer, if someone provided it, a state-supported ideology which separated economics from ethics and declared the individual to be free from all non-economic bonds, ties, obligations and traditional encumbrances.

According to this creed, economic behaviour was best controlled by contract between supposedly free, equal and self-determining individuals each seeking to maximise his own interests in the open market. Some central agency was required to enforce contracts and suppress fraud, but otherwise men should be governed by impersonal market forces. In practice, of course, no society could operate fully, or even mainly, by such principles and mechanisms. In particular, contract theory alone could never have carried the weight which the practice of free enterprise capitalism put upon it. The unfettered, unquestioned control over their employees sought by business entrepreneurs – not necessarily successfully – could never have been derived from an application of pure contract doctrine. The damaging implication of the pure doctrine for the employer would have been that it could not allow him to be the sole judge of whether his rules were arbitrary or exceeded the scope of his authority. Certainly, even under contract doctrine he might be granted – by the contract – the right to make rules, but he would not have the unrestricted right to decide whether the rules he had made or proposed to make were consistent with the contract. Contract theory included the notion of appeal by either party to some outside adjudicating body in the event of behaviour claimed to be inconsistent with the contract. This incipient threat to so integral a part of everyday control as their wide discretionary powers over the workforce would have been intolerable to employers. Contract, as the pure doctrine defined it, could not, therefore, be seen by the property-owning classes as an adequate foundation for governing the employment relation. Their needs were met by infusing the employment contract with the traditional status law of master and servant, which vested almost total prerogative in the former and the duty of obedience in the latter (Fox, 1974, pp. 184–90; Selznick, 1969, p. 135). Burke was among the later theorists who saw that evolving capitalism 'was still heavily dependent on the acceptance of status' (Macpherson, 1980, p. 69). Contract doctrine was bolstered, in other words, by law which, because it embodied the traditional hierarchy of power and control, could be used to underpin the economic exploitation of the weaker by the stronger. This did not, however, deter the prophets of a burgeoning economic individualism from presenting it as a free and open arena within which equal individuals contracted with each other on a basis which excluded all non-economic forces and considerations.

Although, as much of this implies, individualism is often taken to be – and was often intended to describe – a situation in which every person acts alone in competition with all others, this obscures an important distinction which emerged in practice. Individualism is not necessarily to be opposed to collectivism. There are, of course, many examples of collective organisation – churches, fighting units, sports teams – whose members may see the collective entity as embodying a cause transcending their own individual interests, which they may therefore be prepared to subjugate to the higher good. This 'organic' collectivism must be contrasted, however, with an 'instrumental' collectivism which commands the adherence of its members only so long as it serves their self-regarding individual interests more effectively than they could serve themselves standing alone as atomistic and isolated persons. The individualistic impulse remains dominant but is pursued through collectivist means because this is deemed more effective. In this case, the collective possesses no transcendent significance and should it fail to serve the individual interests of its members it will be abandoned or bypassed – unless it develops powers to coerce them into retaining membership.

English Paternalism: Guilds and Statutory Regulation

Strains of both paternalist control and individualism were evident in English society from early times, but attempts towards the former strengthened during the sixteenth and early seventeenth centuries. On labour questions both elements of the paternalist equation – authoritarian control and some profession of solicitude – were visible: the first more obviously than the second. Whether or not the superior was punctilious in discharging his own obligations, inferiors were held to theirs. The Statute of Artificers of 1563 – little more than an attempt to apply, on a national scale, laws, guild rules and municipal regulations going back to the Middle Ages – applied, among other things, the medieval notion of the universal obligation to work by making labour compulsory when employment was offered (Minchinton, 1972, p. 11). It also enabled local justices to punish by imprisonment craftsmen who 'left work unfinished' – a convenient counter to strikes. Vagrancy legislation was particularly revealing of the control element. The essence of the whole paternalist strategy as a mode of social control was that everyone must come under the tutelage, guidance, responsibility and control of some person of superior status. 'No man without a lord' was the phrase which expressed this principle whereby all subjects of the realm were bound within a pyramidal structure of reciprocal obligations of protection and obedience. Given such a conception, 'masterless men' – that is, men lacking any personal and reciprocal bonding of submission to a superior – were a threat to social order and discipline, for they were outside that network of responsible dependencies which was deemed to hold society together. They were accordingly legislated against with extreme ferocity. Successive statutes from the sixteenth century decreed, for 'sturdy beggars', vagrants and men refusing to work, such punishments as whipping, branding, imprisonment and, during one period, slavery and death (Marx, 1976, Vol. 1, pp. 896–9). These statutes, which sought both to compel the idle to work and to force them back into the structure of control, remained legally binding until the beginning of the eighteenth century.

The protective aspect of the strategy is exemplified in the fact that

> Tudor and early Stuart governments generally tried either to stem the course of agricultural change or at least to soften the involuntary hardships which the poor experienced; to control prices in the interest of 'plenty'; to maintain the output of cereals; and to discourage what were seen as excessive shifts in land-use towards sheep-rearing – which required less labour. (Coleman, 1977, p. 175)

Statutes of the mid-sixteenth century had also sought to prohibit the gig-mill, which threatened to convert the wool croppers 'almost overnight from an elite into "an order of men not necessary to the manufacture"'

(E. P. Thompson, 1968, p. 572). Another of about the same date had tried, among other things, to uphold guild regulation by limiting the number of woollen looms owned by persons outside the corporate towns. These and other attempts at regulation sought to grapple with economic changes which were 'upsetting old social relationships, and creating new classes of persons who no longer fitted into the old, ordered hierarchical system. There were now very much larger numbers of ruthless entrepreneurs who were disturbing public order by their thrusting materialist drive for economic gain . . . and very much larger numbers of helpless and dangerous poor . . . ' (Stone, 1972, p. 87). Little was achieved by such regulations, administrative structures being quite inadequate to secure enforcement.

Nevertheless the conception itself ranged wide. The Statute of Artificers also sought to maintain order through an elaborate industrial code which attempted not only stringent controls over work behaviour but also the enforcement of apprenticeship regulations. 'It shall not be lawful to any person, other than such as now do lawfully exercise any art, mistery, or manual occupation, to exercise any craft now used within the realm of England and Wales, except he shall have been brought up therein seven years at the least as apprentice.' This was to remain for centuries a major symbol for the journeymen and apprentices of the craft trades, 'an essential supportive notion of legitimacy' (Rule, 1981, pp. 96–7). As such, it was to prove of great significance in the subsequent development of English trade unions and their strategies. The apprenticeship system was a fundamental survival of medieval corporate control by the guilds, which existed among many craft trades and occupations in towns throughout the country. Wielding their powers under warrant from the crown, they were 'not in themselves units of functional economic organization so much as methods of association and control or social foci of civil ceremony and ritual' (Coleman, 1957, p. 20). Guild regulation sought to control entry into the particular craft or trade, preserve local monopoly, and generally limit competition and uphold customary standards of reward and status. 'The normal method of regulation was to insist upon apprenticeship as a path to full membership of the guild' – which included both the master craftsmen and the journeymen artisans they employed. Guild membership might be 'the only formal path to the "freedom" of the town and thus the right to carry on business there' (ibid.). At the height of their powers, guilds were not only legalised closed shops but also legalised governments with popular assemblies, legislatures, courts, executives and authority to enforce fines and even the imprisonment of those violating guild rules (Commons, 1957, p. 225).

Even by the early sixteenth century, however, much guild regulation was on the decline. It could only expect to be effective if economic conditions were relatively static. If the labour supply or the demand for particular craft products increased substantially, then either pressure for entry would mount irresistibly or production would expand outside the guild limits of regulation. The quickening of trade and production was having just these effects – indeed had exerted them long before in clothmaking. Other trades began to follow it into rural areas where an unregulated economic life then developed which the urban-based guilds were unable to control. This was precisely the sort of situation, threatening in its implications for social order, which fostered the explicit formulation of Tudor paternalism. Hence the renewed statutory rules of 1563 on apprenticeship and other issues, designed to bolster or replace the declining authority of the guilds. The Statute of Artificers ranged further than this, however, by attempting, in its own words, to secure 'unto the hired person both in time of scarcity and in time of plenty a convenient proportion of wages' (Coleman, 1977, p. 180). To this end, the local justices and town authorities were required to make annual assessments of the wage rates to be paid in a range of enumerated trades and occupations in their district – a fresh version of long-standing attempts by the state, dating from the fourteenth century, to regulate wages. As before, these rates were to be not minimum but maximum rates, and given that the assessors were landowners, employers, or parsons it might be supposed that the pious phrases of the statute were merely the façade of a crude class tyranny. In the event, justices sometimes chose to lay down minimum rates, or rates which were to be taken as both minima and maxima (Kelsall, 1972, pp. 168–9). For the most part, however, they were more than ready to interpret their function as that of prescribing maxima. Nevertheless, even here the statute expressed well the paternalist system of control. On the one hand, the principal aim was to prevent any local labour shortage, particularly in agriculture, driving up wages beyond the level considered socially 'reasonable'. On the other hand, whereas previous enactments had subjected the local assessing authorities to a statutory maximum for each trade fixed by Parliament, the new one allowed them discretion to fix their own maxima – the impression conveyed being that these would now have to be higher. The reason for this was that a price rise of unprecedented proportions had borne severely though unevenly upon the lower orders and a single centrally fixed maximum for each trade no longer necessarily guaranteed them subsistence. The paternalist system sought to meet the case by combining the principle of upper limits with the principle of adjustments by which local rulers could temper the rigour of local circumstances by whatever degree they considered necessary to avoid socially disruptive suffering and grievance.

Policies towards the destitute revealed the same combination of control and some minimal care. After 1563 the parish could levy a poor rate – 'poor relief was necessary to subsidize wages', given the economic pressures of the time, 'if the lower orders were not to be forced into revolt by mass starvation' (C. Hill, 1969b, pp. 5–8). A national tax-supported poor relief system got under way on a systematic scale in about 1600 and served the old, the sick and the growing numbers of unemployed. 'For reasons we do not fully understand, the English propertied classes realized very early on that the financial cost of poor relief was a small price to pay for the domestic tranquillity and social deference that resulted. The welfare system was the only viable alternative to a local bureaucracy and a standing army as an instrument for social control' (Stone, 1972, pp. 76–7). A price was exacted, however, for subsistence; a price which must also be included in the category of social control. The receipt of poor relief became socially defined as depriving the recipient of status – a definition which, accepted even by the Levellers, has been carried forward vestigially to the present day.

The question as to how much was achieved by these interlocking policies of poor relief, labour control and social policing does not require a judgement here and, in any case, conclusive evidence is hard to come by. Wage assessment and its enforcement, for example, were undoubtedly effective in some districts and in some periods, but on Tawney's evidence, which though meagre has received support from more recent investigation, 'the legal rate often differed considerably from the market rate, and usually fell short of it' (Tawney, 1972, p. 85; Minchinton, 1972, p. 26). There is certainly some confidence that this was true at least after the mid-seventeenth century (Kelsall, 1972, p. 119). More relevant for the present purpose, however, is the opinion of a leading specialist on the period that perhaps the most important quality of these acts of state lay in their embodiment of the attitude of mind of the political nation.

> 'Plenty' had not only to be balanced against 'power' but seen to be; social control was imperative but had to be balanced by social obligations; the submerged third, quarter, half – whatever the varying proportion may have been – who were the poor, that other entity, had to be regulated, succoured, defined for varying treatments, controlled, prevented from causing trouble – but not eliminated. Without them the economy would have collapsed. (Coleman, 1977, p. 184).

Contributing to this 'attitude of mind of the political nation' was a body of social ethics owing much to religious doctrine. 'When the sixteenth century opens, not only political but social theory is saturated with doctrines drawn from the sphere of ethics and religion, and economic phenomena are expressed in terms of personal conduct ...' In other words, economic behaviour was viewed as needing to be infused with moral, religious and social obligations. Such ideas were of medieval origin – 'Society was interpreted ... not as the expression of economic self-interest, but as held together by a system of mutual, though varying obligations' (Tawney, 1938, pp. 24, 39). Tawney acknowledged that in the great medieval commercial centres there could sometimes be found a capitalism as inhuman as any the world has seen, and Thomas More, in the early sixteenth century, certainly turned a savage pen upon some of the conditions of his day:

> ... when I consider any social system that prevails in the modern world, I can't, so help me God, see it as anything but a conspiracy of the rich to advance their own interests under the pretext of organizing society. They think up all sorts of tricks and dodges, first for keeping safe their ill-gotten gains, and then for exploiting the poor by buying their labour as cheaply as possible. (More, 1965, p. 130)

Tawney nevertheless argued that conditions were such that an ethic of mutual aid was not wholly impossible: 'Whatever emphasis may be laid –

and emphasis can hardly be too strong – upon the gulf between theory and practice . . . the fact remains that, on the small scale involved, the problem of moralizing economic life was faced and not abandoned.' Men called avarice and greed 'by their right names, and had not learned to persuade themselves that greed was enterprise and avarice economy' (Tawney, 1938, pp. 69–71). It scarcely seems rash to hypothesise that within such a framework of judgements and expectations some men, at least, were likely to feel constrained to avoid the more nakedly self-interested economic behaviour. It was important that outside comparatively small sectors of the economy the prospect of gain was as yet contained within relatively modest limits, and given those limits a medieval economic morality had some chance of being observed. Such conditions presented a sharp contrast to those – now beginning to grow – where the prospect of gain seemed unlimited, where men were playing for higher stakes, and where this generated pressures that burst through the none-too-strong inhibitions painfully constructed by medieval religious doctrine. It was important, too, that this older doctrine had another consequence to which Tawney did not draw attention. It lent itself to being used as a legitimising ideology which explained away economic oppression as the exceptional behaviour of sinning individuals, leaving the oppressed with great diffi-culty in formulating a systematic account of their grievances.

We may sum up, however, by quoting from a recent study of English paternalism.

> The writings of the Tudor humanists and the legislation of the Tudor parliaments thus led to three important developments: (1) the emer-gence of paternalism as part of the rhetoric and theory of the age, (2) the growth of the ideal of an educated, Christian, and virtuous gentry and nobility performing the duties of property, and (3) the establishment of a state paternalism not equalled until the twentieth century. (D. Roberts, 1979, p. 12)

The first and the third were to have little impact upon the industrial relations system in its nineteenth-century formative stages, but the second, expressed through a middle- and upper-class ideal of service, was not to be without its effect.

English Individualism: Capitalism and Labour as Commodity

Yet men of affairs were divided. While some feared the effects on social stability of the gathering economic tempo, uneasy at the ways in which a sharpening individualistic thrustfulness might disrupt long-habituated relationships of command and obedience, others welcomed the prospect of faster-growing national strength and private gain. The latter were apt to decide that they must pursue their courses umhampered by traditional strategies of social stability and order and other current state preoccu-pations. It was not inevitable that they should prevail. A powerful state bureaucracy with undivided convictions that the traditional patterns of control must be preserved might have chosen to enforce them. Tudor and early Stuart bureaucracy had neither such power, however, nor such undivided convictions. Unlike some Continental counterparts, for example, the English state did not seek to rejuvenate the guilds. In its attempts to limit the spread of industry to the rural areas it gave the crucial powers of jurisdiction not to the guilds, but to local justices, whose concern to uphold, for example, formal apprenticeship was never as strong as their concern to maintain employment in the interests of social order (Coleman, 1975, p. 22).

Given a weak state apparatus and divided counsels, the paternalist strategy was being eroded even as attempts were made to reinforce it. The individualism which was increasingly breaking through the efforts to uphold or renew traditional economic regulation is usually described as having emerged from the Reformation, the Renaissance and the break-up of feudalism in the fifteenth and sixteenth centuries. Many of the strands of political, religious, ethical, economic and other types of individualism are traced to Hobbes, Luther, Calvin and other post-fifteenth-century notables. As against this, it has recently been argued that individualism was far from being this new to the English scene. 'Within the recorded period covered by our documents it is not possible to find a time when an Englishman did not stand alone . . . Since at least the thirteenth century England has been a country where the individual has been more important than the group . . . ' (Macfarlane, 1978, pp. 196–7). Macfarlane uses the term 'individualism' in the same sense as adopted here.

> . . . that a central and basic feature of English social structure has for long been the stress on the rights and privileges of the individual as against the wider group or the State . . . It is the view that society is constituted of autonomous, equal units, namely separate individuals, and that such individuals are more important, ultimately, than any larger constituent group. It is reflected in the concept of individual private property, in the political and legal liberty of the individual, in the idea of the individual's direct communication with God.

He seeks to show the essentially individualistic nature of many English practices and institutions since (at least) the thirteenth century – for example, that the legal and ideological framework for individual, as against family, ownership in land was then already well developed; that the 'devices of gift, sale and last testament were all expressions of the fact that the society and the law recognized that, ultimately, ownership was in the individual and in no larger grouping' (ibid., pp. 5, 86). In this respect, as in others, English law diverged sharply from law elsewhere in Europe.

Macfarlane's attempt to identify individualism in a wide range of English institutions has met criticism from those who argue that he sustains his case only with respect to family structure. It remains of interest, however, to note his quotation from a picture of England offered, towards the end of the fifteenth century, by Sir John Fortesque, Lord Chancellor to Henry VI. He saw it as an association of free men, self-bound and held together by mutual contracts, ruled by a limited monarchy bound by the same laws. This incorporation of themselves into a kingdom was 'only to the end that thereby they might with more safety than before maintain themselves and enjoy their goods from such misfortunes and losses as they stood in fear of' (ibid., p. 180). The significance of this picture of 'instrumental collectivism' rests not so much on any supposition that Fortesque is giving us valid information about the nature of the social bond in the England of his day, but on the fact that he should offer this kind of interpretation at all. It reminds us of the contrast between conceptions of the state which see it as having a transcendent existence and therefore 'needs' and 'interests' of its own over and above those of the individuals within its boundaries, and conceptions which see it as no more than a set of instrumental agencies designed to serve, for all or some persons, individual interests which they cannot so effectively secure by themselves. It could be expected that a society containing such marked individualistic characteristics as England would throw up theories and doctrines which presented the state as merely an instrumentality for the benefit of individual citizens and which insisted on the importance of institutions that provided defences against the state abusing or exceeding this role.

The encroachment of these individualistic and market characteristics was certainly becoming increasingly evident by the sixteenth century even in that sector of the economy where paternalism might have been expected to offer total resistance, namely the agrarian sector. The landowning aristocracy and gentry were not so committed to the paternalist control system that they could resist the prospect of the financial gains now available through the adoption of the alternative style. In this connection it is important to recall that

> what a good deal of recent research shows is that because of various peculiarities in English agriculture and society *capitalism and capitalists developed within the rural sector*. Certainly recent work has shown that by the early sixteenth century English agriculture was largely a specialised and market-orientated agriculture, literally dominated in parts of the west country by large-scale capitalist farming. (Neale, 1975, p. 92, italics in original)

This has produced the observation that 'the English landowner and capitalist farmer experienced a substantial dose of embourgeoisement well before the bourgeoisie existed and before the emergence of the concept at least as Marx envisaged it ... landowners and the landed aristocracy, within a commercialised agricultural sector, led the transformation of England in the eighteenth century' (ibid., p. 94).

This sixteenth-century growth of a capitalist agriculture strongly infused with individualistic values and assumptions was a significant factor in weakening the alternative conception of society: 'On the land there was a massive shift away from a feudal and paternalist relationship between landlord and tenant, towards one more exclusively based on the maximization of profits in a market economy.' By the seventeenth century there was no other major country in which the relations between landlord and tenant were 'so much governed by the laws of the market place rather than by the customary relationships of service; in no other country had private property rights encroached so extensively on the commercial rights of the village . . . economic developments were dissolving old bonds of service and obligation and creating new relationships founded on the operations of the market'. Nor was it only into agriculture that the landed classes were bringing this profit-maximising market spirit. In no other country 'were the landed classes so extensively involved in investments in overseas trade and settlement . . . In few or none were the great landowners more actively engaged in exploiting the mineral resources of their land [coal and iron] or in developing their urban properties' (Stone, 1972, pp. 68, 71, 72). It was to prove crucial to England's social and political development that no simple and clear-cut distinction could be made between 'landed' and 'industrial' interests.

Stone's formulation greatly exaggerates the speed of the movement away from paternalism, which as a technique of control remained widespread in some areas until the late nineteenth century and even beyond. Nevertheless, the beginnings were visible. They were not confined to the landed classes. One might suppose the traditional paternalist mode of control to be surviving strongly in the then still predominantly small-scale milieu of manufacture and commerce. There can be little doubt that in many places it did. Yet the verdict of one specialist is that in many other places it did not. 'The business man of the sixteenth century' – by which Hill means 'the small merchant or craftsman or farmer who was beginning to give employment to a wider circle than his own family and an apprentice or two' – 'had a very different outlook from that of the feudal landlord . . . he grudged every penny spent over and above the minimum necessary to induce men to work for him. And since they chose "voluntarily" to work for him, he felt no responsibility for them in hard times. If they did not like what he offered, they might go elsewhere . . . ' (C. Hill, 1968, p. 217). It is a perfect statement of the individualist, contractual market relationship; of the repudiation by the master of any responsibility for the servant; of the divorce of economics and ethics; of the 'cash nexus'.

This emergence of the treatment of labour as a commodity to be bought and sold like any other, though not yet elevated to the status of a formally acknowledged proposition in received economic doctrine, became specially apparent in the widespread 'outworking' industries, such as clothmaking, the metal trades, footwear, and others. In these might be found quite sizeable establishments, though large numbers worked in their own homes or in small workshops heavily dependent upon a principal employer or large-scale merchant. This was the outcome of strong economic pressures bursting the bonds of urban monopoly and promoting the growth of so-called 'domestic' industry in the countryside beyond the reach of guild authority. Dean Tucker was not the only cleric and man of affairs who, glad to see employment opportunities increasing for his surrounding rural flocks, was led to support the 'free spirit' of national commerce 'unrestrained by monopoly' on the part of guilds and chartered trading companies.

The growth of individualism had differing impacts upon the dependent lower orders. For those still contained within a traditionally regulated, custom-dominated sector, it might seem only a distant, though potentially disruptive, threat. For those who had come to be directly controlled by it, it could often appear as a disastrous deviation from traditional patterns of personalised control – an abandonment of that diffuse bonding by which, as a reciprocal of their coming under the employer's comprehensive governance, there could be pinned upon him some degree of responsibility for their general welfare. Even though it might be demonstrated that paternalist obligations were more ignored than honoured, there remains significance in the expectation, which bulked large in popular consciousness, that certain social duties of property would be discharged. Men of spirit reacted collectively with outrage when their masters failed them, appealing to principles of 'time immemorial' as leverage against authority and not invariably failing.

What was never abandoned, of course, was the employer's demand for their obedience in the workplace, where the courts invariably supported him. But it was a feature of the growing free labour market, increasingly pervaded by a sharper and more specific conception of contract, that it should be undermining the old notion of each person being contained within a linked pyramid of tutelage, control and diffuse responsibility. Employers were increasingly disposed to throw off such traditional encumbrances in so far as they had survived – for given the English strand of individualism and the lack of a forceful state apparatus to uphold them they had long been more precarious than in some Continental countries. These beginnings of an abdication by those of superior status of their paternalist social control never ceased to disturb some sections of ruling-class opinion and were to excite vocal alarm in the nineteenth century when large-scale consequences began to become apparent. Long before that, they violated the expectations of substantial groups of artisans who appealed to Parliament, town corporations or justices for protection under paternalist statutes and customs only to have quoted at them the tenets of market individualism. But even for them there was not only loss. Instructed by their masters to become independent, many of them took the lesson to heart and became so – not as isolated individual agents, as intended, but as collectives, culturally and socially as well as economically. In these ways the changing English scene was unintentionally weakening, for some groups of workers, such habituated bonds of obedience and deference as there were. Repudiation by their masters of paternalist responsibility left a larger social space within which they could construct a larger independence of spirit and aspiration.

Individualism and the Common Law

The division of opinion within the ruling Establishment as to the desirability of the increasingly individualistic modes was illustrated by divisions among lawyers. Individual employers who sought to overcome or bypass monopolistic regulation often found a powerful ally in English common law. Common law offered them a supportive resource of a kind existing in no Continental country. Its significance for our theme is, however, far wider than this. It is centrally relevant to Britain's history, including that of her industrial relations system, that support from the common law had also long been available to those members of the gentry who sought to resist arbitrary encroachments by the crown or nobility upon their funds, rights, or property.

A convenient way into this topic is offered by J. R. Commons's reference to two 'apparently opposite theories of law . . . According to the one view law is *made* by the command of a superior to an inferior. According to the other, law is *found* in the customs of the people' (Commons, 1957, pp. 298–9, italics in original). The first conception, which sees law (civil law) as resulting from the exercise of prerogative, obviously accorded well with the absolutist monarchies of the Continent. The second (common law) accorded ill with absolutism, for if law derived its legitimacy not from the crown but from 'the people', absolutism was denied. Civil law had made no progress in England but the common law had flourished. And in the process of serving their well-to-do clients, common lawyers 'found' certain principles which limited the crown's power and ever since the fourteenth century had periodically used them to erect defences against royal absolutism (Loades, 1974, pp. 16–17).

This was not the only weapon of defence: Parliament was another. Between them they ensured that the law could not safely be rejected in principle in England even by monarchs; such doctrines as the divine right of monarchy and other absolutist doctrines met fierce – though certainly not universal – resistance. 'Although all the Tudor monarchs had been prepared to tamper with the law in their own interests, only Mary had not been consistently respectful of its forms, and none had ever claimed to stand above it' (ibid., p. 329). Prominent writers on the royal prerogative insisted unanimously upon its limitation by the law.

English common law, which supposedly had come down from 'time immemorial' and which was not the creation of kings or legislative bodies but had evolved out of the needs of peoples; was seen by its practitioners and supporters as being bound up with the 'ancient constitution' and the 'rights' and 'liberties' of Englishmen. Given the established fiction that common law had not to be invented, but was 'discovered' by learned lawyers uncovering its relevance for, and application to, particular situations, its potency as a resource in the hands of those who could successfully claim to be its true practitioners is manifest. 'From the Middle Ages the lawyers had inherited a set of rules and conventions which they could, and eventually did, use to erect barriers for the protection of private property, private interests, and private persons against the encroachment of a centralizing state. These defences were based on the medieval concept of liberties . . .' By the early seventeenth century the ideology of the common law was becoming a powerful independent force. Chief Justice Sir Edward Coke and his fellow Parliamentarians, including other common lawyers, exploiting the myth of Magna Carta, promoted belief 'in the existence of an ancient constitution which predated, and was somehow immune from, the royal prerogative (Stone, 1972, p. 104). Common law was an essential feature of it.

Given the circumstances of common law origins and growth, it was primarily Protestant and secularist; 'profoundly steeped in the beliefs of English empiricism'. Law was seen not, as on the Continent, as embodying a set of logical principles and ideas worked out deductively and systematically in a spirit of rationalism, but as 'an essentially pragmatic art to be left to practical lawyers and judges who, as men of the world, will know what to do'. Thus derived the 'piecemeal creation of law from precedent to precedent' (Lloyd, 1979, p. 223).

The ideology of common law and the 'ancient constitution' became immensely important in the complex seventeenth-century struggles between, on the one hand, the crown, the bishops and large sections of the nobility and, on the other, large sections of the Parliamentarian gentry, common lawyers and some of the nobility. The latter made use, too, of the myth of the Norman Yoke, which had implications that became significant for English political culture. From the seventeenth century the form it took presented the early Anglo-Saxons as free and equal citizens, who governed themselves through representative institutions. The Norman Conquest deprived them of their liberties and imposed upon them a tyranny of alien kings and landlords. There were many variants, but one version much invoked during seventeenth-century struggles 'stressed the unbroken continuity of common law, which had carried Anglo-Saxon liberties into post-conquest England' (C. Hill, 1968, p. 64, see also p. 67). Royalist theories of absolutism based on conquest were seen as threatening this inheritance.

The supposed Anglo-Saxon liberties were bound up with the idea of individual freedoms (needless to say, for independent men of substance only), with the defence of property, with relief from arbitrary taxation and with the upholding of representative institutions. 'A defence of Anglo-Saxon liberties was also a defence of property against the state.' (ibid., p. 73). By the seventeenth century Protestantism, too, had been brought in to counter the religious and political threat of Stuart Catholicism. And since patriotism is invariably a useful card to play, the 'patriotic appeal was always a strong feature of the Norman Yoke theory . . . Liberty, property, and patriotism were inseparable' (ibid., pp. 67, 70). And all were bound up with the common law. Few passages make these points more tellingly than one by Coke, doyen of the common lawyers and hero of seventeenth-century parliamentary opposition to the crown: 'the ancient and excellent laws of England are the birthright and the most ancient and best inheritance that the subjects of this realm have; for by them he enjoyeth not only his inheritance and goods in peace and quietness but his liberty and his most dear country in safety' (ibid., p. 72).

A profoundly significant linkage of ideas had therefore been forged within the English political scene. The defence of representative institutions and of a common law tradition upholding individual rights against the state – a tradition bound up with a legal order independent of the crown – had become closely linked with the liberties of England and the birthright of Englishmen. This meant that patriotic 'Englishness' was being defined in terms of aversion to, and protections against, any threat of the absolutist state.

This link between Englishness and resistance to absolutism became strengthened by the connection between foreign absolutisms and Roman Catholicism. Many of the English nobility and gentry who had profited from the Reformation sale, gift, or appropriation of ecclesiastical land had strong economic as well as religious reasons for being determined to resist the restoration of 'popery', linked as it was with an external threat from royal absolutist regimes. They were active in promoting and disseminating among their dependent ranks the notion that absolutism, tyranny, Roman Catholicism and external threats were bound up together. Absolutism was foreign, and patriotic Protestant Englishness lay in resisting it. In brief, therefore, within the English political culture there was now a powerfully backed and thrusting element which defined quintessential Englishness and the state as being separate and distinct phenomena. We may contrast this with a situation in which an absolutist state succeeds in imposing a concept of patriotism defined in terms of identification with, and total submission to, the 'needs' of the state.

There are three further points to be noted. Circumstances and events had given 'freedom' and 'liberty' a largely negative connotation in English political argument. What was debated was always freedom against some dominating force – crown, aristocracy, bishops, feudal monopoly, or courtier's privilege. Secondly, the link between Englishness and liberty, and the fact that even for substantial sections of the higher classes liberty was defined in terms of wariness towards the central state apparatus, meant that for many Englishmen the state would not be able to appropriate solely to itself the patriotic impulses suffusing the notion of Englishness. Finally, the contemporary eulogies of the common law may convey to the modern reader the false impression that law then was comparable with the 'rule of law' as we have come to understand it since. Much deliberate and far from inevitable effort and struggle, however, had yet to be directed towards fashioning the law into the shape with which we are familiar. Up until the seventeenth century and well beyond, powerful individuals manipulated and exploited both law and lawyers as a private resource with which to subdue rivals, destroy enemies and aggrandise their own families and estates. And as between the method of securing the conviction of an offender by building up a case against him on the evidence of others, and the method of extracting a confession by means which might degenerate into bullying, trickery, or torture, it was, 'in the seventeenth century . . . , touch and go which system would prevail in England'. The 'basis of our British system (mingled as it is with defects peculiar to itself) which must be reckoned among the bulwarks of our liberty is the recognized right to refuse to submit to interrogation, or to go into the witness box' (Brailsford, 1976, pp. 82–3). This right was placed irreversibly on the political agenda by the Levellers.

'Liberty' and 'Liberties'

The fact that the common law, by its very nature as being allegedly discovered in the customs of the people, lent itself to manipulation by the gentry and their lawyers as a weapon of defence against royal power, made it also a useful weapon for those with an interest in attacking grants or privileges held under royal concession. In other words, common law could also be pressed into service to advance the purposes of those whose individual economic interests called for an attack upon monopoly franchises awarded by the crown to favoured courtiers or sold to the highest bidder; upon the privileges enjoyed by exclusive guilds, closed town corporations and chartered companies under royal warrant secured perhaps at a large fee; or upon the restricting encumbrances of old statutes, antiquated customs and traditional institutions. Such attacks were pressed home in the name of individual 'liberty', and since the practices at which they were levelled were themselves often referred to as 'liberties', there emerges here in its sharpest form the ambiguity surrounding these terms. The manner in which powerful political forces contrived an adroit shift from one set of meanings to another diametrically opposite is not only fascinating in its own right, but also points to ambiguities which still, in a certain form, lie at the heart of British society – including British trade unionism.

In Magna Carta, 'liberties' did not mean individual personal or economic liberty. It meant, 'in general, the feudal or other special privileges, immunities, jurisdictions, charters, or franchises, either granted directly by the crown to the subject or claimed by prescription, which pre-supposed a grant'. Even the granting of a trade monopoly, a practice which had expanded massively under Elizabeth, was included, as was also, of course, the exercise of restrictive and regulative powers by a guild. Each of these became a recognised exercise of the royal prerogative placed for certain defined purposes in the hands of the grantee, and each carried the implicit promise that the courts and the executive would not interfere, or allow anyone else to interfere, with the grantee's proper exercise of his privilege, whether it be tenure of land, enjoyment of a monopoly, exercise of guild or corporation power, or whatever.

Thus, when the barons of 1215 presented their Magna Carta, or feudal lords defended their lands against encroachment, or a guild claimed the right to restrict their trade to guild members, or a grantee of the king demanded observance of his monopoly, they were claiming 'liberties' in the sense of privileges or exclusive rights. But men of enterprise were now, in the sixteenth and seventeenth centuries, increasingly asserting their right to conduct their business free of such impediments and restrictions. And because these impediments had their legal origins in the royal prerogative, an attack on them inevitably took on some of the flavour of an attack on crown power. This alone was enough to draw many common lawyers eventually into supporting the claims of 'free' enterprise, especially when they became engaged in a far wider political conflict with the Stuart monarchy and its aspirations towards absolutism. But what principle of common law were they to 'discover' in mounting their defence of entrepreneurial 'freedom'? They were to discover that 'restraint of trade' – monopoly and other forms of restriction on individual economic behaviour – was contrary to the 'liberty' of the free-born Englishman. Thus was born an individualistic legal concept which was to have immense significance not only for the economy but also for the trade unions.

For the moment, however, it was those 'legalized closed shops', the guilds, which were affected. In 1599 the London Guild of Merchant Tailors, under a charter granted by the crown, attempted to restrict their trade to members of the guild. The relevant by-law, however, was declared void by a common law court as being against the 'common right and public good' and 'against the common law' on the ground that, being an attempt at a monopoly, it was 'against the liberty of the subject'. There followed similar cases of common-law 'abhorrence of all monopolies', as at Ipswich, where in 1615 a court resolved that at common law 'no man could be prohibited from working in any lawful trade'. Restraint was 'against the liberty and freedom of the subject', and this was against the common law and the common wealth. Thus was opened up another arena of conflict between crown and major sections of Parliament, with whose cause many common lawyers were in alliance. Here the conflict was joined with the king's own 'prerogative courts', which naturally sought to uphold the privileges or liberties granted in the monopolies, franchises, or charters. To yield to 'the demand for liberty and power on the part of the small but aggressive merchants and manufacturers outside the guilds' might not only threaten stability and order but would also undermine the lucrative royal practice of selling 'liberties' – sales would soon come to an end if royal power proved unable to deliver their privileges (Commons, 1957, pp. 48, 51, 225, 226, 228, 307).

In these ways, along with others, the common law concepts of personal rights, property rights and the liberty of the free-born Englishman came into conflict, during the reigns of Elizabeth and the Stuart kings, with the prerogative of the monarch. There were born, as a consequence, the two contradictory meanings of 'liberty'. Liberty in the sense of a grant of some privilege out of the royal prerogative stood for a relation of superior to inferior; liberty in the common law sense stood for a relation of equality between members of the same class. The latter was to generate socially explosive meanings far beyond the imaginings of seventeenth-century common lawyers.

Meanwhile the diametrically opposed meanings of 'liberties' and 'liberty' illuminate the grievances of many small and middling-scale masters and lesser merchants of the craft trades, urban as well as rural. Out of these conflicts, often infused with religious and social as well as economic significance, there developed alliances which were to reappear in modified forms in later centuries and to have a profoundly formative effect on the social and political behaviour of the upper working class – and indirectly on their trade union behaviour. In clothmaking, for example, the lucrative export business was in the hands of the great monopolistic London trading companies operating under royal charter who, under crown encouragement, dominated provincial merchants and imposed quality regulations which master-producers found burdensome. Such grievances, which mounted during the early and middle decades of the seventeenth century, were

... aspects of a wider and more fundamental conflict of interests between the industrial small producers in general and the merchant-capitalists in general. The merchants had established an economic and political domination over the craftsmen, and were constantly enforcing and reinforcing it to the great resentment of the craftsmen. This domination was achieved and maintained by control of the government of the towns and with the help of the crown. (Manning, 1978, p. 162)

Urban shopkeepers, too, were apt to feel exploited by the merchant-capitalists who monopolised town government.

In addition, from among the ranks of small producers in a range of craft trades there was emerging a new thrusting capitalist class – larger-scale employers who relied far more on hired labour; who put out work on sub-contract to smaller masters, and who were extending their operations towards the supervision of all the stages of production and towards the marketing of the finished product (ibid., p. 170). These were the beginnings of a trend – already established in clothmaking – which was eventually to depress many smaller masters to the status of dependent wage-earners. A similar movement was taking place among small farmers. Typically, these worked their land with family labour, employing no outside workers and producing primarily for subsistence rather than for the market. Now bigger ones were emerging who employed wage-labourers and produced primarily for the market. Both groups could suffer as a result of agrarian rationalisation pursued for profit by the rich and powerful. In the early 1640s 'there was a rising tide of protest and riot in the countryside. This was directed chiefly against the enclosures of commons, wastes and fens, and the invasions of common rights by the king, members of the royal family, courtiers, bishops and great aristocrats' (ibid., p. 140).

The 'Middle Sort of People' and Puritanism

As yet, all these groups – the small craft masters, the larger masters who were drawing the smaller into dependent status, the larger yeoman farmers and the small peasant family farmers – were still categorised, along with shopkeepers, as 'the middle sort of people'. They were considered, and certainly considered themselves, to be fundamentally superior to labourers, servants, beggars, those without a trade and with no independence and no prospect of any. Independence of some kind or description was the key to positive status. It is of particular importance for our inquiry to note the stratum of wage-earning journeymen artisans, destined to grow as eighteenth-century developments undermined the independent status of many small masters and self-employed. Within the established and acknowledged crafts, even journeymen and apprentices, though usually included in the category of 'servants' by virtue of their dependent status, were more likely to identify upwards with their small or larger masters than downwards with the inferior poor. An apprenticeship was a form of property, conferring rights and a certain minimal standing.

From this stratum a peculiarly English form of craft unionism was to emerge. It was a craft unionism which has left to this day a deep imprint upon union methods extending far beyond their original boundaries; upon the whole texture of industrial relations and upon the politics not only of the Labour movement but also of the wider political nation. Both in what has gone before, and in what follows, we see major clues to the nature of the society which threw up this pattern of worker protest.

The 'middle sort of people' were an increasingly restive category, conscious of not only economic, but also fiscal, social, political and religious grievances. For a century there had been a steady shift of the tax burden from the larger to the smaller taxpayer right down the social scale. Socially, the better-off 'middle sort' found their upward mobility blocked, in ways explicitly approved by the king during the 1630s, by the established élites of nobility and gentry in town and country. Politically, the claims of yeoman and peasant farmers, craftsmen and shopkeepers to vote in parliamentary elections and have a voice in local community affairs – sixteenth-century inflation had qualified a considerable number to claim the necessary financial qualification – were resisted by the king and Privy Council, by many of the nobility and gentry, and by the rich merchant oligarchies of the towns. Upon these grievances were superimposed those of religion, more especially Puritanism.

Puritanism and the habituated perceptions, dispositions and alliances which it bequeathed to subsequent generations also have a central relevance to our theme. Puritanism is a portmanteau term of many meanings; it is used here 'to mean no more than a generalized conviction of the need for independent judgement based on conscience and bible reading' (Stone, 1972, p. 99). It was to prove an explosive force in religious, political and social life. Who were the Puritans? The answer is important for the present argument. They included a section of influential gentry, some staunch supporters among the common lawyers, some big merchants and even some nobles. But Puritanism appealed especially to 'smaller employers and self-employed men, whether in town or country, for whom frugality and hard work might make all the difference between prosperity and failure to survive in the world of growing competition' – small master-craftsmen (both employing and self-employed), journeymen artisans and apprentices, shopkeepers and yeomen (C. Hill, 1969a, p. 131). Without the backing of large numbers of these, Puritanism could never have challenged the crown and bishops, and certainly the Civil War could never have been fought and won. Nor can there be excluded from this list of allies the larger farmers and industrial employers who were emerging from the ranks of peasants and craftsmen. These constituted a new 'middle' or capitalist class. Although there were 'inherent conflicts of interests and open antagonisms between these bigger farmers and the mass of small peasants, and between the greater craftsmen and the mass of small craftsmen', the government of Charles I and the existing political, social and religious regime antagonised both levels. Consequently, the higher ranks among 'the middle sort' felt more in common with the lesser artisans, small masters and peasants than with the governing order and ruling class. 'They assumed the leadership of "the middle sort of people"' in opposition to king, lords and bishops' (Manning, 1978, pp. 170–1). Craft trades therefore displayed, in social, political and religious matters, a 'vertical' bonding between higher and lower levels which contrasted sharply with the conflict relations that they sometimes manifested in economic matters. Shared hostility to superior economic, political and religious power overcame, for some purposes, the fact that the middle people were in other respects very divided. Their rising and more ambitious members looked forward in a mood of economic aggression, seeking to break the old order of traditional regulation and restraints. The smaller masters, the self-employed and the journeymen often sought protection rather than opportunity, exhibiting defensiveness rather than aggression and hoping that the dynamic forces which threatened stability and security could be contained. Some of them, idealising the past and invoking the myth of the Norman Yoke, wanted a 'return' to a small-scale society of modest property-owners without great distinctions of wealth and power. These provided the bulk of the Levellers' movement.

Puritanism as a creed gave no support to such notions. It leaned much more towards 'the preservation of the traditional social and political hierarchies and ... the preservation of traditional values' (Stone, 1972, p. 102). But its precepts were such as to threaten those hierarchies, nevertheless. Prominent among them was a stress on the individual conscience and a thrust towards moral improvement and holy zeal in every aspect of living.

Puritanism often represented, in practice, as fierce an individualism in personal religious life as many of its adherents were demanding in economic life. In the latter, the challenge was to higher authorities deemed responsible for economic grievances – the crown, privileged courtiers, bishops, monopolist chartered companies, rich merchants. In the former, it was to those who interposed their authoritarian interpretations and practices between the individual and his God – symbolised in the episcopal hierarchy. The two groups were closely connected. Bishops were major figures in the ruling-class alliance of great merchants, landowning nobility, high-level clerics and the crown.

The assertion of individual rights and individual judgement against authoritarian domination was therefore important on many fronts. No doubt there was a strong elective affinity between the 'middle sort of people' and the central perspective of Puritan creeds. For them it was a highly attractive and, above all, immensely supportive perspective. It braced them, however, against inferiors as well as superiors. Above them were noble rentier landlords, merchants and gentry; below them were labourers, servants and the very poor. Economic and social threats both from above and from below rendered them receptive to doctrines and ideologies which offered a special legitimation of their position and function, which celebrated their particular virtues and which inspired sustaining claims and aspirations. Puritanism in its varying forms satisfied these needs. It 'inspired a concept of godliness that helped to create a self-conscious middle sort of people. It distinguished them from the poor on the one hand and from the rich on the other' (Manning, 1978, p. 78). The distinctions were moral as well as social and economic. The rich, besides being arrogant and domineering, yielded to drunkenness, swearing and vanity. But there was also the ignorance, superstition and profanity of the multitude, which presented its own threats. The 'middle sort of people' wasted no sympathies on the very poor, whose inferiority was seen as deriving from economic and social dependence. It was no part of their purpose to strengthen the voice of this lowest stratum. Theirs was a cry not for a universal freedom which would ennoble the life of all, but for a strictly particularist freedom which would release only their own aspirations. The 'saints' were few and to be found among neither the rich nor the poor, but in the middle rank – 'freeholders and tradesmen are the strength of religion and civility in the land', declared one of their spokesmen. 'Puritanism', writes Manning, 'taught the middle sort of people to think for themselves and to assert their independence against king, lords and bishops. Godliness gave them status and the ability to express their identity as a separate class; and it enabled them to formulate and dignify their hostility towards the ruling class' (ibid., pp. 179–80). It must be remembered, moreover, that members of an acknowledged craft shared the 'mysteries', rules and ethical principles of a craft culture which gave them an identity, a certain status and the degree of confidence which these bestowed. It is not surprising that Puritanism found particularly fertile soil among the urban artisans, both small masters and journeymen.

It was therefore of immense significance politically and socially as well as religiously, providing the Revolution with a conviction of the rectitude of the opposition cause and with a sense of moral indignation at the wickedness of the established authorities. Thereby it injected into English political life a great strengthening in the self-confidence of oppositional modes and dispositions. It also introduced or strengthened political concepts, a political vocabulary and political justifications for opposition which were available for use later by groups with purposes not dreamt of by many seventeenth-century Puritans. The very questions it posed could be seen as subversive: 'What if the Elect of God are not identical with the political leaders of the State? What if the Anglican church is not part of the Covenant? Are there limits to the obedience a godly person owes to a sinful magistrate?' (Stone, 1972, p. 100). Men who had been rendered stubborn and self-righteous by total inner conviction and who asked questions like these were unlikely to bend easily to the dictates of authority and, even more important, they set dangerous precedents. Without absolute confidence in the rightness of their cause the revolutionary leaders would have been incapable of levying war against their king, still less of beheading him.

Along with this independence of individual moral judgement about the religious and political hierarchy went another equally subversive element. Passive acceptance of the status quo and of obedience to the established authorities of church and state was also threatened by a belief among some Puritans in the possibility of a new earth as well as a new heaven. They no longer hoped to receive this earthly millennium at the hands of the established authorities and turned instead to religious radicals, thereby rejecting both the inevitability of the status quo and the leadership of those presiding over it. There were demands for a stronger voice in such matters as lay choice of minister and participation in church government. The implications often exceeded their intent. 'They attacked the legitimacy of the bishops with no thought of attacking other institutions of social order. But both Elizabeth and the Stuarts regarded the abolition of episcopacy as but the prelude to the abolition of hierarchy in society' (ibid., p. 102).

Equally important for our present interest are those further unintended consequences of Puritanism which provided precedents, procedures and training for later grass-roots movements. They created an embryo organisation out of which grew true radicalism. Classes and congregations, for example, practised guided democracy with wide participation in discussion. Popular literacy was encouraged in order that the Scriptures could be read; and popular preaching in order that they be 'correctly' interpreted. The results were the politicising of yeomen and urban artisans and the consequent mass petitioning, mob behaviour and popular movements such as the Levellers and Diggers.

The Levellers

The Levellers have passed into socialist legend as early pioneers of equalitarian principles but this needs much qualification. They represent a lower-middle-class democracy which attacked legally supported privilege and not social or economic inequality as such. They 'included many working craftsmen, cobblers, weavers, printers, and lead miners, together with some well-to-do tradesmen and an occasional professional man ... The bolder and more thoughtful of the journeymen also were sympathisers' (Brailsford, 1976, p. 314), as were also many small rural proprietors. Large numbers of them, perhaps the majority, were members of Dissenting sects. They expressed, not class conflict between 'bourgeoisie' and 'proletariat', for society was not yet structured on those lines, but conflict between the rich and the 'middle sort of people', between the stronger and sections of the less strong, between the rulers and sections of the ruled. They linked together, in a comprehensive indictment of the whole ruling class, the chartered companies' monopolies in exports, monopoly of religion by the ordained clergy, powerful oppressive landlords, monarchical and oligarchical domination by king and Parliament, and oligarchical domination in local government by mayor and aldermen. Also under attack was the law; many Levellers seeing the monopoly of law by the lawyers and its abuse by the rich and powerful as a sign that it, too, had become corrupted by Normanism instead of remaining 'the surviving pledge of Anglo-Saxon freedom' (C. Hill, 1968, p. 86). These were all grievances of long standing which were not created but simply given expression by the Levellers and other radical groups.

There is no evidence that they sought equalisation of property or the levelling of social distinctions (Sabine, 1963, p. 482), but plenty of evidence that many of their leaders were men of some substance and status who hated the rich but also feared the very poor (Manning, 1978, pp. 337, 339). Certainly, there were ambiguities in the message as delivered by different sections of the movement. The achievement of their reforms depended on a sympathetic Parliament, so the degree of their democracy hung on their conception of the franchise. And while this conception certainly brought in the tenant farmers and small master craftsmen, it excluded women and those receiving poor relief – which meant the old, the sick and the unemployed. More significantly, wage-earners, too, often seemed to be excluded, though occasionally not. Such uncertainties helped to weaken the movement, for they frightened off the more prosperous and 'godly' supporters who looked to a more authoritarian regime of the virtuous and talented, while at the same time failing to satisfy and inspire the more radical groups. Given these and other weaknesses the movement proved vulnerable to resolute action by Cromwell and the army.

It is probably fair to say that on the dominant view the equality sought was equality before the law and equality of political rights especially for the class of small property-owners. It was the viewpoint of what was later to be thought of as radical, democratic liberalism; individualist rather than socialist in its philosophy and political rather than economic in its aims. The Levellers' creed built on principles that already enjoyed long-standing and growing strength in English society, being bound up with notions of the Englishman's birthright of traditional individual liberties. Besides making use of a version of the Anglo-Saxon past 'they also moved forward to a conception of natural rights, the rights of man. It is a momentous transition: from the recovery of rights which used to exist to the pursuit of rights because they *ought* to exist' (C. Hill, 1968, p. 81, italics in original). The Levellers 'interpreted the law of nature as endowing human individuals with innate and inalienable rights which legal and political institutions exist only to protect'. It followed that the only justification for society and the state 'is the production of individual advantages'. Government was but a necessary evil. The individual and his rights form the basis of the whole social structure (Sabine, 1963, pp. 484–5). The significance of this has already emerged; we have noted the profound gulf between that view of society and the state which sees them as being only instruments for the securing of individual rights and benefits, and that view which sees the state as a superior entity in its own right transcending the interests of individuals.   ·

The securing of individual rights was to be pursued through the drastic reform of, and wider participation in, political institutions that already existed. 'The Leveller and allied radical agitations were inspired by the belief that if the small man had a vote and a share in the conduct of affairs his social and economic grievances would be redressed and his aspirations would be satisfied. This was the central issue and the dynamic of the English Revolution . . .' (Manning, 1978, p. 340).

Their programme, like their grievances, struck chords familiar to later radical liberal movements. Along with proposals for shifting the burden of taxation from small property-owners to the rich, for breaking monopolies in the export trade, for the abolition of tithes, and for containing the power of landlords with respect to rents and enclosures, the Levellers demanded a new constitution, with a parliament subject to redistribution of seats, annual election by the people and free of limitation by lords and crown. There were also demands from the more radical followers which added up to massive decentralisation – to a society of self-governing local communities marked by a high degree of voluntarism. But, in the main, the Levellers expressed 'with remarkable distinctness the modes of thought and argument which were to characterise revolutionary liberalism in the eighteenth and early nineteenth centuries' (Sabine, 1963, p. 478). It seemed to them acceptable and realistic to seek redress of grievances through admission to a political nation that already existed in terms of essential institutions. There was a franchise of sorts giving access to a parliament which was manifestly increasingly effective in checking crown, court and nobility. That there should have been, at this stage, a consciousness among aggrieved groups that certain embryonic representative institutions and traditions existed which, suitably extended and enlarged, would enable oppositional political pressures to be exerted with at least some possibility of success is a fact of considerable consequence.

Some Relevant Outcomes of the Civil War

All the forgoing themes and issues became absorbed into the wider struggles of the Civil War between Parliamentarians and Royalists, but there is no need here to explore further those extraordinarily complex events, still the subject of conflicting analyses and interpretations. It is, however, worth noting that the policies of church and state which angered and frightened so many of the English gentry accorded closely with those widespread throughout the Continent, where men of affairs would have seen the objectives and methods of Charles and his political and religious advisers as being

> precisely those in which the future lay. The strengthening of the links of Church and State, the suppression of dissidents on all fronts, the creation of an overwhelmingly powerful Court, the acquisition of extensive financial and military powers – these were the basis of the all-but-universal growth of royal absolutism in Europe. If the trend of the times led anywhere, it was in the direction marked out by Charles and his advisers.

Their aim was 'a deferential, strictly hierarchical, socially stable, paternalist absolutism based on a close union of Church and Crown' (Stone, 1972, pp. 126, 132–3). This conception by no means died with Charles. Debates within Cromwell's own army had revealed not only 'the new conception of the nation as a mass of free individuals, cooperating from motives of self-interest, and making its law in the interest of individual freedom', but also reiteration of the older assumption that the community 'is an organization of permanent interests, particularly the landed interest, held together by customary privileges and exactions' (Sabine, 1963, p. 488).

The stratum of journeymen artisans, from which was to emerge the craft unionism that led the formation of Britain's Labour movement and shaped it in so many essential ways, looked in some respects backward to the older conception and in some respects forward to the new. Reared in the traditions of vertically integrated, restrictive, pre-industrial guild structures, this stratum had already learned to fear the consequences of the intensifying competitive, individualistic, unregulated free enterprise. They were no strangers to workplace conflict. Yet there were social, political and religious grievances which many of them shared with their masters, and because these grievances could be presented as having their origins in social, political and religious monopolies upheld by crown, Established Church, landowning aristocracy and rich merchants, an attack on them seemed to require an anti-monopolistic demand for equality of individual rights. An individualist tradition and ideology of the Englishman's rights lay to hand, strongly supported by the common law.

Even the religious impulse among the 'middle sort' often clothed itself in the individualism of Puritanism. Its active figures, while not seeking social transformation, sought a foothold in the structure of religious decision-making that bore upon them. In the course of these struggles, journeymen artisans, many of them under economic pressure, experienced reinforcement of their capacity for organisation and independence of spirit.

Thus was formed, in embryo, a combination of stances that was to play a considerable part in shaping the British Labour movement. Rejection of unregulated market individualism was combined with a strong attachment to individualism on other matters; an individualism which was suspicious and wary of the state even though prepared to invoke its assistance, and which showed absolutely no disposition to invest it with transcendent significance. Thus was initiated, too, the possibility that while relations at the workplace might be conflictual, this did not exclude co-operation between master and men on social, political, or religious issues. Vertical alliances were possible in which small masters, self-employed craftsmen, journeymen and apprentices might make common cause with larger-scale employers against the crown, the landowning aristocracy and the Episcopal Church. For the bigger masters, however, such alliances had their dangers; they sometimes stimulated independent and dangerously radical lower-rank demands which then had to be subdued, as in the case of the more radical Levellers, the Diggers, and others. Yet even the Levellers' creed was individualistic, and its programme implicitly acknowledged the value of some existing political institutions, principally Parliament, drastically reformed though it would have to be.

The complexity of the social forces at work is also demonstrated by the fact that it was not only at the manufacturing handicraft level and among the merchants who often dominated it that the values and behaviours of economic individualism were more and more encroaching upon the paternalistic system of control. As we have seen, among the landed aristocracy were some who themselves were adopting more market-orientated, profit-maximising behaviour, either in relation to their land, or through the pursuit of commercial and industrial enterprises, or through the development of their urban properties.

The outcomes of the Civil War, which included destruction of the monarchy, the House of Lords, and the Episcopal Church, duly followed by a barely disguised military dictatorship, were themselves overthrown, of course, by the restoration of those three great social foundation stones in 1660. Yet despite this, and despite the fact that 'reforms of the electoral system, the law, the administration, the Church and the educational system were completely blocked for nearly two hundred years'; and that 'the social structure became a good deal more hierarchical and immobile after the Revolution than it was before, something nevertheless survived'. It survived the further convulsions leading up to the 1688–9 Settlement, so that when England's long continuity of political stability began early in the eighteenth century there persisted, from these shifting and complex power struggles, political devices which 'effectively restrained the repressive powers of the executive, and, together with further gains won by the common law judges, made the personal and political liberties of the English propertied classes the envy of eighteenth century Europe'. The 'establishment of these ideas as the common property of the political nation . . . prepared the way for the extension of these privileges down the social scale at a later date' (Stone, 1972, p. 147). It was to require long periods of struggle, however, before the more advanced political ideas of the Levellers, such as government 'by consent' on the basis of an extended franchise, reform of parliamentary constituencies, and supremacy of the Commons, became realised, and even longer before the relevant principles became extended down to the upper ranks of labour. Certain of other Leveller interests, such as the right of an accused person to refuse to incriminate himself, contributed rather sooner to the fashioning of the rule of law, itself a crucial condition of successful agitation against superior power. Ideas and ideologies had been introduced which might lie dormant for long periods but which were susceptible of being quickened into vitality and power if and when they came into their time. Many of them were embedded in the complex intellectual and spiritual world of the Dissenting sects, some of which harboured inclinations that were later to lead towards rationalistic and deistic conceptions of the universe and thereby to support notions of 'natural rights' for all men. Republican and libertarian impulses, generated by the political and religious struggles, also for long lay mainly beneath the surface but continued to reveal their presence through a few bolder spirits until fired into new life in the later eighteenth century, when very different circumstances would again evoke cries against king, Established Church and an 'alien' landlord aristocracy.

2

The Eighteenth Century

The System in Embryo

As commerce and industry quickened further during the eighteenth century and approached the 'take-off' point of self-sustaining growth, they did so within the context of those forces that had emerged triumphant from the power struggles of the preceding century. Out of their interaction with those forces was forged the social configurations and motivations from which there later emerged Britain's industrial relations system. Under a monarchy contained by a landowning class exercising its influence through Parliament as required, there was slowly fashioned a regime of constitutionalism and the rule of the law. In its policy towards the lower orders this dominant class followed the logical implications of its preferred strategy of rule, at least to the extent that, despite legislation against worker 'combination', its minimal coercive powers and its self-legitimations precluded any sustained absolutist repression. In its absence, collectivism gathered experience and confidence. Artisans in the lower strata of the 'middle sort of people' increasingly asserted their protective restrictionist job regulation by appealing to custom, tradition and precedent, just as their social betters pursued their own protection through that common law which upheld 'English liberties'. They often drew inner support in this from their identification with another feature of the heritage: that assertion of religious independence from ecclesiastical hierarchy which took the form of the older Dissent and the newer Nonconformity. Their access to creeds which had these unintended consequences of strengthening the spirit of independence was itself furthered by the policies of an Erastian state which on expediency grounds yielded a grudging toleration of religious dissent.

Towards the end of the century, wage-earning artisans showed a renewed readiness to join with manufacturers, small masters, shopkeepers and professional men in demands for a foothold in the political nation. Thus was reproduced a version of that vertical political, social and religious bonding between strata of the 'middle sort' which in the preceding century had campaigned against crown, landed aristocracy and the episcopacy. It heralded the nineteenth-century Liberal–Labour alliance that attracted much of the craft artisan class and indelibly marked the Labour movement. Meanwhile, however, the same strata were being brought increasingly into industrial conflict with each other by the gathering tempo, growing scale and individualistic perspectives which both sides brought to bear; perspectives that had long been evident in English culture, high and low, and that were driving out the paternalism with which it had coexisted. By the end of the century certain essential ingredients and characteristics of the later industrial relations system may already be discerned. Among the interacting forces that produced them, the most salient were constitutionalism, the ideology of law and a strategy of rule which, having chosen to operate with only minimal coercive instruments, had to supplement its shedding of blood with subtler skills if it was to maintain its ascendancy.

The 'Historic Constitution'

For the next two hundred years after the 1688 Settlement the political philosophies which were to resonate most sympathetically with the predominant realities of English political behaviour and attitudes were those that emphasised individual rights and the limited role of the state.

> From Coke, in the beginning of the seventeenth century, to John Locke, at the close of that century, from ... Adam Smith in the eighteenth century down to Herbert Spencer in the nineteenth ... flow this individualistic notion of the state as a mere sum total of individuals on the one hand, and an abstract entity, on the other – [the latter] an artificial creature existing only in contemplation of law. (Commons, 1957, p. 151)

Locke 'fastened on social theory the presumption that individual self-interest is clear and compelling, while a public or a social interest is thin and unsubstantial'. It was not only Locke who sought to rationalise an emergent status quo. 'The individualism of all social theory between Locke and John Stuart Mill depended less on logic than on its agreement with the interests of the class that mainly produced it' (Sabine, 1963, pp. 529, 531).

What was the nature of this status quo? The 'historic Constitution', which common lawyers affected to believe they had simply rescued from the absolutist encroachments of the Stuarts, rested upon a limited monarchy controlled by Parliament upon lines fixed by the results of the Civil War. A central component of the rule of law was affirmed by the 1689 Declaration of Rights, which pronounced illegal the suspending of laws by royal authority without the consent of Parliament, and the power to dispense with laws. After the settlement of the succession in William and Mary there could never again be a doubt that the crown was in the keeping of Parliament if it chose to exert itself. This was not a parliament of the people seen as free and equal individuals even in the limited terms predominant among the Levellers: none of the changes in representation that had seemed pressingly probable in 1650 had materialised. Rather, it was a parliament of the 'interests', particularly the landed interest, with the growing mercantile and financial sectors serving, not the role of 'bour-geois' opposition to a 'declining' landed aristocracy, but of auxiliaries to a powerful section of a landowning stratum which was divided within itself.

Such divisions and factions made Parliament a turbulent arena to control for the purposes of carrying on 'the king's government'. Eighteenth-century Whig rule succeeded, however, in exploiting to the maximum the opportunities for control offered by the presence in the House of many MPs who received sinecures, pensions and other places of profit under the crown. A massive manipulation of patronage fused the interests of executive government with those of an aristocracy whose tap-root was in land but whose side-roots reached out to commerce, industry and finance. Walpole extended the process to embrace the bulk of the landed gentry.

> By doing so he put the nobleman and gentleman back at the heart of English political society. This was to be of tremendous importance for England's future development. The seventeenth century had witnessed the beginnings and partial success of a bourgeois revolution that came near to changing the institutions of government. In this, however, it never succeeded . . . . The power of the land and of commerce fused to create a paradise for gentlemen, for the aristocracy of birth; it thus became much easier for England to adopt an imperial authority, to rule alien peoples, and to train its ruling class for that purpose, rather than to adjust its institutions and its social system to the needs of an industrial society. (Plumb, 1979, p. 187)

England settled into a form of government which was certainly class government and which, during the eighteenth century, exhibited some of the worst abuses of class government. This does not mean that governments expressed, directly and crudely, the interests of the ruling class as its members saw them. Those moments 'in which governing institutions appear as the direct, emphatic, and unmediated organs of a "ruling class" are exceedingly rare, as well as transient' (E. P. Thompson, 1978b, p. 48). In many respects, they represented a complex of predatory interests and hangers-on from which many members and families within the ruling class were excluded. But they did not pursue their plunder unrestrained. The 'historic Constitution' served to prevent England becoming an absolutist monarchy. There was 'a genuine relationship between law and freedom' which the political settlement of 1688 had helped to preserve; there 'was no powerful bureaucracy; there was no English *droit administratif*, no *raison d'état* to override the common law or to intimidate judges and jurymen; there was no torture; above all, there was a permanent and stalwart parliamentary buffer against despotism and a House of Commons which was never at any time empty of elements of opposition' (Briggs, 1959, p. 91).

The most important long-term result of the Civil War had been the clear separation between the state and an independent sphere of private interests and the subordination of the former to the latter. 'For the first time a state had been created whose policies and activities were shaped in response to the needs and movements of civil society'. England saw the continuing development of an individualistic market order and the redefining of public interest to mean the safeguarding of private interests and the liberation of private energies. If the object of the state was to preserve liberty and promote the conditions in which civil society would flourish, then the private realm had to be respected and its major interests, whatever they were, had to be recognised as the legitimate interests of the state. In other words, the state responded 'to the movements and interests and pressures of civil society rather than seeking to lead it or dominate it' (Gamble, 1981, pp. 67, 74). It is a conception which to this day has shaped the attitudes of many senior state servants towards 'planning'.

There was nothing inevitable about the emergence of this pattern of state and society. There were still influential resistances to it. The City, for example, had long been divided; many of the great merchants who dominated the aldermanic bench in the later seventeenth century had been 'drawn to authoritative and patriarchal concepts of society, and a monarchy *à la française* would have held no terrors for them' (Plumb, 1979, p. 24). But the forces against them, both material and ideological, were gathering power with increasing speed.

Law as Legitimation and Ideology

Of towering importance in the England now emerging was the law. Accustomed as we are to seeing economics as the synthesising element in the study of society, and to emphasising economic factors in both the maintenance of stability and the generation of change, a certain imaginative effort is required when we 'return to the Age of Law and the dominance of lawyers inside and outside parliament, in the service of the country house and in the ambit of government' (Briggs, 1959, p. 91). The reason for this exceptional pre-eminence of the law is not far to seek. The law had played a major role in the long struggle against royal absolutism and now emerged as the central legitimising ideology of the eighteenth-century governing regime. 'Justice' had become an evocative word. The constitutional struggles of the seventeenth century

> had helped to establish the principles of the rule of law: that offences should be fixed, not indeterminate; that rules of evidence should be carefully observed; that the law should be administered by a bench that was both learned and honest. These achievements were essential for the protection of the gentry from royal greed and royal tyranny, and for the regulation, in the civil side of the courts, of the details of conveyancing, entailing, contracting, devising, suing and releasing. (D. Hay, 1977, p. 32)

'Take law away, and the royal prerogative, or the presumption of the aristocracy, might flood back upon their properties and lives; take law away and the string which tied together their lands and marriages would fall apart' (E. P. Thompson, 1977, p. 264).

Since the authenticity and legitimacy of the regime rested so heavily on the rule of law, supporters were committed to defending it and propagating its principles. Immense efforts were made to project the image of a ruling class which was itself subject to the rule of law, and whose legitimacy rested upon the equity and universality of those legal forms (ibid., p. 263). To match reality to the image took some time. 'The power of the seventeenth century gentry was sanctioned by violence – riding out against their enemies, hamstringing their neighbour's dogs, beating their farmers' sons, or shooting down their riotous neighbours' (Plumb, 1979, p. 21). This style persisted well into the eighteenth century, but by the end was no longer the style of the true gentleman. There were further implications. Governments that rested their legitimacy on the rule of law could not afford to be too nonchalant towards charges of 'one law for the rich, another for the poor'. Slowly there developed the notion that England's governments must project an image of being evenhanded between the classes. Given the growth of 'principled' Opposition, governments began reluctantly to act by this notion, sometimes only nominally, but sometimes, as we shall see, in practical terms that enlarged the scope for collective action among wage-earners.

The law itself, however, was not without its problems. However strongly Coke might assert, early in the seventeenth century, 'the inviolable supremacy of the Common Law' as against 'innovating statutes', Parliament was hardly likely to agree and there continued into the eighteenth century a controversy in the law books concerning 'the relative supremacy of parliament on the one hand, and on the other the fundamental law of the land as handed down in the Common Law' (Webb and Webb, 1963, p. 457). Parliament won, but the fact that there remained two sources of legal pronouncement, of legal judgement and of legal innovation – statute and judge-made – was to prove of central importance in the later evolution of trade union and labour law. Meanwhile the stature of common law, the fundamental role it had played in England's historical development, and its significance in particular for the landed classes who emerged as politically dominant, had resulted in its imparting its own special character to the English political style and language. Central to this was the automatic respect granted to precedent. 'By invoking customary rights the British had long been used to defending themselves against the claims of sovereigns or of churches which would have deprived them of their liberties (or of their privileges) in the name of some higher good' (B. W. Hill, 1975, p. 55). It was a defensive style that had never been confined to the landed classes, and now reached down to the artisans and small masters of the traditional crafts.

The Strategy of Rule: Attitudes to Army and Police

As against common law, civil law was making little progress. By Continental standards England barely had anything recognisable as a central governing presence and state apparatus and, as already noted, the dominant preference was heavily against active interventionist rule. The central bureaucracy was small, sketchy and 'so riddled with sinecurism, parasitism and clientage that it scarcely offered an independent presence' (E. P. Thompson, 1974a, p. 403). In any case, its writ did not run far in the localities. Early Stuart attempts to create a monarchical bureaucratic machine had foundered on the rock of local rule by the gentry, and a summary end to 'arbitrary interference' with 'local liberties' had been one of the results of the dismissal of the Stuart dynasty. For more than a hundred years from that date, crown and Parliament adopted a policy of indifference as to what the various local governing authorities did or abstained from doing, with the result that during the eighteenth century there was 'nothing that could be regarded, either in theory or practice, as a system of local government', simply 'a confused network of local customs and the common law, of canon law and royal decrees or charters, interspersed with occasional and unsystematised parliamentary statutes' (Webb and Webb, 1963, pp. 351, 353). Presiding over this network in the rural areas were unpaid spare-time justices of the peace, who usually combined economic, social and political power in their localities. The mode of social control exercised by them and their fellow gentry still contained much that could be called paternalist. Though some of it was a matter of mere gestures, postures and rhetoric, there could still be found, in varying degrees, a measure of genuine protection and patronage. Limited though it might be, it was important in helping to maintain the structure of habituated authority relations – a structure illustrated in Flora Thompson's *Lark Rise to Candleford*, which captures, in a late-nineteenth-century example, the full picture of, on the one side, assumptions of superiority, rightful power and 'duty' and, on the other, a complex, contradictory and often alternating mixture of deference and scepticism, respect and resentment.

The caring side of the paternalist equation presented itself to the landowning nobility and the greater and lesser gentry – and indeed to some of those who ran manufacturing businesses – as one of the obligations bearing upon those of higher rank. These obligations were strictly practical and down-to-earth. There was little in the empirical, common-sense texture of English institutions and culture to encourage grand metaphysical theorising about transcendent state purposes to which individuals must submit in a realisation of their 'real' selves. Yet in trying to characterise English society, emphasis on that pursuit of individual self-interest which was being more widely unleashed must not obscure the fact that the English technique of rule needed some spirit of obligation if it was to work. The institutions of a limited monarchy needed aristocrats and gentry to man the Lords and Commons, conducting the king's government but containing him if necessary at the same time. Gentry rule in the localities needed squires and parsons to discharge the unpaid functions of the bench of magistrates. There were, of course, fat pickings for some at the higher levels of this structure, in terms of patronage, place and sinecure. It was Walpole's skill in handling such sanctions that contributed greatly to the stability which, the longer it persisted, made gentlemen increasingly hesitant to put at risk a system which had demonstrably succeeded in preserving their property and status. Yet there were not sufficiently attractive pickings for everyone, and a significant number of the country gentlemen disdained even to pursue them (Namier, 1957, pp. 4–6). Something more was needed. If aristocracy and gentry were to govern themselves and the country, they had to keep each other up to the mark in terms of active participation. Building on old traditions of service due from those holding land under the king, they sought to promote among themselves a sense of the public responsibilities bearing upon men of status and property, especially landed property. The ethic passed from existing members of the ruling class to new entrants, and from fathers to sons. A renewed and refurbished notion of service was to have its effect on the development of working-class organisation late in the next century.

Meanwhile, parochially based and parochially directed as it was, the rule of the country gentry rarely had direct links with the central state powers or with the armed forces of the crown, and thereupon hangs an important point. Some kind of collective control over the army was considered by many of the gentry to be essential for persons of their rank. Those who had felt the need to turn out and fight for their Parliament against the king's forces did not wish to have to do so again and, especially after the experience of Cromwell's professional army under near-dictatorship conditions, were resolved to retain reserve powers. They achieved this with, *inter alia*, the Mutiny Act of 1689, which funded the army but had to be renewed by Parliament each year, thereby preserving a legal fiction that there was not, strictly speaking, a standing army but one engaged and paid for one year only. The fact that annual endorsement became virtually automatic and sanctioned a standing peace-time army does not detract from the significance of the reserve power, which was always available for use if required against any dangerous renewal of royal presumption. Moreover

> an ineradicable prejudice forbade the quartering of the troops in barracks. That the separation between the life of the soldiers and the life of the civil population might be minimized, British soldiers throughout the whole of the eighteenth century were billeted in private lodgings . . . This was one of those peculiar usages which distinguished England from the rest of Europe and satisfied the nation it was free. (Halévy, 1961a, pp. 70–1)

The system of purchasing commissions and promotion, introduced in the early eighteenth century and not abolished until 1871, was felt to render the maintenance of a standing army 'much more safe than it would otherwise be' by keeping its control in the hands of established men of property and out of the hands of mere careerist and possibly independent-spirited professionals (Guttsman, ed., 1969, p. 270). Taken along with the structuring of the local county militia (Halévy, 1961a, pp. 67–71), these were indications that whereas the navy was regarded as constitutionally inert – it 'could neither defend a government against rebellion, nor cause a revolution, nor effect a *coup d'état*' – the army was viewed with a suspicion that had already hardened out into an anti-militarist tradition. It was a tradition cherished at all social levels. Not until the Napoleonic Wars was there any weakening in the popular cries of 'No barracks' and 'No standing army' – at least if a standing army was indispensable it must not be a large one (ibid., pp. 47, 73).

The subject is of considerable importance for the present inquiry, for if major sections of the ruling order were anxious, in their own interests, to restrain the executive's access to coercive forces and were in no way concerned to build up the army's role, prestige and identification with the state, there were implications for the ruling order's strategy of control over the 'plebs'. Especially was this so since the suspicion of large military forces was reinforced by obstinate resistance to the organisation of a state police throughout the country. England 'had an almost perversely in-effective system of police' (Hayter, 1978, p. 1). By their struggle against the king and his ministers

> and their final reduction of the central government to almost nothing, the landed gentry had at the same time deprived themselves of the help of the central government to suppress popular disorder. Without the assistance of a large and well-organised body of police, what force was at the disposal of the magistrates isolated on their several estates, and swamped in the mass of agricultural labourers or factory hands? We have but to read Wesley's diary to realize how impotent were the guardians of law and order in the English country districts. (Halévy, 1961a, pp. 43–4)

This is, perhaps, a sweeping judgement, but even a milder version has important implications for the technique of rule. These can be explored by recalling an earlier discussion. To the extent that the dominant party in a paternalist control system fails to honour its self-assumed obligations it sacrifices any hope of evoking reciprocal obedience – a hope which, in any case, assumes that the dominated party accepts and legitimises the relationship. If domination continues to be its purpose it must lean on straight coercion, swathed about, perhaps, with paternalist rhetoric to assuage the consciences of itself and influential onlookers. The eighteenth-century English regime was therefore in a cleft stick. Full and genuine reciprocal paternalism – that is, something a good deal more than 'limited observance' – would be expensive and burdensome. Yet coercion required a domestically deployed army and police on a scale which stirred distaste even among the rulers themselves. What was the escape from this dilemma? It has been suggested that in certain kinds of situation a different form of 'structured reciprocity' emerged.

To the eighteenth-century populace, 'the larger outlines of power, station in life, political authority appeared to be as inevitable and irrever-sible as the earth and sky'. This did not preclude them from reacting against the 'immediate daily humiliations of dependency' with resentment, surreptitious acts of protest or revenge, and sometimes popular disturbances (E. P. Thompson 1974a, p. 388). Thompson argues that eighteenth-century rulers sometimes showed a surprising degree of indulgence towards the turbulence of the crowd; of permissiveness towards a 'robust, unchristian popular culture' and of caution in handling popular disturbances. This, in his view, indicated a readiness to grant the lower orders a certain leeway of disorderly behaviour and independent culture through which they could release tensions and grievances and thereby come to terms, of a sort, with life as they found it. In other words, the price paid by the aristocracy and gentry for a limited monarchy, a weak state and inadequate mechanisms for enforcing order and conventional cultural norms was the 'licence of the crowd'. This was the central structural context of reciprocity between rulers and ruled. It appears to come from a similar cast of mind as that which, in Tudor times, believed a welfare system, albeit minimal and grudging, to be 'the only viable alternative to a local bureaucracy and a standing army as an instrument for social control' (Stone, 1972, pp. 76–7).

The licence of the crowd was one thing, however; quite another were rioting 'mobs' on the rampage in response to food shortages and high prices, or in conflicts with employers over wage rates. Denied any other satisfactory form of settlement, artisans might well turn to violence against employers' property, in the process dubbed by Hobsbawm 'collective bargaining by riot'. Here much depended on the temper of the local magistrates and the availability in the neighbourhood of armed forces. Lacking such resources, and given the absence of an effective police, magistrates could do little but read the Riot Act and hope for the best. A determined group of magistrates with a troop of horse quartered nearby, however, might turn promptly to repression, with shooting of rioters, hangings and sentences of transportation. But often there were equally prompt reductions of prices and the issue of licences to import wheat. Even the availability of troops did not guarantee the effective enforcement of control.

> For every vigorous, respected, or over-zealous magistrate in English disturbances, there could usually be found another whose fatuity, arrogance, timidity or caution would estrange supporters or confuse and paralyze the constables and military commanders at his disposal. Moreover, the antiquated machinery of order, in particular the anomalies surrounding the operation of the Riot Act, led to endless confusion; and the Englishman's boasted 'right of resistance' to oppression, particularly when the parliamentary opposition chose to exploit it, might almost be construed as a right of rebellion. (Rudé, 1981, p. 263)

These were important formative influences upon the nature, strength and self-confidence of labour protest. Also relevant was the remarkable anxiety exhibited by politicians, magistrates and army commanders as to the legality of using troops against civil disturbance. From the early years of George I's reign, and into the nineteenth century, the Secretary at War repeatedly sought assurances from the law officers of the crown on the legality of using the military and on the limits of their power in confrontations with rioters. Riot duty was detested both by lower ranks and by their officers, in some cases from sympathy with the rioters, but more especially because of the legal uncertainties and because neither the common soldier nor the officer had been trained for it. 'There was no profit or glory in it, but rather a good chance of being insulted in the press, attacked in parliament, or pursued in a court of law for his actions' (Hayter, 1978, pp. 3, 4, 29). These were not the ways to create a cowed and submissive populace.

There was, however, another form of social violence different from rioting over food prices, wages, turnpike tolls, or press gangs: a form against which a landed ruling order could be expected to be particularly savage and vengeful. This struck symbolic as well as practical blows at landed property and sense of security. The hunting of deer, the poaching of hares and fish, the burning of hay-ricks, the malicious wounding of cattle – these and similar acts against the landed order were countered in 1723 with the Black Act. This created fifty new capital offences (and lasted for a hundred years), thereby constituting some evidence of the long decline in the effectiveness of old methods of class control and discipline and their replacement by others. In place of the whipping-post, the stocks, manorial and corporate controls and the physical harrying of vagabonds, economists advocated the discipline of low wages and starvation, and lawyers increasingly 'the sanction of death' (E. P. Thompson, 1977, pp. 206–7).

Yet the actual application of this punitive code, and of others like it, shows how even in a violent and brutal century, the strategy of rule embodied mitigating features which avoided straining vertical social bonds to the point of breakdown. Administration of these new codes was less bloody than their letter. Legal authorities from the justice of the peace to the high court judge made frequent use of the discretionary prerogative of mercy and pardon as part of the tissue of paternalism. It was an important self-justification of the ruling class that once the poor had been chastised sufficiently to protect property, it was the duty of a gentleman to protect 'his people'. The political and social power of England's ruling class 'was reinforced daily by bonds of obligation on one side and condescension on the other, as prosecutors, gentlemen and peers decided to invoke the law or agreed to show mercy . . . the power of gentlemen and peers to punish or forgive worked . . . to maintain the fabric of obedience, gratitude and deference' (D. Hay, 1977, pp. 47–9).

Evidence also reveals that precisely because the law was of massive importance as ideology and as legitimation of the regime in eighteenth-century England its principles and logic sometimes had to be upheld in ways which limited the regime's power. Of course, in general 'the law did mediate existent class relations to the advantage of the rulers; not only is this so, but as the century advanced the law became a superb instrument by which these rulers were able to impose new definitions of property to their even greater advantage.' Yet it was inherent in the very nature of the weapon which they had selected for their own self-defence against royal absolutism that it could not be reserved for the exclusive use of their own class. The law entailed principles of equity and universality which had to be extended to all sorts and degrees of men if the ideological appeal to the majestic impartiality of the law was to remain convincing. Again and again legal forms imposed inhibitions upon the actions of rulers. Not only were the rulers (indeed, the ruling class as a whole) inhibited by their own rules of law against the exercise of direct unmediated force (arbitrary imprisonment, the employment of troops against the crowd, torture, and those other conveniences of power with which we are all conversant), but they also believed enough in these rules, and in their accompanying ideological rhetoric, to allow, in certain limited areas, the law itself to be a genuine forum within which certain kinds of class conflict were fought out. (E. P. Thompson, 1977, pp. 264–265)

This strategy and style of rule was hardly a characteristic of English rulers *per se*. It was not conspicuous in, for example, Ireland and distant colonial possessions. It was the product of a total social system and its history. Yet within the bounds of that system, as Thompson points out, it was not without its effects on ruling behaviour. These effects were reinforced by the very existence of that independent legal order called forth by the rule of law. The profession of the law had its practitioners at every social level from the middle to the very highest social and political ranks, and to describe them as consciously deploying humbug in a calculated strategy for upholding a particular regime is to fall victim to reductionism. Such was already the force and indeed almost mystical quality of the ideology of law that the self-respect and deepest convictions of many practitioners had become bound up with it, and in such a situation a legitimising ideology can become a free-wheeling social force in its own right. Judges, magistrates and law officers of the crown might sometimes feel in particular cases that an assertion of the integrity of the law, to which they were personally and professionally committed, must take precedence over the immediate convenience of particular employers and property-owners.

It might be replied that some evidence of independence was precisely what was necessary to establish the rule of law, biased as it normally was anyway in favour of the rich and powerful, as a legitimising force. Supporters of the status quo could point to it as a just and fair system, while in fact its many shams and inequities enabled exploitation to continue behind a façade of impartiality. Power was thus consolidated, legitimacy enhanced and revolutionary movements inhibited. The argument is valid, yet incomplete. The consolidation and validation of the regime were, after all, being secured through a genuine extension of constitutional limitations on power; limitations which time and effort might succeed in extending further. The English situation had begun, in other words, to demonstrate how a regime that seeks to maintain its ascendancy with the legitimising aid of such concepts as liberty, individual rights and due process of law will be likely to find these concepts being used as rallying cries against itself by aggrieved groups among those it is ruling. Only a determination to ignore these actual and potential gains can depict the eighteenth-century situation as one of purely cynical and totally effective upper-class hegemony.

The paradox is of an importance which can hardly be exaggerated for English development, for the same points will be relevant again later when we discuss the emergence of political democracy and of trade unionism and collective bargaining. We must say of these what we must say of the rule of law. Only to the degree that they were seen and experienced as genuinely limiting the power of dominant groups and securing some protection and satisfaction to the dominated could they serve a valuable ideological and legitimising function. Yet what this function ultimately served was the protection of the essential core structures of the status quo from revolutionary attack.

The 'Free-Born Englishman'

The price that had to be paid for this protection has already been partly indicated. Concepts central to the rule of law could be turned against individuals and groups within the ruling class by the relatively powerless. But the legitimations invoked by the eighteenth-century regime ranged, as we have seen, wider than this, and these too were filtering down in ways relevant to our main theme.

By the end of the century the notion of the 'free-born Englishman' and his birthright had fully passed into the stock of the common man's political and social ideas. Belief in the equality of rich and poor before the law appears to have been a source of authentic popular congratulation. There was also a consciousness of limits 'beyond which the Englishman was not prepared to be "pushed around", and . . . limits beyond which authority did not dare to go . . . The stance of the common Englishman was not so much democratic, in any positive sense, as anti-absolutist. He felt himself to be an individualist, with few affirmative rights, but protected by the laws against the intrusion of arbitrary power.' The freedoms and the protections were not negligible. Contained within the rhetoric of liberty and the 'birthright' were notions

> which Old Corruption felt bound to flatter and yet were to prove dangerous to it in the long run. Freedom from absolutism (the constitutional monarchy), freedom from arbitrary arrest, trial by jury, equality before the law, the freedom of the home from arbitrary entrance and search, some limited liberty of thought, of speech, and of conscience, the vicarious participation in liberty (or in its semblance) afforded by the right of parliamentary opposition and by elections and election tumults (although the people had no vote they had the right to parade, huzza and jeer on the hustings), as well as freedom to travel, trade, and sell one's own labour.

Given this political and legal structure and the culture and ideology which percolated down and fused with the plebs' own culture, there need hardly be surprise that the common people shared, though from a more personal point of view, the distrust of militarism manifested by their masters. 'No institution was as much hated, in the eighteenth century, as the press-gang. A standing army was deeply distrusted . . . The profession of a soldier was held to be dishonourable.' Similarly, 'resistance to an effective police force continued well into the nineteenth century . . . any centralized force with larger powers' was seen as a system of tyranny and the destruction of liberty. In a 'quite surprising consensus of opinion . . . local rights and customs were cherished against the encroachment of the State by gentry and common people alike' (E. P. Thompson, 1968, pp. 86–90).

Versions of the Norman Yoke myth retained their potency. Since these were couched in terms of an alien ruling aristocracy imposing itself upon Saxon freedoms it was as easy and natural for late-eighteenth as for seventeenth-century radicals to use as a rallying cry the concept and rhetoric of patriotism: '"our country", because we work it with our hands'. And along with the many other grievances and resentments against the aristocracy went the charge that they were tainted with cosmopolitanism. Nearly two centuries later an influential English social-ist, standing in the line of an indigenous English strain represented by such men as William Morris, Robert Blatchford and R. H. Tawney, only more Puritan and Jacobinical than they, was to show himself keenly alive to these distant voices of an old patriotic radicalism (Orwell, 1982, pp. 35–70, and Crick's introduction, p. 19).

Customary Rights and Plebeian Independence

The popular notion of the free-born Englishman is important in recon-ciling the fact of a still-significant application of paternalist control with the abundant evidence that 'popular traditions of independence and dissent were deeply rooted in the cultures of many localities'. Labouring people were certainly, in some respects, deferential towards authority and resigned to their positions of subordination. But it is in full accordance with the theory of paternalist control that if the expected behaviours are not forthcoming from superiors, subordinates feel released from their own obligations of deference and submission. In eighteenth-century England the legitimacy of authority of gentlemen, 'both in their own eyes and (especially) in the eyes of the people, depended heavily on the performance of certain paternalist duties that were still widely assumed to be inherent in the exercise of power'. Whether, given the collapse of this legitimacy, the subordinated groups express their release from obligation in their actual behaviour depends partly on the spiritedness of their resentment and partly on the disciplinary and coercive powers at the disposal of superiors.

The uncertainty of the latter has already been noted. The spiritedness of the plebs, on the other hand, when they deemed their rights and custom-ary expectations to have been denied was often considerable. It is here that traditions of the free-born Englishman become important. They provided artisans and the labouring poor with a frame of reference that nerved them intermittently, or even much of the time, to assert a spirit of independence against their masters.

Much of the irreverence, unruliness and insubordination that gentlemen complained of was found in London, where theft, violence, street mugg-ings and the insolence of the lower orders were constant preoccupations of the respectable. But manufacturing towns were coming to resemble it and in many country districts, too, 'the exercise of established authority was tenuous, uncertain, and often ineffectual'. In such communities as small market towns and 'closed' parishes dominated by a single large landowner 'we detect evidence of firm social discipline, outward deference and quiescence', but elsewhere 'we uncover a social reality of dissent, frequent social conflict and plebeian independence'. Nowhere could be reckoned to be wholly free from the possibility of disorder and tumult, focusing on such issues as 'the alleged abuse of magisterial authority, the destruction of certain traditional popular liberties or the imposition of some new claim on the individual by the state (Malcolmson, 1981, pp. 109–11, 132).

A frequent cause of popular protest was the failure of those in authority to discharge what were deemed to be their paternalistic duties, particularly with respect to the supply and price of food – the most common precipitant of social conflict in eighteenth-century England. Local justices were expected to uphold the traditional conventions of market relations, especially at times of scarcity, that is, 'to protect the interests of the small consumers, to seek out and punish malpractices in marketing, to enforce the laws against profiteering and, if necessary, to regulate the prices of essential foodstuffs'. Some did so; many did not, either from simple neglect or because a 'free' market in agricultural produce, unmoderated by moral or social considerations, was extending its range. But if the authorities refused to recognise 'the rights of the poor to a basic subsistence and to protection against the threat of hunger', what could be done? According to the plebs, 'it was legitimate to take direct and unofficial action in order to ensure that justice would be done and that the proper procedures for the marketing of food would be duly observed'. Hence the 'food riot', aimed primarily at seizing supplies and imposing 'just' or 'reasonable' prices. The view from above saw these collective actions in the marketplace as simply undisciplined, formless and lawless risings, a stance adopted by many historians for whom they have ranked only as blind instinctive reactions to hunger or the fear of it. But the character of this collective behaviour 'was vitally determined by custom, inherited expectations and moral evaluation'; its objectives usually, though not always, selective and clearly defined and pursued in a disciplined and reasonably discriminating manner. At its heart lay 'a keen sense of justice – a sense of correct morality being violated, and of injustice being tolerated or encouraged' (ibid., pp. 116–22).

This ability of subordinated groups to sustain an independent set of moral and social criteria which they brought to bear upon the behaviour of their masters was a central factor not only in food riots, pro-smuggling activities, anti-game law tensions, enclosure disturbances and resistance to turnpike tolls, but also in the emergence of robust and spirited collective action in the world of work. In sustaining these independent criteria they drew support from traditional English freedoms, from a wider body of popular culture within which they were embedded, and from the general force exerted within this common law society by precedent, custom and practice, or what could plausibly be presented as custom and practice after a judicious rewriting of history or redefinition of terms. The popular culture of the plebs was in many important ways 'substantially independent of the culture of polite society', but in other important ways drew upon it. It included customary practices which were a powerful source of discipline and moral regulation within their own stratum, and also many which were directed outwards towards their rulers, including employers. Such practices assumed special importance in those spheres of life in which law, official priorities, or formal provision failed to satisfy the needs or values of plebeian life and experience. 'Most customs were both restrictive and permissive: they specified what could be done and . . . helped to clarify the boundaries between what was acceptable and what was unacceptable . . .' Above all, custom 'provided a critical source of self-defence in a highly unequal society, for it was one of the normative weapons of the weak against the strong, one of the ways in which power was disciplined and concessions enjoyed. Customary practices, in short, were vital components of the people's cultural repertory' (ibid., p. 106).

As we shall see (pp. 63–7), the apprenticed artisans of recognised crafts especially benefited, in terms of self-protection at work, from this body of independent-spirited customary justice, for it supplemented and reinforced an already strong heritage relating to their own crafts. These were the combined advantages that enabled them, in many cases, to sustain a collective presence and even continuous formal organisation. Workers in those plebeian occupations that lacked craft status and privileges were rarely, as yet, strong enough for that, so their spirit of customary justice could only express itself in the form of intermittent protests against specially unacceptable policies imposed from above – though these were apt to be accompanied in the more capitalistic trades by the sort of continuous zero-sum relations described by Tucker (see pp. 1–2 above).

Despite what some have seen as a considerable degree of cultural assimilation later by Victorian middle-class values, the British organised working classes never lost this capacity for the collective assertion of customs and principles which diverge sharply from those preferred by their masters. Already, in their nationalist pride at being free-born Englishmen, together with their disinclination to accept full integration into the values and priorities of their masters, the artisans and other active groups of workers were exhibiting traits which much of the British wage- and lower-salary-earning classes have continued to display ever since.

The Decline of the Paternalist System

Customary economic morality among sizeable sections of the plebs covered not only the supply and price of foodstuffs, but also the level of pay. There was, along with the 'just' price, the 'just' wage which should provide certain minimum standards of subsistence. According to this view, labour should not be seen as a commodity, and market forces of supply and demand should not be allowed to determine, without limit or restraint, the level of wage rates. As we have seen, there had long been statutory provision covering the local fixing of rates and this, along with kindred legislation now passing into disuse, had become invested with a heavily idealised aura and even misinterpretation as the practice and ideology of unregulated private enterprise gathered vigour during the century. Two sharply contrasted moralities had long been in conflict: 'a traditional medieval catholic economic morality on the defensive, a Protestant and capitalist ethic on the offensive' (C. Hill, 1968, p. 215); and the latter gained strength from the outcome of the power struggles of the seventeenth century. Yet the former was still far from dead. The very fact that the expanding capitalism of commerce, finance and industry was now being assimilated into a polity still dominated by the landed aristocracy and country gentry meant that the paternalist and patriarchal control system must continue to carry some weight, even if sections of the aristocracy were deeply involved in that capitalism – though usually at a fastidious distance. Paternalism therefore persisted, being in some eyes too valuable a mode of control to dispense with lightly.

Nevertheless, continuing signs of decay were visible – for example, in the gathering disappearance – or translation into monetary payments – of non-monetary rewards and favours, still 'widely pervasive in the early part of the century'. 'This is the century which sees the erosion of half-free forms of labour, the decline of living-in, the final extinction of labour services and the advance of free, mobile wage labour' (E. P. Thompson, 1974a, pp. 382, 384). Such non-monetary forms had been a major support of paternalist control in that they appeared not so much as economic relations between contracting parties but rather as social relations between persons. Statutory regulation, too, became moribund. Wage assessment by local justices and town authorities was applied in parts of the country fairly regularly down to the 1700s, less frequently down to the 1760s, and hardly at all after that. The reasons for decay of the system remain under debate (Minchinton, ed., 1972), but since evidence suggests the increasing difficulty experienced by legal rates, after the mid-seventeenth century, in restraining market rates, it would not be surprising if justices increasingly came to feel, as market pressures percolated more widely throughout the country, that their task had become, quite simply, futile. Moreover, there is evidence that legal decisions in the late seventeenth century deterred justices from making and enforcing assessments (Kelsall, 1972, pp. 192–3), and these may well have been the outcome of common law courts pursuing their long-standing disposition to regard all guild and statutory regulations as unacceptable hindrances to freedom of individual contract and enterprise.

Nevertheless, successive groups of artisans in a range of industries who came under growing competitive pressures invoked the old legislation, petitioning for the authorities to fix a 'convenient proportion of wages'. Needless to say what they sought were not maxima but minima, and there had been enough ambiguity about the intention and the local application of the old statutes – certainly as wishful popular interpretation saw them – to add conviction to the attempts. Sometimes they were successful, but diminishingly so as the century wore on. Among them were the Gloucestershire clothworkers, who after a brief success in 1756 lasting only one year suffered a vigorous counter-attack by the employers which resulted in 1757 in the industry being specifically exempted from wage assessment.

It was an important stage in a long dying fall, yet although the turning tide of influential opinion was unmistakable there remained an undertow of older dispositions which could still have its effect, more especially when serious disorder threatened. No doubt, too, the accidents of attendance in the House could, given the divided state of opinion, result in apparent inconsistencies. These included a parliamentary majority, eleven years after the clothmaking exemption, for regulations governing the wages and working hours of London journeymen tailors, and five years later (1773), for protection of the Spitalfields weavers, who after some particularly serious rioting enjoyed a measure of protection from imports and a floor to earnings. Even in the eighteenth century there were 'special cases'. But it is relevant that, as yet, the House of Commons was largely innocent of any forceful theoretical and ideological construction which supported and legitimised the emergent trends, and in such a situation public men were more open to the continuing influence of traditional policies, especially when social stability and public order seemed immediately at stake.

Parallel with this decay of wage assessment went the further decline of guild and statutory regulation over the craft trades with respect to apprenticeship and related matters. 'The town authorities no longer cared to enforce the old guild regulations and the bench showed much indulgence to transgressors' (Mantoux, 1928, p. 463). Here again, the common-law courts were usually only too ready to speed these processes of decline. In a judgement of 1756 Lord Mansfield described the Elizabethan Statute of Artificers as 'a penal law in restraint of natural right and contrary to the common law of the kingdom' (Marshall, 1950, p. 17). Common lawyers had always disapproved, in particular, of the apprenticeship clause; Blackstone considered it bad law and in a series of case law decisions its use had become progressively restricted. Eighteenth-century justices were encouraged to adapt it to the newer 'needs' of an expanding economy and it was not applied at all to trades which did not exist in 1563 (Rule, 1981, pp. 107–8). Yet here, too, the old statutes were not being allowed to die. As with downward pressure on wages, any example of the degradation of apprenticeship and other craft conditions was seen by the plebs as failure on the part of the authorities to discharge their regulative obligations; as failure to respect popular rights. And if gentlemen forgot their duties they must be reminded of them. 'What happened was that, as each trade in turn felt the effect of the new capitalist competition, the journeymen, and often also the smaller employers, would petition for redress, usually demanding the prohibition of the new machines, the enforcement of a seven years' apprenticeship, or the maintenance of the old limitation of the number of boys to be taught by each employer' (Webb and Webb, 1920, p. 53). Should the authorities persist in their neglect men felt justified in taking matters into their own hands and exerting direct collective pressure upon the masters. And if peaceful approaches failed, a certain amount of violence to property was felt to be in order, such as window-smashing or damage to employers' houses and work premises. Such was the tendency, for increasingly typical of authority's responses to petitions for redress was that of the parliamentary Committee of Inquiry of 1753 which declared that the statutes of the

Company of Stocking Frame Knitters, imposing the standard seven-year apprenticeship, forbidding the employment of foreigners, and laying down other restrictive conditions had become 'contrary to reason and derogatory to the liberty of English subjects'. Such statutes were 'tending to a monopoly', were 'discouraging the manufacture and destroying the trade of the kingdom' (Mantoux, 1928, p. 465; Kellett, 1958, p. 392).

Adam Smith and the Individualist Creed

The self-confidence of the emergent forces was reinforced by the publication in 1776 of Adam Smith's *Essay on the Nature and Causes of the Wealth of Nations*. What lent this book its impact was its systematic integration and formulation of ideas and lines of thought that were not in themselves new; but which Smith brought together in a powerful theoretical framework. This gave his readers an interpretation of their society that often accorded with their values and that crystallised, sharpened and rationalised their perceptions of the way it was developing. It gave them a picture of an economic sphere in which the rational pursuit of self-interest was the predominant motivation of every individual. These individuals related themselves to each other through free and fair market mechanisms which eventuated in contracts and ensured that the outcome of this individualistic competition was beneficial to all. As Reisman suggests in his commentary on Smith, the impartial market excluded all the traditional enemies of thrusting, private-enterprise English entrepreneurship – 'the whim of tyrannical lords, superstitious priests, despotic monarchs or inefficient bureaucrats' (Reisman, 1976, p. 179). It was the adumbration of an economic liberalism which was hostile to state interference because it inhibited the full realisation of material possibilities, and which separated economics from ethics because their juncture meant the imposition of rules fatal to individual success. Spokesmen for the new order popularised – and often vulgarised – these ideas in articles, pamphlets and lectures.

Adam Smith's authority has been invoked on innumerable occasions – even by modern Conservative Cabinet ministers – to legitimise the modern economy of massive industrial corporations and the immense power they wield, so it may seem puzzling as to why the liberal thrust of which his work was one expression should have captured a growing following that included not only the promptings of material self-interest but also the aspirations of an idealistic quest for human liberation. The answer is that the 'motive and inspiration of the liberal movement of the eighteenth century had been the attack on privilege; and when its main ideas were being hammered out, that attack was the one supremely necessary thing'. Smith and the other great individualists of the century 'shot their arrows against the abuses of their day, not of ours . . . when they formulated the new philosophy, the obvious abuse was not the power wielded by the owners of capital over populations unable to work without their permission; it was the network of customary and legal restrictions' which impeded the entrepreneur of relatively modest size who sought to exercise his abilities. 'The grand enemy of the age was monopoly; the battlecry with which enlightenment marched against it was the abolition of privilege; its ideal was a society where each man had free access to the economic opportunities which he could use and enjoy the wealth which by his efforts he had created' (Tawney, 1961, pp. 22–3).

It was an enlightenment which crystallised its ideas while the new industrial order was still young and its effects unknown. Included among those ideas were not only doctrines of private property and freedom of individual contract which would later be manipulated and twisted beyond recognition by joint-stock corporate enterprise and legal attacks on trade unionism, but also doctrines of self-realisation and human dignity which would inspire generations of radicals seeking emancipation, for example, from the social, civic and educational disabilities bearing upon Dissenters and Nonconformists, radicals and freethinkers. Unless we appreciate the width and richness of the liberal cause we may find difficulty in understanding how there came to march behind its banners not only employers and professional men but also wage-earning artisans and other workers attracted by principles as well as by material interests in, for example, free trade. However much wage-earners might look back to a supposedly golden age of guild or state protection when they contemplated their workplace predicament, there were many respects in which they looked forward to a condition of individual rights and liberation.

The Labour Market as a Coercive Instrument

Smith was not as successful as many others in deceiving himself about some features of the emergent society that he was seeking to describe and interpret. His views as to whether there could be said to be an objective exploitation of the labourer by the capitalist and landowner have been described as ambiguous (Reisman, 1976, pp. 167–73). There was no ambiguity, however, about his appraisal of the subjective responses offered by the wage-earner to the economic and social system in which he increasingly found himself. Smith fully expected him to have a sense of exploitation. The observation is important as indicating how a perceptive and knowledgeable observer saw the emergent state of labour relations. As Reisman comments, for all the supposed fairness of the market mechanism 'the worker might still refuse to look upon his employer as his brother. Instead he might insist on perceiving society as a Hobbesian jungle in which relative shares depend not on (marginal) productivity or some other absolute criterion, but simply on power.' To use Smith's own words, all trade is 'a species of warfare . . . What are the common wages of labour, depends everywhere upon the contract usually made by those two parties, whose interests are by no means the same. The workmen desire to get as much, the masters to give as little as possible' (ibid., pp. 178–9).

Down to our own day there have always been certain situations and certain levels of discussion in which particular employers or their spokesmen have been prepared to make this frank avowal of a clash of class interest. But because it appears to justify class conflict it could never be part of any considered ideology of the status quo. Nor were the dominant strata likely to build into their ideology Smith's recognition that the power advantage in wage bargaining clearly lay with the capitalists. In his words, the law 'authorizes or at least does not prohibit their combinations, while it prohibits those of the workmen. We have no acts of parliament against combining to lower the price of work; but many against combining to raise it.' And he argued, too, that the capitalist was more strongly placed than the worker in industrial disputes (ibid., p. 179).

What was plucked from Smith, therefore, were those sections which offered systematic intellectual and moral justifications of policies, practices, values and relationships which had been hardening out for some considerable time. By the end of the century those who seized eagerly on these justifications were rewriting history so as to associate traditional English liberties with Smith's explicit identification of individual and general interests. Typical of many petitions presented to Parliament was one from employers in the wool industry in 1794. The wool combers had appealed for protection against a new labour-saving combing machine. In their counter-appeal the employers declared it to be

> the general right of the subject, which the wisdom of the legislative has for ages admitted, that he be at liberty to exercise his art and profession in that way which appears to be the most conducive to his interest, nor offends against the law or the right of others; that of his interest he is himself in all instances the fittest judge, and that from this unfettered and well directed pursuit of individual interest has arisen, and ever will arise, the greatest aggregate of national benefit. (Mantoux, 1928, p. 417)

The statement reveals how those seeking to exploit expanding economic opportunities had seized upon certain long-standing features of the English institutional, religious and cultural scene in search of legitimation and support. Themselves partly shaped by these features in their attitudes towards their fellows, their work and the state, they were developing and sharpening them and making them increasingly explicit.

By the end of the eighteenth century such utterances were coming to be commonplace among those who deemed themselves in the vanguard of economic practice or theory. Edmund Burke, in 1795, was only presenting such commonplaces when he wrote that

> labour is a commodity, and, as such, an article of trade . . . when any commodity is carried to market, it is not the necessity of the vendor, but the necessity of the purchaser, that raises the price . . . The impossibility of subsistence of the man who carries his labour to a market is totally beside the question, in this way of viewing it. The only question is, what is it worth to the buyer? (Bendix, 1956, p. 75)

In this treatment of labour as a commodity to be bought and dispensed with like any other, employers were repudiating the paternalist notion that lower-level employees had any claim upon them other than the contracted level of wages – which the law increasingly assumed was the outcome of a purely economic contract between free and equal parties.

Further doctrinal support for those who deemed their interests to lie in repudiating the paternalist system came from Malthus. The proposition that 'the "higher classes" are not and, in fact, cannot be responsible for the employment of the people or for the relief of the poor' (ibid., p. 73), received powerful systematisation and elaboration in his *Essay on Population* (1798). Such doctrines became sufficiently widespread within the world of work and employment to generate deep unease among those well-to-do observers who feared their disintegrative impact upon the bonds of responsibility, deference and obedience. Still more, as we shall see (pp. 102–11), were such doctrines deplored when applied to the wider spheres of politics and government. Some version of paternalist doctrine has always persisted within the Tory Party; it was to surface successively in Tory Chartism, in fanciful Disraelian visions of One Nation, in Tory Democracy, in social imperialism and in Cecilian and Baldwinian conceptions of class and industrial relations. It has appeared also in vestigial uneasiness towards the policies of the Thatcher governments.

Meanwhile the open and growing liberal disavowal of traditional doctrine cannot be dismissed simply as having no more significance than the abandonment of paternalist pretence. The ideology, rhetoric and, on occasion, practice of paternalism had always served to muffle the realities of exploitation and to heighten the difficulties of the exploited in getting to grips with their situation. The more open and undisguised the exploitation, in what was now the growing scale and accelerating pace of manufacturing industry, more especially cotton, the easier it was for the exploited to mobilise their sentiments and perhaps their practical defences against it. Even as Adam Smith was publishing *Wealth of Nations*, technical and organisational changes were not far off which would transform Lancashire cotton into a great machine factory industry displaying bitter class enmity. The Industrial Revolution proper was now under way. In Lancashire, as soon elsewhere, increasingly reluctant compliance on the part of operatives evoked more emphatic coercion on the part of employers.

> Here we come to the real cause of the evils attributed to machine industry, namely the absolute and uncontrolled power of the capitalist. In this, the heroic age of great undertakings, it was acknowledged, admitted and even proclaimed with brutal candour. It was the employer's own business, he did as he chose, and did not consider that any other justification of his conduct was necessary. He owed his employees wages, and, once those were paid, the men had no further claim on him: put shortly, this was the attitude of the employer as to his rights and his duties. (Mantoux, 1928, pp. 427–8)

The upshot can be summarised by quoting from another study of the early Industrial Revolution.

> Because of the nature of eighteenth-century British society within which modern industrialism arose, because of the bitterly competitive nature of the market facing the typical manufacturer, because of the

alienation from work involved in the change, and because after all, they faced the employers as enemies within the distributive system of a capitalist economy, the modern industrial proletariat was introduced to its role not so much by attraction or monetary reward, but by compulsion, force and fear . . . The marks of its origins largely determined the atmosphere within which the management of labour was attempted. There are few records of co-operation, and they appear almost eccentric. The typical framework is that of dominance and fear, fear of hunger, of eviction, of prison for those who disobey the new industrial rules. (Pollard, 1968, p. 243)

This picture needs qualifying with a recognition of those employers who found a more generous patriarchal style compatible with satisfactory profits. Their policy rested entirely, however, upon their own personal judgement and, as Robert Owen's experience showed, received support neither from most of their fellow employers, nor from the state, nor from the new economic doctrines and the ideology informing them. For the rest, the repudiation of paternalist obligations was revealing ever more clearly, as it had in the earlier examples, such as clothmaking, that the labour market itself, given the growing disparity of power between employer and individual worker, was an instrument of coercive duress. Of this fact the courts refused to take cognisance. In other spheres of contract the courts had come to accept that 'a contract made by duress or extortion – that is, by actual or threatened violence or imprisonment – could not be upheld'. This was seen as valid morally as well as legally. But ever since 'the devastating analysis by Marx it has been generally realised that this definition of duress as consisting only of threatened violence or imprisonment is impossibly narrow. The formal freedom of the contracting parties can conceal a fundamental inequality of bargaining power which can effectively restrict freedom of choice, even though no physical duress is employed.' The common law courts of the seventeenth century had already made sure, however, that no charge of coercive duress could be read into the dependent position of the individual wage-earner *via-à-vis* his employer. By concentrating solely on physical coercion the courts made 'no allowance for the various forms of economic coercion which might lead a man "freely" to contract for work for low wages or to pay high prices for food, when loss of life was as much the alternative as it would have been had the agreement been made at the point of a pistol' (K. Thomas, 1965, p. 233). In such ways did the old hierarchical structure of power continue to exert itself within what was increasingly proclaimed an open market order of free and equal agents.

It had always been clear, however, in the industries where capitalist organisation had proceeded furthest that market contractualism in the English context was by no means a perfect solution for employers. Ideally, they would have preferred the advantages of both paternalist and market systems of control with the disadvantages of neither. The reciprocal obedience offered within a genuinely paternalist relationship was attractive: the obligations involved in sustaining it were less so. This was especially true for that growing class of small merchants, manufacturers and farmers for whom Puritan individualism had special appeal and who were making their way in a competitive society in which God helped those who helped themselves; in which thrift, accumulation and industry were the cardinal virtues and poverty very nearly a crime (C. Hill, 1969b, p. 129). Conversely, the convenience of being able to draw upon a market of free mobile labour and return it promptly to the market when no longer required was likewise attractive: less so was the consequence that labour viewed its master with the same self-interested indifference. The 'characteristic complaint' of the eighteenth century was the growing indiscipline, irregularity and insubordination of labour (E. P. Thompson, 1974a, p. 383). The strategy mainly preferred by the emergent industrial pioneers was to promote free mobile labour, abandon the obligations of the paternalist mode of control and attempt to make good the resultant shortfall of obedience with the coercions of the law and of the market. The fact that much use continued to be made of the ideology and rhetoric of paternalism simply illustrates the uses ideology can serve in salving the consciences and justifying the behaviour of participants and observers.

The transition was slow and never complete. There remained, during the eighteenth century, situations where authoritarian paternalism was the preferred mode of control. There were situations, too, where vestiges of paternalism coexisted with contractual market individualism and where paternalist rhetoric intensified the difficulties experienced by the dependants in getting to grips with their situation or even seeing it clearly. Finally, there were situations where neither vestiges nor pretence survived and where capital and labour faced each other in the alignments of the class war.

English Capitalism and its Control Strategy

A crucial question to be asked at this juncture is why the rising economic classes in England predominantly chose the control strategy they did. Neither capitalism nor industrialisation *per se* necessarily calls for it. In both Japan and Germany, capitalism and industrialisation proceeded successfully with a very different strategy of control. There is reason to argue, indeed, that England has been in this respect not the standard but a freak model of capitalism.

Certain facts are especially important for the explanation. There was the fact of a weak state, deliberately kept so by a landed class jealous of its independence of the central executive power; a state which was in no position to promote economic growth by active initiative and intervention, or to impose, even assuming it wanted to, a pattern of authoritarian paternalism. It revealed instead a growing preference for rigorously defined market relations. There were, too, the strong and long-standing elements of individualism and a powerful common-law tradition which supported them. There were the Dissenting creeds which helped to sanctify and stimulate these private individualistic impulses towards growth, profit and capital accumulation, and which came, in practice, to stress the morality of self-help within the rigours of the market rather than the virtues of a diffuse paternalistic concern for one's employees (C. Hill, 1968, p. 217). These early stages of industrialisation were therefore developing within 'a nation where the social structure and the cultural environment were far less favourable to paternalism than elsewhere' (Joyce, 1980, p. 152).

The upshot was that when there developed the economic 'take-off' of self-sustaining growth it developed within a society and culture already well advanced towards a new type of society. Much of the new growth occurred in sectors of the economy where contractual market relations had already been evolving over a long period. Lancashire cotton, for example, the first industry to undergo transformation, had seen 'the evolution of a capitalist class and an experienced [wage-earning] work force for nearly two centuries before the first water-powered cotton mills were built in the area' (Chapman, 1972, p. 13). Growth came, too, from employers who were ignorant of the whole paternalist style and of how to maintain the balance between coercive domination, rationalising rhetoric and the occasional sweetening gesture or concession. In both of these categories a fierce individualism was prevalent, widely intensified now by the higher stakes, the growing competition and the need to dragoon workers into the tighter work disiplines considered necessary for the new factories. The makings of an alienated industrial working class were already in evidence.

Had there been a thorough-going, undiluted, state-supported cultural tradition and institutional practice of paternalism there is reason to believe that English entrepreneurs and the English governing classes generally would have utilised that tradition and practice as an instrument of order and control during the industrialising process, both within the enterprise and at the level of state policy, just as their German counterparts did a century later. Even in the absence of such a tradition, a strong state which successfully asserted itself as the embodiment of some higher transcendent purpose could have exploited that purpose, through the media of army, police, education and religion, to subdue the individualistic consciousness of its citizens and render them more susceptible to the values and leadership of higher authority. Prussia, and later Imperial Germany, followed both courses. England could do neither, given its decaying paternalism, its individualist tradition too strong to be subdued, its too few 'nationalist' anxieties and insecurities to have access, as the German state had, to nationalism and national identity as a higher purpose (Fox, 1978; Currie, 1979, p. 20); and its state deliberately kept too weak and circumscribed to be capable of vigorous leadership in anything. England was increasingly free and open in her economic life to individualistic impulses that were bridled neither by the Established Church, nor the higher morality, nor the state. The jealousy which guarded the Englishman's liberty and 'liberties' was fed from the same springs of motivation and attitude as now sought to exploit the opportunities opening up for economic expansion and gain. It was the individualistic elements in English society that asserted the growth impulse.

Perhaps it was too much to expect that employers, economists, politicians and publicists would allow themselves to realise that the alienation of growing sections of wage-earners was an understandable and rational response to the system increasingly imposed upon them. Instead the predictable alternative was followed. It must not be the nature of the system that was blamed, but the moral inadequacies of the workers. From the mid-seventeenth century, attitudes towards the wage-earning stratum became noticeably harsher than those generally held in the first half. They were asserted to be by nature an inferior breed, idle, irresponsible and improvident, and this assertion was then used to justify the existing patterns of work organisation and coercive treatment (Tawney, 1938, pp. 240–1). 'You can keep a secret in a German factory, because the workers are obedient, prudent, and satisfied with a little', declared a French observer in 1788, 'but the English workers are insolent, quarrelsome, adventurous and greedy for money' (Chapman, 1972, pp. 44–9).

A set of attitudes had emerged, in fact, towards the working classes which was to prove especially characteristic of the British scene and to persist until the present day. Dean Tucker exemplified it. Deploring the 'want of subordination in the lower class of people', he condemned the tendency of journeymen to combine 'to extort exorbitant wages', charging them that they 'do not labour as cheap, and are not content to live and fare as hard' as the workers in other countries, with the result that 'their merchants can afford to sell their goods at the market cheaper than ours'. Nevertheless, he was prepared to accept a distinction between the 'deserving' poor – the respectable, honest, hard-working, ambitious working man – and the undeserving idler who, improvident and feckless, became a burden on the ratepayers. Moreover, he remained firm in his defence of liberty 'even at the risk of licentiousness', and for this reason, among others, expressed unease about 'the effect of a large body of men in arms on British liberties' (Shelton, 1981, pp. 40, 47, 52, 54, 57–8).

A self-reinforcing circle of interaction had therefore been set up. The harshness of individualistic market contractualism, with its open and doctrinally supported disapproval of any wider concern for one's workforce, evoked alienation among workers which was then adduced to justify the treatments specially characteristic of individualistic market contractualism. This intensified a feature of class relations especially marked in Britain. It was simply that the extension of capitalist organisation was beginning to bring into sharper focus the economic classes of propertied and propertyless, of employers and employed, of profit-receivers and wage-earners. The relations between these classes were already beginning, in some areas, to take on a quality that was to remain a significant feature of the British scene. This was a quality of mutual class indifference and independence. It is not an easy quality to define. Obviously we are not referring to economic independence. We are referring rather to the way in which growing sections of the governing classes were cutting the painter and viewing the expanding wage-earning stratum not as one which must be marshalled within their own personal and patriarchal tutelage, protection and control, but as a market stratum whose members must make their own way in a difficult world and, in the last resort, be allowed to construct their own plebeian culture.

Plebeian Independence and its Supports

Substantial numbers among the plebs responded by making positive and creative adaptations to the system imposed on them. Many constructed their own protective organisations – friendly societies among artisans might be barely distinguishable from trade unions – and there was a plebs culture of folk songs, entertainments, ceremonies, rituals, and the symbolism of corn dollies and the rest.

From where did they derive the spirit and confidence for such creativity? Local tradition and custom helped to support much. There were some sub-cultures where the tradition of the common Englishman's individual liberties helped to sustain them, particularly of course in protest movements. For leadership and activists in such movements they might look to either of two traditions which had some of their more distant roots in the struggles of the seventeenth century, particularly among the small masters, artisans and shopkeepers. One was the rationalist secular republicanism, prominent among the Levellers and other radicals, which might be either atheist or, in the eighteenth century, adopt forms of deism that removed God to a remote role as designer of a universe open to man's rational investigation and control. The other 'goes back directly to that seventeenth-century revolution which was still fought out in terms of religious ideology', but which received its main impetus from the Methodist revival (Hobsbawm, 1968, p. 373).

Religious toleration emerged during the eighteenth century not as a result of applying theories about freedom of conscience, but through a policy of expediency in allowing Dissenters and Nonconformists virtually to contract out of the national church. They might in certain respects become second-class citizens but they were not forced to conform. Many Dissenters – Quakers, Baptists, Presbyterians and Unitarians – driven from the corporate towns by the Anglican Restoration of Charles II's day had taken refuge in what were to become the growing industrial cities of the Midlands and the north, where new opportunities arose for holding civic office and for accumulating wealth.

The national church itself had been tamed. 'By 1740 more than two centuries of conflict and change had left the Church dependent on the State, the parson subordinate to the squire, and once-powerful ecclesiastical courts bankrupt of independent coercive power' (Gilbert, 1976, p. 4). But although the Anglican clergy had witnessed the gradual erosion of their traditional independent authority over the moral and religious behaviour of their parishioners, they often remained in a position to dictate religious norms by virtue of their alliance with local ruling élites. Squire and parson combined between them a high degree of economic, social and religious control, both through formal dependencies and informal influence. Preservation of the existing order and maintenance of social harmony was the *raison d'être* of the Church of England as a religious Establishment. Integral to the effective discharge of this function was the system of paternalism and deference. This was, as we have seen, partially corroded and undermined by the solvents of market individualism, yet in many areas it was still able to maintain control with the assistance of habit, inertia, the occasional patrician gesture and the difficulty experienced by the lower orders in breaking out of traditional relationships upheld 'time out of mind' by wealth, power and the awe they inspired, however reluctantly and resentfully.

Yet there were areas where market individualism had been unbridled for so long that the ancient writ had long ceased to run. The coincidence had been close, for example, between Puritan creeds and those artisan out-working groups long exposed to the depredations of merchant capitalist clothiers; small masters fearful of being dragged down into the same dependency; yeoman farmers personally aware of the profit-maximising forces working within the rural economy through the medium of enclosures, rising rents and the reinforcement of old exactions with new legalisms. There were other groups, too, among whom the paternalist control by squire and parson had never secured the same foothold as in most of southern England, such as the coal and iron workers, seamen and lightermen of the north-east, the communities of the Potteries, the tin-miners of Cornwall and workers in ports and fishing villages.

Among these groups the attenuation of the personalised control system and the mutual alienation between the classes produced by the growth of market individualism could be measured in terms of personal psychological needs as well as of breakdown in social cohesion, 'for individuals and families the personal security which came from integration in a stable community often gave way to anomie in the new and relatively unstructured world of the industrial shanty town or the industrial city' (Gilbert, 1976, p. 77). For some of them, this passage into a world where the strategies of predatory economic self-interest were unabashed and lauded as near-divine revelation was accompanied by nostalgic backward glances at a past already becoming idealised. But for many others it led to a process of emancipating themselves, at least partially, from the mental and physical habits of deference and of constructing within themselves a spirit of self-respecting independence. For this they needed a new framework of ideas and principles within which they could sustain a certain dignity and status, even if these were bestowed only by those who shared that framework and were treated dismissively by the higher orders. Both these and other needs, such as for a vision which brought consolation against an uncomfortable and insecure present, rendered these sections of the small master, journeymen and other strata especially open to the evangelical Nonconformity which mobilised such large numbers during the eighteenth century. The figures available to us apply to the period from 1800 to 1837, and they reveal that nearly 60 per cent of all Nonconformists were described as 'artisans' – always a broad category embracing, as it did in the seventeenth century, self-employed craftsmen, small masters, outworking artisans and other skilled workers. Colliers, miners and 'labourers' added another 17·4 per cent. Bearing in mind the sharp social division between artisan groups and the unskilled, we can appreciate the observation that the strictly proletarian element in eighteenth-century Nonconformity has sometimes been 'grossly exaggerated' (Field, 1977, p. 216).

This was part of a wider evangelical revival which also permeated the Church of England and the Old Dissent. Important for our purpose is the fact that the evangelical impulse which expressed itself through independence of the Established Church had consequences which strengthened emancipation from paternalist control. These were hardly intended. 'At one level the reactionary – indeed odiously subservient – character of official Wesleyanism can be established without the least difficulty.' Official Methodism clung to Toryism and had considerable utility as a work discipline. From the outset Wesleyan leaders served 'as apologists for an authority in whose eyes they were an object of ridicule or condescension but never of trust ... Luther's doctrines of submission to authority might have served as the text for any Wesleyan Conference in the years after 1789 ...' (E. P. Thompson, 1968, pp. 45, 385, 399 and 1976, p. 388).

In these and other ways, Nonconformity helped to ease substantial sections of the plebs – though its ideology had its appeal also for employers and professional men – into the rapidly industrialising order. But it was also bringing consequences likely to afford supporters of the status quo more ambiguous feelings. There is a familiar and well-supported argument that Methodism was indirectly responsible for a growth in the self-confidence and capacity for organisation of working people. Thompson quotes Robert Southey, who in 1820 referred to 'the manner in which Methodism has familiarized the lower classes to the work of combining in associations, making rules for their own governance, raising funds, and communicating from one part of the kingdom to another' – for Southey one of its 'incidental evils'. Although, as Thompson stresses, most of the contributions of Methodism to the working–class movement came in spite of, and not because of, the Wesleyan Conference, 'all throughout the early history of Methodism we can see a shaping democratic spirit which struggled against the doctrines and the organizational forms which Wesley imposed. Lay preachers, the break with the Established Church, self-governing forms within the societies – all these questions Wesley resisted or temporized or followed after the event. Wesley could not escape the consequences of his own spiritual egalitarianism' (E. P. Thompson, 1968, p. 46). 'People in the process of gaining emancipation from the system of paternalism and deference ... found in extra-Establishment religion a legitimation for their aspirations' (Gilbert, 1976, pp. 84–5).

The other main supportive tradition for leaders and activists was rationalist secular republicanism. As expounded by Thomas Paine in the 1790s this tradition received considerable intellectual elaboration from the eighteenth-century Enlightenment and immense stimulus from the French Revolution, but its roots can be traced back to the Civil War when political and religious forms were inextricably linked and when to attack the one was to attack the other (Royle, 1974, p. 23; C. Hill, 1975, p. 410). Obscure local societies of freethinkers kept the tradition only barely alive during the eighteenth century; nevertheless, when Painite enthusiasm erupted in the 1790s it was seen by many as a revival of an old fire, not the birth of a new one. This explains a comment in the *Annual Register* for 1794 on the clash between Burke and Paine: 'These two famous performances revived, as it were, the royal and republican parties that had divided this nation in the last century, and that had lain dormant ... They now returned to the charge with a rage and animosity equal to that which characterized our ancestors during the civil wars ...' (Royle, 1976, pp. xvi, 6–7, 153).

Painite radical thought, with its hatred of kingship and priestcraft, was not a class analysis but a system of individualistic natural rights and belief in the absolute sovereignty of reason. As presented throughout the nineteenth century by Richard Carlile, George Jacob Holyoake and Charles Bradlaugh, the tradition did little to encourage proto-Marxist thinking about the class basis of power in society. Like Methodism, it appealed to, and supported, those 'who were willing by thrift and sobriety to raise themselves from the irrational state of wilful poverty' (ibid., p. 153). Neither did it offer a role for the state which could be taken up by later socialists. This tradition saw government as but a necessary evil needing to be kept within narrow limits wherever there was danger of it interfering with the exercise of the individual's natural rights. It looked to a widened franchise in a rationally reformed secular republic for the cure of social ills.

The stratum for whom this structure of thought had special appeal was the same as that which had supplied the Levellers with so many supporters. The small master, skilled journeyman, or shopkeeper typically

> did not want an economy of limitless expansion, accumulation and technical revolution, the savage jungle pursuit which doomed the weak to bankruptcy and wage-earning status. His ideal was the secular dream of all 'little men', which has found periodic expression in Leveller, Jeffersonian or Jacobin radicalism, a small-scale society of modest property-owners and comfortably-off wage-earners, without great distinctions of wealth or power ...

They were the people for whom Thomas Paine wrote, 'self-made, self-educated, self-reliant men as yet not finally divided into employers and hired hands' (Hobsbawm, 1968, pp. 2, 13).

Paine's demands included representative government based on a democratic political equality which included this stratum, together with proposals for a tax on landed property for the financing of old-age pensions and the public provision of education. Both had considerable appeal. Among radically minded artisans and small masters the landed classes had always been a *bête noire*, and there were longstanding links between Dissent and aspirations towards parliamentary reform, which offered a means by which Dissenters could seek relief from the social and civic disabilities bearing upon them. As we have seen, Parliament had long been perceived as an arena where, despite a limited franchise, grotesque anomalies of representation and manipulation by patronage, genuine political pressure might be exerted. This made it, in the second half of the eighteenth as in the seventeenth centuries, the focus of radicals who saw that if reformed it could be an effective instrument of influence.

That this Paine-inspired movement, heedless as it mostly was of the slum-dwelling 'residuum', was no socialist-style doctrine seeking emancipation of the entire lower orders is already evident. There were also other campaigns for parliamentary reform which were even further removed from what we would now regard as a universalistic democratic ethos. Robbins 'has emphasised the continuity of an intellectual tradition current among parliamentary reformers of the late eighteenth century which runs back to Locke and Sydney and beyond. In this tradition the machinery of representation was seen as the barrier against authoritarianism on the part of the executive . . . It was in fact the whig political theory' (quoted in Christie, 1970, p. 216). As such as it was designed to protect men of property against executive threat, real or imagined, not to enable the humbler orders of the 'middle sort' to remould society a little nearer their hearts' desire. Similarly, the demand by a minority of London's well-to-do commercial community for a larger share of parliamentary representation was based on the principle that as a rising 'interest' they should have proportionate strength in spokesmen and voting power – a demand later to be taken up by the rising industrial middle classes in the northern and Midland regions. Set alongside these other currents of reform, the Painite movement which developed after 1789 among Dissenters, Nonconformists and freethinkers manifestly carried some echoes of seventeenth-century Leveller radicalism, thereby presenting a sharp contrast with the character of other agitations that had emerged during and after the 1760s.

Artisans and 'Vertical Consciousness': Foundations of an Historic Alliance

Nevertheless, these contrasting currents derived benefit from each other. Men of high status voiced slogans which time was to prove could not be monopolised by those of their own class. There was an embracing of

> extreme notions of political egalitarianism by powerful sections of the Opposition Whigs who had no reason to suspect that egalitarian ideas might next invade the field of property rights. The Chartists of the nineteenth century were never tired of proving that all their six points of Ultra-Radical Reform had been elaborated by Opposition Whigs in 1780. (Maccoby, 1935, pp. 14–15)

Well-to-do reformers, given such slogans in common, could often mobilise their social inferiors in joint agitations and demonstrations. 'In London, during the 1760s and 1770s, there stemmed from the City's radicalism the wider movement that rallied to the cause of John Wilkes; and "Wilkes and Liberty" became for a dozen years the political slogan uniting the diverse activities of City merchants, Middlesex freeholders, and the small shopkeepers, craftsmen, and workmen in the London streets and boroughs.' Those who rioted on Wilkes's behalf during the 1760s and 1770s in his defiance of king, Parliament and administration, and who rioted in 1780 against the removal of some of the disabilities imposed on Roman Catholics were not slum-dwellers, criminals and vagabonds. They were predominantly 'journeymen, apprentices, waiters, domestic servants, and labourers; a smaller number were petty employers, craftsmen, or tradesmen'. The most riotous parts of London were not the crowded rookeries and shadier alleys, but 'the more solid and respectable popular districts' (Rudé, 1981, pp. 52, 61).

It was within this general context that in 1776 Major John Cartwright published his case – supported by claims to Anglo-Saxon precedent – for adult manhood suffrage, annual parliaments, equal electoral districts and payment of Members; a case which four years later a Whig Reform Committee, likewise quoting Saxon 'rights', addressed to the gentry, clergy and 'middling' householders of Westminster. The appeal which this type of programme possessed also for the lower ranks of the 'middle sort of people' became manifest again in 1791–2, when 'corresponding' or 'constitutional' societies for parliamentary and electoral reform began to spring up in London, Sheffield, Derby, Manchester and many other towns and cities. Their social composition was weighted heavily with craftsmen, small masters and shopkeepers. The London society was 'above all, a society of artisans'; in Sheffield the membership was based on the journeymen and small masters of the numerous cutlery crafts (E. P. Thompson, 1968, pp. 170, 172).

Paine's writings and the excitement they generated soon drove a wedge for a while between the 'middle sort' and their higher-rank allies, but at least there had been demonstrated a continued capacity for vertical bonding on political issues not only between journeymen and the smaller masters from whom they might in some trades be scarcely distinguish-able, but also between journeymen and men of palpably superior rank. Such alliances were always more likely to prosper, other things being equal, to the extent that the artisans conveyed an impression of sobriety and respectability. Disparagement of the inferior poor had been prevalent among seventeenth-century radical leaders and activists and did not abate now. Along with a degree of political sympathy with their masters there often went an anxiety to assimilate to them socially.

There was far more to this than the intrinsic satisfactions of status. The relationship between status and material reward was, as it is today, one of interaction: reward helped to determine status but status also carried implications for what was deemed a fitting reward. Standards of 'respect-ability' status were now rising; the onset of so-called 'Victorian respect-ability' began revealing itself long before the Victorian age. By the end of the eighteenth century the 'concern for moral "improvement", refined manners, and orderly conduct . . . were accorded appreciating value by polite society; and consequently popular and genteel tastes became increas-ingly disassociated from each other', with plebeian culture receiving markedly less tolerance from the respectable classes (Malcolmson, 1981, p. 147). The stratum of journeymen artisans was uneasily poised in this situation. Its more aspirant members could not afford to ignore the spread and rising level of gentility. As early as the 1750s some trade societies 'were stressing the need for sobriety' (B. Harrison, 1971, pp. 54, 387). Methodism and Evangelicalism later contributed to the moral sobriety of the artisan's world, but it was also 'a product of the Radical and rationalist agitation itself; and owed much to the old Dissenting and Jacobin tradi-tions . . . A general moral primness . . . was, particularly, the ideology of the artisan or of the skilled worker ... ' (E. P. Thompson, 1968, pp. 813–14). Needless to say, in practice the demon drink and more boisterous behaviour often broke through, including violence in trade disputes; nevertheless, there was no tendency for the status gap to close between the – increasingly politically conscious – journeymen artisans and the lower strata of the plebs.

The vertical bonding between journeymen, self-employed craftsmen and masters on certain political issues therefore bore some similarity to that which in the previous century had pressed comparable interests in very different circumstances. There might be a shared commitment to a Dissenting or Nonconformist religious sect, membership of which was defined by aristocracy, gentry and Established Church as carrying the stigma of inferiority and second-class citizenship. Employer and journeyman might therefore feel a common detestation of domination by the big battalions: a domination which presented itself not only in religious but also in social, political and – especially when the big battalions included the merchant and finance capitalist – economic terms. Partly on the basis of that shared stance there was to develop, in the middle decades of the nineteenth century, the uneasy coalition that was Liberalism, expounding a wide-ranging liberal creed which attacked on many different fronts the common enemies of monopoly, privilege, social arrogance and authoritarian exclusiveness.

Alternatively, the bond might rest on a shared disposition towards a freethinking secular republicanism which, fostered by Carlile and Holyoake out of Paine, developed into 'an alternative infidel culture' of anti-clericalist rationalist thought and individual self-improvement. It was a culture 'which appears to have gripped a considerable minority (or even a majority in some places) among the artisans, tradesmen and respectable working folk of London and the industrial regions' (Royle, 1976, p. xvi). This, too, with its individualism and libertarianism which both responded to, and fostered, existing characteristics in British culture, was to contribute to Victorian Liberalism.

Artisans and the Competitive Market: Foundations of an Historic Workplace Conflict

Even at the workplace, journeymen artisans and other skilled workers might have some interests in common with the smaller masters. These lay in preserving the identity and integrity of their particular craft or trade. Theirs was largely a vertical consciousness directed towards the exclusion, if possible, of whatever threats presented themselves, whether 'illegal' men, 'illegal' masters, or new cost-cutting methods or machines. Yet alongside, or alternating with, the possibility of co-operation was the likelihood of conflict, especially in the larger urban centres, where the rigours of market competition exposed workers to extreme economic insecurity and might threaten craft identity and all its protective devices. The Webbs, describing a situation of the late seventeenth century which later overtook a number of crafts, instanced the expanding London entrepreneurial tailor, employing 'in his own workshops, dozens or even scores of journeymen, who were recruited from the houses of call in times of pressure, and ruthlessly turned adrift when the season was over' (Webb and Webb, 1920, p. 31). Such middle-rank employers might rail against large-scale merchants and predatory capitalists, but they were increasingly driven themselves by quickening economic forces and were often as ready when occasion seemed to require it to practice an individualistic market contractualism devoid of paternalistic overtones.

Dignified now by theoretical formulation and increasingly receiving official recognition, this market contractualism presented men as *individuals* striking their bargains as free and equal agents. No allowance was made for the manifest fact that the employer and the individual wage-earner were increasingly unequal in bargaining strength, and none was made, therefore, for attempts to redress this imbalance through combination among wage-earners. Combinations for this purpose came under repeated legislative interdict applied to one trade after another during the eighteenth century. For the authorities it was a problem with a long history. Ever since at least the fourteenth century there had been examples of journeymen's associations, some lasting for years. Often these were no more than social fraternities auxiliary to the main system – the regulative code maintained by guild statute or masters' convention. Some, however, had mobilised in active conflict with their masters and had often been put down by the law. It was not until the later stages of the seventeenth century that evidence emerges 'of continuous associations of wage-earners for maintaining or improving the conditions of their working lives' (ibid., p. 22). The emphasis on 'continuous association' is less important, however, than the continuous collective labour presence in most skilled crafts which might remain dormant for considerable periods but spring into active life when occasion demanded. Traditions of this collective presence, intermittently supplemented by overt formal organisation, might go back to Tudor times. As the eighteenth century progressed, employer complaints and petitions against combinations among craft workers multiplied, usually to be followed by counter-petitions from the craftsmen. From the middle of the century evidence pointed to the existence of such combinations in most of the craft trades. Their fortunes were often far from peaceful. The history of some of them is intermittently marked by violence, the destruction of tools and materials, and bloody brawls with constables and soldiers (Mantoux, 1928, pp. 79–84). It was not to be expected, in a violent and brutal age, that labour disputes would be any less so. Intimidation, machine-breaking, arson and 'collective bargaining by riot' were not infrequent, workers – and perhaps even small masters – seeking to coerce employers through attacks on property (Rule, 1981, pp. 151, 184–5; Hobsbawm, 1968, pp. 5–22). Certainly, there were also displayed many characteristics of present-day disputes – peaceful collective bargaining, arbitration, the organised strike with strike pay. Few features of modern industrial disputes cannot be traced to pre-industrial times. 'Most institutions and procedures to handle industrial conflict . . . were rehearsed in the reign of George III: only the terminology remained to be invented' (Dobson, 1980, p. 152). Yet 'the typical form of social protest at this time, even among wage earners, was the food riot rather than the strike'. Even on specifically industrial issues, disputation tended to develop into riot, though attacks on workshops and machinery were usually favoured over assaults on persons and private dwellings (Rudé, 1981, pp. 37, 70).

The Webbs were concerned to stress that it was in the craft trades that more stable combination was to be found.

> ... it is not among the farm servants, miners, or general labourers, ill-paid and ill-treated as these often were, that the early trade unions arose ... The formation of independent associations to resist the will of employers requires the possession of a certain degree of personal independence and strength of character. Thus we find the earliest trade unions arising among journeymen whose skill and standard of life had been for centuries encouraged and protected by legal or customary regulations as to apprenticeship, and by the limitation of their numbers which the high premiums and other conditions must have involved. (Webb and Webb, 1920, p. 44)

Early unionism was predominantly a response not by those at the bottom of the industrial pile, but by those who were a significant distance from the bottom and who hoped to preserve their relative advantage. It is still necessary to remember, however, that formal organisation was far from being the only significant expression of labour protest. In addition, temporary combination and 'collective bargaining by riot' could be found outside as well as within the craft trades. Domestic weavers subordinated to merchant-capitalists have Dean Tucker as their witness for the south-western counties, and in Lancashire in 1758, 'several thousands having left their work and entered into combinations for raising their wages ... formed ... a committee ... and established boxes and fixed stewards in every township for collecting money' (George, 1953, p. 142). Intervention by troops against north-east mining disturbances in 1765 brought many indignant letters to the London newspapers. 'Impartial people', declared one, 'think the masters have brought this upon themselves by endeavouring to break through an old custom', and 'in a country which boasts its liberty it is an odd way of deciding differences between masters and servants by dragoons' (Hammond and Hammond, 1979, pp. 13–14).

The Craft Heritage

There was much in eighteenth-century combinations and other expressions of a collective presence that remained redolent of the guild outlook. The emphasis within local journeymen's trade clubs and societies was on the vertical principle of commitment to, and protection of, their particular craft and its restrictive and exclusive traditions, customs and practices. Thereby it was hoped to preserve the occupational identity, and the accompanying status and privileges, of its members. In these respects there was still much to preserve. Now and for a long time to come, an apprenticed journeyman of one of the higher recognised crafts belonged to the lower levels of the same broad social grade as the smaller-scale master and employer. The struggle to maintain this superior status might involve conflict with him; the primary purpose being to uphold practices which sought not only to regulate the pace and rewards of work but, above all, to restrict entry by excluding the unapprenticed – a weaker and poorer stratum wholly without standing and respect.

The craft tradition was strongly suffused with this determination to maintain a privileged status and to identify with the middle stratum just above, rather than with the despised labourer below. The appeal to ancient statute was, of course, part of this struggle; the very terminology of 'illegal' men, that is, interlopers who had not served their apprenticeship, was to survive until the late nineteenth century, long after the 1563 statute itself had been repealed. Obviously in these circumstances it was the restrictive rather than the training functions of apprenticeship that loomed large.

Many craft groups failed to preserve their identity and privileges but many succeeded and thereby kept alive as an active force in England's industrialising economy the traditions and practices of pre-capitalist, medieval, corporate control. That the old traditions could prove a valuable resource for group protection in a rapidly changing world was of great significance. Traditions do not necessarily survive – they perish unmourned unless enough people have an interest in preserving them. Many craftsmen found the 'custom and practice' of the trade – suitably updated where necessary – very effective in defending their status and conditions against unwelcome changes that threatened to undermine them. Thus the seventeenth- and eighteenth-century journeymen's clubs and societies were the direct forerunners of the craft unions of the nineteenth century, which carried over into modern industry what has been called a 'Bastille of customs, institutions, and rules whose spirit was and is as far away from that of capitalist market economics as from that of the Marxist class struggle' (Kahn-Freund, 1979, pp. 32–62). For Kahn-Freund, this marks 'a fundamental contrast between the historical background of trade unionism in this country and on the Continent'. The 'tradition which originated in craft rules and institutions does not in Continental countries play the dominant role it does here'. There was nothing particularly British in the fact that the crafts were the cradle of trade unionism; the same was commonly true all over Europe. What marked the British scene was an emphasis on restrictive and demarcative regulation which was later to be widely emulated where possible by occupational groups with no background of craft tradition and apprenticeship. Given this emphasis, not only doctrines of economic liberalism but also later doctrines urging a mass horizontal unity of the whole wage-earning class were working against much of the grain of British trade union instinct, inclined as it was towards seeking security through exclusion of labour market competitors rather than emancipation through class unity. The emphasis was on controlling the labour market and the labour process within the existing order rather than on aspiring to gain control over all productive resources.

This emphasis was virtually total among the craft combinations of the eighteenth century. The language of class only began to develop among publicists during the latter decades (Briggs, 1967). Although there was an objective class reality underlying much eighteenth-century social conflict, the country's industrial structure was not yet such as to promote a consciousness of massed class ranks of capital and labour arrayed against each other in structurally induced confrontation. Even in the capitalistically organised outworking industries, where the cash nexus and mutual aggression were often stark and unmitigated, labour protest was likely to use the language of 'rich' and 'poor' and the failure of the former to discharge their obligations to the latter.

We have noted that English craft outlook and strategy expressed dispositions and emphases that were much less marked elsewhere. Kahn-Freund points to a legacy of demarcation and restrictionism that is widespread throughout the whole structure of English professional and commercial activities. For the antecedents of this we turn to evidence offered by Plumb, who in a reference to the seventeenth and eighteenth centuries speaks of 'the strong individualism created by chartered rights, liberties, and freeholds, all centuries old, and sanctified by law as well as time'. A university fellowship, an armed forces commission, a church benefice; these and innumerable others were seen as 'freeholds', as 'property'. England was littered with them: 'myriad marks of status, of possession, of profit: stewards of hundreds, precentors of cathedrals, beadles of corporations'. Usually held for life, enjoying their degree of status, and mostly carrying a vote, they bred 'independence, truculence, a willingness to fight and litigate that bordered on neurosis' (Plumb, 1979, pp. 18–19, 26–7). Apprenticeships, too, were property, and in a society marked as widely and deeply as this by traditional and prescriptive rights it is hardly surprising that journeymen of recognised crafts were both motivated and nerved to demand preservation of their own craft 'rights', customs and practices, some medieval, others recent. They were manifesting one expression of a widespread stance which already offered, and was to go on offering, fierce resistance to some of the economic, social, professional and administrative innovations and adjustments which might be thought to be 'needed' by a society in major transition. They were fortified by the fact that the same style marked the conduct by aristocracy and gentry of the country's high political culture. 'The plebs were aware that a ruling class that rested its claim to legitimacy upon prescription and law had little authority to over-rule their own customs and rights' (E. P. Thompson, 1978a, p. 158). It was an indication that English society and culture, though in some respects offering a hospitable climate for the forces of industrialisation and rapid growth, in other respects offered a deeply inhospitable one.

Craft tradition was to leave its mark on British industrial relations in yet another way – in the practice of 'direct democracy'. In their original guild association, masters and journeymen had been members of a self-regulating corporate body whose success in upholding the regulation from which all derived benefit depended, at least partly, upon the vigilance of all in detecting and checking transgressors. This consciousness of a shared fate in which all had a responsible place lost nothing of its strength for the journeymen when the guild structure weakened and finally became moribund. They might now see themselves alone as the ultimate repository of the craft's integrity and traditions which they must defend not only against powerful exploiters, predators and unskilled labourers beyond the workplace but also against possible subversion or betrayal within. Links between the workshops of the locality needed underpinning with an alert consciousness among the collective labour presence within each individual shop, for the strength of the craft position depended upon day-to-day observance of actual working rules. Wariness and vigilant suspicion, always necessities for successful guild regulation, became likewise built into the journeymen's trade societies.

They had been reinforced by the artisans' access to seventeenth-century ideas and aspirations relating to 'liberty' and self-determination. The artisan of a recognised craft had always been a member, however humble, of an 'estate of the realm', and as such had participated in the tradition of the 'freeborn Englishman' with his liberties and rights – and, of course, was supported in this by the native strand of individualism. When they brought this consciousness to bear upon the economic, social and religious oppressions increasingly visited upon them by the rich and powerful, the outcome was the conviction expressed in its extreme form by the Levellers, whose 'Agreement of the People' declared that 'useful experience found the prevalence of corrupt interests powerfully inclining most men once entrusted with authority, to pervert the same to their own domination, and to the prejudice of our peace and liberties'. Safety lay in 'a society of self-governing local communities, with a large degree of voluntaryism', with election of all officers and with short periods of service (Manning, 1978, pp. 324, 328). The dream faded, but reappeared in English Jacobinism as formulated by radicals among the small master and artisan stratum. Later still, it was to contribute much to Chartism.

Meanwhile it is easy to understand why, with longstanding dispositions like these, seventeenth- and eighteenth-century artisans felt, when they formed their trade clubs, that they must depend on nobody ·but themselves. Accordingly, each local club was

> a democracy of the most rudimentary type, free alike from permanently differentiated officials, executive council, or representative assembly. The general meeting strove itself to transact all the business, and grudgingly delegated any of its functions either to officers or to committees. When this delegation could no longer be avoided, the expedients of rotation and short periods of service were used to prevent imposition or any undue influence by particular members.

The Webbs could barely understand, still less sympathise with, these preferences, which they termed, in a revealing phrase, 'primitive democracy'. In this 'earliest type of trade union democracy we find, in fact, the most childlike faith not only that "all men are equal", but also that "what concerns all should be decided by all" (Webb and Webb, 1902, p. 8). They hardly bothered to conceal their irritation with this downgrading of the official and the expert, and with the fact that only 'slowly, reluctantly and incompletely' did British trade unionists move towards the idea of a representative assembly appointing and controlling a standing executive which, in turn, controlled a salaried, professional staff of experts. We limit ourselves here to the observation that native traditions of individualism, liberty and wariness towards authority – traditions greatly strengthened by the politicising effect of seventeenth-century struggles – had become structured into the attitudes and behaviour of wage-earners even towards their own protective organisations. Along with the craft tradition of aiming at a regulation not only of terms of employment but also of access to jobs and of supply in the labour market, direct democracy was to remain a deeply rooted hankering among the rank and file membership of Britain's trade unions. Though not unknown abroad, both were specially significant features of the British heritage.

It is a heritage that reveals the fallacy, still widespread and perpetuated in much journalism, that the adversary, restrictionist postures of organised labour, with its 'them and us' frame of reference, originated in proletarian sufferings during the Industrial Revolution. They have their roots in far older traditions.

3

Alternatives and Choices
the 1790s to the 1840s

During this period the ruling political order became increasingly faced with the need to make choices and answer questions arising from the gathering industrialism and the varied pressures and dilemmas which it generated. How far was the state to yield to those – including many among its own leaders and officials – who pressed for formal abandonment of what vestigially remained of state regulation? In particular, was there any surviving value in the much-decayed tradition of statutory wage and apprenticeship regulation, and in the local paternalism of poor relief? How far, and on what terms, should the ruling order help those employers who wanted to subdue or even destroy worker combinations – especially if such help involved prejudicing the regime's legitimation and ideology of constitutionalism, political freedom and the rule of law? Could concessions safely be made to demands by the rising commercial and industrial classes for inclusion in the political nation? Were there dangers in a thorough-going adoption of the sort of contractual market society favoured by the political economists, with its liberal individualism and rejection of the paternalist system of social control?

To these and related questions the national and local ruling order returned divergent and sometimes confused and contradictory answers. There was no total and consistent overthrow of one pattern of society and values by another. Some features of the old order were swept away. Others faltered but then took on fresh strength. Others appeared to suffer abolition but in fact remained. Still others showed no sign of going and fused with the new to create a society which exhibited features of both. For example, old Tudor statutes governing wages and apprenticeship were repealed, though not before a number of contradictory and uncertain responses. For a time the ruling order seemed sufficiently repressive towards labour organisation as to appear to put at risk its own boast of constitutionalism and freedom, but there were always limits to its heavy-handedness and in the end it drew back. It then confirmed that boast, and thereby rendered more difficult any future withdrawal, by conceding political rights to middle classes hitherto excluded. The old poor law appeared to be swept away in favour of a new and far harsher one but in practice survived much more widely than was once supposed. Finally, the principles and behaviours of liberal individualism made great headway in economic life, where they clashed with labour collectivism, but the paternalist approach remained very much alive in politics, though mostly in its weaker version.

Choices were therefore being made which, now or later, through interaction with the cultures and organisations of labour, shaped the courses of trade unionism and industrial relations. In some respects the shaping was direct: what was to be the legal status of the unions and of collective workplace practices? In other respects it was indirect: what was to be the political and social texture of the society within which they operated – its values, class relations and dispositions towards a range of issues relevant to the unions' interests?

Repeal of Paternalist Legislation

As the eighteenth century wore on, the spreading incidence of worker combination, temporary or longer-lasting, mainly among artisans but also on occasion among such groups as miners, seamen and lightermen, represented a considerable nuisance not only to the particular employers concerned but also to the vision taking shape of a fully free market order. This required not only that such restraints of trade as monopoly and kindred market privileges and impediments be swept away, but also that all guild and statutory intervention and regulation be allowed to lapse or, if necessary, positively discouraged. The threat presented to this emerging vision by worker combination was apparent. Combinations were also helping to keep alive those statutes, customs and traditions to which they made appeal in the effort to uphold their status, security, craft identity and standards of living – efforts which in the eyes of their critics impeded enterprise, challenged the authority rights of property, and presented obstruction to beneficial change.

It was in the attempt to subdue such threats and challenges that during the century more than forty statutes were directed against combination in specific trades. They were not the only legal resource that lay to hand. The common law of criminal conspiracy could always be invoked, though this was costly, time-consuming and difficult. Old statutes providing sanctions against those who 'left work unfinished' – a legitimate enough protection in the days of small-scale dealings – could be manipulated for use against strikers in the very different kinds of industrial structure now emerging.

Despite these deterrents, which were applied for the most part capriciously and unsystematically, combination survived and spread – though of course particular combinations might wax or wane. One of the difficulties confronting their enemies was that as long as the old paternalist legislation remained on the statute book, and as long as there remained individuals and groups within the political and legal Establishment who for one reason or another could still be reached by an appeal for parliamentary or magistrate regulation – especially if disorder threatened – a combination could, if careful, claim legality on the ground that its only concern was to petition for observance of the law.

No small embarrassment was caused, during the first decade of the nineteenth century, by the vigorous continuation of such petitions and by the confusion they produced among different groups within the Establishment. It had clearly been the case during the preceding century that, whatever the intentions of the original statutes – which had been varyingly interpreted at local level – the aim of petitions from artisans and often the smaller masters was to secure, either from magistrates or Parliament, *minimum* wage rates (or the enforcement of apprenticeship and other protective statutes). This remained the purpose. The reception they received indicated that, despite the gathering force of the new economic doctrines, there were still doubts in some high quarters. As subsequent debates were to show, the abandonment of paternalist control was seen by many as a serious misjudgement. Moreover, the wails of upstart factory owners against regulation did not necessarily arouse instant sympathy among landowners, gentry and professional men. There was sometimes, as we shall see, a calculation among the latter groups that the enforcement of a minimum wage in their locality might reduce the burden of poor rates, since parish relief was often forthcoming for families whose income fell below current notions of subsistence. Finally, there could sometimes arise among large-scale manufacturers the belief that an established minimum wage might do something to limit the more cut-throat predatory forms of competition which operated through downward pressure on wage rates – a method not always relished by men of prominent status or conscience.

Whether the demand was for a minimum wage or for some other form of regulation, its reception was therefore sometimes less than clear cut. A petition by woollen workers in 1802 for enforcement of the old statutes was met by a series of Acts suspending their application to woollen manufacture. Outright repeal did not come until seven years later and the delay owed something to genuine puzzlement and uncertainty at the Home Office and among ministers (Hammond and Hammond, 1979, pp. 145–6). There was other evidence of ruling-class confusion. Between 1805 and 1808 cotton manufacturers, 'some of the most wealthy in Bolton', later joined by some of their fellows in other Lancashire towns, 101 in all, 'most of them very wealthy', took the initiative in a joint approach with workers' representatives to secure a statutory minimum wage covering handloom weavers. London merchants joined forces and subscribed money to the proposal for a joint board to fix wages under the presidency of a magistrate. The number and status of its backers appear to have caused a certain amount of embarrassment in the House, embarrassment shared by some of the backers themselves. Sir Robert Peel, having subscribed thirty guineas to the movement, then spoke against it, after which the Bill sank without trace. Serious riots followed, but the 'Crown was clearly anxious not to press the charges' (ibid., pp. 56–61).

This was not the end of ruling-class uncertainties. After a House of Commons Committee of 1808 had decided against a renewed effort by handloom weavers to secure a statutory minimum and limitation of apprentices, the Edinburgh Court of Sessions in 1812 held that magistrates were competent to fix a scale of wages for the cotton weavers of Glasgow. Presented with a scale prepared by the weavers' combination the magistrates declared the rates reasonable but made no order enforcing them. There followed a mass strike which was broken by the arrest and imprisonment of its leaders and the disintegration of the union. It was the sharpest practical expression of the clash between the old conceptions and the new. The events which possibly most concentrated the minds of the Establishment occurred, however, in London, where between 1810 and 1812 a number of trade societies prosecuted masters for employing 'illegal men' and in a few cases for setting up in business without themselves having 'served their time'. There were even some convictions (Webb and Webb, 1920, p. 59). It was clearly time, in Establishment eyes, for the old statutes to go and go they did; the wage-fixing clauses in 1813 and the apprenticeship clauses a year later, though not without much petitioning and counter-petitioning and some anguish within the relevant House of Commons Committee, which declined to make a recommendation.

More expressive of the triumphant doctrine was a Select Committee of the House of Commons which reported in 1811 that 'no interference of the legislature with the freedom of trade, or with the perfect liberty of every individual to dispose of his time and of his labour in the way and on the terms which he may judge most conducive to his own interest, can take place without violating general principles of the first importance to the prosperity and happiness of the community'. Sentiments which had received fierce but limited expression two centuries earlier were on the way to becoming the received conventional cant among those who considered themselves the men of the future. A term whose French origins lay deep in the eighteenth century received an early English mention in 1812 by Lord Liverpool in the House of Commons. *Laissez-faire*, infrequently used before the mid-nineteenth century, is an expression of many varying meanings, but 'more frequently' it has 'been used as a convenient shorthand for the general prescriptions of the classical economists and in particular for a belief in the efficacy of a free market economy'. The members of the classical school never committed themselves rigidly and dogmatically to the cruder versions of *laissez-faire*, but 'to all, except perhaps John Stuart Mill in his later years', intervention by the state was always an evil even if a necessary one, and 'every interventionist act needed its own specific justification' (A. J. Taylor, 1972, p. 24). Supporters of the new political economy were apt to bend the term to suit their own needs. They included members of the landed aristocracy, Whig and Tory; larger manufacturers, merchants and professional men; a growing number of men of affairs; and even some of those who occupied that – to modern eyes – ambivalent ground shared by superior journeymen and employer, a category which included such figures as Francis Place.

The opinions and activities of Place remind us that, outside cotton and woollen clothmaking and certain other trades which, if not yet factory industries, were nevertheless organised on capitalistic lines, there was a large sector of small- and middling-scale urban enterprise in which master and better-placed journeymen were not sharply differentiated class categories. The latter might still aspire to be considered among the 'middle sort of people' and were socially deeply separated still from that stratum which consisted of 'hands', farm labourers, unskilled workers, servants and other categories of the lower poor. Their anxiety not to be down-graded in the manner of workers in the capitalistic industries often lent them desperation in their – not infrequently violent – resistance to competitive pressures. These pressures, operating with varying degrees of severity, threatened to depress the small master into sub-contracting dependency and virtual wage-earner status, his journeymen into mere 'hands', and his apprentices into cheap boy labour. There were, of course, always some at this small master level who were thrusting aggressively above the ruck and whose trade interests might differ accordingly; never-theless, they might well, as already noted, continue to share political and possibly religious sentiments with their more defensive fellows. Should they be of the self-improving, socially aspirant mould they could be attracted to a stratum, not too far above them, which included a more securely established middle-class group of manufacturers, professional men and politicians who as radicals embraced the new political economy and sought parliamentary and electoral reform for the benefit of the 'middle sort'. Their association with these middle-class radicals did not necessarily result in the loss of their craft consciousness and the assump-tions, attitudes and values which tended to go with it.

Within this broad profile can be fitted such men as Francis Place, apprenticed breeches maker, union organiser and later master tailor making profits which rose to well over £3,000 in 1816 and enabled him to retire from business the following year at the age of 46 (Wallas, 1918, p. 38). Place and an associate, Joseph Hume, economist and Radical Member of Parliament, contributed actively to the campaign for sweeping away the apprenticeship clauses of the Statute of Artificers, and when the framework knitters, led by Gravener Henson, had sought protective legislation in 1812 Hume opposed it 'on Dr. A. Smith's grounds', wrote Henson, 'of letting trade alone'.

Yet Place and Hume were to be instrumental also in securing the repeal of a statute which attempted the general prohibition of worker combi-nations in all trades. This renewed and enlarged attempt at suppression began in 1799 but was followed by an amended measure in 1800. Since repeal in 1824–5 was the first stage in the long and continuing struggle by British trade unions for legal protection and security it is of obvious importance for our present purpose. But, in addition, Place's role is worth noting as bearing an early approximation to one which was to play a major formative part in the later growth of the movement and its politics. He combined support of trade unionism with close sympathy for an emergent Liberalism which embraced parliamentary reform, hostility to the Estab-lished Church and to the landed interest with its corn and game laws, and acceptance of the new political economy with its pressure towards free trade. The word 'approximation' is used advisedly; relatively few self-improving artisans became prosperous employers and few would have been so eager to please economist friends by helping to kick away the statutory props of apprenticeship. Yet he does offer something of a Liberal–Labour profile which was to endure throughout the more drama-tic excitements of Owenism and Chartism to become a decisive influence.

This does not exhaust the significance of the Combination statutes. A study of these Acts and of the nature of their enforcement and circumstances of repeal is deeply instructive of ruling-class dispositions and strategies of rule. The lessons they learned, the responses they made and the conceptual language in which they expressed them, constitute crucial evidence for understanding the history of British trade unionism, for the decisions and choices made by rulers during this episode helped to commit them to certain courses of action later. Further insight into the predominant ruling-class stance can be derived not only from the Chartism of the 1830s and 1840s but also from the earlier case of the Tolpuddle Martyrs in the 1830s; a case which has taken on massive legendary force in the hagiography of the Labour movement. Attention to certain of its features which have so far received little or no appraisal will reveal a more complex strategy and technique of rule than emerges in most treatments.

The Combination Acts, 1799–1800

The deepest significance of the period between the 1790s and the 1840s is that it brought the first major test of the ruling-class commitment to law, liberty and constitutionalism as the central legitimising props of their regime. Could these survive revolution and violence on the other side of the Channel and the obvious threat that disaffected elements at home might also become tainted and seek to subvert property and power?

Associations and combinations which had for their object any kind of challenge to authority or proposal for political reform were bound to come under special scrutiny, but alarm did not end there. However limited and apparently non-political the purpose, independent organisation among the plebs was ever likely, it was felt, to be captured and manipulated for subversive ends by agitators who exploited the people's foolishness and gullibility. Any kind of mobilisation of those below the ranks of gentleman was cause for unease except when led by those unequivocally committed to the existing ruling order. Such fears were immensely heightened by the phenomenal success of Paine's *Rights of Man*, there being few places in Britain where his name did not rapidly become a household word. This alone was enough to galvanise the 'panic, and the counter-revolutionary offensive, of the propertied in Britain'. But these alarms were greatly heightened by the rapid radical-isation of the French Revolution after September 1792 and by 'dangerous signs of confluence between the revolutionary exhilaration in France and the growing Jacobin movement at home' (E. P. Thompson, 1968, pp. 116–17, 121).

Home Office papers, which contain 'extraordinarily few references' to combinations before 1790 (Aspinall, ed., 1949, p. ix) – they were a matter for the localities – suddenly begin to include letters between Home Secretaries, local magistrates, district military commanders and the law officers of the crown about the growing menace. In terms of what was actually happening on the ground these papers give only a partial and distorted view, yet they are valuable in revealing the officially received reasons and attitudes which the various parties wished to see entered on the record as explanations of their conduct. In addition, of course, a judicious reading between the lines yields much of value.

No reading between the lines is necessary to identify the opinion of Wilberforce, who in 1799 proposed to the Commons that since combinations were 'a general disease in our society' they should now come under a general statutory prohibition. No serious possibility was raised that they might be dealt with by any other means than the normal procedures of legislation. Given the desirability of suppression it must be sought through the agreed due processes of constitutionality and law. As earlier evidence has indicated, this did not mean that the English ruling classes were any more squeamish than others in defending their property and privileges. Legal technicalities did not necessarily bother country gentlemen in their localities when they came to try poachers and those who paid off old grievances and resentments by damaging crops, cattle, or game forests. 'For as M.P.s they passed a mass of legislation that allowed them, as J.P.s, to convict offenders without the trouble of legalistic indictments or tender-minded juries' (D. Hay, 1977, p. 59). There is other evidence, too, that anxieties about legal or constitutional punctilio were apt to be more in evidence at national than at local level. This owed something to the fact that local civil powers of enforcement were often weak. A relevant example relates to truck – the payment of wages in kind. Attempts to ensure payment in coin of the realm date from the fourteenth century, but industrialisation found truck still common in some industries, with men virtually forced to take payment in the form of inferior and high-priced goods. 'The fact that the law was not carried out is established ... from the frank admissions of the magistrates, who, for the most part, seem to have taken it for granted that if the masters would not obey the law nothing could be done to enforce obedience.' But entering into this disposition was also a simple disinclination 'to carry out legislation that was obnoxious to the masters' (Hammond and Hammond, 1919, pp. 66–7).

Rulers at national level felt a need to present a more rigorous face than this. Here a major anxiety within the ruling class is unmistakable – to preserve a legitimising picture of the law as a majestic edifice dispensing justice equally to rich and poor alike, and entitled by that very token to demand the allegiance of all men to a social and political order which subjected itself to unbiased and independent legal and constitutional procedure. It was a strategy of rule which called for experience and a sure instinct.

> The gentry managed to maintain order without anything resembling the political police used by the French, but it was order that often seemed to rest on precarious foundations. The common Englishman was renowned for his riots, and also for his dislike of standing armies. Although the ideology of justice could be used by gentlemen to quiet a mob, and with success, words sometimes lost their magic. Then the discretion embodied in the law allowed the authorities to use terror with great flexibility. (D. Hay, 1977, p. 49)

They did not always and everywhere have the opportunity, however. The dislike of standing armies was still cherished not only by the common Englishman but also by his masters. 'A new type of anti-militarism was now growing up, based entirely on economic – not, as formerly, on constitutional grounds. A large army cost dear ...' (Halévy, 1961a, p. 94). Officers who sat in Parliament were also landowners and tax-payers, more attached to their class than to their profession. In Britain 'there was no privileged noble caste, and the army was a backwater rather than a great national institution' (C. Barnett, 1967, p. 17). The police fared no better. 'In the climate of opinion which prevailed in England, from the Restoration at any rate, the idea that a main function of the police was the gathering of information about public opinion ... was anathema', and upper-class alarm at popular unrest was never strong enough to overcome distaste for a powerful police force (Tobias, 1972, pp. 203, 204). Resistance to any effective kind of police force had continued into the nineteenth century. In what Thompson calls a 'quite surprising consensus of opinion', Tories, Whigs and Radicals alike saw 'any centralized force with larger powers' as a system of tyranny and the destruction of liberty (E. P. Thompson, 1968, p. 89).

Even if troops were on hand when disorder erupted there was still no guarantee of their being used with the alacrity and vigour that employers might be seeking. For every commanding officer who relished a little blood-letting as useful practice there was another who viewed support for the civil power with considerable distaste when directed towards upholding the interests of factory owners. Among several examples was General Maitland who, during the Lancashire Luddite disturbances of 1812, observed that 'if we were to give way to individual feeling every manufacturer in this part of the country would have wished to have his own property defended by the military, and have made the military probably the means of lowering the labour of his workmen even below their present level' (Hammond and Hammond, 1979, p. 244). Nor could the troops themselves always be relied on. The practice of billeting them among the people instead of in barracks – now more a matter of economy – was apt to rebound on ruling-class heads. During Nottingham industrial disorders in 1815–17 the town clerk urged the building of barracks, 'for otherwise they are mixed up with the mob, and cannot be kept in a state of regularity and discipline ... The constant state of association with the town's people has had a very pernicious effect upon the spirit of the men if attempted to be brought into action against the people' (ibid., p. 194).

Though it was important for the ruling order that a show of force be sufficiently impressive there was also a need for it not to be so brutal as to outrage the beholders and damage the mystique of justice. The system required both ferocity and benign leniency; both penalty and indulgence. Britain's rulers, national and local, spent much time weighing this delicate balance; and the fact that they sometimes got it wrong is less significant than the fact that they often, from their own point of view, got it right. Right or wrong, they expected loyal support from fellow-members of their own class for whatever decision was taken; the gentleman who betrayed his class and its chosen instrument of rule by playing on mob emotions or publicly calling in question the justice of the law or the soundness of a particular course of action was not forgiven. 'The gentry were acutely aware that their security depended on *belief* – belief in the justice of their rule, and in its adamantine strength' (D. Hay, 1977, p. 51). An appreciation of this ruling-class stance is a pre-condition for understanding not only the Combination Acts themselves but also the nature of their application and the repealing legislation of 1824–5.

The Act of 1799 was a hastily contrived and hurriedly passed measure which was modified within a year as a consequence of organised craft pressure taken up by Whig MPs eager, for their own reasons, to embarrass the Tory government. With petitions coming in from up and down the country, the Act offered them plenty of rhetorical scope for orotund speeches denouncing its gross bias. Among other things it declared against combinations of workers but not against combinations of masters; virtually withheld the right of trial by jury; placed the power of summary jurisdiction in the hands of 'one or more' local magistrates, failing to exclude the possibility that he (or they) might employ the men being charged; and for all practical purposes excluded the right of appeal. These features and others were attacked by MPs like Sheridan, who declared the Act 'pregnant with the foulest injustice' and 'replete with the grossest aggressions against the principles of the law of the land and against the right of the subject' (quoted in Aspinall, ed., 1949, p. xiii). He and his supporters had no wish, however, to make combinations of workers legal; the resounding rhetoric issued less from sympathy with the craftsmen than from the itch to score parliamentary points by declaiming Whig principles of law and liberty.

There followed a certain amount of foot-shuffling and the critics were appointed to a committee for the purpose of drafting an amending Bill. This declared against combinations of masters as well as of workmen (though imposing only a £20 fine for the former offence compared with three months' imprisonment for the latter). According to Hunt, 'a few' combinations of masters were in fact prosecuted (Hunt, 1981, p. 199); presumably by workers, since the crown lawyers indicated their own unwillingness. The new Act also required that *two* or more magistrates must preside, none of them to be employers in the trade affected; and provided for the right of appeal to the Court of Quarter Sessions. Legal decorum restored, it was carefully maintained by successive Home Secretaries and law officers of the crown until its repeal in 1825. Though it remained, in Aspinall's words, 'an odious piece of class legislation', neither 'Sheridan nor any of his Whig friends made the slightest attempt to repeal the amending Act of 1800 when they came into office again six years later, nor did they subsequently raise the matter in Parliament during their long period in opposition' (Aspinall, ed., 1949, pp. xiii, xiv). It had been the first, though far from the last, occasion on which parliamentary debate about trade union rights had been shaped as much by party political expediency as by personal conviction. The episode confirmed, nevertheless, that organised pressure from groups among the plebs could exert influence provided the pressure could be usefully exploited by effective figures in the parliamentary game.

Given that severe common law weapons against combination already existed why was there thought to be a need for statutes carrying much milder punishments? The answer lay in the desire for more speedy and exemplary summary justice of which it was hoped employers would more readily avail themselves. Just how uncertain their use of the new Act could be, however, was progressively revealed over the next quarter of a century, a period during which the British ruling class learned lessons that were never forgotten and identified problems that dog employers and governments to this day when they seek to apply legal sanctions to workplace behaviour.

Many of these problems are revealed when the question is posed: who was to bring the law into action? Who was to initiate prosecutions? Home Office records demonstrate a government determination not to be drawn into this role. The reason for this reluctance is revealing both of the Act's nature as a piece of class legislation, and of the anxiety in ruling circles to avoid its class quality being so starkly delineated as to mock the myth of government even-handedness between rich and poor and provide leverage to the radical Opposition. Urged by the London boot and shoe manufacturers in 1804 to initiate a government prosecution against a trade union currently troubling them, the Home Secretary sought the opinion of the law officers of the crown. The Attorney-General replied that if the government conceded this precedent 'similar applications must be expected from every other trade, and it will lead to an opinion that it is not the business of the masters . . . who feel the injury to prosecute, but . . . the business of Government'. This would have a number of disadvantages. If Government shouldered the burden it would only encourage the present 'inertness and timidity' of masters – soon to become a stock lamentation in Whitehall – and, in any case, the masters were better able to collect evidence. More pregnantly, he suggested that 'the impartiality of Government would be awkwardly situated if, after undertaking a prosecution at the instance of the masters against the conspiracy of the journeymen, they were to be applied to on the part of the journeymen to prosecute the same masters for a conspiracy against their men'. Approached shortly after to comment on another and similar proposal, he repeated the view that the consequences would be 'extremely inconvenient', and proposed a 'middle course' whereby the Solicitor of the Treasury might give a 'respectable' local lawyer 'the necessary assistance' and defray the costs of the action. 'This, though not wholly free from all the inconveniences of a more avowed prosecution by the public, is from the circumstances of its not being attended with such notoriety, exposed to fewer of them and in less degree' (Aspinall, 1949, ed., pp. 90–5). In brief, the objection was not to class bias – manifested in the fact that the government had no intention whatever of prosecuting masters for combination – but to its being made public and overt in a way which would greatly weaken the government's assertion of even-handedness. Employers were to be left to their own uncertain and often somewhat nervous courses, and it became clear that, deprived of whole-hearted state support backed by fully effective coercive forces, they lacked the stomach, the resources and the unity for any attempt at the total destruction of worker combinations. These stances taken up by the state and by the general run of employers were to remain constants of Britain's industrial relations system.

Government disinclination to take the initiative in prosecutions had a parallel in its disinclination to involve itself in what it defined as private quarrels between master and man. In a ruling class of landowners there often seemed little sympathy with the labour problems of manufacturers – and often a certain waspish impatience with examples of their shortsighted greed or stupidity when these threatened public peace and the social order. 'Government and the magistracy must ever discountenance combination', declared a letter from Whitehall to a Manchester JP in 1818, 'but they have much to complain of in those who give rise to the combination by relying on the support of the law instead of considering the justice of the demands made on them' (ibid., p. 272). But there were more fundamental reasons for government ambivalence. The status quo, its property rights and its hierarchical authority structure, must be upheld. Yet intervention in the confusing local minutiae of wage rates, costs and profit margins was utterly beyond the competence – and interest – of ministers and their officials; nor was there the slightest intention on their part of incurring the expense – and threat – of a specialist bureaucracy for overseeing industry and its problems. Such practicalities reinforced the argument that intervention in these complex matters where, in the Attorney-General's words, there were always 'complaints on both sides', would destroy the claim of the civil powers to be impartial and that the preferable course was for governments, as far as possible, to remain aloof. The ideology of *laissez-faire* provided an invaluable rationalisation for keeping clear of such vipers' nests, which is what authority would have wanted to do anyway. 'The striking of workmen is certainly to be considered usually as a business of a private nature', wrote the Whig Earl Fitzwilliam, Lord Lieutenant of the West Riding, to the Home Secretary in 1802. 'The public has nothing to do in disputes between master and man, where breaches of contract, or some circumstances of that nature' – such as a threat to public order – 'does not bring the case within the cognisance of magistrates.' And in another example among many, a different Home Secretary in 1818 agreed with the Nottingham magistrates that 'it is not fit for them to interfere' in a current strike of local workers 'until there is danger of the peace being broken' (ibid., pp. 62, 348–9). Nor were governments disposed to override the advice of the law officers when, with their image of the law to protect as well as their consciousness of equally rigorous protectors in Parliament, they invariably cautioned ministers against applying for new powers or stiffer penalties. Conceding that there were often difficulties of evidence and proof in applying the Combination Acts, they yet 'dare not recommend' relaxing the rules of evidence, 'or venture to suggest that less should be required than would be thought necessary to warrant a conviction for any other species of misdemeanour'. Ministers and their officials always, in official documents and letters, urged strict adherence to the law. A Home Secretary tells the mayor of Liverpool in 1792 that he should pursue 'every legal and constitutional means' of suppressing combinations, and the Foreign Secretary calls upon the Durham magistrates 'to take all proper and legal methods' towards the same end (ibid., pp. 3, 15, 216–17). During the 1818 Manchester spinners' strike, employers applied to magistrates for warrants under the Combination Acts against strikers who stood about 'in clusters' in the streets. Asked for advice, the Solicitor-General replied that if the 'persons assembled ... conduct themselves peaceably and quietly, and there are no circumstances attending these meetings of actual force or violence ... I do not think the magistrates will be justified in interfering to disperse them'. The warrants were refused (Hammond and Hammond, 1979, p. 82).

Justices who stretched the law could not expect official encouragement. In 1823 Somerset magistrates pursued vigorous action, under pressures from employers, to take possession of cloth – the employers' property – from the looms of outworking weavers on strike. Under warrant not authorised by law, constables forced their way into cottages and riots ensued which were subdued only by yeoman cavalry. Robert Peel's reply to the magistrates' report was bleak, 'however desirable it may be to preserve the property from deterioration, it is vastly more important that the magistrates should act strictly within the line of their authority ... the tendency of the measure you adopted is rather to foment than to allay the existing discontents' (Aspinall, ed., 1949, p. 376).

Ministerial and Whitehall views were shared by many magistrates themselves, with the result that they, too, were often hesitant and cautious about applying the Act. There were, of course, magistrates possessed of such anti-Jacobin and anti-combination hatreds that they used the law as if it were a personal and private resource. Yet ruling calculations and instincts at national level found many echoes on the local bench. In 1817, for example, the Nottingham town clerk told the Home Secretary, *à propos* a strike by framework knitters, that 'the magistrates have no *power* to interpose – and as individuals they do not conceive that they have any *right* to become parties. Their duty is, as they conceive, to watch the public peace and to preserve it – being ready, nevertheless, at all times to receive complaints and to enforce the laws relating to combinations etc.' (italics in original). Sentiments of this kind – 'the desire of a strict adherence to the principle of non-interference between the master and workman' (1821) – were widespread among magistrates. Sometimes they made the reason for this explicit, revealing thereby a calculation similar to that made by the law officers of the crown. James Norris, a Lancashire magistrate, described to the Home Secretary in 1818 how Manchester cotton-spinners and dye-workers on strike were parading through the streets daily in a manner which, while orderly, 'tended to alarm' by its novelty. 'My brother magistrates and myself', he added in a specially revealing comment, 'did not think it right on this account to interfere in their practice, in order that the lower classes might see distinctly that we kept aloof from any question between them and their employers as to the advance of wages, and in order that they might pay a greater respect to any judgement which we might be called upon to pronounce in case the masters proceeded against any of them under the Combination Act' (ibid., pp. 239, 253, 254, 349).

In some areas magistrates were especially keenly aware of the fragility of the civil power and of how important it was not to bid up group tensions to a point where their bluff might be called and their authority revealed as resting far more on acquiescence than on coercive ability. A deputy adjutant-general reported to the Secretary at War in 1792, for example, that in Sheffield 'there is no civil power'. The Cutlers' Company purported to regulate 'some part of the manufacturers'; otherwise there were only two JPs who came in fortnightly to 'settle any differences' that might arise. One of them lived fourteen miles away; the other, 'having made some efforts during the riots last year relative to some enclosures, the populace burned a part of his property, and since that time he has been very little in the country'. In the north-east, 'South Shields', wrote a Durham MP in 1792, 'has risen so rapidly, from the spirit of commerce, as to contain at least 14,000 inhabitants without a single magistrate to control it. None of its inhabitants are of a description to qualify for that office, and few would be active or hardy enough to undertake so penible a situation. Not a single soldier is there to protect a great and increasing property ... The magistrates of Newcastle are either diffident of their power, or unwilling to exert it . . .' The experience 'of near thirty years' had convinced Tyneside shipowners 'that no reliance could be placed on the magistrates of the river Tyne for the protection of their property, or on the County's magistrates for the protection of either persons or property'. Magistrates in the Blackburn area in 1818 had only a single troop of horse to call on for a district of more than 200 square miles (ibid., pp. 5, 10, 12, 300) and other examples of a similar nature could be given. Property owners could, of course, always be relied on to exaggerate their vulnerability to the depredations of the 'mob', yet even when full allowance for this is made there is clear evidence of how quickly strained the civil and military powers become when presented with a challenge of any size.

Such factors – which did not exclude an understandable concern for their own skin and property – reinforced the disposition of magistrates in many cases to proceed with caution, conciliation and 'mercy'. Their tendency to be concerned above all to preserve stability and public order by minimising action which might aggravate tensions often earned them the opprobrium of local employers and, somewhat unfairly in the circumstances, the impatience of Whitehall. The occasions on which they pursued – or allowed to develop – a policy of active legal or military aggression, as in the incident and aftermath of the Peterloo Massacre in 1819, left deep scars on the social fabric and entered into the historical memory and ideology of the organised working class. But the evidence suggests that they were outnumbered by the occasions when magistrates were accused by employers of being inert, supine and over-indulgent towards the lower orders. At about the same time as the Peterloo Massacre, the Coventry ribbon-weavers were passing a vote of thanks to the local magistrates for their 'kind attention' to the weavers' claim for a wage increase 'and particularly for their requisition to the masters to take the case into their immediate consideration' (ibid., p. 322).

There are further qualifications to be made to any picture of a simple class-war line-up. Workers pursuing industrial action through combination not infrequently received sympathy and help from local populations, thereby enjoying a greater chance of avoiding prosecution. The impulse prompting this support was not necessarily a disinterested pursuit of social justice. Workers with low bargaining power of whom employers took advantage were a burden on the poor rates. In Derbyshire in 1817 a manifesto signed by 'freeholders, farmers, and tradesmen', including a vicar, a churchwarden and two poor-law overseers, declared co-operation with local framework knitters in their struggle for a living wage. Nottingham overseers expressed similar sentiments. In Leicester, between 1819 and 1824, a friendly society for framework knitters, initiated by a parson, openly favoured by the lord-lieutenant of the county, and in receipt of a £100 grant by the Leicester Corporation and subscriptions from the local gentry, sought to protect standard piece-rates from undercutting employers by paying out relief to workers who refused employment at cut rates. The industry's historian, Felkin, 'notes the great effect of this enterprise on the poor rates' (Hammond and Hammond, 1979, pp. 199–200). Another effect, of course, was acrimony between employers and other local gentry who were accused of undermining the spirit of subordination.

In this situation, where all the parties blamed each other, none suffered blame more than the employers themselves. For while, in the eyes of Whitehall and many local magistrates, it should be the employer who initiated legal action against combinations, he often enough found reasons for abstaining. Rival manufacturers were often quick to take advantage of his embarrassments and there were many incidental disadvantages. Prosecution not only involved trouble and expense but also required hard evidence which was often difficult to collect; the employer had to live with the long-term consequences of animosity, ill-will and loss of skilled labour; and in an ill-policed society, violence and wilful damage to property were additional hazards. Consequently, 'a combination was usually let alone until some employer was sufficiently inconvenienced by its operations to be willing himself to set the law in motion. In many cases we find employers apparently accepting or conniving at their men's combinations' (Webb and Webb, 1920, p. 74). Most combinations of this period were of skilled artisans who could at times bring considerable pressure to bear, and until some great stake or strategic issue was involved the employer might well decide in the meantime to tolerate the union and even find positive value in it if it imposed equal conditions on his rivals and thereby limited competition. Nottingham hosiery employers exemplified this interest by agreeing in 1811 'to give the men unabated wages, provided they would join in bringing up the under-paying masters to the same standard' (Hammond and Hammond, 1979, p. 211).

It was unwise, however, for unions to rely on any of these responses. Together with the common law as interpreted and developed by the courts, the combination statutes offered a potent instrument of punishment to any employer who, out of expediency or mood, chose to use it. One example of the arbitrary and capricious application of the law is provided by the London master printers, who negotiated collective agreements with a journeymen's combination at intervals after 1785 but in 1798 secured an indictment of five of its members for conspiracy, for which they received two years' imprisonment. Many unions went on negotiating openly and steadily with their employers during the whole period of repression; others suffered damaging legal attack – often not under the Combination Acts but under common law. It was in the new textile industries, however, that the weight of the Combination Acts is said to have been chiefly felt, being experienced as 'a tremendous millstone round the neck of the local artisans' (Webb and Webb, 1920, p. 81). Even here there is counter-evidence worth noting. During the long lead-up to the Peterloo Massacre, Lancashire witnessed bitter strikes and disturbances among weavers, spinners, building workers and dye-workers. Radical reformers fished hopefully in troubled waters, disseminating, in the opinion of W. R. Hay, a prominent local clerical magistrate, 'the most poisonous and alarming sentiments'. These were beginning to gain ground and 'in consequence the working classes have become not only more pertinacious but more insolent in their demands and demeanour'. Yet despite mounting fears among the gentry and middle class during 1818 that 'demagogues' would 'avail themselves of the present temper of the working people to throw this populous district into disorder and . . . rebellion', the 'magistrates here came to a determination on the question, not to put themselves forward in it – it was . . . one between servants and employers . . . their sole object being to preserve the public peace' (Aspinall, ed., 1949, pp. 257, 259). Ministers and Whitehall officials joined them in complaining constantly about the 'want of spirit in the master manufacturers'. Yet for all the growing anxiety at both national and local levels the legal proprieties were maintained. A suggestion by a magistrate's clerk that striking spinners be designated 'rogues and vagabonds' under a Tudor statute and punished accordingly met the reply from the under-secretary of the Home Department: 'There must be proof of poverty and of refusal to work' (ibid., p. 277).

But with disturbance renewed in 1819 local emotions among the respectable classes were deeply stirred by sworn accounts of military-type mass drilling among the workers, and in July a committee resolved 'that government having signified their approbation of an Armed Association, an offer be immediately made by this Committee . . . of an Armed Association in aid of the civil power, and for the protection of the towns of Manchester and Salford' (Bamford, 1841, Vol. 1, pp. 182–3). These mounting tensions of class war were ignited by a mass working-class assembly for parliamentary reform held in St Peter's Field, Manchester on 16 August 1819. In an attack by mounted forces, 11 were killed or died of wounds and at least 421 suffered injury, mainly at the hands of the local Yeomanry Cavalry – Manchester manufacturers, merchants, publicans and shopkeepers on horseback – whose class fears and frustrations exploded in a panic of violence. Regular troops also in attendance did far less damage, according to Bamford's eye-witness account (ibid., pp. 205–11).

Our concern here, however, is not with the incident itself but with what it reveals of national and local policies. There is still argument as to how far government ministers were parties to an advance decision by the Manchester authorities to use violence. The probabilities seem to support Thompson's opinion that while the latter intended to use some force – though how much is problematic – the former were certainly 'unprepared' for the extent to which it was applied. Significant for our present purpose is Canning's reaction. 'To let down the magistrates', he wrote, 'would be to invite their resignation, and to lose all gratuitous service in the counties liable to disturbance for ever. It is, to be sure, very provoking that the magistrates, right as they were in principle, and nearly right in practice, should have spoilt the completeness of their case by half an hour's precipitation' (Brock, 1941, p. 112). Lord Liverpool, the Prime Minister, declared the magistrates' action 'substantially right', though not alto-gether 'prudent'. 'There remained no alternative but to support them' (E. P. Thompson, 1968, pp. 750–1). These are precisely the verdicts we would expect from those who sought to apply the strategy of control examined earlier. The troops' behaviour had, perhaps, been overemph-atic, had blurred the desired image of authority as rigorously firm but never blood-thirsty, had run the risk of bidding up class tensions to a level inconvenient for the authorities. But the operational men on the spot had made their decision, had run personal risks to uphold order and the status quo, and the code demanded that they be supported. They were, accord-ingly, publicly praised, while Earl Fitzwilliam, who protested publicly against the massacre, was dismissed from his Yorkshire lord-lieutenantcy, an extremely rare event.

The Heritage under Strain: State Repression

Peterloo occurred during a period when Britain's rulers seemed to come somewhere near to abandoning the general strategy of rule developed, for the most part skilfully and effectively, over the past century, and adopting instead the techniques, widespread elsewhere, of arbitrary rule backed by overt coercion. All over Europe events in France had sounded the alarms for nobility and gentry and Britain's were no exception. Much fear was generated by the blaze of interest fired among the artisan, small master and professional strata by Painite radicalism, with its political egalitarianism and its animus against the landed classes.

Riots, disorder and particularly the more organised forms of challenge to authority and the status quo were liable to be met with the mood of a ruling order that feels itself under threat and a string of repressive statutes made their appearance. The 'constitutional' and 'corresponding' societies pursuing mainly pacific agitation for parliamentary reform and the 'rights of man' found their leaders on trial for high treason in 1794, with the Habeas Corpus Act in suspension; followed in 1795 with a Treason Act and a Seditious Meetings and Assemblies Act which imposed restrictions on freedom of utterance, public meeting and political discussion. Naval mutinies in 1797, during which some leaders used revolutionary phrases to adorn a list of material demands and induced sailors to swear dramatic oaths of commitment to the common cause, were followed by the Act against Unlawful Oaths – though it is worth noting that 'the Cabinet was obviously anxious to punish as few as possible' (Halévy, 1961a, p. 56). A Newspaper Act of 1798 was designed to counter written as well as spoken propaganda. After the 1799 Combination Act came the Unlawful Soci-eties Act of the same year, which sought the complete suppression of a number of the leading radical societies, and a further Seditious Meetings Act followed in 1801. An Act of 1812 made Luddite machine-breaking punishable by death.

One form of machine-breaking had been a familiar tactic since the seventeenth century as an expression of 'collective bargaining by riot' – a way of bringing pressure to bear upon employers especially in trades where formal and continuous organisation had not yet developed or where employers refused recognition. It implied no special hostility to machines as such. The other main form was directed against labour-saving machinery that directly threatened the jobs and status of the workers involved or against old machinery now turned to new and threatening uses. It was these forms that were specially prominent in the Midlands and north between 1811 and 1813, with further outbreaks in 1816 (Hammond and Hammond, 1979, chs 9–11; Hobsbawm, 1968, ch. 2; Musson, 1972, p. 14). 'The distinguishing mark of the frame-breaking in 1811–12 was that it was not a wild outburst of popular anger, but a well-planned and organized policy.' As so often, alongside the ferocity of sentiments expressed in Parliament supporting the death sentence there was the usual readiness of the crown's law officers to squelch the enthusiasm of over-exuberant magistrates. Some of these had proposed to hold responsible the occupants of houses containing rented machines when these were smashed by persons coming in from outside, but the law officers rejected this as illegal unless gross negligence could be proved (Hammond and Hammond, 1979, pp. 213, 217). The difficulties of applying a really rigorous policy of repression were compounded by the fact that local opinion was often sympathetic and juries were unwilling to convict if the consequence was hanging. Smaller manufacturers, too, might be only too glad to see the keener forms of competition violently discouraged. The wider significance of Luddism, and the reason why it is likely to remain permanently controversial, lies in the debate as to whether it bears interpretation as evidence of a revolutionary strand in British working-class history. Some accounts seem eager to support such an interpretation; others convey the impression that all working-class behaviour which did not contribute towards the evolutionary civilised development of modern political democracy and collective bargaining through disciplined trade unionism must be regarded as regrettable deviations of no historical significance. Thompson gives support to the former; the Hammonds are accused of supporting the latter (Rule, 1979, p. xxi). Ruling-class fears, at least, are sufficiently explained by Rudé's judgement that 'there were moments when Luddism might overlap with, or impinge upon, a movement whose object was to remove, though not to overthrow, the government', but that these 'occasional political overtones' were 'intrusive rather than intrinsic' to the movement (Rudé, 1981, p. 90). They certainly demonstrate, however, that along with those artisan leaders anxious to co-operate with middle-class parliamentary reformers and to heed the veteran Major Cartwright's injunction to 'hold fast to the laws', there were leaders of depressed occupational groups, such as framework knitters and hand-loom weavers who, in their economic desperation, were prepared to use insurrectionary language of a kind likely to give fright to the ruling classes.

A fresh surge of legal repression followed the acute distress, unrest, disorder and renewed radicalism which ensued after the Napoleonic Wars, when ministers were told that the 'higher classes' in Lancashire and Yorkshire 'fully expect a revolution'. The government turned again, reportedly 'with some reluctance', to strong measures (Brock, 1941, pp. 117, 118). There seems no reason to doubt Halévy's judgement that it was 'distasteful, almost humiliating', for British rulers to have recourse within three years of Waterloo, the final triumph in a long campaign supposedly to defend liberty, to special legislation for the maintenance of law and order. Never, since 1688, except in Ireland, had methods outside the ordinary process of the law been used to put down revolt (Halévy, 1961b, p. 20). There was further suspension of Habeas Corpus, renewed Treason and Seditious Meetings and Assemblies Acts in 1817 and, two years later, Acts prohibiting unlawful drilling of a military character, imposing even more stringent restrictions on public meetings, laying down heavy penalties for publication of blasphemous or seditious matter, and extending the heavy stamp duties upon newspapers – designed to discourage a popular press – to all pamphlets and printed papers.

This sequence of repressive measures is significant because it expressed the authoritative – and authoritarian – reactions of responsible men in high office. There had, of course, been earlier occasions when individual members of the ruling class at both national and local levels had urged policies which dangerously threatened the British heritage of constitutionality and the rule of law. When, for example, in 1791, 'Church and King' mobs in Birmingham had rioted against wealthy local Dissenters who were campaigning for parliamentary and electoral reform and full toleration for Dissent, 'certain of the justices, . . . declared opponents of dissent and political reform, acted with criminal negligence or even directly incited the rioters to act'. A few members of the nobility also had 'thought them a suitable example for others to follow', and the king himself seems to have expressed some support (Rudé, 1981, p. 146). Not until now, however, did it become practically demonstrated that British governments, as against individuals, could be sufficiently politically unnerved as to press systematically and dangerously hard against much-vaunted British freedoms. Plainly those freedoms enjoyed no inevitable stability and a further period of sustained external or internal threat might have extinguished, or at least severely damaged, them for ever.

Throughout the period, however, there remained effective political forces which, from principle or expediency or a mixture of both, continued to uphold that 'integral part of the national traditions', the right of the British people to assert 'resistance in the last resort'. The Whig *Edinburgh Review* never wearied of reminding its readers that 'The great and ultimate barrier against corruption, oppression, and arbitrary power must always be raised on public opinion – and on opinion so valued and so asserted as to point resolutely to *resistance*, if it be once insulted or set at defiance' (Halévy, 1961a, pp. 148–9, italics in original). Government ministers themselves, only a few years after the last of their repressive measures reached the statute book, showed that in relation to the

Combination Acts they were sufficiently in command of themselves to draw some highly pragmatic common-sense conclusions. The case for the Acts seemed a good deal weaker now than it had done in 1800. However much they might serve to relieve the feelings of particular employers and to punish particular workers' leaders, they could never be an instrument for the general suppression of trade unions. And there was a further point that was not lost on Britain's rulers. Repressive legislation aimed directly and specifically at the unions, while it could not destroy them, sometimes drove them underground where they could not be observed, and where secrecy fostered extremism. If their existence was to be seen as inevitable they might more safely and conveniently be allowed to pursue it in the light of day. Other law was no more generally successful than the Combination Acts. Penalties for 'leaving work unfinished', for swearing unlawful oaths, and for the common-law crime of conspiracy had all been applied during the same period and had likewise failed as universal deterrents. It was the Combination Acts, however, which were most blatantly class-biased, most immediately provocative to the artisan classes, and most threatening to the rulers' self-image both inside and outside Parliament.

With respect to the rulers' self-image it is not irrelevant that during the early decades of the nineteenth century the occupation of politician was becoming both more professional and more reputable. The patronage system was on the decline as an effective means of party organisation and the government was more vulnerable to outside opinion expressed through a large independent section of Parliament. Ministers themselves were becoming professionals who were expected to show some capacity for hard work and a readiness to serve an apprenticeship in the lower ranks; the days were past when the hereditary leader of a 'connection' could claim high political office as a matter of prescriptive right. These changes, along with such influences as the evangelical movement, were raising the standards by which many politicians felt it prudent to measure their public reputations. During the long premiership of Lord Liverpool from 1812 to 1827,

> an imperceptible change took place in one aspect of English manners: at the end of the eighteenth century, and in spite of Pitt's great name, the average Englishman endorsed Adam Smith's verdict upon that "insidious and crafty animal, vulgarly called a statesman or politician"; by the time of the great Reform Bill there is already found the alliance between politicians and the respectable middle class. Victorian governments would have been utterly different in character had not politics become the profession for honest men as well as the recreation of landed aristocrats. In the eighteenth century an honest politican had been, in the public eye, an extraordinary and praiseworthy exception to a general rule; in the nineteenth century the corrupt time server was singled out for reprobation because he was an isolated case and not the symbol of a class. (Brock, 1941, pp. 30–1, 77–8, 151)

Such was the context of structure and opinion within which the campaign for repeal of the Combination Acts was pursued.

Repeal of the Combination Acts, 1824–5

The story of repeal was told by Francis Place in a way which presented it as virtually a single-handed campaign with himself as the hero who manipulated the Radical MP Joseph Hume. This is known now to be an exaggerated account. While Place's achievement 'was a remarkable feat of intelligent wire-pulling and of enormously industrious and well-informed lobbying', others were also active in mobilising the unions – in particular Gravener Henson, the framework-knitters' leader, and Peter Moore, Radical MP for Coventry (E. P. Thompson, 1968, pp. 564, 566). More important for our present context, however, than the minutiae of the campaign is the fact that it revealed the beginnings of a conception of trade unionism on the part of influential sections of the Establishment which has persisted in certain major respects to this day.

Much has been written of how Place and Hume packed and managed a Select Committee and, without either debate or division, hustled a strong Bill through 'a House full of gentlemen who found trade union matters boring, some of whom had made of *laissez-faire* an unquestioned dogma, and most of whom were confused or indifferent as to the issue' (ibid., pp. 564–5). This Bill of 1824 not only repealed the Combination Acts and freed workers from restrictions on collective action with respect to wages and hours, but also protected such activities from common-law conspiracy prosecutions.

Because repeal was followed by a burst of economic prosperity and a sharp rise in the cost of living there ensued 'an outbreak of trade unionism and strikes. From one end of the country to the other masters and men were engaged in industrial conflict' (Wallas, 1918, p. 218). Under pressure from, among others, the shipowning and shipbuilding interests, Huskisson, MP for Liverpool and President of the Board of Trade, along with Peel, reopened the whole issue with a new Select Committee and the initial intention of pushing through a Bill, drafted by the shipping interest, that would make trade unions and even friendly societies virtually impossible (Webb and Webb, 1920, pp. 105–6). According to Place the Attorney-General shrank from its legal implications and this strengthened their position when he and Hume went into action again. After much busy lobbying they secured a shift in the balance of committee opinion against Huskisson, and the Act of 1825 're-established the general common-law prohibition of combinations, but specifically excepted from prosecution associations for the purpose of regulating wages or hours of labour' (ibid., p. 107).

Although many legal battles had yet to be fought on the issue of union security and rights the 1825 Act was of great significance, not only in its substantive content but also because it represented a major occasion on which parliamentary constitutional procedure secured for organised labour important concessions manifestly against the wishes of powerful groups within the ruling class. For this reason considerable interest attaches to the arguments and sentiments which were considered relevant and appropriate to the subject in the House of Commons.

Speaking in the House on the first Bill in 1824, Hume plainly felt on

strong ground in being able to play upon British sensitivity about legal
equality. Employers might combine against their workmen and 'determine not to give them more than a certain sum for their labour' but the
workmen could not 'consult together about the rate they ought to fix on
that labour, without rendering themselves liable to fine and imprisonment'. This gross inequality in the law had been a source of perpetual
dissatisfaction. 'Some of those persons who were well satisfied with the
state of things, without knowing exactly what that state was, professed to
feel pride that, in the eyes of the British law, all were equal – that high and
low, rich and poor, were alike protected.' This might be the case in theory,
but practice was different (Hume, 1824a, cols 145–6). In a later speech
Hume emphasised that the Combination Acts had not only failed to
prevent combinations but had also, 'in the opinion of many of both
parties', given them 'a violent character' and rendered them 'highly
dangerous to the peace of the community' (Hume, 1824b, col. 812). This
early opinion that repression, far from eliminating what was seen by many
as a social threat, aggravated it by driving unions into the role of a
semi-secret, semi-underground movement was to be remembered for a
long time and revived at a time of important legal change for the unions.

Speaking on the weaker, amending Bill of 1825, Huskisson, despite
having come under strong pressure from major employer interests,
declared that many of the Combination Acts were 'oppressive and cruel in
their operation on workmen; and he had always advocated the principle of
allowing every man to dispose of his labour to the best advantage, which
principle they, in very many instances, had directly violated'. He did not
wish 'to interfere with the meetings or combinations' of workmen 'so far
as related to the amount of their own wages. They were at liberty to take
all proper means to secure that remuneration for their labour to which they
conceived they were entitled – considering the circumstances of a greater
demand for labour, or a greater expense incurred in the purchase of
provisions.' He did not want a return to the Combination Acts 'or to any
measure that would not give equal protection to the employed as well as to
the employer'. Unions could therefore properly be formed and could
'reasonably ask for larger wages'. Unfortunately, however, unions were
apt to go a good deal further. Huskisson then proceeded, by reading to the
House extracts from union rules, to construct a picture of powerful
instruments of control which sought to dictate to their masters how they
should conduct their business in such matters as apprenticeship, which
men should be employed, and the principle of uniform wages for all
(Huskisson, 1825a, col. 1288 and 1825b, cols 354–5). Wallace, Master of
the Mint, reiterated that the Bill permitted men to meet for the purpose of
obtaining a wage increase, but if they went beyond this they were going
too far.

> The permitted combinations for workers were those for the 'sole
> purpose' of agreeing on *their own* hours and wages, and nothing else.
> Another section . . . set out at length a series of vaguely worded criminal
> offences in respect of pressure brought in industrial conflict by violence,
> 'threats', 'molestation', 'intimidation', and 'obstruction'. This Act, plus

the judges' interpretations of the common law, remained the basic law until the reforms of 1871–5 . . . '. (Wedderburn 1971, p. 307, italics in original)

'The right of collective bargaining . . . was for the first time expressly established' (Webb and Webb, 1920, p. 108). Yet it was hedged round with qualifications that were full of legal danger for trade unionists as soon as they applied the threats, pressures and sanctions inseparable from effective bargaining.

The motives of Place, Hume and other Radicals in supporting the unions' campaign for repeal have never been convincingly demonstrated. What did they believe themselves to be doing in securing repeal? Place's argument, accepted by his biographer and the Webbs, that paradoxically combinations were being kept alive only by legal repression and would realise their own futility in the face of economic forces when repression was lifted, does not square with his own behaviour as organiser and secretary of several craft societies (Wallas, 1918, pp. 19, 199, 219–20). Yet the fact that economists often asserted the unions' inability to defy successfully the laws of political economy did not necessarily mean there was no acceptable role for them. Huskisson's remarks are compatible with a view that repeal was commensurate with a number of measures taken during the first half of the century which aimed at 'clearing the markets' – that is, at removing such legislative or other impediments as might seem to impede the wholesome and progressive operation of market forces. Other examples were the removal of statutory wage assessment and apprenticeship regulation, of restrictions on the emigration of skilled artisans and the exportation of machinery and, of course, the abolition of the corn laws and the progressive introduction of full free trade. So long as the unions were kept vulnerable to the law if they attempted coercive pressure upon employers they might have a legitimate place in political economy. This would lie not in doomed attempts to defy market forces but in contributing to their smoother operation. By being free to deal with the employer or employers as a collective, workers could improve the workings of the labour market by helping to register more clearly the forces of supply and demand. Such an approach implied a sharp distinction between two types of union activity. On the one hand, was this regulatory market function which could be deemed useful even though it might, for some or all of the time, be bitterly resented by the employers themselves. On the other hand, were the restrictionist attempts by unions or unionised workgroups to encroach on the employer's prerogative in his disposition and handling of the resources at his disposal, which were deemed, by economists and employers alike, to be both an economically pernicious obstruction to the proper and universally beneficial pursuit of profit, and a socially unacceptable imposition upon the authority and status of a property-owner. The 1825 Act could be seen as designed to permit peaceful negotiations about the market price of labour, but to ensure that as soon as workers applied coercive sanctions or brought their collective pressure to bear upon issues other than wages and hours, such as apprenticeship, production methods, output, hiring and firing, or the closed shop, they put themselves at risk. The Act might therefore have been defended by its supporters on three counts. It served a purpose deemed useful by the economists. It could be used by employers to uphold their prerogative in the areas where it was most important. And it served a conscience-salving and ideological purpose by lending itself to the assertion that legal equality between rich and poor, a central item in the ruling-class self-legitimation, was being maintained – though in fact the equality was merely formal.

Nevertheless, it must be recalled that the initial objective of Huskisson and Peel had been to create conditions which, it was hoped, would make possible the suppression of trade unionism altogether. The fact that they were deterred from this purpose by a combination of external agitation, parliamentary procedure and the evidence of a Select Committee, gives point to the following judgement by E. P. Thompson, though he extends it to the whole period from 1790 to 1832, the year of the first increment of parliamentary reform. The oligarchs and great gentry of the eighteenth century had been

> content to be subject to the rule of law only because this law was serviceable and afforded to their hegemony the rhetoric of legitimacy. This paradox ... was ... at the heart of eighteenth-century society. But it was also a paradox which that society could not in the end transcend, for the paradox was held in equipoise upon an ulterior equilibrium of class forces. When the struggles of 1790–1832 signalled that this equilibrium had changed, the rulers of England were faced with alarming alternatives. They could either dispense with the rule of law, dismantle their elaborate constitutional structures, countermand their own rhetoric and exercise power by force, or they could submit to their own rules ...

In their handling of some of the challenges with which they were confronted, 'they took halting steps in the first direction. But in the end, rather than shatter their own self-image and repudiate 150 years of constitutional legality, they surrendered to the law' (E. P. Thompson, 1977, p. 269).

They went forward with an official conception of trade unions which, arrived at partly by luck and partly by shrewd judgement, was to serve their own class ideology and propaganda well. We have noted that at this first stage in the legal development of modern unionism there had emerged already the ruling-class distinction between union participation in regulating the market price of labour, and union 'interference' in the employer's authority with respect to the deployment of resources at the workplace. This distinction has to this day lain at the heart of policies and attitudes brought to bear upon trade unionism and collective bargaining by influential sections of the Establishment and middle-class opinion. They have often found it relatively easy to tolerate – and even to encourage – a restrained and peaceful union role in the regulation of the labour market. Few, however, have hesitated to condemn not only strikes and other forms of collective pressure at the workplace, but also regulations and practices which obstructed the employer's total freedom to do as he pleased with respect to technology, work organisation, hiring and firing. The popularity of the distinction is easy to understand. By identifying an aspect of trade unionism that could be supported it soothed consciences, expressed perhaps a genuine measure of concern and reinforced legitimation of the system; by identifying what was inadmissible it asserted the absolute imperative of progress, the sanctity of property rights and the 'freedoms' of the individual worker on such issues as the closed shop. Men could put their hands upon their hearts and profess full sympathy with the legitimate aspirations of working men while regretting that so many of their present aspirations and behaviours were illegitimate – such as wilful obstruction of beneficial change, intimidation, violence and encroachments on individual liberty.

With this distinction between a legitimate and an illegitimate trade unionism now beginning to emerge, the ruling classes fumbled forward with a growing consciousness among some of their influential members that constitutionality and the rule of law must be extended to such labour movements and organisations as showed signs of keeping within the law themselves. The application of this policy was neither universal nor consistent – there were always to remain instances of the law being cynically manipulated, bent, or stretched to breaking point. Yet on the whole the policy held. For illustration of all these tendencies we may select a *cause célèbre* in Britain's labour history – the case of the Tolpuddle Martyrs.

The Tolpuddle Martyrs

The case of the Martyrs of Tolpuddle bulks large in Labour movement myth and legend. The most extravagant claims for its importance are those made in a centenary commemoration volume published by the Trades Union Congress in 1934. There it was described as a central key incident both in the inspiration and growth of trade unionism and in 'a sequence of events which led, through Chartism, to the second Reform Act of 1867, the creation of the Trades Union Congress, and the formation of political parties as we know them today' (Henderson, 1934, pp. 187, 197). It would not be difficult to construct an argument which demoted the incident to very much smaller significance than this. Yet a slippery element in any such construction would be the difficulty in gauging the effect upon subsequent generations of Labour movement activists of the *belief* that the Tolpuddle case was an immensely important milestone, and the consequences in terms of their convictions and behaviour. There is no necessity here, however, to attempt any evaluation on those lines, for the present purpose is rather to examine the case for what it reveals of ruling-class dispositions and commitments.

The essential facts, though soon told, must be seen in context. The farm workers of the southern counties had long been in a mood of resentment and riot. The especially bad year of 1829 had been followed by outbursts of machine-breaking, rick-burning and hunger rioting which ran through the counties like a prairie fire. Such factors as 'tithe, rents, wages, pauperism and poverty, agricultural depression, poaching and the game laws, and radical agitation may all have played a part' (Rudé, 1981, p. 150). But the triggering cause was the example of France, where, on the occasion of the replacement of a despotism with a constitutional monarchy, widespread popular movements had included the destruction of property by peasants. In some areas, notably Kent and Sussex, an important feature 'was the sympathy of other classes with the demands of the labourers'; farmers and magistrates often being less united and eager to crush the riots than government urged. Even where the will existed, troops were often thin on the ground. There was much hand-wringing by the big landed proprietors and for once they were probably not exaggerating. It was a 'far more general and more serious' rising than those of 1795 and 1816; 'several counties . . . were in a state bordering on insurrection . . . The terror of the landowners . . . is reflected in such language as that of the Duke of Buckingham, who talked of the country being in the hands of the rebels, or of one of the Barings, who said in the House of Commons that if the disorders went on for three or four days longer they would be beyond the reach of almost any power to control them' (Hammond and Hammond, 1945, pp. 44, 54).

When the riots were subdued reprisals were savage. Nearly 2,000 rioters or suspects were brought to trial before special commissions or county quarter sessions, 9 being hanged, 644 imprisoned and 481 transported. 'It was the largest batch of prisoners ever transported from England for a common crime, thus underlining the enormity of the labourers' offence in the eyes of government and magistrates.' Radicals and Dissenting ministers had played some part in the disturbances and there were certainly Nonconformists among those transported. One justice noted also that the participants included many whose wages placed them 'far above want' – 'blacksmiths, carpenters and artisans, and men in a superior condition of life'. Most of those transported were 'settled family men' of 'high moral character' and a good standard of literacy (Rudé, 1981, pp. 150, 155).

There was plenty in all this to concentrate the minds of the ruling order, particularly fearful as they were of what seemed systematic principled campaigns of violence and disorder against rural property and landed authority. There was felt to be a special significance, too, when leaders of local protest were identified as Nonconformists. Evangelical Nonconformism emphasised 'the natural equality and essential moral inadequacy of all men before God', propagating 'a spiritual status system which, while not radical in any political sense, cut across the hierarchical structures of the contemporary society'. The Duchess of Buckingham had sensed more shrewdly than Wesley an essential truth about the broad ideological and social implications of Methodist doctrines when she described them as 'strongly tinctured with impertinence and disrespect . . . towards superiors, in perpetually endeavouring to level all ranks, and do away with all distinctions'. It was monstrous 'to be told that you have a heart as sinful as the common wretches that crawl on the earth' (Gilbert, 1976, pp. 82–3). For a Nonconformist to take part in active social protest was to proclaim himself in principled organisational hostility to the landed classes, the episcopacy and the alliance of squire and parson.

It is against this background that Tolpuddle must be viewed. Only a year after the trials had concluded it was reported in 1832 to Lord Melbourne, then Home Secretary, that more than half the labourers in Hampshire were contributing to local trade unions, that the movement was spreading and that wages were being forced up. In Dorset in 1833 a group of Tolpuddle men formed a society and established contact with Robert Owen's Grand National Consolidated Trades Union. They were Methodists, two of them itinerant preachers – 'sedate and serious peasants, anxious to improve their lot but equally anxious to observe the law. Their standards were high – no swearing, no obscenity, above all no violence – but some mumbo jumbo of secret oaths was gone through by new members . . . ' (Ziegler, 1978, p. 160).

Besides being trade unionists and Methodists, the Tolpuddle men laboured under an additional misfortune. The MP for the county, W. S. Ponsonby, a local landowner, was Melbourne's brother-in-law. On taking office in 1830 Melbourne had been warned by Peel that the growth of the unions was the most disturbing threat he faced – though Peel probably included in this category the 'political unions' currently agitating for parliamentary reform. Consulted for advice in 1831, Nassau Senior, Professor of Political Economy at Oxford, offered the opinion that the 1825 Act repealing the Combination Acts could not itself be repealed, but that union rights should be tightly restricted, with picketing prohibited, employers given power to arrest men without warrant and, if necessary, union funds confiscated. Melbourne decided it would be impossible to get such proposals through Parliament (Clynes, 1934, p. 160), and abandoned the idea of fresh legislation. A biographer attributes to him the opinion that unions were 'evils to be lived with . . . people had a right to unite and . . . government could only properly seek to curb them if they were acting in some way subversive to the state' (Ziegler, 1978, p. 155). He was supported in this stance by the belief, confidently put about by the classical economists, that trade unions could not in the long run survive if they attempted to defy inexorable laws of political economy.

He now received from his brother-in-law a request for help and advice; a request soon reinforced by heavy pressure from James Frampton, local squire and magistrate. There followed some flurry in Whitehall as crown lawyers cast around for a suitable statute for use against the Tolpuddle unionists. Melbourne's first suggestion to Frampton was the 1817 Seditious Meetings and Assemblies Act, but having had doubts he consulted the crown lawyers, who reported that the case would probably not stand up. Eventually someone remembered the secret oaths, which appear genuinely to have frightened Frampton and his fellow squires as proceeding 'from some general directing authority'. The dust was accordingly blown off the Mutiny Act of 1797, originally directed against disaffection in the armed forces. Melbourne knew he was on thin ice and urged Frampton to get the men to trial as soon as possible, wanting a quick conviction before too much public attention was aroused.

The trial (18 March 1834) was presided over by John Williams,

previously Whig MP for Lincoln, a friend of Melbourne's who was 'ambitious and eager to please'. It was his first assize, held before a packed jury of
local farmers. After what seems to have been a travesty of a trial the six
men were sentenced to seven years' transportation. They were in the hulks
before the end of the month and had sailed for Botany Bay before the
middle of April. Speed did not, however, avail. There were nationwide
meetings, demonstrations, petitions, questions in the House. Passionate
principle and political expediency combined in an extensive and protracted condemnation of the government. Much political advantage was
squeezed from the situation by its critics with the slogan 'One law for the
rich and another for the poor' – Freemasons, too, it was pointed out,
conducted secret oaths, as did Orange lodges of Anglo-Irish landlords,
whose Grand Master was the Duke of Cumberland (Citrine, 1934,
pp. 1–101).

So far the Tolpuddle case reveals ministers conducting their repressive
activities within the formal framework of law and parliamentary procedure but nevertheless stretching the law in the process. Their behaviour
now revealed a growing unease that the stretching had gone too far, that
important legitimising principles had been badly dented, and that no more
hostages must be given to fortune. Following the trial Frampton was eager
to complete the rout and inquired of Melbourne whether the local farmers
should dismiss all the men who had joined the union. Viscount Howick
replied that Melbourne thought it 'very doubtful whether it would be
prudent, on the part of the Justices of the Peace, to recommend the farmers
to discharge those of their labourers who may have joined the union,
merely upon the ground of their having done so, and without any
unreasonable demand having been preferred on their part or any overt act
of menace and intimidation having been resorted to'. Melbourne himself
also wrote on the same day (26 March 1834), privately and confidentially,
so that its substance would not 'find its way into the newspapers'. The
government, he told Frampton, believed that trade unions were legal
provided no violence, forced intimidation, or illegal oaths or acts were
resorted to. Given this, could government or magistrates advise farmers
to 'discharge their men for doing that which may be not only legal but just
and reasonable?' Would they not 'incur much odium and subject themselves to observations which it would be difficult to reply to?' Moreover,
would such a policy be successful and effective? It had always been found
difficult to obtain co-operation among manufacturers, and farmers were
even more 'timid, more disunited, more attentive to their particular
situation and individual interests'.

Melbourne then asked rhetorically: 'are we then to wait with our arms
folded whilst this combination spreads itself throughout the peasantry? I
am compelled to answer, that in the present state of the law and of the
public feeling I see no safe or effectual mode of prevention.' Melbourne
was telling Frampton what he was also telling the king, who, much
disturbed about industrial and political unrest, had written that 'there
must be something in the law of the country which is inadequate and
defective'. Melbourne indicated that 'no remedy can be applied . . . the fire
cannot be extinguished, but . . . must burn until it burns out'. To

Frampton he predicted that the unionism probably *would* spread into the agricultural areas, but were it to become dangerous 'the immediate peril will probably at once suggest and reconcile the public mind to the necessary measures'. None of this satisfied Frampton, who replied that the farmers themselves would probably take the initiative and responsibility of refusing to employ trade unionists. Melbourne's final word on this issue was an indication of approval, provided that the farmers had 'themselves acted justly, and have not generally attempted to reduce the wages of their labourers below the fair and natural level'. He added, for good measure, that it was doubtful if a labourer discharged for being a unionist could be refused parish poor relief.

Meanwhile, coming under pressure in the House of Commons, he had occasion, in his turn, to pester Frampton. Frampton had notified him that two of the Tolpuddle men had been active in the 1830 riots, and that another had been convicted of stealing iron in 1829. Melbourne pressed for hard evidence as 'it is most material to avoid error in a public statement' ('The Frampton–Melbourne Correspondence', in Citrine, ed., 1934, pp. 171–85). Far more important for the transportees, however, was Melbourne's elevation, in July 1834 and again in April 1835, to the premiership, which in the latter year brought to the Home Office Lord John Russell, whose Whig conscience about freedom was somewhat less elastic than Melbourne's. Much fussed over the 'one law for the rich and another for the poor' charge, he reduced the judge's sentence, writing to Melbourne: 'To be sure the Duke of Cumberland' and others 'are far more guilty than the labourers but the law does not reach them, I fear.' Melbourne resisted further clemency, but Russell now began to express doubts as to whether the trial itself had been fully legal and finally, in March 1836, the agitation still persisting, the Tolpuddle men were given a free pardon, remitted the rest of their sentence and were eventually brought home (Citrine, 1934, pp. 71–6).

What is revealed by the Tolpuddle episode, and by the nature, the enforcement and the repeal of the Combination Acts is the growing nervousness of British governments about the political capital that could be made by their enemies and critics both inside and outside the House of Commons from any government behaviour that could be represented as violating freedom, constitutionality, the rule of law and the even-handed-ness of government between the classes. The modern constitutional role of parliamentary Opposition was not yet forged, but the emergent beginnings of a principled, as against a merely factional, independent presence in the House were making the old legitimations more rather than less important for governments. Two corollaries may be added. The effectiveness of principled Opposition depended not only upon the exist-ence outside the House of a growing 'public opinion' among the expanding commercial, manufacturing and professional classes to which appeal could be made, but also upon the existence among significant sections of this opinion of political aspirations and convictions which sought expression through universal ideals of 'freedom' and 'justice'. In the absence of such convictions there would have been no leverage to exert against governments. And, secondly, the logic of the situation was already indicating clearly that individuals and groups who hoped to benefit from the ruling order's commitment to freedom must take care themselves to keep within the law, for under the implicit contract any attempt to subvert the system or public order at once released the state from its obligation to respect their liberties.

The 1832 Reform Act

By the time of the Tolpuddle case the British political and constitutional system had already passed its greatest and most significant test by assimilating the Reform Act of 1832. This had been 'at once the victory of a political group – a group of great Whig families – and the victory of a class – the vast middle class electorate, the farmers, bond holders, manufacturers and shop-keepers, who henceforward enjoyed the franchise on the same terms throughout the entire country' (Halévy, 1961c, p. 61). Most artisans, and certainly all those below them in the pecking order, remained excluded.

The political scene with respect to parliamentary reform had changed significantly since a few Whig patricians had manœuvred with somewhat reckless stakes in the eighteenth century. For some groups of wage-earners reform in the accepted sense now seemed hopelessly inadequate. There were, in the rapidly expanding textile towns of the northern counties, growing numbers of factory operatives who, denied as yet any systematic method for influencing their terms and conditions of work, were open to exhortations to seek far-reaching political solutions. Alongside such slogans of the old liberal-radicalism as 'the people versus the aristocracy' were arising new ones generated by the rising factory industrialism, such as 'labour versus capital'. These were offered by leaders such as John Doherty, who in 1829 launched a federation of cotton-spinners that, given the support of Robert Owen and others, broadened out into the short-lived Grand National Consolidated Trades Union (GNCTU) of 1833–4. Doherty preached doctrines developed by, for example, Thomas Hodgskin (to whom Marx, in *Capital*, acknowledged a debt) and popularised by William Thompson, to the effect that the whole product of labour should be distributed among the workers, 'manual or mental'. There were visions of using the GNCTU as a means to this end, but it was never anything more than an unsuccessful attempt to organise efficient strike relief (Musson, 1972, p. 34). Nevertheless, among a small minority there was a genuine revolutionary thrust of which the main northern centre was Manchester, where as early as the 1780s writers were lamenting a 'growing gulf' between rich and poor and where by now 'extremists were too active to allow the moderates room to manœuvre' (Briggs, 1968, pp. 89–91). Bred in this atmosphere, 'Operative Ultra-Radicals of the class-conscious school wanted universal suffrage at once so that a working-class majority might be obtained for the widest alterations in the social and economic fabric of society' (Maccoby, 1935, p. 33). But London, too, was another revolutionary focus, where artisans deeply read in Paine and Cobbett had gone on to revolutionary notions about the economic organisation of society that were derived from Owen and confirmed by Hodgskin's lectures at the London Mechanics Institute.

The leaders and activists of this and other movements for social transformation came under the strong disapproval of men such as Francis Place who in this, as in his ardent support of sober trade unionism, the abolition of the corn laws, free trade and artisan respectability was a recognisable forerunner of influential later leaders among the labour aristocracy. He and many like him, determined and resourceful in their pursuit of rights which were intended to advance the welfare and status of their class without threatening the social order in any fundamental sense, had been able to work with middle-class reformers for many years, albeit with intermittent friction and mutual doubts. Even the northern factory districts demonstrated some capacity for vertical alliance. These were 'the strongest home of a commercial Radicalism whose central principle was hostility to the corn laws. Divided on so much else, masters and men agreed on the fundamental inequity of the corn legislation which kept bread dear so that rents might be high for the landlord class that dominated Whig and Tory party alike' (ibid., p. 34). Of course middle-class aspirations ranged wider than this. Their pressure for fuller admission to the political nation had mounted as their stake in the economy grew and as their demand for full social and religious emancipation and recognition grew with it. Among the dominant landed classes, by contrast, the Tories wished to concede nothing and the Whigs, much divided, veered and backed with shifting political circumstance.

The temperature of the reform movement had been sharply and decisively raised by the July Revolution in France, which despatched the despotic Charles X and raised an approving storm of popular feeling in Britain. At first it was shared, though more temperately, by the ruling classes. But in the parliamentary election of that year the constitutional issue took precedence. 'It was the privileges of the aristocracy which were the object of attack, the excessive influence it was in a position to exercise over an unduly restricted electorate.' In every constituency where the elections were more than a form the candidates found themselves virtually obliged to promise a review of the franchise (Halévy, 1961c, pp. 5–6). The easy success of the French overthrow not only gave a strong impetus to the movement for reform but also helped to decide the particular form it took during the next two years. 'The first French Revolution had completely discredited in England any policy of forcible resistance to Government. Now, however, an organized rising began to seem not only a reasonable, but a virtuous and tolerably safe method of solving constitutional difficulties' (Wallas, 1918, p. 244). As the alternating ruling parties manoeuvred and counter-manoeuvred and it seemed as if the Duke of Wellington's government and the House of Lords might stand pat against reform, plans were made by powerful sections among the middle and artisan classes – and to some extent put into effect – for the organised disruption of commercial and financial life. There was no doubt as to the existence of a total determination to secure change. What remained open was the response of the last-ditch resisters. Everything now depended on the choices made by a relatively small number of men. The doctrines of the constitution, Place pointed out, could now be turned against them. 'The theory of "the Constitution" was against them; the elucidation by "constitutional writers" was against them; the whole doctrine of checks was against them; that beautiful system so lauded by Whigs and Tories, and believed by almost everybody, as constituting the very essence of the best of all possible governments, was against them . . . ' (ibid., pp. 289–90).

It hardly needs saying that their decision to concede must not be viewed in the light of our hindsight knowledge of a subsequent century and a half of peaceful democratic 'development', with, in the words of Tennyson, freedom broadening 'slowly down from precedent to precedent'. From their point of view the uncertainty was racking. At what point did an apparently judicious and timely concession become a signal to restive challengers that rulers had lost the will and nerve to govern and could safely be totally overrun? There seemed plenty of potential challengers. Property-owners in the southern counties had not yet recovered from the alarms of the 1830 labourers' revolt. New and ominous combinations of factory operatives were arising in the north. Dangerous doctrines put about among artisans in the capital were spreading far from their origin. Ruling groups have decided on less evidence than this that the time has come to enforce their command with some exemplary demonstrations of blood-letting. It would have been a comprehensible decision in 1832.

The rulers of Britain did not, on balance, so decide. If we may recall Thompson's words – 'They could either dispense with the rule of law, dismantle their elaborate constitutional structures, countermand their own rhetoric and exercise power by force; or they could submit to their own rules . . . ' (E. P. Thompson, 1977, p. 269). Some of them, now as later, were prepared to choose the first, but could not prevail over those who urged the second. We may hypothesise that by now the sheer enormity of 'destroying' the system, and the terrible burden of responsibility that would bear upon those sharing such a decision, had by themselves become powerful deterrents – deterrents that reinforced such doubts as existed about the likely success of a wholesale resort to force. They may even have felt that the task of designing, operating and raising the money for the authoritarian system that would have been needed to subdue growing sections of the middle as well as the lower classes was simply beyond them. 'The methods of continental absolutism were unintelligible to the English gentry' (Halévy, 1961c, p. 6).

The hypothesis offered above assumes that a political system which is tolerably successful in maintaining stability will gather cumulative resilience against fundamental disturbance the longer it persists. Every successive policy pursued or decision made to preserve, nourish and uphold it increases its inertia and the social investment embodied in it, thereby raising the threshold of frustration, fear, or discontent which has to be reached before powerful groups put it at risk. Such policies and decisions had been made by the British ruling class over a very long period and some of the more recent ones were having an increasingly significant bearing upon the official attitude towards trade unions. Along with the repression, the harshness and much local cruelty there was beginning to emerge an awareness that certain minimal forms of protocol and legal punctilio must be observed even towards these feared and detested organisations. The first stage had been the very minor semantic expression of ruling-class legal even-handedness embodied in the amending Combination Act 1800. This had been followed by a more weighty manifestation when it was decided that the state must not itself initiate prosecutions of worker combinations since this would highlight its refusal to prosecute employer combinations. A further stage was reached when, on the occasion of repeal, ministers of Huskisson's persuasion felt it expedient to express publicly, as he did in 1825, that he did not want a return to 'any measure that would not give equal protection to the employed as well as to the employer'. Unions were still in danger whenever they exerted the sanctions integral to effective trade unionism and collective bargaining, and were to remain so for another half-century. But they could no longer be attacked merely for existing; a fact which emerged even from the fumbling botch of Tolpuddle. There was now a tiny legal base on which to build.

The New Poor Law

Halévy has been accused of dangerously underestimating the changes wrought by the 1832 Reform Act in the social and political composition of the House of Commons (Maccoby, 1935, p. 75). All that we need to register here is that the presence of middle-class Radicals and economists certainly helped to ensure the passage of the Poor Law Act of 1834. The nature, reception and political impact of this statute are relevant for the present analysis, for it played a major part in intensifying doubts about the new industrial order and renewing a public debate about the relative merits of authoritarian paternalism as against *laissez-faire* market contractualism.

It was noted earlier that the local, non-professional administration of the old Elizabethan Poor Law had in many areas made of it something more than simply a means of relieving destitution and suppressing vagrancy – 'its constructive aims suggested an interpretation of social welfare reminiscent of the more primitive, but more genuine, social rights which it had largely superseded'. Even at the end of the eighteenth century the poor law represented 'the last remains of a system which tried to adjust real income to the social needs and status of the citizen and not solely to the market value of his labour' (T. H. Marshall, 1950, pp. 22, 23). It was applied in some areas as a 'by no means . . . unenlightened policy' for 'dealing with the problem of surplus labour in the lagging rural sector of a rapidly expanding but still underdeveloped economy' (Blaug, 1974, p. 143). A notable feature was the readiness to distribute outdoor relief in money or in kind – outside, that is, the workhouse or poorhouse – not only to the disabled or chronic sick but also to the able-bodied unemployed or those whose work incomes were insufficient for subsistence. This early version of Family Income Supplement existed, for example, in Leicestershire where, according to a local magistrate, master-hosiers concerted 'to keep down the prices of the workmen so low that the parishes are obliged to make up the earnings of the workmen, so as to enable them to support their families and thus carry on their trade in some measure out of the poor rates'. The same practice was applied to domestic wool spinners in Norfolk, Suffolk and Essex (Hammond and Hammond, 1979, pp. 124, 198), as well as to some agricultural labourers.

It was this extra-market aspect which attracted the doctrinal hostility of the economists, who saw the poor law as obstructing and distorting the proper workings of the labour market by interposing non-market considerations. Worse, it tended to corrupt the lower orders' will to work and 'infect the honest working man and destroy his character'. Rising expenditure on poor relief brought a marked resurgence after the Napoleonic Wars 'of the belief that any kind of charity, over and beyond relief in cases of dire necessity, tended to encourage idleness and vice' (J. D. Marshall, 1968, p. 15). Edwin Chadwick, Nassau Senior and their colleagues on the Royal Commission on the Poor Laws, 1832–4, played on such fears – 'the allegedly demoralising effects of the old poor law were wildly exaggerated by the propagandists of the new poor law of 1834' (Rose, 1972, p. 8).

The link between, on the one hand, the economists, Utilitarians and their conceptions of *laissez-faire* and of clearing the markets and, on the other, the governing classes of mainly landed aristocrats, was Lord John Russell, who instead of reading classics at Oxford or Cambridge had read political economy at Edinburgh at the hands of key figures of the Scottish Enlightenment. 'Russell was the only member of the ruling classes, the only man in really high office, who understood what Bentham and the economists were driving at.' It was Russell who introduced the new poor law; Russell 'the man of the transition, the link between the old order and the new, belonging to the old order by birth, carried over to the new order by his ideas' (A. J. P. Taylor, 1976, pp. 67–8, 71).

The symbolism embodied in the new poor law was arguably of greater significance than its practical effects, which fell far short of what was expected. Seen as a final solution to the problem of pauperism which would work wonders for the moral character of the working man, it was understandably welcomed by many members of the superior classes. Outdoor relief for the able-bodied destitute was to be abolished, and they were to be offered instead maintenance in a workhouse in which their lives would be regulated and – with segregation of the sexes – made less acceptable than those who chose to stay outside and fend for themselves. The test of 'less eligibility' would ensure that while those in dire need would be constrained to accept the workhouse rather than starve, those not so reduced would prefer to remain independent 'and thus avoid contracting the morally wasting disease of pauperism' (Rose, 1972, p. 8).

In the event, the new system provided no final solution to the problem of pauperism; nor did it do much to improve either the material or the moral condition of the working classes. It was certainly less inhumane in its application than its opponents alleged; contrary to some half-serious expectations the skins of old pauper women who died in the workhouse were not used to provide chair covers for the Poor Law Commissioners (ibid., p. 9). It has long been established that outdoor relief to the able-bodied continued in the industrial north, where unemployment and hardship were more obviously a function of the trade cycle than of individual moral fibre, but recent research had shown also that even in the rural south, where the new system was long believed to have been effective, outdoor supplements to wages continued to be available to the able-bodied, ostensibly in aid of sickness (Digby, 1975, p. 69).

The implications of the new approach, however, were massive and were seen to be so at the time. A relatively recent comment is that 'By the Act of 1834 the poor law renounced all claim to trespass on the territory of the wages system, or to interfere with the forces of the free market. It offered relief only to those who, through age or sickness, were incapable of continuing the battle, and to those other weaklings who gave up the struggle, admitted defeat, and cried for mercy' (T. H. Marshall, 1950, p. 23). Taylor goes so far as to call it 'the most revolutionary economic measure of the early nineteenth century. The new poor law swept away the old principle of the right to work or maintenance, the idea that society had some responsibility for its members; it substituted the idea ... of treating human beings as individuals who must struggle for themselves or else succumb ... ' (A. J. P. Taylor, 1976, pp. 71–2). It was 'an aid ... to capitalism because it relieved industry of all social responsibility outside the contract of employment, while sharpening the edge of competition in the labour market' (T. H. Marshall, 1950, p. 35).

Before we focus on the contemporary debate we may usefully remind ourselves of an important point about the terms in which the debate was conducted, then and since. It was a feature of the ascendant ideology, as soon both by its defenders and its attackers, that the new poor law was a further stage in the process of clearing the labour market – the dismantling of regulatory statutes being earlier stages. That master and man were to make their own contracts as free and equal agents within a free and unencumbered labour market was at once the boast of the 'new' men and the accusation of the 'old'. The language of 'dismantling' and 'clearance' is, however, profoundly misleading. Workers made their employment contracts and performed their tasks within a controlling structure of power and status, ultimately enforced by the courts, which was every bit as 'artificial' as the regulatory statutes and which left them even weaker against the forces of capital. Not for nothing did the terminology of Master and Servant law persist until 1875 (Corrigan, 1977). Taking into account also the strength of ascription – the tendency for class and family origin to' determine social destination – it is clear that the system of free-enterprise capitalism embodied large quantities of unfree labour, not as 'feudal relics' but as an integral part of the system itself.

Needless to say, such considerations played no role in the poor law controversy, which became absorbed into a wide and searching debate that had begun early in the nineteenth century, not about whether the rich and powerful should continue to control and extract a surplus from the poor and weak, but about how they should do it. The 'new' view – new only in the sense that it was becoming more widespread, overt and explicitly formulated – saw control in terms of extracting the surplus by economic means via the market and the wage contract – in other words, via that supposedly 'equal' exchange between 'free' agents which in fact reproduced hourly and daily an exploitation based on a grossly disparate power relationship. On those occasions when that power relationship was challenged, the common law could be relied upon to exact the obedience and respect due to property-owning status and impose acceptance of the rules constantly being developed to govern economic activities. For the opposing school the key feature of the new conception was its explicit repudiation by the superior classes of responsibility for the welfare and behaviour of the lower orders. This, it was argued, would have fatal consequences. With upper-class tutelage, guidance and personalised control withdrawn, the independence of the working classes would be strengthened and the social bond weakened, with predictable consequences for property, social stability and the civilised virtues. Subjected to the economic disturbances of the new industrialism, substantial sections of the population would, under the regime of the economists, suffer such depredations as would render them susceptible to revolutionary agitation.

Manifestly the old conception accorded better with a view of society as an organic unity of interdependent and integral orders each with its own special duties, rights and status, governed by prescription and tradition, than with the view which saw society simply as an aggregate of individuals each seeking his own enlightened self-interest within a system of free contracts, governed by market forces. These differences had emerged during the early days of the debate in such writings as those of Coleridge and Southey.

The Debate on the 'New' Social Order: Coleridge and Southey

The context within which they and many others thought, wrote and acted was one of romantic reaction, beginning in the late eighteenth century, against the assumptions, values and attitudes of the Age of Enlightenment. Many disparate factors fostered it, among them the loss of the American colonies, the French Revolution and Napoleonic Wars, the rise of political radicalism, the increasing significance attached to labour agitation and social distress, and the religious revival known as evangelicalism which sought a re-examination of personal and social morality.

Anglican evangelicalism made some headway within the governing classes and was later to influence education, factory reform and the abolition of the slave trade. Seeking not to attack the status quo but – in their view – preserve it by substituting for individualism and *laissez-faire* a new code of social morality based on a more personal Christianity, evangelicals such as Wilberforce promoted a wide variety of good works which included the Society for Bettering the Condition and Increasing the Comforts of the Poor (1796). The evangelical message had a distinctly Germanic flavour. 'Class divisions were the work of divine Providence, and there must be no "abatement of a just subordination", but if the poor must learn frugality and patience, the rich must recognize a sense of charity and responsibility, and must set an example to those less fortunate than themselves. In this way class hatred will be eliminated and all people will be brought together in brotherhood and charity' (R. W. Harris, 1969, p. 136). It was a message which, carried through to the end of the nineteenth century and beyond, was to shape the policies of influential men towards the working classes and their organisations.

Evangelical utterances tending towards the unctuous, it was left to writers such as Coleridge and Southey to introduce a more astringent note. Like many others moved by social injustice, Coleridge welcomed the French Revolution in its early days but was alienated by the subsequent violence and came to reject individualism, Utilitarianism, political economy and the growing tendency 'to look at all things through the medium of the market and to estimate the worth of all pursuits and attainments by their marketable value' (White, 1953, p. 197). This stance he expounded forcefully in writings between the 1790s and the early 1830s. Accepting the analogy of the state with an organism, Coleridge argued that 'an overbalance of the commercial spirit' was producing social misery which disrupted organic harmony and threatened to 'undermine the foundations of the social edifice'. The remedy lay in a new attitude to social relationships.

> If . . . you say to a man, 'You have no claim on me . . . In a state of nature, indeed, had I food, I should offer you a share from sympathy, from humanity: but in this advanced and artificial state of society, I cannot afford you relief: *you must starve*' . . . What would be this man's answer? He would say, 'You disclaim all connection with me; I have no claims upon you? *I can then have no duties towards you*, and this pistol shall put me in possession of your wealth.'

These were the relationships which must change.

> Our manufacturers must consent to regulations; our gentry must concern themselves in the education as well as in the instruction of their natural clients and dependants, must regard their estates as secured indeed from all human interference by every principle of law and policy; but yet as offices of trust, with duties to be performed in the sight of God and their country. (R. W. Harris, 1969, pp. 223, 226–7, Coleridge's italics)

Burke and Coleridge, it has been said, provided the philosophical basis of much nineteenth-century conservatism and certainly Disraeli and some of his successors bear the marks. But Robert Southey was among many others who, over the same period, were also urging the resumption of authoritarian paternalism. At present, Britain had a population

> exposed at all times by the fluctuations of trade to suffer the severest privations in the midst of a rich and luxurious society, under little or no restraint from religious principle, and if not absolutely disaffected to the institutions of the country, certainly not attached to them: a class of men aware of their numbers and of their strength; experienced in all the details of combination; improvident when they are in receipt of good

wages, yet feeling themselves injured when those wages, during some failure of demand, are so lowered as no longer to afford the means of comfortable subsistence; and directing against the Government and the laws of the country their resentment and indignation for the evils which have been brought upon them by competition and the spirit of rivalry in trade.

Writing in 1812 he reminded his readers that

> in this country, journeymen have long been accustomed to combine for the purpose of obtaining higher pay from their employers; each trade has its fund for such occasions, raised by weekly or monthly payments; the different trades assist each other in their combinations, and the business is managed by secret committees ... Such are the means which the disaffected part of the populace have in their hands ... These are fearful circumstances.

Rulers must draw the obvious conclusions. Pursuing the theme of paternalist reciprocity, Southey argued against Malthusian doctrines and especially against Malthus's remedy for over-population, which was simply to abolish the poor rates and starve the poor into celibacy. Malthus had written that nature had laid no place at the feast for those without subsistence, and that they had no right to expect one: 'A plan for the abolition of the poor rates as practicable as it is humane! The rich are to be called upon for no sacrifices; nothing more is required of them than that they should harden their hearts. They have found a place at the table of nature, and why should they be disturbed at their feast?' (ibid., pp. 265, 267, 279–80).

Unlike many who otherwise shared the same stance, Southey acknowledged that the new industrialism was 'a necessary stage in the progress of society' and was productive of great benefits. This makes him a far more interesting figure. Much of the righteous indignation being generated had its origins in nothing more disinterested than a fear and detestation of the implicit challenge posed by the new industrialism to old structures of power, status and culture. Southey, however, was posing the question: how could the social benefits of industrialism be retained and the social evils avoided? The answer: through the active and constructive intervention of the state. The duties of the rulers are patriarchal and paternal. Their first objects must be to consider the moral improvement and discipline of the people, rich and poor alike, to establish a religion, to train the whole community in that religion, and to treat all dissenters as enemies. Southey also urged a programme of public works to maintain full employment, a system of national education, and a systematic scheme of imperial expansion and settlement. A similar programme was to have its appeal a century later.

Coleridge and Southey had considerable influence on men such as the evangelical Ashley, later Lord Shaftesbury, a leading figure in factory reform. Ashley, who took up 'the factory question' as much 'from dislike of the mill-owners as from sympathy with the mill-workers', was 'deep in correspondence with Southey from 1831 onwards, and was undoubtedly much under Southey's influence'. There were plenty of conservative writers besides Coleridge and Southey 'making similar analyses of current economic, social, political and intellectual tendencies, and coming up with the same sort of findings ... Society ought to be stable, peaceful, harmonious, the lower orders looking up to the higher for protection, guidance and betterment, and the higher conscientiously providing it ... This was the ideal: aristocratic, paternalistic, community-spirited, religious ... ' (Best, 1975, pp. 88, 91).

If Coleridge and Southey could be said to represent a major brand of British Toryism, Macaulay could be said to do the same for Whiggism. Macaulay lost no time in replying to Southey's *Colloquies* (1829) with a review essay for the *Edinburgh Review* in 1830 that constituted a statement of the current Whig philosophy, emphasising the inevitability of progress, the importance of liberty, and the suspect nature of all government, especially paternalistic government. Nothing would be more galling to a people like the English,

> not broken in from the birth to a paternal, or, in other words, a meddling government ... Our fathers could not bear it two hundred years ago; and we are not more patient than they ... Our rulers will best promote the improvement of the nation by strictly confining themselves to their legitimate duties, by leaving capital to find its most lucrative course, commodities their fair price, industry and intelligence their natural reward, idleness and folly their natural punishment, by maintaining peace, by defending property, by diminishing the price of law, and by observing strict economy in every department of the State. Let the Government do this: the People will assuredly do the rest. (Macaulay, 1967, Vol. 2, pp. 205–24)

Sentiments like these were underpinned by the analyses of the Philosophical Radicals. While German philosophers such as Hegel were still constructing systems which presented the nation, rather than the individual or any group of individuals, as the significant unit, British Utilitarians developed further the long-standing British tradition of assuming 'for practical purposes ... the primacy of individual rights and the desirability of leaving to individual freedom as large a scope as was compatible with public order'. Bentham 'assumed that utility refers to the advantage or disadvantage of the individual members of a society, the community itself being a "fictitious body" which has no interests other than those of its members' (Sabine, 1937, pp. 648, 653). Government exists only 'so that citizens can pursue their private ends without getting too much in each other's way ... Men compete and also co-operate, but whichever they do they care only for their own personal advantage or for that of other individuals for whom, for one reason or another, they happen to be concerned'. The 'public good is merely a sum of private goods or a means to private goods' (Plamenatz, 1963, Vol. 2, p. 245). Benthamite Liberals had a consistent programme of legal, economic and political reform which they traced back to the ethical principle of the greatest happiness of the

greatest number. Though often identified with *laissez-faire* they were not
in fact its doctrinaire advocates. The test of policy was its effect on human
happiness, and though there was an explicit presumption that over a wide
field state interference was inadvisable it was not ruled out *a priori*.
Government was evil, but was justified if it excluded a greater evil (Hart,
1974, pp. 203–4).

The Debate and the New Poor Law

The debate was intensified by the introduction of the new poor law and its
political consequences. Alarm on the part of its opponents had begun
early. 'A High Tory periodical, *Blackwood's*, had consistently opposed all
attempts to reform the old poor law, which it saw as a fundamental part of
the old paternalist order of society' (Rose, 1972, p. 9). Concern widened
when working–class outrage against the new poor law became a contributory factor to Chartism in the late 1830s and early 1840s, thereby sharpening the edge of the more general controversy. While some of the critics
would have been hostile to industrialism in whatever institutional and
cultural forms it was clothed, others, such as Southey, acknowledged its
importance and were concerned only to attack the existing forms as being
destructive of the social bond and upper-class control. And both sets of
critics, far from supposing themselves to be doomed and forlorn voices,
clearly believed the social situation to be open in a way that made choice
still possible.
    Carlyle, in 1843, declared that

> our life is not a mutual helpfulness; but rather, cloaked under due
> laws-of-war, named 'fair competition' and so forth, it is a mutual
> hostility. We have profoundly forgotten everywhere that cash-payment
> is not the sole relation of human beings; we think . . . that *it* absolves and
> liquidates all engagements of man. 'My starving workers?' answers the
> rich mill-owner; 'Did I not hire them fairly in the market? Did I not pay
> them, to the last sixpence, the sum covenanted for? What have I to do
> with them more?' (Carlyle, 1971, pp. 277–8)

This, Carlyle had already decided in 1840, constituted 'an abdication on
the part of governors'. Given *laissez-faire* practices and policies, 'a
government of the under-classes by the upper on a principle of *Let-alone* is
no longer possible in England'. And this was becoming disastrous. 'The
working classes cannot any longer go on without government; without
being actually guided and governed . . . ' Of all the 'rights of man', the
'right of the ignorant man to be guided by the wiser; to be, gently or
forcibly, held in the true course by him, is the indisputablest' (ibid.,
pp. 187–9).
    Carlyle's call was to the existing holders of power – the aristocracy and
'captains of industry' – to fit themselves for leadership in the reorganisation of society, to take up the role of a highly cultivated and responsible
minority concerned to define and emphasise the highest values at which

society must aim (R. Williams, 1958, pp. 80–1, 84). In the second half of the century many big employers in cotton, coal and iron were to heed his words yet fail to reverse the directions predominantly taken by industrial relations in British industry. In his later work Carlyle looked to a different solution whereby the heroic superman leader would inspire reverent obedience among the masses. Either was bound to appeal to those who were more specifically concerned with the implications of the situation for middle- and upper-class power than for the higher values of the national life.

The distinction between idealism and *real politik* was not, however, the distinction between theorists and 'practical' men. This was not a debate confined to the study and the obscure journal. Few were more busily active in the dusty arena than Richard Oastler, the Tory Radical who campaigned during the 1830s and 1840s for factory reform and against the new poor law. Supported by a motley group of clergymen, philanthropists, small squires, Tory MPs and publicists, Oastler was driven by a vision of a supposed social harmony of the past in which 'statesmen had conceived their main task to be the regulation of the multifarious activities of society to the end that the general welfare of the whole might be secured'. Into this English Eden had crept the serpents of individualism and *laissez-faire*. In the name of freedom, the country's statesmen were deliberately abnegating that solemn responsibility.

> The Demon called *Liberalism* [he wrote] who is stalking through the land scattering absolute want in the richest cornfields, and the deepest distress among the busy rattling of our looms – assuming first one name and then another: March of Intellect, Political Economy, Free Trade, Liberal Principles, etc., but always destroying the peace of the cottage and the happiness of the palace – this Demon will be found to have been the enemy of true religion and of the prosperity and well-being of man.

The country had to return to the principle that we are members one of another; to the idea of an organic social harmony in which 'none was allowed to trench upon or invade the rights of another; the whole system of the old British Constitution being a series of guards, checks and counter-guards, intended to prevent competition and undue expansion' (Driver, 1946, pp. 295, 425).

Underlying all this was a theory of consent and legitimacy which lay also at the heart of much unease felt by many whose concern was more self-regarding than Oastler's. Every man had a 'natural right to live well', Britain's governmental institutions were intended to secure this right, and 'denial of this right automatically destroys any claim to allegiance. When a government repudiates the obligations to the common man that these principles impose upon it, Oastler asserted, "it has by its own act and deed put him without the pale of the Commonwealth, and he is morally justified in taking care of his own life and the life of his family"' (ibid., p. 302).

This fear, expressed with evangelical fervour, comes through clearly in the editorials of *The Times*, which returned repeatedly to the issue in passages nicely blended of moral sentiment and political calculation. 'Utilitarianism and political economy have tried their hands at the management of the social system, and have made a wretched and disgraceful failure', it declared (11 January 1844). 'Some great new moral impulse' was required. The new poor law was the 'greatest social revolution England has yet seen, and the greatest break into existing law, and rule, and precedent' (4 April 1844). '. . . we cannot bring ourselves to understand on what principle the landed gentry – the Conservatives, as they profess themselves – of England could sanction a law which tends . . . to snap the delicate but powerful links which bind society together . . . We warn them . . . that . . . they have paved the way for a domination of vulgar democrats, mushroom agitators, and sectarian railers . . . ' (26 January 1844).

In a discussion of the campaign to limit by statute the length of the factory working day to ten hours, *The Times* warned 'legislators of the infallible result of their not carrying out the protective character of Government. They may think there is danger in restricting labour, but there is certainly more danger in telling labour to shift for itself. Tell the British labourer that he must fight all his battles, and make all his own conditions, without help from the state, and what sort of feeling is he likely to have towards that state, towards its head, and its aristocracy?' (9 May 1844).

In an early expression of a concern which was to bulk large half a century later, another editorial asked what value economic growth offered if it bequeathed to the future 'a noble race degenerated – diminished, enfeebled, diseased frames, occupied by abject slavish souls? . . . And what could compensate to a future age, if we left to them – the whole paternal character of government and national humanity forgotten – a mere multitude of rich and poor, everyone making the best bargain for himself, bringing his strength and skill to the best market allowed him by the insatiable avarice of a few. . . ?' (11 March 1844).

There were gloomy analyses on the lines of 'mass society'.

> Instead of an infinite number of small people, some mere labourers, and some rather better, sub-divided into distinct and different groups and classes, and tied to persons, places, and interests, we now have 'a labouring population' – one uniform unencumbered living sea of labour. Every breakwater has been smoothed down, and now we see a great lagoon before us. What follows? The storms of passion and the currents of desire will now have absolute sway on the vast unbroken surface. A breath will raise it into billows . . . All this is, of course, exactly as it should be to the political economist. He has labour at his command without any restriction; but so has the speculator – so also has the agitator. (22 March 1844)

The picture was more fantasy than fact but the fears were real enough.

If the state intended this condition of society to persist and even to develop further along the same lines it must, declared *The Times*, say so: 'If the state is to disown entirely those parental obligations, let it be clearly understood.' Those who still saw the state in terms of paternalism, 'much as they may inwardly grieve over the condition of the working classes . . . feel still more the duty of not sympathising with popular acts of self-vindication' and self-help. 'By force of ancient habit they look to the state to set things right. Combinations, strikes, delegates, committees and such democratic productions they consider mere sedition . . . ' They must now be disabused. 'Let parliament plainly inform them that it leaves the million to make its own terms with the employer . . . ' They will then feel very differently about strikes and agitations. 'They will think it no longer misprision or treason to lend an ear to the demands of operative unions . . . ' They would also take a different view of the legislature. Authority which had hitherto been 'carefully collected and concentrated in the Sovereign and the Parliament will seem to be thrown back, as it were, to the people' (14 May 1844). Authority was, of course, the crux. It comes out clearly, too, in the writings of Ruskin, another active figure in the debate. Though often described as a socialist forerunner, his principles of 'design' and 'function' supported an authoritarian idea which included a strongly asserted hierarchy of classes and the notion of a paternal state (R. Williams, 1958, pp. 140, 146).

The idea that a revival of chivalric *noblesse oblige* was the solution for the nation's social ills briefly inspired Disraeli and a handful of young Tory aristocrats to initiate, in the early 1840s, the 'Young England' movement. Drawing upon Sir Walter Scott's glamorisation of medievalism and the social theory of men such as Coleridge and Carlyle, it depicted a modern aristocratic party dedicated to serving society. His reference in the novel *Sybil* (1845) to the 'two nations' was based on a speech by a friend and fellow MP, W. B. Ferrand, in 1843, who declared that 'We are now divided, as nearly as possible, into two classes – the very rich and the very poor . . . ' No country could long survive such a gulf. 'We must have the intermediate links, amalgamating into each other, descending with a regular and even gradation; in order that the monarch on the throne and the peasant in the cottage may alike enjoy the privileges and blessings of our free and glorious constitution' (Butler, 1980, p. 12). Disraeli's proposal was to unite the workers and their noble protectors against the supposed common enemy: the commercial and industrial middle classes – a proposal which glossed over the extent to which the aristocracy's interests were bound up with commerce and industrialisation. The alliance was to be effected, of course, through the constitution of the paternalist control system.

Disraeli makes clear in his novel that he wanted paternalism applied in the realm of work as well as in the political and social spheres. Interestingly, it is the younger son of an old landed family, now turned manufacturer, who is depicted as exemplifying the desired strategy. 'He felt that between [employer and employed] there should be other ties than the payment and the receipt of wages.' Trafford provides housing, public baths, schools and gardens. The control aspect is well in evidence. All the work is carried out in one great room, an arrangement which not only secures improved health, avoids accidents and reduces fatigue, but also facilitates managerial observation and inspection, 'the child works under the eye of the parent, the parent under that of the superior workman; the inspector or employer at a glance can behold all'. Workers must be protected from their well-known weaknesses; 'the expensive and evil habits which result from wages being paid in public houses' are prevented by paying them at the mill. Visitors lament that this strategy is 'not so common as we could wish', but suggest that it must be expensive. Trafford replies, 'I have always considered that there was nothing so expensive as a vicious population'. More significantly, he continues that although 'I should find an ample reward in the moral tone and material happiness of this community . . . viewing it in a pecuniary point of view, the investment of capital has been one of the most profitable I ever made . . . ' (Disraeli, 1980, pp. 224–6, 230, 243). All the elements of the full paternalist control conception are present in this picture, which owes much to Robert Owen.

It is worth noting that shrewd Whig observers were far from seeing an aristocracy–worker political alliance as beyond the bounds of possibility. 'Political energies were in an extremely fluid condition and there was no certainty about the moulds in which they would finally become set . . . since the boundaries of affiliation were not fixed, genuine alternatives seemed available' (Driver, 1946, p. 112). Disraeli certainly appears to have helped the Chartists, but in ways that smack less of *noblesse oblige* than of short-term political expediency. That indefatigable Radical, George Jacob Holyoake, alleged that Disraeli gave many Chartist leaders money to finance their attacks on the Whigs: 'Francis Place showed me cheques paid to them to break up Anti-Corn Law meetings, because that cause was defended by Whigs. I saw the cheques which were sent to Place by Sir John Easthope and other bankers, who had cashed them.' Disraeli was also said to have given money to the Chartist leader, Ernest Jones, for his *People's Paper* (Holyoake, 1906, pt 1, p. 85, pt 2, p. 249).

On a more principled basis the Tory–Radical alliance seemed to offer a certain credibility during the 1830s and 1840s. For evidence we must look neither to the Conservatism of the metropolitan and party organisation scene, nor to that of the great aristocratic landowners and financial interests. These were increasingly accepting the leadership of men such as Peel who sought to reconstruct the party on the basis of sympathy with the manufacturing interests. 'Whatever the scruples of provincial Tories, the Conservative Party sought to ensure its future by an alliance with the industrial interest' (R. L. Hill, 1929 , p.181). We must look rather to the old Toryism of provincial and country gentry and clergy who supported Factory Short-Time Committees and the agitation against the new poor law. 'The Tory whose little world of rank and station was being overturned in the march of progress, and the Radical whom the march of progress had rendered desperately hungry, together looked to the past, to a half-legendary paradise when there was no machinery, no Political Economy, no Huskisson and no Ure. This ill-defined but powerful sentiment, half-resentful, half-bewildered, transcended class and party' (ibid., p. 31).

Some socialist thinkers used the same terms as some conservative thinkers not only for criticising *laissez-faire* society but also for indicating the idea of a future superior one (R. Williams, 1958, p. 140). Prominent among these shared terms was 'organic', which in its minimal sense conveyed, in contrast to the individualistic atomism and enligtened self-interest of liberal society, the idea of interdependence and a mutual sense of responsibility and obligation. William Morris and those he inspired after the middle of the century used the principles which they abstracted from an idealised medievalism to shape an egalitarian socialist vision for the future – albeit one which excluded industrialisation and extreme division of labour.

As we have noted, some conservative critics looked to a future that included industrialisation but located it within an organic society and paternalist control system which fully upheld class hierarchy while stabilising it by accepting responsibilities towards the lower orders. It proved for many to be an attractive vision in that it appeared to promise stability and social peace with the minimum of disadvantageous structural change. It was still attracting some leading Conservative politicians eighty years later.

Paternalism Renewed?

Within the context of such moods and sentiments the early Victorian period saw attempts by some landlords, clergy, politicians and industrialists to revive the paternalist control system. Practically speaking, paternalism made considerable strides under the early Victorians (D. Roberts, 1979). John Stuart Mill wrote in 1845 that

> the stream at present flows in a multitude of small channels. Societies for the protection of needlewomen, of governesses – associations to improve the buildings of the labouring classes, to provide them with baths, with parks and promenades, have started into existence. Legislative interference to abridge the hours of labour in factories have obtained large minorities . . . In the rural districts, every expedient, practicable or not, for giving work to the unemployed finds advocates; public meetings for the discussion and comparison of projects have lately been frequent; and the movement towards the 'allotment system' is becoming general.

Mill surveyed the movement with an analysis which combined shrewd practical observation, clear insight and total lack of humbug. If these schemes were ordinary charity 'they would not fill the large space they do in public discussion', being 'made familiar to every reader of newspapers by sedulous inculcation from day to day'. But it was 'not in this spirit that the new schemes of benevolence are conceived. They are propounded as instalments of a great social reform. They are celebrated as the beginning of a new moral order, or an old order revived, in which the possessors of property are to resume their place as the paternal guardians of those less fortunate; and which, when established, is to cause peace and union throughout society . . .' (G. L. Williams, 1976, pp. 281–2).

Mill noted the basis of all this as being the theory of dependence, according to which 'the lot of the poor, in all things which affect them collectively, should be regulated *for* them, not *by* them. They should not be required or encouraged to think for themselves, or give to their own reflection or forecast an influential voice in the determination of their destiny. It is supposed to be the duty of the higher classes to think for them, and to take the responsibility of their lot . . . ' (italics in original). The relationship, besides being authoritative, is also amiable and caring – 'affectionate tutelage on the one side, respectful and grateful deference on the other'.

He made short shrift – perhaps too short shrift – of the notion that this relationship was ever an historical reality:

> . . . no times can be pointed out in which the higher classes of this or any other country performed a part even distantly resembling the one assigned to them in this theory . . . All privileged and powerful classes, as such, have used their power in the interest of their own selfishness, and have indulged their self-importance in despising, and not in lovingly caring for, those who were, in their estimation, degraded by being under the necessity of working for their benefit. (Mill, 1878, pp. 334, 336)

Nevertheless, many among the then well-to-do were reviving the myth, for a mixture of motives which included 'conscience and philanthropy' and 'fashion', but also the 'ever-strengthening demands upon their sense of self-interest'. Carlyle was receiving support, wrote Mill in 1845

> from those whom a spirit of reaction against the democratic tendencies of the age had flung off with the greatest violence in the direction of feudal and sacerdotal ascendancy . . . men who look back with fondness to times when the poor had no notion of any other social state than to give obedience to the nearest great landholder, and receive protection; and who assert, in the meantime, the right of the poor to protection in hopes that the obedience will follow. (G. L. Williams, 1976, p. 280)

But it was too late, in Mill's opinion, for 'the patriarchal or paternal system of government' was one to which working men would 'not again be subject' (Mill, 1878, p. 337). This pattern of social relations was not only an historical myth; it had ceased to be even an adequate ideal. In 1848 Mill wrote (at Harriet Taylor's bidding, according to his biographer) that 'The poor have come out of leading-strings, and cannot any longer be governed or treated like children . . . Whatever advice, exhortation or guidance is held out to the labouring classes, must henceforth be tendered to them as equals, and accepted by them with their eyes open. The prospect of the future depends on the degree to which they can be made rational beings' (Packe, 1970, p. 307). 'The working classes have taken their interests into their own hands, and are perpetually showing that they think the interests of their employers not identical with their own, but opposite to them. Some among the higher classes flatter themselves that these tendencies may be counteracted by moral and religious education, but they have let the time go by for giving an education which can serve their purpose' (Mill, 1878, p. 337).

In support of his conviction that present trends were irreversible, Mill offered impressions of the prevailing pattern of employer–worker relations which, in the absence of any systematic contemporary inquiry, must be considered important evidence, for Mill was an acute and wide-ranging observer. His appraisal presents a situation which now displayed almost universally those characteristics identified by Dean Tucker in the clothmaking industry a century earlier. In a comment which expressed precisely a conception of prevalent labour relations as a zero-sum game, Mill referred to the absence of any 'sense of co-operation and common interest' and to a situation, instead, 'of hostile rivals whose gain is each other's loss'; a '*sourde* animosity which is universal in this country towards the whole class of employers, in the whole class of the employed' (G. L. Williams, 1976, pp. 291–3). 'The relation is nearly as unsatisfactory to the payer of wages as to the receiver. If the rich regard the poor as, by a kind of natural law, their servants and dependants, the rich in their turn are regarded as a mere prey and pasture for the poor; the subject of demands and expectations wholly indefinite, increasing in extent with every concession made to them.' Within this 'standing feud between capital and labour', the working classes' 'sole endeavour is to receive as much, and return as little in the shape of service, as possible' (Mill, 1878, pp. 342–3, 373).

Mill saw all this as understandable. Under the present system the labourer was 'a mere bought instrument in the work of production, having no residuary interest in the work itself'. It was

> not an age in which a man can feel loyal and dutiful to another because he has been born on his estate. Obedience in return for protection is a bargain only made when protection can be had on no other terms . . . Obedience in return for wages is a different matter. They will make that bargain, too, if necessity drives them to it. But good-will and gratitude form no part of the conditions of such a contract. The deference which a man now pays to his 'brother of the earth', merely because the one was born rich and the other poor, is either hypocrisy or servility'. (G. L. Williams, pp. 292–3, 295)

The paternalist revival of the mid-century was therefore a response to the realisation that if the rich and powerful were declared by official ideology to have no responsibility for the poor except through private philanthropy – even this being often deplored – then the working classes would be driven to assert even more aggressively a self-protective independence in forms which included, to name two current alarms, Chartism and trade unionism. Chartism does not concern us directly here, but it is worth noting that even towards a movement seen as 'enemies of property and public order', governments trod warily and preserved a strong commitment to law, constitutionality and political freedom (Mather, 1959, pp. 374–402).

The Trade Unions: Industry and Politics

It was hardly to be expected that they would be any less circumspect in their policy towards trade unions. Unions might be detested as nuisances, but although there were always some individual unionists to be found participating in advanced political movements, including the most militant, it was clear to many observers that the main thrust of union organisation, as such, was towards securing or maintaining a foothold in job regulation of some kind or another. Where this was tolerably successful, and looked like remaining so, those who acted and spoke for the union *per se* were more likely to settle for the half-loaf than put it at hazard by reaching for what might be seen as dangerously ambitious political solutions. They might bring their unions into support of 'moral force' Chartism, seeking by peaceful, moderate, constitutional and gradualist means to secure the six points of manhood suffrage, annual parliaments, the secret ballot, equal electoral constituencies, payment of MPs, and abolition of their property qualifications. But it was the weaker and less superior unions who were likely to offer support for 'physical force' Chartism, with its militant impatience and disposition to talk, and sometimes act, in terms which alarmed local magistrates, employers and Whitehall. The upper strata – printers, engineers, iron-founders and cotton-spinners, for example – damned by the militants as 'the pompous trades and proud mechanics who are now willing forgers of their own fetters', held aloof, and the Miners' Association, too, 'was at all times careful to avoid association with "physical force" Chartism' (Hunt, 1981, pp. 229, 231). These and others with an aspiration towards status often did not care to prejudice it with too intemperate a participation in local agitations that might be viewed with disfavour by local worthies. It was still true, and was to remain so to some extent for the rest of the century, and beyond, that many members of these relatively favoured groups identified far more strongly with the lower middle class than with those 'beneath' them. 'Indeed the term "lower middle class" was sometimes used to include the aristocracy of labour" (Hobsbawm, 1968, p. 273). Their individualism, independence and contempt for the world's losers were a craft and cultural inheritance, not the invention of Samuel Smiles. Groups like these kept their heads down, pursued job regulation by whatever seemed currently the most viable methods and might actively dissociate themselves from causes which threatened to prejudice those methods. A campaign by engineers in 1851 against systematic overtime and piece-work was presented by a hostile press as 'anarchism' and 'revolution', and when Ernest Jones, the Chartist leader and Marxist socialist, attempted a public speech in their support they booed him off the platform, fearful that his presence would give further leverage to their enemies (Jefferys, 1945, p. 38).

For the most part, industrial action by the crafts and such non-craft groups as could muster the strength, though often publicly condemned by the ruling order as a threat to property rights or progress or both, was not regarded as worth undermining the ideology and legitimacy of a whole regime for. We need look no further for an explanation of why the state launched no systematic and concerted efforts to smash the unions.

Behind the dramas and excitements of Chartism, therefore – and of earlier working-class political movements – many relatively privileged groups continued to be assiduous and successful in strengthening their conservative pursuit of purely sectional interests. Such distinctions and continuities must not, however, be overdrawn. Individual activists within even the most superior of craft unions, and sometimes the unions themselves, became caught up in these expressions of an awakening political consciousness, which could hardly be without their effect on the frame of reference through which the activists and their successors viewed the industrial as well as the political scene. Yet it is equally clear that it will not do to convey the impression, as did the Webbs and later observers, that the entire active working class first, during the 1830s and 1840s, adopted class-conscious, militant and radical political aims, and then, in 'disillusionment' for a period after the mid-century, 'accepted' capitalism through a strategy of respectable, cautious and sectional trade unionism. Both forms had coexisted since at least the early part of the century and both had expanded during the period. The latter was destined to gain ground at the expense of the former during the 1850s and 1860s when living standards for many workers rose somewhat and when circumstances tipped the balance towards social and legal toleration of the unions. There remained, however, an undertow of political radicalism, taking varied forms, that spared the union movement from becoming solely an affair of 'business unionism' totally bereft of any wider and more generous idealism.

Nevertheless, the thrust towards prudent accommodation to middle-class values and manners was increasingly apparent from the 1830s onwards. Leaders of strongly organised groups, conscious of having something to lose, were often prepared to accommodate to growing Victorian demands for good order, decorum and respectability in so far as these were compatible with the union functions deemed essential. This did not necessarily involve a sharp break from earlier styles. As we have seen, some craft leaders and activists had long demonstrated a certain strain towards sobriety and respectability even amidst the violence and brutalities of eighteenth-century England, and as Victorian decorum asserted itself more and more widely it had its effect on union methods and styles as on other forms of labour protest. Food riots, collective bargaining by riot and Luddism were dying out; pre-industrial direct action was giving way to more organised forms. Some union violence continued but it was increasingly confined to the 'more old-fashioned trade clubs, especially in declining trades, where trade unionism was weak and men were sometimes desperate' (Musson, 1972, p. 14). Avoidance of disorder and law-breaking was increasingly seen by many union leaders as a functional necessity, including those of the coal-miners and northern factory operatives.

Here, as in other respects, a simple distinction between, on the one hand, the skilled, well-organised traditional crafts and, on the other, the newer factory workers will not do. For one thing, in some of the old crafts, such as tailoring and shoe-making, though artisans of the higher levels of the trade were holding their own, the cheaper ranges had long been increasingly subject to division of labour and degradation of conditions, with the weakening or even destruction of craft control. For another, some old crafts or their modern offshoots, such as steam-engine makers, pattern makers, fitters and turners, were moving into the factories, where they became a new élite applying traditions and techniques of craft control which they inherited from their predecessors. Yet again, some newer groups within the factories, such as the cotton-spinners – all men – found it possible to establish effective restrictions on entry which elevated them nearer to the higher craft category than to 'factory operatives' as ordinarily understood. A comment on Manchester spinners in 1830 has a distinctly craft ring: they 'insist', wrote an army commander, 'not only on the masters giving them such wages as they demand, but that they regulate the whole work in the factories in all its details, in the manner which the union prescribes' (Hammond and Hammond 1979, p. 103). The picture is overdrawn but indicates the direction in which aspirations lay: aspirations which could not have been entertained by weavers.

Both craft and non-craft unions, therefore, might seek respectability status. Elizabeth Gaskell, from her close personal observation of the Manchester cotton industry in the mid-nineteenth century, captures the point precisely in her novel, *North and South*. The daughter of a union leader who is currently leading a strike explains to a visitor that 'there was to be no going against the law of the land. Folk would go with them if they saw them striving and starving wi' dumb patience; but if there was once any noise o' fighting and struggling – even wi' knobsticks – all was up, as they knew by th' experience of many and many a time before.' Provided they kept the peace there was hope of carrying the rest of local opinion with them. The Strike Committee 'didn't want to have right all mixed up with wrong, till folk can't separate it'. They wanted to show the world that the real leaders of the strike were not noisy rioters and lawbreakers 'but steady thoughtful men; good hands and good citizens who were friendly to law and judgement, and would uphold order' (Gaskell, 1970, p. 259).

The background to such sentiments was the alacrity of the courts to pounce punitively upon worker behaviour that could be presented as being in restraint of trade or in breach of contract, or as criminal conspiracy, or as 'leaving work unfinished', or as being any of the vaguely defined forms of conduct prohibited by the 1825 Act, such as 'intimidation', 'molestation', 'obstruction' and 'threats'. Governments were not prepared to attempt to destroy the unions, or to give practical or moral support to employers to do so. The courts, however, were often prepared to harass and oppress them, punish their leaders and activists, deny them social and legal validity, and withold legal protection for their funds.

In such a context, union restraint, preservation of good order and promotion of respectability were becoming, in a society moving towards an increased outward propriety, no more nor less than possible contributors to effective action. The effects could be direct and crucial. Were local shopkeepers prepared to allow credit to strikers' families? Much might depend on the state of surrounding gentry opinion. For mass stoppages of miners and factory operatives, especially, the maintenance of public sympathy was an important element of strategy and the leader who was capable of commanding a non-violent and orderly campaign ranked, paradoxically for the employers, as both a more welcome yet more formidable opponent.

But the effects were indirect as well as direct. Violent or riotous behaviour so alarmed the local middle class and gentry that whatever sympathy there may have been for the strikers became swamped by anxiety about possible threats to life and property. In such an atmosphere, employers felt able to justify using their economic power to the utmost, police to justify harassing pickets with special zeal, and magistrates and judges to justify applying, and if necessary stretching, the law with particular vigour. The insistence by strike leaders on restraint and good order was designed, therefore, to ensure that the strike would not be closed down prematurely and that they would be left free to exert such degree of market strength against the employers as they could muster. Of course, market strength – or sheer strength of feeling – might, in some instances, be great enough to inspire the confidence or will to ride out all harassments for perhaps a long period. We are not dealing here with automatic responses but with probabilities – probabilities great enough, nevertheless, to give a functional significance to the anxieties experienced by substantial sections of the organised working class about respectability.

The old aspirations among artisan leaders towards sobriety, order and self-improvement were therefore now pursued more widely and systematically. The London Compositors urged members in 1835 to 'show the artisans of England a brighter and better example; and casting away the aid to be derived from cunning and brute strength, let us, when we contend with our opponents, employ only the irresistible weapons of truth and reason'. The Ironmoulders and Stonemasons were speaking with similar voices in the mid-1840s. 'How often have disputes been averted by a few timely words with employers! It is surely no dishonour to explain to your employer the nature and extent of our grievance.' Reason and intelligent communication must be reinforced by self-improvement. 'Let us earnestly advise you to educate', the *Flint Glass Makers' Magazine* urged its readers in 1850: 'get intelligence instead of alcohol – it is sweeter and more lasting' (Webb and Webb, 1920, pp. 198–9). Such unction was aimed at socialising and controlling the behaviour of the membership, not at committing the leadership necessarily to either sweet reason, industrial peace, or temperance.

Changes in union organisation strengthened this impulse among some union leaders towards securing a more disciplined membership. A movement towards amalgamation or federation of local societies into wider districts or national unions had become widespread in the late 1820s and early 1830s and was followed by a similar movement in the mid-1840s. Head office leaders and officials, distant from many of their members in the field, and anxious to conserve funds and minimise headstrong action in the localities, sought to enhance their control by preaching caution, restraint and conciliatory tactics. There were few other means available than exhortation. Craft strength was underpinned by rank and file vigilance at the workplace, buttressed by strong traditions of local self-regulation, and there was little scope here for authoritarian direction from afar.

Regulative methods were, in essence, much as they had long been for the better-placed societies. Union branches enforced their own restrictive rules as far as they could and supported members in their strikes and other hardships out of carefully husbanded funds. They sought to preserve craft rules as non-negotiable, but if collective bargaining was desirable - to negotiate about piece-rates or a local wage increase – the employers were approached verbally or by written memorials, now usually 'respectfully', and invited to meet union representatives. A strike might be necessary but there was 'no wish to undergo the hardships of unemployment or the rigours of the law, or to risk their meagre funds and imperil their friendly benefits without good cause, and the typical "craft" societies generally deplored mob violence' (Musson, 1972, p. 15).

Outside the craft trades, and those newer groups which were finding it possible to adopt craft-type methods, collective bargaining was the only means available to workers for securing a foothold in the regulation of terms and conditions of employment. In some districts and trades a foothold was hardly necessary where custom still exerted a widespread writ that was taken for granted by both sides. But where conditions were more volatile there were more choices, and employers often fought bitter defensive actions against any encroachment on their freedom. No universal proposition along these lines is possible, however. In some trades, during some periods, employers came, as we have seen, to interpret their circumstances as favouring a view of worker combinations as possible partners in labour regulation and control – though partners to be watched suspiciously and hit hard whenever they ventured beyond the limits of the role cast for them.

Despite all this there was little basis, at the end of the 1840s, for confident predictions of a strong future of mass growth for the unions and collective bargaining. Groups of the relatively privileged were doing well, but then they had always done so, and the gulf between them and the rest of manual labour – mostly regarded as unorganisable – was as great as ever. Governments had their own reasons for not mounting a frontal onslaught, but the courts seemed to have adequate resources for keeping collective action among workers within tolerable bounds and were manifestly ready to use them. Employers and magistrates often seemed to Whitehall to be regrettably craven, but the former at least were showing themselves capable of organising against the union threat when it became too obtrusive. The working-class struggle for a foothold in the political nation – a foothold which could be used to improve this unfavourable environment – was being contained. For all the manifest and latent terrors common among the rich and powerful towards the relatively poor and weak, it would have been possible for a sober voice to argue that there was not too much to worry about.

If the future for a mass union movement seemed doubtful, it was the case for some observers that the situation was open with respect to other relevant variables. There were those for whom it seemed by no means certain that organised labour would hitch its wagon politically to the rising Liberal star, and the idea of an alliance with a Tory paternalism could not be laughed out of court. There was not even a felt universal certainty that the Liberal star would or should continue rising so far as economic liberalism was concerned. The possibility of reversing, or at least stemming, the advance of industrialisation, political economy, *laissez-faire* and the cash nexus was entertained by not a few sober men of affairs. Others thought that industrialisation must continue but not within an individualistic social system.

One thing would have been agreed by most. It would require a threat to the status quo of really major proportions to goad a British government into abandoning the constitutionality, political freedom and rule of law that were now publicly venerated as sources of the nation's stability and well-being. This stance, widely shared by a large and politically alert middle class, coexisted with keen awareness of an emerging class polarisation that was publicly discussed with candour by many of those on both sides of the gulf. Consciousness of these beginnings of a more systematic class dissociation and antagonism strengthened during the 1820s and 1830s with the growing division between large-scale capitalists and large aggregates of full-time, life-long wage-earners organised into trade unions. 'The stormiest political decade of early nineteenth-century English history, that which began with the financial crisis of 1836 and the economic crisis of 1837, was the decade when class terms were most generally used and "middle classes" and "working classes" alike did not hesitate to relate politics directly to class antagonisms' (Briggs, 1967, p. 49).

Yet a careful observer would have noted that workplace grievance and conflict translated only very partially and imperfectly into political class conflict expressed in terms of 'labour versus capital'. Large numbers of workers, such as farm labourers and domestic servants, who constituted between them over a third of the workforce in 1830, were, like many other rural and urban poor, in work situations which might well supply them with grievances but not with the facility to see their fate in systematic terms of class power, exploitation and conflict. A further impediment to uniform class perceptions was that these levels of the working classes were as riddled with fine status distinctions as were the 'pompous trades and proud mechanics'. Engineering labourers, for example, regarded themselves as superior to bricklayers' labourers who, in turn, looked down on general labourers. Though they, like most other workers, might be too poor, weak and unconfident to organise themselves into trade unions, they were far from seeing themselves as an undifferentiated proletariat.

Nor were most of those who were capable of union organisation likely to perceive themselves as members of a class with common interests in opposition to a dominant class. In many industries and trades the workforce was divided not, or not only, into craftsmen and labourers but also into petty masters and underhands. This was the sub-contracting system, in which the leading member of the small operational work group or team himself employed and paid the others as subordinate labour and thus had a direct personal interest in controlling them and keeping their wages down. The system was widespread in coal-mining, shipbuilding, cotton spinning, building, iron and steel, boot and shoe manufacture, clothing, furniture, the diverse metal trades of Birmingham and the Black Country, and many lesser trades. Trade unionism developed first not among the subordinate labour but among the sub-contractors, who had no interest in promoting it among their own hands.

The system reinforced the tendency of craftsmen to perceive such higher status and rewards as they might enjoy as resting upon their sectional ability to exclude other workers from their own ranks and so heighten their own scarcity value – a divisive notion born not of some docile acceptance of classical economics but of centuries-long experience and tradition. The much greater significance of exclusionist strategies for British craftsmen than for their Continental counterparts rendered the leaders and activists among them more susceptible to doctrines of liberal individualism and instrumental sectional collectivism than to doctrines of class unity. Neither Painite Jacobinism nor Cobbettite radicalism, with their cry of 'people versus aristocracy', offered frameworks of thought appropriate to the conception of workers collectively as a class getting to grips with industrial class society and its rising power structures, and their influence persisted long after the class shape of the new order had started to emerge. Derivative doctrines of secularism, rationalism and republicanism, which continued to attract a significant following among the active and organised working class, were individualistic and libertarian in ways which presented obstacles to the spread of socialist ideas and to notions of an active interventionist state. Within Chartism there were activists pursuing 'physical force' preparations, but also substantial elements which drew their political programme not, as did the Paris craftsmen, from a new stock of socialist ideas but from the radical parliamentary reformers of the past. When William Lovett and the London Workingmen's Association, aided by Francis Place, drew up the six points of the 'People's Charter' in 1838 they were largely repeating what the Westminster Reform Committee had drafted fifty-eight years before. In cities such as London and Birmingham, 'cities of ancient crafts and petty workshops, much of the enthusiasm for the Charter sprang from the disappointment of radical craftsmen with the failure of the Whigs to give them the vote by the Reform Bill of 1832. To such men, the campaign for the Charter was a stage in a long and protracted struggle not to win something new but to reclaim ancient and "natural" rights' (Rudé, 1981, p. 179).

Other substantial sections within Chartism were attracted by the message of individual self-improvement (Rudé, 1980, p. 162), or by the Owenite ideals of education, morality and the co-operative community, or by Anti-Corn-Law League lecturers preaching the inestimable benefits to all of free trade, or by middle-class reformers seeking factory legislation or attacking the new poor law. The careful observer would also have registered how many middle-class members of the league ventured into 'the remarkable movement of 1841–2' which aimed at reconciling middle-class and working-class Radicalisms on the basis of 'complete suffrage' (Maccoby, 1935, pp. 212, 228). With its basis in Radical Dissent, the movement attracted support from many varied species of Chartist leadership and membership, artisans prominent among them.

The same observer might reasonably have concluded that if economic fortunes continued to favour the upper levels of labour they were unlikely to abandon their trade unions – all experience suggested that prosperity strengthened the impulse towards organisation – but that they might be the more amenable to political co-operation across class boundaries. Some leading Tories hoped that what co-operation there was might be with them, but 'there were already powerful forces at work tending to bring the upper ranks of the trade society world more and more into a large acceptance of the middle-class Radical attitude towards politics and society'. Franchise reform, free trade, the temperance movement and persistent echoes of a shared ancient hostility towards aristocratic land-ownership, monopoly and privilege were among the bonding elements. A mass-circulation commercial literature which reinforced these dispositions proved widely acceptable to 'some of the solidest in the trades' (ibid., pp. 406–7).

Yet this widespread disinclination among significant groups within the active working class to adopt the full stance of class war was not due to the total absence of appropriate theoretical frames of reference. From the 1820s Hodgskin wrote (and preached at the London Mechanics Institute) about doctrines of class struggle and the elimination of capitalists and landlords. Other theorists included Ernest Jones, whose socialism, after 1848 at least, was that of Marx. All commanded some following, and most urged that only through their own collective efforts as a class, exerted both industrially and politically, could workers achieve full emancipation from domination by capital and receive the whole product of their labour. Yet such doctrines never secured the adhesion of the more stable unions, nor of substantial sections of their members. Mediating between working-class experience of conflict in the workplace and much influential working-class political behaviour were social, political and religious values often shared with substantial elements of the middle class. It was a sharing which, though fostered by middle-class indoctrination, had its principal roots in much older and deeper structures of circumstance. These shared values ensured that a considerable amount of economic conflict was only to a very limited degree translated into political class conflict. This seemed particularly the case where union organisation or a collective spirit at the workplace maintained a tolerably satisfactory regulative presence with respect to terms and conditions of employment. Whether particular sections of workers responded positively to programmes for social transformation or not seemed to correlate inversely with their sectional ability to regulate their own immediate job conditions, either unilaterally or through negotiation with employers. Some capacity for regulation during the everyday basic experience of work appeared to act as a species of lightning conductor. It defused the scene and acted as a facilitating condition which made possible the creation of political links across the gulf of ownership and control.

To sum up: while it could be said that, in the objective sense of 'class', a class structure was certainly emerging, the question of what the workers' subjective consciousness was of this structure, and how it shaped their protest ideologies and activity, permitted of no simple answer. Some leaders and activists looked back to a supposedly better world that might possibly be recaptured. Others, looking forward, corresponded with Marx and visualised the transformation of the new industrial society into socialist terms. Still others, mostly in the established and more successful craft or non-craft occupations, kept their eyes on the protection of their special advantages – by peaceful means if possible, by militant means if necessary – and politically found much to sympathise with among middle-class radicalism.

The states of consciousness of their respective groups of rank and file followers are less penetrable. Members of a group conscious of workplace conflict with their employers might well, as it were, look sideways and see other groups similarly placed. They might, if there seemed a prospect of reciprocity, help them with funds. A very few might take the further considerable step of abstracting from these experiences and internalising general concepts of structural class conflict and structured class war. In so far as this appeared to them to call both for industrial action and political class action at the national level they might be regarded as having full working-class conciousness in the Marxist sense. In situations and periods of special grievance, excitement, or frustration, they might command the ear of their fellows who, while not internalising the analysis in any committed sense, would find that it spoke to their mood – for as long as the situation lasted at any rate. Suitably intense and prolonged, a situation of this kind is as much as revolutionaries can hope for. If successful revolutions depended on mass understanding and internalisation of revolutionary analysis and doctrine the world would have seen few indeed. The crucial question is: are the rank and file in sufficient numbers sufficiently frustrated and desperate to follow advanced leaders to the further political extremities – in terms of either slogans, or action, or both? There seems no reason to doubt that particular groups within the working class reached this stage at certain periods during the first half of the nineteenth century. There is equally no reason to doubt that such responses were too patchy, uneven and ephemeral to enable great claims to be made for the growth of full working-class consciousness of the kind that acknowledged a need to make common cause in a political struggle against the exploiting classes.

Among the many reasons for this must be included, along with sectional exclusiveness and the other factors already mentioned, a more pervasive feature of Britain's culture. This was individualism, either atomistic or collectivist. A full ideological and emotional commitment to one's class in a class-war context required as a necessary condition the ability to relate oneself to an abstract concept of class which signifies interests universal to all its members whether they realise it or not, and which bespeaks a higher good which may require individual or group sacrifice. The culture of Britain has never equipped its citizens for this kind of abstraction. Small minorities manage it; most do not, thereby perpetuating the nation's reputation for 'pragmatism' and 'empirical commonsense'. Even those whose structural work situation lent itself to such analysis were mostly led away from it by deeply-rooted cultural dispositions as well as by sectional self-interest, status satisfactions and a measure of vertical bonding with sections of the middle class. Such impediments caused fracturing even of that more modest class consciousness which lay in awareness of workplace interests shared with others similarly placed. Some clearly felt it; many equally clearly did not. We must also include, in any appraisal of working-class dispositions, 'the views of most of those beneath the artisans, those who manifested the "flag-saluting, foreigner-hating, peer-respecting side of the plebeian mind"' (Hunt, 1981, p. 239). No doubt some of these impediments would have been greatly weakened had the next quarter-century been a period of economic disaster or had the state and employers combined in attempts to smash the trade unions. Instead it was a period of relative prosperity whose consequences enabled many groups of employers and prevailing groups within the ruling class to take up a cautiously permissive stance towards the unions and towards certain of their political aspirations.

4

The Emergence of the System

The 1850s to the 1880s

By the mid-1870s the legal, and in certain respects the social, political and industrial situation of organised labour had become transformed. A wide diversity of social forces, some of them fortuitous, some of them persistent historical continuities, were converging to create what was beginning to be recognisable as an industrial relations system. Of these, fortuitous but crucial was a quarter of a century of national economic buoyancy which underpinned a mood of social optimism and assumptions of continuous moral and material progress. This had three decisive consequences. First, economic growth brought betterment and increasing 'respectability' to the upper strata of labour and sufficiently stimulated the expansion and strength of their unions to ensure that repression became even less of a practical political option than at the beginning of the century. Secondly, economic well-being, social stability and assumptions of continuous progress made it possible for the ruling classes to relax their fears of revolutionary disorder and to maintain their commitment to constitutionalism, the rule of law and representative institutions – and even to admit the urban worker to the franchise, thereby exposing themselves to successful political pressures for a major recasting of trade union and labour law. Thirdly, the same social optimism favoured a vision, propagated by a group of highly influential middle-class reformers, that an increasingly enlightened trade union movement would come to co-operate with employers through the collective bargaining process to promote class harmony, 'responsible' joint regulation and continued economic growth. By the time these assumptions of continuous economic, social and moral progress were faltering, organised labour had secured a body of industrial and political rights that could be severely dented but not destroyed except at the cost of an authoritarian overturn of Britain's entire political and economic system.

The period therefore saw a considerable extension of collective bargaining, conciliation and arbitration procedures; a revolution in trade union law; and a marked quickening of union participation in organisational politics. The Parliament that assembled after the 1874 election contained the first two working-men MPs, both miners and both Liberals supported by Liberal–Labour votes. It was to be only a decade later that the Prince of Wales would receive a group of trade union leaders at Sandringham, conduct them personally on a tour of the royal residence, and consider it judicious to express a hope that having seen how 'I have attempted to discharge some of my duties as a country gentleman', they would be convinced that 'I have not been unmindful of my obligations as a landlord and employer of labour' (Magnus, 1967, p. 252). The organised working class now had both feet planted on the stage of history, and the recognition among informed observers that they could not be dislodged was confirmation that the heritage of constitutionalism, civic freedoms and the rule of law was to be allowed to pursue its course provided that current expectations about working-class behaviour were fulfilled. Those expectations were, as will be seen, an important part of the story.

Mid-Victorian Prosperity and Consolidation of the 'New Order'

The economic prosperity which supported these changes owed something to events outside as well as within Britain itself. Circumstances combined to secure that for a quarter of a century industry and agriculture prospered together on an unprecedented scale. The year 1850 saw the beginning of a great global boom. 'What followed was so extraordinary that men were at a loss for a precedent. Never, for instance, did British exports grow more rapidly than in the first seven years of the 1850s.' Cheap capital and a rapid rise in prices brought high profits, and the 1851 Crystal Palace Exhibition symptomised a mood, at once buoyant, optimistic and arrogantly confident of limitless progress, which seems almost to have been born in that year. 'The political consequence of this boom was far-reaching. It ... wrecked the hopes of the revolutionaries ... In Britain Chartism died away, and the fact that its death was more protracted than historians used to suppose did not make it any the less final.' The depression of 1857 proved 'merely an interruption of the golden era of capitalist growth which resumed on an even larger scale in the 1860s and reached its peak in the boom of 1871–3' (Hobsbawm, 1977, pp. 44–6). Other historians offer a more muted account of growth in this period, but Hobsbawm conveys the sense of wonder felt at the time.

Seeking to understand this remarkable upsurge, contemporaries included among many factors the contribution made by 'the liberation of private enterprise, the engine which, by common agreement, powered the progress of industry. Never has there been a more overwhelming consensus among economists or indeed among intelligent politicians and administrators about the recipe for economic growth: economic liberalism' (ibid., p. 50). At the same time there began to emerge evidence, for those aware of it, that might well have seemed reassuring, at least at first sight, to the social critics of preceding decades, with their charge that economic liberalism was undermining the ruling class's powers of control.

Alongside the usual flow of fear and mistrust of the lower orders there now began to develop a current of approval towards the rising standards of behaviour increasingly observed among the upper strata of the working classes and a belief that they would eventually overtake the lower strata also. The critics might well have inferred initially from social developments in much northern factory industry that their admonitions were being taken to heart, for there now began to develop a new paternalism which carried a good deal further and more widely the movements described by Mill in the 1840s and which was to remain effective until late in the century.

A New Paternalism

Among the larger and more secure employers in the coal and iron industries of the north-east and south Wales, but especially those of the spectacularly booming Lancashire cotton industry, there was a growing consciousness of industry's civilising mission. 'Carlyle and Ruskin's elevation of the employer as the Captain of Industry was taken seriously by the big employers ... '. Contributing to it were religious notions of duty and accountability, an urge to vindicate economic power, a desire to buttress social superiority and the notion of re-creating community. These expressed themselves partly in terms of deliberate community-building but more in the piecemeal provision of churches, schools, baths, reading rooms and the promotion of community sense at the workplace. Such measures were also expected to create a loyal, attached and grateful workforce, and certainly in some industrial towns and villages there appears to have developed a vertical bonding between employer and employed that was more genuinely internalised by the lower orders than in many earlier situations, where the deference had been more calculated. It was facilitated by the pervasive dominance of factory or mine in neighbourhood life, and in Lancashire cotton, Joyce suggests, by the symmetry between local occupational and family structure (Joyce, 1980). The spirit engendered within these industrial neighbourhoods was to some extent expressed in attitudes towards work and employer–worker relations. In Lancash' e cotton, spokesmen on both sides, as the 1860s moved into the 187(and 1880s, became ready to laud the industry's prevalent spirit of co-operation, class harmony and sense of common interests.

All this might seem to add up to the formula for class control and social peace which critics had been urging upon industry for some considerable time. How far did it in fact conform to their vision? Was the Lancashire cotton industry during the second half of the century offering a pattern of relations which might have served as a model for the rest of British industry? Joyce makes clear that there was a great deal which was fortuitous about the growth of paternalism in Lancashire cotton. But he also indicates that, in any case, Britain's ideological and cultural context set important limits to this paternalism, in terms both of what was offered and how it was received. Much of it developed 'within the matrix of strongly held *laissez-faire* notions of what the relations of employer and worker should be' (ibid., p. 138). Principles of thrift, hard work and self-reliance were valued by both sides, and the virtues of individualism were currently being hymned throughout Britain possibly more palpably than ever before. 'Every society has its propagandists who try to persuade their fellow-citizens to develop a special kind of social character which will best serve the needs of the day', and the literature of individual striving and success was 'more common in the middle of the nineteenth century than has usually been recognized' (Briggs, 1965, pp. 124, 310). Samuel Smiles, whose first major work, *Self-Help*, appeared in 1859, stressed the importance of directing diligence, perseverance, determination and thrift towards the objective of individual self-improvement, 'it was still generally believed that a benevolent and ... invisible hand was directing individual action, along lines suggested by Adam Smith, to produce social gain' (ibid., p. 134). This, along with the prevalent and long-standing British conception of the nation-state as no more than an aggregate of individuals, could lead Smiles to write that 'national progress is the sum of individual industry, energy, and uprightness' (ibid., p. 133).

More significant than all this for our present purpose, however, is the fact that the new paternalism fell crucially short of the 'strong' version advanced by the critics as the key strategy for social control. From Southey to the leader-writers of *The Times*, they had urged the reassertion of an authoritarian paternalism, practised and encouraged by the state, which obviated all need and justification for independent organisation among the lower orders. The maintenance of unbroken organic links between the ranks and classes, and the exploitation of those links for the purposes of control and social peace, were the essential notions of the bond they sought. This was a version of paternalism which saw it as the necessary alternative to independent organisation among subordinates.

Yet the development of the new paternalism in the industrial north after the mid-century was accompanied by the considerable growth of a trade unionism whose methods of unilateral regulation and/or collective bargaining were pursued through independent organisation which challenged employer prerogative. The two were far from being necessarily opposed. There were certainly some among the anti-union employers who applied the full authoritarian paternalism as a strategy for excluding a union presence, and one Lancashire firm was recently studied which maintained until the Second World War this combination of paternalistic benevolence and autocratic suppression of trade unionism (Martin and Fryer, 1973). Much of the union recognition and collective bargaining in Lancashire cotton and north-east coal and iron, however, was owed to those very employers who led the move towards paternalism (Joyce, 1980, p. 71; Nossiter, 1975, p. 40).

It was therefore paternalism in the 'weak' sense that was being applied. The recognition by the employer of his employees' right to organise themselves independently of his authority, to define their own interests, to formulate their own grievances and to have them represented and processed through collective institutional machinery, is incompatible with the full paternalist assertion that father knows best and must impose that knowledge upon his children. Nor was the trade unionism even of paternalist Lancashire cotton docile and biddable. Though there was much talk of identity of interests, this 'was understood in terms of a common commitment to the means of production as the source of a livelihood and a future', and only very infrequently 'to an acceptance of *laissez-faire* doctrine'. For all textile labour 'the lesson of the capitalist market place was that of the unavoidable divergence of economic interests' (Joyce, 1980, p. 65). For the more pessimistic observers these were developments full of dangers for property, progress, order, individual liberty and civilisation.

Union Growth and Job Regulation

As the mid-Victorian period wore on, however, the optimistic voices strengthened. At least the workers' organised industrial power was not being directed towards dangerous political theories. 'Average English workmen', wrote one informed observer in 1871, 'are not so political as continental ... workmen are ... They have not the type of mind for which theoretical or philosophical politics have fascination . . . ' They seek to improve their position 'by strikes and the strengthening of trade unions – and not by the establishment of entirely new social systems' (Cronin, 1982, pp. 78–9).

Lancashire cotton was prominent among those industries in which organisation on both sides was accompanied by a considerable degree of harmony and even co-operation – 'a degree of social calm perhaps unique in English industrial society' (Joyce, 1980, p. 90). Among employers, prosperity brought some mitigation of *laissez-faire* rigour; among factory operatives some alleviation in a lot which, though still marked by poverty and hardship, offered a little betterment and hope of more to come. Together with the paternal policies of many larger employers, this provided a material basis for the vertical bonding which extended to politics and greatly affected voting according to whether the employer was Tory or Liberal.

The craftsmen fared even better. It is likely that real wages as a whole rose by at least a third during the third quarter and the lion's share went to the upper stratum of the working class – which included some better-paid operatives other than craftsmen. An absolute improvement in the living standards of the working classes as a whole was occurring at the same time as a relative improvement among the labour aristocracy *vis-à-vis* the rest. The social distance between many craftsmen and many non–craftsmen increased and craft unionism 'attained a heightened self-confidence' (R. Harrison, 1965, pp. 5, 15, 25, 30), projecting itself into a major position of leadership which extended into the political field and left important imprints upon the whole later movement.

The most widely publicised demonstrations of this craft leadership emanated from a group of union head offices located in London, but among the significant events of the period was the convening of special union conferences by provincial trades councils to deal with urgent issues of common concern – Glasgow Trades Council in 1864, Sheffield's in

1867. 'But the credit of initiating the idea of an annual conference to deal with all subjects of interest to the trade union world belongs to the Manchester and Salford Trades Council . . . ' (Webb and Webb, 1920, p. 280). Thus was born in 1868, the Trades Union Congress (TUC), which became and remained the one national centre. It has proved of major significance for Britain's trade unionism and industrial relations system that they have never suffered the disruptive effect of having two or more rival national centres, as in America and Continental countries, where political or religious differences or both expressed and aggravated weakening divisions. In this the national tradition of religious toleration undoubtedly played its part. The effect remained and the TUC has continued to express and maintain the relatively high degree of homogeneity within the British movement.

Within the favourable economic environment union membership grew rapidly. That of the Amalgamated Society of Engineers, for example, rose from 5,000 at its formation in 1851 to 35,000 in 1870 and 45,000 in 1880, and comparable rates of growth were achieved by other craft and by non-craft unions. The Operative Cotton Spinners, founded in 1853, had 11,000 members by 1870 and 17,000 by 1888. Cotton-weaving unionism expanded comparably. Such growth rates could probably not have been achieved unless prosperity had been accompanied by a more accommodating stance among the wider public and the employers towards the more sober and 'businesslike' unions. Middle-class opinion generally came to take a somewhat less censorious attitude towards strikes – even a stoppage by engineering craftsmen in 1852 against systematic overtime, piecework, and the employment of 'illegal' men on certain machines aroused less hostility than might have been expected.

> Thanks to the currents of thought set up by J. S. Mill and the Christian Socialists, the 'public' now contained influential elements ready to show sympathy for a body like the engineers, who refrained from 'outrages', held great and orderly meetings, issued reasoned social explanations of their conduct, and made punctual disbursements of strike pay. Indeed, in 1853 the 'public' was to show almost a general tolerance for the great 'wages movement' of that year, though it led to much varied striking. Part of the tolerance was, of course, due to the great rapidity with which the wealth of the upper and middle classes was growing, and proved quite unable to withstand the onset of depression. But part was a permanent gain, the result of a dawning appreciation of the immense cultural advances which had been made by large sections of the artisan class. (Maccoby, 1935, pp. 408–9)

Both parts were to make possible the securing of the franchise for that class and of legal protections for their unions.

Industrially, prosperity made it easier for many employers to perceive that provided a union could become strong enough to discipline its members into orderly and peaceful procedures for dealing with disputes and grievances, and to ensure that competing employers all paid the same price for labour, thereby limiting the more cut-throat forms of

competition, it might be acceptable as a partner in labour regulation –
always assuming it did not proceed to use its strength in ways offensive to
the employer. Among these ideas, that of seeking to take the price of
labour out of competition was not new – Lancashire cotton manufacturers
had, after all, joined with weavers' spokesmen as early as 1805 to seek a
statutory minimum wage, thereby embarrassing both the government
and themselves. Now the larger cotton employers were making most of
the running in developing collective bargaining in the rapidly growing
industry. A similar hankering was evident elsewhere for some form of
regulation which increased the chances of industrial peace and of establishing a floor to the more predatory forms of competition. With statutory
intervention now inconceivable, there remained regulation through the
medium of the union. But there was a gradation of offences which would
render a partnership with the union unacceptable. It might be excessively
militant in its wage demands. It might encroach upon employer prerogatives in even more fundamental ways by seeking to impose its own
regulations on labour utilisation, technology, hiring and firing. Policies of
this kind could sometimes generate employer fantasies that the union's
object was to seize productive resources and expropriate the present
owners by direct industrial action. This, the most crucial issue, involved
the question of whether trade unionism was prepared to operate a role akin
to that of loyal and 'legitimate' Opposition in Parliament. Obviously the
analogy was highly imperfect: the union would never be allowed to
become the government as could the Opposition in the political context.
Indeed, to be a loyal Opposition in industry meant abstaining from any
such aspiration and being prepared instead to work within the established
system of property relations and ownership rights along with the basic
conventions of authority, status and reward. What the political and
industrial concepts of loyal Opposition had in common was the readiness
of the Opposition to allow itself to be contained within a pattern of
constraints which ensured continuance of the system in its basic essentials
– as these were defined by those whose interests disposed them to conserve it.

Obviously employers could never give themselves a final and definitive
answer on this question, for there could not be one. Nor could they be
expected to speak with one voice at any one time. At any particular
moment the employers in some industries might be conducting a bitter
struggle with organised labour; in others the scene might be relatively
peaceful, with employers feeling that there was something to be said for
dealing collectively with their employees through representative spokesmen. A few years later the situations might be reversed.

Given such qualifications, other industries besides cotton found many
employers prepared to experiment with the union as regulative partner.
Established by A. J. Mundella in 1860, the Nottingham Hosiery Joint
Conciliation Board 'regulated the many piece-prices of the industry as
well as settling works disputes', and soon similar boards covered Leicester
and Derby. As in cotton weaving, the attractions for employers were the
prospects of containing competitive wage cutting and of maintaining
peaceful dispute procedures (Clegg, Fox and Thompson, 1964, p. 24).

Mundella himself, later Liberal politician and government minister, declared support for trade unions, provided they were 'conducted on moderate and reasonable principles', on the ground that they 'afforded the only machinery for getting at the workmen of any trade *en masse* with a view to arbitration and conciliation' (Mundella, 1871, col. 273). He claimed the Nottingham Board as the first of its kind, but in fact from the 1830s onwards similar attempts were being made in a diversity of trades and localities, including the Scottish textile trades, Staffordshire potteries, Macclesfield silk, north-east shipbuilding, printing, tailoring, lace-making, the Midlands building trades and various others (Amulree, 1929, ch. 7). And from '1867 to 1875 innumerable Boards of Conciliation and Arbitration were established at which representatives of the masters met representatives of the trade unions on equal terms' (Webb and Webb, 1920, p. 337).

The casualty rate was high. Unions often lacked or lost the strength to discipline their members or to enforce the standard terms on the more predatory employers, especially when competition became especially intense. They could therefore offer the employers nothing in return for recognition. Other arrangements ran into trouble when the union ventured beyond its allotted role. In the newly mechanising boot and shoe industry, union membership and strength rose rapidly during the 1880s and the leading employers' trade journal observed in 1889 that

> never in the history of the trade has [trade unionism] been so powerful, and never, on the whole, has it exerted so much influence for good . . . Among manufacturers, too, the movement is in the same direction . . . And the progress is in both instances a satisfactory sign of the times . . . It is to the advantage of all concerned that chaos should be reduced to order, and that, as far as possible, uniformity of wage and practice should be attained. Every manufacturer today feels that he has an interest in the settlement of the wages paid by his competitors, and although the workmen were the first to point this out, yet now that the principle has been acceded, employers are eager to carry it to its logical issue whenever a dispute arises.

Within a few years this idyllic picture had changed dramatically. The union was bitterly resisting labour-saving technical and organisational changes and imposing restrictive rules, while at the same time socialist militants were finding a receptive audience among a membership fearful of threats to jobs and status. Alarmed at both developments, the organised employers smashed these union pretensions and restored the previous and relatively innocuous relationship (Fox, 1958, p. 129, chs 4 and 5).

'Conciliation' and a Middle-Class Vision

Despite difficulties and failures there developed around the idea of 'conciliation' a vision ardently pressed by a number of influential middle-class reformers. Conciliation was a term that was to undergo several shifts of meaning. The Webbs were to write in 1897 that 'there has been until quite recently no clear distinction drawn between collective bargaining, conciliation, and arbitration. Much of what is called arbitration or conciliation in the early writings . . . amounts to nothing more than organized collective bargaining' (Webb and Webb, 1902, p. 223). And indeed the practical form of conciliation as middle-class reformers promoted it lay in regular and systematic meetings between equal numbers of employers' and workers' representatives, and since this eventually became a major form of collective bargaining in Britain, it would be easy to assume that what all the proselytisers of conciliation were urging upon industry was simply collective bargaining as the British scene came to know it – namely, the wary, mutually suspicious, arms-length, zero-sum relationship as it has been seen by so many observers.

In fact some of them hoped for, and confidently expected to materialise, something very different. There was some evidence to support their hopes. Cotton and hosiery offered examples of co-operation between employers and unions which suggested to many observers that a modern, enlightened age of industrial relations was dawning. In cotton, where technical improvements had earlier been 'the subject of furious strife between masters and men', the unions after the mid-1860s felt sufficiently secure to 'meet the innovating employers halfway' by accepting change while insisting that the operatives concerned gained a share in, but not the whole of, the resulting financial benefit (ibid., pp. 408–10). Few union policies can have been more heartening to the Victorian middle-class observer. It cast, for the time being, a wholly favourable light on what might otherwise have been seen as an ominous sign – the development of rigorous bargaining of a highly specific and keenly focused kind which involved the application at workplace level, by salaried professional specialists representing both sides, of mathematically complex formulæ for applying and adjusting piece-rates. In the context of prosperity and relative class harmony, this, along with the unions' accommodating stance towards technical innovation, appeared to some observers, including the Webbs in the 1890s, as the rational and progressive next step in industrial relations.

The present antagonism between capital and labour, Henry Crompton wrote in 1876, was destined to die away; harmony would be restored 'as employers and employed gradually cease to be opposed, and meet together and co-operate in mutual trust, equally animated with the conception of peaceably working out the great ends before them'. The 'mutually predatory' system of hatred and suspicion in which there was no real contact but merely trials of strength when depression changed to boom and vice versa would give way to constructive reconciliation.

There was much here that relied on an assumption of moral education and moral progress. By the time Crompton was writing this assumption was of many years standing. ' . . . the improved education of masters and men, there is good reason to hope, is doing more to avert collisions between them than any mere arrangements could accomplish', declared a report of 1860 by the Committee on Trades' Societies, prepared for the National Association for the Promotion of Social Science. This was a major consideration for middle-class Christian Socialist and Positivist supporters of the unions, but it did not lead them to ignore 'mere arrangements'. Thomas Hughes, one of the former, and a member of the committee, argued in the same year that 'the present disastrous state of feeling between employers and employed can never be improved, will only become worse, while the unions remain unrecognized by the law, and misrepresented, hated, and feared by all classes of society except that great one of which they are exclusively composed, and whose ideas and wishes they do, on the whole, faithfully represent and carry out' (Shuttleworth, 1860, pp xx, 187).

The principal arrangement for promoting constructive reconciliation was to be the joint board of conciliation, supported by strong organisation on both sides. 'Increased organization, whether of masters or men, or both, means decreased war ... There is no way of binding the men to accept the decision of the board, unless there are unions or some other organization among them that would have the same power over them.' Such boards 'have already shown that they are capable of being employed to promote industrial progress, apart from the more special object with which they were originally established' (Crompton, 1876, pp. 23, 34–48, 164).

What was envisaged was a positive-sum relationship from which both sides, as well as society at large, would derive benefit. Underlying and inspiring it was a belief that rising living standards and the spread of education were bringing great changes in the condition of large sections of the working classes – changes towards increasing refinement, sobriety, self-respect and self-control. The third quarter of the century had seen 'a great intellectual and moral progress among employers and employed'. The assumptions here were a far cry from the paternalist-dependence system which, as these observers saw it, had now gone for ever. 'Individually and collectively, the workmen have assumed a new position. The old relationship of masters and men is shattered.' Employers would have to seek to reconstitute their authority, but they must do so on the basis of accepting their workers' independence. Far from undermining their own position this would strengthen it. Worker independence was 'the only sure foundation for a higher and nobler authority' (ibid., pp. 3, 9, 10–11, 13, 14). Secure and confident in their own strength and self-respect, workers would feel able to accept and co-operate with the employer's leadership in a joint pursuit of economic progress, and would do so within a joint regulative structure which 'develops the higher human qualities of each'. In effect, conciliation so defined would bring the unions into an accommodative posture with respect to the organisational and technological innovations generated by market competition, but the posture would derive dignity from being an outcome not of coercion but independence. This conception of the future of the industrial relations system and the unions' role in it was to be offered as a confident prediction by, for example, a leading economist, Jevons, in 1882 (see pp. 159–60 below) and by the Webbs in their *Industrial Democracy* in 1897 (pt 3, ch. 4).

The aspect of independence was taking on increased prominence in the syndrome of qualities that defined respectability, though needless to say it had to be an independence exercised within understood boundaries and aspirations – namely, those that could be welcomed, or at worst reluctantly tolerated – by the middle classes. What 'the old-fashioned Liberal ... liked in trade unionism', wrote the Webbs at the end of the century, 'was the voluntary spontaneity of its structure and the self-helpfulness of its methods; even when he disbelieved in the possibility of its objects and disliked its devices' (Webb and Webb, 1902, p. 808).

The Positivists and the Labour Aristocracy

Crompton was one of a group of Positivists – that also included Frederic Harrison, Godfrey Lushington and E. S. Beesly – who strongly supported trade unionism but were far from uncritical of some of its aims and methods. Positivism had a strong appeal for lapsed evangelicals who retained a sense of social duty. They were not socialists, but were conscious of inequities and inefficiencies which they believed – as Crompton's words illustrate – could be eradicated by moral reform and a change of heart among businessmen, administrators and others in positions of leadership, and influence, especially union spokesmen. Their creed provided the young Sidney Webb with a transitional stage on his journey from reformist Liberalism to socialism, and they transmitted to the Fabians their belief that 'more good might be done by working through existing organizations than by opposing them' (MacKenzie and MacKenzie, 1979, p. 61). Their support of the unions was therefore quite compatible with deep doubts about certain aspects of their policies, even those of the craft unions with whose leaders they were most in contact.

It would have been quite impossible, for example, for a middle-class Victorian in public life to allow himself to feel approval or even sympathetic understanding either for violence, intimidation and coercive pressures on non-unionists, or for the dogged obstruction which strongly organised craftsmen could present to technical or organisational 'progress' which threatened jobs, pay, status, or craft identity. The notions of individual liberty, industrial progress and that social violence was totally unforgivable bore such a sacred aura that to slight them was to remove oneself from rational discourse – even George Eliot, Charlotte Brontë, Elizabeth Gaskell, Charles Kingsley and Dickens felt totally unable to cross this line in their industrial novels for all their manifest sympathy with the lower orders.

The close co-operation with middle-class reformers brought certain craft unions and their leaders the extremes of both approval and disapproval, depending on the bias of the observer. Yet despite subsequent portrayal as vehicles of a uniquely selfish sectionalism and the labelling of their leaders as 'the servile generation' (Postgate, 1923, ch. 9), the misleadingly termed 'new model' unions of the 1850s and 1860s were, as we have noted, only continuing trends already well established. The largest of the unions which came together in the Amalgamated Society of Engineers (ASE), formed in 1851, was itself an amalgamation of Yorkshire and Lancashire engineering craft societies which had united in 1838 and pursued centralisation of administration through a full-time salaried general secretary. In other ways, too, the new model organisations 'merely maintained the traditional characteristics of the old skilled craft unions: restriction of membership to apprenticed craftsmen, payment of high subscriptions and provision of friendly benefits' (Musson, 1972, p. 50). The centuries-old exclusivist sectionalism remained the central thrust of trade policy, as Samuel Smiles noted in 1862. 'They, in fact, constitute an exclusive body, whose principal object is to keep as many as possible out of their particular trades, and especially to shut out the poor and unskilled from participating in their peculiar advantages' (Phelps Brown, 1959, p. 147).

For all their unctuous protestations of peace and sweet reason, the craft societies were sometimes forced into the open by a concerted challenge from the employers. For the most part, craft restrictions were enforced by withdrawing small groups or even single members from the individual 'defaulting' employer, a comparatively unobtrusive method which persisted as long as employers generally were prepared to tolerate craft regulation, whatever the frustration. Every so often, however, the employers might feel goaded, with respect to some particular issue or in some particular set of market conditions, to offer a collective challenge. No sketch of the craft culture is therefore complete without some examples of the tenacious struggles in which they could become involved. A campaign by the ASE to eliminate systematic overtime and piece-work and prevent the employment of 'illegal' men on certain machines provoked a lockout in 1852 by the Manchester and London employers, who issued a resolution which contrasted the old order with the new. 'That while this nation, by its representatives in parliament, has abolished guild privileges, exclusive charters of corporate handicrafts, restrictions on the export of machinery or the free egress from the realm of skilled workmen, and all monopolies', the demands of the ASE were 'an attempt to ignore the right of every British subject to dispose of his own labour or capital according to his individual views of his own interest' (T. Hughes, 1860, p. 180). The employers' legal advisers saw very clearly the pre-industrial antecedents of the craftsmen's demands.

They were forced back to work on terms which implied the destruction of their union; every man being required to sign a declaration forswearing support of any society which 'professes to control or interfere with the arrangements or regulations of this or any other manufacturing or trade establishment'. But there was no follow-through and the employers were soon acquiescing once more in the union presence in their workshops. Membership and funds quickly recovered; the 'declaration' was forgotten and it was the employers' organisations that disappeared (Jefferys, 1945, pp. 42–4). Other major craft clashes involved the formation of the Midland Association of Flint Glass Manufacturers in 1858 to defend its members against a series of strikes aimed at controlling the number of apprentices. In the following year the London building contractors together defeated a demand for the nine-hour day, and in 1866 master tailors in London, Manchester, Birmingham and other major cities combined to oppose the demands of their craftsmen. The often bland and pacific utterances by

top-level craft leaders were therefore misleading. 'They are very nice people
if they have their own way', said a Manchester foundry owner of the ASE in
1868, 'but if they have not they will fight, and they can fight anything and
anybody, they are so strong' (Clegg, Fox and Thompson, 1964, pp. 5, 9).

Among these 'very nice people' was John Burnett, who became general
secretary of the ASE in 1875, and who serves as a representative figure of his
kind. A committed Liberal who lectured for Joseph Chamberlain's
National Education League and later became the first Chief Labour
Correspondent of the Board of Trade, he led a tenacious and successful
twenty-week strike of the Tyneside engineers in 1871 for the nine-hour day
– 'one of the most significant industrial disputes of nineteenth-century
Britain' (Allen *et al.*, 1971, p. 98). Burnett

> always preferred methods of negotiation and conciliation to outright
> conflict in industrial disputes. While very well aware of the injustices
> and irregularities which abounded in contemporary society, he sought
> to remedy them not by revolutionary subversion, but by making the
> maximum possible use of the opportunities for improvement made
> available in practice by the existing structure of society. He believed . . .
> that it was possible to move significantly towards a more just and equal
> society by a policy of co-operation with the more enlightened elements
> among the contemporary privileged and influential groups. (ibid.,
> p. 107)

Robert Applegarth, general secretary of the Amalgamated Society of
Carpenters and Joiners between 1862 and 1871, was in the same mould.
Along with many others like him, Applegarth urged temperance, chas-
tity, self-education and hard work upon members of his class, but
combined with this a capacity for passionate defence of independent trade
union organisation – defence which included close co-operation with
middle-class sympathisers. 'When he looked to the future, Applegarth did
not see a utopia but a land of more equal opportunity, where unionists
were full, responsible citizens, exercising an active influence in national
affairs and building with care and vision a cooperative commonwealth'
(Briggs, 1965, p. 204).

Here were leaders expressing in Victorian terms a long-standing disposition of artisan activists to combine strong solidarity among members of
the same craft with strong commitments upwards to certain groups
within the middle class. There were, of course, strands within the trade
union movement markedly different from this and, then as now, some of
them gave 'moderates' like Burnett and Applegarth a stressful time on
occasions. Yet they set the tone that was, in general, to predominate, and
at no time was this tone more important and influential than during the
third quarter of the nineteenth century. For within the context of
economic buoyancy, profitability and rising living standards that was
fostering expectations of steady moral as well as material progress, union
leaders like these appeared to confirm those expectations. This eased the
passage of legislation favouring the unions; a process which, in seeming to
promise continued amelioration by constitutional means, consolidated an

already strong political system by securing the attachment of the Labour movement. The trade unions, having already shown themselves pre- pared to play the role of loyal Opposition in industry, were being further encouraged by events to accept the same role in politics.

The Echoes of an Old Alliance: Social Identity and Political Attachments

Historical continuities help us to understand why that role of loyal Opposition in politics took the form predominantly of attachment to the Liberal Party. There were, of course, certain structural reasons why trade unionists could not expect to be politically effective if they attempted to stand alone – there was simply not the electoral basis for a large-scale party founded on the working classes. Though the exten- sions of the franchise in 1867 and 1885 are usually acclaimed as the most important electoral reforms in Britain's history they left only 28 per cent of all adults with the vote, and until 1918 about 44 per cent of all males of 21 and over – mainly working class – and, of course, all women, were without it. By December 1910, the last general election before the war, the total electorate had grown only from about 5 million after the 1885 Act to 7½ million (Chamberlain, 1973, pp. 476–7).

But this lack of an adequate electorate for a mass independent working-class party was not the only reason why most working-class activists had chosen to work through the Liberal Party or in alliance with it. We have noted that much working-class radicalism had long been capable of establishing a vertical bonding with middle-class radi- calism; a bonding with deep historical roots that might have as a central element a shared religion and an associated cluster of social and political attitudes. After the 1860s, when the two mass parties began to be formed, the

> basic line of political cleavage in the political market for the middle classes, and for the newly enfranchised workers as well, was religion ... Dissent became associated with Liberalism, the Established Angli- can Church with Toryism. This was true too for the working classes. The pattern was not uniform; in Lancashire, for instance, the Tories captured the Orange anti-Catholic vote. But it does seem to have been the dominant pattern. Membership of a religious community tied men to a particular party, and made them responsive to different sets of political attitudes and ideas. Party affiliation from the beginn- ing was more a consequence of social identity than of rational deliberation ... Social identity is not, however, dependent upon the preferences and values of the sovereign individual. On the contrary, it determines them. Different social identities arise from the way in which the structure of society distributes men into groups, classes, and communities, and determines the framework of their opportun- ities and experiences. (Gamble, 1974, pp. 202–3)

The early links between religion, social identity and political affiliations had left the Victorians with a legacy of structural religious conflict which both expressed and reinforced fundamental divisions between the older and the newer forms of economic, social, political and religious authority and interests (Gilbert, 1976, p. 205). This continuing conflict was, of course, only made possible by the persistence of a popular, Dissenting, extra-Establishment religion rivalling the quantitative size of the Church of England. And though nineteenth-century Liberalism was more than Nonconformity, the organisations of religious Dissent continued to provide major definitions of a social identity which was associated with support for a liberal-reformist political movement prepared to work within the broad framework of established social and political structures. This takes on great significance when contrasted with such facts as that no such extra-Establishment religion emerged, for example, in Germany. Dissent and Nonconformity reared generations of upper-working-class leaders and activists, many of whom eschewed violence and direct action in favour of a strict constitutionalism yet at the same time fought for an extension of their class's rights within the established framework. The doctrines and values clustering around political liberalism during the nineteenth century provided a rationalising and educative democratic ideology, too, for the pragmatic strategies and techniques of rule which the traditional landed aristocracy and gentry had been evolving by trial and error since the late seventeenth century. It educated those in the lower as well as those in the upper ranks. In this way, major movements of religious Dissent which, for all their bitter grievances, were gradually achieving religious equality by constitutional means, were serving as vehicles for a political dissent which was likewise being encouraged by events to work within the limits and constraints of constitutionalism.

When, therefore, leaders and activists of the upper working class pursued their Lib–Lab connections they were acting within a social identity that had a long history. For many of them, if not most, that identity was to be little affected by the revival of socialist doctrines in the 1880s.

> Neither the members of the Parliamentary Committee of the Trades Union Congress, with the exception of one or two, nor the tiny group of working men whom the miners had begun to return to parliament as their representatives, Burt for example, and Fenwick, pious Methodists and local preachers, universally respected for their earnestness and virtues, had the least wish to be considered Socialists. They persisted in regarding themselves as the heirs of great Liberal tradition, the sworn foe of protection, socialism, and war, the tradition of Cobden, Bright and Gladstone. (Halévy, 1961d, p. 213)

This social identity was central to their self-image, their social standing and their achievements.

The commitment to constitutionalism and 'respectability' which was a central element in this identity received intermittent and grudging but nevertheless adequate reinforcement. There had already been a precedent in 1825 that Parliament could be moved, against the obvious preferences of the courts, to make a favourable change in the status of trade unions, and the 10-hours campaign had managed a qualified success with statutes of 1847 and 1850 which established the 10½-hour day. Events during the 1850s and 1860s reinforced the evidence that external and internal pressures upon Parliament could induce a further divergence from the common-law values embodied in hostile legal judgements, and that union lobbying could be effective in this process.

Parliament and the Courts: an Increasing Divergence

Given the independence of the judiciary there was no way in which parliamentary or governmental pressure could reliably be brought to bear upon the courts in the interests of expediency or changing social principles; if the state of the law was to be changed it had to be by legislative statute. In 1859 the Molestation of Workmen Act was passed 'without discussion or comment, probably with reference to some recent judicial decision' (Webb and Webb, 1920, p. 277). It excluded from the definition of 'molestation' or 'obstruction' (and therefore from criminality) the mere agreement to seek an alteration in wages or hours, and also the peaceful persuasion of others, without threat or intimidation, to stop work in order to secure the wages or hours aimed at (provided it did not induce any breach of contract). It had little effect in protecting pickets from prosecution and its interest lies in the additional small evidence it offers of Parliament being prepared to set aside the courts' ingenuity in finding ways of crippling effective collective action among workers – some judges had ruled, for example, that the freedom to combine conferred by the 1825 Act existed only when 'men were not in the employ of any master' (ibid., p. 277).

The first notable success of union lobbying came in 1867. Under the old Master and Servant Act, workers who wilfully broke their contracts of service (for example, by striking without giving due notice or by 'leaving work unfinished') were guilty of a criminal offence and liable to three months' imprisonment, whereas an employer breaking a contract of service (for example, by underpaying wages) was guilty only of a civil offence for which he was liable to a summons or a suit for damages. Given the fact that over 10,000 cases of breach of contract of service came before the courts in a single year (ibid., p. 252), the issue was a sensitive one. A union campaign to remedy this inequality originated in Glasgow in 1863 and was extended to include nationwide representation which eventually focused on London and some well-organised lobbying of the House of Commons. After a Select Committee of 1866 had reported favourably, a piece of legislation in the following year 'remedied the grossest injustice of the law ... The Master and Servant Act of 1867 ... the first positive success of the trade unions in the legislative field, did much to increase their confidence in parliamentary agitation' (ibid., p. 253). Perhaps this understates the case. Perhaps one can scarcely exaggerate the significance of this modest success, showing as it did that useful gains of practical relevance for people's working lives could be made by peaceful constitutional means. Taken along with the proven usefulness of collective bargaining it demonstrated that through their own political and industrial initiative and organisation working people could improve their everyday lot. A future of continuous improvement seemed even more plausible given the current prosperity and the doctrine of progress.

The debate on the Act is important in revealing a belief that it took a further significant step towards placing employer and worker on a basis of legal equality. Such sentiments had been prominent in the 1824-5 debates on the repeal of the Combination Acts, and were an important feature of an official ideology that was increasingly important in asserting the legitimacy of the regime. But how far could civic equality be taken? Were members of the working classes fit and proper persons for the full exercise of political rights, or would they use those rights to attack property, debase standards and undermine culture and civilisation?

The Working Classes in Politics – a 'Loyal Opposition'?

The issue of whether the working classes would accept the role of loyal and civilised Opposition if admitted to participation in the political system underlay much discussion about working-class behaviour. Matthew Arnold, in *Culture and Anarchy*, spoke for the fear haunting many educated well-to-do Victorians that barely beneath the surface lay the threat of mob violence and the destruction of civilised values as well as property. But by the late 1850s many practical men of affairs could be found hailing the spread of self-improving respectability within the upper strata of the working classes. Indeed, this became one of the political clichés of the period. Some of this talk was no more than the platform flattery of the hack politician or part of the fulsome exchanges customary between master and men during the annual works outing. But the fact that it could be lavishly indulged in during parliamentary debates without being met by instant ridicule was an indication that, however many might inwardly demur, the sentiment was too publicly acceptable to be openly derided. Labouchère in 1858 commented on the 'great increase in the intelligence and moderation of the working classes' (Labouchère, 1858, col. 533), and in the following year Mackinnon suggested that 'everyone must perceive how their manners, their temperance, and their general conduct had improved' (Mackinnon, 1859, col. 1274). Men of affairs were encouraged in such sentiments by subsequent evidence that, for many among the working class, possession of the vote was coming to symbolise acceptance of the existing system rather than the first step towards radically transforming it (Royle, 1974, p. 3). The apparent continuity implied by the persistent working-class focus on Parliament and the franchise was misleading; after the mid-century the campaign was for a foothold from which to pursue ameliorative piecemeal reform, not for an instrument with which to overturn the present order.

In 1860 Lord John Russell, introducing one of several abortive attempts during the 1850s and 1860s to enlarge the franchise, compared their times with the early years of the century when governments introduced measures of 'severe repression . . . I think that according to the system of government then pursued, such measures may be considered necessary. But looking at the state of the country in 1860 I find a generally prevailing spirit of loyalty to our institutions – a spirit that wishes to preserve and extend, not to destroy them'. It had been said

> that the franchise in boroughs was in 1832 purposely framed to exclude the working classes from the right of voting; but to that statement I cannot subscribe, although I am ready to admit that it was framed with the view generally of giving weight to the middle classes in this country, whose information and character appeared to us at that time to be such as to entitle them to obtain that vast accession of power which they then received. I own, however, that I think it would be a great evil if we were to continue much longer to exclude from our representative system that large number of the working classes who, by their knowledge, their character, and their qualifications, are fitted to exercise the franchise freely and independently.

Were a 'certain number of those working men best qualified for the privilege' to be admitted to the franchise, 'they would thereby be induced', Russell added delicately, 'to set a greater value on the benefits which the constitution confers' (Russell, 1860, cols 2050–2053). Some Conservatives were manifestly anxious not to be left behind in this parade of compliments. Baxter rejoiced that 'Physical force Chartism and revolutionary ideas had gone down, and had given place . . . to a firm confidence that political rights would be surely though gradually conceded to the people'. There had been amazing progress 'of late years' in the education of the people, and the 'higher class of artisan' were now just as intelligent, sober and worthy as the shopkeeping class – an opinion repeated by others. 'It was among the working class that the Conservatives wished to spread the roots of the constitution' (Adderley, 1860, col. 1066). As early as 1851 Disraeli had 'declared that he had no fear of the artisan class: he was confident that they would not vote Radical, but would support the Monarchy and the Empire' (Blake, 1969, p. 396).

Behind the compliments lay party anxieties about a parliamentary situation of great confusion. Party lines were fluid and uncertain and on both sides party managers were prepared to contemplate an extension of the electorate which naturally they hoped to capture for their own side and which, equally naturally, they believed would present, so far as could be judged, no threat to property and other crucial features of the status quo. None could be certain about such matters, however, and sanguine references to growing moderation and respectability vied with the darker counsel of men like Arnold.

In the event it was party political expediency as much as principle which led some parliamentarians to select the favourable rather than the unfavourable judgements and use them as arguments for franchise extension. It is not surprising, therefore, that the timing and precise nature of that extension was determined more by Disraeli's opportunism and improvisation than by careful long-term strategy. Yet a precondition of his success was a sufficiency of belief among the politically influential that a certain degree of risk in this direction was acceptable and must not be burked. This emphasis was not confined to politicians eager to convince themselves that what they were hankering to do was based on sound arguments. In his introduction to the second edition of *The English Constitution* in 1872, Bagehot referred to 'an idea – a very prevalent idea when the first edition of this book was published (1867) – that there then was an unrepresented class of skilled artisans who could form superior opinions on national matters, and ought to have the means of expressing them' (Bagehot, 1963, p. 272). And a year later the Cambridge economist, Alfred Marshall, argued that 'progress' would 'go on steadily, if slowly, till, by occupation at least, every man is a gentleman'. By 'gentleman' Marshall meant 'civilised'. He believed he saw evidence 'that the skilled artisans, whose labour was not deadening and soul-destroying, were already rising towards the condition' which he foresaw as the ultimate achievement of all. They are 'steadily developing independence and a manly respect for themselves and, therefore, a courteous respect for others; they are steadily accepting the private and public duties of a citizen ... They are steadily becoming gentlemen' (T. H. Marshall, 1950, pp. 4–5, 7–8). The concepts of progress and social evolution undoubtedly encouraged many Victorians to see not only science and technology but society generally as moving along an upward gradient of civilisation and achievement.

The 'Labour Aristocracy' Controversy

Disraeli's opportunism granted the vote to more members of the working classes than that upper stratum whose alleged steady growth in 'sobriety, industry, providence, good taste, good morals, and good habits' had been celebrated by so many during the middle decades. It was this stratum, however, which continued to supply the higher classes with such evidence as they found encouraging. Its nature and origins are controversial. Evidence presented in preceding chapters favours the view that there was little essentially new in the structures, stances and aspirations of this labour aristocracy. Certainly, it was growing in the sense that some better-placed non-craft groups were taking craft status and styles as their model, and this was to prove of great significance with the later widening of union membership. But the existence of a labour aristocracy had emerged over centuries out of the small-scale craft manufacture from which it had drawn its traditions. Some historians, however, have seen its aspirations and anxieties about respectability as a mid-century invention on the part of a newly developing stratum. The Webbs emphasised the supposed novelty of the new model union with its centralised administration, elaborate friendly benefits, non-militant emphasis on conciliation and caution, and reaction against the alleged reckless, utopian, revolutionary aggression of earlier decades (Webb and Webb, 1920, ch. 4). Subsequent writers who saw the labour aristocracy as largely a product of the third quarter of the century have often linked its emergence with Britain's gathering prosperity as the dominant economic power. Marx and Engels sought systematically to trace a relationship between, on the one hand, accommodative and opportunist strategies within the Labour movement and, on the other, the imperialist features of British capitalism – the vast colonial possessions and a monopolistic position in world markets (Marx and Engels, 1975). Imperialism was seen as conferring economic privilege upon not only the bourgeoisie but also a small stratum of workers who felt able in consequence to identify with the system and share in bourgeois respectability and bourgeois prejudices. Lenin, too, argued that an 'exceptional monopolist position created in England relatively tolerable conditions of life for the *aristocracy of labour*, i.e. for the minority of skilled and well-paid workers' (italics in original). This aristocracy 'isolated itself from the mass of the proletariat in close, selfish, craft unions' and in all their political activities followed the Liberalism of their bourgeois masters. When Britain's monopoly position was broken by America and Germany the economic basis of petty bourgeois trade unionism and working-class Liberalism was destroyed and socialism 'again raised its head' (Lenin, 1969, pp. 99, 118). Other interpretations see the labour aristocracy in terms of 'economic bribery' by the ruling class: bribery which rendered it open to ruling-class ideas and values which it then transmitted to the wider working-class movement (Reid, 1978).

These accounts perform a service inasmuch as they direct attention to the ways in which mid-Victorian prosperity furthered and consolidated certain trends already at work, but they do a disservice if they distract attention from social continuities and traditions which had their roots in a very distant past. A perspective that goes back to the seventeenth century impresses at least as much with its persistent features as with the changes it reveals. Certainly, some of these persistences were taking new forms and a new language. We have noted Thompson's judgement that for all the many expressions of violence and disorder in the eighteenth century, 'a general moral primness . . . was, particularly, the ideology of the artisan or of the skilled worker who had held his position in the face of the boisterous unskilled tide' (E. P. Thompson, 1968, pp. 813–14). His predecessors might well have exhibited a fierce Puritan strain of self-righteous virtue; his successors included many who took eagerly to the temperance movement, which became 'a central component of the cult of respectability' (Tholfsen, 1976, p. 238). Its appeal to the concept of respectability 'was powerful enough to attract an important section of the working class and to bind them together with employers, Nonconformists and others to form a pan-class reforming movement' (B. Harrison, 1971, p. 395).

Much can be made of the ways in which this vertical bonding delayed – some would say prevented – the emergence of a distinctive working-class ideology and strategy. The appeal of respectability and the cult of individual improvement probably rendered many working men 'vulnerable to assimilation to cultural patterns determined by the middle class' (Tholfsen, 1976, p. 239). In other words, the transmission of political and social ideas from higher to lower levels was facilitated by the vertical bonding produced by a shared chapel Nonconformity and hostility to

Anglicanism, by a shared faith in free trade, by deep distrust of the landed interest with its history of agricultural protection and 'dear food', by the appeal of temperance, and by artisan convictions that their material interests still lay in staying close to the middle class. Yet the process can hardly be described as one of simple indoctrination and docile acceptance. From the seventeenth century the artisan class had been cherishing for itself political ideas marked by individualism, libertarianism and a principled suspicion of the state; ideas whose practical expression included extension of the franchise. The slowness in growth of any distinctive ideology and strategy embracing the whole of the working class was due not to some calculated capture and imperialist bribery of a new labour aristocracy, but to a long-standing tradition of social justice which excluded the unskilled poor and which persisted because the structural basis for it persisted – namely, a situation in which artisans saw their interests in terms of preserving and not closing the social distance between them and the bottom ranks. Unquestionably the present middle classes were now playing upon this tradition as a method of social control, and this was contributing towards the promotion of peaceful 'conciliation' in industry and constitutional methods in politics. Middle-class approval and assistance were strictly conditional upon 'good behaviour'. But this is not to say that either the labour aristocracy or its strategy were inventions of the ruling class. All that need be said is that members of that class were simply making the most of what resources lay to hand in their struggle to assert control, just as workers were making the most of the heritage of constitutionalism in their struggle to challenge them.

Similar considerations can be applied to the practice and ideology of individualism. It is safe to say that for most British trade unionists the collectivism which they expressed, willingly or under pressure, through membership of their union was of a strictly instrumental kind. A report of the National Association for the Promotion of Social Science in 1860 offered an interesting choice of words in its definition of a trade union, seeing it as 'a combination of workmen to enable *each* to secure the conditions most favourable for labour' (Shuttleworth, 1860, p. viii, italics added). Individualism was expressed now in the language of Samuel Smiles rather than that of the free-born Englishman kicking against the Norman Yoke. A sketch of William Inskip, general secretary from 1886 to 1899 of the National Union of Boot and Shoe Operatives, whose members were on the fringes of the craft world, conveys the flavour.

> In general, he accepted the economic framework of the society in which he lived, looking rather to a strong trade unionism for ameliorations than to any fundamental change in that economic structure. In general, too, he accepted its social values. He was contemptuous of egalitarianism, and convinced that progress required the generous rewarding of individual ability, thrift, and energy. Like most Victorian artisans with any pretensions to 'respectability' and skill, he drew a sharp distinction between men of ability, thrift, and energy and the idle, unscrupulous, and improvident. The former must be rewarded, the latter must bear the consequences of their sins and weaknesses. Inskip

tended to think of skilled artisans, with their trade unions, robust independence, and policies of 'self-help', as falling into the first group, and unskilled workers and labourers, with their more acute poverty, disease, and notorious inability to form stable trade unions, as falling into the second ... These attitudes were very much middle–class Victorian attitudes and there is no doubt that Inskip saw himself closer in interests and sympathies to the middle classes than to the unskilled 'unorganizable' labourers'. (Fox, 1958, pp. 120–1)

As rising living standards and the beginnings of gentility began to elevate other operative groups they too looked to the craft and lower–middle-class strata as the model. Keith Burgess has pointed out that 'the leadership of the Lancashire cotton operatives was adamant that improvements must derive from workers' own efforts, from individualism rather than collectivism' (Fraser, 1981, p. 28). This ambiguity of attitude towards collectivism, an attitude which rigorously defined and limited its place in working-class life, was expressed also in attitudes towards the poor law. On the one hand, it was feared and hated. On the other, it drew a decisive dividing line between the failures and the respectable and provided the latter with reasons for self-congratulation and pride mixed with pity and contempt for the former. The poor law was manifestly underpinned by the philosophy of bourgeois individualism. 'In separating the destitute from the merely poor, in dividing the deserving from the undeserving, the poor law explicitly extolled the virtues of self-help and individualism.' There is no reason to doubt Fraser's judgement that 'labour attitudes to the poor law do give some credence to the view that the values of individualism did not have to be imposed from above, but grew naturally in the working-class milieu' (ibid., p. 27).

Working-Class Individualism and Attitudes to the State

This all-pervasive individualist self-help creed – which in the wider political world 'prevailed almost as much in the Conservative as in the Liberal party' (Blake, 1969, p. 554) – revealed aspects less appealing to the fastidious, especially when manifested by the working classes. Matthew Arnold's social criticism testifies to prevalent dispositions and institutions as seen by a highly knowledgeable observer. 'Of all the nineteenth-century prophets who pronounced upon the condition of England', writes Dover Wilson, 'Matthew Arnold knew his England best.' Arnold's work as HM Inspector of Schools from 1851 to 1886 'took him all over the country and made him intimately acquainted with every class of society' (Arnold, 1971, p. xv). His writings are evidence of the persistent characteristics that underlay Britain's social and political institutions and the theory used to justify them.

Arnold wrote in 1869:

Our prevalent notion is ... that it is a most happy and important thing for a man merely to be able to do as he likes ... the central idea of

English life and politics is the *assertion of personal liberty* . . . We have not
the notion, so familiar on the continent, of *the state* – the nation in its
collective and corporate character, entrusted with stringent powers for
the general advantage, and controlling individual wills in the name of an
interest wider than that of individuals. We say, what is very true, that
this notion is often made instrumental to tyranny; we say that a State is
in reality made up of the individuals who compose it, and that every
individual is the best judge of his own interests.

Arnold distinguished between men's 'ordinary' self and their 'best' self,
which expressed their 'higher' or 'right' reason. This right reason should
be embodied in the idea, at present lacking, 'of the nation in its collective
and corporate character controlling, as governments, the free swing of this
or that one of its members in the name of the higher reason of all of them,
his own as well as that of others'.

Arnold saw little hope in Britain for the enthronement of 'right reason'.
Worse:

> . . . not only do we get no suggestions of right reason and no rebukes of
> ordinary self, from our governors, but a kind of philosophical theory is
> widely spread among us to the effect that there is no such thing at all as a
> best self and a right reason having claim to paramount authority, or, at
> any rate, no such thing ascertainable and capable of being made use of;
> and that there is nothing but an infinite number of ideas and works of
> our ordinary selves . . . pretty nearly equal in value, which are doomed
> either to an irreconcilable conflict, or else to a perpetual give and take;
> and that wisdom consists in choosing the give and take rather than the
> conflict . . .

Hardly any Englishman had

> the idea of the *State*, as a working power. And why? Because we
> habitually live in our ordinary selves, which do not carry us beyond the
> ideas and wishes of the class to which we happen to belong. And we are
> all afraid of giving to the State too much power, because we only
> conceive of the State as something equivalent to the class in occupation
> of the executive government, and are afraid of that class abusing power
> to its purposes.

Arnold's fears ran specially deep when he contemplated the working
class's recent emergence on the stage of history; the working class being
'the very centre and stronghold of our national idea that it is man's ideal
right and felicity to do as he likes'. The system might have worked
conveniently enough when only the higher orders enjoyed the scope to 'do
as they liked', but when the general populace 'wants to do what it likes too'
the result must be 'productive of anarchy'. So far from the working class
'having the idea of public duty and of discipline, superior to the individual's self-will, brought to their mind by a universal obligation of
military service', such as existed in France, '. . . the very idea of a

conscription is so at variance with our English notion . . . that I remember the manager of the Clay Cross works in Derbyshire told me during the Crimean War . . . that sooner than submit to a conscription the population of that district would flee to the mines and lead a sort of Robin Hood life under ground' (Arnold, 1971, pp. 74–6, 81, 94–5, 120–1, italics in original).

Supporting these long-standing dispositions were doctrines which included rationalist, secularist and republican themes stemming from Paine and which 'appealed especially to a considerable section of the skilled craftsmen in the older, hand working crafts, and, under their leadership, to a part of the urban proletariat in the industrial areas' (Cole, 1954, p. 391). 'I am addressing an audience', Professor E. S Beesly told a meeting of trade unionists in 1868, 'which, whether it calls itself republican or not, has, I am sure, a thoroughly republican spirit . . .' (Frow and Katanka, eds, 1968, p. 171). After Chartism, radical republicanism, on its secularist side, had developed largely into an individualist libertarian movement deeply suspicious of socialism. Bradlaugh, with his substantial following, was in the tradition of Paine himself, who had written 'Society is produced by our wants, and government by our wickedness . . . The first is a patron, the last a punisher . . . Government, even in its best state, is but a necessary evil . . .' Beesly, at the same meeting, referring to 'the various schemes of Socialists and Communists which have found so many supporters on the Continent', noted that while they differed widely 'they all agree in demanding that the state shall intervene, more or less, in the direction of industry. Now that opinion has never found much favour in England, nor is there at the present time any large body of workmen who support it' (ibid., p. 156).

The Strategy of Rule and the Franchise Reform Campaign

Contributing to Arnold's distaste were the public demonstrations and excitements of the campaign for further extension of the franchise, culminating in a massive meeting in Hyde Park in May 1867 said to number from 100,000 to 150,000, when railings were uprooted and the military made to look foolish despite much government blustering and elaborate military preparation designed to deter attendance. John Bright had already headed impressive demonstrations in the Midlands, the north and Scotland, and their success convinced Disraeli 'that the country had determined to obtain Reform' (Briggs, 1965, p. 277). Large public demonstrations were still feared and disliked, and not only by fastidious intellectuals such as Arnold. A few months before the Earl of Dudley had complained in the House of Lords of an imminent mass demonstration by trade unionists in favour of franchise extension, 'undoubtedly the great question of the day'. Proclaiming himself 'the last man to . . . deny the right of the people to meet and discuss any political grievance under which they deemed themselves to be suffering', he nevertheless feared that this was designed to bring undue pressure on Parliament and produce 'an effect on the clubs and the West End' (Dudley, 1867, cols 137–8). The Earl of

Derby replied for the government, which had already consulted the crown lawyers in July 1866. They had advised that 'there is not for any practical purpose a legal authority to disperse by force a meeting of the kind proposed'. Derby agreed that the demonstration was very inconvenient, mischievous, injurious and might well induce breaches of the peace. Yet it was 'strictly within the law'. Though the demonstrators sought manhood suffrage and the secret ballot – which combined 'would absolutely and entirely overthrow the Constitution of this country' – its leaders were, he believed, sincere in having 'the most peaceable intentions' and the government would 'entirely confine themselves within the limits of the law'. Derby indicated awareness of the political risks involved in any drastic repression. He hoped that a change in the law would not be made necessary by constant repetition

> because we know that such an alteration of the law, however just or necessary, would meet with very great resistance and might be thought an undue interference with the liberties of the people – an interference which could not be justified except by a general feeling on the part of the country, that these demonstrations had become quite intolerable, and a source of evil and mischief so grave as to render the interposition of parliament imperatively requisite. (Derby, 1867, cols 139–143)

In other words, governments must now hesitate long before overtly breaking a tradition of political freedom so strong and sacred that even Engels acknowledged its existence. 'For a hundred years already', he had written in 1844, 'England has known no fear of despotism, no struggle against the power of the Crown; England is undoubtedly the freest, that is, the least unfree country in the world ... and as a result the educated Englishman has a measure of inborn independence of which no Frenchman, let alone a German, can boast.' English liberties included freedom of opinion ('nowhere is there a more extensive freedom of the press'), the legal principle of Habeas Corpus, freedom of association, and freedom of assembly ('a right no other people in Europe as yet enjoys') (Marx and Engels, 1975, pp. 32–3, 49).

The implications of the Hyde Park 'Great Surrender' were recognised at the time by Frederic Harrison. 'To have used the army would have been the end of the British constitution', he wrote in 1868.

> The fact is that our political organism of the constitutional type was based on a totally different theory from that of force at all. The governing classes never pretended to rely on force. They trusted to maintain their supremacy by their social power and their skill in working the machine. Local self-government, representation of the people, civil liberty, was all the cry, until at last the tone of English public life became saturated with ideas of rule by consent, and not by force. Very excellent theories of a certain kind – but you must abide by them, and never dream of force, for you have cut yourself off from the right to appeal to it. The least suggestion of force puts the governing classes in an outrageously false position, and arrays against them all the

noble sentiments of liberty on which they based their own title to rule.
(F. Harrison, 1975, pp. 183–4)

Such ruling-class doubts as there were about this strategy of rule – and
every testing situation found belligerent voices eager to put the workers
forcibly in their place – were increasingly confronted by evidence that
constitutionality among the rulers was promoting constitutionality
among the ruled. There was still, of course, much violence, brutality,
deep poverty and despair which all had to be rediscovered in the 1880s.
But men were currently more impressed with economic and social
betterment and their effects in spreading procedural order and organisational restraints. In the hectic boom and labour shortages of 1870–3
many groups, even of workers hitherto deemed incapable of solidarity,
managed to sustain a temporary organisational unity, but strictly for bread
and butter purposes. Surveying the scene in December 1873, Harrison
dismissed any 'notion that our working classes of any kind cherish designs
against society and property' as

> the very delirium of ill-will and ignorance ... Go where you will
> amongst workmen in town or country, in trade unions, in clubs, and
> 'mass meetings', and their talk is about Bills and Petitions and the
> sections of an Act, commissions of inquiry, and deputations to
> ministers. They are saturated with the parliamentary dye, and an
> indignation meeting of costermongers will be sticklers for all the
> formulae in Hansard, and will call 'order' and stand by the chair.

There was nothing here of revolution.

> Stormy meetings of sailors ask only for a few new clauses in an Act; and
> a union of a hundred thousand miners have agitated for years for a few
> more stringent provisions as to truck, weighing, and inspection. In a
> few weeks there will meet in much-maligned Sheffield a parliament
> chosen by 700,000 skilled artisans, and, amidst many things which the
> rich dislike exceedingly, there will be heard what in that parliament has
> been heard before, neither visions about reconstructing society, reform-
> ing property, or regenerating the state, but a solid attention to
> business, a discussion of Bills and Acts, and of bringing certain facts to
> the knowledge of parliament. It may be well-done, or ill-done; but there
> will be nothing about 'social liquidation'. (ibid., pp. 246–8)

The Royal Commission of 1867

Less benign and sanguine appraisals were widespread in both political
parties. Lord Elcho, leader of one parliamentary group, claimed to speak
for 'men acting with the fear of a coming democracy and trades union
tyranny before their eyes' (Briggs, 1965, p. 289). 'Democracy' was still a
term of abuse. When Disraeli's 1867 Reform Act gave the vote to the
urban male householder and £10 lodger, thereby enfranchising many

workers in the boroughs, there were many both inside and outside the House who were 'assuring the world that the end was at hand' (F. Harrison, 1975, p. 162; Bagehot, 1963, p. 273). Robert Lowe, one of the bitterest critics of the Act, stressed the 'great danger that the machinery which at present exists for strikes and trade unions may be used for political purposes . . . [the working classes] therefore have in their hands the power, if they know how to use it, of becoming masters of the situation' (McKenzie and Silver, 1968, p. 5). It was clear that no simple connection existed between party leaders' behaviour and what their party followers considered to be in the interests of their class. In Bagehot's view, 'many, perhaps most, of the intelligent Conservatives were fearful of the consequences . . . but as it was made by the heads of their own party, they did not like to oppose it, and the discipline of party carried them with it' (Briggs, 1965, p. 296).

Dark fears nevertheless remained vocal: the theme of self-improving working-class respectability met the counter-theme of democracy's gathering encroachments on property, civilisation and order. Though the 1867 Act increased the electorate by only 1½ million – from 7 per cent to 16 per cent of the adult population – it nevertheless strengthened claims to which some attention would now have to be paid. The third Marquis of Salisbury became convinced, by 1883, that the policy of concession to democracy and to the demand for social reform would have disastrous and irreversible consequences for British government. His reasons reveal how prominent ruling-class leaders defined that government in terms of evenhandedness. The increasing domination of the House of Commons by men without property would result in law and government assuming a class character. Government would cease to possess the main characteristic of a civilised age: that of impartiality. 'Our ruler is no longer an impartial judge between classes who bring their differences before him for adjustments; our ruler is an assembly which is itself the very field of battle . . .' (O'Sullivan, 1976, p. 107).

Industrial disorder, too, could always be relied on to inspire gloom. Strikes, picketing and demonstrations, then as now, provided the respectable classes with alarums and excursions enough. The 'moderates' of the new model unions, though influential, were far from dominating the movement – or even the London section of it. It was George Potter, leader of the smaller, more militant London societies who, together with provincial union leaders, eventually created the Trades Union Congress in 1868, summoned by the Manchester and Salford Trades Council. Potter was a major figure, too, in the great London building trades strike of 1859 – to which Bagehot offered reactions, in *The Economist*, which are a good example of the blood-curdling picture of trade union power that men of affairs were apt to terrify themselves with (Stevas, ed., 1974, pp. 15–18). But it was violence, of course, which most rapidly chilled the blood, and the unsavoury reputation of Sheffield workers, for example, in this respect led eventually to a Royal Commission on Trade Unions being appointed in 1867.

However, in a period marked by economic buoyancy and social optimism, dominant party influences felt disposed, as we have seen, to stress the more favourable picture, anxious to capture for themselves the votes of those being improved. There was some receptiveness, therefore, offered to the moderates when they mobilised their influence to meet the potential threat embodied in the Royal Commission. No direct representatives of either employers or unions were to be included, but Thomas Hughes, a known Christian Socialist sympathiser of the unions was appointed, and Frederic Harrison, the Positivist, also familiar as a supporter, was accepted as a 'special representative' – the employers likewise being allowed their equivalent. The unions had vital reasons for wishing to present a reassuring picture of themselves. The Friendly Societies Act of 1855 had included a clause enabling a society established for any purpose not illegal to have disputes among its own members summarily dealt with by the magistrates. Since the 1825 Act had done nothing to give the unions legal status, as such, or enable them to take proceedings as corporate bodies, several of the larger unions registered under this clause in order to be able to take action against officials who embezzled or absconded with the funds. The widespread belief – even at government level – that this gave union funds protection was shattered in 1867 when the Queen's Bench confirmed a magistrate's decision that trade unions were outside the scope of the Friendly Societies Act, giving the additional reason that union objects, though not actually criminal, were yet so far in restraint of trade as to render the union an illegal association. 'Thus the officers of the great national trade unions found their societies deprived of the legal status which they imagined they had acquired, and saw themselves once more destitute of any legal protection for their accumulated funds' (Webb and Webb, 1920, p. 262).

Had it not been for the unstinting support and legal expertise given by the Positivists, both on and outside the Royal Commission, the unions would have made some serious errors in their campaign for statutory recognition and protection, with the possible result that the subsequent history of the movement might have been significantly different. The group of union leaders who were organising the campaign – Applegarth among the most prominent – had been demanding the complete legalisation of the unions, and the Positivists had to explain that this would expose them to endless litigation and end in crippling them (R. Harrison, 1965, p. 287). Harrison and Hughes included, in their Minority Report, recommendations for protecting union funds against theft or fraud 'while retaining to the full the exceptional legal privilege of being incapable of being sued or otherwise proceeded against as a corporate entity' (Webb and Webb, 1920, p. 271).

The Majority Report, an inconclusive and somewhat inconsistent document, is nevertheless of interest in that it embodied the conception that had begun to take shape in the 1825 Act and had developed since: namely, that there were two species of trade unionism, one acceptable, the other not. Legal protection of funds should be made available but only to unions whose rules were free of restrictive practices on such matters as the employment of apprentices, the use of machinery, piece-work and subcontract. It was also to be withheld from unions whose rules authorised 'sympathetic' support of disputes in other trades. Further, unions were to be exempted from prosecution for being in restraint of trade but only if they excluded 'acts which involved breach of contract' and refusal to work with any particular person – a reference to disputes arising from non-unionism and exclusive closed shops.

By implication, unions which confined themselves to joining with employers in regulating terms and conditions in the labour market could be tolerated, though in the Majority Report's opinion they could be of no real economic advantage to their members. Unions which sought to encroach on employer freedom and prerogative in the workplace, whose members invaded individual liberty by refusing to work with non-unionists or non-members of the craft, or who lent their muscle to support other trades, must be condemned. This distinction had long been, and long remained, the limit of most enlightened and progressive middle-class opinion. The 1860 report of the Committee on Trades' Societies, for example, had acknowledged that whereas the 'capitalist has the advantage of past accumulations in striking his bargain', the 'labourer unassisted by combination has not', so the object of a union was 'to put him on more equal ground in competing with the capitalist'. This was a marked advance on the popular cant of political economy which, ignoring the less convenient propositions of Adam Smith, treated employer and individual worker as free and equal bargaining agents. The report had even gone so far as to assert that in some respects the unions did not violate the strict laws of political economy – even 'many' employers believed 'that without combination, workmen in their trades could not secure the fair market rate of wages'. Unions could therefore contribute towards the economically rational working of the labour market. Nevertheless, masters believed that unions were 'the greatest social evils that now exist in society . . . worse than plague, pestilence, and famine'. Any attempt, however, to 'return to the old policy of prohibiting combinations', though desired by some, 'would be most mischievous'.

For the committee – composed of academics, lawyers and businessmen – the unions' possible contribution to labour market rationality exhausted all possibilities of approval: '. . . there are still, in many trades' societies, rules . . . which interfere with the freedom of the masters, and of the men within as well as without the bodies that impose them, and which persons of all schools in political and social economy must utterly condemn'. Workmen could not 'too cautiously abstain from interfering with the methods by which the employer conducts his business'. The committee feared also 'that in too many instances the rights of non-society men are not respected, and that they are subjected to unjustifiable persecution . . . public opinion in a free country will never tolerate any infringement of the liberty of the subject' (Shuttleworth, 1860, pp. viii–xix, 600).

The Majority Report shared much of this thinking. Harrison's Minority Report, signed also by Thomas Hughes and the Earl of Lichfield, trusted to moral progress and offered a complete charter of union liberty. By the beginning of 1869 Harrison had drafted a comprehensive Bill embodying all his legislative proposals, and Mundella and Hughes then introduced it to a predominantly hostile House of Commons and Liberal government. Beesly and Crompton directed the union lobby outside, while at the

Home Office Godfrey Lushington, later permanent under-secretary, was soon to be drafting what became the Trade Union Act of 1871. Other influential figures in this group of 'candid friends' included J. M. Ludlow, Christian Socialist, later Registrar of Friendly Societies; Professor Neate, formerly holding the Chair in Political Economy and then MP for Oxford; and Sir Fowell Buxton, MP. Their activities were strongly supported in the field by newly enfranchised workers in every part of the country who put pressure upon MPs and organised demonstrations. The government finally agreed to bring in a Bill, meanwhile hurrying through a provisional measure giving temporary protection to union funds. Much further pressure had to be exerted, however, before the full Bill materialised.

The Trade Union Legislation of the 1870s

To the accompaniment of vehement complaints from employers, the 1871 Trade Union Act laid down that no trade union, however wide its objects, was henceforth to be illegal merely because it was 'in restraint of trade', and a registration process gave the union complete protection for its funds. More fully, the object of the Act, in the words of a later Royal Commission on Labour, appears to have been, while freeing trade unions from the last remains of their character of criminal conspiracies, and giving full protection to their property, (1) to prevent them from having any legal rights against their members, or their members against them; and next, (2) to prevent their entering into any legally enforceable contracts as bodies with each other or with outside individuals, except with regard to the management of their own funds and real estate (C–7421, 1894, p. 116). 'These were assumed to be all the cases that could arise' (Webb and Webb 1920, p. 602).

But in other respects the Act fell far short of Harrison's charter of union rights. A lengthy clause summed up and codified previous legislation and judicial decisions by declaring criminal a range of activities described as molestation, obstruction, threats, intimidation, and the like, all of which had proved their utility for judges anxious to deter trade unionists from the methods necessary for effective negotiation or industrial action – in 1851, for example, the posting of placards announcing a strike had been held to be intimidation of the employers. Thus a strike was lawful, but anything done in pursuance of a strike was criminal. After strong and bitter pressure from the unions the government finally agreed to embody this clause in a separate Criminal Law Amendment Act and the struggle to secure its repeal proved the dominant preoccupation of the trade union world for the next four years of the Liberal government until its defeat in 1874. Gladstone had neither sympathy for, nor interest in, organised labour – Morley's biography of 1,500 pages devotes over 200 of them to the period from 1867 to 1874, but they contain not a single reference to the Royal Commission on Trade Unions, the Trade Union Act passed by his government, the four-year campaign by the unions, or indeed to the unions themselves, their problems, and the questions they posed for the

Establishment. Gladstone's most recent biographer makes passing reference to the 1871 Act, but is compelled to dispatch it in five lines (Magnus,
1954).

Frederic Harrison referred after the government's defeat to the Liberal
Party's tendency to assume that labour was their natural ally and needed
no courting. 'The hard-and-fast party man . . . has been wont to smile at
the vision of the Conservative working man. Perhaps he smiles no
longer.' Certainly 'the great bulk of the skilled artisans will undoubtedly
be found to have voted for the Liberal cause, though in the cotton and
textile trades . . . the Conservative working-men may be found in
masses'. Moreover, not all the urban workers receiving the vote in 1867
were skilled artisans and this was important. It was still true, and was to
remain so into the twentieth century, that

> perhaps throughout all English society there is no break more marked
> than that which in cities divides the skilled from the unskilled
> workmen. In temper, interest, and intelligence, they are separated by a
> deep and invariable gulf. The political aptitudes and proclivities with
> which in 1867 it was the fashion to credit the workmen were truly
> credited to the skilled workmen, but not accurately, or but partially, to
> the unskilled. The Whigs forgot if Mr Disraeli remembered that when
> you pass below the skilled workmen you come upon a stratum of
> casual employment, low education, and habitual dependence, where
> political action is dormant, and the influences of clergyman, publican,
> wealth and mere ostentation, are almost paramount.

This stratum of town labourers 'the genius of Mr Disraeli' had secured
for the British Constitution (F. Harrison, 1975, pp. 272–5). Recent
studies have tempered 'earlier views of Disraeli as a self-conscious
prophet of working-class Conservatism and put much greater stress upon
the improvisatory and opportunistic character of his policy in sponsoring
the Second Reform Bill of 1867. But they leave essentially unchanged his
distinctive position as that Tory leader most predisposed to discern and
credit the possibilities of working class Conservatism' (McKenzie and
Silver, 1968, p. 8).

Harrison also noted that the Conservative Party had 'become as much
the middle-class party as the Liberal used to be, as much and more . . .
The great merchants of London, the great spinners of Manchester, are
Tories of the Tories; and the small merchant and tradesman has begun to
follow the fashion' (F. Harrison, 1975, pp. 272–5). For this reason the
readiness of Disraeli's government of 1874–80 to give the unions more
than they hoped for cannot be explained in terms of Disraeli's youthful
One Nation conception of an aristocratic alliance with the working
classes. Neither can this serve to explain the sequence of social reform
measures covering public health, housing, friendly societies and factory
conditions – 'the biggest instalment of social reform passed by any one
government in the nineteenth century'. None of this can convincingly be
seen

as the product of a fundamentally different political philosophy from that of the Liberals, or . . . the fulfilment of some concept of paternalistic Tory democracy . . . adumbrated by Disraeli . . . The forces of property, commercial and industrial as well as landed, were by 1874 too deeply rooted in the Conservative Party to make it politically possible for the party to pursue the idea of an aristocratic anti-middle class alliance with the working masses even if it had wished to do so.

In any case, the contribution of Disraeli himself was small. 'Some of it was already in the Civil Service pipeline, some flowed naturally from the publication of official inquiries, some was of the codifying nature which would probably have been passed by any government then, and much of it was due to the hard work' of R. A. (later Viscount) Cross (Blake, 1969, pp. 553, 555).

Cross it was, as Home Secretary, who astonished trade union observers in the House of Commons by declaring for total repeal of the Criminal Law Amendment Act and carrying through the rest of Harrison's charter of union rights. The Conspiracy and Protection of Property Act of 1875 'invented a golden formula which became the bedrock of British workers' rights to organize and take effective industrial action' (Wedderburn, 1971, p. 312). No collective act taken in 'contemplation or furtherance of a trade dispute' was to be treated as a criminal conspiracy unless the act itself was criminal, whoever did it. Peaceful picketing was expressly permitted. The old words 'molest' and 'coerce', which had proved so potent in the hands of punitive magistrates and judges, were omitted, and violence and intimidation were dealt with as part of the general criminal code. Another measure of the same year, in a significant shift of nomenclature, substituted the Employers and Workmen Act for the Master and Servant Act 1867 and removed the remaining taint of criminality from breach of contract by workers – henceforth employer and employee became, in strictly legal terms, equal parties to a civil contract.

It was the ultimate triumph of the Positivists who, though their influence was on the wane by the early 1880s, nevertheless 'played a decisive part in securing a satisfactory legal basis for trade unionism. They formulated the unionists' demands and – in the end – the Government's own measures. They played a vital part in shaping the strategy which workmen followed in pressing their case home, and they made an important contribution towards changing public attitudes towards that case' (R. Harrison, 1965, p. 277). These measures, together with a further statute of 1906, created the basic framework of Britain's trade union law.

Yet, in terms of their wider hopes for the trade unions, the Positivists had failed, and the failure is instructive. They were the latest group of middle-class reformers to attempt to capture the unions for purposes which they deemed higher and nobler than mere workplace struggles for better conditions and protection against arbitrary rule. Robert Owen and his followers had sought to win them over to his campaign for co-operative communities. The Christian Socialists, often ready to give vigorous practical support to the unions, did so with the *arrière-pensée* of bringing them into schemes of producer co-operation. Now it was the turn of the Positivists, who

> believed that the corrupting influences of Protestantism and mammon worship had made the least headway among workmen. Of all classes in modern society, the workmen were best prepared to receive large principles and to grasp the truth of the proposition that wealth, which was social in its origins, ought to be used in socially beneficial ways. Their trade unions were the elementary schools of a higher morality and they would, in close conjunction with the Positivist teachers, help to 'moralize' the capitalists and institute the new order in which private rights were subordinated to social duties. (R. Harrison, 1967, p. 209)

No such vision materialised and the unions went their own ways. If it was not the first, it was certainly not the last occasion on which the unions accepted practical help from wherever it came but declined to follow courses mapped out for them by their betters.

How Was the Legislation Justified?

What were the Conservative government's motives in yielding this degree of legal emancipation? 'As a result of the Act of 1867 it was electorally necessary to make some concessions to working-class demands ...' (Blake, 1969, p. 553). Yet the 1875 legislation went far beyond what was thought acceptable by most employers or judicious by most lawyers, the trade unions would have been tolerably satisfied with less, and Cross had to overcome resistance from the rest of the Cabinet. The major explanation is that Disraeli believed these measures would 'gain and retain for the Conservatives the lasting affection of the working classes'. He took a keener interest in them than in any of Cross's other measures and backed Cross against his Cabinet opponents. 'Since they involved neither interventionism nor public expenditure, and since they gave the unions almost everything which they wanted and had been denied by the Liberals, it is not surprising that the party was jubilant' (ibid., p. 555).

In one respect Disraeli's calculation went awry. He had tapped a vein of conservatism that perhaps was specially rich in the lower working class (McKenzie and Silver, 1968; R. Roberts, 1973, pp. 177–9, 183–5; F. Harrison, 1975, p. 274), but much – though certainly not all – of the upper working class developed more fully its attachment elsewhere. It had only been the refusal of Gladstone's government to repeal the Criminal Law Amendment Act that 'had prevented the full alliance with the Liberals towards which most of the union leaders were impelled by their Radical predilections and connexions. Thereafter, despite Disraeli's satisfaction of their immediate demands and the continued blandishments of the Conservatives, they took their place among the groups that made up the Liberal Party ...', though they retained some independence and continued to work for specific trade union representation in Parliament (Clegg, Fox and Thompson, 1964, p. 50).

Private political calculation was one thing: not necessarily the same were the propositions, opinions and sentiments publicly voiced by men of affairs during the period between 1867 and 1875 to explain and justify the legal concessions made to trade unions and the workers. Whether or not these revealed – or fully revealed – private opinions, they are important in registering dominant strands of ruling-class ideology and the arguments which its members gave themselves and each other for behaving as they did. These were arguments which they believed legitimised the social and political system and their place in it, but through which they also gave hostages to fortune. As we noted with respect to the eighteenth century and the conception of law, legitimations of a certain kind are difficult to confine to the service of one particular class. The concept of equality, for example, quickly escapes from Pandora's box, and this played a prominent part in the current debates.

Of the three themes which emerge, two showed strong continuity with those stressed by the Radical reformers of 1825 and acquiesced in by some influential leading politicians of that period. The first focused on the impossibility of suppressing the unions and indeed the inadvisability of even attempting to do so. H. A. Bruce, Home Secretary under Gladstone, told the House of Commons when recommending legalisation of unions in 1871 that the period of the general Combination Acts, 1800–24, had seen 'more cases of outrage and violence . . . than at any subsequent period' and worse relations between masters and men than formerly (Bruce, 1871, col. 259). The nature of the argument is more important for our present purpose than the validity of its implied conclusions. They were shared by many of influential views. Bagehot, in *The Economist*, had argued in 1867 that unions must be legalised and their rules made public; otherwise they would remain secret and oppressive bodies. 'Persecute a sect and it holds together . . .' (Bagehot, 1867, pp. 468–9). Two years later: 'Everyone is agreed that . . . in fact you cannot put them down; they are part of the real forces of the industrial world which the law did not make, and which it cannot unmake . . . we are all now agreed that you cannot put down strikes by law . . .' (Bagehot, 1869, pp. 802–3). Better by far, declared Thomas Hughes in a successful appeal to the Commons in 1869, 'to bring the sympathies and interests of the members of these great organizations into entire conformity with the interests of the country. If they did so, they would effect a change in the feeling of those societies, making it a much more cordial one towards the Government and the laws . . .' (Hughes, 1869, col. 1537).

If unions could not be suppressed by coercion, what was the alternative? The alternative was to hope that their teeth could be drawn – or at least filed down to a safe bluntness – by granting them a partial integration into the legal and social structure. Integration was to take the form of offering the unions, not without some unction and self-congratulatory fanfares, 'equality' with the employers. This theme, too, demonstrated continuity with the principles of 1825. Robert Lowe, Home Secretary under Disraeli, told the Commons in 1875:

Everybody must feel that it was extremely desirable that there should be one law for both the rich and the poor, and that there should be no ground given for the accusation or the suspicion that they were passing laws for their poorer fellow-countrymen to which they themselves would not be willing to submit ... it was very important to teach the working men to consider that they were not a class apart from the rest of the country ...

They must be given 'thoroughly to understand that they should be treated with the most perfect equality and justice' (Lowe, 1875, col. 1342). There was clearly a strong feeling in favour of Lowe's sentiments (Holms, 1875, col. 1738). Mundella assured MPs that whereas socialism had great appeal for working men in foreign countries it had none for those of the United Kingdom.

Why was that? Because our workmen had strong common sense and respect for property, and all that they wanted was that masters and workmen should stand on equal bases of right: and if this parliament would only put them on an equality in that respect, and contrive means for settling disputes amicably, the results would be the best possible for the interests of capital and labour and for the promotion of the general harmony. (Mundella, 1875, col. 674)

Collective bargaining was becoming more widely seen as the most acceptable practicable answer to a palpable problem. With growing scale and complexity of operations, there was increasing need for more systematic regulation of the terms and conditions of employment. Who was to do it? Governments had long made it plain that in their view this was no function for the state and the law. Bruce told the House of Commons in 1871 that the law could not and should not try to prescribe and impose solutions to the contentious issues arising between masters and men. Not by penal enactment could such problems be tackled. 'It was rather by making the law neutral between both parties; by taking care that it should in all respects be just and equal; by promoting in every possible manner a good understanding between them; and by leading them to arrange, so far as that could be done, their disputes among one another rather by force of reason than by force of law' (Bruce, 1871, col. 269).

In other words, though the employer would, ideally, rule his own roost, the unions existed and the ruling class would damage itself badly by attempting to suppress them. It was better to make a virtue out of necessity by proclaiming how collective bargaining itself embodied the holy precept of procedural equality. Some spokesmen argued that such equality was morally desirable and that collective bargaining achieved it. Terms like 'fairness' and 'fair play' made their appearance. Sir Charles Adderley told the House in 1871 that 'employers of labour were in themselves a great combination, and there ought to be a countervailing power permitted to the employed to guard their own interests' (Adderley, 1871, col. 2039), and Mundella had asserted earlier that if workers faced their employer as a trade union 'they were a body equal to himself, and a bargain could be made on equal terms' (Mundella, 1869, col. 1374). Such statements were the small change of the crucial debates between 1867 and 1875.

But there were major loose ends to be tied up. What would be the consequences for civilisation and national prosperity of these emancipating measures? Mid-Victorian optimism about the inevitable march of enlightenment came to the rescue to supply a rationalising reassurance. Bruce admitted in 1869 a 'universal agreement' that in their restrictionist encroachments on employer prerogative the unions had not been wisely advised. 'But the unions were becoming wiser every day, and some of the best of them were abandoning principles which had brought discredit on them' (Bruce, 1869, col. 1380) – a proposition which anticipated by nearly thirty years a major argument of the Webbs, and which was echoed by other speakers. On a more specific level there was a readiness to underline points put by Bagehot in *The Economist*. Unions were seen as having economic disadvantages, but by acting as representative bodies 'sometimes enable the masters to get into new and extremely beneficial relations with the men', imposing control and order (Bagehot, 1867, pp. 468–9).

But it was left to Auberon Herbert in 1871 to make the most candid expression of the fundamental ruling-class justification of what they were doing. They 'ought to be obliged to the trade unionists' for teaching them 'how to carry out the principles of arbitration amongst the working men' (arbitration being a term often used interchangeably with conciliation to refer to collective bargaining). 'If there was any reason why the danger of revolution was less with us than it was with other countries, it was not that the condition of our working people was better than the condition of others, but because our working people had a well-grounded belief that in these associations, by their own efforts, they were working out for themselves a better state of things' (Herbert, 1871, col. 1176).

Such was the prevalent mood that these sentiments and arguments commanded wide assent on both sides of the House and few spoke against them. This is indicative of the fact that the social standing and legal safety of the unions have never been constants, but depend heavily not only upon the disposition of the courts but also upon the fluctuating moods and opinions among the more influential sections of the middle and upper classes, for many of the same spokesmen expressed themselves very differently at other times and in other places – across the dinner table, for example. And, of course, outside Parliament, now and at all times, could be found many who were bitterly opposed to all the sentiments and arguments that have just been examined.

Nevertheless, the predominant parliamentary and public mood of 1867–75 continued to receive expression by prominent men of affairs, often infused by those assumptions of progress and social evolution already noted. Such assumptions affected even orthodox economists, censorious though they usually were of the supposedly pernicious economic consequences of trade unionism. Alfred Marshall's observations of 1873 have been mentioned (see p. 142), and those made by another leading economist, W. Stanley Jevons, in 1882, have special interest in that they anticipate by fifteen years – in style as well as content – predictions made by the Webbs in their *Industrial Democracy* as to the general direction in which the trade unions would develop.

> The existing great trade societies only need to be let alone and they will probably degenerate from their original trade purposes. But inasmuch as those trade purposes were against the public good the process of degeneration will probably bring them more nearly into consonance with public interests. What were, under the Combination Laws, mere midnight conspiracies, are developing and will develop into widespread philanthropic bodies, headed by Members of Parliament, meeting in large halls before a table full of reporters, gradually giving up their selfish and mistaken ideas. No one could have read the proceedings of the Trades Union Congress in London in 1881 without feeling that recent wise legislation was bearing good fruit. Instead of machine-breakers and midnight conspirators, the working men met as the members of a parliament to discuss the means and ends of legislation with dignity and propriety at least equal to that recently exhibited at St. Stephens. No longer entirely devoted to the pet fallacies and interests of their order, their deliberations touch many of the most important social questions of the day. The more extensive the federations of trades which thus meet in peaceful conference, the more wide and generous must of necessity become their views ... It is impossible not to accept the general views of Mr Henry Crompton, that as working-men gradually acquire their full rights, their leaders will turn to the noble task of impressing upon them the duties of citizenship. (Jevons, 1894, pp. 129–30)

Parliament and the Courts: Renewed Divergence

There was a striking contrast between the behaviour and sentiments of legislators and members of the executive in Parliament, and the utterances of some magistrates and judges up and down the country in cases, large and small, involving trade unions and trade unionists. In 1871 seven women were imprisoned in South Wales for hooting at a blackleg. Innumerable convictions took place for the use of bad language. A year later some London gas-workers received twelve months' imprisonment, having been found guilty under common law of 'conspiracy to coerce' or molest their employers by simply concerting a simultaneous withdrawal of labour. The law officers of the crown exhibited some embarrassment in the House of Commons at this interpretation, the Solicitor-General going so far as to dismiss it out of hand and being supported by a number of eminent lawyers. Eventually the Home Secretary intervened to reduce the sentences to four months (K. D. Brown, 1982, p. 118).

This divergence between different elements within the state apparatus had begun to open up in 1825. At its heart lay the judges' interpretations of the common law tradition with its emphasis on individualism and individual rights. To this day, 'the fundamental institution' to which 'the English lawyer ... is forced to return again and again is the individual contract of employment ... the common law sets up a model of an individual contract which is a "voluntary relationship into which the parties may enter on terms laid down by themselves within limitations imposed only by the general law of contract"'. Such labour law as developed in Britain rested heavily, therefore, upon 'that legal phenomenon, the individual contract of employment, in which the two sides (the employer and individual employee) are looked at by the law as equals to a legally enforceable agreement' (Wedderburn, 1971, pp. 15, 51). And the rules of law dealing with the individual contract were largely judge-made.

The availability of this strongly individualist common law tradition had been highly convenient for those who saw trade unionism as, at best, a pernicious obstruction to economic progress and, at worst, a collectivist vehicle for subversion. The notion of 'availability' is important; there was nothing inevitable about common law being so applied as to ignore the great disparity of power of the two parties – and the consequent importance for employees of collective institutions and collective relations; an importance which the courts persistently failed to acknowledge. The common law was applied as it was because judges chose that mode of interpretation, and their principal instruments were, as we have seen, the doctrines of conspiracy and restraint of trade.

It was when Parliament's accessibility to working-class pressure became significantly increased by the 1867 franchise extension that the divergence from the courts widened dramatically. Collectivist needs and values, communicated to Parliament through electoral and lobbying pressures, vied with the strong individualist tradition manipulated and exploited by the courts in a series of counter-attacks against labour organisation. The struggle is not over, for after a long period of truce it was resumed in the 1960s.

The manner in which franchise concessions that were extracted from one major element within the state apparatus were used to counter, by statute, the disabilities imposed by another major element through common law (and statute) is of obvious practical and theoretical significance. The effects of this see-saw upon the growth of trade unionism and collective bargaining must not, however, be exaggerated. The unions did not depend on the law for their existence and functioning. They had continued to exist under the Combination Acts, and the upsurge in membership of the 1850s and 1860s 'was not prevented by the many legal disabilities under which the unions then suffered. This phase of growth reached its peak in 1874 when the Criminal Law Amendment Act was still in force, whereas complete emancipation (as it appeared) in 1875 was followed by many years of decline in trade union membership and power' (Clegg, Fox and Thompson, 1964, pp. 46–7).

Trade Union Law and the Language of 'Immunities'

The nature of the see-saw between executive and courts is central to an understanding of the somewhat peculiar form in which trade unions in Britain secured the necessary conditions of statutory law that enabled them to protect their funds and pursue those activities – including the imposition of sanctions on employers and members – which were integral to their chosen function of job regulation. These conditions were secured not in the form of positive stated rights (for example, the 'right to strike') but in the form of 'immunity' from judge-made doctrines, such as that unions were illegal through being 'in restraint of trade' and were in themselves criminal conspiracies. 'The doctrines themselves (apart from their effect on trade unions) are not affected by the statute; but a special "immunity" is, in form, provided by the statute as a protection. In substance, behind the form, the statute provides liberties or rights which the common law would deny to unions . . . The "immunity" is mere form' (Wedderburn, 1971, p. 314).

This method of providing trade unions with the rights necessary for their functions, along with the language of 'immunities' in which it is customarily described, has served as a powerful ideological weapon in the hands of those wishing to see union rights curtailed. In a culture so deeply rooted in the idea of law as the British, it has been easy for lawyers and non-lawyers alike to confess themselves aghast at the spectacle of these 'over-mighty subjects' enjoying 'immunities' denied to the rest of the crown's subjects, and the part which this stance can play during periods when the unions are in danger as a result of specially marked unpopularity has been considerable. Yet in the view of Wedderburn and other specialists in labour law, 'the apparent "privileges" or "immunities" of our law of industrial conflict are often no more than the British way of providing modern collective liberties for workers on their side of the bargaining table' (ibid., p. 400).

How did it come about that the legal framework of Britain's industrial relations took this form? It is relevant that industrial organisation among workers, and their securing of the franchise, long pre-dated independent political organisation among them. Trade union leaders and activists, helped by sympathetic but cautious lawyers and pragmatic Positivists, were concerned not to construct a comprehensive system of positive and explicit rights but to squeeze as much as they realistically could out of two bourgeois parties on whose good will they were ultimately dependent. They were not without leverage, of course. The urban householder vote of 1867 was demonstrably effective, and the ruling classes manifestly felt constrained to heed their own ideology of equality before the law, 'fair play' and 'the liberties of the people' – more especially when the prevalent mood among the higher classes was in favour of judicious concessions to the lower orders. But there was obviously a point beyond which resistance to over-ambitious working-class demands would have become more immediately pressing for the ruling class than the servicing of their own class legitimations.

This explains why the unions, concerned to mitigate the existing system rather than transform it, and always conscious of the limitations on their strength, worked towards piecemeal modifications by whatever means were available. But it does not explain why governments of the time made no attempt, as did some governments elsewhere, to construct a comprehensive framework of industrial relations law with explicit statements of rights and obligations. To understand this we need to recall the nature of the British political system, the role of the state and certain character-istics of the British style of limited politics.

Out of the political settlement of the late seventeenth century there had been growing, not by conscious plan and principle but by much fumbling and trial and error, a system subsequently dignified and rationalised as a two-party parliamentary democracy. It was fortuitous that the overall benefits of political compromise and peaceful transfers of power between different groups within the higher classes were such as to outweigh the disadvantages for each group of having to submit to rule by its rival. Relevant to this situation were the facts, first, that in Anderson's words, there was '*no fundamental, antagonistic contradiction between the old aristocracy and the new bourgeoisie*' (Anderson, 1965, p. 18, italics in original); and secondly, that given this basic consensus on essentials within the dominant classes, groups within it were able to refrain from pushing their opponents too far either in applying a policy when in power or in resisting one when in opposition. The consensus made possible by the disposition of material forces was too valuable to risk damage through the over-zealous pursuit of partisanship in lesser matters.

Also relevant was the more general view of the role of the state implied by this system and its accompanying ideology. Dominant groups defined the state as having only a minimal role, under which it might have to intervene but only to meet particular *ad hoc* contingencies. It coped with problems as it went along. Its role did not include formulating long-term major plans or strategies for particular social institutions. Social policy on such matters emerged, usually unwittingly, by incremental stages as an outcome of responses to short-term contingencies, often as the result of pressures and counter-pressures from free associations of individuals. This style of limited politics expressed the long-standing British suspicion of government which Bagehot commented on in 1867. He observed that

> one of the most curious peculiarities of the English people is its dislike of the executive government . . . our freedom is the result of centuries of resistance . . . to the executive government. We have, accordingly, inherited the traditions of conflict, and preserve them in the fulness of victory. We look on state action, not as our own action, but as alien action; as an imposed tyranny from without, not as the consummated result of our own organized wishes.

The notion 'that the government is an extrinsic agency still rules our imaginations; a notion that accorded well with the inbred insubordination of the English people' and with their 'natural impulse to resist authority' (Bagehot, 1963, pp. 262–3).

This wariness towards 'positive government' and a preference for piecemeal accommodations to particular pressures marked the develop-ment of trade union legislation. The successive statutes conferring so-called 'immunities' were *ad hoc* political responses designed to offset the hostility of the courts towards institutions that now, from the parlia-mentary point of view, had some political clout. A comprehensive and

internally consistent industrial relations code embodying explicit rights
and obligations would have required, in effect, the formulation of a
philosophy of society – something quite alien to the British political style.
The absence of will meant an absence of means; there was no sufficiently
influential group in the service of the British state who understood or even
cared enough about industrial relations to be capable of producing such a
comprehensive code.

Trade Unions: the Behaviour and Language of 'Accommodation'

The system that was now developing, both industrially and politically,
rested upon a considerable measure of procedural and substantive consensus and upon the participants valuing the system sufficiently to be
prepared to set aside threatening differences and focus on what could be
made negotiable. The acceptance of 'accommodative' postures towards
the broad social structures of wealth, power and status did not mean that
all working men were necessarily reconciled and fully assimilated to those
structures. It did, however, mean that in order to secure modifications in
what most directly affected them and their families they considered it
necessary to avoid challenging the basic foundations of their society.

The successful operation of such a system required the cultivation of
certain skills, style and language, and attracted into its service those who
had or could acquire them. They lay in the ability to negotiate compromises; to find forms of words and action which pushed specially intract-
able problems into the future for solution or further postponement by a
later generation; and to sense whether pressing a particular line of argument or principle would open up an unbridgeable gap and whether,
therefore, certain arguments or principles must be fudged and certain facts
ignored. These skills have been curiously defined as demonstrating an
incapacity for logic, a long-cherished British boast. But if the object of the
exercise is the discovery of a course of action which two contesting parties
are prepared to accept without violence, nothing is more practically
logical than the avoidance of behaviour, ideology and language which
sharpen differences rather than muffle them. The failure of certain patterns
of political thought and vocabulary to take root in British industrial and
political relations has been due less to intellectual *naïveté* or an inability to
grasp complex foreign ideas than to the fact that they have had no
functional usefulness for the practitioners.

Trade union leaders and employers did not have to invent this muffled
language and style of fudge and compromise, for it had long existed
already in the society around them. It was the language and style of the
social and political culture into which they were born. Isaiah Berlin has
referred to the British 'tendency towards instinctive compromise,
whereby sharp edges are not indeed planed away, but largely ignored by
both sides in a dispute if they threatened to disrupt the social texture too
widely, and break down the minimum conditions for common life'
(Berlin, 1980, p. 55). So long as it served the purposes of its users this style

was perpetuated and helped to shape the perceptions and habituated structures of thinking inherited by successive generations. It did not serve everyone's purposes. Soon there were to emerge groups on the far left and far right who did not value the consensus and the institutions based on it and who forged a sharper-edged language. For the rest it was, and has remained, the received language and style of industrial and political conflict. When organised labour took up its own accommodative role within this system, its leadership likewise developed – not necessarily against the preferences of either the leaders themselves or their constituents – the muffled vocabulary which avoided the sharp edges of economic class relations and exploitation. 'Englishmen do not like Marxian terms', observed Lenin (1969, p. 102). And H. M. Hyndman, in his memoirs, made the same point. 'Accustomed as we are nowadays, especially in England, to fence with big soft buttons on the points of our rapiers, Marx's terrible onslaughts with naked steel appeared so improper that it was impossible for our gentlemanly sham-fighters and mental gymnasium men to believe that this unsparing controversialist and furious assailant of capital and capitalists was really the deepest thinker of modern times' (Hyndman, 1911). Both comments cover organised labour. Halévy notes that while 'in England, as everywhere else, the trade unions were organized for the class war' – in the sense that 'their arrangements implied that a state of war was the normal relation between the two classes' – 'there was not a country in the world where revolutionary catchwords had less power over the organized workers than in England' (Halévy, 1961d, p. 215).

Had organised labour – and the later working-class political movement – suffered consistent repression and denial of even the smallest foothold in decision-making they would have been forced to adopt a sharper and fiercer ideology and language. Nothing less would have represented their world as they saw it; nothing less would have enabled them to explain it to themselves; nothing less would have nerved them for a class struggle both palpable and unmitigated. As it was, the growing readiness of the dominant classes to concede the organised working class a marginal influence in decision-making represented a limited mitigation of the class encounter which depended upon an implicit contract – upon working-class readiness to reciprocate by not developing the practice and theory of full class war. Collective bargaining and electoral parliamentary democracy, precisely because they embody the mutual concession by each of the other's survival, cannot rest upon an ideology and language of class struggle. By the canons of the liberal-democratic institutions that were developing, this is dangerous language; inflammatory language that stirs primitive resentments and aggressions; language that makes more difficult those self-restraints, concessions and compromises that are central elements in the game, that – from the leadership point of view – stimulates feelings and aspirations among the rank and file which may strengthen rival grass-roots leaders or movements. For publicly accommodative relations, a publicly accommodative language is a functional necessity. And as this language develops it helps to shape the consciousness of successive generations who use it and are affected by its use, thereby constituting one factor in the continuation of the system of which it is a part. It could not by itself determine continuation. There could be events or decisions of a significance so great as to change the material and cultural basis that made working-class accommodation possible, and the ideological language of accommodation would give way under such an impact. Yet short of such an extremity, this language and the whole social perspective that it embodied almost certainly helped to raise the threshold level at which discontent and grievance could pass into fundamental challenges to the system.

The ways in which major sections of the working classes were demonstrating by their behaviour that, far from wishing to overthrow the social order, they sought only, by a mixture of collective and individual effort, to improve their position in it were evoking conflicting opinions from foreign observers. 'The oldest and strongest unions' were becoming 'so orderly that continental statesmen regarded them with envy as bulwarks against socialism and anarchy' (Nicholson, 1896, p. 29). At the opposite end of the political spectrum, Engels, writing from London in December 1889, the year of 'new unionism' and socialist excitements, was able to point to characteristics of British social structure that were far older than the 'bourgeois' label he gave them.

> The most repulsive thing here is the bourgeois 'respectability' which has become part of the flesh and blood of the workers. The division of society into innumerable gradations, each unquestionably accepted, each with its own pride but also its native respect for its 'betters' and 'superiors', is so old and so firmly established that the bourgeois still find it pretty easy to get their bait accepted. I, for instance, am not at all sure that John Burns is not secretly prouder of his popularity with Cardinal Manning, with the Lord Mayor and the bourgeoisie generally, than of his popularity with his own class ... And even Tom Mann, whom I regard as the finest of them, is fond of mentioning that he will be lunching with the Lord Mayor. (Lenin, 1969, pp. 78–9)

With his reference to 'innumerable gradations ... each with its own pride' but also 'its native respect for its "betters" and "superiors"', Engels was pointing to working-class ambivalences of the sort that Joyce has documented in detail in the case of Lancashire cotton, where trade unionism and certain kinds of 'deference' were not only compatible but complemented each other (Joyce, 1980).

Given all this, there was every reason for the ruling class, buoyed up by mid-Victorian prosperity and optimism, to see its best policy as one of taking a calculated risk and conceding legal recognition to the unions and the franchise to the urban worker. With luck, this would bond the respectable working class even more firmly within the constitution, and would consolidate legitimation of the system by giving formal recognition both to an extension of equality before the law and to the pursuit of equality of bargaining power in the labour market.

The Whig Version of Industrial Relations History

Nobody questioned the assumption that combination and collective bargaining among workers created an approximate parity with employers; an assumption that plays a major part in legitimising the system to this day. It can, of course, be argued that they do nothing of the kind; that ultimate power continues, despite some appearances to the contrary, to lie predominantly with the owners and controllers of economic and political resources. The argument is complex and cannot be dealt with here (Castles *et al*, eds, 1971, pt. 3; Fox, 1974, ch. 6; Clegg, 1975; Hyman, 1978). It remains true, however, that beliefs about collective bargaining restoring equality to the labour market have contributed to the interpretation of British society as an example of fully pluralist liberal democracy.

That interpretation, in its widest sense, once took the form of the so-called Whig version of history which portrayed a steady growth of representative Cabinet government supposedly stemming from the Glorious Revolution of 1688, and which assumed that the only aspects of Britain's history worthy of study derived from the gradual but steady and apparently inevitable unfolding of enlightened liberal principles and institutions. This perspective, out of favour so far as general political history is concerned, showed greater staying power in the field of industrial relations. There was a tendency to view the growth of strong trade unions and systematised collective bargaining as an evolutionary triumph of liberal principles and civilised restraints, with workers coming gradually to 'learn' what was required of them in this best of all liberal worlds. Organised labour, after a turbulent and irrational period, grasped the wisdom of rational, peaceful negotiation and fashioned systems which took their place in the emerging panoply of civilised institutions, with alternative strategies deservedly sinking down into the dustbin of history as pathetic and doomed digressions. Even in T. H. Marshall's classic presentation of the gradual emergence of 'citizenship' in Britain (T. H. Marshall, 1950), the development of trade unionism and collective bargaining – 'a sort of secondary industrial citizenship' – appears to carry with it some of the Whiggish flavour of liberal inevitability – though this was certainly not Marshall's intention (Halsey, 1984).

An Alternative Version

An alternative view would see collective bargaining in a very different light. Groups of workers fumbled their way towards it as the most promising way of reducing the uncertainties of their immediate work experience; employers reacted in the light of their particular interests and exigencies. Sometimes it was they who led the fumbling; in a few cases it was they who pressed it upon self-regulating groups of craftsmen. Both groups were affected in their behaviour by a complex of influences – including their own traditions and culture – but the most palpable was the structure of power relations. For workers who turned to collective bargaining it was not the peak achievement of liberal-democratic aspiration; it was simply the best means available for self-defence against superior power and arbitrary rule. They might, indeed, have no more ambitious aspirations, but even if they did these had to be suppressed, shrunk or distorted to fit the requirements of whatever bargaining relationship the employers ultimately found tolerable.

The emerging system of industrial relations was therefore the outcome of, on the one hand, the way in which some relatively favoured sections of the working class sought to make the best of a bad job and, on the other, the way in which the dominant classes reacted to these initiatives. But if the system cannot be seen as a predictable unfolding of liberal enlightenment, neither can it be seen as simply a new and cunningly devised system of social control. If the workers were improvising and feeling their way, so were the dominant classes. Legalised trade unionism and collective bargaining, supplemented by historical continuities and state welfare provisions, certainly proved to have the hoped-for result of preserving the social fabric and encapsulating the economic class war within a vertical bonding of political influence and power that has lasted to this day.

Yet major points remain to be added. The first is that the dominant classes, as on other occasions in Britain's history, paid a price for putting social stability and cohesion at the top of their priorities. That price was the encapsulation into their society of an organised Labour movement strong enough to be able to manifest, on the whole, indifference or active mistrust towards employer interests and towards the favourite employers' notion that a joint co-operative pursuit of higher profits would make possible higher wages. On the whole, the stronger the union, the more it directed its efforts not towards a high-productivity, high-profits, high-wages policy but to a policy of restriction designed to limit employer control over technical change and utilisation of labour. This adversary stance was itself an outcome of historical continuities and ruling-class control strategies. By encapsulating it the governing classes were, in effect, though not in intention, acquiescing in the disadvantageous consequences of their own strategy of rule. How was it possible for them so to acquiesce? Here we come to a consideration of major importance for the appraisal of that strategy as it had developed during and since the eighteenth century. The British governing classes might well have felt unable to maintain their grudging tolerance of oppositional working-class organisation had their most politically influential elements been totally dependent on the domestic economy and domestically generated wealth. The growth of foreign trade and of London as a world financial centre, however, significantly reduced that dependence. A margin of economic slack had been created which enabled dominant political elements the more easily to pursue their preferred strategy of rule. Here lies the significance of imperialism and the support it gave to Britain's foreign trade. The important effect was less the direct one on particular groups of favoured workers than the mitigation of political ruling class hostility towards oppositional working-class organisation.

The State 'Holds the Ring'

In the absence of that margin of slack, a ruling class totally dependent on a surplus extracted from the domestic economy might have reacted differently. They might have estimated the long-term consequences of a restrictionist, adversarial and growing trade union movement, and mobilised their collective strength to smash it. In the event, it remained as true at the end of the nineteenth century as at the beginning that the political ruling class was not prepared, outside situations of extreme crisis, to put its coercive apparatus at the disposal of employers for use against organised labour except within the framework of the law – stretched and strained though this might have to be.

Some practical consequences of this relationship between business and the state can be illustrated by a comparison between Sir William Armstrong, manufacturer and supplier of arms to the Admiralty and War Office, and Krupp, his equivalent in Germany. 'In the last quarter of the nineteenth century the Ruhr barons, discovering that they were indispensable to the Second Reich's martial might, drew up their own terms for coexistence with Berlin.' Policies of repression and harassment against socialism and active trade unionism – usually identified with each other by the big industrialists – would have been pursued in any case; 'nevertheless there is little doubt that the vehemence of the repression owed much to *der Grosse Krupp*' (Manchester, 1970, p. 173). The material and moral backing given to heavy industry by the German state and its agencies in the fight against working-class movements was manifest through to 1914 and beyond.

Armstrong enjoyed no such support. When, in 1871, he placed himself at the head of the engineering employers' resistance to the Tyneside strike for the nine-hour day, the government and the relevant state departments stood by and watched him fight hard and expensively for nearly five months before going down to defeat. Yet Armstrong, far more than most industrialists, 'had powerful and influential connections in high places', and a 'striking feature' of the company's activities 'was the frequency with which men in high positions in the British Admiralty took up key managerial and executive positions within Armstrong's, and men previously in the employ of Armstrong's passed from the firm to positions of prestige and responsibility in the Admiralty' (Allen *et al.*, 1971, pp. 22–3). Friends at court did not avail. In Germany they assuredly did: Krupp was told by the Kaiser that the work of the Krupp family was 'God-given'. Armstrong received, not messages of congratulation from a monarch grateful for his patriotic stand against this monstrous subversion of the sacred national mission, but only an offer from A. J. Mundella to mediate in his capacity as Vice-President of the Capital and Labour Committee of the Social Science Association.

There are different explanations on different levels for this situation. A reduction in working hours was a popular cause with articulate sections of the middle classes, as increasing the leisure opportunities for moral and cultural refinement – strike leaders assumed pained expressions in public at the suggestion that their followers were more interested in longer overtime at premium rates of pay. Moreover, Armstrong had led the resistance in a manner so provocatively heavy-handed as to make even *The Times* feel uncomfortable. Official support for him would have received a bad press. But there was a more fundamental reason why the political ruling class had to affect to be above the battle. This was the now familiar one that it was boxed in by its own legitimations and chosen strategy of rule. Far more congenial as well as expedient was the 'settled conviction of the individualists', to use Beatrice Webb's words, 'that government should be limited to keeping the ring clear for private individuals to fight in'. It was a notion that gained in plausibility as organisations developed on both sides and groped towards methods of joint settlement. By minimising direct intervention and at the same time claiming to pursue a progressive equalising of the legal and organisational conditions within which the two sides conducted their relations, a weak state could both avoid involvement in a confusing and distasteful arena and strengthen traditional legitimations that still served it well.

The Emerging System

The argument presented here, therefore, is that the system of industrial relations now emerging represented neither the dawning of liberal enlightenment among a hitherto turbulent and irrational working class, nor a calculated strategy of control imposed by employers and state upon a passive workforce. It was the outcome rather of responses by employers and state to working-class initiatives and strategies. These initiatives and strategies were not new. Unilateral job regulation and collective bargaining went back, as we have seen, a very long way. But during a quarter-century of growth and optimism they expanded as the preferred strategies because they seemed to offer the better-placed workers a degree of immediate relief that proved more appealing than ambitious long-term plans of social transformation. They were more fortunate than workers elsewhere. A mixture of luck and shrewd judgement had led Britain's dominant classes into shaping social institutions and values in such a way as to make possible a degree of working-class participation in decision-making. Though the fundamental brute facts of power, status, control and privilege remained, there developed marginal adjustments to the balance of power and new syntheses of behaviour, relationships and institutions. Participation at the place of work took the form of struggling to secure a foothold in the making of decisions about pay, working hours, overtime, and the like, and to wrest from management as much control as possible over the job itself and its arrangements. Participation was now extending into the political field and on the same terms; its methods those of lobbying, persuasion, electoral pressure and skilful manipulation of concepts integral to the regime's own legitimations.

This interpretation implies that the working class had to choose between active pursuit of a millenarian vision and the pragmatic pursuit of piecemeal improvement, and in one sense a choice did have to be, and was, made. The working-class foothold in existing institutions would not have survived a widespread conviction within the ruling order that it would be used as a jumping-off point for social transformation. Any working-class behaviour that could be defined by their social and industrial superiors as revolutionary, subversive, irresponsible, or simply feckless weakened their position, in the sense that these charges could be used to justify resistance to their claims, harassment of their organisations, and repression by the police, government and the law. It was within such a context that the concept of 'respectability' becomes specially significant. Yet the idea of a choice being made needs a little elaboration. By the 1880s the old-style ultra-radicalism marked so heavily by Painite doctrines of individualism, rationalism, freethought and republicanism was looking old-fashioned: Bradlaugh died in 1891 and had no real successor. In their place were revived socialist ideas. As against the individualism and suspicion of the state that pervaded so much of the old radicalism, the new socialism asserted the class basis of power in society and argued that it could only be overcome by state ownership and control. Such ideas can hardly be said to have fallen on fruitful soil. The individualism that had become embodied in habituated behaviours, institutions and traditions proved powerfully resistant. To this day, the British are always prepared to accept state support or intervention when it suits their sectional purposes, yet only in dire national emergency do they invest it with 'national' meaning and give it the willing submission which such an investment implies. And as far as socialism itself was concerned, it was the very accessibility of piecemeal reform through existing institutions which blunted the appeal of social visions. For most of the men and women coping with the everyday struggle for existence it was the potentiality for relief in the immediate or foreseeable future that beckoned most strongly.

Yet, as this reasoning implies, there was nothing inevitable about the continuance of these mutual accommodations. They were vulnerable to a major shift of fortunes, perceptions, or aspirations on the part of either the dominant or the dominated classes. From the point of view of the latter, for example, any substantial and prolonged check to the system's ability to deliver at least minimal amelioration would be likely to render more attractive the prospect of total transformation. The timing and severity of such checks, however, were all-important, for with every decade the system acquired ever-accumulating institutional inertia and vested interests. Not only did rank and file members become increasingly conscious that they had something to lose. Even more directly personal were the benefits accruing to those who led, officered, staffed, or otherwise played an active role in the trade unions, the collective bargaining procedures, the structured relationships with employers, the systematic participation within political institutions. Congenial employment, personal satisfactions and career prospects became bound up with the survival and further development of these creative initiatives by the organised working class. Institutional inertia and vested interests could not guarantee that survival, but they raised the threshold at which dissatisfaction with outcomes was allowed to threaten the system.

Had the system offered only prolonged and total frustration or been threatened with attack by state or employers the result would probably have been a greater transcending of the sectionalism which conspicuously marked the movement. The unions had already shown, in the legal struggles of 1867–75, that what brought them together most reliably were shared interests in achieving and maintaining a secure environment within which to exercise their functions. The degree of unity then achieved was never to be wholly lost. The rise of socialist doctrines in the 1880s came nowhere near creating a socialist Labour movement, but a vague spirit of class solidarity was beginning to affect many activists. There was a growing practical base to support it. As union organisation spread, the possibility of a mutually helpful solidarity between different sectional groups grew with it. In such ways, collectivist ideals and tactical needs supported each other in some small measure. This was no more than an enlargement of possibilities long visible in aid between trades, in attempts towards larger groupings, in historic aspirations towards 'the one big union'. Yet, as before, these were far less palpable than narrower group self-interest. As the Webbs were to write in 1894: the basis of association was

> primarily sectional in nature. They come together, and contribute their pence, for the defence of their interests as boilermakers, miners, cotton-spinners, and not directly for the advancement of the whole working class . . . The vague general collectivism . . . has hitherto got translated into practical proposals only in so far as it can be expressed in projects for the advantage of a particular trade. (Webb and Webb, 1894, p. 477)

One emergent property of the system that provided a massive benefit for the ruling classes was that it kept the organised working classes sectionally divided.

If the system involved costs for those members of the Labour movement who entertained the larger hope, in that the movement had to contain its actions within limits defined by its social masters, then it also involved costs as well as benefits for the masters. As we have seen, sections of the ruling classes viewed with great foreboding the rise of democracy, with its organised working-class movements to which concessions had to be made in terms of the franchise, supportive legislation and social policy. The very nature of the system to which they had thus far committed themselves was now even requiring them occasionally to discipline their own over-exuberant defenders. Sir Charles Warren, appointed Chief Commissioner of the London Metropolitan Police in 1886, banned all (labour) demonstrations in Trafalgar Square and tried to enforce the ban with police and military violence. There was a public outcry which the Home Secretary considered it judicious to heed, but which Warren did not. When he refused outright to accept the Home Secretary's instructions 'he was forced, with the *douceur* of a KCB, to exchange the command of London for the command of Singapore (1889)' (E. P. Thompson, 1980, p. 155).

There was another price to be paid. The trade union movement, which had received statutory acceptance and protection under this regime, possessed characteristics which, though far less threatening for the ruling class than ideas of social transformation, nevertheless caused alarm and hostility enough. It was a movement which, while choosing to assimilate to the broader principles of the status quo, displayed strong restrictionist and adversarial tendencies underlying a veneer of respectability that could sometimes mislead middle-class social optimists. Even in Lancashire cotton, which of all the major industries offered the most evidence of workers' readiness to perceive common interests with their employers, collective relations between employer and unions were fully as commercialised, specific and unyielding as elsewhere, and experiments in 1885 to increase the number of looms per weaver met immediate union resistance which was largely successful (Clegg, Fox and Thompson, 1964, p. 118).

The integration of trade unionism into the social and legal fabric left it with its heritage of restrictionism and zero-sum conceptions untouched. Not disposed to contemplate struggling towards transformation of the capitalist order, organised labour was so structured and shaped as to preclude also the strategy of co-operating to make British capitalism more successful in the hope of fatter crumbs from the rich man's table. If there was a sense in which the dominant classes were boxed in by their own history and structured ways of proceeding, there was also a sense in which the organised working classes, too, were showing signs of being boxed in. They were predominantly rejecting ideas of attempting to transform the system, and they were also rejecting ideas of co-operating to make it more productive for their own advantage. The latter rejection was an expression not of mere perversity, but of the postures of arms-length wariness and mistrust generated among both sides by the historical development of the system.

5

Challenges to the System
The 1890s to 1914 (Part I)

An Emergent System of Industrial Relations

By the 1880s it was possible to discern the emergence of a 'system' of organised industrial relations in Britain, based on autonomous sectional collective bargaining between representative associations of employers and workers. Authoritative declarations by ministers had made clear that for governments this was the preferred method in which they had no intention of interfering. The state's professed role was to 'hold the ring', maintaining what was asserted to be legal even-handedness between the contenders and intervening only to uphold law and order. For the employer the system required recognition of the relevant union, acceptance of its representative character, pragmatic acknowledgement that his workers were conscious of grievances and claims of their own defining, and readiness to negotiate through mutually agreed procedures. For the union it required observance of the basic laws, principles and conventions governing ownership, status and reward, and an eschewing of the 'political' strike, that is, an acceptance that the collective industrial power of members would not be directed towards what were deemed political ends – a tactic which would eventually have destroyed the implicit understandings on which the system depended. These patterns of behaviour were felt to have been facilitated by the legislation of the 1870s. Employer organisation had never suffered attack by the courts; worker organisation had been scarred by it but had now, it was felt, been freed from the worst consequences of criminal liability. Also supporting the system was the elevated status of the upper working class as a consequence of rising living standards and widening education. Their existence and *raison d'être* acknowledged by the future king, the unions not infrequently heard observations like that of a prominent employers' leader in the boot and shoe industry in 1892. 'The day is long since past and gone when we can afford to look upon the officials of the union in any other way than occupying an authoritative position . . . It is a manifest absurdity to expect to receive these gentlemen in any other way . . . under the changed conditions of labour' (Fox, 1958, p. 59). That they might be received as authoritative did not, of course, necessarily mean they were welcomed, though even this was possible. But though personal relations between spokesmen at the negotiating level were often amicable and might become friendly, they continued generally to express, on both sides, structured dispositions towards arms-length, win–lose attitudes which were at best more restrained versions of those described by Dean Tucker in the eighteenth century.

Outside the relatively favoured circles of union recognition, collective bargaining and tolerable living standards – the first two likely to be as much an effect as a cause of the third – there were millions living too deep in poverty and oppression to be capable of sustained organisation or even the confidence to attempt it. The last febrile boom of British capitalism's golden age in the early 1870s had swept into the organised ranks many groups hitherto dismissed by the labour aristocracy as unorganisable, but the depression which followed appeared to confirm their scepticism when many of these efforts collapsed yet again. The picture changed for good, however, in the so-called 'new unionism' of the late 1880s, when a combination of boom conditions, socialism and an alerted social con-science created favourable conditions for what proved a more persistent foothold for groups such as the dockers, gas-workers, tramwaymen and unapprenticed labourers in craft trades. These, too, suffered damaging losses and counter-attacks, but enough survived on which to build. Although even this enlarged beach-head left massive numbers unorgan-ised the essential shape of the system was emerging even more clearly.

Yet during the period to 1914 it came under a series of counter-attacks and challenges from many diverse directions which sought to undermine it or to change its nature in one or more crucial respects. They came from the courts, from groups of employers and from wider social and political movements, including movements among the workers themselves. None of them succeeded. It is possible to argue – against some interpreta-tions which suggest the 'strange death' of Liberal England (Dangerfield, 1936) – that in 1914 the system was more securely installed than ever before.

None of the attacks on the unions drew much weight from aspirations to destroy them outright. By the time Britain's threatened economic position was prompting considered judgements among significant groups of organised employers that union restrictionism was near the top of their agenda, trade unionism had become too strong for its destruction to be a serious proposition except among a rabid minority. Its growth during the eighteenth and nineteenth centuries had benefited from a weak state and the predominant governing class strategy of rule, and on those foun-dations had been built a powerful legalised structure during the period of exceptional economic and social optimism from the 1850s to the mid-1870s. By the 1890s no government was likely to incur, if there was a possibility of avoiding, the damage to its electoral chances and to the constitutional structure that would follow an overt destructive attack on the unions, and most employers revealed by their behaviour that they were not prepared to mount a decisive attack on their own. Ideas of this sort had come much too late – if indeed there ever had been a fitting time for them.

The Economic Context: the 'Great Depression' and After

The tempo of mid–Victorian prosperity enjoyed by industrial, commercial and agrarian interests alike appeared to reach a high–water mark in the early 1870s. The decades that followed have been widely regarded both then and since as a period during which Britain began to be overtaken industrially by Germany and America, revealing an emergent backwardness which provoked much anxious inquiry and heart-searching. Agriculture also – more especially corn-growing – throughout Europe was exposed to severe competition from America and Russia, but in Britain alone remained unprotected. The fact that corn-growing interests could not mobilise the political strength to defend themselves against the policy and ideology of free trade – now invested with something like religious as well as material significance for many at all social levels – led to severe decline in major sections of the traditional economic base of the land-owning ruling class. But new bases had been long in the forging, including manufacturing industry itself. Even more important, however, were the various forms of finance capitalism – banking and merchant banking, insurance, the capital and money markets and related activities – which had provided auxiliary support to the landowning class for some considerable time. Given the upward surge in world industrial production and commerce, and the phase of renewed imperialism which consolidated and reoriented Britain's vast inheritance of previous colonisation and overseas trade, the opportunity was open for a great expansion of City-based money-making. The opportunity was duly taken. Having 'ceased to be able to command an abnormal share of world trade in manufactures', Britain temporarily maintained her balance of payments by achieving an abnormal share of the world's financial, insurance and shipping services (W. A. Lewis, 1949, p. 77). Private wealth could be maintained by applying talent, vigour and resources not to the 'modernisation' and reorienting of British industry, but to the development of London's financial eminence. 'Naturally, City institutions monopolized the outstanding talents and energies of the business class; in addition, they exerted virtual hegemony over the state in virtue of the élite social solidarity so strongly rooted in English civil society' (Nairn, 1977, p. 23).

The period between the mid-1870s and the mid-1890s saw prices and profits under pressure, a slackening in the growth of exports and a faltering of productivity growth in some industries. 'But the home market expanded, there were important developments in terms of the balance of production of goods and services, and foreign investment and the sale of services overseas boomed. Only with respect to the period from the 1890s to 1914 is there *general* agreement among historians that the economy had slowed down sufficiently to speak of a critical phase' (Supple, 1977, p. 10, italics in original).

Yet dispassionate and statistically supported appraisals by historians may bear little relation to the moods of the time, to the selective perceptions prompted by those moods and to the behaviour deriving from them. Many informed and articulate observers, their expectations checked by rapid economic growth among Britain's rivals, believed they saw in the so-called Great Depression a major sign of national reverse and instability, and the term itself would hardly have gained currency had they not recorded a sense of unease that was in fact widespread. Accompanying these economic doubts was a revival of social debates that had been somewhat muted by the long period of optimism. These took place against the background of what many identified as the beginnings of a shift from a relatively individualistic to a more collectivist society. Industrial combines and cartels – limited though these were by comparison with elsewhere, political parties, urbanisation, the beginnings of social legislation on health and housing, the growth of the unions – these were taken as signs of fundamental changes in the social order.

For some these were changes to be opposed and if possible reversed. For others they were changes to be encouraged but moulded in certain directions; there was a renewal here of doubts about the quality of liberal society in the form proclaimed by its mid-century prophets, with its extreme individualism, its preference for the minimal state, its assumption of progress and its reliance on the market as the harmonising mechanism. Such doubts were most strongly felt in other countries, particularly Germany, but they were present in diluted form even in Britain. Three differing conceptions developed. Socially concerned members of the rising Establishment generation, fired by evangelicalism or Oxbridge influences, or both, pursued one or a combination of them. The first was a new concept of active and enlightened empire combined with a domestic statutory structure of social welfare designed to eliminate class conflict and to unify and improve an imperial race. The second was a 'new' Liberalism, ranging far beyond Gladstonian retrenchment and the minimal state, designed to enlarge and enrich individual opportunity for self-development and communal participation by means of collective provision. The third was a socialist collectivism which went beyond the second in its acceptance of state intervention in the constitutional and decision-making structures of economic life. Neither the second nor the third was necessarily incompatible with a measure of the first. What all three conceptions shared was detestation of *laissez-faire* individualism as represented by the old Liberalism. What had happened, in fact, was that social criticism, partly muted by the long period of economic buoyancy, had resumed its stridency. The hostility towards liberal individualism voiced by Coleridge, Southey, Carlyle and Ruskin, and on a different level by such men as Owen and Oastler, re-emerged in new forms. Some were, like Southey's or Carlyle's, unequivocally conservative; others, like Owen's, bore the marks of an ambiguous paternalist socialism that revealed an anxiety to maintain order, control and leadership by qualified élites. Yet all these, along with the egalitarian socialism propagated by William Morris and later Tawney, looked to a renewal of community through the rejection of competitive individualism. The gaps between these various collectivist conceptions were therefore more readily bridgeable than might be supposed. The socialist Tawney and the imperialist Leo Amery could to some extent talk the same language; both Amery and his fellow arch-imperialist Milner at one stage toyed with socialism; and Sidney Webb's analysis of 1901 could be supported by many who by no means shared his prescriptions. Gladstonian Liberalism 'visualizes the world as a world of independent Roundheads with separate ends, and abstract rights to pursue those ends'. This older Liberalism had been 'a great instrument of progress' by 'wrenching away the shackles – political, fiscal, legal, theological and social – that hindered individual advancement'. But during the last twenty years

> its aspirations and its watchwords, its ideas of daily life and its conceptions of the universe, have become increasingly distasteful to the ordinary citizen . . . Its reliance on 'freedom of contract' and 'supply and demand', with its corresponding 'voluntaryism' in religion and philanthropy, now seems to work out disastrously for the masses, who are too poor to have . . . an 'effective demand' for even the minimum conditions of physical and mental health necessary to national well-being . . . We have become aware . . . that we are not merely individuals, but members of a community . . .

A conception of the 'higher freedom' of corporate life was now being opposed to Gladstonian Liberalism, with its characteristically Whig conception of the citizen's contribution to the expenses of the social organisation as 'a bill paid by a private man for certain specific commodities which he has ordered and purchased for his own use' (B. Webb, 1948, pp. 221–2; Morgan, 1978, p. 128).

In opposition to these three groups who were prepared to accept and promote the growing collectivism were groups determined to check and if possible reverse it. These passionately resisted the critique of individualism and viewed the drift towards a more corporate society as pernicious. Seen through modern 'welfare state' spectacles they appear as reactionaries trying to put the clock back. From their viewpoint, however, it was the collectivists and others favouring a more active state who were the reactionaries in that they sought to return to Tudor and Stuart preferences for economic and social regulation. They themselves were the true progressives who upheld the individualism that had made the country great, and who sought to roll back those frontiers of the state which had shown signs over several decades of inching forward.

As atomistic individualists they could be expected to view the advancing collectivism of the working classes with special hostility, and the intensity of their responses was heightened by some of the many diverse new currents generated in the last quarter of the century. The apparent checks to economic progress, the rise of a new and initially noisy and militant trade unionism among groups hitherto regarded as unorganisable, the emergence of socialism, social legislation involving state intervention – the proper response to all these was an even more ardent reassertion of the individualist creed. Some forms of this reassertion were, or were designed to be, direct in their effect upon trade union activities, others were indirect in that they sought to reverse trends and opinions throughout the wider society. Those in the former category enjoyed a powerful ally in the common law, itself the supreme embodiment of individualism in British life.

While the challenge offered by extreme individualism to the collectivist institutions of the industrial relations system is obvious, there were also forces within all the three groups with collectivist leanings which were by no means disposed to allow that system to continue in its present pattern, style and temper. All hoped substantially to change it – in some cases beyond recognition. This list of threats and challenges has also to include direct confrontations with groups of organised employers, some of whom, for short periods at least, aspired not only to smash the unions with which they were directly involved but also to draw employers generally into an overtly aggressive stance towards the union movement as a whole. The present chapter and the next examines these diverse threats and challenges, beginning with that traditional enemy of labour collectivism, the courts, and the atomistic individualism with which they were allied.

Counter-Attacks against Labour Collectivism: the Courts

Those who sought to assert individualistic against collectivist principles could always expect to receive support from the courts, more especially when the working classes were concerned. Laski has referred to

> the persistent inability of English judges to understand the very nature of trade unionism. Historically, its activities lie, in the eyes of the common law, so near to the boundaries of criminal conspiracy, that any judge who does not take the greatest care to guard himself against bias may easily find himself interpreting the issues of a labour case upon assumptions which condemn trade unionists before the issue is heard. The common law has at its foundation what Mr. Justice Holmes had called an 'inarticulate major premiss' about trade unions which even statute law can hardly overcome. (Laski, 1934, p. 150)

The 1871 and 1875 statutes certainly failed to overcome it. The courts remained concerned to interpret them – and common law – in ways which sought to check and subdue a growing labour collectivism seen by the courts as threatening property, freedom of contract, economic progress and individual rights – all issues on which the common law had cut its teeth and established its great prestige centuries earlier. Legislation having been conceded by governments to relieve the growing unions from the worst consequences of criminal liability, the judges turned to the development of civil liability. If an action was brought by those who could convincingly argue that union officers or members had maliciously conspired to injure them, or to interfere with their freedom of contract, the courts could, according to their newly developed doctrine of civil conspiracy, award damages. The class bias was manifest. 'In 1895 unionists who posted a "black list" of blackleg workers were made liable for a "conspiracy to injure"; in 1892 and 1902 the circulation of lists of strikers and trouble-makers by employers' associations was held not unlawful because the employers were defending legitimate self-interest' (Wedderburn, 1971, p. 27).

The heaviest blow was yet to come. It was supposed during the 1890s that such damages could only be awarded against union officers and members as individuals, and not against the union and its funds as such. The prevalent view, in the absence of a decision by the House of Lords to the contrary, was that the 1871 Act had not given the unions a corporate legal personality which enabled them to sue and be sued. As we saw, the Positivist adviser to the unions, Frederic Harrison, had realised that full incorporation would have dangers for them, and the 1871 Act, while giving their funds legal protection against defaulting or embezzling officials, had been drafted – so it was long believed – in such a manner as 'to prevent their being sued or proceeded against in a court of law' (Webb and Webb, 1920, p. 276). The 1894 Majority Report of the Royal Commission on Labour had expressed some dissatisfaction with this position, but the Minority Report, signed by four of the six trade union members (though mostly written for them by Sidney Webb), was alert to the fact that corporate legal personality would render union funds vulnerable to civil actions and thus leave the unions open to destruction by a series of employer-mounted law suits. Although the Majority Report itself made no recommendations on these points, a small but influential group of commission members – employers, lawyers, prominent politicians – had suggested that unions and employers' associations should be free, if they chose, to acquire full legal personality and thereby become able to enter into legally binding collective agreements – and suable for damages in the event of breach of contract (Clegg, Fox and Thompson, 1964, p. 311).

Subsequent events in the 1890s hardened the mood. Middle-class candid friends as well as enemies expressed renewed alarm at the effects of workplace restrictionism upon British industry's ability to hold its own against German and American competition, at the encroachments of union activities upon individual liberty, and at the economic damage done by stoppages – a coal dispute in 1893, for example, by far the largest the country had ever seen, had lasted nearly four months, had brought out 300,000 miners, and cost over twenty-one million working days. Socialism was seen as intensifying the worst tendencies in trade unionism. Among the proposals generated by these alarms the most threatening came from *The Times*, which demanded that 'unions should cease to be extra-legal in character . . . The time has come . . . for placing upon the unions a proper amount of corporate responsibility for illegal acts which inflict injury upon employers or upon non-unionists' (29 January 1898).

Three years later this demand was met. In 1901 the unions had full legal personality imposed on them by the House of Lords in the historic Taff Vale case, Lord Halsbury, the Lord Chancellor, presiding. Henceforth all unions which registered under the 1871 Act in order to secure legal protection for their funds were open to claims for damages resulting from the actions of their officers and members.

So far the series of adverse decisions by the courts as they fashioned their doctrine of 'conspiracy to injure' had not greatly influenced the course of union development.

Now it seemed that a case could be brought on the grounds of almost anything that might be done in a trade dispute, not only against the members and officers but against the union itself; and there was no clear limit, short of an empty treasury, to the damages which could be awarded against a union's funds. Had the unions been disposed to make light of Taff Vale a series of subsequent decisions in which heavy damages were awarded against them pressed home the lesson. (Clegg, Fox and Thompson, 1964, pp. 315–16)

Few voices of power and influence were raised against this decision. The Conservative press fully approved and even the Liberal newspapers spoke with two voices (Halévy, 1961d, p. 274). In Parliament, the leading lawyers of both parties expressed resistance to any idea of reverting to the previous position. Especially ominously, middle-class supporters, including the Webbs, took the same line. There had long been a conception in the minds of such sympathisers, already noted, of the ideal trade union which would be strong enough to protect its members from oppression and to educate them in 'responsible citizenship' but not so strong – and misguided – as to be capable of 'dictating' to employers, obstructing 'necessary' change and 'tyrannising' over the individual. The Taff Vale judgement appeared to offer a useful curb on excessive union pretensions. But what was likely to disturb rank and file union activists most of all was that many union leaders, too, were willing to consider whether the Taff Vale decision might not yield them some advantages. If central union funds were to be answerable for all action taken in the localities, would this not require and justify a far more rigorous control and discipline by top leadership over the members? It was a far from disagreeable prospect for general secretaries or presidents harassed by militants and unofficial action. 'There are those in the labour movement', wrote one of them, 'sanguine enough to think that the decision ... will be a blessing in disguise, and will tend to strengthen executive control and minimise, if not entirely kill, irresponsible action in the localities' (Clegg, Fox and Thompson, 1964, p. 319).

This makes it probable that if the Conservative government had moved swiftly it could have carried the union leaders with it in promoting a Bill which, while protecting picketing and abolishing the doctrine of civil conspiracy with respect to trade disputes, retained something of the corporate responsibility and liability of the unions. But this possibility was lost by the delay imposed by the appointment of a Royal Commission, by the punitively heavy damages finally awarded in January 1903 in the Taff Vale case and, finally, by the overtaking of events with a general election in 1906. It was a delay which some later Conservative leaders were to regret. Baldwin, who entered the House of Commons in 1908, always 'deplored the open exultation with which the Taff Vale decision had been received by the employers and their sympathisers, and to the end of his life considered that Balfour's Government should have struck in to restore the nineteenth century status of the unions which had been Disraeli's gift'. His verdict was that 'the Conservatives can't talk of class war: they started it' (Middlemas and Barnes, 1969, p. 99).

Meanwhile, although opinion within the unions differed as to what kind of legislation was to be sought, there was hardly any doubt about the need for legislation of some sort to clarify the confusion into which trade union law had been plunged. This concentrated minds rapidly on the subject of independent labour representation in Parliament. Already there had been restiveness among the more socialist leaders and activists of the Labour movement against the long-standing attachment of working-class MPs, in both doctrine and practice, to the Liberal Party. Leaders like Keir Hardie, of the Independent Labour Party, had always hoped to harness the mass forces of the trade unions to the political cause of socialism. This strategy now began to achieve a modest success. The year preceding the Taff Vale judgement saw the formation of the Labour Representation Committee (LRC), which included spokesmen of the unions, the Independent Labour Party, the Social Democratic Federation (though only briefly) and the Fabian Society (which took little interest). The conference of 1900, initiated by the Parliamentary Committee of the Trades Union Congress and setting up what was to become the Labour Party in 1906, indicated certain broad preferences. A proposal to found a party based on the principle of the class war and with a programme of unqualified socialism was defeated. Yet the conference 'refused to be content with a mere group of trade unionists, free if they pleased to remain members of the Liberal Party. It therefore decided in favour of a group which, without being committed to a particular economic theory, would nevertheless present in every respect the character of a "party", politically independent' (Halévy, 1961d, p. 262). This distinct Labour group would have its own Whips and agree upon its own policy, while being ready to co-operate with any party promoting legislation in the direct interests of labour. What the unions sought from the LRC 'was not any long-term alternative to Liberalism, but a sufficiently strong bargaining position to force the next Liberal government to repeal the effects of the Taff Vale judgement' (Hinton, 1982, p. 33). Although Lib–Labs showed no enthusiasm for the new move, some indeed being bitterly hostile, they did not mobilise to kill it. Among them were many who by no means offered unqualified commitment to the status quo; many who, though 'less violently opposed to the existing social and economic structure than [the socialists], nevertheless wanted government action taken to maintain full employment, eliminate the trade cycle, and reduce inequalities of wealth' (Fox, 1958, pp. 197–8). Differences were, in fact, less sharp than the more strident voices on both sides cared to acknowledge.

Yet the ardour vested by the unions in parliamentary representation and political activity generally had always tended to wax and wane according to whether there figured on the political agenda some issue closely affecting union security and interests. For twelve months after the election of 1900, the early and very modest union affiliations to the LRC rose hardly at all. The Lords' judgement in the Taff Vale case, however, and the subsequent award of punitive damages, proved powerful recruiting agents. By 1903–4, well over half the TUC's affiliated membership was affiliated also to the LRC. As MPs gathered after the 1906 election and began business there seemed plenty of evidence of the Labour movement's increased political effectiveness. There were now no less than forty-seven MPs with a clear organisational link with the Labour movement, thirty of them LRC-sponsored. With gathering union alarm about the implications of Taff Vale, the time for saddling the unions with any degree whatsoever of legal liability had long passed so far as the TUC was concerned, and a demand for complete immunity from actions for damages had been the movement's policy since September 1903.

At first the Liberal lawyers, fortified by the arguments of a recent Royal Commission and supported by the law officers of the crown, sought to impose corporate responsibility and declared complete immunity to be a legal monstrosity. But rumours of dissension within the Cabinet encouraged the LRC MPs to press on with their own Bill, especially since many Liberal MPs had pledged support during the election campaign. To the disgust of most of the legal profession the Labour Bill received the royal assent within the year. Thus was passed the Trade Disputes Act of 1906, which relieved the unions of all the legal dangers with respect to civil conspiracy and picketing created for them by adverse court judgements over the past decade, and which specifically included a section repealing the Taff Vale decision by ruling out actions for damages against trade unions for civil wrongs committed by officers or members.

Lawyers among the Conservative Opposition were the principal critics of the Bill during the Commons debate on the third reading, though arguments were also heard that it would complete the destruction of British trade and irretrievably damage the working classes. But the Opposition leader, A. J. Balfour, noted that an alleged 'great dislike of this measure among the employing classes' had not found expression in the debates and in any case, it was 'too late to change the Bill' and 'too late to reject it' – it must be accepted. 'His best hope was founded on the fact that Englishmen had on the whole shown themselves so far capable of exercising great powers with moderation. There was a natural good sense and moderation about the race in its corporate dealings which might be able to resist the temptation given even by a wide Act of Parliament' (Simon, 1926, app. 4).

Not even all prominent lawyers declared themselves affronted. Lord Loreburn, Lord Chancellor in the Liberal government, who introduced the second reading in the House of Lords (4 December 1906) spoke resoundingly in its favour. Language almost failed Lord Halsbury, however, who had presided in the Lords, sitting judicially, when the Taff Vale case was decided. 'Anything more outrageously unjust, anything more tyrannical, I can hardly conceive' (Halsbury, 1906, cols. 704 ff.). The outrage was felt to lie principally in the fact 'that if a man does wrong to another in the course of a trade dispute the courts are to have no jurisdiction'. It was considered the ultimate surrender with respect to granting 'immunities' and has scandalised many lawyers ever since. Viewed within a purely legalistic context their shock was understandable. But in the wider social context it had begun to seem that if the tenacious traditions of English common law and its individualistic bias were allowed to prevail, the collectivist ethos and behaviours of trade unionism might be at least subdued, at most crushed. For those whose thinking could get beyond the prevalent legal traditions, the issue hinged on whether or not the unions were to be allowed to survive, to grow and to develop their functions.

This becomes of crucial significance when we attempt to assess the motives and calculations of the leading politicians of the day. Party political considerations unquestionably played a part. The attachment of organised labour was something that the Liberal Party still hoped to retain and the Conservative Party, restaking 'their historic claim to the allegiance of the Tory working man', still hoped to capture (Middlemas, 1979, p. 40). The Conservative leadership had throughout shown little keenness to oppose the measure and in the House of Lords, at the very moment when their lordships, under Lansdowne's leadership, were engaged in garrotting the Education Bill, he offered them the bland argument that 'the country had spoken, that if they sent back the Trade Disputes Bill it would be returned to them in a more embittered spirit, and therefore that the only possible course was to pass it' (Halévy, 1961e, p. 98) – an argument that notably failed to occur to many of them during the constitutional crisis over their own functions in 1910.

Once more, therefore, the political influence of organised labour, exerted at the parliamentary level, had reversed a class-biased attack by the courts. But the courts had by no means finished with the unions. The successful campaign for the 1906 Act had revealed a reviving political will and – given the predominant stance of governments and parties – political effectiveness. And in the eyes of many lawyers this had resulted in a shocking capitulation which had weakened the impartial majesty of the law by awarding to one form of social organisation 'privileges' yielded to no other. But in the opinion of the Webbs and other historians and legal commentators, more was involved in the attitudes of lawyers than outrage at the violation of legal principles.

'The progress of the Labour party was causing a quite exaggerated alarm among members of the governing class' (Webb and Webb, 1920, p. 626). In December 1909 the House of Lords upheld an injunction taken out by a member of the Amalgamated Society of Railway Servants, W. V. Osborne, restraining the union from spending its funds for political purposes. Osborne's aim had not been to prevent political action as such, but to contest the union's right to enforce a political levy and subscribe to the funds of the Labour Party. Here he spoke for many trade unionists – including the general secretary of his own union – whose commitment to the Liberal or Conservative Parties was sufficiently strong to generate resentment at seeing a compulsory levy, tiny though it was, support the parliamentary position of so-called 'socialists' – though 'given the history of the L.R.C. there was never any likelihood that the new Labour Party ... would assume the character of a militant and independent opposition, with distinctive, let alone socialist, policies' – rather was it simply a 'more or less radical appendage of the Liberal Party' (Miliband, 1973, pp. 21–2). The House of Lords, however, declared all political action by unions to be *ultra vires*, as not being included in the purposes of a trade union defined in the Trade Union Acts of 1871 and 1876. 'The historical novelty of the decision is often underestimated ... There can be no doubt that *Osborne* marked a new and determined departure to control the unions . . . two influences played a part, namely the desire to treat unions as corporations, and the feeling that they were still illicit, probably dangerous, associations' (Wedderburn, 1971, p. 414). The judges 'were really affirming their view that trade union rights are purely the creation of statute law and that trade unions themselves are artificial bodies created by statute to perform certain functions'. This implied a conception by which all their rights and powers were derived from the state (Cole, 1972, p. 10).

Yet again political pressures and calculations produced a path divergent from the courts. Whatever party spokesmen thought and said in private, they did not choose, when they acted and spoke for the public record, to follow the predominant line of the legal profession. ' . . . it is quite impossible', declared Winston Churchill in the House of Commons (30 May 1911), 'to prevent trade unions from entering the political field'. The spheres of industrial and political activity always overlapped and were sometimes indistinguishable, so representation in Parliament was absolutely necessary. Churchill then registered an opinion about the courts that came rarely from Establishment figures.

> The courts hold justly a high and, I think, unequalled prominence in the respect of the world in criminal cases, and in civil cases . . . but where class issues are involved, it is impossible to pretend that the courts command the same degree of general confidence. On the contrary, they do not, and a very large number of our population have been led to the opinion that they are, unconsciously no doubt, biassed . . . It is not good for trade unions that they should be brought into contact with the courts, and it is not good for the courts.

Churchill continued with observations that struck a chord with long-standing features of British political culture. They were expressed also by other critics of the Osborne judgement who argued that trade unionism was 'not a creature of statute law, but a natural form of human association, and therefore capable of growth and the assumption of new purposes'. Such arguments embodied a conception by which the rights and powers of associations did not derive from the state, but belonged to the associations 'by virtue of their nature and the purposes for which they exist' (Cole, 1972, p. 10). 'We know perfectly well,' said Churchill, 'that the trade union movement ought to develop, ought not to be stereotyped, ought to have power to enter a new field and to make new experiments . . . We wish to set the trade unions free to develop their efforts . . . ' (Milne-Bailey, 1929, pp. 380–1).

Several years passed, however, before public men found themselves having to choose their words on the subject of the Trade Union Bill which reversed the Osborne judgement and it was February 1913 before Haldane, Lord Chancellor, moved the second reading in the House of Lords. The Act which resulted established the unions' right to engage in political activity, subject to membership ballot, but stipulated that every member must be free to contract out of the political levy.

Haldane's observations reveal much about the terms of public discourse which 'reasonable' people were currently expected to share when they discussed the trade unions. Outlining the argument that it was 'impossible for an individual workman to hold his own against an employer in a far more powerful position' and that it was 'only by combining for the purpose of negotiating on a footing in which the parties are more evenly matched that it is possible for the working man to drive for himself a fair bargain', he felt able to say that this, though 'hotly contested in the past', now 'seems to us elementary'. Bad things had been done by trade unionists in the nineteenth century, such as the inflicting of 'outrages upon their fellow-workers', 'but there grew the conviction in the minds of reasonable people that, if these things happened, there was some excuse for their happening by reason of the laws to which trade unions were subjected and the little power which the members . . . had to protect themselves'. Here Haldane was still demonstrating the act of faith, observable among some Liberals and some Conservatives since the mid-nineteenth century, that given 'fair' and 'just' treatment – as they defined it – trade unions would increasingly assimilate to the best behaviours already apparent among them and could therefore increasingly be accepted into the full structures and conventions of the constitution. No doubt there was a mixture here of wishful thinking, of genuine convictions about social progress – an idea not yet extinguished – and of a search for rationalisations of what seemed convenient for party interests.

The present Bill, Haldane explained, sought to remedy what the unions felt to be 'a very great injustice'. For a while there had been 'a good deal of controversy . . . but a happy spirit of give and take appears to have prevailed in the latter stages . . . and the three parties concerned appear to have found themselves completely at one'. The facts bore him out. In the House of Commons there had been no division on the third reading and Bonar Law, Leader of the Conservative Opposition, had underlined Liberal sentiments towards the Bill. 'As regards its general principle there has not been from the first any dispute. I think everyone in all quarters of the House recognizes that the Osborne judgement left trade unions in an invidious and I think an unfair position. They ought to have been able, if they wished, to carry on political action under fair conditions.' In his opinion the Bill represented a satisfactory method of giving effect to principles on which there was general agreement (Emden, ed., 1939, Vol. 1, pp. 77–8, 80–1).

Counter-Attacks against Labour Collectivism: the Employers

The passage of the Trade Disputes Act 1906 and the Trade Union Act 1913 owed much to party political calculation, but it is doubtful whether the politicians would have been able to indulge their calculations had the mass of employers as a class been determined to retain and exploit the original legal judgements for the purpose of destroying the unions as an effective industrial and political force.

The 1890s had seen several ventures by specific groups of employers which revealed a serious intention of smashing the particular unions confronting them. Scarcely had the upsurge of the 'New Unionism' in 1889 begun to take effect than some employers were mobilising against it. In 1890 George Livesey, the militantly anti-union chairman of the South Metropolitan Gas Company, broke the union in his own works with a combination of 'free' (that is, non-union) labour – strongly protected by the police – and a profit-sharing scheme. In the same year Ben Tillett's union was eased out of the London docks and in other ports Free Labour Associations were formed which reduced the unions to a nullity. Ship-owners formed the Shipping Federation under the general managership of G. A. Laws, opened free labour registries and undermined the seamen's union. What was significant in these and similar events was not the attempt by particular employers or groups of employers to destroy the union or unions facing them. Such attempts were as old as collective action itself. Nor was it the attempts at systematic organisation of free labour – a Free Labour Registration Society operating from London in the 1860s had sent strike-breaking workers to distant parts of the country (Clegg, Fox and Thompson, 1964, p. 5). What was especially noteworthy was that active in these counter-attacks were prominent men in prominent industries who appeared in one or more of a range of anti-labour organisations with far-reaching political programmes that sought to reverse some of the most important recent social and political trends.

Meanwhile the industrial counter-attack extended to the crafts. 1890 saw references to a possible 'understanding' between the Shipping Federation and the engineering and shipbuilding employers and it was not long before the engineering industry itself began moving towards a classic craft conflict. Competition was quickening both at home and abroad and American and German rivals had already overtaken the British lead. At home new methods of production in some firms were destroying craft customs and privileges and forcing other firms to follow suit. New specialist machines lent themselves to the employment of unapprenticed labour and as improvisation gave way increasingly to planning the craftsmen found themselves hedged about by 'detailed specification, close inspection, and tighter supervision, while speeding-up was encouraged by the growth of payment by results' (ibid., p. 139). Shop-floor resistance to these trends led eventually to the formation in 1896 of the Employers' Federation of Engineering Associations, with the object, in particular, of asserting themselves 'against combinations of workmen seeking by strikes or other action to impose unduly restrictive conditions upon any branch of the engineering trade'. The Federation took the occasion of a union demand for the eight-hour day in 1897 to lock out 35,000 workers, though the crucial issue was the unions' attitude towards technical change and its consequences.

The temper of the dispute on the employers' side was undoubtedly heightened by a belief that the union challenge was stiffened if not inspired by socialist militancy. Leading figures uttered sentiments exemplified by Alexander Siemens and Colonel Dyer of Armstrong-Whitworth, who informed *The Times* that Federation members were 'determined to obtain the freedom to manage their own affairs which has proved to be so beneficial to the American manufacturer'. Their first declaration of settlement proposals gave strong support to the view that their aim was to crush the unions, and a number of public protests followed which included one from fifteen Oxford dons who described the Federation ultimatum as 'a deliberate attempt to overthrow the principle of collective bargaining', a judgement in which Beatrice Webb concurred (B. Webb, 1948, p. 54). Alfred Marshall, on the other hand, gave the economists' verdict by declaring, from Cambridge, that he wanted the unionists to be 'beaten at all costs'. In the event, the unions retained the right of collective bargaining, but had to sign away all craft claims to encroach on managerial freedom with respect to machinery, work organisation, piece-work, overtime, apprenticeship and the employment of non-unionists. What mattered here, however, was not the text of top-level agreements, but how far employers found it expedient to confront craftsmen in their own workshops on such issues, and what responses were forthcoming. Whatever impact defeat might have had in the short run, by 1914 there was still 'an extensive body of custom and vested right in regulations that could . . . be held to "restrict production or employment" and which were considered by the unions, and recognized by the Government, as of first-rate importance' (Goodrich, 1975, p. 181).

Similar struggles over craft control took place in printing, tailoring, footwear and building, among others. Some employers looked hopefully, as always, to 'free' labour, but although this had served a purpose in 'new unionism' conflicts on the docks, in shipping and in gas and other affected industries, it could do little to help employers in the craft trades and made only a limited and ineffectual appearance in the engineering dispute. Among a number of organised sources of non-union labour was the National Free Labour Association, set up by William Collison in 1893 and backed by George Livesey and the shipping and dock interests. The interest of these ventures lies, paradoxically, in how little they affected the development of the trade union movement and the industrial relations system, despite being considered an important feature of strategy by several anti-labour organisations that sprang up between the 1880s and 1914. These will later receive some attention, for the nature and development of any labour movement is obviously affected by the strength of the resistances offered to it. The relative weakness of these organisations is important evidence of the predominant temper of Britain's ruling and employing classes and helps to explain why the labour movement suffered no concerted onslaught.

The limited appeal of this particular direction of attack is demonstrated by, among other things, the way in which the same names tend to turn up under different organisational umbrellas. The Free Labour Protection Association, with a force of ex-policemen and soldiers to protect free labour when required, was established in 1897 at a meeting attended by, among others, George Livesey, G. A. Laws of the Shipping Federation, Colonel Dyer and Alexander Siemens. The chairman was Lord Wemyss, previously Lord Elcho, who in his earlier incarnation had demonstrated some sympathy with working-class needs (see p. 194) but who had become a doctrinaire individualist after 1880. Even in his extremity, however, he was too alert to middle-class queasiness about political violence to encourage street-brawling. Despite being perhaps the most persistent advocate of free labour, he apparently 'objected to the open warfare of strike-breaking'. Lord Dysart shared this objection 'and hoped that educational methods would suffice', while 'Lord Avebury . . . conducted a long correspondence with Collison on whether strike-breaking could be avoided' (Clegg, Fox and Thompson, 1964, p. 173). This demonstrates that for some of the prominent backers of the free labour movement the central issue was less strike-breaking *per se* than the reassertion of individualism in the labour market. The perceived menace was the growing 'tyrannical' collectivism which, increasingly tainted with socialism, encroached on the 'freedom' of both employer and worker, 'distorted' economic forces, and impeded 'progress'.

Even employers directly facing this menace often had little stomach for what one union leader described as the American-style 'Boss system, with its attendant unrestrained brutality and lawlessness'. After the engineering lock-out the Employers' Federation of Engineering Associations invited Lord Wemyss and the Free Labour Protection Association to a conference in 1898 to 'consider a proposal to accept into the Federation . . . all cognate trades having . . . grievances with tyrannical trade unions'. The intention was to maintain 'absolute freedom of contract between employers and employed' and 'the right of managing their . . . business without interference from trade unions'. But there were many indications that the Federation was not representative of the employers even in the engineering and shipbuilding industries. The proposal for a link-up with the Free Labour Protection Association fell through because in the words of one commentator, 'many . . . firms . . . did not at all care about being tied to the tail of Wemyss and Co'. The conference resolved instead on the more modest aim of forming a Parliamentary Committee (later Council) to watch over legislation 'affecting the interests of trade, of free contract, and of free labour' (ibid., pp. 174, 175). The employers who were active in it, however, were 'few and unrepresentative' (Phelps Brown, 1959, p. 272). Outside these industries there were even clearer signs that the employing classes were deeply divided on the issue of whether to attempt to destroy the unions or try to work with them. The mid-1890s saw the first of a number of occasions on which the eruption of highly publicised conflict was followed by employers and union officials of other industries coming together in attempts to re-knit the social fabric with a public display of conciliation and class goodwill. In 1895 an Industrial Union of Employers and Employed was established 'in the belief that there was a need for an association which, while adopting as a fundamental principle the recognition of combination, would "emphasize the underlying common interests of both classes . . . and cultivate the feeling of goodwill on both sides".' Participants included David Dale, the prominent ironmaster, Edward Trow, an ironworkers' union official, and W. J. Davis, perhaps the best-known figure of Birmingham trade unionism. The Industrial Union faded out in 1896, but in 1900 the more impressive National Industrial Association was established – 'a National Association of Employers' Associations and Trade Unions', with much the same objects and likewise attracting support from prominent leaders on both sides (Clegg, Fox and Thompson, 1964, pp 175–6). Their interest lies not in their activities or achievements, which were meagre enough, but in the evidence they offered that leaders who in their time conducted robust struggles with each other were concerned to demonstrate that industrial conflict was to be contained within a framework of mutual survival and not to take the form of testing the opponent to destruction. In this they were probably nearer the bulk of middle-class opinion than the bellicose voices that surfaced in the editorials of *The Times* during this period and in the more combative wings of the various free labour movements.

In the light of these divisions within the employing classes it is clear that, in the absence of a mass determination among employers to exploit the Taff Vale judgement and prevent it being reversed by legislation, politicians had elbow room within which to calculate party advantage – and their own. There were, of course, some employer attempts in the expected direction. Suits were brought, and the Parliamentary Council of militantly anti-union employers tried to persuade peers to amend the 1906 Trade Disputes Bill. But if we are to gauge the predominant mood of employers we must look both wider and closer than this. At first sight the evidence might seem to suggest that while the Taff Vale and other adverse legal judgements applied, the unions were quelled into submissiveness. Certainly, there was a period of industrial peace from 1899 to 1907, 'unparalleled between 1891, when adequate strike statistics start, and 1933, when a comparable period began', and it was long customary for historians to explain this with the reasoning that since a strike 'might lead to legal action on a number of counts, and union funds were now liable to suffer . . . trade union officers and committees avoided strikes whenever they could'. Union action was supposedly paralysed by fear of employer retaliation.

There is some evidence to support them, but a closer analysis reveals other factors at work. Had

> British employers wished to be rid of trade unions, the depression years of 1902–5, with the Taff Vale precedent valid in every court, were as favourable an opportunity as ever presented itself. There are, however, relatively few instances of organized employers taking advantage of it to attempt to weaken or destroy the unions. This was not because employers were inactive. Important new employers' organizations were founded . . . Moreover, in some industries the employers were willing to take the initiative, and where they did so, as in building and printing, it was to strengthen and extend systems of collective bargaining and to enlarge the scope of joint regulation. (Clegg, Fox and Thompson, 1964, pp. 326, 362–3)

This suggests that although employers were ever ready to grumble about the unions and represent them as responsible for most of their industry's ills, enough of them drew back from anything in the nature of a knock-down, drag-out fight. As we shall see in more detail later, this was no doubt partly due to the fact that there was nothing in the predominant stance of governments and the senior civil servants most directly involved to suggest that much support would be forthcoming from those quarters. Far more likely would be a studied appearance of 'neutrality' and attempts by prominent and influential persons to 'heal the breach' through mediation and conciliation.

Another factor at work in shaping employers' responses was that individualism and sectionalism were as strong among them as among their workers. They might stomach organisations in their own particular industry, and even accept leadership from a particularly strong figure, but there was widespread wariness towards ideas of any larger grouping and no attempt at it had flourished. A central authority among employers, and that only of a strictly circumscribed kind, was not to come until the First World War – relatively late, considering Britain's early industrialisation. A strong central organisation formed in the 1890s and charged with the task of formulating a long-term strategy for employer interests might have been able to affect events, but probably not its members' disinclination systematically to exploit the Taff Vale judgement. The evidence indicates that despite that judgement the majority of organised employers preferred to make a serious attempt to work with the unions. Given these policies prevalent among employers, governments, the relevant higher civil servants and the political parties, it is not surprising that resistance to the idea of reversing the adverse legal judgements proved, except among lawyers, half-hearted and unconfident. And lawyers had far less of a role in Britain's system of government and administration than, for example, in Germany's. Unions were thus able to win so-called 'immunities' which amounted, in effect, given the English legal context, to a charter of rights enabling them to pursue collectivist ends through collectivist means.

Wider Challenges to the System: Atomistic Individualism

The attacks by the courts and by particular groups of employers were aimed directly at the legal rights and the activities of trade unionists, and at the legal vulnerability and even existence of trade unions. Inasmuch as a certain pattern of unionism and union behaviour was an integral part of the emergent system of industrial relations, such attacks were a direct threat to that system. But the system also came under indirect threat from wider social and political initiatives which, while they hoped to change the industrial relations system in fundamental ways, went beyond that in a more comprehensive attempt to reassert what were deemed vital but threatened principles in the national life. Among these initiatives were movements which, despite the still-dominant part played by the individualistic creed in British life, considered that it was endangered by certain collectivist trends which must be reversed. There was more to this reaction than the simple conviction that individualism and self-help were what had made Britain great. In so far as collectivist tendencies and 'positive' government led to greater public spending they increased the burden of taxes or rates. Rigorous government economy was popular among the better-off, and so were doctrines which appeared to make it a virtue. Principled conviction and private interest combined to view with alarm those departures from *laissez-faire* which, along with working-class organisation and working-class political participation, seemed to threaten wealth, progress and individual liberty.

Specially prominent in these movements was Lord Wemyss. Wemyss would have had no further place in this account had his concern been solely with the introduction and protection of free labour for purposes of strike-breaking, for the free labour movement possessed only a variable and fluctuating vitality. Collison's National Free Labour Association was called in on a few occasions by railway companies, who fought one of the most tenacious rearguard actions against union recognition and collective bargaining that this country has seen, and other lesser examples can be found during the early twentieth century. But the Free Labour Protection Association was put to little use and was moribund by 1904. This is not to say that it exerted no influence upon the industrial relations system. Then, as now, picketing was ever a subject of controversy and the Association's joint first step had been to distribute among leading employers, magistrates and chief constables throughout the country copies of a handbook by W. J. Shaxby, *The Case against Picketing* (1897). Frederick Millar, the Association's secretary, told the 1906 Royal Commission on Trade Disputes and Trade Combinations that as a consequence 'a more wholesome and satisfactory method of interpreting the law [towards picketing disturbances] was adopted . . . Imprisonment with hard labour soon became the rule' (Clegg, Fox and Thompson, 1964, p. 173).

Just how long this more punitive policy prevailed is not known: in any case, the introduction and protection of free labour for strike-breaking was only the lesser purpose of men like Wemyss. He and a number of other aristocratic and middle-class leaders devoted considerable money and energy to organisations whose principal purpose was to roll back the frontiers of collectivism and assert the principle of individualism in its pure and extreme form. This was the form under which individuals not only pursue their own enlightened self-interest, which they define for themselves, but do so with no concerted action between them, each acting as an atomistic, independent and self-responsible unit and being treated as such. This may be termed for convenience 'atomistic' individualism, which enables us to distinguish it from the form described earlier as 'instrumental' collectivism in which individuals, while still using perceived self-interest as their criterion of judgement and action, find it expedient to concert with others on those issues where collective action yields better results. The current tendencies which were seen as most violating the principle of atomistic individualism were militant and 'socialistic' trade unionism, a politicised working class, an interventionist state – especially in the field of social legislation – and the movement away from the extreme rigour of the 1834 legislative principles in administering poor relief.

In this reassertion of liberal individualism a political paradox had become evident: a paradox produced by the shift of political affiliations among many well-to-do in the industrial, commercial and financial worlds. In transferring their allegiance from the Liberals to the Conservatives they did not necessarily leave their economic liberalism behind. As a consequence, the structure of Conservative dispositions was changing. Earlier the Conservative enemy had been especially the individualism of radical liberalism, seen as, among other things, undermining authority, habits of obedience and respect for the cohesive value of traditional social bonds. Now the principal threat to Conservative values and the structure of power and interests which they supported seemed to be collectivism among the working class and the danger of a permanently cemented alliance between its organisations and what was left of the Liberal Party. As will be seen, some Conservative thought and action, seeing collectivism as irreversible, sought ways of rendering it harmless by incorporating it into a society unified from above by imperial glory, economic protectionism and statutory social welfare. But alongside them now in the Conservative camp were groups which made a different appraisal. For them, atomistic individualism was too much a key factor in Britain's greatness or in the preservation of their own interests to permit of further encroachments. The tendency of Britain's workers to pursue their individual interests by collective means and to tempt the Conservative Party, for electoral reasons, to engage in collectivist social provision, must be checked.

Wemyss typified those who still hoped to reverse or at least stem the trend, and who threw their weight behind the cause of atomistic individualism. In terms of resistance to positive state intervention in the shaping and directing of the economy they spoke for a strong tradition which has survived in Britain to this day, and their propaganda may even have contributed a little to that result. In terms of resistance to state intervention in social welfare and to the growth of collectivism in industrial relations they ostensibly failed, yet these trends have been accompanied by a persistent underlying individualism which continues to affect legislation and behaviour. Both the success and the failure tell us something about the emergent industrial relations system and the society within which it operated.

Wemyss's Liberty and Property Defence League, founded in 1882 when he was still Lord Elcho, had as its frame of reference an amalgam of *laissez-faire* economics, Herbert Spencer's extreme individualist philosophy and Whig fears of popular democracy. Its ethical system harmonised doctrines of evolution, natural selection, science, individual liberty, efficiency and progress. Elcho remained its mentor and major financial support until his death in 1914. Alexander Siemens was another charter member, and Lord Halsbury, who presided over the Lords sitting judicially on the occasion of the Taff Vale appeal, was a League sympathiser whose appointees during his period as Lord Chancellor 'displayed a noticeable free-contract bias' (Soldon, 1974, p. 224). Holding office for seventeen years between 1885 and 1905, Halsbury made thirty appointments to the High Court of which fourteen were politicians, ten of them Conservative – six of these being considered 'bad appointments' (Griffith, 1981, pp. 24–5).

By 1893 150 trade associations had affiliated to the league, including mining, shipping and licensed victuallers, but its individual membership never rose much above 2,000. Its wooing of the working man is, however, a reminder that Samuel Smiles had many admirers among organised as well as unorganised labour. 'Officers of friendly societies and co-operatives, policemen and soldiers, civil servants, thrifty workmen, and deacons of dissenting chapels were always profoundly conscious of the wickedness of the thriftless poor and were often more conservative than members of the Primrose League' (Soldon, 1974, pp. 210, 214, 215). Earlier, of course, alignments had seemed even less clear and this open situation had made it possible for Elcho, on the one hand, to see front-bench Liberal radicals, the Reform League, the Reform Union and the London Trades Council as an 'urban bloc determined to destroy the power of the landed aristocracy, its supportive institutions and the commonsense truths of Adam Smith and Samuel Smiles' and, on the other, to befriend Alexander Macdonald, president of the National Union of Miners, with whom he co-operated, along with the Glasgow Trades Council, to liberalise the Master and Servant law (Kauffman, 1974, pp. 184–5, 189).

The league's strategy of rallying opinion to its atomistic individualism, weakening trade unionism by encouraging the free labour movement and setting up free labour registries, and promoting a more punitive policy by the courts towards picketing, was supplemented by attempts to promote a sense of common interests and active co-operation at the workplace through co-partnership and profit-sharing. These aims were pursued through the Free Labour Protection Association; the Parliamentary Council; the league's unofficial journal, *Liberty Review*, edited by Fred-erick Millar, the league's secretary; and support for the Labour Co-Partnership Association, an 1884 foundation given this name in 1902. There were even hopes of a 'free, independent, unofficial, *bona-fide* Conservative Party in the House of Commons; Wemyss suggested Rose-bery as leader of an Independent-Individualist grouping (Soldon, 1974, p. 227).

These purposes attracted a widely varied assortment of supporters – landowners fearful of middle-class radicalism operating through the legislature, employers hoping to stem trade unionism and state interven-tionism, ideologues of individualism, and – in the field of co-partnership and profit-sharing – employers and others hoping to woo labour into a co-operative stance. The league also recruited Thomas Mackay, vice-chairman of the council of the Charity Organisation Society (COS), formed in 1869 'to reawaken the obligation to work among the poor who had been demoralized by an excess of impersonal charity'. During the 1870s COS ideas had become fairly widely accepted. Poverty was the result of character defects, and the administration of the poor law, now grown too lax and indulgent towards outdoor relief for the able-bodied, must be rigorously tightened to avoid weakening self-reliance. Mackay, who had absorbed Malthusian ideas about population and Spencerian ideas about a Darwinian struggle for existence, represented a considerable body of opinion inside and outside the COS when he denounced the drift away from the spirit of the 1834 Act as 'reactionary'. In his writings for the league he 'represented the face of the COS in an age of direct confrontation with collectivist and socialist ideology', urging a reconstructed individual-ism and a return to the minimal state (Mason, 1974, pp. 291, 294, 297–8).

The league attracted other formidable adherents, among them W. H. Mallock, its most vigorous pamphleteer, who wrote a forceful analysis of socialism emphasising the function of capitalist 'great men' as creators of wealth – and thereby of social stability (Ford, 1974, pp. 318, 319).

The league was far from monopolising its field. The British Constitution Association (BCA), formed in 1905 and also attracting an ultra-individualist amalgam of Spencerians, orthodox poor law administrators and Conservative free-traders, shared the league's hostility to state interventionism and its aim of fostering self-reliance (K. D. Brown, 1974, p. 239). Neither of these organisations satisfied those who formed the Anti-Socialist Union (ASU) in 1908 in response to the 1906 Liberal victory, the rise of the Labour Party, the Trade Disputes Act and the growth of social legislation. The ASU (with Mallock on its steering committee in 1907), likewise upheld self-reliance, thrift and individual responsibility, but made much play with the argument that the league and the BCA were too negative and were engendering socialism by their wholesale opposition to all proposals for the people's welfare. Despite this the ASU itself, funded by business and financial interests and brandishing banners which included social reform along with patriotism, empire and industrial peace, opposed almost all reform proposals. One of its very few positive policies was the encouragement of that favourite device of anti-union, anti-socialist campaigners – profit-sharing.

These and similar organisations, such as the Middle-Class Defence League (1906), which lasted only a few years, and the British Empire Union, heavily funded by business and finance and which had a much longer life, exerted no small propagandist effect. Their efforts were reinforced by other publicists such as William Lecky, whose *Democracy and Liberty* (1896) argued that a new type of working-class leadership was demanding further state restrictions on freedom of contract and trade, not, as earlier, out of humanitarian motives, but from a desire to reintroduce the restrictive and anti-individualistic economic organisation of the Middle Ages. This danger of a new feudalism arose from their 'ideal . . . to restrict by the strongest trade union regulation the amount of work . . . to introduce the principle of legal compulsion into every branch of industry, to give the trade union an absolute coercive power over its members, to attain a high average but to permit no superiorities' (O'Sullivan, 1976, p. 110). We may note here, in passing, the familiar phenomenon among social critics of the ever-receding golden age. In the 1980s observers refer back to the 1930s, when the unions pursued the noble task of defending the poor and weak; in the 1930s they cast back to pre-1914; in the 1890s the vision is falling back into an even more distant past. But what is significant about Lecky's writings is the way they exemplify the major change of direction in British Conservatism. Now that the Conservative enemy is no longer Liberalism but socialism, Conservatism begins to adopt and defend the liberal values and ideology it had formerly opposed and Lecky views with dread the very medieval structures for which Coleridge and Carlyle expressed so much nostalgia half a century or more earlier.

Such interpretations told many people what they wanted to hear. They helped to sustain the individualism long present in Britain's culture and to some extent no doubt heightened middle-class feelings against socialism, trade unionism and social legislation – often seen as virtually synonymous. Yet during the period when all these individualist organisations were coexistent and active, social legislation took considerable strides forward, while trade unionism not only retained its liberating legislation but overcame the last obstacle in 1913 against the efforts of Lords Robert and Hugh Cecil, who personally financed the campaign of W. V. Osborne (by then chief clerk of the BCA) to prevent the legislative reversal of the Osborne judgement (Bristow, 1974,p. 284). Beatrice Webb's struggle, conducted through the Royal Commission on the Poor Law (1905–9), to secure wider recognition that unemployment and destitution owed far more to social structural causes than to individual moral weakness, received support in the Majority as well as in the Minority Report written by herself. The effective resistance to reform of the poor law system was less that of the BCA – regarded by the reformers as 'comparatively unimportant' – than that springing from the institutional interests of the existing Boards of Poor Law Guardians and from county councils who often had no wish to be saddled with 'onerous and expensive functions' (McBriar, 1966, pp. 267, 272). As for socialism, its failure to sweep the British working classes was certainly not due to the efforts of these organisations, which remained small and essentially marginal in their impact.

The reasons for their limited effectiveness were several. For one thing they proved unable to unite despite the similarity of their aims. Lord Robert Cecil tried in 1911 to amalgamate them into a Citizens' Union which would bid for mass support and become the 'centre' party that he wanted. There was a flurry of interest inside and outside Parliament, but the outcome fell far short of hopes and the idea was never as widely canvassed again (Bristow, 1974, p. 284). The fact was that any such loose federation of threatened interests offered no steady foundation for a political party; the messages they peddled were essentially negative and by their nature could hardly be otherwise. However appealing their ideals were in the abstract to businessmen, financiers, administrators and ideologues, they no longer met the practical needs of the big battalions or the problems and pressures with which institutions and political parties had increasingly to come to terms. Collectivism, regulation, mass organisation and attempts at mass manipulation were not arbitrary choices but responses to pressing practical constraints. Appeals to atomistic individualism, free contract and self-reliance might influence behaviour at the margins, but the basic shape and direction of social institutions and policies were being moulded by different forces.

Another reason for the failure to unite in what might have been a more effective political force is that the temper of the participants in these movements varied widely and the variations threw up conflicting emphases with respect to strategy and tactics. At one extreme were militant anti-socialists and anti-unionists of proven bellicosity who fought the class war openly and with gusto and relish, such as Sir George Livesey of the gas industry. At the other were fastidious aristocrats like Lord Robert Cecil, who told Austen Chamberlain, ' . . . you must remember that I was brought up to think that a class war, whether the class attacked be landowners or Labour, is the most insidious form of national disintegration' (Cowling, 1971, p. 60). Cecil's impulse was therefore towards class reconciliation rather than open and provocative challenges. This led him into, among other things, the strenuous advocacy of profit-sharing and co-partnership, an interest which he shared with pioneers of industrial welfare like Seebohm Rowntree and class warriors like Livesey. Cecil was active in the BCA which, along with the ASU and the Tariff Reform League, came out strongly for co-partnership during 1911–14. Mixed in a few cases with some rather more benign intentions, the central thrust behind such devices was the attempt to undermine or abort trade unionism by attaching workforce loyalty to the enterprise through profit bonuses. They met the suspicion, distrust and, in some cases, open hostility of trade unionists, socialist and non-socialist alike, and many schemes foundered on this alone. But even given a clear run the benefit for the employer in most cases was highly elusive. The bonus was too small, remote and uncertain to sustain increased commitment and there was a steadily high failure rate of over 50 per cent. Hope continued to spring eternal, but only a totally committed few could seriously believe that profit-sharing was a means whereby capital could significantly modify the industrial relations system in favour of the employers. Meanwhile, the distinction between the Cecilian strategy for preserving the status quo and the strategy of open and unabashed militancy against working-class organisations remained important and was to become massively so after the First World War, when the choice that was eventually made had the effect of determining the nature of Britain's industrial and class relations and much else besides.

One last comment may usefully be made about the organisations just examined. The core characteristics they shared of emphasising atomistic individualism, free contract and self-reliance led them to perform one function of great significance for the growth of Britain's institutions, not least its industrial relations system. They rallied many of the alarmed, disgruntled and worried elements among the rich and powerful not to a programme of authoritarian rule and state worship, but to the propagation of principles which were at the opposite extreme to such a programme. From the point of view of trade unionism, of the politicisation of the working classes, and of the enlargement of the state role in social amelioration, these organisations had nuisance value in that they promoted hostile propaganda and a hostile atmosphere, but they could not mobilise the resources for a destructive practical onslaught. That would have required the creation of a powerful authoritarian state, and on such an issue substantial numbers among their own membership would almost certainly have faltered. They served, therefore, rather as lightning conductors for fears and grievances which might have been harnessed to far more threatening social and political forces.

Yet although the atomistic individualism of Elcho and his kind was in process of becoming, for some practical purposes, anachronistic, it betokened, as we have seen, an interesting transfer of doctrines between parties. As many larger-scale property-owners of industry, commerce and finance moved over to the Conservative from the Liberal Party they took some of their old liberal-individualist doctrines with them, while the 'new' Liberalism showed increasing hospitality to collectivist principles. Given the growing collectivism among the working classes, liberal individualism became more and more important for many Conservatives as a positive differentiating ideology which both gave them something to say and served as a defensive principle against pressure for unwelcome social legislation. These dispositions had to coexist, however, with that long-standing and significant strand of opinion within the Conservative Party which, though fully committed to capitalism and to its property and class relations, feared the disintegrative effect upon the social bond of an excessively crude, predatory, individualistic capitalism which alienated the working classes and aggravated class conflict.

Paradoxically, it was this strand of opinion which nourished another set of movements, policies and ideas that offered a greater threat to the emerging industrial relations system than atomistic individualism. They were more threatening precisely because they were more consonant with the nature of the problems and pressures of the age. These were not of a kind that could be effectively grappled with or brought under control by reiterating slogans of atomistic individualism. The emergence of fiercely competitive foreign industrialisms, the struggle for world markets and raw materials, the widening of the electorate, the advance of large-scale labour organisations, the rise of socialism, the growth of parties, lobbies and pressure groups – these were the characteristics of a new social pattern: collectivist or 'mass' society which offered scope for new forms of political manipulation and new styles of political leadership.

It becomes relevant to our account at this point to note that the potential new styles of leadership included the possibility of creating a broad popular electoral base which might prove resistant to pendulum swings of favour. There appeared on the scene the vision of the great 'centre party' wielding permanent political power. It was a vision that was liable to present itself to a leader with the motivation, the appeal and ability to break out of established political conventions, prevailing party boundaries and accepted party programmes. Such permanent power could derive from his being able to attract and bring together a variety of widely disparate social and political forces, aspirations and grievances under a largely personal leadership, perhaps being enabled thereby to transcend parliamentary constraints and the pendulum of alternating party rule. Leadership of this kind, which might feel no attachment to any particular interest, doctrine, or class, could present a considerable threat to party, to sectional organisation, even to 'due process' and to the notion that a contained degree of institutionalised industrial and political conflict is inevitable, even desirable. The threat is the greater at times of crisis, emergency and tension when there is a widespread desire for strong leadership and when disagreements and conflicting interests can be presented as undermining 'national unity'.

It is instructive to note, in the light of this model, the attempts of Joseph Chamberlain and Lloyd George (and later Oswald Mosley). During the late nineteenth and early twentieth centuries there was offered to the British people by a wide diversity of publicists and prophets a range of policies and programmes that added up to an approximation to a British national socialism. Compared with the varieties since displayed elsewhere it was a muted and expurgated version. Nevertheless, had these policies and programmes made sufficiently widespread and strong appeal they could have engendered a head of political steam susceptible of being exploited by Chamberlain or, after his removal from the scene in 1906, by Lloyd George in 1910. Had this occurred, the future of the industrial relations system, of trade unionism and of its political expression would certainly have been different, whether to a greater or lesser degree is beyond judgement. Some attention should therefore be given to these ingredients of a modest national socialism, for in trying to trace why the British people in the main rejected them we can hope to gain further insight into the strength of their institutions and dispositions during this period.

Wider Challenges to the System: the Vision of Social Imperialism

It had been a flight of Disraelian rhetoric in 1872 which had set up the three great objects of the Tory Party as being 'to maintain the institutions of the country ... to uphold the Empire of England ... and to elevate the condition of the people'. The inclusion of empire was a marked departure from earlier Tory attitudes. It had been unwittingly prescient. The imperialism of the late nineteenth and early twentieth centuries was to be one major element in a wider movement of action and ideas within the powerful industrial nations which found brief or lasting favour according to the predominant traditions and institutional texture of the nation concerned. The long-term fruitfulness of Germany's social context for imperialism, militaristic nationalism and socialism has received ample attention. In America the imperialistic acquisition during 1898–9 of Hawaii, Cuba and the Philippines, bitterly and articulately opposed by an Anti-Imperialistic League, was accompanied by proclamations from an up-an-coming politican named Albert Beveridge to the effect that 'We are a conquering race. We must obey our blood and occupy new markets and if necessary new lands ... In the Almighty's infinite plan ... debased civilizations and decaying races' were to disappear 'before the higher civilization of the nobler and more virile types of man'. God has been preparing 'the English-speaking and Teutonic peoples for this mission for a thousand years' (Tuchman, 1980, pp. 153, 164).

The British people, too, during this period, were offered by a mixed bag of their fellows at different social levels a conception of their social and political future which contained similar ingredients. No doubt was left even at the time as to the model from which this conception was drawn. A number of prominent men of affairs were turning admiring though increasingly fearful eyes towards Imperial Germany, 'What modern democracy has to face', wrote Hobhouse in 1911, '... is no mere inertia of tradition' but 'a distinct reactionary policy with a definite and not inco-herent creed of its own', an 'ideal which in its best expression ... is certain to exercise a powerful attraction on many generous minds – the ideal of the efficient, disciplined nation, centre and dominating force of a powerful, self-contained, militant empire'. The vision came in several versions with differing emphases but, predominantly, held that the governing classes of Britain were to assert themselves; promote a comprehensive thrust towards national and industrial efficiency; re-establish the church through doctrinal education; consolidate and extend the empire; teach civilisation and the law to the 'sullen, new-caught peoples' abroad; bind the colonies to the mother country by ties of fiscal preference; establish the great industrial and commercial interests on the basis of tariff protection; apply the revenue from this trading policy to finance programmes of domestic social welfare; and further consolidate the attachment of the working classes with factory acts and regulatory wage boards, meanwhile rigor-ously playing down both practically and ideologically any conception of class conflict. Thereby they would ensure social stability, undercut social-ism and rear a healthy imperial racial stock. 'They were to make an efficient and a disciplined people. In the idea of discipline the military element rapidly assumed a greater prominence' (Hobhouse, 1911, pp. 215–17).

Many different strands of interest and conviction contributed to, sup-plemented, or modified this broad conception. The most powerful thrust was in response to Britain's declining economic strength relatively to Germany and America. Joseph Chamberlain, in his crucial 1903 speech on Tariff Reform and Imperial Preference, was among other things respond-ing to the profit needs of the industrial Midlands, threatened by foreign, especially German, competition. His reason, according to some observers, for breaking with Gladstone in 1886 over Home Rule for Ireland and taking the Birmingham Liberals into the Conservative Party had been that Home Rule threatened the loss of still another market to hard-pressed British manufacturers (Semmel, 1960, p. 85). That social imperialism, with its combination of tariff reform, a managed economy integrated with empire markets, and social welfare legislation, should derive one of its major sources of inspiration from Birmingham was not simply a result of the political personality of Joseph Chamberlain. The area had long been characterised by small-scale industrial structure and organi-sation of a kind which had so far precluded militant trade unionism and facilitated a considerable measure of vertical bonding between master and artisan, who often shared also a strong Liberal Nonconformity. Traditions had been created which survived to support the arch-social-imperialist, Leo Amery, in his Birmingham seat for thirty-four years from his entry into Parliament in 1911. They survived, too, to give the area special significance in terms of support for Mosley in the parliamentary Labour Party in the early 1930s (Skidelsky, 1967, p. 274). Amery himself was later to expound a quasi-fascist corporatism.

Meanwhile, however, Chamberlain's public nailing of colours to the mast in 1903 produced equally public division between protectionist and free trade imperialisms. These corresponded broadly, on the one hand, to the imperialism of some less secure sections of industry which sought stable markets and raw materials and, on the other, to the imperialism of sections which made more confident assessments, together with the imperialism of finance, which needed, for the most part, full freedom of international payments in and out of London in the form of dividends and interest; shipping and insurance commissions; capital and money market fees. The issue was whether national policy should 'aim to maximise the opportunities and the returns for British companies, banks, and workers by maintaining the greatest possible degree of openness to the world economy, or whether it should be subordinated to a national assessment by public agencies of British interests, British welfare and British security' (Gamble, 1981, p. 170). The distinction barely made sense in Germany, where finance capital was virtually taking over industrial capital, but in Britain it created powerful allies for the Liberal cause of free trade, which was to remain a strong force in British politics for another thirty years. Financial interests were, therefore, represented by the Liberal Imperialists – Rosebery, Asquith, Haldane, Grey – who, according to Beatrice Webb, were 'desperately in awe of the City'.

Beatrice herself, along with Sidney and some other, though far from all, Fabians, came to be persuaded about tariffs after their previous attachment to free trade (McBriar, 1966, ch. 5). They were prepared to see either Rosebery or Chamberlain lead the new political thrust they had in mind. Since their preoccupations were chiefly domestic until 1913 their vision took concrete form largely in this field. The vision was essentially corporatist, in one sense of that diffuse term, and envisaged unions, employers and state coming together in a collaborative, problem-solving alliance for the modernisation of British industry – a vision not unlike that offered by Scientific Management, especially as shaped by German social structures and traditions. They wanted

> to invite the larger unions, the captains of industry, and the bureaucratic state to conclude a species of *concordat*. They called upon the workers to abandon all regulations or claims made by their unions which in any way hampered the progress of machinery, and upon the employers to accept in return the principle of a regulation of labour which might extend to the legal enactment of a minimum wage, and they urged both alike to get rid of their liberal prejudices and submit to the authority of the State whose protection they enjoyed. It was a 'Prussian' rather than a revolutionary programme. (Halévy, 1961, p. 230)

This or something comparable was widespread among the social imperialists, who saw tariff-financed social welfare as eliminating class conflict and thereby enabling all social levels to transcend the petty strife of liberal political economy and work together for 'national' ends.

The fear of open, organised class conflict and of 'confiscatory socialism' played an important part in much social imperialist thinking. Leo Amery, a committed and passionate expositor of that thinking, offers a good example of the logic. The basic belief was that, in a world economy increasingly invaded by efficient and predatory rivals who employed protectionist policies, Britain would not be able to maintain the necessary economic growth if she remained committed to free trade and *laissez-faire* individualism. From this great dangers sprang. The working classes were increasingly organising themselves, industrially and politically. A regressive or even stationary economy with 'heavy and continuous unemployment' would not be able to meet their demands without the imposition of an ever-growing burden of taxation and public support which would weaken economic incentive, evoke resistance from the well-to-do and sharpen class conflict. 'The one thing I dreaded . . . ' was 'a political cleavage based on class, on the desire for the material gain of one class of the community at the expense of others and of the banding together of those others in defence of their possessions'. The grimness of this prospect for Amery and others of his class who thought like him was that if, as they assumed, political democracy remained, an organised working class driven into alienation and class conflict was bound to win 'by sheer numbers in the end'. 'If my long political life has had any meaning it has lain in my constant struggle to keep the Tory Party true to a policy of Imperial greatness and social progress, linked with a definite economic creed of its own, and to prevent it drifting into becoming the party of a mere negative *laissez-faire* anti-Socialism' (Amery, 1953, pp. 254–5). For this reason, along with others, the economy must be kept fully employed and progressive. Some of the elements in this structure of thinking were to play a decisive role in postwar politics and to shape the predominant long-term Conservative Party policy towards the industrial relations system.

The Webbs, with their hankering after Prussian efficiency and strong leadership, went a long way with the social imperialist vision. They shared with Bernard Shaw a 'lofty and public-spirited Imperialism' which, while excluding the vulgarities – and worse – of jingoism and exploitation, would carry the 'higher civilization' of Western Europe to the 'lower', 'backward' – and especially the smaller – nations. Beatrice, with her fierce, fastidious puritanism, echoed a mood of revulsion, shared by others, against what they felt to be a widespread overpreoccupation with the flesh-pots. 'To us', she wrote in 1900, 'public affairs seem gloomy; the middle classes are materialistic, and the working class stupid, and in large sections, sottish, with no interest except in racing odds, while the government of the country is firmly in the hands of little cliques of landlords and great capitalists, and their hangers-on.' Amateurism, the neglect of science, absence of national purpose, the failure to secure the breeding of any better stock than those 'myriads of deficient minds and deformed bodies that swarm in our great cities' (B. Webb, 1948, p. 83) – all this was no way to achieve the necessary national regeneration and the breeding of an imperial race, with its high moral qualities and lofty-spirited duties. Darwin's conclusions, declared Sidney Webb, did not reinforce individualism and *laissez-faire*, rather they demanded the planned evolution of human society, through state initiative and organisation – dimensions along which, for Webb, Germany was demonstrating its superiority (Bowle, 1963, pp. 422–3).

Such views had their strong adherents in government departments. Among them was the young W. H. (later Sir William, eventually Lord) Beveridge (Balliol and Toynbee Hall), who by 1905, when he entered the

Board of Trade, was already a leading figure in London social administration. The setting for his convictions was his imperialist belief that the 'progressive' nations must increasingly dominate the underdeveloped. Liberalism and democracy were not the appropriate creeds for this destiny. The individualism of the former was often selfish, whereas what was needed was a system (which he called 'socialism') that 'would simply subordinate the interests of individuals to those of the nation at large'. This could only be done by a strong and 'remorselessly unsentimental government' which gave more power to non-elected experts. Expressing what became a lifelong mistrust of all forms of direct democracy, Beveridge declared his belief in a centralised, enlightened and impartial administrative state. But national progress required national social cohesion, and this called for a social policy which minimised political and class conflict and fostered feelings of identification with a benevolent state. The working class, especially, must be deliberately integrated into the system by, among other things, profit-sharing, but also by reforms devised not piecemeal but in a 'grand design of welfare'. By such measures as minimising unemployment and eliminating overwork the state would be defending the future of the race (J. Harris, 1977, pp. 64–107).

Beveridge was influenced, practically, by his study of the social institutions of Imperial Germany, and theoretically – though he professed a deep suspicion of theory – by T. H. Huxley and the Spencerian conception of social evolution. Yet some of his central dispositions struck sympathetic chords with current criticism of Spencerian individualism. The Cobdenite ethics of self-interest, and the Spencerian principle of a progressive identification of individual self-interest and the interest of society, found prominent critics among publicists, theorists and active men of affairs whose leanings found philosophical underpinning in works by neo-Hegelians like Bosanquet. 'The English neo-Hegelians . . . refused to regard society as a mere collection of individuals. Far from it being true that society existed in virtue of individuals and for their sake, individuals existed only in virtue of society and for the sake of society – that is to say, in so far as society was the embodiment of the ideal ends – science, art, religion, whose pursuit alone gave value to the individual' (Halévy, 1961d, p. 18).

Contributing to the same theme were Social Darwinists, who saw progress as the outcome of an evolutionary competitive struggle not between individuals, as Herbert Spencer had seen it, but between groups, tribes, races, or nations. Benjamin Kidd's *Social Evolution* (1894), which ran to nineteen editions in four years, argued that the quality bringing superiority and victory over rivals was not reason, a critical and destructive faculty, serving only as the instrument of self-seeking individualism, but faith, which inspired social discipline, devotion to duty and readiness to subordinate individual interests to the larger national and racial needs. Karl Pearson, who had studied in Germany, was a national socialist who urged 'veneration for the State', eulogised class unity in the interests of a homogeneous nation organised for struggle, sought the application of eugenic ideas to raise the quality of the racial stock, and regarded war as a contribution to the evolutionary weeding out (Semmel, 1960, pp. 34–43).

Both Kidd and Pearson were influenced by Hegel, and their disparagement of democratic institutions and procedures expressed in extreme
form attitudes which often lay barely beneath the surface in many others
responding to the mood.

The myth of race found influential followers. John Ruskin, lecturing at
Oxford in 1869, had been among those who preached a new expansionist
vision of empire bearing strong racial overtones. Cecil Rhodes, one of his
hearers, helped to extend the vision towards 'the extreme racial faith of
subsequent generations of imperialists, personified by Alfred Milner and
Leo Amery'; a faith which included the notion of inescapable 'responsibility and toil' (Rhodes James, 1978, pp. 24, 25). 'Powerful groups in
Germany and England', where 'the concept of race, conjoined with
imperialism, rose to a peak', adopted 'the arguments of the racial theorist
to suit their own political ends'. Rhodes, Rosebery, Chamberlain, and
others propagated the Anglo-Saxon race myth with its semi-mystical
destiny of world duties to perform (Hayes, 1973, pp. 24–5).

H. G. Wells, who was caught up both socially and politically in these
movements of opinion, offers an involved-observer's portrait of the times
in his novel, *The New Machiavelli*, published in 1911.

> There were some very fine personalities among them: there were the
> great peers who had administered Egypt, India, South Africa . . .
> Cromer, Kitchener, Curzon, Milner . . . for example . . . They wanted
> to arm and they wanted to educate, but the habit of immediate necessity
> made them far more eager to arm than to educate, and their exper-
> ience of heterogeneous controls made them overrate the need for
> obedience . . .

He portrays 'men of all parties' forming a dining club to 'discuss the
welfare of the Empire in a disinterested spirit', and notes of those whom he
came to know best that they were 'very keen on military organisation,
and with a curious little martinet twist in their minds that boded ill for that
side of public liberty' (Wells, 1946, pp. 246–7, 268). The evidence supports
him. Milner has been described as not 'a democrat at all, but a despot and an
ideologue, who could be enlightened yet also at times dangerously
limited' (Grigg, 1973, p. 257). He revealed his contempt for parliamentary
democracy in phrases which carry an ominous ring for Western twentieth-
century liberals. British party politics were 'rotten', involving 'weakness
and compromise' (Pakenham, 1982, p. 64). Amery was ever critical of the
'general individualist fallacy' which assumed that 'individuals know better
than the State what is in their own interest' and that 'the common interest
will be best served if they are allowed to exercise their individual economic
activities without interference by the State'. As against this, Amery argued
that the 'object of all legislation, in fact, in the economic field, as in any
other, is to influence the individual so as to make his interest and his
activities coincide with the public interest' (Amery, 1953, pp. 247–8).
Those whose conception of 'the public interest' might not coincide with
Amery's might well be alert to an authoritarian strain in the new currents
of thought. The Webbs themselves, though careful in their written work

to emphasise the indispensability of popular control, cherished a worship of the centralised, bureaucratic, professional expert which pressed hard against their acknowledgement of the democratic decencies. Their portrayal by Wells as Oscar and Altiora Bailey in *The New Machiavelli* has Oscar, 'glib and winking, explaining that democracy was really just a dodge for getting assent to the ordinances of the expert official by means of the polling booth' (Wells, 1946, p. 256). It is a plausible picture. Shaw's – and some other Fabians' – growing doubts about democracy and his espousal of the Superman notion are well known and he, along with the Webbs, came to look with deep admiration upon the USSR (MacKenzie and MacKenzie, 1979, pp. 406–8).

As is already evident, militarism was a frequent element in the picture, albeit of a far more restrained kind than its German counterpart. Even the Fabians, with their careful rejection of jingoism, favoured compulsory military service to promote 'the growth of social consciousness'. Lord Roberts, popular hero of the relief of Ladysmith, established the National Service League in 1901 and in 1904 took up the campaign for a mild form of conscription. In a letter to *The Times* in 1911 he expressed his social imperialist creed. 'The conditions amid which millions of our people are living appear to me to make it natural that they should not care a straw under what rule they may be called upon to dwell, and I can well understand their want of patriotic feeling.' He demanded education in patriotism, order, obedience and discipline, but argued that the country could appeal to men to do their duty with far more confidence if within the nation and empire they could live nobler and fuller lives than elsewhere (Semmel, 1960, p. 221). The league had 200,000 members and adherents in 1914, drawn from the ranks of Conservatives, Anglicans, Orange and Tory working men. Its more ambitious members such as Milner 'saw the League as a potential vehicle for a new Bismarckian politics in Britain'. They called for conscription because this demand 'was subversive of old notions of liberal individualism, and involved the subordination of the individual to the collective interest as represented by the state' (Summers, 1976, pp. 114, 116–17).

Certain leading academics combined a number of these ideas. A few days after a group of prominent economists – including Marshall, Bowley, Edgeworth, Pigou and Cannan – had denounced the Chamberlain programme in *The Times* in 1903, H. S. Foxwell drew its readers' attention to the fact that 'with scarcely an exception, the historical group of English economists declined to sign the manifesto'. Shortly after, the leading economic historians, one by one, announced their adherence to tariff reform and their support of Chamberlain's campaign. W. J. Ashley, a disciple of the German historical school, had close ties with members of the *Verein für Sozialpolitik*, with its rejection of Manchester individualism and its reliance on the state as guardian of the national welfare. He argued that trusts and cartels were necessary for the national economic interest and, in a 'characteristically German' way, linked protection and social reform (Hayes, 1973, p. 98). W. Cunningham, of Cambridge, anti-union and anti-Semitic, was greatly influenced by Germany in his ideas about order, discipline and anti-individualist methods of strengthening the state's power internally against particularist institutions and externally against other states (Semmel, 1960, pp. 150, 202–3). Holding a conservative conception of a strongly unified state founded on a modernised version of what he saw as Tudor and Stuart paternalism, he also displayed 'the xenophobia which was so characteristic of those who supported nationalist economies' and 'was not afraid of being called a chauvinist militarist or rabid nationalist'. Both Ashley and Cunningham came to advocate economic self-sufficiency and a species of state socialism; Ashley being described by Schumpeter as closer 'than any other English economist to the German professional type of that time' (Hayes, 1973, pp. 97–8). Another academic, W. A. S. Hewins, whom Sidney Webb had chosen in 1895 as the first director of the new London School of Economics, resigned in 1903 to become secretary to the Tariff Commission which was to develop and organise Chamberlain's propaganda. Even more prominent in the movement was H. J. (later Sir Halford) Mackinder, the Oxford geographer, who was also favoured by Webb later with the directorship of the LSE. Mackinder, a 'Bismarckian Darwinist of the purest Milnerian water' (J. Harris, 1977, p. 264) began as a Liberal free trade imperialist prepared to accept that while the relative importance of industry might decline the role of the City could continue to grow. In 1903, convinced that a day of reckoning with Germany must come, he switched to Tariff Reform imperialism, adopted the doctrines of the protectionist economist, Friedrich List, took up the Anglo-Saxon race myth, and urged the need for 'a great and efficient population' (Semmel, 1960, pp. 168–9, 173). Others fed into this same general conception ideas about the desirability of encouraging early marriage and large families, along with the need to promote the people's effectiveness for industrial or military pursuits.

Few came to combine certain of these ideas in a more unorthodox combination than Robert Blatchford, ex-army NCO turned journalist and propagandist, who founded the socialist Clarion movement with all its many off-shoots – glee clubs, cycling clubs, rambling clubs, clarion scouts, and many more. His book, *Merrie England* (1893), far outsold any other socialist work of the time with its wide popular appeal and his weekly, *The Clarion*, not only appealed to 'intelligent artisans . . . with a craving to "improve" themselves' but also 'made its mark on a whole generation of M.P.s, town councillors, journalists, clergymen, moulders of public opinion in the years before . . . the First World War' (L. Thompson, 1951, p. 130). Blatchford's socialism was compounded of deep ambivalences. Susceptible to the tug of conflicting ideas, visions and principles, he could strike resonances with a very varied audience. Hatred of the gross inequalities of wealth, power and life chances surrounding him existed alongside deep respect for the hierarchical order, discipline and efficiency that he saw in Germany. Hankerings for peace and a cosy Little Englandism struggled with pride in the empire, with a determination to defend it against rivals, and with a longing to see for this purpose a regenerated nation. Admiration for Germany, a nation of patriotic soldiers ruled by an autocrat, vied with exasperated love for his own country of unpatriotic 'divided, ragamuffin democrats' who did 'not want to pay', did 'not want to drill', and did 'not want to fight' (ibid., p. 214). An earlier opposition to conscription because he did not trust the ruling classes gave way to approval of it because he did not trust the lower ones. As he moved into the twentieth century, and particularly after 1906, Blatchford's pronouncements hardened out in favour of social imperialism and against the kind of socialism favoured by many of his readers on the left, who moved away in consequence. But for a while, until the imperialist mood itself waned, he continued to speak for those attracted by his dislike of 'Manchesterism' and free trade; the factory system and its destruction of the 'balanced' economic structure of 'old England'; liberal cosmopolitanism and its parliamentarism and party system; pacifism and its resistance to heavy rearmament.

These examples illustrate the development during this period of a set of economic and political forces, and an array of economic and political ideas, which together constituted something approximating to an incipient, indigenous national socialism with exponents and adherents at all social levels. 'By the early years of the twentieth century, a form of economic national socialism had secured a firm grip on a large section of the intellectual community and in some cases had even caught the imagination of the general public' (Hayes, 1973, p. 97).

Both Chamberlain and Lloyd George were fired by the possibility of forging out of these diverse ferments a new mass following of interests, ideals and moods from all classes; a following roused by a synthesis which transcended present party programmes and which, because it offered a 'national' perspective, might retain a national long-term stability – and long-term power for its leaders. Chamberlain was removed from the scene by paralysis in 1906, but Lloyd George two years later made a visit to Germany where 'the striking achievement of Bismarckian social legislation deeply impressed him', as did 'the emerging military might of Germany, and the way in which its national strength was directly related to an enlightened welfare programme'. In 1910 he made his 'extraordinary proposal for an all-party coalition', which would unify the empire for both commerce and defence, introduce compulsory national training, promote the state role in assistance to trade and commerce, develop agriculture, and deal with education, housing, unemployment, national insurance, drink, the poor law and other matters affecting 'the health, the vitality, the efficiency, and the happiness of the individuals ... that dwell in these islands'. The scheme illustrated Lloyd George's 'illusory passion for a transcendent national synthesis that would soar above partisan strife – the kind of grandiose vision of leadership that attracted him to Joseph Chamberlain in his youth, later on to the "New Nationalism" of Theodore Roosevelt in the United States, later still to Milner's Prussian "efficiency", and in the 1930s to ... Hitler'. Some leading members of both parties were attracted, but the 'English political culture, and its deep-rooted alignments, would not be extinguished by the blandishments of the Welsh apostle of coalitions, and Lloyd George's plan abruptly failed' (Morgan, 1978, pp. 43, 47, 48, 150–6). Issues that he dismissed as non-partisan were in fact intensely controversial, being bound up with decades of traditional conflict and genuine cleavages of interest and opinion. The structure of party boundaries, loyalties and interests therefore survived Lloyd George's attempt to subvert them.

The Conservative leadership had reason to be wary, and not only on account of Lloyd George's demagogical, populist past. A divergence between traditional paternalist Toryism and economic liberalism was now built into the Conservative following, and this, quite apart from anything else, was bound to arouse conflicting responses to any such 'national synthesis' as was now being mooted. It was often a divergence of emphasis rather than of clear-cut differences and many people combined within themselves features of both sets of dispositions. One set stressed the value of individualism, competition, the market principle in all spheres of life, rolling back the encroachments of the state, self-reliance and self-help, individual liberty, a punitive approach to society's casualties and losers, and a policy of ever seeking to combat and weaken organised labour and disparage its leaders. The other set derived from the conviction that all these dispositions, if applied too overtly, emphatically, or blatantly, were potentially dangerous for social cohesion and ultimately therefore for property and order, especially since the ruling class had so far committed itself to political liberalism and the numbers game. They needed to be moderated as occasion demanded by the necessary measure of collect-ivism, protectionism, mitigation of competition and the market principle, readiness to compromise on certain expressions of individual liberty, a somewhat less harsh response towards poverty, and a rather more accom-modating stance towards organised labour, not to mention better manners towards its leaders.

The first set of dispositions was to be forcefully expressed by leading members of the Coalition government of 1919–22 and to be among the reasons why the Conservative Party withdrew from the Coalition, thereby ushering in the Baldwin regime which moderated the expression of those dispositions during the interwar period. They were to assert themselves intermittently after the 1950s and finally to receive their verbal apotheosis under the Thatcher administration. For the time being, however, they were restrained by a Conservative stance which still hoped to deprive the Liberal Party of its working-class vote, but found many reasons, soon to be examined, for not embracing a thorough-going social imperialist programme, still less a national socialist one.

Despite, therefore, the existence in Britain of some of the elements of a national socialism, elements promoted by many influential voices, they never became fused under a sufficiently powerful leadership group with strong economic and political backing. No existing set of economic, social or political grievances or aspirations were of a scale great and intense enough to gather up these elements in a flood-tide and to use and be used by them in a common campaign under a common banner. It would certainly have required a major struggle of revolutionary proportions, aided by many powerful allies at the very top, to carry through what was seen by its exponents as a comprehensive programme of national eff-iciency and reconstruction. The fact however, that there was no body of grievances or aspirations sufficiently powerful and desperate to provide the engine for such a programme should not be taken to imply that this would have been a sufficient condition for its fulfilment. Given the distinct nonchalance revealed by some of its prominent adherents towards democratic institutions it would have met keen resistance along that dimension alone, and not only from working-class and radical organisations. Had it been successful, however, in transcending the existing party structure, the political stage would certainly have offered room for policies, values and personalities which might well have presented the Labour movement with unfamiliar and difficult challenges. The industrial relations system could scarcely have remained unaffected.

To point to Lloyd George's failure prompts a further stage of questioning. What were the resistances offered by British society to the various individual ingredients of this national socialist vision – economic protectionism, imperialism, militarism, a dynamic drive to eliminate class conflict and maximise industrial efficiency? Pursuit of this question raises central issues about the British working classes as well as other social strata during this period – their attitudes to their society, their employers, and each other. It also introduces a long-standing debate about the motivations of the employers themselves. Finally, it leads to an examination of the way in which some of the sources of the impulses towards imperialism, national efficiency and more authoritarian rule also, paradoxically, fostered impulses which helped to humanise the industrial scene and legitimise and support trade unionism and collective bargaining.

Resistances to the Vision: Economics and Race

Some of the resistances were generated out of long-standing characteristics of the British political and social scene; others arose from more fortuitous circumstances. The timing of Chamberlain's protectionist campaign proved to be inopportune. With the country just about to begin its last and greatest campaign of capital export, protectionist pessimism about short-run prospects for the British economy were falsified. Even given the usual cyclical setbacks, the fortunes of the great staple industries – coal, cotton, wool, heavy engineering and shipbuilding, all with a considerable dependence on exporting – showed through to 1914 a buoyancy which subdued protectionist arguments about underlying weaknesses. Given that there were powerful sectors of the economy which, in and out of season, were committed, by the nature of their interests, to free trade – such as the City – the cause of protection needed to be able to call upon a strong and determined impetus from other sectors if it was to mobilise decisive economic power behind the political campaign. As yet, however, the relevant big battalions were too engrossed in profitable business.

On the political level the cause was certainly in need of powerful allies since it faced considerable opposition. 'To the officials of the Liberal Party and the leaders of Nonconformity and trade unionism', the organised working class and the internationalist socialists of the Independent Labour Party, free trade remained 'something more than a scientific conclusion', rather was it 'a sacred tradition invested with a sentimental and semi-religious halo, like the kindred principles of peace, liberty, and the brotherhood of man' (Halévy, 1961d, p. 343). These were the forces which brought the massive 1906 electoral victory to the Liberals, still in power in 1914; a victory in which the free trade issue was a major factor.

Even if the industrial forces behind protectionism had been strong enough, and we assume their ability to translate economic power into political terms, there is no guarantee that they could have found common cause with tariff reformers when the time came to define practical policies. Mackinder and Hewins, for example, offered economic benefit only in some vague long run, if at all, and thought rather in terms of the political stability and defensive power of the empire (ibid., p. 349). Political victory over the principle would have promptly been followed, on the practical and concrete level, by arguments with protectionist manufacturers interested only in the profit and loss account.

Other elements of the potential national socialism package faced no easier a run. Opposition to racialist ideas came from scientists, traditional Conservatives, and radical and socialist groups, and was much stronger and more articulate than in Germany, where the voices of traditionalist liberals were raised in vain (Hayes, 1973, p. 26). Nevertheless, it is worth noting that within the organised Labour movement in Britain there existed a latent racialism which sometimes became manifest and which might have been susceptible to large-scale mobilisation had economic and social circumstances favoured it. In the general election of 1900, held during the South African war, the 'anti-semitic campaign instigated by Lloyd George was eagerly echoed by John Burns and Keir Hardie. Burns declared that the British Army had become "the janissary of the Jews", and he, Hardie, and eighty-one executive officers of the trade union movement signed a resolution that blamed the war not only on the capitalists and the press, but on the fact that they were "largely Jews and foreigners"' (Rhodes James, 1978, p. 201).

Resistances to the Vision: Imperialism and Militarism

In the event, neither racialism nor imperialism became caught up in any specifically 'national' movement. The former remained for the most part relatively subdued; the latter did not destroy party boundaries but was contained as an important element in both. Though it was a central feature, in fact, of Conservative faith and an influential force in the Liberal Party, the material and moral shocks of the South African war greatly weakened it as a cause capable of rousing the nation. Conservative governments 'had pursued too systematically the policy of diverting popular feeling to imperial questions. The British public was heartily weary of their policy of national honour and expensive victory, and this weariness ... contributed ... powerfully to the Liberal victory of 1906 ...' (Halévy, 1961e, p. 52). Most trade union leaders and activists, whether under the influence of socialism or of the older Liberalism, had always been deeply distrustful of foreign adventuring, and the Independent Labour Party and the Social Democratic Federation were ardently anti-imperialist. The Webbs, with their high-toned imperialism, spoke for the most part to the middle-class intelligentsia. But relevant here are not only the policies of small socialist minorities and organisational leaderships, but also what can be gleaned of the dispositions of the wider rank and file working class. Historians are at variance. Price, for example, is concerned to refute the opinion that the Boer War revealed any significant working-class 'attachment' to imperialism, claiming to detect apathy instead (Price, 1972). Pelling, too, argues that 'whatever spontaneous and temporary enthusiasm developed in the course of the South African war, there is no evidence of a direct continuous support for the cause of Imperialism among any sections of the working class' (Pelling, 1979, p. 99).

Blanch, on the other hand, offers evidence for believing 'that imperialism and nationalist sentiment obtained real roots in working-class opinion, in Birmingham at least' (Blanch, 1979, p. 119). Roberts offers impressionistic personal evidence about working-class Salford: 'Compulsory state education had been introduced with overt propagation of the imperialist idea: especially was this so after 1880', and 'once instructed . . . the indigent remained staunchly patriotic'. Unsure whether the empire was good for trade or trade good for the empire, they nevertheless 'knew the Empire was theirs and they were going to support it' (R. Roberts, 1973, pp. 143–4). He notes the jingoistic and chauvinistic propaganda of popular newspapers which 'filtered into lower-working-class minds, already imbued with the imperialistic teachings of school days, and found enthusiastic welcome there . . . Our district, like all industrial ghettoes, showed itself immensely patriotic . . . ' (ibid., pp. 142–4, 179–81). Rudé's judgement is that imperialism gave many British workers a sense of security and superiority over their fellow-workers overseas' (Rudé, 1980, p. 163).

Yet the precise nature of this patriotism needs examination. Anderson agrees that 'the existence, maintenance and constant celebration of the Empire affected all classes and institutions in Britain; it could not have done otherwise . . . A general internalization of the prestations and motifs of Empire undoubtedly occurred'. But this 'did not necessarily mean that the working class became in any direct sense committed to imperialism'. Contrary to the Marx/Engels attempt to trace a systematic relationship between imperialism and the 'opportunism' of the British Labour movement, Anderson argues that it is 'very doubtful whether the working class of this period benefited materially from colonial exploitation'. The primary impact of imperialism was at the level of consciousness. 'The British working class was not in any profound sense mobilized *for* imperialism . . . but it was, undeniably, deflected *from* undistracted confrontation with the class exploiting it' (Anderson, 1965, pp. 22–4, italics in original).

Among the more important indications that the working class was not 'in any profound sense' mobilised for imperialism was that imperialist consciousness did little to change popular – or for that matter official – dispositions towards militarism, an issue of great significance for imperialists, as we have noted. The tradition of the free-born Englishman had always contained elements of chauvinism and insular disparagement of foreigners: these were now inflated by the knowledge of British rule over all that was red on the map. But the free-born Englishmen had also shown no respect for official militarism and this feature, too, remained. Imperialism created no mass love for warrior virtues which could be exploited by politicians seeking to promote a spirit of national efficiency, purpose, pride and assertion. Kipling and Blatchford knew and publicly bemoaned the fact that the army was still far from being the admired and privileged caste that it was in Germany. In some measure it remained outside society; uniforms were rarely seen and military bands rarely heard. Enthusiasts for a larger military establishment 'were treated with a kind of indulgent contempt by the influential sections of government and society', and constituted no more than an eccentric fringe. Although there were moods of militarist excitement, 'on the whole the public never accepted for any lengthy period the argument that it was necessary for England to be armed to the teeth and to inculcate military virtues in all her able-bodied citizens' (Hayes, 1973, pp. 78, 86). The moderation of Lord Roberts' proposal for military training 'did not exempt it from ... the hostility arising from the widespread feeling among all classes that conscription was somehow "un-British"' (Semmel, 1960, p. 216). The National Service League had no electoral presence, met professional opposition in many quarters of the government, army and navy, and found little support in either of the parties.

Even more revealing is the fact that alongside, and at one time in opposition to, official militarism there had long existed a popular militarism whose nature is worth noting. 'Liberal, popular, and independent', 'utterly different from Prussianism', this was an integral part of the liberal political culture and integral also to much of Anglican and Nonconformist Christianity. It was to be found in such organisations as the National Service League itself and in the Volunteer Force, precursor of the Territorial Army. This popular militarism was not about fighting and killing, but about fellowship and citizenship, physical and spiritual exercise, social control and industrial performance. The failure of the league's day-to-day practice and propaganda to emulate the fierce German professional tradition irritated Milner intensely and he can hardly have been reassured by the Volunteer Force. At least 70 per cent of its membership came from the working class, and in many places its rank and file were 'drawn more from unionised and unionising trades than from those ... which might be thought to embody deferential attitudes and aspirations towards gentility'. This voluntary movement had come to play an important part in social and recreational life, and earlier the popular enthusiasm for militarism as a sporting pastime had often gone 'hand in hand with a deep aversion to the forces of the Crown'. Especially in mid-Victorian years it had been underpinned by a strong liberal, even radical, commitment. Here, in fact, was a radical patriotism which extended back to the seventeenth century and was to find forward echoes in mid-twentieth-century Orwellian socialism. 'Many Volunteers felt that their weekly drill sessions served an anti-authoritarian, or at least an anti-aristocratic cause . . . ', and it was politically possible and respectable 'to preach the ideal of a citizenry united in defence of the homeland while simultaneously decrying the imperialistic adventures of the Regular Army'. Beneath the surface an even older tradition had currency and meaning. 'The literary revival of interest in Oliver Cromwell at the end of the century is evidence of the deep continuity of nonconformist and radical memories and images of militarism.'

By now attitudes within popular militarism were in some respects changing with a shift from evangelism and Nonconformity to a greater respect for professionalism and the beginnings of an acceptance of the army as 'a truly national institution' (Summers, 1976, pp. 105–21). Yet the resistances remained strong. Popular militarism remained staunchly liberal, and Roberts declares of pre-1914 Salford that 'with us, as with the rest of the working class, "regulars", ex-regulars and their families stayed unquestionably "low"' (R. Roberts, 1973, p. 181). And the attitudes at all social levels towards conscription have already been noted. Politicians who looked hopefully for a sustained upsurge of militarism which could be harnessed for 'national' ends by 'national' leadership found little in all this to encourage them.

Nor was the state educational system apparently doing anything to remedy these deficiences. 'The young man or woman', wrote a 'German Resident' to the *National Review* in June 1905, 'leaves the primary school in England with no idea of duty, and no knowledge . . . that war is still one of the means by which the progress of the race is maintained'. Social imperialists were only too ready to agree that the British people were failing to respond to the call, and that this betokened an inability to rise above purely personal ends. There was much talk of 'lack of moral purpose and conviction', of the absence of 'steady individual sacrifice for the attainment of a common end', of the inability to 'generate any real spirit of every-day devotion to the common good' (Shadwell, 1909, p. 658). The industrial fortunes of Germany were linked in the eyes of contemporary observers to its educational system – not only in its 'inculcation of the requisite skills at all levels for industrial progress' but also in its instilling of 'a sense of duty, a national will and determination' (Roderick and Stephens, 1978, p. 158). 'Milner was indeed right to come to the conclusion that democracy was no way to run an Empire' (Pelling, 1979, p. 100).

Resistances to the Vision: Industrial Efficiency

If social imperialists felt frustrated by the persistence of widespread convictions about free trade, and disappointed by the failure of the British people to translate such emotions as they might derive from imperialism and racial pride into practical support for militarism, conscription and national purpose, they were hardly likely to be compensated by evidence of working-class readiness to respond to the appeal for greater industrial efficiency. Evidence suggests rather that the tendency at the workplace, wherever men had the strength and confidence, was to maintain, overtly or covertly, the sort of restrictionist stance and pre-capitalist values so noticeable in other areas of national life and economy. The observations of

Plumb and Kahn-Freund, for example, on the earlier period have been noted (see pp. 64, 65) and it was still true that the very modes by which a British profession typically defined itself set its members off from the world of capitalist values. 'The process of incorporation, acquisition of an expensive and palatial headquarters in central London, establishment of an apprenticeship system, limitation on entries, and scheduling of fees, are all manifestly designed to "gentrify" the profession ... This aspect of professionalisation is profoundly anti-capitalist ... ' (W. D. Rubinstein, quoted in Wiener, 1981, p. 16).

Similar dispositions were widespread throughout manual wage-earning. The Webbs thought that they saw labour abandoning earlier restrictionist tactics against innovation in favour of rational bargaining over the terms of its introduction, and their whole vision of the future sketched out in *Industrial Democracy* (1897) rested upon that belief. Yet the new tactics could be just as restrictive as the old if labour pitched its terms high enough, and in the very year the Webbs' book appeared the engineering industries were convulsed by a prolonged conflict over this issue. More importantly, the Webbs were misled by heeding too much the statements of national leaders, and too little the quiet but unremitting defence of 'custom and practice' by work groups on the shop floor. National leaders were well aware, from the public relations point of view, on which side the union's bread was buttered. They could often truthfully declare that such and such a practice was 'not union policy', and back it up with resounding sentiments about economic progress. What mattered were sentiments and union strength at the workplace. Llewellyn Smith, in 1902, as Commissioner of Labour in the Board of Trade and no enemy of the unions, was prepared, like many other commentators at the time, to attribute the loss of British cost effectiveness in world markets to wage-push inflation and the retardative effects of restrictive practices upon technical innovation (Davidson, 1978, p. 585). And as we have seen in another context, with the outbreak of war in 1914 and the emergence of a direct government interest in expanding production through the greatly enlarged use of unskilled, unapprenticed labour on more simplified machinery, the strength of long-standing craft resistances became clear. The Munitions of War Act of 1915 was to provide that in 'controlled establishments' in munitions industries 'any rule, practice or custom not having the force of law which tends to restrict production or employment shall be suspended'. Evidently, then, comments Carter Goodrich, 'there was an extensive body of custom and vested right in regulation that could at least be held to "restrict production or employment" and which were considered by the unions, and recognized by the government, as of first-rate importance' (Goodrich, 1975, p. 181).

This was not confined to the craft trades. The 'new unionism' was 'associated with the systematic extension of the old practice of deliberately restricting output (ca' canny) in the hope that what was left undone would provide work for the unemployed' (Hunt, 1981, p. 336). A later pamphlet, *Industrial Democracy for Miners* (1919), would concede that 'the disastrous grasping policy of the mine owner has had the result of causing the workmen to erect a code of customs and rules, designed to protect their wages and conditions. These act directly in restraint of production, as well as of the owners' greed' (Goodrich, 1975, p. 184). Frederick Taylor, pioneer of the Scientific Management movement that was to prove so successful in America and Germany but met such a discouraging reception in Britain, had to deal in Pennsylvania in the 1880s with British immigrant steel workers. He was staggered by the assortment of restrictive practices which they brought with them, and, 'never understanding the source of [their] customary habits of self-protection', remained forever convinced that they were born masters of the art (Merkle, 1980, p. 220). Given anything less than a strong entrepreneurial drive on the part of the employer, British labour's dogged defence of custom and practice in the face of proposed innovation wherever strength permitted can safely be assumed to have been daunting. True, there had been, and were to continue to be, isolated occasions when groups of British employers were brought to a pitch where they were prepared collectively to challenge this near-instinctive restrictionist culture of the shop floor – which was often older than formal trade unionism. But even an immediate victory was less important than what happened after the workers on the shop floor had licked their wounds and recovered their spirits, when a quiet resumption of old habits as soon as trade became brisk appears to have been widespread and tolerated.

Of considerable importance also beyond the craft trades was the widespread incidence of what was referred to earlier as the 'adversary relationship': that disposition of labour to respond with a wary arms-length stance which regarded all workplace conditions and changes in them as potential issues for manifest or tacit bargaining. Bargaining about the terms on which change was to be introduced was, of course, the Webbs' recommendation, but given their belief in social as well as economic progress they assumed an onset of enlightenment in which unions would co-operate with the forces of change and seek only to ensure that members secured their 'just' and 'rightful' protection. This was not how it looked to many an employer facing an effectively organised work group. He might well fear that any attempted change in techniques or organisation would be accompanied by a prolonged harangue, followed at best by a settlement which cancelled out much of the benefit, at worst by a bitter dispute and soured relationships thereafter. Arthur Shadwell, in the early 1900s, carried out an exhaustive study of British and Continental industry and education. Unlike some inquiries, such as the anti-union diatribe prepared concurrently by Edwin Pratt, a correspondent of *The Times* backed by the ideologues of the Liberty and Property Defence League (Pratt, 1904), Shadwell's inspires some confidence, if only because, unlike Pratt, he was capable of distinguishing between the union *per se* and workplace shop-floor culture: 'Restriction of output and opposition to machinery are much older than the unions... ' He was also capable of seeing that what for him was the greatest service of the unions – 'the establishment of more stable relations between employers and employed' – was neither an artificial arrangement imposed from above, nor simply the product of an abstract idea or sentiment, 'but an organic growth sprung from the interaction of needs and circumstances, and, therefore, a real thing possessing vitality and adaptability'.

Union influence he found to be on the whole, a moderating one – the leader's task came to be

> more and more the composing, not the fomenting, of disputes. His difficulty is not in stirring the men up, but in keeping them quiet . . . He must satisfy an exacting, suspicious and often insubordinate set of men; he must reconcile impossible aspirations with the facts of life; he must be conciliatory with employers while firmly maintaining the interests of his clients; he must keep an eye on public opinion; and all the time he is liable to have the ground undermined beneath his feet by jealousy and intrigue.

Shadwell found little evidence that the unions, as such, promoted restriction of output, opposition to machinery, or hostile relations with employers. Behaviour and relationships developed by the workers themselves, however, were a different matter. As with most other observers before and since, domestic and foreign, the features which struck him most forcibly were still, in essence, those emphasised by Dean Tucker in 1757. 'There is suspicion, deep and abiding, between employers and employed – particularly in the industrial north . . . Whatever its origin may be, the habit of distrust is both a sign and a source of weakness in industrial matters . . . The standing objection of workmen to innovations and improvements is rooted in it, and a very large proportion of the disputes between labour and capital can be traced to nothing but mutual mistrust.'

Shop-floor resistance to innovation was stressed by Shadwell – 'the introduction of new methods has been more effectively resisted by the workmen in England than elsewhere'. Relationships between men and management bedevilled British industry as they did not on the Continent. In many industries he found that the manufacturers 'fully recognize the necessity of keeping abreast of the times', whereas the workmen 'dislike and resent change, and even ridiculed foreign competition'. He noted as the background to all this the fact that although Britain 'led the way in model settlements, as in most industrial matters, the sense of duty towards the employed has never been so generally developed here as in Germany. If it had been, trade unionism would not have been forced into existence so early or would not have displayed such unquenchable vitality and such vigorous growth . . . ' Paternalism was less evident than in Germany, where he found 'welfare institutions much more common' and where the 'more general good-will of employers towards their employed . . . has certainly retarded the development of trade unionism'.

Shadwell might have added that much British paternalism had, in any case, been accompanied by employer recognition of trade unionism and collective bargaining, the outstanding case being Lancashire cotton. The overt and frequently publicised acceptance by cotton workers that they shared common interests with their employers, together with a period of accommodating union attitudes towards technical improvements, had caused cotton-weaving unionism to seem the nearest approximation yet to that ideal form for which middle-class candid friends yearned. Rational and businesslike; peaceful and respectable; joining with employers to improve the workings of the labour market by means of intelligent, statistically supported negotiations; accommodating to innovation in ways which both stimulated the employer to undertake it and the workers to accept it – this ideal dated back a long way and had been the vision of Positivists, some leading economists, the Webbs, and others who still thought in terms of evolutionary social progress and enlightenment. Yet even in Lancashire cotton the vision had faded. By the end of the century, the family firm was giving way to the joint stock company and paternalist impulses were shrivelling. The limited companies brought innovations of technology and method that pointed forward to twentieth-century rationalisation and the more impersonal structures proved unable to take the strain. The history of industrial relations in the limited companies 'was a history of bitterness and suspicion' (Joyce, 1980, p. 340). Vertical neighbourhood bonds with employers were being broken by other changes – by developments in transport and urban growth which separated home and work, and by a popular press and spectator sports which also weakened the neighbourhood dominance of the employer. These changes, besides sapping the influence-politics of Conservative and Liberal employers and promoting an independent labour consciousness, left the workplace scene increasingly open to the impersonal relations of union and management. The great paternalist family employers, especially during the years leading up to 1914, 'bowed out of local life to reap the fruits of their labour in the sunnier South' (ibid., p. 340).

Given the very different texture of German industrial paternalism, almost wholly as it was of the strong authoritarian version, there can be no surprise at the German employers' 'hate and dread' of trade unions; a marked contrast with Shadwell's observations in Britain. 'Nothing has struck me more in the course of this investigation than the remarkable difference of attitude displayed, in private, by employers in this country and in the others.' He had heard not a single word in favour of unions from any employer in Germany or America, whereas in Britain he had received 'far more often' from employers and managers 'fair and even friendly expressions of opinion' (Shadwell, 1909, pp. 5, 7, 336, 426, 552–9).

Much of the essence of what Shadwell presented was echoed by other observers. One of the shrewdest, the American sociologist Thorstein Veblen, noted in a publication of 1915 that the German workmen had recently 'grown difficult and discontented in some degree, but not after the refractory fashion in which they have tried the patience and narrowed the gains of their capitalist-employers' in Britain. Here the workers 'had no whole-hearted interest in the efficiency of the work done, but rather in what can be got in terms of price', while the employers lacked interest 'in the well-being or even in the continued efficiency of the workmen. From which follow, on the one hand, inhibiting trade-union rules, strikes, lockouts . . . and, on the other, an exploitation of the human raw material of industry . . . in the way of over-work, under-pay, unsafe and unwholesome conditions, and so forth.' Veblen located these comments within a context of references to the 'characteristic English philosophical work' which had been 'of a sceptical temper on the whole', leaning greatly 'on principles of self-interest and serviceability to human use, with its moral premises and precepts strongly impregnated with utilitarian and pragmatic, not to say materialistic, conceits'. He sharpened the contrast with Germany in the observation: 'A loyalty which raises the question, What for? comes far short of the feudalistic ideal and of that spirit of enthusiastic abnegation that has always been the foundation of a prosperous dynastic State.' He saw in Britain a subordination 'of a sullen, unenthusiastic character, tending more and more to a grudging disloyalty ... the alienation between the two classes, the workmen and their owners, is nearly complete in all that bears on the conduct of the industrial system' (Veblen, 1954, pp. 103, 124, 134, 196–7).

The Debate about Relative Decline

These characteristics, usually presented as the invention of trade unions who imposed them on their members, were often argued to be the main, sometimes the only, cause of Britain's relative industrial decline. They receded in prominence somewhat as the debate about the nature and causes of that decline widened to include a greater diversity of variables. The debate continues and remains inconclusive (Payne, 1974; Roderick and Stephens, 1978, ch. 7). The argument that the effects of workplace restrictionism were significant was bound to carry some intuitive persuasiveness. Equally apparent to all but the blinkered, however, is the argument that workplace cultures and management–worker relations cannot be the only variables affecting growth. And once it is accepted that a variety of factors are at work, the possibility exists that these particular variables may be either reinforced or offset by others, thereby making it virtually impossible to know whether or how far they are affecting the outcome.

Among the other factors bearing upon economic growth must be included the entrepreneurial function. How important were the skills, vision, aspirations, single-mindedness and ruthless determination of those making the relevant decisions? This, like the others, has waxed and waned in terms of the importance attached to it, with the usual inconclusiveness. Yet the argument needs to be noted, since it has relevance for the shaping of the industrial relations system and its law. The literature of entrepreneurial performance in 1870–1914 is littered with examples and counter-examples.

Of course, it could be argued that individual British business men were behaving perfectly 'rationally' in the late nineteenth century – maximizing profits and adjusting with smooth effectiveness to the spur of the market – but that the successful pursuit of private gain was inimical to the maximizing of a *social* return. So far the only version of this argument to be widely accepted is the one which holds that British business men were too slow to adapt staple industries, too half-hearted in the expansion of chemical, electrical, and vehicle industries, too content with good profits and neglectful of the long-run competitive future, too reliant on overseas investment and the international sale of services. (Supple 1977, p. 14; see also Mathias, 1983)

The picture of private 'rationality' conflicting with, and triumphing over, some conception of a 'social' or 'national' good is, of course, one that we would expect in a country which expressly repudiated the notion of an active interventionist state shaping economic growth along lines suggested by long-term national needs. 'Liberal political economy treats the nation as an association of individuals pursuing their own separate purposes within a framework of law. The nation has no purpose other than the purposes of the individuals who compose it ... For national political economy, there is a national interest beyond the purposes of individuals, which it is the task of the permanent agencies of the state to identify, formulate and secure.' The concern of national political economy was less with the market than with production and with the role of public agencies in making good deficiencies in markets (Gamble, 1981, pp. 168–70). British governments, however, worked to no model of a strong active state stimulating and mobilising industrial strength for the enhancement of national power and glory. They moved mostly in response to pressures from organised interests, reformist groups and opinion lobbies. Attempts at masterful dynamic state leadership in a society where individualism and instrumental collectivism were rife, and where cultures and sub-cultures gave little support to conceptions of a 'higher national good', were likely to split parties without really mobilising a mass following.

Yet doubts were being expressed about the ability of private industry itself to generate the desirable drive towards innovation and long-term planning for growth. Arguments were heard that the social context of British industry was such as to blunt the edge of its entrepreneurial and managerial thrust and to deprive it of the nation's best talents. The debate is complicated, as we have seen, by uncertainty as to how far, in any given situation, economic performance is determined by the quality of entrepreneurial skills and motivation. Yet the arguments, greatly reinforced subsequently, have persisted and are relevant to our main theme in several ways. If, as a consequence of this social context, British industry was insufficiently powered in the sense of having significantly less of the entrepreneurial will and single-minded vision that was evident, for example, in Germany, this could be among the reasons why the ingredients of any incipient national socialism never fused to become an independent political force. In particular, it would help to explain why most employers, consulting no doubt not only their own dispositions but also the probable responses of the wider society and the state, felt that it made better sense to try to work with the unions than to attempt to destroy them. The arguments about the social context of industry are important, therefore, in that, if valid, they help to explain why, at a time when the unions were arousing specially strong hostility from some industrialists and from the courts, there was no concerted mass attack on them – through the Taff Vale judgement, for example. Instead, the politicians were left free to compete for the unions' favour – and a group of civil servants were left free to encourage and promote union recognition and collective bargaining. These issues we pursue in the next chapter.

6

Challenges to the System
The 1890s to 1914 (Part II)

Entrepreneurship and the Public Schools

At its most fundamental, the argument about the social context and its effect upon entrepreneurial behaviour needs to begin by recalling that Britain had not witnessed, and was not witnessing now, the political and social ousting of a patrician ruling class by a thrusting and modernising industrial bourgeoisie. Neither was there, as in Germany, a situation in which such a bourgeoisie, socially excluded and despised by an aristocratic, militarist and nationalist landed ruling class hostile to industrialism and parliamentary institutions, was denied aristocratic assimilation and instead concentrated all the more fiercely on realising their ambitions through their own bourgeois values of wealth, industrial power and domination of their local community. Effective power at the national level was willingly surrendered to leadership by the traditional ruling class, a leadership checked only marginally by a largely impotent Reichstag. In Britain, by contrast, a landed aristocracy which had developed both parliamentary institutions and a large stake in industrialism was assimilating, and putting its imprint on, the upper ranks of a bourgeoisie which was only too eager to be assimilated. The result was a partnership with considerable political and social strength and homogeneity. Enough influential members of Britain's patrician élite had, or were able to develop, strategic footholds in industry or finance to allow them to survive the transition to an industrial society within which the City represented not only a growing economic asset but also its social apex in terms of status. The relative ease of this assimilation which, while admitting powerful new aspirants to a re-formed upper class, allowed influential groups of the old to retain their status, wealth and values, facilitated the role of the public schools in transmitting to the rising bourgeoisie a culture bearing a heavy aristocratic, patrician imprint. 'Old values and patterns of behaviour lived on within the new, whose character was thus profoundly modified. The end result of the nineteenth-century transformation of Britain was indeed a peaceful accommodation, but one that entrenched pre-modern elements within the new society and gave legitimacy to anti-modern sentiments' (Wiener, 1981, p. 7). It was not only at the levels of manual and professional labour, therefore, that the governing class strategy of rule resulted in the encapsulation of pre-modern techniques, values and traditions. The re-formed upper class was based, not upon a powerful modernising bourgeois revolution, but upon the conservative containment, taming and even partial humanising of such a revolution – a humanising derived to some extent from disinterested concern but predominantly from the practical experience of upholding a class rule in the British context.

The rule of public school education in this process was central, and the context of that education was not such as to encourage the development of ruthless, thrusting entrepreneurial qualities. 'They took the fees of the textile magnate and the lawyer, and in return . . . exposed their sons to the full public service traditions of the aristocrat and the country squire . . . the public school bias that preferred government service to private profit-making was all part and parcel of a gentleman ideal.' There is no evidence, however, that recruitment itself suffered inordinately from the low prestige that public school values conferred on business activities. Public schoolboys, and able public schoolboys, did take up positions of direction, management and control in business, however much more gentlemanly the church, the army, or the civil service might seem (Wilkinson, 1964, p. 118). A quantitative analysis yields the judgement that

> By the turn of the century, amongst the larger industrial organizations, we see the emergence of a national economic élite, whose background and educational experience does not differentiate them in any obvious way from that of those men in the dominant positions in the spheres of politics, the Civil Service, and the Church. Certainly some economic sectors, particularly banking, remain ahead of most others in these terms; but this does not alter the general picture. (Stanworth and Giddens, 1974, p. 101)

Much depends, therefore, on what style, standards and quality of industrial leadership were predominantly characteristic of this élite drawn from the public schools. The charge both then and since has been, first, that not enough of the highest talent chose industry as a career, 'the best of the brains of our upper classes', wrote G. B. Dibblee, editor of the *Manchester Guardian* in 1902, 'will go anywhere but into industry – into a bank or a merchant's office, perhaps, but not into horny-handed manufacture' (Dibblee, 1902). Those making careers at the upper levels of finance and merchanting entered a world 'decidedly richer, more powerful, and possessed of a more distinguished historical pedigree' than that of northern manufacturing, and one far more readily accepted by the old landed élite. The City, especially, 'with its centuries-old traditions, its location near the heart of upper-class England, and its gradually woven, closely-knit ties to the aristocracy and gentry, enjoyed a social cachet that evaded industry' (Wiener, 1981, p. 128). This made for strong and tenacious links and continuities at the apex of society between the old wealth and the new, but they were links and continuities from which manufacturing industrialists were apt to be excluded. In the realm of social structure as in that of values, the impact of the industrial revolution in Britain was muffled.

Those going from public schools into manufacturing industry

'regarded it as second-best', not a truly fit activity for a gentleman. They therefore 'treated it as second-best and, in the end, parts of it tended to become second-best' (Catherwood, 1966, p. 21). The reason why Britain 'did not become a business society' therefore lay not only with the aristocracy, the gentry and the higher civil servants who likewise absorbed the public service tradition; it lay also with the business men themselves, many of whom 'were deferential rather than rebellious, snobbish rather than independent', cherishing visions of a country estate and the life of an English gentleman (Briggs, 1965, pp. 19–20).

> The image of an essentially rural, traditional England, and the distrust of materialism and economic change that went along with it, had practical effects upon business ... Social prestige and moral approbation were to be found by using the wealth acquired in industry to escape it. This myth of England both diverted talent and energies from industry and gave a particular 'gentry' cast to existing industry, discouraging commitment to a wholehearted pursuit of economic growth. (Wiener, 1981, p. 127)

It is worth noting, too, that this gentry disdain towards single-minded dedication to material gain and growth also influenced the attitudes of the professional middle class towards trade unionism and socialism. The background that produced the Milners and the Amerys also produced the Tawneys, who rejected capitalist industry as a vulgar materialism which sacrificed every human aspiration to the pursuit of riches, and argued that it must be replaced by the organisation of industry as a professional service. In a sense, therefore, British working-class socialism, much influenced by this creed, among others, joined with the public school and university imprint to disparage competitive, profit-seeking industry. Even middle-class professionals who could not go this far and who remained, as most of them did, fully committed to capitalism not infrequently revealed only a tepid commitment to capitalists. As will be seen, higher civil servants in strategic positions often turned as dispassionate an eye upon manufacturing employers as had their counterparts early in the century when they suspected shortsightedness and greed. It was a stance which encouraged the suspicion that conflict might not always be the workers' fault and that trade unions might be necessary nuisances.

We have yet, however, to pursue the fuller implications of the gentry imprint. There is plenty of support for Wilkinson's judgement that even if 'the public school system did not starve industry of recruits, it did tend to induce unsuitable traits in those who entered industry. Public school life militated against entrepreneur qualities – creative imagination; friendliness to innovation . . . ' Moreover, the public schools 'probably' starved the development of science and technology; 'certainly they supported a type of leadership which failed to *implement* new technical ideas' (Wilkinson, 1964, pp. 4, 118–19). Ward supports this judgement. The public schools were 'committed in their ideals, character and curricula to the training of youth in a direction that pointed away from success in commerce and industry. Those who did go into their family firms were apt to see business simply as a means of earning money for the kind of life they wanted (D. Ward, 1967, pp. 49, 50, 52; see also Briggs, 1965, pp. 18–20). It was hardly a formula for dynamic and adventurous entrepreneurship. It was, however, a formula which could be expected to contribute to the possibility of a mutual accommodation between industrial employers and organised labour. Thrusting, innovating, dynamic and adventurous entrepreneurship puts a strain on management–worker relations in so far as it disturbs existing work organisation and job structure, with consequent threats to people's security and expectations. Public school tradition and training had been distilled from a long political experience that had come to put stability before innovation if this was bitterly contested. Within the emerging industrial democracy that was Victorian Britain, such dispositions 'provided an anchor in the midst of turbulence, a force for social cohesion offsetting centrifugal tendencies in the environment . . . Against the competitive individualism of the Industrial Revolution they kept alive the traditional gentleman's assumption that private privilege means public duty.'

The public schools also cemented 'that reliance on traditional wisdom' which 'is a deep-rooted element in the British social character . . . tempered it a little with ideals of restraint and moderation and left it fundamentally unquestioned'. Included also was an emphasis which 'implied moderation, compromise, and self-restraint'. Politically, these characteristics 'seemed best suited to a minimal concept of government', an outlook which 'saw the ruler as guardian rather than innovator' (Wilkinson, 1964, pp. 21, 58, 62). Jenks, pointing out that aristocratic values were never displaced by specifically Utilitarian values, compares, on the one hand, the imaginative Utilitarian conception of politics as an exercise in problem-solving and in the exploration of opportunities for innovation with, on the other, the aristocratic emphasis on loyalty and duty and the view of problem-solving as an exception rather than the rule (Jenks, 1977, p. 494). 'New ideas and methods nearly always appear to disrupt . . . Certainly the guardian outlook on government was well in tune with the public school prefect's style of leadership: the prefect's main task was to keep order rather than initiate major new schemes.' But keeping order in a changing world implies, on one level, a certain flexibility, and the style included an ability to make 'piecemeal adjustment to changing factors and circumstances. When new forces arose to threaten the old order – in the Empire, forces of nationalism; at home, forces of democracy – the prevailing instinct of British leadership was to accommodate and contain rather than suppress' (Wilkinson, 1964, p. 62). This needs to be supplemented with a reminder of the readiness to spill blood which lay well within this governing style when it was deemed desirable. Yet what is being said here suggests that the public schools elaborated, reinforced, stylised – and, above all, disseminated throughout the rising industrial, commercial and financial bourgeoisie – a strategy of control and leadership which had its consequences for a predominant style of industrial as well as political rule.

It needs to be noted, however, that none of the foregoing necessarily implies that the general level of entrepreneurial performance *deteriorated* after the 1870s. Payne concludes a survey of the debate with the suggestion that 'with the development of competitive economies, British entre-preneurial errors and hesitancies, *always present*, even in the period of the classic Industrial Revolution, became more apparent' (Payne, 1974, p. 56, italics in original). They were revealing themselves more damagingly in the failure adequately to exploit new industries and inventions; a failure owing much, perhaps, to the relative neglect of science and scientific education.

The Social Nature of British Capitalism

What options were forgone when Britain's manufacturing bourgeoisie chose this path? Another of the suppressed alternatives of British history is the possibility that the radical reformism of the Benthamite Utilitarian school might have extended widely enough and lasted long enough to create a more receptive and stimulating environment for the 'second industrial revolution' which began in the last quarter of the century. The thrust of the Philosophical Radicals had been 'an intellectual force of enormous practical importance' in the first half of the century, disseminat-ing ideas in the light of which 'a vast amount of antiquated political lumber was swept away, and legislation, administration, and judicial process were made both more efficient and more democratic'. Bentham, 'convinced of the importance of institutions in determining behaviour', had campaigned 'to sweep away traditional government and establish a rational regime which would deliberately condition character'. He revealed in the process his 'exasperation with tradition, his desire for efficiency … his brisk intolerance, his faith in reason, and his rejection of historical myth' (Bowle, 1963, pp. 55, 65–6; Sabine, 1963, p. 697). These were precisely the qualities that would have been needed later for a comprehensive drive towards what may be summed up for convenience as 'industrial moderni-sation'.

They can hardly be subsumed under the conventional categories of Liberalism. The Utilitarian thrust included 'a doctrine of authority which looked to the deliberate and in a sense the scientific interference of government to produce a harmony of interests'. This drive towards a strong, centralized, interventionist state 'had aroused among Conserva-tives and ordinary Liberals alike the opposition only to be expected where for a century and a half the national tradition had demanded a state so weak that its existence was barely felt' (Halévy, 1961c, pp. 100–1). Admittedly, in true pragmatic spirit, a sufficiency of the country gentlemen had been prepared to accept administrative centralisation where it suited their direct personal interest, as in the case of the new punitive and more economical poor law. But an 1833 Benthamite scheme for a national centralised scheme of compulsory education, based on the Prussian model, which would, among other things, lay down syllabuses, sank without trace under concerted attack by the whole House.

These resistances persisted. It is conceivable, in their absence, that industrial capital might have harnessed the workers' movement in an alliance to fight for 'a fundamental reconstruction of the state and civil society aimed at the abolition of social privilege and exclusiveness and the inauguration of a genuine democratic republic of equal citizens, a more egalitarian bourgeois order, a more energetic and mobile civil society' (Gamble, 1981, p. 81). The six points of the Charter offered the basic programme for such a democratic republic, and Bentham himself favoured, *inter alia*, annual parliaments, the secret ballot, female suffrage, and abolition of the monarchy and the House of Lords (Plamenatz, 1949, p. 82). Included in such a reconstruction would have been the creation of a national secondary and higher education system, established on merito-cratic lines, which favoured science and technology and operated an aggressive search for innovation and the practical application of research.

There is no reason to dismiss such a possibility had the attempt been made, say, in the 1850s. There was no inevitability about independent working-class political organisation, still less about socialism. An account of socialist ideas and organisations after the 1880s is apt to convey a greater sense of their practical impact upon the working class than they warrant. The Social Democratic Federation and the Fabian Society (1884), William Morris and the Socialist League of the same year, the Independent Labour Party (1893) – the detailing of these organisations, their doctrines and their internecine conflicts can easily distract attention from the fact that within the working classes themselves, pioneers with egalitarian dreams

> formed only a very small part of the working-class intelligentsia. The Liberal-voting skilled worker . . . easily maintained ascendancy as the purveyor of progressive ideas, ideas in which there was, in fact, little place for true equality with those beneath him. Until 1914 the members of this élite generally, as far as class values were concerned, stayed almost as conformist and establishment-minded as their Tory counter-parts. Together they stood, the great bulwark against revolution of any kind. (R. Roberts, 1973, p. 179)

A middle-class-led campaign in the 1850s towards a society based on the greater encouragement of individual merit and an attack on aristocratic values and institutions might have had more appeal for the upper working class. Yet middle-class fears even of this stratum were at least as strong as the optimism. To invite it to participate in a joint pursuit of social and political modernisation would have carried the same dangers that frightened their seventeenth-century forebears. Radicalisation on this scale might have released forces of much wider – and for them damaging – social change. In any case, they were getting much of what was most important to them. Divisions within the landed interest had secured them admission to the political nation in 1832 and free trade in 1846. In addition, the landed aristocracy had shown itself ready to admit them – or rather their sons and daughters – to its society, to its marriage market, and to its mystique of the gentleman and the lady. The combination proved irresis-tible. The young Utilitarians 'were in the end forced to admit that the aristocracy exercised a fascination which was proof against all their arguments, particularly among that prosperous middle rank which James Mill had said had the decisive influence over public opinion' (W. Thomas,

1979, p. 448). The appeal of the Benthamite creed was not sufficiently widespread to prevail against this fascination. The 'prime reason' why Benthamism 'never became the official philosophy of the radical left as Marxism did on the continent' was that 'English radicals and Whigs alike opposed a strongly centralized state, tended to prefer cheap to efficient government, and until remarkably late in the century, left the solution of pressing social problems to the operation of private philanthropy' (ibid., p. 452).

What the 'prosperous middle rank' gave up, 'apart from a democratic republic free of the aristocratic ethos and rituals which continued to shroud most national institutions, was the chance to forestall the working class organizing itself industrially and politically as a class'. What they chose was 'the path of accommodation with landed property and its political arm, gradual reform of the state to make it more effective in protecting the market order and aiding capital accumulation within it, and gradual concessions to working-class demands' (Gamble, 1981, p. 81). In the place of Utilitarianism, in both middle and upper classes, was a spirit of piecemeal adaptive reform underpinned by a paternalist fusion of aristocratic *noblesse oblige* and the evangelical doctrine of service and duty now receiving expression in varied forms, including Oxford Idealism and what Beatrice Webb called 'consciousness of sin'.

The consequence was a capitalism significantly unlike that of either America or Germany. For one thing this mutual class accommodation preserved the structure of social privilege and exclusiveness both in attitudes and institutions, and this was one factor blocking practical application of the sort of extreme individualism urged by Samuel Smiles and Herbert Spencer and supported by the Liberty and Property Defence League and kindred organisations. Another consequence was a failure to develop 'the educational system essential for national efficiency'. It has been argued that whatever the causes of Britain's initial industrial pre-eminence, education 'could have had a key role in the maintenance of the pre-eminence as the favourable circumstances disappeared one by one'. It played no such role. 'The philosophy of the English educational system was class-based as opposed to the meritocratic ethos pervading the German system. The products of the English system were imbued with such attitudes as to reinforce and strengthen the class bias of the central philosophy. This philosophy was inimical to industrial progress in an international competitive situation' (Roderick and Stephens, 1978, p. 172).

Yet another result of the class accommodation was the final consolidation of an independent-spirited working class with its own culture and organisations committed to resisting individualism in the labour market and in management–worker relations, and carrying a restrictionist inheritance of suspicion towards innovation and profit-seeking in competitive markets. The growth of an open, egalitarian, meritocratic and mobile bourgeois society was inhibited, therefore, both by the traditional exclusiveness and anti-business culture of an aristocratic order and by the partial repudiation on the part of the organised working class of some of the central tenets of such a society. Both obstructions were far less evident in the United States. On the other hand, such limited thrust as there was towards the German model was also blocked in its most important respects. There were no authoritarian institutions, traditions and culture making possible a strong nationalist state leadership towards industrial modernisation and a close partnership between government and business. Any developments along those lines were ruled out by the preservation of essential features of the traditional political order, particularly with respect to relationships between the individual and the state, the limited conception of government, and other concomitants of liberal civil society.

Modernisation could have been more vigorously pursued under the auspices of either model, as the experience of Britain's two major rivals indicates. Britain, however, 'failed to move strongly in either direction, and it was this failure which lies at the root of the hundred years decline' (Gamble, 1981, p. 84). Other consequences were continuance of the traditional strategy of rule and, along with it, continuance of the policy of contained concessions to the working class and its organisations. This offers support for Nairn's suggestion that the category of such terms as 'moderate', 'orderly', 'decent', 'tolerant' and 'peaceful', and the category of such terms as 'backward-looking', 'insular', 'class-ridden' and 'inefficient' are opposite sides of the same coin (Nairn, 1977, pp. 44–5). Or, in Wiener's words, 'potentially disruptive forces of change were harnessed and channelled into supporting a new social order, a synthesis of old and new. This containment of the cultural revolution of industrialization lies at the heart of both the achievements and the failures of modern British history' (Wiener, 1981, p. 158).

Some Consequences of the Non-Interventionist State

Although the anti-enterprise culture has bulked large in the preceding discussion, it cannot stand by itself as a social factor contributing to the relative weakness of Britain's entrepreneurial drive – a weakness that might be seen as playing a part not only (problematically) in economic backwardness but also in the relatively ready accommodation of trade unionism and collective bargaining. The anti-enterprise culture was only one element in a cluster of characteristics which continued to be displayed by Britain's political system and which, in certain respects, mark it to the present day.

First and foremost was the practice of non-interventionism by the state in economic affairs and reliance on market forces for settling the shape and directions of the economy. One of the more plausible economic generalisations is that while market forces may be successful in achieving short-term marginal adjustments they contain no mechanism for assessing long-term needs and initiating the movements of research, resources and capital investment required to satisfy those needs. Hence the distinction drawn between 'liberal' and 'national' political economy. There is no necessary connection, however, between a widespread anti-enterprise culture and a liberal political economy which eschews the active, interventionist state with its direct and indirect promotion of long-term strategies. The weakness of the anti-enterprise culture argument, used by itself, is that an equally impressive array of similar sentiments could be assembled to describe dispositions in France up to the present day. What France has, however, which Britain has not is a tradition of interventionist state centralisation and a readiness to apply planning and policy discrimination between firms and industries which the ruling order in Britain has always found distasteful. This seems to suggest that it was the combination of an anti-enterprise culture with the persistence of free trade and the deep-rooted aversion to positive and constructive state intervention in the economy that spared Britain's employers and trade unions the pressures of a more thorough-going modernisation. Many men of talent and idealism sought public service: had they defined public service in terms of pro-moting the long-term interests of the national economy and establishing a high-status civil service planning technocracy, the anti-enterprise culture would have met bracing opposition. At the same time, governments and state agencies would have had far greater difficulty in preserving the image of the impartial state dealing even-handedly with the interests and the classes.

We thus arrive at a reformulation of a proposition noted in the preceding pages. The British state could, to some extent, afford to allow the unions to remain, in Churchill's words, later echoed by Baldwin, 'a natural form of human association, and therefore capable of growth and the assumption of new purposes' – though within limits defined by the ruling-class need to protect property rights and the social hierarchy of wealth, status and power. But even these were wider limits of freedom than would have been possible had the state itself been a direct participant in deciding the directions, tempo and changes of economic activity. The milieu in which the unions and employers were left to fight out these issues in their own way was also a milieu in which the anti-enterprise culture was left unchallenged by the state. Thus was muted what could have been a far more intense phase of class conflict resulting from a keener drive towards modernisation; with what consequences for the industrial relations system is open to speculation. This was a potential challenge that failed to materialise.

We have already noted threats that did materialise. There were direct counter-attacks and also wider challenges which threatened the system, partly directly and partly indirectly, by seeking certain changes in domi-nant social values and national political purposes. In few cases was the threat considerable. Some industrialists, aspiring to destroy the unions and assert an unfettered prerogative and individual bargaining, sought to draw fellow-employers into an aggressive industrial and political cam-paign, but found few supporters. The unions had long demonstrated their great tenacity of purpose where their own existence and functions were concerned, and few British employers had shown that they had the stomach for a fight to the death, particularly since governments usually affected 'neutrality' in trade disputes. 'The Board of Admiralty', replied its First Lord to a parliamentary questioner during the great engineering stoppage of 1897–8, 'will adhere to the same strict impartiality between the two parties as they have observed on similar occasions' (Goschen,

1897, col. 899). There was little to be hoped for there. The counter-attacks from the courts were immensely more threatening, but again the political system lent itself to the reversal of hostile legal judgements through political mobilisation by the unions.

The continued freedom of the unions to pursue a measure of joint regulation with employers and to employ in the process a diversity of industrial and political weapons and sanctions owed much to the determination of the unions themselves. But that determination was bringing success because it was exerted within a relatively favourable social context which generations of working-class activists, inside and outside the unions, had played a part in creating. The whole inheritance of constitutionality, rule of law and political freedom, profoundly flawed though it was by class privilege, prejudice and gross inequalities of power, provided footholds and leverage for organised groups among the working class, provided they showed no intention of using them to overturn the social system.

It was this same political, economic and social context that proved strongly resistant to those wider challenges which, if successful, could hardly have failed to affect the industrial relations system in fundamental ways. The attempt to assert atomistic individualism in the fields of poor relief, social legislation, the labour market and management–worker relations could not seriously hope to prevail against the many and growing manifestations of collectivism. Nor could it prevail against such political necessities as ensured that governments could not attempt drastically to remodel the social order in the face of popular, organised political forces and the compulsion to attract votes.

If it was the collectivism of the industrial relations system that was challenged by the forces of atomistic individualism, it was its tacit acceptance of open economic class conflict that was challenged by the forces of social imperialism and national socialism. While prepared to accept collectivist corporatism as a means of social control, these forces saw class conflict as one of the most serious elements weakening the nation. Underlying their declared intention to heal the rift between capital and labour and establish a new spirit of class harmony and collaboration there lay authoritarian militaristic impulses which, if given their head, would hardly have stopped short at persuasion. Neither set of challenges ever showed signs of achieving its ends; the British people, their institutions and the power structure informing their society showing themselves, on the whole, resistant to both. This resistance included the employers. Although both sets of movements attracted money from business and financial interests, the public school élite which dominated most major sections of the economy showed few signs of being adequately seized by either.

The Industrial Relations System and Social Reform

Our examination of these wider challenges has identified certain aspects of the economic and political scene which facilitated the continued development of the industrial relations system on the lines visible by the 1880s. The aspects identified so far, however, were largely negative or permissive in nature. Political democracy only enabled, it did not compel, the unions to mobilise themselves politically. The predominant style among employers was not in favour of a concerted mass attack to destroy the unions. Atomistic individualism and social imperialism failed to mobilise enough support to be a real threat.

But in addition to these negative factors a number of positive forces were also at work. On the face of it, one of them might seem to be social reform legislation – as helping to maintain that basic social cohesion and stability within which trade unions and their members would be prepared to operate both industrially and politically within the broad structures of the existing system. Certainly, both major parties acted as if they believed that social reform was important for capturing the allegiance of the working classes, especially their organised sections. The partial shift of Conservative ideology towards liberal individualism did not prevent Conservative governments acknowledging what they saw as the facts of political life and offering, or acquiescing in, piecemeal concessions to the working classes. They introduced the Workmen's Compensation Act 1897; the Unemployed Workmen Act 1905, which gave local 'distress' committees powers to use some portion of rating income for finding employment and settling the workless on farm colonies; and the Aliens Act 1905, which, in response to earlier TUC pressure to prohibit the immigration of destitute aliens, set up a control system of port examination. 'These two Acts of 1905 ... could be regarded as ... a bid ... however timid ... for the support of labour, made over the head of the old Liberal Opposition' (Halévy, 1961d, p. 375). The Liberals, however, soon outbid them with old-age pensions in 1908; the Trade Boards Act of 1909, which provided for compulsory collective bargaining to establish minimum rates in selected chronically ill-paid 'sweated' trades; the Labour Exchanges Act of the same year; and the beginnings of health and unemployment insurance in the National Insurance Act of 1911. The Conservative-dominated House of Lords, usually eager to emasculate Liberal legislation, was far more cautious about measures which touched the trade unions and the working classes.

At least as significant as the substantive benefits conferred by these statutes were the procedural methods laid down for their administration. Legislation on the trade boards, labour exchanges and national insurance all provided participation in some form by representatives of the trade unions, thereby knitting them further into the structure of public recognition, office and status. This was specially important for national insurance. Lloyd George had been impressed by the German system when visiting that country in 1908 and two years later sent a young civil servant, W. J. Braithwaite (New College and Toynbee Hall) to investigate. Braithwaite later wrote that whereas the German scheme had been 'imposed on a clear field ... in England it had to be superimposed on a great variety of existing organizations. Friendly societies, trade unions and commercial insurance companies had already developed the idea of insurance against such misfortunes as sickness, accident, death and, in some cases, unemployment. They formed a powerful vested interest ...' Lloyd George duly appeased them by building them into the administrative structure as 'approved societies' (Rose, 1972, pp. 48–9) – though it has been argued that the Act subordinated 'the participatory democracy of the most successful of all nineteenth-century working-class institutions – the Friendly Societies – to the bureaucratic procedures of the commercial insurance industry' (Hinton, 1982, p. 36).

If social legislation is to be seen, however, as serving indirectly the underpinning of the industrial relations system, it must be regarded as exerting its effects not in crude terms of satisfying certain immediate and explicit demands of organised labour, but rather through a long-term humanising of the economic order which, though at first little appreciated by the working classes, helped to prevent industrial conflict becoming translated into political conflict. There is some evidence that significant numbers among the labour rank and file long remained suspicious of statutory welfare. Many 'seem to have had strong reservations' about German legislation, and 'it has been argued that the leaders of the workers would support state welfare legislation only when their hold over the loyalty of the working class was secure; otherwise they would tend to oppose what they saw as state competition for that loyalty' (R. Hay, 1981, p. 110).

There is said to be 'clear evidence' from by-election reverses in the autumn of 1911 that the health insurance scheme 'was doing the government no good, electorally, in England'. Working men with the vote tended to be 'of that section of the working class from which the members of friendly societies were predominantly drawn'; men who were 'the natural *clientèle* of . . . institutions which embodied the Victorian ideal of self-help while also appealing to the traditional British taste for social exclusiveness'. They 'might not feel very enthusiastic about being obliged to contribute to a scheme from which people less virtuous and thrifty than themselves would benefit'. Lloyd George was up against 'the Victorian – and specifically Liberal – ideology of individualism, by which all classes were affected . . . Samuel Smiles's philosophy had in some degree influenced all British working men' (Grigg, 1978, pp. 316, 346, 347). Pelling offers the verdict that 'the pressure for social reform from the working class was politically negligible in the years before the First World War' (Pelling, 1979, p. 16), and even during that war 'a substantial section of the labour movement' was to see 'government social welfare as a thinly disguised form of coercion by a repressive state' (J. Harris, 1981, p. 260).

If social reform legislation cannot be seen as a simple response to working-class pressure, neither can it be viewed in terms of a comprehensive programme of social compassion resting on a concept of the welfare state. Many of the reforms were devised as specific remedies for specific problems (Briggs, 1961, pp. 221–58), and were pressed not only, for example, by Fabians but also by non-Fabians leading non-party, *ad hoc*, public opinion pressure groups (McBriar, 1966, p. 263). The Webbs themselves often expressed not so much social compassion as impatience and disgust at the disorder, inefficiency and waste created by competitive market society; responses shared by Wells, Shaw and many others who demanded constructive social intervention. Another contributory factor was the belief that social reform – and the resulting public expenditure –

had to be endured for the sake of social stability and the pre-emption of the socialists. Bismarck was only the earliest example of leaders of modern states who, conspicuous neither for democratic nor for compassionate motives, have promoted programmes of social welfare.

Social Cohesion and the Spirit of 'Service'

Yet informing some of the impulses behind the movement in Britain were ideals and principles which expressed themselves not only through the 'new' Liberalism but also through imperialist consciousness. Since this, too, played a part in maintaining a certain basic social cohesion it needs some examination within our present context. In fact the impulses towards social amelioration and the idealist element in imperialism received much stimulus and inspiration from the same sources. The ancient universities, with their disparagement of applied science, technology, industry and money-making confirmed dispositions inculcated by the public schools. Certain of their most influential figures, such as Benjamin Jowett of Balliol, applied the principle that the offspring of the manufacturing classes should be led towards superior purposes by higher education – and this at a time when Max Weber was complaining that the German social system 'directs all major talents for leadership into the service of capitalist industry' (Jenks, 1977, p. 495). Jowett, whose influence 'was very great indeed: much greater than has been generally understood', believed in a dedicated élite whose members, working within an 'aristocratically framed society', accepted that 'privilege, whether inherited or acquired, meant responsibility, and that responsibility meant hard work' (Faber, 1957, pp. 24, 40, 41). The idea of service, described by Raymond Williams as 'the great achievement of the Victorian middle class ... deeply inherited by its successors (R. Williams, 1958, p. 328), is relevant to our interests in that it helped to shape the social context within which the working-class movement developed. Whether at home or overseas – where it fostered a certain style of colonial rule – it could sometimes be expressed in something more than simply a concern for the queen's peace, national security, law and order, the public weal. It could mean acceptance of responsibility for improving the condition of the lower orders. Improvement was, of course, pursued within a framework regarded, in terms of its principal institutional structures, as inviolate; the idea of service was nothing if not supportive of the status quo. Yet it was not narrowly exclusive. One of the many forms of service was the promotion of opportunities in education, industry, and elsewhere for individuals of lowly origin to ascend the ladder – opportunities seized by many working-class leaders. This conflict of values by which the self-serving individualism of bourgeois liberalism faced the opposing concept of service was thereby carried over into the working-class movement, where leaders who strove to promote solidarity among their members – on one level a challenge to bourgeois individualism – were also dazzled by the bourgeois ideal of 'bettering oneself' (ibid., pp. 329–31).

The ideas of service, including that of improving the condition of one's social inferiors and of helping the abler and finer spirits among them to rise to 'better' things, strongly reinforced the ruling-class strategy of conceding limited reforms to groups whom it was currently deemed safe to admit to the political and social nation. As expressed, for example, by the Christian Socialists and Positivists, these impulses had significantly shaped the nature and timing of the trade union legislation of the 1870s. Such dispositions, now and for some time to come, helped to humanise a competitive market society and, by a process of social recognition, to relieve the frustrations of energetic and ambitious working-class leaders whose counterparts in other countries were being accorded only pariah status.

These stances played a considerable part in the 'new' Liberalism in so far as politicians believed they saw in them a means of capturing the votes of a widened electorate, and the Conservative Party, too, for the same reason could not afford to ignore them. Accordingly, there entered into social imperialism, too, the conception of increasing public expenditure to bear the social costs of free market competition in the interests of social stability. This became 'part of the general political consensus', duly 'appropriated by other political forces fully committed to maintaining free trade, especially the "New Liberals" and social democrats who came increasingly to dominate the policy discussions of the Labour movement' (Gamble, 1981, p. 174).

The contribution of Jowett's Oxford to all this was important for imperialism as well as for social welfare. Movements of ideas at Oxford and Cambridge were no mere unworldly irrelevancies. It was there 'that the official symbols and intellectual justifications of Church and State were fashioned, conserved and disseminated' (Richter, 1966, p. 15) – sufficient explanation of why any reference to 'reforming' them aroused great passions. We may note in passing – since it connects with earlier discussion of how the thrust of Utilitarian 'modernisation' petered out with the inter-penetration of aristocracy and bourgeoisie – that the 'philosophy of duty' was used to justify Oxford's existence and spare it the rigours of Utilitarian reform towards the 'needs' of an industrial nation. It was at Oxford, especially, that there developed a widely persuasive set of influences which did much to soften and humanise some of the abrasive forces of a competitive, acquisitive and highly contractual economy, and which took the view that Parliament was less significant as a power for good – or evil – in social welfare than private voluntary influence 'and those forms of mutual aid developed by the more prosperous working men' (ibid., p. 12). This was Oxford Idealism, which between 1880 and 1914 superseded Utilitarianism as the most prominent school in British universities. Since it is revealing of what the British temper, tradition and style made of German Hegelianism, and of the way in which the outcome affected the industrial relations system, it calls for some attention.

Jowett introduced Hegel into Oxford – indeed, into Britain – where he had been virtually unknown, in the 1840s, and from this source the Oxford Idealists such as T. H. Green, Edward Caird, Bernard Bosanquet and F. H. Bradley, who between them spanned the later decades of the nineteenth and the early twentieth centuries, learned their Hegelian alphabet (Faber, 1957, pp. 177–86). For our purposes the relevant aspects are those concerning the nature of society, the state and their relationships to the individual. Green and the many others who reacted against the social consequences of economic individualism and *laissez-faire* attacked the conception of society as simply an aggregate of individuals, and the conception of the state as merely a coercive apparatus for the enforcement of contracts, the suppression of wrong-doing, and the maintenance of defence. Some based their arguments on candid expediency. Professor Goldwin Smith, urging in lectures and pamphlets from the 1860s onwards the need for a reinterpretation of Christianity as a universalist 'Love thy neighbour' ethic, argued on the unashamedly instrumental basis that this was necessary if a crisis of French Revolution proportions was to be avoided. Christianity must be transformed into a purely rational moral doctrine if 'the social system peculiar to Britain – premised on the statesmanlike qualities of a small élite' – was to survive (Jenks, 1977, p. 491).

Others were manifestly motivated more by principle. Concerned as they were to restore to political thinking the concepts of community and the mutual involvement and creative moral purpose of its members, the Oxford Idealists experienced Hegel's ideas as in certain respects sympathetic. The important influence was Hegel's searching critique of individualism and his general assertion that human nature is fundamentally social. Thus reinforced, they argued that the collective will of society, exerted through the state apparatus, and the private will of its members, exerted through voluntary effort, should seek to create a society in which every person could enjoy the positive freedom of pursuing material and moral self-development, not through predatory attack on or manipulation of others, but through responsible participation in a context of mutual respect.

Hegel's glorification, however, of the authoritarian state, seen as an end in itself with rights totally transcending those of the individual, fell on stony ground so far as the British Idealists were concerned, with the partial exception of Bosanquet and the handful of publicists referred to in the preceding chapter. 'The anti-liberal bias of Hegel's political theory was so remote from the realities of English politics that it passed almost unobserved' (Sabine, 1963, p. 667).

One of Green's disciples, L. T. Hobhouse, in an authoritative statement of the 'new' Liberalism in 1911, emphasised that 'Society consists wholly of persons. It has no distinct personality separate from and superior to those of its members' (Hobhouse, 1911, p. 127). Not the least revealing contrast between Britain and Germany is apparent here. Upon those foundations of theory represented by the idea of community and the positive state, Hegel, responsive to a persistent German tradition, erected a superstructure which gave the state a transcendent and absolutist reality – ideas later distorted and exploited by others as ideological supports for an aggressive, imperialist, racialist regime glorifying militarism and war. Upon the same foundations, but against a background of British empiricism and the evangelical movement, some upper-class spokesmen developed a political theory that supported their impulses to knit the classes together with a practical programme of enlarging the life chances of the poor and deprived.

Green was a representative figure in the practical application as well as the theoretical elucidation of these ideas, and his role extended far beyond academic analysis into public policy. Green himself died in 1882, but he and others like him moulded a considerable number of serious young men dedicated to reform not only in politics and the civil service but also in social work, philanthropy and adult education. While far from rejecting the need for an interventionist liberalism, Green preferred to reform motives rather than structures of government. British patterns of social relations and voluntary effort gave him and the members of his school and their numerous successors some scope for doing so. 'In contrast to the alienated European intelligentsia to which Marx and Herzen belonged, the Idealists had ready access to both the world of voluntary organizations and that of party organizations.' This vitally affected attitudes and strategy. Marx and Herzen respected only those parties which had an oppositional ideology and engaged in direct action, whereas the Idealists believed that the strongest motive for reform was to be found not in anger, but in guilt – in the discrepancy between ideals and performance. Seeking, among other things, to close the gap between the classes, they fostered cohesive relationships of respect and confidence with active figures in working-class organisations and, with their manifest sincerity, convinced at least some of them that the philosophy of duty, moral responsibility and a humane constitutionalism was not, in their cases – as it certainly was in others – a façade of cant covering exploitation and cynical indifference. 'Many of them were to spend their lives in improving the school system, establishing or working in settlement houses, reorganizing charity and the Poor Law, and contributing to the movements for adult education and making access to the universities possible for classes hitherto excluded.' Toynbee Hall, Oxford House, the London Ethical Society, the Fabian Society – these were part of a reformers' universe which had links with Westminster and Whitehall and which, as we shall see, helped to shape state policy towards trade unionism and collective bargaining. 'To an impressive degree they affected their country's social and political arrangements by transforming the way in which one part of its ruling class viewed itself and its obligations' (Richter, 1966, pp. 4, 12–14).

Green's liberalism could be bent towards conservatism, but it was more resonant with liberal forms of socialism which eschewed class conflict and which, though embodying 'many of the ideas that go to make up the framework of Socialist teaching . . . also emphasize elements of individual right and personal independence, of which Socialism at times appears oblivious' (Hobhouse, 1911, p. 211). No sharp difference of principle separated Green's liberalism from Fabian socialism, but there is no reason to suppose direct influence by Green upon the Fabians: there were many separate and independent expressions of a ground-swell in late Victorian political opinion. It was a ground-swell produced by a mixture of ideas, sentiments, impulses and motives. Some of the middle-class reformers who moved into the Fabian Society had been influenced by the Positivists – it was Frederic Harrison who reminded Beatrice Webb in 1893 that the

Positivist Programme of 1872, 'which called for improved housing, sanitation, land usage and the conditions of work, had long anticipated certain socialist ideas' (F. Harrison, 1975, p. vii). It was Harrison, too, who first convinced her during the 1880s of 'the economic validity of trade unionism and factory legislation' (B. Webb, 1938, Vol. 1, p. 169). Positivism had been one outcome of a fusion, after the middle of the century, of two major strands of thought and feeling – first, the belief that it was by science and science alone that all human misery would ultimately be swept away, and secondly, an impulse of self-subordinating service fast becoming secularised in the sense of being transferred from God to man. The result was a 'religion of humanity', served through the glorification of science, with its synthesis of observation, hypothesis, experiment and verification.

But also at work was the freshly stimulated motivational thrust of the evangelical – or ex-evangelical – conscience, together with the ambition of men of affairs who hoped to mobilise the mood for their own political purposes. Beatrice Webb, posing the question: 'Why this demand for State intervention from a generation reared amidst rapidly rising riches and disciplined in the school of philosophical radicalism and orthodox political economy?', did not find the answer in pressure from the working classes. 'The origin of the ferment is to be discovered in a new consciousness of sin' – by which she meant not personal but collective or class sin – 'among men of intellect and men of property' – whom she traced as far back as Shaftesbury and Oastler. 'This class-consciousness of sin was usually accompanied by devoted personal service, sometimes by open confession and a deliberate dedication of means and strength to the organization of society on a more equalitarian basis' (B. Webb, 1948, pp. 203–6, 208).

We have resumed contact here with certain themes examined earlier – in particular the idea of service and the paternalistic conception of concern for social subordinates and inferiors. Largely excluded from industrial and commercial relations, where individualism and low-trust contract were on the whole the predominant principles, paternalism was increasingly potent in the widening field of social policy. Many social activists would have fiercely denied it – Green and the whole generation of liberals to which he belonged were 'nervously fearful of "paternalism" and the undermining of individual responsibility by social legislation' (Sabine, 1963, p. 735). And it is true that some varieties of the New Liberalism, such as that purveyed by George Cadbury and his associates, made a point of emphasising the supreme value of collective and independent self-help among working men. Yet there has always been a tendency within British middle-class Liberalism, and to some extent within British middle-class socialism, to express the utmost sympathy with working-class aspirations but only so long as the workers themselves abstained from militant and assertive action to realise them, or so long as the aspirations were such as the middle classes felt able to approve. Militancy and 'inappropriate' aspirations have often caused a rapid shift from sympathy to hostility, revealing in the process that the sympathy embodied an essentially paternalistic stance.

Nevertheless this array of reformist, paternalist, humanitarian and philanthropic impulses is of great significance in the interpretation of Britain's social and political structure and the place within it of her industrial relations system. In the first place, the unique pattern of social cohesion which Britain's governing circles still found too valuable and – short of compulsive last-ditch necessity – too politically sacrosanct to put at hazard, rendered them more open to proposals for reform now that the working classes were becoming soberly and respectably organised and articulate within the established framework. Piecemeal reform, appropriately delayed and whittled down to the minimum acceptable, was after all a crucial element in the strategy. It was therefore of great importance for social cohesion that, at a time when electoral needs were inclining party managers towards cautious consideration of inexpensive social measures and concessions, there was developing outside state boundaries an array of constructive initiatives available for adoption by political agencies. 'It may be said that this novel concentration of attention on the social condition of the people was due neither to intellectual curiosity nor to the spirit of philanthropy but rather to a panic fear of the newly-enfranchised democracy. But this is looking at the same fact from another standpoint' (B. Webb, 1938, pp. 174–5). It was, nevertheless, a crucial standpoint, for it greatly reinforced the incentives to action. If 'the people' were to be entrusted with the weapon of trade unionism and, through the ballot box, with some influence over the nation's wealth and overseas dominions, was it safe for so many of them to remain poor and uneducated?

In the second place, and more important, the promotion of social cohesion was only to a very limited extent pursued through formal action by the state. Much was pursued by organisations and movements quite outside the official state structures of national and local government, enforcement and socialisation. Many of these responded to the new mood by initiating, or being receptive towards, policies which embodied concern with 'the social condition of the people'. As a consequence, the 'changed position of labour', as contemporaries experienced it, expressed itself in many more ways than legislation. In his 1894 introduction to the third edition of Stanley Jevons's *The State in Relation to Labour*, Michael Cababé commented that

> The progress of the Labour movement during the last twelve years can be traced but imperfectly from the statute book. Legislation . . . has proceeded much on the old lines, and has mainly consisted in extensions and improvements of the Factory Acts and the Mines Acts. Indications indeed of a new departure may be found in the Acts attempting to regulate the hours of railway servants and of shop assistants, and to improve the lot of the rural labourer by means of allotments and small holdings; but, on the whole, the fact that a new spirit has arisen, or that old ideals have been dimmed, is as yet only faintly to be traced in Acts of Parliament. (Cababé, 1894, p. xiii)

Social Cohesion and Imperialism

Among those forces promoting social cohesion which owed relatively little to formal state action were the multitudinous influences fostering and propagating imperialist consciousness. For some understanding of how this came to be so potent we must return to the Oxford of Jowett and Green, where idealism and the spirit of service took other expressions besides R. H. Tawney, Toynbee Hall, the Workers' Educational Association and the support of trade unionism and collective bargaining. 'These elevated, fundamentally religious, minds with their neo-Greek, neo-Puritan, creed of self-rewarding morality, their careful charitable lives, their strong social conscience, were guarded by the fleets and guns of the greatest naval power in the world' (Bowle, 1963, p. 279). Beyond the Oxford cloisters were fierce capitalist competition, the armaments race and, above all, the struggle for empire. But even here the philosophy of duty and service played its part. Jowett's Oxford stimulated and focused 'the sense of world-wide responsibility which took possession of the young men's minds' and, through one of Jowett's pupils, Alfred Milner, 'gave impetus to a new philosophy of empire. This sense of responsibility sprang from a general conviction that in England more than anywhere else in the world, the great problems had all been resolved or were well on the way to being resolved – in particular the problem of serving both God and Mammon' (Faber, 1957, pp. 29–30).

Given that the impulse towards the ameliorative promotion of class harmony and the idealistic element in imperialism had certain common sources, it is not surprising that in some members of the middle and upper classes they went together, the mixture contributing much to social imperialism. Milner 'was a man of the Left whom circumstances later forced into association with the Tory party . . . in many ways he had less mental kinship with bourgeois democrats . . . than with Fabian Imperialists such as the Webbs' (Grigg, 1973, p. 257). Something of the same mixture appeared in, for example, Leo Amery. Strongly influenced by an evangelical mother, Amery went from Harrow to Balliol; developed a detestation of *laissez-faire* individualism with its celebration of blatant self-seeking to the detriment of larger purposes; toyed with socialism and helped to form Oxford's first Fabian Society; served a stint at Toynbee Hall and soon settled on a life-long and passionate commitment to empire unity, imperial preference and the principle of 'armed strength as the guarantee of peace' (Amery, 1953, p. 57). Men such as Milner, Amery, Curzon, and a host of lesser pro-consuls helped to humanise the imperialist thrust, and to create the favourable elements within the deeply ambivalent feelings with which British imperialism is viewed by her sometime possessions, particularly of course India. But more important domestically was the fact that innumerable hack journalists romanticised and glorified the myth of empire.

In trying to assess the nature of this consciousness it is necessary to recall the close association between the Victorian spirit of service and the mystique of the public school and the English gentleman. Some of the ingredients in the national socialism package were by no means ignoble

and the imperialist element, for example, could not have awakened 'the
enthusiasm of the masses if it had been nothing more than a manifestation
of commercial greed, and had not contained a very considerable element
of idealism' (Halévy, 1961d, p. 18). Milner, Amery, Roberts, Ashley,
Cunningham, Blatchford, the Fabians; none had any interest in promoting
the interests of capitalist acquisitiveness as such. Certainly the Webbs, like
H. G. Wells and Bernard Shaw, thought not in terms of supporting a
leisured class in its privileges but in terms of disinterested experts pursuing
national efficiency within a system of state control and carrying the same
civilised order to the world's backward regions. The literary figures, too,
who were more important in popular dissemination – Stevenson, Conrad,
Henley and, above all, Kipling – spoke not to self-interest but to adven-
ture, endurance and heroism in distant lands, the experience of battle and
glory, service under the white man's burden. The picture of men enduring
tedium, discomfort, and perhaps danger in the service of what was then
seen as a noble ideal – that of administering the greatest empire the world
had yet seen and carrying a superior culture to inferior ones – was an
obviously attractive theme for countless speakers, writers and publicists.
And, as Roberts has noted, the educational system systematically reinforced this ideological dissemination.

It is not easy to convey the full nature of this dissemination to those born
after the mid-1930s. From the late nineteenth century to the Second World
War, popular culture was suffused with an awareness of empire which was
not necessarily explicit or obtrusive but which was never less than a
permanent backdrop to the national life. Images of empire sank deep into
the British consciousness. Only for a small socialist minority were they
images of domination and exploitation: of workers at bare subsistence
level producing primary commodities at knock-down prices for the rich
industrial powers. For the majority they were images of 'kith and kin'
courageously subduing nature in far-distant lands; of district officers
upholding justice and decency in lonely outposts; of laconic majors
guarding dangerous frontiers. A whole popular literature developed
which linked together the ideas of service within the empire, the public
school mystique, and Clubland heroes who were effortlessly and innately
superior to the lower orders, themselves apt to figure as loyal but stupid
retainers, seedy subversives, or comic relief. Some sections of the working
classes were more resistant to these projections than others, but there
cannot be many who escaped entirely. There have been few attempts to
gauge the effects of this culture on the attitudes of the organised working
class, yet they need to be taken into account in any attempt to judge the
texture of the social bond. The likelihood is that they helped to make the
attitude of organised labour towards the ruling classes extremely complex
in that they added a measure of respect to feelings of resentment, cynicism
and class hostility. They may also have strengthened distaste for those
socialist doctrines seen as foreign and alien. For these reasons the imperialist culture needs some attention.

It could not have developed as it did had it not met some receptive
chords in the hearts and minds of those who received it. We oversimplify
the picture if we paint it in terms of the *tabula rasa* – the blank white sheet

which merely receives ideas imprinted upon it by a designing ruling order. British class relations had taken on some deeply ambivalent tendencies so far as the attitudes of lower to upper classes were concerned. Alongside the dispositions of independence, wariness and cynicism held by many members of the working class towards all forms of authority – including that of their own union officers – there was often a belief that somewhere in the higher ranks of society there existed a superior breed of people capable of deeper, finer feelings. They were not the politicians, employers, magistrates and officials one met in everyday life but they were there somewhere and they were innately superior to one's own kind. In later decades when some local working-class worthy, his wits addled by a lifetime of committees, was pensioned off to the House of Lords, he would be viewed with an undertow of contemptuous scepticism towards his pretensions – 'He's no better than we are'. However fiercely one guarded one's own class pride and traditions, one might well concede in the last extremity that breeding and education were what ultimately counted. Only committed socialists (as against 'labour supporters') were likely to be wholly immune from such sentiments.

This structure of feeling and attitude reached its apogee between the late nineteenth century and 1939, with writers and spokesmen, acting under varying degrees of self-interest, reflecting the ideology back to their publics in a way that heightened it, gave it coherent form, and invested it with the emotion which they were able to generate with their arts and skills. They reached even the working-class young.

> Even before the first world war many youngsters in the working class had developed an addiction for Frank Richards's school stories. The standards of conduct observed by Harry Wharton and his friends at Greyfriars set social norms to which schoolboys and some young teenagers strove spasmodically to conform . . . Through the Old School we learned to admire guts, integrity, tradition . . . The Famous Five stood for us as young knights, *sans peur et sans reproche*. Any idea that Harry Wharton could possibly have been guilty of 'certain practices' would have filled us with shame . . . With nothing in our own school that called for love or allegiance, Greyfriars became for some of us our true Alma Mater, to whom we felt bound by a dreamlike loyalty . . . It came as a curious shock to one who revered the Old School when it dawned upon him that he himself was a typical sample of the 'low cads' so despised by all at Greyfriars . . . The public school ethos, distorted into myth and sold among us weekly in penny numbers, for good or ill, set ideals and standards. In the final estimate it may well be found that Frank Richards during the first quarter of the twentieth century had more influence on the mind and outlook of young working-class England than any other single person, not excluding Baden-Powell. (R. Roberts, 1973, pp. 160–1)

Orwell had earlier, in 1939, offered a similar and greatly extended analysis, noting that even the modern successors to the *Magnet* and *Gem* were more like them than unlike. The aristocrat who drawls and wears a monocle but 'is always to the fore in moments of danger turns up over and over again', and 'no one in a star part is ever permitted to drop an aitch'. Orwell noted also that in terms of ownership the *Magnet* and *Gem* were 'closely linked up with the *Daily Telegraph* and the *Financial Times*. This in itself would be enough to arouse certain suspicions, even if it were not obvious that the stories in the boys' weeklies are politically vetted' (Orwell, 1962, pp. 198, 201).

What was being strengthened by all this was not so much attachment to a set of specific economic and political institutions – these continued to be seen by many in the organised working class as structures of domination, largely inevitable but rendered bearable by increasing possibilities of some participatory influence on decision-making. It was something vaguer and more diffuse yet capable of being a potent influence – a national standard of admired behaviour invested with the glamour of a certain ruling class style: the style of the gentleman. Though it was the public schools which fastened the model upon the national consciousness it was not a public school invention. The outlines of the Victorian – as against earlier – conceptions of the English gentleman were forming in fact by the late eighteenth century. He emerges unmistakably as Mr Knightley, landowner in the great house in Jane Austen's *Emma* (1816): brave but not reckless, sensible but certainly not intellectual, courteous, considerate and, above all, fair-minded towards his social inferiors, ever ready to recognise fine behaviour in the lowest and condemn ignoble behaviour in the highest. We find other portraits in Jane Austen of aristocrats, squires and parsons who are selfish, arrogant, vain, foolish and contemptible. Yet among a dozen of these in real life it needed only one approximation to Mr Knightley to keep the model alive and upon his broad shoulders the model rested until its long slow extinction between the two world wars.

A not unimportant item in the style of the perfect gentleman was his recognition that true gentlemen might be found anywhere in the social hierarchy – there were such things as 'nature's gentlemen'. But these were understandably rare, the lower orders lacking tradition, education and breeding. For the vast majority the consequent sense of exclusion by birth and education only heightened the mystique, a mystique further strengthened by symbols of imputed superiority and inferiority which bore upon working-class experience in a hundred different ways. To some extent this was calculated. The mystique was too valuable a ruling-class asset to be left to chance and its members observed a code designed to sustain it. Its widespread propagation, however, required no conspiracy; writers, journalists and publicists themselves often believed in it and, in any case, had their bread and butter to earn.

Yet it was a difficult and subtle style to apply in practical face-to-face relations, and practitioners, especially in industry, often mishandled it to the disadvantage of themselves and their class. Nevertheless in the wider realm it developed into a powerful governing weapon, and one of its central strengths was the role of duty and service within the empire – the manifest fact that the ruling classes were prepared to educate their sons not only to rule the roost and skim the cream off the labour of the inferior orders but also to sweat and, if necessary, die in far-off uncomfortable places.

The significance of all this for our present purpose is that a popular, visible and constantly publicised imperialism proved to be a fortuitous and timely benefit for the ruling order. Now a fusion of landed, financial and industrial power, it stood in some need of a reinforcement of its mystique. Not that British society was rocking on its foundations – despite the noise of industrial and political conflict, the high degree of consensus about methods of handling it suggested deep roots of stability and considerable reserves of resilience, to which trade unionism, collective bargaining, a widening franchise, and working-class political activity were contributing. Yet men of affairs concerned to maintain the principal framework of the status quo and the civilisation which it supported – including the privileges of its favoured beneficiaries – were right in thinking that a working class with a clear and determined alternative vision could use its growing footholds to vastly greater effect than had been evident so far. This danger would be minimised to the extent that the working class could be brought to accept the mystique of the ruling order – a mystique that included patterns of behaviour in which the ruling classes could be presented as displaying superiority of performance. Yet the difficulties of maintaining this acceptance were increasing. Urbanisation and other changes were emancipating people from small rural and industrial communities where, with a mixture of power, status, self-confidence and paternalism, the landed gentry and the family firms often succeeded for some of the time in imposing their values and vision upon the lower orders – sometimes only in the sense that the lower orders lacked the confidence and perspective to assert alternatives, but often in the full sense that they internalised the mystique of ruling-class innate superiority. Had it not been for the new cult of empire it might have seemed by the end of the century that the traditional agrarian mystique of the landed ruling class was waning with the contraction of its material base (Anderson, 1965, p. 23). And this was important in that industrial governance, too, was manifestly not sustaining the same aura, as the workers themselves were making all too clear with their increasingly confident challenges. However, imperialism and the mystifications and myths constructed around it came to the rescue, infusing fresh legitimation into the whole of the ruling class, now increasingly unified by the public schools. Not all the working class succumbed. But enough of it – and even of its organisations – did so, with resulting internal divisions which mark them to this day.

The peculiar nature of this renewed vertical bonding needs emphasis. It was not a bonding which had much practical relevance for everyday control within the institutions of industrial and political government. On the contrary, the British working class was moving up a rising graph of independent industrial and political action. What imperialism did, along with its associated images and myths, was to create around the higher reaches of the social order a certain aura of glamour, of emotional appeal, of qualities of essential 'British-ness' which only the right breeding and education could fully bestow and only the ruling class fully possess but in which all could to some extent participate. And because it was the

Conservative Party which was most closely identified with these higher reaches of the social order, it was the Conservative Party which was able to exploit this aura of British-ness. 'Being Conservative', said Quintin Hogg, MP, in 1967, 'is only another way of being British.' He was taking his cue from a long tradition to which much was contributed by Disraeli, who declared that 'By the Conservative cause I mean the splendour of the Crown, the lustre of the Peerage, the privileges of the Commons, the rights of the poor. I mean that harmonious union, that magnificent concord of all interests, of all classes, on which our national greatness depends.' This view of the Conservative mission and its right to speak for the whole nation, 'which owes so much to the baroque imagination of Disraeli, has had a profound influence on the course of English politics' (McKenzie and Silver, 1968, pp. 18, 35–6).

Imperialist consciousness thereby enabled the Conservative Party to appropriate the concept and rhetoric of patriotism. This has proved a significant loss for the Labour movement. Embedded in the concept are meanings and emotions which no movement seeking mass appeal can afford to ignore. Certainly, many socialists have always found repugnant that definition which expresses the assertion of one's country *against* others, and still more that which lauds the imperialist imposition of national dominance overseas (A. Barnett, 1982, p. 93). They have repudi-ated the elevation of these definitions in public life and public policy. But there is another definition which a would-be popular movement dispa-rages at its peril. This refers to love of the best in one's country and its achievements, along with the readiness to defend a common identity against aggression. These meanings can be clearly separated, but too easily become blurred in both discussion and action. Labour has often been constrained, in the process of differentiating itself from its political opponents, to condemn patriotism when manifested in its aggressive meanings. But because Conservatism has appropriated the whole concept its residual meaning and attached emotions have been denied to Labour, more especially to socialism. To this day the failure of British socialism to make the necessary appropriation of a natural and legitimate sentiment of radical patriotism remains a potentially divisive one within working–class ranks. Still alive into the 1900s, radical patriotism was almost submerged by 1914 and the war finished off the process so far as its popular expression was concerned. From now on the Labour movement would be fighting a defensive battle on the subject of love of country. Its difficulties in this sphere were heightened by the propagandist identification of socialism with 'alien' and 'foreign' creeds, carefully fostered ever since. Large numbers, even within the Labour movement itself, proved receptive recipients of this identification.

The nature of imperialist consciousness, focused as it usually was upon socially distant and often geographically distant experience and be-haviour, was, as we have seen, of a sort that could not easily be manipu-lated as an instrument of control by employers and managers at the industrial workplace except in a context of established paternalism. In the more frequent context of adversarial postures, the ruling-class style was likely to be counter-productive in the most literal sense. Imperialist consciousness had come much too late to serve generally as a manipulative element in the command systems of everyday life. Detached from these, it became directed instead towards the apex of the social order, the monarchy. This was a highly appropriate recipient. The crown was too remote to be associated with, still less be held responsible for, the trials and tribulations of everyday life. Convention would soon establish that the crown was 'above politics', and in terms of the perceptions of most citizens it was. What more suitable focus, therefore, for the pomp and circumstance of national imperialist vanity; for the vicarious satisfactions of people at all social levels in the glories of empire; for the belief that what was being celebrated was not so much a particular regime, a particular dynasty, or even a particular set of political institutions, but the good fortune of being British? In this way the monarchy came to be presented – and later carefully cultivated – as the supreme symbol of a unity of British-ness. In fact it was the apex of a particular system of rule and domination; a particular ruling-class structure and style. As a result of becoming presented and perceived, however, as a symbol of unity transcending class and conflict it performed, as it still performs, a profoundly ideological function.

What is being suggested here, therefore, is that although the ingredients of an incipient national socialism never cohered into a unified movement, one of the ingredients, imperialism, had the effect of strengthening the existing bonds and institutions of British society with new symbols which included a cult of monarchy. The strengthening was not of the kind which led the British people to vest in the state a significance transcending that of the individuals composing it. They remained highly resistant to all such doctrines. Nor did it even inspire the lesser notion of some supra-party national purpose, leading them to accept some supra-party national leadership. Rather was it a strengthening of that deep-lying resilience and insularity of the social bond which were expressed in, among other things, dispositions of mistrust towards proposals of radical change, resistance to foreign ideas, and – later – an ability to survive prolonged total war. Perhaps the master stroke of British Conservatism 'has been to pre-empt not merely the nation's past but its national symbols and its sense of community as well'. This has included the complementary argument that the party's opponents 'are in some sense a deliberately divisive force in the national community, the champions of sectional rather than national interests ... Few democratic political parties can have so systematically and ruthlessly called into question the integrity, the devotion to the institutions of the country, and the patriotism of its opponents' (McKenzie and Silver, 1968, pp. 35, 48, 49).

Thus developed a ruling-class style which infused imperialist greed, territorial aggrandisement and nationalist arrogance with a spirit of duty and service and a code of admired behaviour successfully presented to the lower orders as quintessentially British. It was within these bonds of strengthened resilience that the severe industrial and political conflicts of the future were played out – and by the help of which they were ultimately contained. Imperialist consciousness did not prevent strikes; nor did it modify the adversary relationship or prompt all working men to vote

Conservative. It was almost certainly, however, among the factors which made foreign socialist doctrines seem to most workers alien and uncongenial, and which made it difficult for them to carry over their experience of workplace grievances and conflict into a critique of the total social order and its ruling classes. In that way, it became one of the forces helping to maintain the industrial relations system in its emergent shape, given that the system depended for its sufferance upon its remaining contained within the basic expectations of the status quo.

Direct Supports of the System: the Role of the Board of Trade

What we have just been examining are certain positive but indirect effects exerted by social forces towards consolidation of the industrial relations system. We turn now to ways in which the system enjoyed certain direct supports. Among them was the 'fair wages' movement. Given public professions by both parties of concern for the working classes, reformers were now using as a test of sincerity the state's treatment of its own employees. Both parliamentary parties felt it judicious 'to set an example to private industry' by accepting a Liberal resolution in the House of Commons in 1891 laying down, under TUC prodding, a government duty 'in all government contracts ... to make every effort to secure the payment of such wages as are generally accepted as current in each trade for competent workmen in the district where the work is carried out'. Though specifically toned down to exclude reference to 'recognized trade union rates', the resolution provided the unions with useful leverage and was strengthened in 1909. Local authorities and public bodies had already begun, under pressure from trades councils, to include similar 'fair wages' clauses in their contracts from 1889 onward.

Major interest in the sphere of direct supports, however, must focus on the Board of Trade and its policies in the labour field between the 1880s and 1914. It yields much that is fascinating and revealing. For among the state agencies it was the Board of Trade that took up and promoted the policies of those sections among the ruling classes which saw trade unionism and collective bargaining as the best means of pursuing three desirable ends. They seemed to offer a method of pursuing industrial peace and regulated order – even possibly of promoting active co-operation between management and workers. They provided a safety-valve that both reduced the working-class threat to property and class relations and offered a means of social control. And finally, they furthered these purposes through organisations and institutionalised procedures which were fully congruent with the whole strategy, legitimation and ideology of rule. All these were fully reconcilable with the overall aim of the Board, which was 'the facilitation, in so far as was consistent with the canons of fairness and freedom, of capitalist enterprise' (Caldwell, 1959, p. 367). That the Board favoured collectivist solutions was bound to bring it the enmity of those sections among the ruling classes that preferred the assertion of atomistic individualism, and the Liberty and Property

Defence League mounted attacks from a viewpoint shared by many industrialists, by the Conservative press, and by much of the Whitehall establishment. The Board was not notably dislodged.

This ability of the Board to pursue its own consistent line stemmed from several factors. There was no serious Cabinet concern with labour questions and industrial unrest before 1911, and this, together with the lack of political consensus as to the best strategy to adopt, ensured that 'government measures . . . were largely initiated by departmental ministers in conjunction with their permanent officials' (Davidson, 1978, pp. 571–2). And the fact that among the relevant departments the Board of Trade came to outweigh both the Home Office and the Local Government Board as the source of official industrial relations policy (Middlemas, 1979, p. 59) has been explained in terms of the Board's long tradition of administrative initiative, inventiveness and drive. This, in turn, has been attributed to the presidency being of low status and carrying a salary of less than half that of other Cabinet ministers, with the result that a high turnover of ministers gave the permanent staff considerable independence (Caldwell, 1959, pp. 369–70). It was also significant, however, that during this period the senior labour establishment was not appointed by open competitive examination but selected for 'peculiar qualifications', a 'specialist' recruitment which was in marked contrast to the 'generalist' emphasis of other departments of social administration (Davidson and Lowe, 1981, pp. 265–6; Davidson, 1982). Whatever the causes, 'an outstanding feature of the growth of social administration in Britain before 1914 was the degree to which the Board of Trade monopolized the formulation, initiation and execution of labour policy' (Davidson, 1972, p. 227). The Home Office, by comparison, hardly counted. 'Much legislation', including one of the great union-liberating statutes, the Conspiracy and Protection of Property Act, 'was initiated by external pressure groups in the face of Home Office apathy' (Davidson and Lowe, 1981, p. 269).

The Board's traditions of initiative and drive would not, however, have persisted automatically and it is possible that it attracted men of the calibre and interests to ensure continuance. There was also, for periods in the 1880s and 1890s, a Liberal President of the Board of Trade, A. J. Mundella, a committed advocate of collective bargaining on Crompton lines in that he believed it could be conducted so as to promote constructive co-operation between employers and employed. Such views were fully consonant with those of the senior labour establishment recruited between 1886 and 1914. These, numbering thirteen, included seven who were specialists in industrial relations and collective bargaining. They included John Burnett, who had impressed Mundella with his conduct of the nine-hours strike on Tyneside in 1871. Burnett, 'a very good example of a kind of working-class leader which has made a crucially important contribution to the way in which modern British society has evolved' (Allen *et al.*, 1971, p. 107), was the first Labour Correspondent and in 1893 became the first Chief Correspondent, a post he held for more than a decade. His appointment presaged a general practice of appointing experienced trade unionists as local labour correspondents.

Five of the thirteen had participated in the University Settlement

Movement, and five had been associated with the 'New Oxford Movement' of the 1880s. Here again we come upon that complex of impulses and ideals that comprised the 'new' Liberalism and the duty of service, particularly as nourished by the Balliol of Jowett and Green.

> ... it was from the Oxford of the 1880s that emerged a new generation of public servants who, in the pursuit of constructive administration, were to combat the prevailing negative attitude to domestic policy within the civil service. Their careers set an administrative pattern as educationally distinctive as the earlier products of Jowett's Balliol, but whereas their predecessors had lacked any very deep commitment to social action and were recruited largely for their academic ability, men such as Llewellyn Smith developed at Oxford lasting involvements that led on to specialized activities ... (Davidson, 1972, p. 239)

Hubert (later Sir Hubert) Llewellyn Smith had been taken up by the Webbs, who had 'the habit of patronizing and promoting the careers of young men who exemplified their notion of efficient public servants' (MacKenzie and MacKenzie, 1979, p. 356). After serving his apprenticeship, like others in the Webb entourage, at Toynbee Hall, he helped to mobilise public opinion in the match girls strike of 1888 and the great dock strike of 1889, worked for agricultural unionism in 1890 and co-ordinated strike action and picketing for John Burns in the London bus strike of 1891. Moving into the Board of Trade, he was Commissioner of Labour from 1893 to 1903, Controller-General from 1903 to 1907, and Permanent Secretary from 1907 to 1919. The specialist labour interest of the Board had begun in 1886 with a Commons resolution calling for 'full and accurate collection and publication of labour statistics', and in 1893 this activity became the Labour Department of the new Commercial, Labour and Statistical section.

For Llewellyn Smith self-reliance was still the professed basis of social amelioration and the 'education of association' was to him a leading motive force in social change – hence the espousal of the 'new' unionism among groups hitherto thought unorganisable. Yet beneath the appeal to self-reliance lay the paternalist assumption, shared by most of the middle-class reformers, that a self-organising working class, led and taught appropriately, would choose those definitions of the good life favoured by the reformers themselves. The Board's stance generally, in fact, on labour issues was one of enlightened paternalism – in the weaker sense – and trade union leaders were consulted primarily to win consent and co-operation rather than to democratise decision-making.

Systematic fact-gathering was a central preoccupation. Himself a keen empiricist, Llewellyn Smith 'shared in the initiation of a new empirical sociology that was to revolutionize the basis of social policy by the creation of a statistical framework' yielding an accumulation of facts from which social legislation might be evolved. Indeed, he was one of a group of reformers who saw in the educative effects of adequate labour statistics themselves 'the means of working-class self-improvement'. No theory was offered. His political philosophy was 'a set of practical alternatives and proposals' (Davidson, 1972, pp. 229, 240, 242, 244).

Standing so centrally within a certain British tradition, Llewellyn Smith was well equipped to apply a departmental policy which he convinced himself and most employers for most of the time was simply common sense. Since it pursued a path which was neither militant pro-labour collectivism nor militant pro-employer individualism it was regarded by many, in the curious British way, as 'impartial' and 'objective'. Needless to say, it was nothing of the kind. Nor was it seen so by relatively small groups of the far right and the far left. To the former it appeared as a vehicle for the new militant unionism and socialism. To the latter it seemed a conspiracy to institutionalise industrial conflict and, through that, to preserve the 'moderation' and servile constitutionalism of the main body of union leaders and maintain orthodox criteria of wage determination. The Board, in its reports, sought to discredit both groups (Davidson, 1982, p. 173).

Given the Board's policy of promoting union recognition and collective bargaining, it is indicative of the prevalent dispositions within British society that the Board's conciliators were able so often to present as simply 'reasonable' the setting up of systematic procedures of joint negotiation and dispute-settlement. The arch-practitioner of this approach, G. R. (later Sir George and eventually Lord) Askwith, was later to deny that the Labour Department 'had any policy. It might be said that they waited upon events' (Askwith, 1920, p. 128). This was simply a case of the British practical man who is unable or unwilling to identify the policy or principles implicit in his actions. By 1911 the power of the state apparatus as distinct from party administrations was increasing, and although this was mostly in negative and often haphazard ways which could not compare with the centralised bureaucracy of Germany, Middlemas suggests that the Labour Department was the one possible exception to the generalisation that 'no single office possessed a departmental opinion . . .' (Middlemas, 1979, pp. 29, 31). It is probable that many ministers in successive governments were scarcely aware of what was going on and that some of those who were aware disapproved. Certainly, the policy can hardly be viewed as a carefully considered and calculated programme consciously backed by major sections of the ruling class. Yet it served to reinforce and continue some central tendencies in the British system of order and control, which is no doubt why the reformers, though on occasion challenged by some powerful sections of society, nevertheless enjoyed enough of a free hand to be able to make their policy the predominant practice of the state. They were little known by the general public. Halévy refers to men in the background of political life who 'played a part probably more important than the great political figures who occupied the stage while they worked in the wings' (Halévy, 1961e, p. 265).

Their policy and practice could not help but embody a view of the proper and desirable relations between employers and workers and between industry and the state. It must not be assumed, however, that in encouraging and promoting union recognition and collective bargaining the Board's officials wanted to further, and believed themselves to be furthering, those adversary, win-lose, arms-length relations which middle-class candid friends so frequently identified – and deplored – as the predominant mode in Britain. There is evidence, some circumstantial, some direct, that certain leading Board officials shared the prediction offered in 1876 by Crompton, the Positivist enthusiast for 'conciliation', in 1882 by Jevons, and in 1897 by the Webbs, that in their responsible maturity the unions would move away from their defensive restrictionist stance towards a role of constructive co-operation with management. We have noted Mundella's promotional role at the Board. Llewellyn Smith was an early protegé of the Webbs and the famous pair wasted little time on those with the wrong views. Under his leadership, the Board was to show concern in 1916 about 'securing industrial harmony and efficiency after the war' and the Whitley Committee which resulted from that pressure made co-operative positive-sum relations the keynote of its recommendations on collective bargaining.

Askwith, assistant secretary in the same department 1907–9, Controller-General 1909–11 and Chief Industrial Commissioner 1911–19, did not, it seems, finally abandon hope until after the war that the two sides could be led in that direction. Throughout his long and immensely varied experience of conciliation and arbitration he consistently pursued, in his own words, a 'policy of peace and construction'. Conciliation, as a term, now covered the activities of someone who intervened in a dispute to bring the parties together for peaceful negotiation and perhaps preside over their deliberations; it also covered, as in 'conciliation machinery', the systematic disputes procedures which Askwith and other 'conciliators' often tried to establish. He made it 'a rule each time as an industrial dispute was submitted to him, to secure the signature by the parties concerned' of a collective procedural agreement establishing voluntary joint machinery for negotiation and dispute settlement. 'He thus built up piece by piece throughout the United Kingdom a vast written code governing the relations between employers and employed . . .' (Halévy, 1961e, p. 265). This fails to convey the predominant extent to which the parties themselves were creating this code under their own initiative – the Labour Department was only seeking to universalise a system which employers and unions had long been evolving for themselves – but it correctly identifies the principal thrust of departmental policy.   ˙

Askwith makes clear, however, that what he sought and hoped for was not adversary-style collective bargaining but conciliation in the earlier sense as conceived by Crompton and others. In a long book published in 1920 which expounds his philosophy and practical experiences, Askwith never once uses the term collective bargaining but refers always to conciliation, which he defines as 'indicating a common interest and effecting better understanding between employers and employed'. His stance emerges even more clearly when he describes how 'the well-known phrase, "Capital and Labour", emphasizes the view that there are in this country two rival camps or armies, acting sometimes in veiled and sometimes in open opposition to each other . . . each evidently regarding the interests of the other as opposed to their own'. This had to end: '. . . the employing class and the workpeople must unite in a common effort and realize that their interests are identical . . . the theory that one side must beat the other has to be thrown out . . . The unity of the two camps is the aim of conciliation'.

Commenting on the 1917 Whitley recommendation that industries should each set up their own permanent, standing joint councils which would range far beyond the present limited stock of contested bargaining issues, Askwith declared that if 'the aim is mutual cooperation and joint effort, and that aim is continuously kept in sight and broadly interpreted, an industry . . . may be improved by the existence of a council'. But if the parties remained mutually predatory the situation would be made worse (Askwith 1920, pp. 67, 84, 489). Askwith appears to have decided, however, that the case was hopeless, for he became leader of the Middle Class Union, an organisation viewed with distaste by Lord Robert Cecil as a strike-breaking body whose object was to persuade 'the smaller trading, propertied and professional classes [to] band themselves together to protect their interests . . . and secure their property . . . from revolution and extreme Labour demands' (Cowling, 1971, pp. 65, 74).

It was within his earlier frame of reference, however, that the Labour Department developed what was unquestionably a collectivist momentum. It 'sought to strengthen the bargaining power of labour in two important respects. It advocated union recognition where the right of labour to combine was still denied by employers, and it advocated the reform of trade union law'. Towards recalcitrant employers in railways, shipping and quarrying, the Board maintained a steady policy; the Permanent Secretary, Sir Courtenay Boyle, declaring that the time was past 'when the right of wage-earners to combine for their protection could be called in question'. According to one specialist, 'it would appear that the shift in the labour policy of many organized employers' towards collective bargaining 'was, if not initially inspired, at least reinforced' by the efforts of the Labour Department (Davidson, 1978, pp. 573, 575, 576).

A policy of this kind was not easy to embody in positive legislation, the Board's concern being to adapt itself to, and in turn help to foster, the essentially voluntarist nature of the system that was developing. 'Although a department of government it did not work primarily through law, but by cajoling, persuading, leaning on the parties to a conflict . . .' It thereby 'contributed to that tradition of avoidance of legalism and the insulation of industrial disputes from politics' (Crouch, 1979, p. 30). Yet at an early stage those constructing this policy felt impelled to bring it the recognition and status which some sort of appearance in the statute book would bestow. After several attempts in the early 1890s that were crowded out by more pressing business, a Conciliation Act was passed in 1896 which expressed approval of voluntary standing disputes machinery by trying – ineffectually – through a system of registration to give it 'a certain status and dignity', and which formally vested in the Board of Trade powers to provide conciliation and arbitration services if requested. 'At the last moment powers to compel attendance of witnesses or disclosure of documents were omitted' (Askwith, 1920, p. 77). 'Apart from giving direct statutory authority for incurring the small expenditure necessary, the Act does not seem to have given the Board power to do anything which it could not do and was not in fact doing before' (Amulree, 1929, pp. 108–9). Askwith was later to give further indication, by his comments on the Act, that his conception of conciliation was essentially that of a co-operative problem-solving exercise. In the course of somewhat disparaging remarks he noted that the Act 'did nothing by itself to reconcile the growing force of labour and the resistance of capital' and did not show 'that any step could be taken to organize capital and labour in any trade as a joint effort' (Askwith, 1920, p. 78).

There were, however, indications that Establishment support for collective bargaining by no means necessarily rested on the co-operative vision. Among them was the Royal Commission on Labour, with John Burnett as one of its two secretaries, appointed by a Conservative government in 1891 and including among its members a number of prominent trade unionists as well as industrialists, lawyers and politicians. Its report of 1894 gives valuable clues to much Establishment thinking. Until recently the reason why trade unionism had for a long time been free of attacks by governments had been partly that the state's coercive apparatus was inadequate and partly that such a policy would have been damaging to a successful system of rule and its ideology and legitimation. Freedom of association, 'fairness' and 'class equality before the law' had been key notions in this presentation. These remained important, but a new key notion was the contribution which trade unionism might make to order and control. Fused with the still persistent idea of social progress, it resulted in a *Fifth and Final Report* (C. 7421, 1894) of which some passages were almost a panegyric of collective bargaining.

> When organizations on either side are so strong as fairly to balance each other, the result . . . is a disposition . . . to form a mixed board, meeting regularly to discuss and settle questions affecting their relations . . . The most successful . . . are those . . . where organizations on either side are strongest and most complete . . . We hope and believe that the present rapid extension of voluntary boards will continue. Authoritative and responsible organisations of workpeople could maintain control over their members' behaviour in a way that legal sanctions could not.
>
> The general conclusion seems to be that the moral sanction or force which at present is alone available to secure respect to the arrangements between bodies of employers and workmen . . . and to the awards of arbitration, can only . . . be relied upon . . . in those trades which are very well organized so as to comprise practically all the workers in a trade, or important districts of it, and which have a strong and efficient form of internal government.

This represented progress.

> . . . just as a modern war between two great European states, costly though it is, seems to represent a higher stage of civilization than the incessant local fights and border raids which occur in times or places where governments are less strong and centralized, so, on the whole, an

occasional great conflict, breaking in upon years of peace, seems to be preferable to continued local bickerings, stoppages of work, and petty conflicts.

In the period up to 1914, dissent from these views, in political terms, lay within rather than between parties. 'Both major parties showed themselves interested in "respectable" trade union activity, and, implicitly, in the formation of powerful formal bodies on both sides of industry.' Conservative Party leaders, as well as others, tended to see working-class votes 'in terms of the class pyramid, and to imply that labour, formally organized in trade unions, could properly be seen as a contributor to social stability and national recovery' (Middlemas, 1979, pp. 39, 60). Given this kind of support for trade unionism and collective bargaining – hedged around though it was by all manner of qualifications – attitudes of unqualified hostility were 'becoming old-fashioned, and by most people, whether employers or not, it was recognized that trade unions had come to stay, and would form an important feature in the industrial life of the country' (Amulree, 1929, p. 105). Clearly no group of employers who tried to smash the unions could expect to receive much active material or moral support from the state and major sections of influential opinion.

Yet the qualifications were important and the Labour Department shared them. Given the Board's pretensions to be an impartial arbiter seeking only to reconcile the conflicting interests of managerial and labouring groups within society, it no more underwrote all union demands on trade union law than it underwrote demands by some propertied interests for the absolute reassertion of unfettered employer prerogative. In seeking to accommodate to the collectivist pressures of a democratic industrialism, it was applying a governing élite's strategy of rule which had long manifested wariness towards too free an assertion of uncompromising dogma, repression, or penal and military sanctions. Yet the strategy decreed that along with accommodation must go containment. Certainly foolish employers must be discouraged from creating a working-class mood receptive to revolutionary socialism, and if the social and economic prejudices of judges threatened a similar danger then legislation must redress the balance. The stance of department officials between 1901 and 1905 was that the law must be clarified 'so as to minimize the scope for judicial review and to secure a "more equitable treatment of *bona fide* union activities in law"'. But this did not mean giving the unions *carte blanche* and, like the Webbs, departmental officials were very reluctant to endorse the protections and immunities granted by the 1906 Act. The legal status thereby bestowed was 'entirely contrary to the advice and social ideology' of the Labour Department (Davidson, 1978, pp. 576, 582, 584). Party pressures generated by the electoral struggle for power could sometimes override more carefully considered calculations.

In other respects, too, departmental officials could not expect to have things all their own way, especially on issues attracting the public eye. C. T. Ritchie, Conservative President of the Board in the early years of the new century, was reluctant to have the Board identified with well-publicised union struggles for recognition, and officials had to tone down some of their reports when attacks from the far right became too virulent (Middlemas, 1979, pp. 58–9). At the other extreme, the bravura opportunist interventions of Lloyd George and Churchill – undertaken despite the preferences of Campbell-Bannerman and Asquith for a minimalist policy of state intervention in industrial relations – were little more to officials' liking and evoked icy comments from Askwith. Nevertheless, Churchill, during his period at the Board of Trade from 1908 to 1910, revealed the influence of his officials by declaring the main function of trade unionism as being to provide the 'necessary guard-rails' and 'social bulwarks' of the capitalist system by fending off the 'barbarous formulas' propounded by extremists and by participating in collective bargaining – the means of securing both social harmony and a living wage. Responsible trade unionism was the antithesis of socialism. These influences soon wore off when he moved to the Home Office, where under different traditions he rapidly acquired in the eyes of organised labour a very different reputation. It was probably Sydney Buxton, President from 1910 to 1914, whose stable personal stance was most consonant with that of his officials. His views 'typified the middle-class consensus idealism of late Victorian progressivism. By securing for the mass of urban workers the benefits of responsible and "informed" collective bargaining, class conflict would be averted. While trade unionism could humanize the capitalist system, it would therefore also provide an invaluable means of social control' (Davidson, 1978, pp. 577–80).

Along with the foregoing positive evidence of active Labour Department support for trade unions as the appropriate representative institutions of the organised working class, we need also to note negative evidence manifested in the fact that the department did not actively encourage other possibilities. One such that was being given state encouragement in certain other countries was the formation of joint works councils more or less dissociated from trade unionism and collective bargaining. In Germany, for example, employers had begun introducing them early in some regions; an industrial regulation order of 1891 had provided for their voluntary establishment; and they had been statutorily imposed in the state-owned railways in 1892 and coal-mining in 1905. Among the reasons for this growth was the strategy favoured by some sections among the ruling order of drawing subordinate classes into a participant role which, within an imposed ideology of organic unity, would strengthen a vertical integration that could then be manipulated from above. Supporting this strategy were long-standing authoritarian traditions and an emerging company law which implied the concept of a 'works community' and defined the duties of management as including concern for the interests of all stakeholders in the enterprise, employees and community as well as shareholders and customers (Fogarty, 1965, pp. 82, 86). The competitive pursuit of profit was thus qualified in ideological and legal ways that were altogether more public and formal than in Britain, where such restraints as there were had their roots only in private conviction, in informal and unorganised sentiment, or in the unions, which hovered on the margins of legitimacy so far as the middle and upper classes were concerned. British company law expressed long-standing practice and ideology by moving in the direction of boards 'being expected to take the interests of shareholders alone as the final test of their decisions'.

This and other features of the British scene constituted unfavourable soil for joint works councils. Here and there employers had set up worker-elected committees, having no connection with the unions and usually excluded from industrial questions, to deal with provident, welfare, canteen and recreative facilities. Others might give employee spokesmen a voice in co-partnership or profit-sharing arrangements. But there were also joint committees or councils specifically for dealing with industrial questions and by 1914 some of them had existed for many years. Although in some cases they were established by employers in strongly unionised plants and might even work in full harmony with the unions – or at least not in definite antagonism to them – the predominant union stance was one of suspicion that their object might be to undermine the union presence and effectiveness by setting up a rival channel of representation more easily brought under management influence. Most, however, 'of the forms of industrial works organization created by employers before the war were . . . largely ineffective . . . At the most, all that had been done in Great Britain up to the time of the war was to make isolated experiments, which seemed most unlikely to lead to any considerable results . . . The great body of employers . . . was entirely unaffected by any of these developments. Only a tiny minority of firms made any organized pro-vision . . . for welfare work'; canteens were still exceptional and sports clubs and provident schemes were growing only slowly. Firms setting out to establish any form of works organization tended to be exceptional in attitude (Cole, 1973, pp. 20–4).

This was hardly surprising. There was little in Britain's history, trad-itions and culture to lead many employers to suppose there was much to be gained from works councils. A social context of *laissez-faire*, individual-ism and self-help, market forces, and emphasis on arms–length contractual relations – together with the forms and dispositions of labour organisation which these evoked – gave little encouragement to either employees or employers to think in terms of a 'works community' which could command the participative loyalty of the rank and file. And there was certainly no prospect of Britain's trade unions following the lead of many German unions. These had come round to supporting works councils very much as a second best in the face of heavy industry's bitter hostility to collective bargaining, and were thereby acquiescing in the early beginn-ings of what was eventually to become a dual-channel system of worker representation. There was no reason whatever for Britain's unions to do likewise. Neither did the state find any reason to encourage them. The state's interest lay in industrial peace and effective joint regulation, and for those the best bet seemed to be a strong and uncluttered structure of union control, despite the various doubts and qualifications that could be entered against it. Already, therefore, circumstances were favouring the single channel system of employee representation.

Challenge to the System from the Left: Syndicalism

We have reviewed social forces which, directly and indirectly, facilitated, underpinned, or actively promoted the system of industrial relations that had begun to take shape during the 1870s and 1880s. Prominent among them has been the disposition within the predominantly influential political groups among the ruling classes to see trade unionism and voluntary sectional collective bargaining as offering the best prospects for labour control and industrial regulation in the British context. We may now note further evidence of this disposition which emerged from their reactions to attempts by small groups on the far left of the Labour movement to change the system in ways which threatened the status quo. These reactions pointed unmistakably to a desire to preserve and support the existing system.

The circumstances of these attempts by groups on the left were the booming trade, relative labour shortage and rapidly rising union membership marking the years 1910–14. The evidence of widespread unrest, militancy and frustration is massive. Strikes by seamen, dock workers, railwaymen, miners, cotton-spinners and semi-skilled engineering workers were only the most prominent features of an outburst which sent the figure for 'working days lost' rocketing from under 3 million in 1909 to a peak of nearly 41 million in 1912, the previous yearly maximum since records began in 1891 being 30 million in 1893 (21 million of them due to a coal stoppage). Between 1899 and 1909 the annual figure had hovered mostly around the 2 or 3 million mark except in 1908, when it was nearly 11 million. Trade union membership in the United Kingdom also rose impressively. Having climbed hesitantly from around 1½ million in 1892 to around 2 million in 1899, it hovered about that mark until 1907. After remaining at around 2½ million for four years, it turned more steeply upward to over 4 million by 1913 (Bain and Price, 1908, p. 37).

Other characteristics of this upsurge besides simply its scale produced acute alarm among the middle and upper classes. In many instances strikes broke out spontaneously among the rank and file, sometimes against the wishes of official leadership. Existing collective agreements laying down systematic peaceful procedures for the settlement of grievances and disputes were sometimes ignored. Thirty per cent of the strikers downed tools to protest against the use of non-union labour. There was some local physical violence, arson and looting. Above all, the widespread mass excitement and disorder were often infused with the language of class war. Collective bargaining and the Board of Trade's activities under the Conciliation Act were condemned in the Independent Labour Party and other socialist press as serving only to cripple expression of the workers' industrial power and to impose on them bourgeois criteria of wage-fixing. The slogans of syndicalism enjoyed a brisk vogue. Syndicalists saw the trade union, suitably reconstructed and democratised, as the sole agency of revolutionary socialist transformation, with reliance placed on 'direct action' – industrial militancy and civil disorder – as the means towards establishing the control and administration of industry by the workers. Such slogans touched the deepest fears of those concerned to uphold the existing order. The workers' collective industrial power was to be directed towards revolutionary political change – the most radical departure from the existing industrial relations system that could be conceived. The mood which favoured these ideas, combined with incidents like the rioting and looting in the South Wales mining village of Tonypandy, could be guaranteed to inspire *The Times* of 9 November 1910 to such phrases as 'an orgy of naked anarchy' (Halévy, 1960e, p. 454).

That there was a powerful ground-swell of discontent and resentment is therefore not in dispute. Revolutionaries and radicals – more likely to be found at the local unofficial level – naturally hoped to use the head of steam generated among rank and file membership as a force for advancing their doctrines. They were helped by the fact that habits of obedience by the rank and file of Britain's unions towards their national officers were neither so strong nor so widespread as among their counterparts, say, in Germany. Local and unofficial workplace leaders were followed if they seemed to offer more effective results. Syndicalism was therefore 'able to draw upon, and articulate in novel form, those older traditions of primitive democracy and control over the work process upon which popular sovereignty had once rested. The policy of workers' control, for example, had strong affinities with the traditions of local autonomy and unilateral regulation . . .' (Gore, 1982, p. 68).

In some industries workplace leadership had already begun to be institutionalised. Within, for example, shipbuilding and the engineering industries a number of factors such as growing size of plant, rapid changes in techniques, and the increase in piece-rate and incentive schemes had been encouraging the emergence of workplace shop stewards in some areas, particularly since the late nineteenth century. These ill-defined figures, sometimes no more than union dues collectors, in other cases unofficial negotiators, could find themselves in a somewhat ambiguous relationship with their full-time officials, who might eye them warily as a possible independent source of influence and leadership over rank and file members. There was already something of a tendency for the shop-floor activist seeking election to full-time salaried union office to assume that attacks on the integrity and policies of national officials were an important part of convincing fellow members of his own fitness for their trust. The tendency grew as unions became larger, as amalgamations were achieved, and as head offices became more distant and bureaucratic. When the shop-floor militant moved up the hierarchy and had to grapple with the constraints, compromises and subtleties of high-level conflict-negotiation he, too, found himself in a firing line in which there were attacks from behind as well as from the front.

Shop-floor union organisation, workplace militancy, local activists' challenges to full-time officials, strain on formal disputes procedures – all these were likely to be strengthened by boom conditions and labour shortage. Men who were all too aware of the transitory and uncertain nature of shop-floor strength were keenly alert to managerial delaying tactics and were apt to act accordingly. When to these are added the facts that by 1911 trade union membership was double the 1892 figure – this alone creating the probability that disputes would be on a bigger scale –

and that major groups such as the seamen, the railwaymen and the miners were fighting on issues of principle – the first two for union recognition, the third for a minimum wage – we have enough explanation for the turbulence of the prewar years.

How widely was it informed by genuine revolutionary sentiment of a sort which seriously threatened the industrial relations system? In some industries the signs seemed abundant. Certainly in south Wales, where leading coal-owners had long maintained a venomous doctrinaire hostility towards independent unionism, the struggle for that independence, not achieved until 1898, sowed the seeds of an equally venomous hostility towards coal-owners. The south Wales miners became after 1906 the leaders of a new militant thrust, with an unofficial reform movement arising in 1911 whose members 'held a socialism far removed from the jolly fellowship of Robert Blatchford, the hygienic bureaucracy of the Fabians, or the idylls of Keir Hardie: their analysis they drew from Karl Marx, their strategy from Daniel de Leon in America and Tom Mann newly returned from Australia to preach syndicalism' (Phelps Brown, 1959, p. 320). 'Wales seemed by 1914 to have become the major battleground for the class war; in no other part of Britain was the confrontation between capital and labour more naked and complete' (Morgan, 1974, p. 171).

Yet for an overall assessment we may usefully turn to an observer whose instinctive sympathies lay with the militants. '. . . it must be admitted', wrote G. D. H. Cole in 1913, 'that there is at present very little real revolutionary feeling in this country . . . Of real syndicalism there is . . . practically none' (Cole, 1919, pp. 33, 39). The theorists, 'working-class and middle-class alike, who sought to give this movement form and direction and to interpret its vague strivings into a new social gospel, never really captured the great mass of the working class', which 'as ever, was thinking not of Utopia and not even of the class war, but mainly of the immediate issues involved in each separate dispute. If a new temper was abroad, and the moderate leaders found their control of the movement seriously threatened, this did not imply a wholesale conversion of the British working class to revolutionary doctrines' (Cole, 1927, pp. 70–1).

Continental revolutionaries were apt to deplore the weakness of class theory among British labour. Lenin, though in principle ever hopeful of Britain's 'masses', was often ready to acknowledge what for him were regrettable deficiencies in their Labour movement. He renewed Engels' complaint that there was still a fatal inattention to, and lack of interest in, theory, and referred to a resolution at the 1912 Independent Labour Party Conference being 'drawn up in the pure "English" manner: without any general principles (the English pride themselves on their "practicalness" and their dislike for general principles . . .)'. Along with this went mere 'spontaneous' opportunism. He quoted Martynov's comparison of Robert Knight, general secretary of the Boilermakers, with Wilhelm Liebknecht, one of the founders of German Social Democracy. The latter offered a 'revolutionary explanation of the whole of modern society'; the former 'attached more significance to the forward march of the drab, everyday struggle' and 'formulated the immediate demands of the proletariat and . . . the manner in which they can be achieved' (Lenin, 1969, pp. 83–4, 100).

Even of south Wales it has recently been argued that many writers 'have overstated the prevalence of syndicalism and of other theories of "direct action", and misinterpreted their influence upon events'. The Plebs League, preaching Marxism and the class war, was 'almost entirely confined to the Rhondda valleys'; by the summer of 1914 the Unofficial Reform Committee was 'largely disbanded'; and the 'turmoil of the years 1908–14 ended with the official union leadership firmly in control of events . . . Despite the class conflict . . . "lib–labism" remained a dominant and unifying creed in industrial south Wales down to the outbreak of war in 1914'. Almost in spite of themselves, Independent Labour Party activists 'became symbols of the official processes of collective bargaining, of constitutionalism and the imperatives of the "progressive alliance".' Welsh Liberalism remained strong, almost untouched by the new London and Manchester version of the creed, and still looking to that old deep-rooted conception of 'class harmony of the productive classes against the feudal pretensions of the bishop and the squire'. In 'narrowly political terms', even in industrial south Wales 'it was Labour rather than the Liberals who felt themselves to be on the defensive' in 1914 (Morgan, 1974, pp. 162, 171–3).

Similar evidence was emerging from the wider union movement. Under the Trade Union Act 1913 any union wanting to undertake political activity had to secure a majority in a ballot of the membership. In most cases the activity desired was strictly constitutional and moderate in nature but yet independent of the two main parties. Even this was more than many trade unionists could stomach. Coal-miners and cotton weavers, two of the largest blocs in the movement, provide examples. 194,800 miners voted against compared with 261,643 for; among the cotton weavers 75,893 voted against and 98,158 for (Clegg, Fox and Thompson, 1964, p. 418). Despite the possibilities in Britain for socialists to fish hopefully in troubled waters, the evidence of 1911–14 seems to indicate that for the majority the waters which were troubled were industrial and not political. Neither for the first nor for the last time, some men of affairs stood aghast at the remarkable industrial solidarity of which the British working class was capable and read it as having political significance. What has been suggested before in these pages can bear being repeated – that the majority of the working class, however fiercely they were prepared to fight for their organisations and for what they currently deemed their rights, did not translate these struggles into revolutionary or even radical political terms.

With respect to industrial action also, alarms among the more fretful ruling-class quarters ran far ahead of the facts. The Triple Industrial Alliance, formed in 1913 by the Miners' Federation, the National Union of Railwaymen and the National Transport Workers' Federation, was invested by its more militant supporters with hopes that it would serve as a leviathan of 'direct action' in the use of industrial power for political ends. Many middle-class observers feared the worst. Yet Bagwell's judgement is that 'only a small minority of the leaders ever considered that the purpose of the Alliance was to bring about revolutionary change'. The predominant idea was that 'each of these great fighting organizations, before embarking upon any big programme, either defensive or aggressive, should formulate its programme, submit it to the others, and that upon joint proposals joint action should then be taken', though each retained 'complete autonomy' to take action on its own behalf (Bagwell, 1971, pp. 102–4).

Support from the Establishment: the Industrial Council

Although Establishment opinion was deeply disturbed by the Triple Alliance, by syndicalist slogans, by the large-scale stoppages, and by the many spontaneous unofficial strikes that were sometimes also 'unconstitutional' in the sense that they violated agreed procedure for settling disputes, the predominant governing policy leaned not towards destroying labour organisation but towards strengthening the control of its official leadership over the rank and file. 'I should like to see the trade unions become stronger', the Conservative leader Bonar Law told the Commons in 1912, 'because I think that, as a rule, they tend to the diminution of disputes' (Law, 1912, col. 1124).

Many influential and representative employers were prepared to agree. In 1911, prompted by the industrial disruption of that year, Asquith and the President of the Board of Trade, Sidney Buxton, after 'numerous conferences and consultations with leading employers and workers with a view to strengthening the official machinery for dealing with labour questions', set up the Industrial Council. Its origins were in accord with the precedents of 1895 and 1900 (see pp. 189–90), when prominent industrialists had come forward at a time when the social fabric was under strain and promoted conciliatory public demonstrations designed to mobilise 'moderate' opinion. The Industrial Council was intended to bring together all those on both sides of industry who sought to substitute 'co-operation for antagonism in the relations between employers and employed'. It comprised thirteen spokesmen of each side, 'all actively engaged as officials of employers' and workmen's associations', chaired by Sir George Askwith, Chief Industrial Commissioner, with the brief of 'considering and of inquiring into matters referred to them affecting trade disputes and . . . taking suitable action'. Soon proving of no use for the purposes of conciliation and arbitration, it was allowed to lapse after 1912. It did, however, produce a report published in 1913 (*Report of the Industrial Council on Industrial Agreements*, Cd 6952) in response to two questions referred to it, on its own suggestion, by the government: (1) What is the best method of securing the due fulfilment of industrial agreements? and (2) How far, and in what manner, should industrial agreements made between representative bodies of employers and workmen be enforced throughout the particular trade or district?

The terms of reference are significant. Their very narrowness showed that the government was envisaging no radical divergence from the general lines of development so far. The council's *Report* indicated that no radical divergence was envisaged either by the employers' associations and trade unions pursuing those developments. For those with any knowledge of post-Second World War controversies their discussion conveys a powerful sense of *plus ça change*. The idea of legislating penalties against strikes which violated procedure agreements was considered and rejected – penal clauses would only endanger the great body of voluntary machinery now in existence. Repudiated likewise was all desire to interfere in any significant way with existing machinery for conciliation and arbitration, though among other supplementary notions the principle of what has since become known as a 'cooling-off' period was recommended. In other words, between the exhaustion of procedure and a stoppage there should be opportunity for further review by the parties and for the voice to be heard of some authority representing 'the interests of the community'. The report responded to a great majority of witnesses by recommending that, on application from both sides, an agreement should be capable of extension – and legal enforcement – over the whole of the trade in a district, including employers who were not party to it – though it stipulated that there was to be no stoppage or change in conditions until after investigation and pronouncement by some agreed tribunal. These and other modest conclusions reflected an apparently strong conviction, voiced neither for the first nor the last time, that there was little wrong with Britain's system of industrial relations that could not be cured by more powerful control wielded by the top-level leaders of its representative organizations: '. . . we find that where agreements are the outcome of properly organized machinery for dealing with disputes they are, with very few exceptions, loyally observed by both sides'. Council members were prepared, in other words, to put their signatures to an overall verdict similar to that offered later by a well-qualified academic observer: '. . . before the war we had in this country reached a fair working solution of the problem. I do not forget the fears that the strikes and threats of strikes of 1911–14 excited. Such fears are a normal concomitant of the problem, because any agitation for better conditions is in the eyes of the more comfortable classes a sign of imminent revolution' (Clay, 1929, pp. 10–11).

Given the circumstances in which their conclusions were formulated and voiced, and the air of apocalypse projected by some of the other public pronouncements of the day with respect to 'disorder' and 'anarchy', it is significant that Industrial Council members clearly did not think they were exposing themselves to ridicule with their calm and moderate reference to 'the rare cases in which agreements are broken' and their conviction that the vast majority were fully honoured. Moreover, they did not allow their narrow terms of reference to preclude them from a resounding declaration in favour of voluntary collective bargaining. 'The desirability of maintaining the principle of collective bargaining – which has become so important a constituent in the industrial life of this country – cannot be called into question, and we regard it as axiomatic that nothing should be done that would lead to the abandonment of a method of adjusting the relationships between employers and workpeople which has proved so mutually advantageous throughout most of the trades of the country.' Leading spokesmen of employers and unions were in effect telling the government: 'Hands off!' Underlying their day-to-day zero-sum game was a consensus on the rules of the game and a demand that they be free of state interference unless either side or both chose to invoke it.

There seems no reason to dispute Charles's judgement that 'the main practical significance of the Council is that it helped to consolidate the mass of moderate opinion – which was ultimately as predominant on both sides of industry as it was in the country generally – behind the belief that the main immediate task was to give the maximum possible encouragement to collective bargaining and the trade unionism on which it depended' (Charles, 1973, pp. 71–2). That this 'moderate opinion' was indeed widespread is suggested by the fact that the council, having served its immediate purpose, was allowed by the government to expire. Meanwhile many smaller trades and industries were joining larger ones in moving towards collective bargaining rather than away from it. At a time when 'the system of collective bargaining and conciliation boards . . . was widely believed to be in jeopardy', the number of such boards known to the Board of Trade rose from 162 in 1905 to 293 by the end of 1911 and 325 by the end of 1913, having been 64 in 1894 (Halévy, 1961e, p. 477). The activities of the Board of Trade under the Conciliation Act were not seen by the majority of union negotiators as hostile. Its officials were highly regarded in union circles as 'progressive' administrators with a genuine commitment to social reform, including union recognition (Davidson, 1982, p. 172). There is little support here for such judgements as that only war 'providentially aborted a potentially explosive situation . . . when . . . working-class militancy threatened to escape the control of a faltering and reactionary trade union leadership (syndicalism)' (Anderson, 1965, p. 27). Halévy is more convincing: 'To read the lamentations of the middle class one might believe that the structure of "social peace" based on reciprocal concessions freely accepted, hitherto the boast of British society, was a thing of the past. In reality nothing could be more untrue' (Halévy, 1961e, p. 476).

Rank and File Restlessness

There is, however, more to say if we are to gauge the full nature of the system that was evoking this kind of support from union leaders, employers' spokesmen, and the currently dominant political forces. The idea that the desirable handling of industrial relations required strong organisations headed by powerful leaders with plenary powers who could commit their members to collective agreements and ensure that they were carried out – a species of corporate solution – was understandably upheld by many middle- and upper-class observers, not to mention the organisational leaders themselves, but it found far less favour with many active members of the trade union rank and file who had their own criticisms of the way things were developing. Larger workplaces, centralised unions, more distant bargaining, top leaderships who saw more of top employers – and even Cabinet ministers – than of their own members, a parliamentary Labour Party whose general stance was still that of a Lib-Lab pressure group, the flunkeyism displayed by too many leading Labour spokesmen towards wealth and power – these helped to stiffen socialist and syndicalist ideas among an activist minority, and to goad even the majority rank and file into kicking over the traces at times when labour shortage made it possible. Some middle-class socialists, such as G. D. H. Cole, reacting against what they considered the bureaucratic and over-centralised collectivism predominant in the Labour movement, hoped to see the working classes move towards some form of 'workers control'. Hitherto most socialists had assumed not syndicalism but what *Punch* called Sidneywebbicalism; 'an impartial State, controlling and organizing industry, securing for the worker an adequate share in the wealth he produces, laying charges on industry for benevolent State services for the benefit of the weak and incapable . . . carrying on production much as it is carried on now, with a State Department in place of a Trust and a bureaucrat in place of a managing director' (Cole, 1919, p. 7). Large-scale, centrally planned production, shorn of the wastes, inefficiencies and neglect of human capital characteristic of competitive private enterprise, was taken for granted as the most efficient. This essentially Fabian vision saw the social problem as first and foremost a question of distribution, of efficiency, of man's interests as a consumer. Cole and other Guild Socialists wanted to see, and sought to promote, a growing consciousness among workers of their interests as producers; of their capability and need to become responsible participants in a new system of de-centralised industrial organisation. This would transform each industry into something approaching a self-governing profession controlled by the unions, co-operating with the state but administering its own internal affairs.

The difficulty here lay in deciding just how far the grass-roots ferment expressed an inchoate impulse towards greater control of the wider decision-making in their industry, and how far simply the impatience of people in a favourable market position with the distant manœuvres of their leaders about immediate bread and butter issues. Were they, by mobilising against the arbitrary class power of the employers, bringing upon themselves domination by the bureaucratic power of the union? As we have already had occasion to note, the rank and file of Britain's trade unions had never been notably deferential and submissive towards their leaders. The movement beginning in the early decades of the nineteenth century towards the amalgamation of regional craft federations and local societies into national unions with centralised finances was followed by 'the growth of the modern phenomenon of large numbers of rank and file trade unionists persistently complaining of the high-handed autocracy of their leaders'. Amalgamations 'were invariably either accompanied or followed by attempts on the part of the rank and file to impose checks on their leaders . . . The ideas of what the Webbs patronisingly called "primitive democracy" remained strongly entrenched, as they still do today' (Lane, 1974, p. 78). Attempts by union head office to dictate trade policy were usually rebuffed. The craft culture, especially, with its central concept of group self-regulation, did not take kindly to attempted dictation from far-distant locations over which rank and file members had little or no control. For the protection of local 'custom and practice' craftsmen had

often relied on an alert union representative in the workplace whose own
functions might be minimal but who turned, in the event of difficulty, for
action and negotiation to the district union official and committee. We
have noted, however, that in recent decades a combination of factors was
beginning to draw workplace representatives into a more active role –
including, in some cases, the negotiating of piece-rates and other shop-
floor issues. These remained, for the most part, however, unofficial
activities which enjoyed little or no formal recognition by either unions or
employers. Moreover, by their very nature as workplace leaders the shop
stewards could sometimes find themselves acting outside the official brief.
And since their role required them to be in the front line, as it were, at the
very 'frontier of control', they tended to need a strength of motivation that
was most likely to be found among socialists and others with a well-
developed spirit of aggression against official authority, including that of
union officials, if need be, as well as employers. If no shop steward
leadership was available when members felt the union was failing them
they might follow a man with no recognised role in the union structure at
all. For many union officials the 'socialist agitator' had come to seem 'a
disruptive influence out to undermine properly constituted authority for
ulterior political ends' (ibid. p. 110).

Shop stewards as individuals were not the only threat. Practical
pressures reinforced by ideological impulses were also beginning to
promote a closer unity of action among the shop stewards of a given
union, who found it convenient to set up workshop or works committees
– though sometimes committees with bargaining functions were set up
independently of the stewards, who retained their minimal official
'reporting' functions. The same combination of pressures was also beginning to bring together, in a works committee, stewards of different unions
within a given workplace. This trend was fostered by the fact that in
almost all industries there were movements of varying degrees of strength
in favour of the amalgamation of rival and overlapping unions into
broad-based 'industrial' unions organising all the industry's workers
regardless of craft, skill, grade, or sex. Sometimes this thrust served
immediate practical needs favouring closer working. Thus the 'inchoate
and unregulated tendency towards workshop organization was naturally
in intimate connection with this amalgamation movement, which was for
the most part a "rank and file" movement of a left-wing character, keenly
critical of the attitude and conduct of the permanent trade union official'
(Cole, 1973, pp. 15–17).

This made officials less inclined to put their energies into stimulating or
attempting to rationalise and co-ordinate workshop organisation, and
little disposed to concede recognition and enlarged powers. There
remained a tendency for the workshop movement to develop along
unofficial lines and in relationships with the union hierarchy which ranged
from close co-operation to outright hostility. And since the widely
received official conception of industrial relations was in terms of powerful organisations on both sides jointly regulating their industry there was
nothing in this workplace restlessness which seemed to call for Establishment encouragement. As a consequence there was, 'in all the manifold

discussions which took place in Great Britain between 1910 and 1914 concerning the basis of trade union organization and policy', very little constructive focus on workplace union organisation and the role of shop stewards except among those 'immediately affected' – namely, union activists and socialist sympathisers. Even at the practical level, workplace interest was far from sustained. In many districts in 1914 the shop steward system 'had fallen almost into desuetude' (ibid. pp. 17–18, 33). Neither the workplace organisation initiated by the workers nor that initiated by employers could have struck many informed observers in 1914 outside socialist ranks as having a significant future.

Nevertheless it would have been possible to draw from the 1911–14 experience of workplace militancy some further conclusions about the nature of Britain's industrial relations system. On the one hand, even by 1910 it was shaping towards centralised unions and 'national' or industry-wide dispute settlement. Only shipbuilding and cotton as yet had national pay agreements, other industries being regulated by district agreements possibly supplementing or superimposed on workplace arrangements. But national agreements regulating disputes procedure were already becoming more widespread – in shipbuilding, cotton weaving, cotton spinning, engineering, footwear and building – with the employers supplying the impetus in all cases but one. On the other hand, it was apparent that these trends were not subduing the workplace spirit of independence. Much depended, of course, on the state of the labour market. At times of recession, members might have little workplace power to assert against the compromises and fudgings of union officers and therefore had to endure them with varying degrees of resignation or cynicism. When labour was in demand, however, it might be a different story, with the local work group either heeding or ignoring its official leaders according to the situation and mood. Moreover, within such a context, the widening spread of negotiated disputes procedures, with their requirement of rank and file abstinence from stoppages while issues were processed through successive stages of joint conciliation, highlighted the problem of labour 'indiscipline' and how to control it. Collective bargaining and formal procedures might be spreading, but neither employers, nor governments, nor union officers could congratulate themselves on a docile workforce which could be relied on to submit obediently to the regulations handed down from above.

Middle-class candied friends of the unions contrasted them in this respect with their German counterparts. Sidney Webb referred with ill-concealed envy to the German rank and file 'recognition . . . of the absolute necessity, in any effective democracy, of centralization as well as local autonomy, of leadership as well as popular control' (S. Webb, 1916, pp. 3–5). In many other respects, as well, the German unions evoked panegyrics from contemporary British observers, though they had achieved nothing like the negotiation coverage or political foothold of British unions. A youthful G. D. H. Cole, writing in 1913, considered them to be 'far better organized against the employer', than their English counterparts and to have achieved 'an almost perfect form of organization', while their members were 'conscious of broad issues behind trade unionism in a manner that is quite beyond the range of the rank and file in England' (Cole, 1919, pp. 169, 172, 182). Sidney Webb wrote of the 'wonderful development of the central trade union offices, with their expert staffs; the skill and wisdom with which they obtain and utilise their own statistical information; their really remarkable efforts for the education of their members; their training schools for trade union officials – all this is in striking contrast with the haphazard methods of British wage-earning democracy'. German trade unionism represented, in fact, the practical realisation of all the hopes that the Webbs had once cherished (in, for example, *Industrial Democracy*) for British unions. Webb manifested disillusion in his judgement that German superiority lay not in organisation *per se* but in brains – ' in the higher level of general education among . . . its members; in the intelligence that recognizes the need for trained officials and also for expert assistance in accountancy, law, and statistics' (S. Webb, 1916, pp. 3–5). Beatrice Webb's earlier experience at an International Socialist Congress had prompted her to describe the British delegates as approaching 'raving imbecility', but the German delegates as 'substantial persons – their intellects somewhat twisted by their authoritarian dogmatism – but with strong sterling character and capable of persistent and deliberate effort' (B. Webb, 1948, p. 134).

Another Fabian with considerable knowledge of the German scene offered a more qualified judgement. He agreed that the organisation and methods of German unions were 'adapted perfectly to the German characteristics of patience, foresight, discipline, submission to expert judgement, and passionate attention to detail'. But they had gains to make 'before they obtained anything like the political and economic influence enjoyed by the English trade unions'. German unionists visiting Britain were 'amazed at the readiness with which English trade union representatives are received and consulted by Cabinet Ministers' (Sanders, 1916, p. 47). Some German methods could be studied with advantage, thought Sanders,

> but it is more than doubtful whether it would ever be possible, or even advantageous, for English trade unions to adopt the strongly bureaucratic form of control which is exercised by the German trade union officials, and on which the success of the highly centralized form of organization largely depends. A people who have grown up under the iron regime of the German military system are capable of a degree of obedience to officials of voluntary organisations which would in England be considered derogatory to individual dignity and liberty. (ibid., p. 48)

Investments in the System: Unions, Employers and the State

If we seek to make analytically explicit the reasons why most of the unions, the prevailing forces within governments and relevant state agencies, and the predominant groups among the interested employers, were prepared to make common cause in upholding this industrial relations system against forces which appeared to threaten it – the courts, groups among the militant left, groups among the militant right, 'indiscipline' on the shop floor – the basic fact emerges that they had all by now made a considerable investment in the system and were concerned to protect that investment. The returns they derived from it were very different; nevertheless a review of them reveals the stable foundations, not necessarily immediately visible, on which the system now rested.

For the union leaders, collective bargaining required the fudgings, the ambiguities, and make-do-and-mend of negotiated compromises, along with the restraints and delays of formal procedure and often much abuse from those they represented. Yet for the long term they could see nothing better. For them, 'collective bargaining had come to stay. Despite its shortcomings, they saw in it the guarantee of union stability, one source of their own power, and the best means available for winning benefits for their own members' (Clegg, Fox and Thompson, 1964, pp. 472–3). By 1914 additional reinforcement had long become apparent: union officers and activists were increasingly enjoying a taste of honey. No Machiavellian calculation was required for middle- and upper-class persons to admit to a widening range of official statutory bodies, trade union leaders and activists who had already demonstrated their acceptance of institutional and constitutional procedures. These were, for the most part, men one could deal with; men with a 'realistic' grasp of the 'practical necessities'; men who understood, for example, that employers, like all rulers, were largely the creatures of circumstance. The results further integrated union activists into civil society.

Henry Broadhurst, a stonemason, had been the first working-man trade unionist to be appointed to high political office when he became under-secretary to the Home Office in 1886, and John Burns entered the Liberal Cabinet in 1906. Individual union experience is exemplified in the National Union of Boot and Shoe Operatives. In 1910, 77 union members held 85 official positions of widely varying kinds.

> There were 5 magistrates, 2 aldermen, 13 town councillors, 27 urban district councillors, 1 county councillor, 10 rural district councillors, 20 poor law guardians, 1 school board member, 2 borough auditors, 3 co-opted members of education committees, and 1 Board of Trade Commissioner. By 1912, 80 members held 100 positions. The additions reflected the emergent beginnings of the welfare state. There were now members of old-age pension committees, members of National Insurance Act advisory committees, a member of a Water Board, and school managers. (Fox, 1958, p. 329)

Neither was there any hesitation about recruiting union officers into the civil service, a procedure which would have been mortally offensive to the dignity of its German counterpart. Trade unionists were appointed to the Factory Inspectorate, one of the favourite hopes of advancement among union officials – Broadhurst's secretary told Beatrice Webb that he did 'not believe there was a single secretary of a trade union' who did not write to Broadhurst 'to ask for an appointment as factory inspector' (B. Webb,

1948, p. 25). And during the Liberal administration of 1892–5 alone, 'about a hundred working men had been appointed Justices of the Peace' (Halévy, 1961d, p. 214). After the social reform measures of the 1906 Liberal government, 'ministers had considered themselves justified in utilizing the practical experience of labour possessed by the trade union officials. It was also a clever move to conciliate by this largess the favour of the Labour party. The Trade Boards Act had necessitated the creation of 800 posts whose salaries reached in some cases £1,000 a year. There was a deluge of applications.' Union officers also took posts as superintendents of labour exchanges and labour advisers at the Home Office, and there were thirty sub-inspectorships of mines and quarries. 'In 1911 the ... National Insurance Bill brought with it another batch of official posts to satisfy the hunger of trade union officials.' The account could be extended (Halévy, 1961e, pp. 446–7).

The unions themselves were drawn into the machinery of the state by the National Insurance Act. Like the friendly societies, they were invited to help as 'approved societies' in administering it. This almost certainly helped to increase – and hold – their membership as well as promote their respectability. 'We are driven to the paradoxical conclusion that during those very years in which revolutionary syndicalism was so vocal, co-operation between the trade unions and the Government became closer than before' (ibid., p. 479).

Further aspects of the relative openness of the ruling class and its contribution to union integration were to be found on the purely social dimension; a fact unlikely to escape the piercing eye of Beatrice Webb. She noted that by the 1870s and 1880s London society and country house life 'differed significantly from other social aristocracies'. In a picture which differed profoundly from the German scene, where barriers of social caste and standards of social honour were rigorously enforced, she described how there 'were no fixed caste barriers; there seemed to be, in fact, no recognized types of exclusiveness based on birth or breeding, on personal riches or personal charm; there was no fastidiousness about manners or morals or intellectual gifts ... To foreign observers it appeared all-embracing in its easy-going tolerance and superficial good nature'. And not even labour leaders were excluded. 'Thirty years before the Labour party became His Majesty's Government there was a distinct desire, on the part of a select politico-social set, to welcome the leaders of the newly enfranchised trade union democracy'. Yet there *was* a test of fitness for membership of this most gigantic of all social clubs. 'It was a test seldom recognized by those applying it; still less by those to whom it was applied. The test was *the possession of some form of power over other people*' (B. Webb, 1938, pp. 68–70, italics in original). Few single facts cast more light on the nature of the British Establishment and how it came to be constructed. It was a network linking people of different classes, backgrounds and objectives who might, on one level, find themselves in keen competition or conflict with one another, yet who, because they all derived some degree of power and status from their location in the system, and might, perhaps, have genuine convictions about its merits, shared at least a common interest in defending its basic framework and assumptions.

The investment made by the employers in the system was in terms of the time and patience required for the relevant committees, conciliation boards, or procedures, and in terms of the slow and often painful learning of negotiating skills and techniques which might prevent or end disruption of a plant, a company, an entire industry. Moreover, they too had to accept restraints, learn a new language, accept shortfalls in expectations. It was an investment which they justified by their belief that the union could be a valuable, indeed necessary, partner in the maintenance of order, regulation and control.

Employers had begun to show an interest in making this investment long before governments demonstrated any positive encouragement – indeed, it was an employer prominent in early ventures, A. J. Mundella, who as a Liberal MP constantly pressed the value of trade unionism and collective bargaining upon the House of Commons. Yet although employers did not have to learn about collective bargaining from the state, it was against the background of a state which showed itself increasingly prepared to underpin and encourage the collective bargaining method that employers had to resolve their ambivalences about trade unionism. Even early in the century governments had made clear that, mistrustful though they were of trade unionism, any group of employers who engaged them in battle were on their own so far as hope of state assistance was concerned. It might be a primary government purpose to defend general capitalist principles of property and class relations, but this did not require the state to intervene to defend particular capitalist interests in every local skirmish. Governments had their own interests to maintain and these must not be put at risk by necessarily backing every group of employers who might get themselves into difficulty by sheer pigheadedness, stupidity, or greed. Indeed, the lesson had already been learned by the ruling class – possibly (*pace* some socialist beliefs) the least stupid ruling class the world has ever seen – that the surest defence of capitalist property and class relations lay in *not* using the state apparatus to enforce capitalist interests on every disputed principle and in every disputed instance.

By the end of the century employers were having to realise that the state was making its own investment in collective bargaining – if necessary over their heads – because despite abundant weaknesses it seemed to serve vital state interests. Many employers agreed. Those who did not – or who passed through periods when they did not – quickly discovered that should they engage a union in battle with the intention of destroying it, all they could expect from the state was conciliatory intervention by the Labour Department, whose eminent civil servants would seek to promote, not an employer 'victory', but an 'amicable solution' with both sides making concessions and agreeing to behave with more civilised restraint in future. Soon government ministers themselves realised that successful intervention in a well-publicised conflict was not without its political advantage. 'After 1906 Lloyd George and Winston Churchill, as Presidents of the Board of Trade, and their officials in the Labour Department, intervened in industrial relations to a degree far beyond the expectations of the majority of the Royal Commission [on Labour] or of the legislators of 1896' (Clegg, Fox and Thompson, 1964, p. 485). Even when a specially aggressive group of employers were prepared to brazen it out with the Labour Department or prominent politicians, they were likely to find other major groups of employers, along with the Liberal press, making anxious and self-righteous noises about the importance of 'cultivating goodwill on both sides'. We have noted three organisational expressions of this tendency in 1895, 1900 and 1911. It was not the sort of social milieu that encouraged the employer to entertain visions of smashing the unions. He could still decide to try, but the chances were that he found less support among the great and the good than he might have expected.

Compared with the large and growing apparatus of formal machinery and procedure created jointly by employers and unions, the investment made by the state – meaning, in this context, governments and their advisers and immediate backers, along with certain relevant state agencies – seems far less palpable. Yet the investment was in fact considerable – indeed, in a sense, crucial. What the state invested was only to a limited extent material – the Labour Department of the Board of Trade hardly called for impressive budgeting. It was predominantly an investment of experience and hope. Experience had taught successive generations and governments of the ruling class that their strategy of rule could cope with successive admissions of new social groups to decision-making processes vital to society – provided these groups could be induced to work within the framework. If this was the investment of experience, the investment of hope was that the crucial qualification would continue to be fulfilled in the case of the new groups of organised labour. Would they continue consenting to be assimilated into a system which offered only *ad hoc*, piecemeal and marginal reforms while preserving the essential structures of power, wealth and status intact? Of course, there was already passing into the legitimation of the system the notion that trade unionism produced something approximating to an *equivalence* of power between employers and workers – perhaps even a bias in favour of the latter. The notion was unconvincing to some, but many worthy men believed it. Trade unionists themselves were likely to be among those who did not. Nevertheless their organisations did offer them something and it seemed the best thing available for coping with the rent, the housekeeping bills and arbitrary management. The hope was that they would go on thinking so. Some officials of the Labour Department entertained the even larger expectation that adversary zero-sum bargaining would mature into co-operative positive-sum 'conciliation' and encouraged union recognition and collective relations on the basis of that vision.

Governments themselves could hardly help being disposed to accept collective organisation on both sides, leave them to adjust their own relations, hope for the best and profess 'neutrality'. If a reputation for impartiality and even-handedness between the classes had seemed important to influential public men in the early years of the century it seemed vastly more so at the end of it. The supreme legitimation of the liberal-democratic state was beginning to take shape. In its later full flowering, it asserted that, with the widening of the franchise, the growth of representative organisations and parties, and the emergence of institutions for resolving conflict and pursuing change peacefully, power was becoming so widely diffused as to leave no class or group with overriding dominance. There was growing opportunity for any aggrieved group to organise, put its case, and be heard fairly. No possible justification existed for political violence. Therefore every possible justification existed for public condemnation and, if thought expedient, active state discouragement or even suppression of any group, movement, or ideology which appeared to threaten this admirably fair system. For since it was so admirable and fair, any attempted subversion of it must necessarily proclaim itself morally suspect.

For those who wished to preserve the existing structures of rule and control basically intact, the value of this legitimation was, and is, inestimable. It has served to justify condemnation of, and action against, all those expressions of protest, from street demonstrations to unofficial strikes and mass picketing, which can be represented as going beyond the legitimate, institutional, orderly and fair procedures. Yet, as already noted, arguments can be advanced that power remains, as it has always been, heavily concentrated and that this inequality perpetuates – and is, in turn, perpetuated by – gross inequalities of wealth, income, status and respect. The significance of the liberal–democratic legitimation now emerges in its full force. In a society which is marked by profound inequalities yet which preserves a conception of proper government as 'national' and even-handed, and which succeeds in upholding, as a consequence, a political culture which excludes violence and contains protest within defined institutional procedures, the basic structures of inequality will come under no serious threat. For within the institutional procedures the established authorities can draw upon great reserve powers of socialisation, manipulation, delay and resistance which, in the last resort, cannot be overcome without violence. The inhibitions against political violence – and political disobedience generally – therefore have crucial importance. They are put under strain if a government reveals itself, on issues of major institutional or constitutional significance, to be consistently and blatantly partial beyond hope of compromise, concession, or compensation. A reputation for a judicious sense of 'fairness' and even-handedness becomes a pearl above price, for it may serve to take strains which, in its absence, would threaten the stability of the whole system.

For governments and the state, therefore, here was a further aspect of the investment. If the gradually evolving liberal–democratic ethos was succeeding in preserving the essential structures of power and property – while providing machinery for the peaceful assimilation of inevitable shifts and changes – it was clearly worth preserving, if necessary at some sacrifice. The upholding of the system appeared to spell out its own logic. When, in Germany, the government, the army, the police, a court, a state agency, or any public figure of importance, chose to repress, punish, harass, deter, condemn, or hold up for public vilification any independent working-class organisation which challenged the official and approved structures of decision-making and authority, such actions were in full congruence with the predominant ideology, which stressed the supremacy of the militaristic unitary state and implied contempt for the constraints, tolerances and compromises of liberal-democratic society. Similar actions in Britain were increasingly incongruent with the regime and the legitimations on which it rested. And if collective organisation among interest groups and their application of pressure upon decision-makers was to be tolerated and legitimised in the political sphere, could such principles be suppressed in the industrial sphere without destroying the whole strategy? Even simple abuse of alleged trade union obstruction of progress would have to be accompanied by assurances that such condemnation did not apply to the more 'enlightened' and 'responsible' unions. Any attempt at total repression would require not a modification of the regime and its legitimations, but a total recasting. The risks attendant upon choosing to destroy a system which had preserved civil peace, power and property for two centuries were appalling and, until proved unavoidable by the manifest failure of the system, senseless.

Such might be the logic. But men do not necessarily follow the dictates of logic and, in any case, the logic rested on 'other things being equal'. There could be no guarantee that issues or personalities might not irrupt into the scene and generate forces and emotions which would override cooler long-term evaluations based on the earlier situation. The years leading up to 1914 included events which demonstrate that the industrial relations system must not be viewed as a settled and secure pattern 'evolving' according to certain 'irresistible trends' within British 'industrial society'. The most important of these events touched upon the whole political and constitutional order within which the industrial relations system was contained. Behaviour within the Conservative Party over issues involving the powers of the House of Lords, the political role of the monarchy, the position of Ulster in a Home Rule Ireland, and army obedience to its political masters put that order distinctly at hazard. Had it been destroyed or seriously damaged the industrial relations system could hardly have remained unaffected. Yet the Conservative Opposition leader, Bonar Law, who in 1913 expressed party support for the unions' right to conduct constitutional political activity, was declaring around the same time that he could 'imagine no length of resistance' to which Ulster people might go in their resistance to Irish Home Rule in which he would not be prepared to support them. 'I said the other day in the House of Commons, and I repeat here, that there are things stronger than parliamentary majorities . . .' (Rhodes James, 1981, p. 57). It is perhaps worth noting, therefore, that the only serious practical threats to Britain's political and constitutional system in the twentieth century have come not from the Labour movement but from major groups among the system's chief beneficiaries.

The other example relates to the industrial relations system itself and Churchill in his period at the Home Office. Earlier, as President of the Board of Trade, he had applied his dynamic energies to social improvement and reform which he saw as desirable and necessary 'not to transform society but to preserve it more effectively'. At the Home Office, during 1910 and 1911, he displayed his wayward personality by applying both the state policy which had contributed to the development of Britain's industrial relations system, and a policy which, systematically pursued, would have seriously threatened it. During the turbulence in the south Wales coal industry in May 1910, Churchill behaved, contrary to the received myth, with restraint and skill. He was 'very reluctant to consider the despatch of troops to cope with violence in Newport, and in the event the situation had been taken under control before the necessity arose'. An even more serious strike in November in the Rhondda brought another appeal from local authorities for troops. These were made available 'but their employment was strictly controlled at Churchill's insistence' – neither police nor military were to be used as strike breakers 'nor were they to be regarded as being at the disposal of the mine-owners'. This stance, for which he received a bad press from Conservative newspapers, followed a long-standing tradition and evoked an approving comment later by a prominent union leader. Of the London dock strike, too, in 1911, the dockers' leader Ben Tillett subsequently declared Churchill's influence to have been 'a moderating and responsible one'. It was quite otherwise in the 1911 rail strike. Despite a regulation that forbade the use of the military unless it was specifically requested by civil authority, Churchill mobilised 50,000 troops without waiting for a request, supplied them with twenty pounds apiece and dispatched them to all strategic points. For this he was applauded by the Conservative press but met a storm of criticism elsewhere, 'some of which was echoed in ministerial circles' (ibid., pp. 48–50). Churchill departed soon after to the Admiralty, and for the most part the established proprieties were otherwise publicly preserved.

All the doubts about the system, however, remained, not only among those with a personal and immediate axe to grind, but also among those who strove for what they believed to be a balanced view of economic and social progress. Opinion was still divided, and not along party lines, on 'whether incorporation of properly motivated trade unionists should be seen as a stabilizing influence; and secondly whether Britain's relative decline ... would be hastened or redeemed by such incorporation' (Middlemas, 1979, p. 36). Britain's industrial relations system had not eliminated the massive trials of strength that caused so much industrial disruption and aroused so much public concern. Neither was it proving an effective instrument of social justice as between better-paid and poorly paid workers. The membership boom of 1889–90 had certainly included groups who until then had been viewed disparagingly by most unionists as being beyond organisational redemption, but for all the boasts by 'new' unionism of being militant, class-conscious and socialist, competitive sectionalism soon reasserted itself. The bigger boom of 1911–14 widened the social base of the movement far more and reached further down among the poorer strata, yet union purposes and methods remained essentially the same. These two periods of growth and what happened in between had in some ways transformed the texture and consciousness of the movement and naturally socialists made the most of the change. Nevertheless, their vision of an all-embracing class movement was no nearer realisation. Large numbers of the poorest remained without protection and the predominant attitude among male trade unionists towards women workers was one of hostility that left little room for assistance in organising. Moreover, in a society whose public value structure attached so much importance to property, contract and individual rights and freedoms over the disposal of one's property or labour in the making and keeping of contracts, it was hardly to be expected that a generalised approval of trade unionism based on its contribution to order and control would be proof against recurrent doubts and fears on just these issues. For trade unions could not, after all, be effective without limiting the freedom of individuals – members, non-members and employers alike – to contract, and without limiting on occasions even the freedom of employers to contract with their customers. Liberal individualist values also seemed violated by the closed shop and by coercive group pressures upon the non-unionist and non-striker. The very collectives which seemed so promising for order and stability appeared even to many whose personal interests were not directly involved to foreshadow that 'tyranny of the mob' whose prospect had alarmed so many Victorian observers from Mill and Arnold onward.

The restrictionism which often appeared to be the essence of union attempts to protect earnings, jobs and shop-floor control was likewise anathema to virtually all middle- and upper-class observers. The rules, regulations, customs and practices relating to hours of labour, overtime, the right of entrance to trades, demarcations of jobs, methods of payment, the regulation of boy labour, manning ratios, the exclusion of women and unapprenticed men to certain occupations, the right to use certain tools – these and the many others like them lay far beyond the range of middle-class sympathetic understanding – especially that of lawyers, whose own restrictive practices were highly successful but never condemned. Finally, there was the question, especially after 1910, of whether top leaders could effectively control their members so as to subdue unofficial rank and file militancy, prevent spontaneous strikes and ensure observance of agreements – crucial questions indeed since if they could not they lost much of what value they had for employers and state alike.

Despite all these doubts the ruling order and the bulk of important employers remained, as we have seen, committed to the system. Taken together with the equally manifest determination of trade union leaders, officials and activists to preserve it, the result was a tacit alliance possessing reserves of power, influence and resource which could be mobilised if necessary to protect the system from de-stabilising pressures whether of the far left or the far right. There is no evidence that this alliance was imposing the system upon the rank and file membership in the teeth of substantial and considered resistance, though it was manifestly imposing it upon a small minority of militant socialists who sought to fight industrial battles untrammelled by the constraints and obligations of industrial procedures. Even for the mainly acquiescent majority the system and the aims it pursued hardly represented the peak of civilised achievement and aspiration, but their experience had taught them that in the face of greatly superior power it was the best they could do, and their own leaders, even more convinced and, in any case, with a great deal to lose, were anxious to assure them that this was so.

Yet because the social forces supporting the system were partially overlaid by the temporary noisy excitements of the period, and because to a considerable extent these supports were latent, with deep roots in historical continuities, it was easy to misread the signs. 'The masses of the English workers', wrote Lenin in 1913 in one of his more hopeful moments, 'are slowly but surely taking a new path – from the defence of the petty privileges of the labour aristocracy to the great heroic struggle of the masses themselves for a new system of society. And bearing in mind the energy and state of organization of the English proletariat, they will bring about socialism on this path much more quickly and firmly than anywhere else' (Lenin, 1969, p. 130).

Observers closer to the scene of operations than Lenin made the same misjudgement. Yet the necessary ingredients were present for a very different assessment which did not need to rest on hindsight. Certainly Lenin would have been able to point to evidence not only of union membership extending to many groups among the semi-unskilled, but also of the growth of a 'movement' which to some extent looked beyond pressure-group sectional interests to a more generous vision of future society. This rested on a measure of class consciousness which could also sometimes express itself in solidarity not only within a group but also between groups in an instinctive urge towards the brotherhood of all labour. But two qualifications were necessary. These visions and solidarities were not a recent product, but had been evident in some measure in the trade union world since the early nineteenth century, though in some periods only vestigially. Secondly, they rarely asserted themselves against the sectional self-interests of the unions concerned. What the Webbs said of trade unionists in 1894 was still true in 1914 – that the basis of their association was primarily sectional in nature and 'not directly for the advancement of the whole working class' (Webb and Webb, 1894, p. 477). Those who observed a growing class consciousness within the trade union world needed also to note that it expressed itself most forcefully when threats were presented to the unions' rights and functions. Those common interests which figured at the top of the unions' agenda were those not of a class unity for replacing the social system with a better one, but of a class unity for defending the rights and functions of the unions themselves. It was a class consciousness directed, paradoxically, towards protecting institutions which sought to maintain wage differentials, demarcations, exclusive closed shops, or other forms of stratification within the working classes and within the existing system. Only for a small minority was it a class consciousness which sought to transcend these understandable sectional responses to a hostile environment with a unified campaign to render that environment a benign one for all. Even the years of unparalleled unrest between 1911 and 1914 had not generated among the working classes any 'substantial public demand for "socialism" – however we define that term. Most of the Labour candidates who stood at by-elections held opinions which would have excited no comment whatever if they had been expressed by Liberal M.P.s . . . The various unofficial socialists who stood from time to time . . . fared, without exception, exceedingly badly' (Douglas, 1974, p. 125). Churchill told his audiences in 1908 that 'trade unions are not socialistic. They are undoubtedly individualistic organizations, more in the character of the old guilds, and lean much more in the direction of the culture of the individual than in that of the smooth and bloodless uniformity of the mass' (Wrigley, 1982, p. 145).

If, therefore, class consciousness was to be measured in terms of the extent and strength of trade unionism it was a concept needing careful definition. Although the definition was likely to worry employers, caught up in their everyday struggles, it was less likely to worry governments, with their concern to preserve a system rather than the fortunes of particular groups of employers. From this point of view, a trade unionism which sought to organise, regulate and control their members sectionally was vastly preferable to the dangers of a mass appeal across the board to all wage-earners *per se*. Against this background it would have been possible in 1914, drawing upon evidence available, to argue that the system of industrial relations as it seemed to be developing would strengthen rather than weaken the basic structures of the status quo.

Trade Unions and the Establishment

Basic to this argument is a general premise that when British ruling groups admitted to a recognised foothold in decision-making such organisations as demonstrated their readiness to pursue their ends within the established constitutional structures, they thereby created new allies in the defence of those structures. For, once admitted, the organisations concerned rapidly developed an interest – provided they derived the necessary minimum benefit – in preserving both the formal rules and the informal understandings by which the system operated. Voluntary associations were, of course, prominent in this process. And British society was rich, at all social levels down to the lower working class, in voluntary associations. Many of them might need and seek no place in the decision-making establishment as such. Others, like the trade unions, needed a recognised legal status for the protection of their funds and their activities, which included a foothold in decision-making in both the industrial and political spheres. Given their vested interest in maintaining key institutions of the status quo, unions, like the political parties, were on the way towards becoming part of the Establishment in the sense that they educated officers and activists, not only in the formal laws and rules governing their functioning, but also in a set of informal and often unspoken conventions and observances necessary for maintaining their standing, reputation and safety with the higher classes. One example was the language and style of 'respectability' examined earlier, which helped to shape the perceptions and assumptions also of the rank and file membership.

In consequence there was developing in Britain, given its long-standing tradition of freedom of association and its culturally induced preference for voluntary effort as against state provision, a network of organisations and associations which, though voluntary in the sense of being independent of the state, educated and trained their members and the public in the rules and conventions of constitutionalism and the status quo. Many of these rules and conventions were none the less effective for being informal;

indeed, their very informality could invest functionaries with that aura of *savoir-faire* and 'being in the know' which strengthened their authority. In many cases informality was unavoidable. The successful operation of organisations such as trade unions, resting on negotiated compromise within a framework of constitutionalism, required tacit understandings with other organisations, such as employers' associations, which could hardly be publicly formalised or codified. Such understandings could nevertheless be strong, for they were underpinned by a common interest in preserving the system; a common interest which might need to be directed against any who sought to overturn it or who, through ignorance or design, threatened its rules and conventions. Thus developed alliances between organisations – perhaps including state agencies – which, though sometimes overt, were often tacit. While these organisations might be, on one level, in rivalry and conflict, they might on a more fundamental level project very similar messages.

   This is the structural basis of what a number of observers have claimed to detect in the British social scene – an intangible network of basic consensus, often latent but capable of expression in practical though usually informal and covert alliances. This network extends between the top levels of organisations that may be political, social, or industrial adversaries; it has also come to include – with the construction of a popular monarchy – highly sympathetic links between Labour governments and the crown. Those involved see themselves as practical realists observing the common-sense necessities of things as they are, and later often expressed baffled irritation when the term 'Establishment', an imprecise word for an imprecise phenomenon, began to be used in the 1950s. Those most sharply convinced of the usefulness of the term include individuals and groups at lower levels who have moved beyond the limits of 'received' or 'acceptable' behaviour or doctrine and have felt the pressures of these tacit alliances between what in other respects are disparate and even opposed institutions. The alliances often involve the withholding or playing down of facts, disagreements, or group gossip which top-level leaders consider it judicious that the lower orders should not be allowed to hear. Such items might provide ammunition for lower-level critics or in some other way embarrass conventional procedures, or the leaders' own positions, or the official policies being pursued. In other words, the system fosters élitism in all those organisations, statutory and voluntary, which are conscious of having a foothold in the higher structures of influence and decision-making. The entry of labour organisations into the Establishment by no means reduced the secretiveness with which British governments had long sought to surround their activities – typified in the fact that only after a long eighteenth-century struggle both inside and outside the courts, for example, had the British public been allowed to read the parliamentary debates of their political masters and 'representatives'. Beatrice Webb's perception of the early stages of this absorption of union élites into Establishment networks was noted in the preceding section (see p. 268).

   Many trade unions were in fact developing a pattern of leadership and authority similar to those characteristic of other British institutions. Jessop refers to findings by Eckstein of a 'remarkable similarity' between the authority structures of government and administration in Britain and those of parties, pressure groups, big business corporations, professional associations – and trade unions. 'The basic pattern is one of strong leadership tempered by constitutionalism – that is, one of a relatively autonomous and secure leadership restrained by a broad and explicit framework of procedural and substantive rules. Democratic participation has only a small part in the overall pattern' (Jessop, 1974, pp. 68–9). Some would describe the leadership as being tempered also by insurgency. At the level of government McKenzie and Silver refer to

> the modest role accorded 'the people' in British political culture. Although it is a commonplace of research on stable democracies that general electorates are typically uninvolved in politics . . . it is only in Britain that this is so largely consistent with the prevailing climate of political values. Though modern constitutions typically locate the source of sovereignty in 'the people', in Britain it is the Crown in Parliament that is sovereign. Nor is that a merely technical point. The political culture of democratic Britain assigns to ordinary people the role, not of citizens, but of subjects . . .' (McKenzie and Silver, 1968, p. 251)

At the deepest level, 'such distinctions are not bourgeois-constitutional trivia (as so many Marxists have held): they manifest the nature of the state, and the whole material history which produced that state' (Nairn, 1977, p. 40). Jessop extends the argument to 'relations between dominant institutions as well as their internal organization. Even where there are severe disagreements on specific issues and policies, for example, the different élites agree to confine bargaining and consultation to the centre and not to include outsiders who might "rock the boat"' (Jessop, 1974, p. 69).

All this co-existed, of course, with much genuine conflict in specific industries over union recognition, wages, working hours and the line defining the frontier of control at the workplace. It also co-existed, as it always had done, with local outbursts of official violence. 'Troops and cavalry, police baton-charges, warships, all became a familiar feature of many large strikes from the 1890s to the 1920s.' Two striking miners were killed and others injured at Featherstone, Yorkshire, in 1893, at the hands of troops called in by a local coal-owning magistrate after much riot and damage to colliery premises – Asquith, the Home Secretary, having transmitted to the War Office, as he was obliged to do, the local authority's request for military support. Twenty years later his meetings were still being interrupted by shouts of 'Featherstone'. There were two more deaths and injuries in similar circumstances at Llanelly in 1911. Followed though they were by much public concern and official inquiries, such incidents were modest by Continental standards. Injuries at the hands of the police were more numerous. 'Frightened police going berserk in baton charges were almost a commonplace during a large strike' (Lane, 1974, p. 78). It had been apparent long before Peterloo that the state's coercive agencies wielded a certain degree of local tactical autonomy which in specific situations was not necessarily exercised in ways deemed judicious by Whitehall. This applied even in the capital, where the Metropolitan Police was not an arm of government, and where the Commissioner, despite his direct responsibility to the Home Secretary, was seen as part of the force and not as a political figure. This autonomy, which could be used in the direction of either leniency or severity, helped the public presentation of the police as a 'neutral' professional force, though such claims have always been found far more persuasive by the middle and upper than by the working classes.

Yet there were certain characteristics of British police forces which marked them off from, say, their German counterparts and which were important for the British strategy of rule and its legitimations. To begin with, they were smaller in scale. Upper-class alarm at popular unrest had still not become strong enough to overcome the distaste for a powerful national police (Tobias, 1972, p. 204). Moreover, police behaviour was still contained firmly within due process of law. The fact that English common law differed from Continental Roman law in placing more emphasis on the rights of individuals put the police, like public officials generally, in a less favourable position. Remedies against them were available through actions for damages, and there were even differences in court procedure which required them to be especially wary. German police, like the English, were called upon to give evidence in court, but German courts were not, and are still not, structured on the full 'adversary system' of the Anglo-Saxon pattern, which exposes them to rigorous cross-examination by a hostile counsel. Consequent habits of caution evolved during the early formative years resulted in law-enforcement agencies keeping a low profile politically (ibid., pp. 203–7). It might not seem so to harassed strike pickets, but in their general role as trade union activists they were a good deal freer from the attentions of the local police than their fellow-unionists in Germany. The paradox was that the British strategy of rule relied on other, and in the last resort more effective, forces of social cohesion and control, among them an Establishment network which was coming to include their own unions.

7

Consolidation and Integration

1914 to the 1950s

The effects of the First World War and its aftermath upon the industrial relations system were, on the one hand, to confirm and extend its existing structures and dispositions and, on the other, to generate sharply contrasting hopes among a number of different groups that the system might be changed in directions which they preferred. None of these hopes was realised, but in examining the reasons for the failure of these suppressed alternatives we shall, by the same token, be revealing how the system came to persist. Among the factors which secured its persistence can be identified some that were fortuitous. These included the personality and emergence to political prominence of Stanley Baldwin. In his hands, the application of the traditional strategy of rule to industrial relations was brought to something approaching an art form. His hope of securing the best of all worlds by containing class conflict and, at the same time, inducing the unions to co-operate in modernisation did not, however, succeed. Moreover, even under Baldwin's quietism the industrial relations system did not escape threats from both left and right. As before, the far left aspired to use the mass membership of the unions as a vehicle for more ambitious purposes than industrial regulation. Corporatism and Mosley's fascism offered their own species of danger. Both threats were contained with ease. Britain's industrial relations system survived a second exercise in total war stronger than ever before. During the 1950s, specialist students were disposed to see it as the 'mature case'.

Unions and Employer Organisation: the Impact of Total War

The acute labour shortages which quickly developed as the economy became drawn into the war effort had their predictable effect upon union organisation and membership, which doubled from just over 4 million in 1914 to over 8 million in 1920. There was a parallel effect upon employer organisation. Among the pressures fostering it was the need of government departments for representative institutions with which to deal for such purposes as organising production, allocating raw materials and drafting wartime regulations. But equally powerful was the logic of wartime wage-fixing. The government's early hope that this, in accordance with long-established tradition, could be left to industry itself soon had to be abandoned. Even stable and well-tried systems of collective bargaining were ill-adapted to dealing with the tremendous pressures and rapid changes generated by the war. More fundamentally, problems were emerging which no one industry's collective bargaining procedure could handle, for they were problems created by the interplay of circumstances, events and bargaining in a number of industries. Problems on this level could only be handled by the state.

They soon presented themselves in abundance. Wage rates throughout the economy constituted an interconnected system in the sense that a change at one point invariably generated – in circumstances of acute labour shortages and the imperative of avoiding stoppages of work – irresistible pressures for change at other points. Traditional comparisons and differentials played a considerable part in such pressures, as did feelings about equity which many wage-earners now had the strength to express. As a consequence the Committee on Production, comprising Sir George Askwith and representatives of the Admiralty and War Office and set up in February 1915 to ensure an adequate and uninterrupted labour supply for the war industries, found itself increasingly drawn into a struggle to co-ordinate wage movements with the aims of maintaining production, minimising inflation and keeping down the cost of the war. Its efforts towards these ends were frequently compromised and undermined by government departments and the Cabinet, who for their own reasons of productive or political expediency often conceded increases without consideration of the wider effects. Despite this the committee had some success. To achieve it required increasing authoritative intervention, albeit through the structures and institutions of collective bargaining, which became greatly extended and centralised as a consequence. By the end of the war the state 'was fixing the rates of wages for large numbers of workers directly by administrative order; it was controlling, or attempting to control, the rates of large numbers of others by compelling them to accept the determinations of official arbitration authorities; altogether a majority of the wage-earning population had their wages fixed by Government in one or other of these ways' (Clay, 1929, p. 20). In the context of a widespread disposition at all social levels to support the government and win the war, these policies not only managed to cope with wartime needs without direct compulsion of labour – a possibility so dreaded by the unions as to be one of the reasons for their accepting the role of partner, if only junior partner, in the conduct of affairs – but also kept down production losses from strikes to a fraction of those incurred during the few years immediately preceding and immediately following the war.

Authoritative intervention required for success far more than the mere issue of decrees. Representative organisations were needed for the negotiation, arbitration, or administrative determination of wage rates just as for the handling of production and distribution problems. Where these did not exist, government departments sometimes had to galvanise employers into organisation purely in order to have spokesmen with whom to deal. Especially between 1917 and 1920, employers' associations, trade associations and chambers of commerce grew in strength and authority. Collective bargaining became greatly strengthened and furthered to include many industries not hitherto covered – including some, like railways and shipping, where employers had until now fought a tenacious rearguard action against it. There was widespread recognition of unions in the civil service and other public sectors, and collective bargaining for public employees became almost universal. With few exceptions the agreements concluded in both public and private sectors were national in coverage.

Among the organisational gaps filled was that of a central employers association; several prewar attempts in this direction having failed. In 1915 the British Manufacturers' Association was created from 200 leading industrial firms specifically to represent manufacturing as distinct from commercial interests, and the following year saw the establishment of the Federation of British Industries (FBI). In view of the FBI's later fortunes it is worth noting that at this stage the FBI declared itself concerned, among other things, with the general industrial relations field, and spoke of its future role in terms of 'organizing and developing industry after the war in co-operation with labour and in conjunction with the government and government departments' (Charles, 1973, p. 234). There was a contrast here with the distinctly harder line followed by the most powerful employers' association, the Engineering Employers' Federation (EEF), whose own policy, in the face of wary, mistrustful and restrictive craft workers, had been to confine dealings with the unions to the minimum. For several years, however, the FBI continued to express the stance of those industrialists who had become attracted by such wartime co-operation as had developed and saw in it the shape of a possible peacetime pattern.

This co-operation between government agencies, employers and the unions was being secured through a greatly increased integration of labour representatives into political and administrative machinery. Arthur Henderson, a trade unionist who had succeeded to the leadership of the parliamentary Labour Party in August 1914 when Ramsay MacDonald resigned against the party's support of the war, was brought into the Cabinet in 1915, nominally as President of the Board of Education but in reality as 'the voice of labour'. Two other Labour MPs received junior office. Henderson continued as a member of Lloyd George's reconstructed War Cabinet after the toppling of Asquith as Prime Minister in December 1916, being replaced in 1917 by another trade unionist, G. N. Barnes, who remained until 1919. This time five other labour leaders were given office, two of them senior posts. Moreover, as the state gradually extended its control over industry and the country's life, national and local committees of a wide variety of kinds proliferated on which sat trade union and labour representatives – indeed the unions were 'to a large extent absorbed temporarily into the State's administrative machine . . .

With dramatic suddenness the . . . movement found itself . . . treated with deference and respect and given large powers in the war-time administration' (Milne-Bailey, 1929, p. 32). It has been argued, indeed, that for Lloyd George, forming his War Cabinet in 1916, 'it was the attitude of Labour that would make or break his attempts to form a government'. Through the mediation of J. H. Thomas, general secretary of the National Union of Railwaymen and a rapidly rising figure, he won, 'by the narrowest of majorities', the support of the union leaders for his proposed labour policy (Morgan, 1978, p. 67).

A Mass Electorate and a Mass Labour Party

This unprecedented admission of labour spokesmen into political and administrative decision-making expressed a recognition that modern large-scale war, resting as it did upon an industrial technology of massive dimensions, required the active co-operation of organised labour. But there was a still wider consideration. If this was to be a mass-participation war, the people must be made to feel that they had a stake in the outcome; that their sacrifices would yield positive gains for themselves as well as for their masters. Talk of postwar social reconstruction was officially encouraged. In this atmosphere the existing limitations to the franchise seemed less and less convincing and the Representation of the People Act of February 1918 conceded the vote to all adult males and to women of 30 and over with a property qualification. The last prewar general election in December 1910 had been based on an electorate of only 7½ million, which excluded about 44 per cent of all adult males – mainly working class – and all women. The 1918 Act, bringing the electorate to over 21 million, provided the necessary condition for the growth of a mass-based working-class party (Chamberlain, 1973, pp. 476–7).

Its basis had already been under construction during 1917–18 in the form of a reconstituted Labour Party. War had both deeply split the Liberal Party between the Lloyd George and Asquith factions and acted as a forcing house upon the aspirations of Labour Party leaders. In place of a loose federation of affiliated organisations, the constitution of February 1918 provided for a centralised, nationally cohesive party, with its own individual members organised in local constituency parties and subject to central party discipline. This has often been referred to as the conversion of a Lib–Lab party into a socialist one, largely through the influence of Sidney Webb who supposedly created the new organisation in the Fabian image. In fact, the programme was largely a piecing together of resolutions from previous annual conferences – though the very fact that this could be construed as a Fabian programme is itself significant. It is true that Webb and Henderson were able to embody in the new constitution a socialist declaration in Clause 4 – though the word 'socialism' was still avoided. This formally committed the party 'to secure for the producers by hand and by brain the full fruits of their industry, and the most equitable distribution thereof that may be possible, upon the basis of the common ownership of the means of production and the best obtainable system of popular administration and control of each industry and service'. This certainly gave the party a modest ideology of sorts which it had hitherto lacked, and created a niche within the party for political intellectuals and experts. But the debates on the new constitution 'emphasized the dislike of the trade union leaders for socialist theory, and their clear intention to make the party, in the words of one unionist leader, "our political arm"' (Rhodes James, 1978, p. 378). Within British society as it had been, and was to become again after the war, this jarred far less on many rank and file socialists than might have been expected. Hardship and poverty were sufficiently widespread for sectional and self-serving struggles to be subsumed within the general struggle for a better society; the former in fact seeming to serve the latter.

It was nevertheless significant that the socialist societies, such as the Independent Labour Party, an Anglo-Marxist sect which had been allowed to affiliate in 1916, saw their power position within the party severely curtailed. They lost their previous separate status and reserved seats on the National Executive Committee and their right to elect their own NEC representatives. All executive members were now to be elected by the annual conference, which could be dominated by the block votes of the unions if they so chose. This was the price paid to secure the continued adhesion of the large unions, whose leaders viewed the social-ist societies with dislike and distrust, and who were now to be required to pay substantially increased affiliation fees to finance the new nationally organised party with its own constituencies. This key struggle over increased union domination was won by the unions with relative ease; Clause 4 being 'a mere sop thrown to the Fabians on the off-chance that there was some electoral appeal in their trust in workers "by hand and brain"' (Hall, 1977, p. 358). Nevertheless, the party had its committed left wing. By early 1921 it was firmly installed as 'a two-faced threat to the established order ... It had the face of Thomas, Webb, Henderson and Clynes: it had the face of Lansbury, Smillie, Williams and Hodges' (Cowling, 1971, p. 44). The first four were not mistaken for dangerous revolutionaries; about the second four there was more doubt.

Moreover, although socialist militancy might be susceptible of being blocked at the national political level it was finding plenty of scope at the workplace, more especially in those war industries where the urgent imperatives of simplified speeded-up production confronted head-on the protective restrictionism of craft workers. Workplace union organ-isation, with its shop stewards and works committees, having shown distinct signs of flagging after the 1911–13 upsurge, leapt into renewed and greatly enhanced life with the appearance of 'dilution'. In 1914 most leaders of the Labour movement had quickly demonstrated a readiness to co-operate in prosecuting the war provided working-class interests could be protected – on 25 August the unions and the Labour Party declared an industrial truce for the duration, and on 29 August the party agreed to an electoral truce and placed its organisation at the disposal of the recruiting campaign. But sharply rising prices soon triggered off demands for wage increases and informal government pressure was doing little for output, so the two major preoccupations of the Committee on Production soon became the maintenance of industrial peace and the promotion of 'dilution'.

'Dilution' and the Shop Stewards' Movement

Dilution was 'the introduction of less skilled workers to undertake the whole or part of the work previously done by workers of greater skill or experience, often, but not always, accompanied by simplification of machinery, or the breaking up of a job into a number of simpler operations' (Cole, 1973, p. 48). Integral to dilution and other methods of speeding up production was the need for skilled workers to submit to the suspension of all those regulations, customs and practices, formal and informal, which they or their predecessors had evolved precisely to defend their skills, status, job control and pay against just such an undermining of their position as was now proposed. Already by December 1914 the engineering employers were applying unsuccessfully to the unions for freedom from craft restrictions on the employment of less skilled labour, freedom to increase the number of machines per man, and freedom from demarcation and overtime restrictions. Some months later, in March 1915, a Shells and Fuses Agreement was concluded between the unions and the Engineering Employers' Federation, but showed few signs of being accepted by those whose consent really mattered, namely, the craftsmen at the workplace. It was overtaken by the Treasury Agreement reached after conferences later in the month between Lloyd George, then Chancellor of the Exchequer, and representatives of the main relevant unions. The latter agreed to 'recommend to their members' that for the purposes of avoiding stoppages and maximising production all disputes which could not be settled by existing procedures should go to arbitration by the Committee on Production or some jointly acceptable alternative, and that present 'restrictive' trade rules and customs should be relaxed 'as may be necessary'. In return, the government undertook to require firms on war work to pay the full 'skilled' rates to the new semi-skilled workers doing diluted jobs and to guarantee the full restoration after the war of whatever trade practices and customs were being suspended. At a further conference the government also promised to limit profits on munitions work 'so that any sacrifices made by the unions should be for the benefit of the country, and not of the shareholders of firms engaged on munitions production'. (Clay, 1929, p. 25; Goodrich, 1975, pp. 194–7). Over a year later the then Minister of Munitions, E. S. Montagu, was to say

> The Government asked Labour to put . . . on one side . . . the whole armour of trade union regulations upon which they had hitherto relied – rules and customs relating to hours of labour, overtime, the right of entrance to trades, demarcation of industry, the regulation of boy labour, and the exclusion of women from certain classes of occupations . . . It was a great deal to ask . . . but with a loyalty and statemanship which cannot be over-estimated, the request was readily granted. The trade unions required, and they were right to require, a scrupulous

record and recognition of what they were conceding. It was promised to them as a right, but they will receive more – not only the restoration of the system they temporarily abandoned, but the gratitude of the army, and of the nation . . . (Milne-Bailey, 1929, p. 396)

The significance of this government stance has received too little attention. There was more in these remarks besides fulsome flattery of what were recognised to be powerful forces needing to be cultivated. The pressures of war had compelled the government to express something approaching official legitimation of trade union 'restrictive practices'. Legitimation did not, of course, imply approval; Montagu might well, if taxed, have manifested the customary Establishment condemnation of 'misguided' and 'wrong-headed' union policies. Yet in guaranteeing their restoration in such terms as he employed, the government was conceding the unions' right to retain them. This was fully in line with previous state practice of acquiescing in the predominantly autonomous development of the unions and industrial relations generally. It was a further development of a stance which brought little cheer and encouragement to any who dreamed of winning positive and material state support for a peacetime campaign of economic modernisation which included the smashing of union pretensions towards job control at the workplace.

Even the negotiated suspension of restrictive practices, however, soon proved inadequate to achieve the speed-up hoped for. Lloyd George, 'with profound misunderstanding', had 'imagined that trade unions and the TUC were bodies capable of making bargains and enforcing them, if necessary, against their members' opposition' (Middlemas, 1979, p. 80). But it was 'one thing to convince and secure the assent of the trade union leaders to the new policy, it was another to overcome the almost instinctive resistance of the rank and file of skilled workers to anything that threatened their established position' (Clay, 1929, p. 25). As shop-floor resistance and resort to stoppages mounted, the government turned to legislative compulsion with the first Munitions of War Act in July 1915 which embodied the bargain of the Treasury Conference. In pursuit of the efficient manufacture, transport and supply of munitions, the Act's purpose was to limit collective bargaining and to extend government control over the worker's normal freedom as far as wartime exigencies demanded and the state of feeling in the labour world would allow. Under union pressure all features in an earlier draft suggestive of industrial conscription or of military organisation and authority had been abandoned, but there remained prohibition of stoppages, compulsory arbitration and suspension of restrictive practices.

Given, however, the shop-floor power derived from acute labour shortages and a spirit of independence which was fully ready to exert this power against pressure and patriotic appeals by management, government and labour leaders, legislation as such proved no more effective. The only feature of the Munitions of War Act which really furthered the government's aims was the limitation on profits in 'controlled establishments'. Even so, change was slow. And because so much of the detailed application of change was specific to each particular workplace, full-time union officials were often able to contribute less than the workplace's own shop stewards, who were also more significant figures for the winning of consent. There developed a rapid growth of workplace representation and leadership by shop stewards, not a few of them militant socialists.

Cole has referred to the government's realisation of 'the certainty that dilution would prove effective only when it was introduced with the consent, and, if possible, the willing co-operation, of the skilled workers affected' (Cole, 1973, p. 50). He goes on to explain the appointment of Dilution Commissioners for the Clyde and the Tyne in terms of this conciliatory introduction of government policy. Against this it has been argued that the commissioners went in not only armed with a carefully planned contingency campaign against the workers, but also conscious that pressure against the employers was also necessary. Unconvinced of the value of dilution, employers feared to 'force it through against the wishes of their men and at the risk of provoking extensive strike action'; and were nervous that their scarce skilled labour might be transferred to competitors (Hinton, 1971, pp. 174, 177).

Left-wing shop steward leadership in the field of dilution did not necessarily take the form of supporting unqualified opposition by conservative, exclusivist craftsmen fearful of losing their status and privileges. Especially on Clydeside, socialist leaders such as David Kirkwood declared support of dilution in principle as a necessary stage in the evolution of machine industry and directed their attack instead into a struggle to control the circumstances of its introduction. For Marxists, the blurring and eventual elimination of craft distinctions represented a necessary stage in the overthrow of capitalism. In the event, however, 'even the revolutionaries could not escape entanglement in the protective reflexes of the craftsmen' (ibid., p. 184).

Both stances were guaranteed in any case to generate numerous and widespread frictions, especially in certain areas such as Clydeside and Sheffield, and a fruitful soil was created for left-wing influence; all the more so since little advice or assistance was forthcoming from national or district officers of the unions. Often preoccupied with the plethora of official committees into which they were increasingly drawn, union officers had all too little time or energy to spare for the rapid, hastily improvised and often unprecedented technical and organisational changes being introduced at the workplace. The opportunities thereby made available were eagerly grasped by shop-floor purveyors of a variety of left-wing revolutionary philosophies whose appeal often sprang largely from the practical leadership and support which they offered to work groups engaged in a deeply mistrustful struggle against higher authority. Prominent among the ideas that gained currency were those connected with syndicalism, guild socialism and other varieties of 'workers' control' (Pribićević, 1959). It was hardly surprising in the circumstances that what had the most immediate appeal was a conception of the organised rank and file under their shop steward leaders using their collective industrial strength for political as well as industrial ends in the process known as 'direct action'. The prospect of the working classes collectively using their only potent weapon – refusal to work – for political purposes was one of the oldest nightmares of the ruling class, and there was more than anxiety about war production in the Establishment's emphatic responses to shop steward militancy in the most affected areas.

Yet although significant political consequences were to flow from this powerful grass-roots fillip to Marxist and other left-wing doctrines, their impact on the shop-floor movement must not be exaggerated. As authority learned to adapt to the exigencies of the changed power relations at the workplace, shop stewards and the works committees they set up became more and involved in humdrum negotiations over the many detailed and complex issues thrown up by what in some industries was an almost continuous process of adjustment and change. As a consequence, although 'the shop stewards' movement rose to fame primarily as a quasi-revolutionary movement, the great mass of the work done by the stewards remained throughout the war period of this essentially unrevolutionary character'. It was not the case that 'the great mass of the shop stewards ever became revolutionaries or even socialists in any theoretical sense' (Cole, 1973, pp. 54, 55). Still less was it true of their constituents, most of whom were preoccupied with their own material interests – which widened to include, as the war ground on, protection on such issues as payment by results, freedom of job movement, and especially the threat of conscription under the Military Service Acts. Nor was it the case that the rank and file became open to left-wing capture as a result of the union hierarchies becoming a mere arm of the state. The notion that the Amalgamated Society of Engineers, perhaps the key union in all the major wartime issues, acted simply as a state agency would have evoked hollow laughter from the harassed officials of the Ministry of Munitions. It consulted its members, took determined stands on a variety of issues, and outside the Clyde largely succeeded, for example, in keeping women off skilled men's work.

But if the wartime workshop movement was not in any major sense captured, shaped, or organised by revolutionary socialist sects, neither was it developed under official union control or for that matter under the auspices of any other external direction or inspiration. Its key feature was its spontaneity. It was the outcome of circumstances common to many different areas, but although attempts were made from time to time to co-ordinate its many expressions, and various organisations such as the Socialist Labour Party made more or less successful attempts to influence its development, on the whole it followed its own course. Local variations developed according to local differences of conditions and organisation. There were variations, too, in the responses of the official union hierarchies. Many stewards were fully and officially recognised by their unions; many professed no allegiance to left-wing leaders. But there were many cases, too, where union officials viewed the new developments with, at best ambivalence, at worst hostility, seeing them as independent bases of power which both challenged their own authority and served as vehicles for doctrines they disliked and mistrusted. Those unions for whom a vigilant shop-floor organisation was a key first-line defence of union standards were anxious to consolidate the wartime gains in shop steward organisation into permanent practice. The widespread *de facto* recognition by employers must be rendered *de jure* recognition through embodiment in formal agreements. Unions in the engineering industries managed to secure a national agreement in 1917, and another more satisfactory to them in 1919 which officially recognised not only the shop stewards but also the numerous works committees set up by them.

This wartime shop steward movement was capable of yielding some important propositions about the growth of Britain's industrial relations system. First, its development on such a scale had been quite unexpected by both employers and trade unionists; prewar experience had been carefully studied for useful guidance but little was found. Secondly, it had revealed an especially powerful potentiality for organised shop-floor resistance to managerial will in that great complex of engineering and metals industries which were becoming, in place of the textile trades, the key group of capitalist industries; a group particularly dependent upon a receptive shop-floor attitude to managerial innovation and experiment. Thirdly, it had constituted the most dramatic reminder yet of the weakness in the grand conception of the Royal Commission on Labour in its *Final Report* of 1894: the conception of large centralised unions and large centralised employers' associations negotiating definitive regulations covering their industry and imposing them upon well-disciplined constituents. There were aspects of Britain's social and industrial structures and culture which rendered this an uncertain prospect and wartime conditions of acute labour shortage had strengthened them.

Individualism and Patriotism

Some observers within the Establishment were concerned to make more general propositions about this point. The Cabinet papers of July 1916 contain a remarkable memorandum submitted by the insurance companies on the conditions for mobilising popular consent. It argued, first, that 'it is impossible to secure the performance of any new duty by the individual member of the population unless the particular act . . . is closely linked up with the personal self-interest of the individual, or with the action which he would normally take in his own self-interest'. Secondly, that 'legal sanctions as to penalties are powerless to secure the general performance . . . of any such duties if divorced from self-interested motives or actions; it is impossible to prosecute the whole population'. And, thirdly, that 'the use of sanctions to enforce the performance of any duty only becomes effective if the persons upon whom the duty is placed are limited in number and responsible in character'. The memorandum denied, in short,

> that the individual . . . can be brought to perform even the simplest operation by being subjected to a legal obligation to do so . . . This is not due to any lack of patriotism or of respect for law, but has its cause deep down in the genius of the nation, the freedom of its private life from

bureaucratic incursions, its unfamiliarity with and distaste for forma-
lities of procedure and 'red tape'. Such a system could only be successful
when enforced, as in Germany, by a rigorous and ubiquitous police
system upon a nation accustomed to be regulated in all the minor
matters of life.

Arrangements in Britain, to be successful, 'must be based upon different
principles' (Middlemas, 1979, pp. 84, 355).

This analysis, based as it is upon the assumption that the society of which
it speaks is strongly infused by individualism of a self-interested kind,
draws attention to the difficulties faced by British governments when they
seek mass support for some 'national' purpose which allegedly transcends
individual or organized group interests. There was plenty of individual
patriotism in Britain. Imperialist consciousness and a dutiful monarchy
had strengthened it with a legitimation, an ideology and an abundance of
symbols. But the social imperialists had been working very much against
the grain of British society in trying to promote a mass readiness to
abnegate private purpose and, above all, private judgement in favour of an
unquestioned authoritarian leadership. Patriotism was emphatically not
unconditional. There was little in it of the semi-mystical submission to
transcendent purpose. The old radical patriotism had even taken the form
of active suspicion towards the ruling class, and although popular collective expressions of it had faded under the onslaught of the Conservative
bid to appropriate the rhetoric of patriotism for their exclusive use, it could
still find expression. H. G. Wells, one of the most influential publicists of
modern times, was not alone in reacting with fury to the bland assumption
of official proclamations that men must flock to the colours 'to serve His
Majesty'. For men and women like the early Wells, His Majesty was not
the supreme symbol of the Britain for which they fought, and his
establishment in that role was a piece of official impertinence.

The Beginnings of Tripartite Corporatism

Within this complex blend of individualism, scepticism towards authority, and an individual patriotism that was strong but sometimes difficult
to tap, the organised interests – trade unions and employers' associations
as well as other pressure groups and lobbies – were structured to operate to
rigorously segmental and particularist definitions of their members' interests. Not for them the broad conception which yielded accommodatingly
to idealistic intangibles or to the promise of diffuse and long-term
outcomes, but rather the narrow and specific focus for which they had
been set up and which was their containing term of reference. When they
dealt with government they brought to bear the same preferences for the
'bargain', the 'mutual arrangement', the 'deal', as they brought to bear on
each other.

British governments were well adapted to this style. They had long
been expected not to exercise bold creative leadership but to cope pragmat-
ically with problems as they arose, picking their way warily through the

minefield of organised groups, lobbies and vested interests. And it was implicit in this style that there should be the possibility of consultation and quasi-negotiations between legislators and such of those affected who had the power to make themselves difficult. Middlemas, noting that British governments began earlier than governments of any other industrial country to make the avoidance of crises their first priority, goes on to register that even before full suffrage they had discovered how to exercise the art of 'public management'. This included extending the state's powers to assess, educate, bargain with, appease, or constrain the demands of the electorate, raising to a degree of parity with the state the various competing interests and institutions to which voters owed allegiance. They sought to avoid, by compromise, crises in sensitive areas, 'abolishing Hobbes' "natural anarchy of competing wills" not by invoking authority (at a time of declining faith and deference) but by the alternate gratification and cancelling out of the desires of large, well-organized, collective groups to the detriment of individuals, minorities and deviants' (Middlemas, 1979, p. 18).

When this process is made public and explicit it is apt to cause alarm in some quarters as 'bypassing' Parliament and subverting its sovereignty. Such alarms are specially apparent when the bargain is with organised labour, as was to be the case in the 1970s, when the deal became known as the 'social contract'. Though regarded by some as a daring and highly suspect novelty, this had several antecedents, the first being the Treasury Agreement of 1915. This represented no more than an explicit extension of an already existent governing style. Its in-built weakness had already been revealed during 1911–13. When labour shortage gives power to workplace union organisation, bargains concluded nationally may face acute problems of observance unless extreme care has been taken to secure the consent of the rank and file.

The Restoration of Pre-War Practices

Shop-floor power had made such problems especially severe with respect to the suspension of restrictive practices and Lloyd George was manifestly anxious to avoid provoking rank and file hostility by delaying their restoration. In early 1919 disaffection in the army coincided with widespread industrial unrest. The miners, railwaymen and transport workers revised the Triple Alliance in February. The engineers were in belligerent mood and in Glasgow a series of stoppages brought violent scenes and tanks on the streets. The mood revealed 'the organized workers to be a live militant force, unrevolutionary in its ultimate aims, but ready for bold leadership on political as well as on industrial issues'. Some government ministers feared far worse, and possibly a great deal 'could have been extracted at the end of the war' from a government that was less confident than its pronouncements suggested and that was not even sure it could rely on the rank and file of the army and police (Miliband, 1973, p. 65). Most union leaders, fearing a loss of control to militants, were more anxious to contain this force than exploit it. There were, nevertheless, certain issues within their more limited pattern of aspirations on which they were prepared to present an implacable face to government leaders. Prominent among them was the restoration of prewar customs and practices in the workplace. Here can be found support for Tawney's assertion that the involvement of the unions in the political arena was essentially negative and mostly concerned with the protection of certain liberties (Hall, 1977, p. 359). Lloyd George had already deemed it judicious to set up, only two days after the armistice, a Conference of Employers and Employed to advise him on the terms of legislation.

The Restoration of Pre-War Practices Act 1919 has so far received only the briefest of passing references in the texts, apparently on the supposition that its passage can be taken for granted. This understates its significance. Restoration can by no means be taken for granted. In the Cabinet Churchill argued against it on the grounds of industrial efficiency, but was overruled. When it came it went further than many might have expected. It not only required the employer, under threat of an admittedly small financial penalty, to permit restoration for at least one year of 'any rule, practice, or custom obtaining before the war'; it also required the employer in any establishment which came into existence or which took up munitions production *during* the war to permit the *introduction* of such practices 'as obtained before the war' in similar establishments. Sir Robert Horne, Minister of Labour, told the House of Commons (June 1919), that there had been some 30,000–40,000 recorded cases of departure from prewar custom and practice. In the debate that followed, several MPs bemoaned the effect that restoration would have on industry's competitiveness – it would be 'tremendously prejudicial' – it was to be hoped it would remain a dead letter. None argued against the general feeling that 'they must redeem the pledge given'.

It did not remain a dead letter. 'Contrary to all expectations', this, like other aspects of the transition to peace, was 'rapidly and almost smoothly carried out', with 'relatively little friction'. Confident predictions 'by many different authorities that the effect of the war-time experience would be a permanent revolution in the methods of British engineering practice' proved false. The engineering employers 'have, for the most part', wrote Cole in 1923, 'reverted largely to their pre-war methods of production' (Cole, 1973, pp. 124–5).

This prompt redemption of the pledge is not difficult to explain. 'The employers and the Government were, during the first half of the year (1919), in a state of alarm lest there should be a labour uprising which would seriously interfere with the resumption of business; and great care was exercised to avoid any disputes.' The employers preferred, 'in face of the immediate demand, to avoid trouble, to revert to the old methods and to get back their former staffs, rather than engage in the hazardous enterprise' of applying mass-production methods to their peacetime markets (Webb and Webb, 1920, p. 643). The very expectation of general friction over the reversion to peace was likely to remind government leaders that craftsmen especially, as they had recently demonstrated, could be remarkably tenacious in defence of what they considered their rights. More fundamentally, the government was likely to be receiving urgent advice that hesitancy over restoring suspended practices would, given the threat from the unofficial far left, further undermine the already weakened standing of the official leaders who had supported suspension in the first place. Even politicians deeply hostile to organised labour could sometimes grasp this principle. 'Trade union organization is the only thing between us and anarchy', declared Bonar Law in 1919, and in the same year Churchill, too, argued that 'Trade union organization was very important, and the more moderate its officials were, the less representative it was; but it was the only organization with which the government could deal. The curse of trade unionism was that there was not enough of it, and it was not highly enough developed to make its branch secretaries fall into line with the head office' (Middlemas, 1979, pp. 143–4).

There may have been voices, too, reinforcing these expediency reasons with another of the sort which Baldwin later considered relevant for Conservative policy during the 1930s. 'The Tory Party should be seen to keep its bargains and perhaps, through that vindication of honour, the Labour party might be restrained from violence and encouraged to resume the strict parliamentary pattern' (Middlemas and Barnes, 1969, p. 803). We can be sure, however, that the reasons for restoration did not include what has to be described rather as one of its unwilled consequences. However emphatically men of affairs might denounce union restrictionism, the fact remained that many standard tactics of job protection had now received statutory acknowledgement and status as forms of property which organised labour had a right to retain – if necessary with the support of state sanctions.

The Whitley Report

Restoration was, however, far from indicating that the Establishment generally was satisfied to see the industrial relations system revert to its prewar pattern, with the only differences being that trade unionism, employer organisation, and joint negotiation on the 'adversary' model were far more widely spread. Wartime conditions had generated a number of alternative conceptions. One of them had stemmed from an official initiative. The Whitley Committee on the Relations between Employers and Employed was an offshoot of a Reconstruction Committee set up by Asquith in March 1916. It comprised officials of leading employers' associations and of large trade unions, and economists and social workers. Some of its members illustrate the kinds of interconnections that had become important in Establishment thought and activity. J. J. Mallon, for example, member of the Independent Labour Party and Fabian Society, had, at the Board of Trade, been closely involved with the setting-up of trade boards for negotiation of statutory minimum wage rates in certain sweated trades and was to become warden of Toynbee Hall. The secretaries, usually the most influential members in this kind of inquiry, were Arthur Greenwood, university and WEA lecturer, and H. J. Wilson, secretary of the Committee on Production, who had been on the staff of Sir George Askwith in the Labour Department of the Board of Trade. The very existence of the committee owed something to prodding by W. H. Beveridge and Llewellyn Smith, of the Labour Department, who had done so much to foster the state policy of support and encouragement of voluntary and independent sectional collective bargaining, though in the hope and belief, shared by Askwith, that it could be brought to move from adversary to co-operative postures.

During 1917 and 1918 the committee presented five reports. The second merely supplied additional support for a Bill, already in draft and passed in 1918, which amended and extended the application of the Trade Boards principle first introduced in 1909. The fourth provided a formal basis for the Industrial Courts Act of 1919, which set up a permanent and voluntary arbitration authority of which the two parties to a dispute could avail themselves if they chose. The fifth largely summed up the preceding four. The first was usually thought of as *the* Whitley Report. It recommended the setting up, in every industry sufficiently well organised, of a permanent, standing joint body of regulation and decision-making called a Joint Industrial Council (JIC) comprising representatives of employers' associations and trade unions. This was to be supplemented by joint district councils and, as recommended in the third report, by a joint committee at each works. Recognised by government as the official and authoritative bodies for their respective industries, as the newly created Ministry of Labour declared in 1917, JICs were to be consulted as 'the normal channel through which the opinion and experience of an industry will be sought'.

They were intended to be more than negotiating bodies. A permanent improvement in the industrial scene had to be founded, it was argued, upon relationships which went far beyond the mere cash basis, and JICs were to discuss all problems of common concern and usher in a regime of harmonious co-operation between employers and employed. The idea was, in fact, that they would continue, in industry, 'the co-operation of all classes established during the war'. The Whitley Report hoped 'that representative men in each industry, with pride in their calling and care for its place as a contributor to the national well-being, will come together in the manner here suggested, and apply themselves to promoting industrial harmony and efficiency and removing the obstacles that have hitherto stood in the way' (Charles, 1973, p. 108). A supplementary report on works committees issued in 1918 (Cd 9001) described them as essential means for enlisting the interest of the workers in the success of their industry and in constructive co-operation at the level of their own workshop or factory. It gave short shrift, however, 'to the idea, sometimes put forward by particular groups of employers, that the constitution of works committees might provide a bulwark against the growth of trade unionism and render it unnecessary ... to recognize the unions' (Cole, 1973, p. 117). Success of the committees, declared the report, 'would be very seriously interfered with' if such an idea existed, and employee representatives on the committees were to be trade union members, duly elected. The whole scheme, indeed, rested upon full recognition of the unions at all levels.

Here, then, was an attempt to revive that long-standing vision of conciliation which had been urged by some of the Positivists and which prominent members of the Labour Department had themselves sought to encourage. We may recall the words of Askwith, now Lord Askwith, in 1920.

> If the aim is mutual co-operation and joint effort, and that aim is continuously kept in sight and broadly interpreted, an industry . . . may be improved by the existence of a council. If the council is used to maintain two camps, and during a period of advancing wages and prosperity only employed for purposes of pressure, with an inevitable deadlock so soon as the demands become greater than the trade can bear, then ultimate disintegration will ensue, and possibly a worse situation than before the advent of a council. (Askwith, 1920, p. 458)

Literally nothing in the First Whitley Report was therefore new. Popularly misread as a concession of 'industrial self-government' to the workers, the report in fact conceded nothing, since no obligation was placed upon anybody to do anything. It left unions and employers' associations free to form JICs or not as they thought best, and offered no new rights or privileges to those who did. Wage-earners were left as dependent as before on their own exertions and the strength of their organisations for securing whatever degree of 'participation' employers could be brought to yield. The report was principally an attempt by officials reared in the old Labour Department tradition to further their positive-sum vision of collective bargaining by capitalising the wartime mood of shared effort. It urged both sides to adopt towards each other a stance which they had always found impossible, given the historically rooted structures, values and ideologies of Britain's productive system. Yet it was these exhortations that caught the popular and amateur attention by suggesting a fundamental innovation in industrial relations which the report's proposals were unable to secure.

Nevertheless, the rhetoric was not entirely empty for those professionally involved. The Ministry of Labour, newly created in 1917, has been described as having 'perhaps more than its share of those who were determined to seek fulfilment of reconstruction promises'. Its officials set about promoting Whitley ideas and structures with an energy which testified 'to a driving conviction rather than a bureaucratic sense of duty' (Charles, 1973, p. 210). Their hope and enthusiasm found many echoes. The Whitley Report had generated an excitement which spread even as far as the United States. It did not exclude those in industry itself. In the main, however, the professionals remained unmoved by such visions. It was highly significant that the fifth and final report had contained a squelching caveat signed by five of the committee members – all of them trade unionists or labour sympathisers – who welcomed JICs 'if through them minimum conditions and common interests could be improved and forwarded', and welcomed, too, the idea of promoting industrial peace. They warned, however, that 'a complete identity of interests between capital and labour cannot thus be effected and that such machinery cannot be expected to furnish a settlement for the more serious conflicts of interest involved in the working of an economic system primarily governed and directed by the motives of private profit'. Here were 'moderates' giving due notice that there could be no prospect of the sort of harmonious problem-solving alliance which the report hoped for. And it was not long before the suspicions of many unions were made manifest even against the idea of regularising and permanently recognising works committees, given their tendency either to develop too much independence *vis-à-vis* the union or too little *vis-à-vis* the employer. 'Moderate' shop stewards likewise had their doubts about works committees on the Whitley model. Their own authority rested on wary scepticism towards managerial intentions and here were bodies to be set up for the purpose of promoting a collaborative relationship. Could not management exploit them to weaken or even eliminate the union presence at the workplace? (Clegg, 1951, pp. 7–8). 'They often held that they could secure better results for their members by preserving their complete independence, and only meeting the management when a question calling for joint consideration arose' (Cole, 1973, p. 120). Revolutionary shop stewards were far more emphatic. For them the Whitley model was anathema; an attempt to restore 'orderly' industrial relations and contain the disruptive tendencies which the war had unleashed (Hyman, in Goodrich, 1975, p. xx). Eschewing alliance or shared control with the employer, the shop steward movement must work towards wresting power from him by 'direct industrial action' at the workplace. Revolutionary industrial unionism would not only create the basis for a revolutionary general strike but would also create the structures through which workers would control their industries once socialism was established.

Many employers also were wary of some aspects of the Whitley proposals. The FBI, while approving JICs, lost no time in declaring its hostility not so much to joint works committees as such but to the idea of works committees with industrial functions. Many employers, especially those in major industries with long experience of arms-length, zero-sum bargaining, found no evidence to support any hope that a major permanent shift in wage-earner attitudes was about to take place. Accordingly, they feared that full adoption of the Whitley approach, with its implication that managements must lower their guard and welcome union representatives into close discussions on, for example, 'processes, machinery, and organization', might be exploited by militants who, far from pursuing constructive collaboration, would pursue a class war. To invite consultation with employee spokesmen over a virtually open-ended range of issues offered management a fruitful prospect if the spokesmen shared management's broad priorities; it offered at best time-wasting frustration if they did not. And managements, faced so often with employee indifference or worse, were disposed to doubt whether their workers could be brought to manifest a sufficient identification with 'company objectives' to make a joint problem-solving approach possible. To many of them it seemed safer, where they had already established their own procedures and conventions of negotiation with the unions, to stick to them. And their opposite numbers among the union leaders and officials often had their own reasons, as we have noted, for remaining with the tried and tested.

As a consequence the Whitley Committee's conception that their system would be applied primarily to industries already well-organised in terms of joint collective relations was only very partially realised. Coal, cotton, iron and steel, engineering and shipbuilding, for example, retained their own forms, though printing, building, railways, the docks, and others with well-established procedures ventured into the JIC pattern. These were considerably out-numbered, however, by industries in which effective bargaining developed only during the war or immediately after. They were mainly lesser industries which, in many cases, submitted only after active persuasion by the Ministry of Labour, whose officials pursued a keen proselytisation campaign throughout 1918 and 1919.

Adoption of Whitley forms did not, however, mean adoption of the Whitley spirit. In a few of the JICs there were exceptional figures who led developments along less conventional lines, but only by those few innovators were any serious and sustained attempts made to establish works councils. 'For the most part the works councils were never set up or were quietly abandoned' (Clegg, 1951, p. 7). Union officials and shop stewards often had their – sometimes contrasting – reasons for not mourning their passing. And by the time reconstruction moods had given way to the onset of postwar depression in late 1920 and to the full return of sectional conflict, most JICs had moved into the standard pattern of win-lose collective bargaining, 'working on the same lines as, though on the whole more successfully than, the older procedures for the settlement of disputes which remained in force in the country's major industries' (ibid., p. 7). Nearly all the seventy-four JICs had been formed during 1918–20; by 1939 only twenty survived, though these were by far the largest and most important. The Ministry of Labour drive quickly petered out after the collapse of the postwar boom and the high levels of government spending. Support for Whitleyism could hardly be separated from support for strong and vigorous trade unionism, and now that the unions no longer had to be courted this was a sensitive issue even among employers committed to joint regulation. Even ministry officials who might be specially sympathetic to trade unions and collective bargaining were likely to be aware that excessive zeal would raise awkward questions for their political masters. Any possibility that the ministry would be able to pursue its encouragement of collective bargaining on a scale larger than that of the old prewar Labour Department was finally removed in 1922, when economy cuts reduced the ministry's expenditure by nearly half – the Industrial Relations Division, whose special section devoted to JICs was 'the heart of the drive', suffering a staff cut from 115 to 20 (Charles, 1973, pp. 204, 210–11).

Nevertheless, the fact that labour shortages persisted through to late 1920 as war demands gave way to a re-stocking boom was important for the industrial relations system. The high level of demand and of labour strength induced the government to pursue policies on industrial relations which were predominantly favourable to the unions, who did well out of collective bargaining during this period both with respect to pay and to their securing of the 47- or 48-hour week. Had the armistice been followed by an immediate economic collapse, Britain's history both industrially and politically might well have been different, just as it would have been different had postwar buoyancy continued for ten or even five years instead of only two.

Rival Conceptions

The deflation of Whitley rhetoric into the hard-headed postures of a collective bargaining limited mainly to terms and conditions of employment disappointed some employers, who had been encouraged by wartime unity and good business, with its easy profits and high wages which could so readily be conceded, to dream of all classes 'pulling together'; of unions casting off their 'obstructive' and 'antagonistic' attitudes and co-operating with employers to maximise the creation of wealth. The vision had attracted some politicians also, among them Lord Milner, who had been in the War Cabinet. Milner had not lost his social imperialist yearning for an active, interventionist state, and wartime experience had suggested the possibility of industrial class collaboration on corporate lines. By 1923 he was deploring the postwar dismantling of state controls, the abandonment of the positive role of government, the lapse of unity and co-operation between management and labour, and the return of 'the old pre-war feud between Capital and Labour'. He saw the best hope for the future in JICs provided they developed 'not chiefly for settling disputes but to associate masters and men in the conduct of their business' (O'Brien, 1979, pp. 377–8). Soon he was supporting an unsuccessful corporatist campaign by a group of JICs to secure statutory powers by which they could impose upon the whole of their respective industries the terms and conditions they had jointly negotiated.

In some cases the collaboration was seen not in expansionary but in restrictionist terms. In the footwear industry, for example, the 'experience of guaranteed markets and guaranteed prices, and the subsequent elimination of competitive stresses, was so pleasant as to encourage some spokesmen on the employers' side to hint at the possibilities of continuing some of its features after the war'. Certain observations by a few prominent manufacturers suggest that they had in mind an industry regulated and controlled as fully as possible by the employers' association and the union acting in close co-operation, with competition eliminated or at least restricted and the way made clear for 'the maintenance of standards', 'a fair profit for capital', and 'a fair wage for labour'. A trade journal congratulated the union on setting the example 'in hanging together' and applauded a union proposal in 1919 to strike against non-unionists: 'trade security and prosperity now lay in having strong representative bodies on both sides' which together could regulate the industry. 'There was a time, not very long ago, when very much would have been said about interfering with the liberty of the subject ... Times and circumstances are changed now ... ' (Fox, 1958, pp. 372–3). This and a few other industries such as pottery and printing therefore hoped to use their JICs for the systematic joint restriction of competition. This type of collaboration, however, has always proved as unstable in Britain as any other, and did not survive the rigours of postwar recession.

For the time being, nevertheless, the mood contributed to the considerable stimulus being enjoyed by the 'industrial welfare' movement. 'Welfare', as a term, was something of a ragbag. It included profit-sharing, co-partnership, joint consultation committees, provident funds, canteens, recreational and sports clubs, medical services, and the attempts to create a pleasant and healthy working environment through attention to such factors as heating, lighting, ventilation and machine design. The diverse factors fostering these initiatives included, besides the 'passion for some sort of social reconstruction', the facts that 'at a time of heavy work during the war the value of welfare in relieving the strain' was realised by certain eminent employers such as Seebohm Rowntree who urged it on the Ministry of Munitions; that 'the workers were becoming restless' and 'all sorts of means had to be invented to meet their demands'; and that the costs of welfare could be deducted from excess profits tax. But as important as any was the growing belief of a few progressive employers that 'to cultivate industrial welfare is to cultivate efficiency' (Lee, 1924, pp. 2, 22).

It was to be expected, perhaps, that the wartime mood would encourage some of the more optimistic spirits to entertain ideas of social reconstruction, especially those that were compatible with good business. It was also to be expected that such speculations would be tolerated, even encouraged, by hard-headed men of affairs who calculated that the war would go better if the people were promised a somewhat larger stake in the society for which they were being required to fight. But there was also evidence of a further set of attitudes which conceded little to such sentiments. Many employers beyond engineering found a voice in Sir Allan Smith, autocratic spokesman for the EEF, who regularly referred to the workers as 'the enemy' and whose forte it was to scent sinister political influences behind their industrial policies. And the 'allegation that "some employers look upon the Military Service Acts, the state control of war industries, and the temporary abandonment of trade union restrictions as an opportunity to establish once and for all the ascendancy of Capital over Labour" was made by a liberal employers' association and in substance conceded by the Federation of British Industries' (Waites, 1976, pp. 43–4).

While the war was in progress, and for a short period after, the FBI's voice was prominent. In its *Report on the Control of Industry* (July 1919) it quoted approvingly Harry Gosling's presidential address to the Trades Union Congress of 1916 in which he asserted labour's right to participate in all decision-making affecting the working lives of wage-earners. But the harder note was never absent and received support from an influential source within the Board of Trade, namely Beveridge. As head of the Employment Department, Beveridge had concerned himself with, among other things, the promotion of industrial efficiency. He had submitted to the Cabinet Reconstruction Committee, in 1916, proposals for the widespread introduction of profit-sharing schemes between employers and unions. These 'would promote solidarity between the two sides of industry, they would discourage strikes and restriction of output, and they would mobilize support among trade union officials for "discipline and efficiency". They would at the same time radically transform the nature of trade unions, turning them from restrictive protectionist organizations into profit-making "business concerns".' He followed this up with a brief to the Prime Minister proposing that 'compulsory profit-sharing' should be widely substituted for voluntary collective bargaining, and introduced in return for the permanent suspension of 'any rule, practice or custom certified by the Board of Trade . . . to be restrictive of output or employ-ment or contrary to the national interest'. Here were proposals for an alliance between state and industry to overcome union restrictionism. Embodied in a draft Bill, they were widely circulated.

They met a bleak reception at the hands of colleagues and friends, from whose proximity Beveridge had obviously learned nothing about British trade unions and employers. Llewellyn Smith, his permanent secretary, with masterly understatement, 'feared that any attempt to evade the restoration of pre-war trade union practices would provoke union hostil-ity' and 'make them suspicious of our good faith'. Vaughan Nash, secretary to the Cabinet Reconstruction Committee, thought that to bring the unions into profit-sharing would be to 'place them in a false position and to weaken their functions as agencies dealing with wages and con-ditions of labour'. The Webbs considered Beveridge's scheme 'both unworkable and undesirable' (J. Harris, 1977, pp. 251–2). In the event, Nash's Capital and Labour Sub-Committee worked along very different lines towards the Whitley approach.

The Struggle over the 'Political' Strike

The rival conceptions examined so far emanated from the centre and right, sometimes the far right, of the political spectrum, but there was another which came from the far left. This was the old dream of using the mass power of organised labour as a means of exerting direct pressure on government for what Establishment figures, including most leading union officials, defined as political ends. Government leaders considered they had good cause to fear revolutionary elements that might succeed in harnessing the power generated by large-scale industrial stoppages.

In terms of a broad-based demand for social transformation the threat was negligible. Labour might now be a mass party destined for rapid rise but this was no measure of a popular base for fundamental change. It was rather the result of a massive increase in the incidence of trade union consciousness and an enlarged desire for independent working-class representation. During the war labour had become more class conscious in the sense of being driven to see leaders of both Liberal and Conservative parties in government as applying, or aspiring to apply, policies deeply threatening to working-class interests. Increased state intervention had often seemed to be on the side of the employers. These perceptions created not a mass demand for a new system, but a greater will to mobilise independently in order to be able to hit harder within the old one.

For many this meant not only independence in the arena of parliamentary democracy but also, on the right issue and if they felt strong enough, direct action. The Establishment nightmare had already raised its head in two minor cases in 1918 but appeared most vividly in connection with the miners' claim in February 1919 for higher wages, reduced working hours, state ownership and 'democratic control' of the pits – the miners having no wish, after wartime state control, to be pushed back to the untender mercies of private ownership. Lloyd George's response was, first, to call a National Industrial Conference of employers and labour spokesmen to discuss ways of improving industrial relations; and secondly, to appoint the Royal (Sankey) Commission on the Mines. The commission soon recommended in favour of higher wages and reduced working hours, and hinted that its final report, due several months hence, would recommend fundamental changes in the present system of ownership and working. This enabled the leaders of the miners, who had voted for strike action if state ownership were not conceded, to keep their members in check, albeit with great difficulty. Meanwhile Lloyd George, who had committed himself to accepting the commission's report 'in the spirit as well as in the letter and to take all necessary steps to carry out its recommendations without delay', was presented with some crucial evidence as to the temper of the Labour movement and its leaders.

At a joint conference of the Labour Party and the TUC in April 1919 the chairman (who was also chairman of the Parliamentary Committee of the TUC) refused to accept a motion which implied direct industrial action to compel the government to withdraw British troops from Russia, end conscription, lift the blockade against Germany, and release conscientious objectors from prison. Further attempts by the left to press the issue were also successfully blocked. Their next opportunity was the Labour Party Annual Conference in June 1919, two days after the Sankey Commission had reported a bare majority (the Labour representatives together with the chairman) in favour of nationalisation, but presenting also various divergent recommendations. The National Executive Committee's report to the conference noted 'many resolutions . . . indicating that there are some sections of the movement anxious that an organized attempt to defeat the Government's political policy by direct industrial action should be discussed by a joint conference representative of both the political and industrial movements'.

The NEC lobbed this ball firmly into the trade union court.

If the British labour movement is to institute a new precedent in our industrial history by initiating a general strike for the purpose of achieving not industrial but political objects, it is imperative that the trade unions, whose members are to fulfil the obligations implied in the new policy . . . should realize the responsibilities such a strike movement would entail and should themselves determine the plan of any such new campaign. (Miliband, 1973, pp. 68–9)

During the subsequent debates the opponents of direct action argued variously that it was unconstitutional and undemocratic; or that it would not receive sufficient mass support; or that it might receive too much, plunge the country into civil war, and 'destroy all their organizations for generations to come'. Using the argument that Baldwin and other public men were to invoke seven years later, they invested direct action with its most extreme meaning of attempted revolutionary overthrow, thereby restricting the apparent available alternatives. Their tactic was to define it, not as direct actionists themselves – for the most part no revolutionaries – defined it, namely as an admittedly unconstitutional but necessary 'means of pressure, for specific and limited purposes, incomparably more effective than parliamentary action', but as a strategy for capturing total power from the government and thereby destroying it. A resolution instructing the NEC to consult the TUC with a view to direct action being taken nevertheless carried the day by two to one.

But plenty of resources remained available to the leadership, now as always condemned by the militants as 'leaders who were too respectable, who did not like to be roasted in the capitalist press, who liked to be called level-headed trade unionists' (ibid., p. 71). Despite the emphatic vote putting direct action on the agenda the NEC created another chance for it to be defeated by deciding to press the TUC for a special conference to discuss only 'whether and by what means direct industrial action should be taken'. A majority on the TUC Parliamentary Committee reinforced this resistance by refusing to convene a conference at all. Henderson added his voice to the resisters by declaring that direct action 'involves the abro-gation of parliamentary government, established a dictatorship of the minority, and might easily destroy eventually all our constitutional liberties'. This did not end the struggle, but Churchill was soon to deflate it in late July with an announcement that British troops were being withdrawn from Russia, in accordance with a decision taken months earlier, and that the remaining issues were also being dealt with.

Certain issues central to the nature of Britain's industrial relations and political systems had been raised during these months and, from the point of view of government and Establishment, had been left dangerously unresolved. The war had brought the government into active intervention in the control and operation of industry. This put under strain the old definitions of 'industrial' and 'political'. Previously there had been no problem. The carefully cultivated liberal distinction between 'economics' and 'politics', a distinction that expressed the essence of *laissez-faire* market society, supplied the answer. 'Political' described what governments did; 'industrial' described what industry did. But what was the position when governments involved themselves in what industry did? Were their actions 'political' or 'industrial'? This was no mere word-play. Trade unions existed to challenge managerial authority in industry and were defined as industrial organisations. Their great legal 'immunities' existed in respect of 'trade' disputes. But what if unions challenged *government* authority when it was involving itself in industry? Was that an industrial or a political act? If the challenge was limited to labour issues normally decided by industrial managers, such as wages or working hours, perhaps it could still be defined as an industrial or trade dispute? For many members of the Establishment even to concede this much was dangerous. The intensity of their reaction revealed that they felt far more under threat from the working class's industrial strength than from its parliamentary strength. To them it seemed safest to define all cases of industrial action against the government as political and therefore unconstitutional in the sense that it was an attempt at mass coercive pressure which by-passed the due constitutional processes. The same issue arose again later in 1919 over the government's negotiations with the railway unions on wages, hours and conditions of work; negotiations which led to a strike damned by government and press alike as essentially political.

The case that all extra-parliamentary industrial pressure against government was unconstitutional was often made to rest upon a grotesquely unreal picture of Parliament and government which presented them as an arena of pure rational and moral thought, totally insulated from, and uncontaminated by, all outside pressures which might distort the god-like, even-handed perspective. Such a picture was not only unreal, in that governments had always had to take into account manifest or latent extra-parliamentary power. It was also class-biased in that, while exhibiting alarm over extra-parliamentary power wielded by organised labour, it chose to ignore all the occasions when governments were affected in what they did by a consciousness of the extra-parliamentary power wielded by, for example, the City, the church, the brewers, the army, or the landed interest.

Despite this, most labour leaders were prepared to accept and operate within these mystifications. It is hardly enough, however, to attribute this solely to timidity, servility, the craving for respectability, or fear of losing their own organisational position and status to the militants if the bidding and the stakes were allowed to go too high. There is the additional consideration that, in a system of rule that had drawn so much strength and stability from the legitimations of legalism and constitutionalism, agents of the ruling order hesitated long before acting coercively against their enemies provided those enemies kept within the conventionally defined bounds of legal constitutionality. Once those bounds were crossed, governments (or their agencies) could pounce with whatever weight they chose to bring to bear. It mattered little that the exponents of direct action might be pursuing only limited and specific objectives. By transgressing what the ruling order and 'public' opinion defined as the bounds of constitutionalism, they freed a government to take draconian counter-measures – and governments and their supporters were strongly placed to influence people on what was 'unconstitutional'.

Such considerations could not by themselves determine the union leaders' case against direct action. Uncertainties existed at crucial decision points – there was no inevitability that any particular direct action venture would bring down government vengeance so damaging as to outweigh any possible gains. This had already been proved by events and was shortly to be proved again. Yet the question of whether, given the broadest and deepest appraisal, the method was worth the candle was open to genuine differences of opinion – and the opinions even of the doubters might fluctuate according to the scale and nature of the issue involved, as events were to show.

By August 1919 evidence was available to Lloyd George that a majority of labour leaders were hostile to direct action, and that although a substantial segment of the organised working class was prepared to follow the left at least for 'limited and specific' objectives it was not powerful enough to override the organisational control enjoyed by the strict constitutionalists. The left might win temporary majorities at conferences, but what told in the last resort was control of the political and industrial machine. On 19 August Lloyd George announced rejection of the Sankey Commission majority report recommending nationalisation of the coal industry. Even among the miners themselves the war-generated sense that long-standing structures could be permanently changed was ebbing away. After a long-drawn-out decline the campaign finally died in March 1920.

On the face of it, the events which developed a few months later over the threat of British military intervention in support of Poland against Russia might seem to undermine the judgements just expressed about the official leadership position on direct action. On this issue the political and industrial wings joined in making threats which were unquestionably an attempt to coerce the government by extra-parliamentary means. The party National Executive Committee, the parliamentary Labour Party, and the Parliamentary Committee of the TUC gave unified initiative and leadership in a campaign to mobilise 'the whole industrial power of the organized workers . . . to defeat this war'. Lloyd George's hasty assurances that no troops would be sent made it unnecessary, however, for labour leaders to substantiate their threats of a general strike. This rendered it easy even for J. H. Thomas, along with other leaders, to glory in the assertion that their action 'definitely challenged the Constitution'. Yet there was a vital difference from other direct action situations. Labour leaders were convinced that they were expressing a national mood and interest, not a class mood and interest (Miliband, 1973, p. 82). Besides rendering their action more legitimate, this could be supposed to reduce the danger of ruling-class reprisal. Nevertheless, the episode demonstrated that the use of industrial action for political objectives must always remain an open question. Nobody could be sure that a government would not on some occasion propose a policy deemed so abnormally damaging by the unions and the party as to override their normal observance of the constitutional conventions. Moreover, the fact that opinions could differ on what was 'abnormally damaging' rendered an agreed boundary line impossible to draw. The situation was likely to leave governments thoughtful.

Meanwhile, given the threat of the political strike, 'military and patriotic people felt the need to create organizations which would counter this threat, maintain public order, and guarantee essential services'. The first of Britain's fascist movements was formed in 1923, 'mainly military, naval, and "county" with the lower ranks consisting of loyal working-class toughs'. The British Fascists committed its members to a struggle 'against all treacherous and revolutionary movements now working for the destruction of the Throne and Empire'. Their title was a misnomer; there was no trace of radical doctrine and a more thorough-going fascist later dismissed the movement disgustedly as mere 'Conservatism with knobs on' (Griffiths, 1983, pp. 86–7).

It was soon clear, however, that, for the time being, at least, the left-wing vision of a militant working class throwing off the leadership of constitutionalist moderates and pursuing a long-term strategy for the eventual seizure of power had broken on the fact that postwar working-class militancy was neither sufficiently widespread, fierce, or persistent enough to prevail against a leadership determined to preserve the industrial and political structures and rights in which they had invested so much. And even among the rank and file the failure of the postwar mood to sustain the necessary level of militant resolve must be reckoned to owe something to history – to a belief that there was much to be lost as well as gained by any radical departure from well-established practices. Yet to these factors must be added an element of the fortuitous if we are fully to account for the failure of the left-wing vision and for the continued – indeed further consolidation – of ascendancy by the official union hierarchies. Economic collapse from late 1920 through to 1923, with its wholesale employer attacks on wages and conditions, ushered in the interwar characteristic of long-term mass unemployment in the old staple exporting industries heavily concentrated in just those areas of the north, Scotland and south Wales where wartime shop steward organisation had enjoyed its principal strengths. The impact on shop-floor activity and militancy, already weakened by the closure of many wartime munitions factories and the disappearance of such issues as dilution and conscription, was profound, resulting at worst in demoralisation and at best in 'uncertainty and defensiveness. For those who remained in trade unions, the growing self-confidence and self-assertiveness of the previous decade was checked, leading to a new relationship of dependence on the union bureaucracies', with 'the focus of power and influence' within the unions shifting upwards to the full-time officials (Hinton and Hyman, 1975, p. 18). Had world economic conditions been such as to maintain in Britain for a decade a high level of activity and employment in the industries and areas where the unions and their membership were strongest there would have been a different story to tell.

As it was, the accession of strength to higher officials not only consolidated bureaucratic hierarchy directly but also permitted a continuation of the prewar and wartime tendency towards industry-wide negotiations conducted at national level – which further enhanced the role of national officers. Coal-miners were to be forced back to district bargaining by the owners, but in nearly all other major industries where the unions were generally recognised national pay agreements became established. Increased union size made its own contribution to these combined effects – which varied widely, however, as between unions. Bureaucratic consolidation affected also the TUC, which had functioned before the war as a talking shop and clearing house for political lobbying. War had brought big changes. The government involved TUC representatives in a wide range of consultative and collaborative machinery, with the result that additional staff were appointed, a committee structure was instituted and the old Parliamentary Committee was replaced in 1921 by the modern General Council. In 1923 the first full-time general secretary, Bramley, was appointed, to be succeeded two years later by Citrine, arch-administrator and bureaucrat. 'His mind was as clean, clear and precise as himself; his office was run to exact schedules; his speeches . . . were models of passionless and convincing argument. Divergencies and rebellions he rebuked, never with a labourer's oath, but with instant reference to the resolutions which they contravened' (Postgate, 1951, p. 289).

It was during this period, when 'the role of the union bureaucracy was more central to industrial relations than in any other period of British labour history', and when 'the scope for rank and file initiative was severely curtailed by the changed economic climate', that the Communist Party 'set out to build a mass party on the basis of rank and file self-activity in the workplace' (Hinton and Hyman, 1975, p. 22). Its failure was evidence of more than the relative lack of revolutionary tinder in the British Labour movement. It further illustrated the organisational control enjoyed by the constitutionalist moderates who largely ran the unions. The Minority Movement, launched by the party in 1924 with the aim of working within the existing unions 'to organize the working masses . . . for the overthrow of capitalism', was designed to 'provide a temporary resting place for union members dissatisfied with orthodox trade union-ism but unready to join the Communist party'. For a couple of years it enjoyed considerable success, though even by 1925 'many trade unionists were beginning to see the Movement as an illegitimate pressure group, an instrument of "outside interference"' (Martin, 1969, pp. 186–7). Union executives who found its independent programmes and personal abuse disruptive soon mobilised their forces against it. Nearly all major unions proscribed Movement or Communist Party members from standing for national or local office; Communists were barred as trade union delegates to the Labour Party Conference, and eventually the party totally excluded individual Communists 'by a system more elaborate than anything known since the repeal of the Test Acts' (A. J. P. Taylor, 1970, p. 259). The end came after 1928 when the Communist International, in a swing further to the left, issued instructions that the party was to sponsor anti-Labour candidates and that the Minority Movement was to work for the creation of new revolutionary unions where possible. This brought out sharply the conflicts implicit in the movement's ambiguous nature. It had attracted many unionists who, while not averse to seeing a ginger group sharply reminding union officials who paid their salaries (thereby continuing a long and hallowed tradition among Britain's trade unionists), had no intention of seeing their unions abandoned or even weakened. They voted with their feet and the Minority Movement faded away. The whole sequence registered another failure in an extended list of attempts, now going back over a century, by outside groups to use the mass strength of the unions for their own purposes.

Emergency Powers and the National Industrial Conference

In the years of political as well as industrial disturbance immediately following the war it was hardly likely to escape the notice of Lloyd George that there was political capital to be made from the bogey of red revolution. Some members of the Coalition government may even have convinced themselves that the bogey was real and Lloyd George was not disposed to discourage them. He told the Cabinet in 1919 that the threatened miners' strike was 'practical and not theoretical Bolshevism, and must be dealt with with a firm hand . . . The whole of the future of this country might be at stake, and if the government were beaten and the miners won, it would result in a Soviet government . . . the real parliament would be at the headquarters of the Miners' Federation . . .' The Parliament elected in 1918 was not of a quality likely to deflate such rhetoric. Rhodes James's judgement is that we may accept 'the overwhelming evidence of contemporaries that this was a hard, selfish, volatile and intolerant parliament' (Rhodes James, 1981, pp. 128, 131).

One outcome was the Emergency Powers Act 1920, which empowered the government to declare a state of emergency in the event of action 'on so extensive a scale as to be calculated, by interfering with the supply and distribution of food, water, fuel, or light, or with the means of locomotion, to deprive the community . . . of the essentials of life'. Under the emergency, such measures could be taken as were deemed necessary for preserving the peace and maintaining supplies. The Act 'made permanent the dictatorial powers which the government had possessed in Defence of the Realm Acts – as big a blow against the traditional constitution as any ever levelled' (A. J. P. Taylor, 1970, p. 194). The years between 1919 and 1922 were later confessed by one government minister, Eric Geddes, to be a period when we 'were all mad; "we had lost all sense of proportion, and I did things of which I am now thoroughly ashamed"' (Middlemas and Barnes, 1969, p. 97). Nevertheless, even during this febrile phase certain due decencies were observed. The regulations had to be approved and regularly renewed by Parliament, and although the powers were extensive they expressly denied the government power to make striking or peaceful picketing an offence, or to use military or industrial conscription to break strikes. There was considerable backstage uneasiness even about the legality of using the armed forces for strike-breaking. The Chief of the Imperial General Staff, supported by the Services legal advisers, considered it illegal for the army to run power stations and the government became extremely nervous of arousing a public debate. Not until 1925 were the army's King's Regulations amended to permit strike-breaking, and until then the use of troops and marines, including the 1924 Labour government's preparation to bring naval stokers into the power stations, 'continued on an unofficial and, indeed, illegal basis' (Middlemas, 1979, p. 145).

Pace Geddes, some ministers did keep a sense of proportion. Evidence to help them in doing so was coming from the National Industrial Conference, launched by Lloyd George in February 1919 to help in stabilising the industrial scene by mobilising organised labour and organised employers to indulge in some expressions of mutual good will. Eight hundred delegates from employers' associations (encouraged in their participation by the FBI), trade unions, trade boards, JICs and the TUC elected a Provisional Joint Committee (PJC) which at once got to work, 'convinced that its recommendations, if approved by the Conference, would become law' (Charles, 1973, p. 249). The second conference met in April 1919 to consider its report. It acknowledged the right of union membership and recommended a statutory maximum 48-hour week, a universal legal minimum wage, improved old-age pensions and sickness benefits, a long list of proposals to cope with unemployment, and an elected jointly representative National Industrial Council which would supplement the existing sectional machinery by focusing 'upon the problems that affect industrial relations as a whole'. Lloyd George sent a message, reinforced by Sir Robert Horne, Minister of Labour, that the report would receive immediate and sympathetic consideration. In an atmosphere of euphoric good will the report was overwhelmingly well received and approved.

When the PJC met the government in May, however, government hedging was soon apparent. There is circumstantial evidence, too, that influential groups among the employers, strongly represented in the EEF, had become seriously alarmed by what they considered over-generous concessions resulting from the FBI stance. It was now that the National Confederation of Employers' Organisations (NCEO), the EEF its backbone, came into existence. There emerged a division of functions by which the FBI was confined to trade matters, while labour relations were handled by the hard-line NCEO. Dominated by the leading representatives of the engineers, the coal-owners and the ship-owners, it 'exercised little control over its constituent organizations', and, 'always fearful of losing any one of them', moved 'at the rate of its slowest and most "reactionary" members' (Garside, 1977, p. 256). Its essential philosophy was expressed by Sir Allan Smith in October 1920 when he warned the government against further interference in labour matters: overseas competition must be met and any attempts to impose minimum standards would put firms out of business and increase unemployment. After August 1919 it was clear that the National Industrial Conference would be allowed to achieve nothing of consequence. Perhaps Lloyd George's only candid moment in the whole exercise came in 1921 when the unions finally accepted that they might as well allow it to lapse. He thanked the PJC for the 'good work it had done to inculcate a spirit of co-operation in industrial relations between employers and employed at a crucial time' and appreciated its role in 'creating a steadying influence' during reconstruction (Charles, 1973, p. 249).

The Downfall of Lloyd George

Lloyd George's nimble opportunist footwork on the great labour issues of the immediate postwar world undoubtedly impressed some members of the Conservative Party on whose support he now rested, but it only strengthened deep and growing suspicions among many others. His combination of immense vitality, personal charm and flair for political unorthodoxy had already shown a capacity for dividing groups hitherto bonded by shared principles, traditions and interests. His displacement of Asquith in 1916 having split the Liberal Party, a growing number of Conservatives, Baldwin among them, feared that he would split the Conservative Party also.

There was already abundant evidence that Lloyd George was committed neither to party, nor to Parliament, nor to any wider aspect of constitutionalism. The wartime experience had fed his 'illusory passion', first exhibited in 1910, 'for a transcendent national synthesis that would soar above partisan strife – the kind of grandiose vision of leadership that attracted him to Joseph Chamberlain in his youth, later on to the "New Nationalism" of Theodore Roosevelt in the United States, later still to Milner's Prussian "efficiency", and in the 1930s to . . . Hitler' (Morgan, 1978, p. 47). By the end of the war he was 'closest in spirit' to 'self-made captains of industry, whose contempt for democracy was often very marked'; it was said that he constantly referred to 'the great services' they had rendered and how they deserved 'the large share of the profits they have taken'. For years 'he had consorted with businessmen and bankers, press lords and bureaucrats, all in their way devotees of a new "national" politics, based on executive power and national unity'. The version sought was a species of 'Nationalism-Socialism' pursued through the 'perpetuation of the coalition on a permanent basis' (ibid., pp. 72, 78, 80, 83, 198).

The implications of this conception for the trade unions and the wider Labour movement were ominous. 'Not since 1848 had such views been exercised in Cabinet as were heard in the years 1919–1922: the only disputes were over the extent of the violent measures to be taken in repression of what was evidently believed to be the first stirring of universal revolution' (Middlemas and Barnes, 1969, p. 99). But there were more grounds for uneasiness than this, known at the time only to those at higher levels. Middlemas has documented the apparatus of lies, trickery, censorship, strike-breaking, deportations and techniques of mass persuasion and propaganda set up under the Coalition government. Lloyd George established his own secret propaganda agency in 1919, financed from industrial sources, chiefly members of the EEF. Fed information by Special Branch and the secret intelligence services, it had MPs and journalists on the payroll whose articles could be placed in over 1,200 newspapers. Lloyd George himself handed over to Sir Vincent Caillard, chairman of Vickers Engineering, secret intelligence material on 'agitators' for use against the shop stewards in his factories. With these and other techniques financed by private and public money the Coalition government 'blurred almost beyond retrieval the distinction between government and party propaganda or public and private morality . . . The octopus they created may, not unfairly, be compared with the Nixon apparatus at the time of Watergate without the dénouement of exposure' (Middlemas, 1979, pp. 129–33, 351–3).

Parts of the apparatus survived the break-up of Coalition under the name of the Supply and Transport Committee which, under Baldwin's instruction, was assiduously elaborated by J. C. C. Davidson as a nation-wide organisation for maintaining essential services and supplies in the event of strikes. What happened when the Labour government took over in 1924 is so instructive of Britain's Establishment and its methods of working that we may usefully indulge a brief anticipatory digression. Urged by a senior civil servant to hand over all plans and papers in confidence to a top-level official, leaving the organisation 'wrapped in temporary obscurity and silence', Davidson passed them instead to the incoming Labour minister, Josiah Wedgwood, 'an old friend', begging him to think in 'national' and not 'party' terms by preserving the organisation and not informing the Cabinet of it. Wedgwood replied that 'he could not continue to build my organization' but promised not to interfere with it. 'On my return [in November 1924] I found that Josh had been as good as his word' (Rhodes James, 1969, pp. 179–80). 'Josh' had blown the dust off the plans himself when instructed by the Cabinet to prepare for a tramwaymen's strike, Ramsay MacDonald declaring that 'major services must be maintained' (Clegg, forthcoming).

To return to the Coalition: there seems little doubt that under the leadership of Lloyd George and his closer colleagues the liberal constitutionalist structure of rule came under severe strain.

> Ministers did not exactly deceive themselves, but by creating a machine for surveillance they highlighted the things they feared. Morbidly aware of the European revolutionary context, already inclined to interpret working-class unrest as subversion, they ... not only programmed themselves to define the Triple Alliance and shop stewards organizations as extremist organizations, but then set out to destroy them in a manner which ensured the downfall of industrial relations reconstruction and of the Coalition itself. (Middlemas, 1979, pp. 129–33, 352–3)

Had the Coalition government enjoyed a sustained period of rule the condition of Britain's industrial relations system and much else besides might well have been very different. Its downfall in 1922 marked a return, however, by Conservative Party leadership to the mainstream policy towards industrial relations and therefore calls for some attention. It was due to a mixture of fortuitous and more enduring factors. The threat of Britain becoming involved in fresh wars in Asia Minor as a result of policies by leading Coalition ministers proved a precipitating cause of revolt. But there were more fundamental sources of unease among influential groups of Conservatives both inside and outside Parliament, and one such source was the Coalition stance towards organised labour and class relations. Few issues more closely touched the nerve of a central and long-standing Conservative tradition now represented prominently by Lord Salisbury. Salisbury had 'a sure touch with the body of the Conservative party', which contained a number of disparate groups, some reactionary, some liberal-minded, for whom his importance 'lay in the confidence felt by all in his intentions' (Cowling, 1971, pp. 70, 76). Like his brother, Lord Robert Cecil (see pp. 196–7), Salisbury 'regarded class conflict as the worst of political evils and the one subject about which discussion should be avoided'. There was continuity here with that prewar Conservative body of opinion which considered that to alienate the working class within a context of constitutionalism and political democracy would inevitably bring about destruction of the ruling order through sheer weight of numbers. The ruling order must therefore constantly seek to promote class harmony, avoid open class confrontation, eschew any impression of being anti-working class, and project an image of the state as being even-handed between the classes.

This, in the opinion of Salisbury and a growing number of other Conservatives, the Coalition government was conspicuously failing to do. They 'expected the unprincipled capitalist ethos generated by the Coalition' and 'the aggressive attacks on trade union leaders with which Lloyd George and Birkenhead had approached the public' to 'play into the Labour party's hands by heightening class tension when it ought to be reduced' (Cowling, 1971, pp. 72, 244). In letters to *The Times* (9 January and 17 January 1920), and in speeches right through 1920, 1921 and 1922, Salisbury's message expressed criticism of Lloyd George's 'opportunism', warned that its want of principle would 'make the triumph of Mr. Smillie's principle inevitable', and called upon ministers 'to re-establish the principle that government stood impartially between Capital and Labour'.

It is important to register that Salisbury's condemnation was directed at means not ends. He was no less determined than Coalition leaders to preserve the economic and social order and no more ready to capitulate to the trade unions. But as Lloyd George, Birkenhead and Churchill 'made their mark on industrial relations, he anticipated a situation in which necessary efforts to deal with direct action would be turned by defects in tone into demonstrations of the power and arrogance of wealth'. The notion of tone is important. Like a lot of Conservative leaders and politicians before him, Salisbury valued capitalism more than he valued capitalists. The Disraelian tradition of 'higher-thinking Conservatives' included a view of 'the Liberal capitalist as a dangerous reactionary' and a belief in 'a natural harmony between the gentry or aristocracy on the one hand and the working classes on the other' (ibid., pp. 72, 90). This harmony was thought to be prejudiced by ostentatious vulgarity of personal life among the rich and by provocative flaunting of personal success and achievement, both of them prominent among certain Coalition leaders. Birkenhead's style of private life aroused detestation among many active Conservatives – and their wives – and he evoked revulsion not only among socialists by his 1923 rectoral address at Glasgow University, with its declaration that 'politically, economically and philosophically the motive of self-interest not only is but must ... and ought to be the mainspring of human conduct ... the world continues to offer glittering prizes to those who have stout hearts and sharp swords'. Christ had not really intended 'him who was rich to ... give ... his possessions to the poor'. The speech provoked shudders down the spines of those Conservatives who

disliked and to a certain extent feared the atmosphere which Austen Chamberlain, Birkenhead, Lloyd George and Churchill had been creating ... They feared it because corruption in the rectitude of the governing authority, deliberate affronts to the working classes and the philosophy of self-seeking propagated by Birkenhead would stimulate among the working classes a reciprocal hostility to the ruling classes which they already thought was dangerous. (ibid., pp. 242–3, 322–3)

In explaining the influence which 'higher-thinking' Conservatives could sometimes exert on their fellows it is relevant that there was still a clearly visible stratum of what by any definition could only be called 'the poor'. Appeals to the duty and conscience of the 'rich' could not easily be shrugged off by denials that the poor no longer existed. This was important inasmuch as whereas the rich and the poor are manifestly two nations, the same is less demonstrably true of 'well-to-do' and 'the less well-to-do', who lend themselves more easily to being seen simply as groups differentially placed within one nation. And whereas claims by the poor against the rich may sometimes evoke compassion, even if only from political prudence, claims by the less well-to-do against the well-to-do can more readily be defined by the latter as class war motivated by envy, and be resisted with all the violence which it is possible to exert against an enemy defined as having no moral case. The fact of persistent and visible poverty therefore affected the attitudes of many Conservatives towards the Labour Party and the unions. 'The decision to be the party of resistance to socialism did not, paradoxically, produce much animus against the Labour party.' The Labour Party was seen as 'the embodiment of a possible view of social and political duty which should be treated with the respect due to a real faith by which people could be moved' (ibid., p. 406).

Given such a stance and all that went with it, much was made subsequently of the notion that the party's withdrawal from Coalition stemmed from a movement to purify the tone of English politics. We must therefore note Cowling's observation that 'the tone and the manner had been accepted so long as they were successful electorally and were questioned only when they ceased to be'. There was no doubting the cause of declining electoral success. In by-elections between 1918 and 1921 the Labour vote increased considerably in over twenty and went down in hardly any. 'These gains marked the beginning of a psephological earthquake which politicians recognized for what it was' and there emerged 'overwhelming agreement amongst all non-socialist leaders that the major problem of the future was to provide leadership and create conditions in which the existing social order could be preserved' (ibid., pp. 25, 26, 414). By late 1922 there was also wide agreement in the Conservative Party that a purely negative anti-Socialist stance was not enough by itself to ensure permanent Conservative leadership of anti-socialist sentiment. Added to this were the fears, already mentioned, that he would split the party. These factors combined to effect his downfall at the famous Carlton Club meeting in October 1922 when it was decided by 185 votes to 88 to withdraw from the Coalition. Lloyd George resigned, never to hold office again: . . . the great dream of the Centre Party, dominated by Lloyd George and in perpetual power, had been shattered' (Rhodes James, 1969, p. 129).

The Signifiance of Baldwin

An important part was played in these events by Baldwin, who as a highly significant figure in the history of Britain's industrial relations system brought to bear a perspective which calls for some attention, since it materially shaped Conservative policies towards the Labour movement during the interwar period. Baldwin had the deepest commitment to that traditional constitutionalism of Britain's political system which included the cautious and controlled admission of new elements into the political nation. He set great store by the 'integrity of party' as the vital principle of the representative system, and saw it as the duty of a party to 'maintain a vigorous and honest parliamentary life'. To fail in that duty would be to threaten dictatorship – the destruction of all parties but one. At the Carlton Club meeting he expressed the fear that under the impact of Lloyd George's political personality – a 'dynamic force ... a very terrible thing' – the fragmentation of the party system would be carried further, leaving him the one dominant figure imposing his will in a disordered landscape (Middlesmas and Barnes, 1969, pp. 96–7, 123).

Baldwin's background, personality and political philosophy rendered him ideally suited to embody and represent traditions and techniques of rule that we have noted as long-standing among Britain's ruling class, especially since he added to these an ability to present himself as the epitome of that 'Englishness' which we have also registered as being the basis of a considerable social cohesion. He was also well within the central English tradition in being able to combine identification with Englishness with a dogged individualist refusal to vest Englishness in abstract political concepts of the state or society. 'There is no national well-being', he declared in 1930, 'which is not the well-being of definite individuals, of John Smith, in fact' (ibidl p. 1081). Every significant element in the syndrome of ruling-class style which has emerged in preceding chapters was present in Baldwin, and for that reason his contribution to the consolidation not simply of parliamentary political democracy but also of Britain's industrial relations system must be considered massive.

He came to the fore when his party faced a choice between three different strategies. It could treat the Labour movement, as Birkenhead and others wish, as the advance guard of Bolshevism and seize every opportunity to smash or weaken it, both politically and industrially. It could seek to transcend class distinctions by creating a national movement with a social imperialist programme of the sort still urged by Amery. Baldwin helped to rally those who saw the first as disastrous and the second as now impossible. They believed that 'the primary task must be to incorporate the Labour Movement within the state by winning its leaders both in parliament and in the trade unions to constitutional methods, to an acceptance of the existing state and the need to govern within its constraints' (Gamble, 1981, p. 92).

The son of a wealthy upper-middle-class ironmaster, from whom he inherited a concept of service – 'a patriarchal Toryism near enough to Disrael's definition of Tory democracy' – Baldwin went from Harrow to Cambridge where he read history. Returning to the family firm from a sense of duty rather than from enthusiasm, he proved a 'diffident decision-maker', interested only in the administrative and accounting side – 'the despair of management experts and costing studies'. The firm appears to have been relatively generous and tolerant towards its employees in a manner which Baldwin recognised to be exceptional, and which he wished to see applied by the Conservatives in national politics.

Given such views, Baldwin was well equipped to apply the traditional technique of rule which pursued compromise, avoided too overt a class confrontation, tempered innovation with caution, and was prepared – in his case, eager – to draw working-class organisations into constitutional frameworks of conflict-resolution, industrial as well as political. Of the latter he declared that 'there was a danger of Labour becoming embittered and extreme unless they were taught the value of the House of Commons'; of the former, that the only alternatives to collective bargaining were anarchy and force – 'but we may rule out force in this country'. By 'the natural evolution of our industrial life . . .', he said in 1925, 'we are confronted today, and shall be more and more, with great consolidations of capital managed by small concentrated groups, and by the great organizations of labour led by experienced and responsible leaders. That position must be accepted.'

Baldwin was true to the tradition in the additional sense that he could turn a ruthless face towards aspirations of transforming the social order. 'If there are those who want to fight the class war we will beat them . . .' It was under his premiership in 1925 that one of Britain's extremely rare political trials was initiated by the Home Secretary, Joynson-Hicks, when after a police raid on Communist Party headquarters twelve leading members received prison sentences for seditious libel. We cannot gauge, however, the extent to which political prudence prompted him to give the hawks their heads on this occasion. What is certain is that he never allowed this hawkish stance to be placed at the disposal of management and employers' associations in the ordinary course of labour relations. Britain's management he strongly suspected of being a widely inefficient and backward class, not least in their handling of labour relations; employers' associations and their officials he positively disliked, especially those like Sir Allan Smith of the EEF (Middlemas and Barnes, 1969, pp. 24, 26, 39, 209, 294, 1037, 1041; Charles, 1973, pp. 252–3).

Managerial 'backwardness', for Baldwin, related especially to a failure to humanise labour relations, heal class divisions and lead organised labour into a collaborative pursuit of greater efficiency. This could only be achieved through voluntary co-operation by the parties themselves. 'If both sides of industry could only talk to each other', he declared in 1925, 'they could face the problems of over-capitalization, defective management, wasted resources, failures in marketing, restrictive practices, demarcation disputes.' These were questions that 'no Government can settle, that no Government can interfere with', so intervention, coercive or otherwise, was ruled out.

Baldwin's own style of rule, however, hardly set an example of dynamic modernisation.

> Baldwin failed to solve the underlying problems of Britain's relative economic and strategic decline . . . Perhaps other responses, authoritarian demands for 'efficiency', for the rule of businessmen or the clean sweep which Churchill demanded in the 1930s might have succeeded. It

must remain doubtful . . . Baldwin's years of political leadership were not unlike those of his business career: he made the machinery work, preferring a little inefficiency to a greater alienation of faith from any form of democratic government, administering with humanity and innovating with caution and in peace. (Middlemas and Barnes, 1969, pp. 295, 1077)

With his accession, after Bonar Law's brief reign, to Conservative Party leadership, and to the premiership for a large segment of the interwar period, there disappeared from practical possibility the last of the alternative futures of industrial relations which the war had generated in opposition to the existing system. Joint restrictive collaboration against market and consumer had never struck firm roots in the British environment. Dreams of expansionist collaboration foundered on the zero-sum adversary relationship which in some sectors had seen a degree of partial mitigation but only 'for the duration'. And now Baldwin was speaking for that predominant Conservative opinion which, viewing the rise of the Labour Party with its fierce left wing, dreaded driving the working classes into permanent alienation. There would be no state repression of the sort necessary to destroy workplace efforts towards restrictive job control. And events suggested that not enough of the employers themselves had sufficient modernising drive or sufficient confidence to mount a wholesale attack in the absence of moral or practical support from the state.

The effect of all this upon a particularly well-informed academic observer was to cause him in 1927 to stress, with respect both to 'the problem of industrial relations with which the post-war world has been faced' and to 'the machinery with which industry handles it', the

> essential continuity of the pre-war with the post-war period . . . Briefly, the organization of trade unions and employers' associations, conciliation agreements and joint boards, which covered a minority of well-organized trades before the war, has now been extended to cover the greater part of wage-earning employment. No change in kind, no innovation in principle is to be discerned, but a wide extension and elaboration, in a single decade, of practices and methods, devised by the empirical wisdom of workpeople and imposed on a few industries by continuous pressure for a century. (Clay, 1929, p. 143)

There was, however, rather more to say than this. For example, in the 1919 Shop Stewards' Agreement covering the complex of industries known as 'engineering', the

> right to carry collective bargaining into the workshops, and to establish definitely trade union machinery in the shops themselves, was for the first time explicitly recognized, in such a way that it would be difficult for the employers, however circumstances might change, to take back what they had conceded. The shop stewards' organization lost, indeed, very greatly in power immediately on the termination of the war, when the shortage of labour which had been the basis of its strength ceased to

exist . . . But the gain represented by recognition was, as far as it went, a solid gain; and the instrument of collective workshop bargaining which was created in war years will undoubtedly be called again into play when a favourable occasion presents itself, and will remain perm- anently as an integral part of the machinery of trade unionism. (Cole, 1973, p. 75 – written in 1923)

Furthermore, Britain was now developing 'its own distinctive form of triangular collaboration in the industrial sphere, between government, trade unions and the business class, just as in the field of parliamentary politics the Labour party grew harmoniously to rival Conservatives and supersede the Liberals'. Already by the end of the war a procedure had developed at the initiative of the Ministry of Labour by which all Bills concerning labour and industry, such as the Industrial Courts Act, and later unemployment insurance, 'were shown by Departments to the NCEO and the TUC, to be vetted before introduction to the House of Commons; and several were amended at this stage' (Middlemas, 1979, pp. 123, 161). Even during the febrile years immediately following the war, when conflict 'created an attitude towards government which made it difficult for trade union leaders to collaborate openly' and when 'the result was a heightening of language even when they did not mean it', there was still at times something resembling co-operation between Lloyd George and some union leaders. J. H. Thomas was not alone in combining leadership of one of the major constituents of the Triple Alliance, a public name as a 'concocter of extreme policies', and a reputation as a negotiator with whom ministers could work. Others also saw Lloyd George secretly at moments of tension, and some lunched with Lord Derby 'searching for help against "the extremists" in the Miners' Federation' (Cowling, 1971, pp. 39–40).

Consultation about legislation, too, continued, despite the tendency of some Labour ministers, *plus royaliste que le roi*, to frown on the practice. A steady *rapprochement* therefore developed between government depart- ments dealing with industry, their official and unofficial advisers, the scientific lobby, large and increasingly co-ordinated groups of employ- ers, and, 'even before 1926, the majority of trade union leaders'. These developments were marked by great caution. The TUC 'learnt to its surprise' that the NCEO and FBI 'feared the same reaction from their members as it did, if they tried to impose central direction'. The TUC only managed to build up a role of authoritative spokesman by accom- modating to the historical idiosyncrasies, differentials and demarcation lines of its affiliated unions – and thereby acting as a highly conservative force. Acting under these limitations, 'big business, trade unions and the state apparatus had acknowledged the importance of a peculiarly subtle and pervasive form of corporate interchange, less and less affected by party hostilities' – corporatist in a far more flexible form than had been implied by the Industrial Council project (Middlemas, 1979, pp. 178, 209, 212, 214, 219).

Large-Scale Business, Public Ownership and the Union Role

Baldwin persisted in his hopes for a more positive collaboration between the two sides of industry, and these struck answering chords with a few top-level union leaders and with some of the large-scale industrialists he had come to know when they were drawn by the war into high political office. The latter were a new breed. There had long been, of course, a movement from business into politics, sometimes to Cabinet level. But with the growth in scale of enterprise there was developing a generation of industrialists who were conscious of being far more publicly visible – and therefore in a sense publicly accountable – than the older-type entrepreneur of small-scale competitive industry. Anxious for a public status commensurate with their power and position, they could hardly help discovering that too overt and personal a preoccupation with maximising profits was not the route to full acceptance at the highest levels; ideally a true gentleman hired others to make his profits for him while he pursued public service. They might not be able to go that far, but, fresh from the Whitehall corridors of power, they could seek to infuse their industrial leadership with notions of service to the broader interests of the nation. One of the new breed, Samuel Courtauld, declared that business leaders 'must look upon themselves as do high officers in an army, as do leading statesmen in a government, as do the great men in the worlds of science and art; as men, in fact, whose first motive is service to the truth of their *metier* and to the community . . . Service, and not exploitation, must be the inspiration of business men . . . ' (Courtauld, 1949, p. 30).

Often their personal links with politicians remained, so despite the rush to dismantle the wartime structure of industrial control, 'the state and business, once joined together, were never afterwards entirely put asunder'. Those at the head of affairs in politics, administration and business, having grown accustomed to working together, never again retired into separate compartments. 'Men like McGowan and Mond in business; like Baldwin, Runciman, and Cunliffe-Lister in politics; like Warren Fisher and John Anderson in the civil service; like McKenna, Weir, and Ashfield in positions overlapping all the rest – all had easy access to each other and continued the wartime habit of consultation and co-operation' (Reader, 1977, p. 241).

These links and the conceptions of business, labour relations and 'national interest' which informed them had important consequences both for the structure of some of the rapidly growing newer industries such as chemicals, electricity generation and London Transport, and for some aspects of industrial relations. Baldwin chose Weir in 1925 to head a committee 'to review the national problem of electrical energy' and, when Weir put up a bold plan to create a Central Electricity Board (CEB) – a state monopoly selling through a national grid – pushed what was 'quite possibly the most important single Act passed between the wars' through a reluctant Cabinet and party in 1926 (Middlemas and Barnes, 1969, pp. 393–4). As a public corporation of the sort later to be adopted by the Labour Party for its own nationalisation measures, the CEB legislation was at least as significant an event as the General Strike. 'In a sense', the roots of this 'chosen instrument for the administration of publicly owned' undertakings

> lie considerably further back than those of the joint stock company; for the corporation in its various forms is one of the legacies of the Middle Ages, when such corporate bodies as universities, guilds and cities enjoyed a measure of autonomy. Through the sixteenth, seventeenth and eighteenth centuries the idea of the corporation survived and developed in various forms, influencing such bodies as the Improvement Commissioners and the Turnpike Trusts. More recently, one can trace a derivation from the Representative Trust, the Ecclesiastical and the Charity Commissions and the Road Board of 1909. (Goodman, 1951, p. 40)

For a short while after the First World War, when public attention was first seriously concerned with the form of control for state-owned industries, it seemed as if this persistent tradition might be abandoned. The Haldane Committee on the Machinery of Government favoured direct management of each nationalised industry by the appropriate government department. The Acland Committee on Forestry, however, advised setting up an independent forestry authority, and although this advice was only partially accepted the modern conception of the public corporation came to prevail. Given the dominance within Labour Party leadership of those forces which sought only marginal modifications of the social order, it is no surprise to find Herbert Morrison, when in 1929 he came to the task of drafting the London Passenger Transport Bill, turning to the public corporation as 'most likely to be consistent with socialist principles and with practical success' (ibid., p. 44).

Another initiative of significance for our present purpose was a suggestion to McGowan in 1926 by McKenna, sometime Chancellor of the Exchequer, now chairman of the Midland Bank, about the possibility of organising the British dye-stuffs industry into a more effective force 'for reasons of national policy rather than commercial profit'. McGowan went much further, under government blessing, with an amalgamation of all the important firms in British chemicals, thus the Imperial Chemical Industries (ICI) was born, deliberately so named to 'lay emphasis upon the fact "that the promotion of imperial trading interests will command the special consideration and thought of those who will be responsible for directing this new company"'. McGowan and Mond, its leading figures, wanted the merger in order to secure weighty standing in the world's chemical industry, especially against the brilliantly successful German company, I. G. Farbenindustrie, but there were present also, especially for Mond, a Liberal Imperialist turned Conservative, 'notions of national policy' (Reader, 1977, pp. 227, 242). Other ICI directors came to include Weir, Anderson, Duncan, who was also first chairman of the CEB, and Ashfield, who was later first chairman of the 1933 London Passenger Transport Board. 'Directors of this stamp might, perhaps, be considered informal trustees for the public interest, and they certainly ensured a close connection between ICI and the world of government and politics.' This example of the growing forms of interaction between matters of state and matters of commerce was symptomatic. 'Questions of ownership apart, the idea that government should take a part in the organization and direction of business and should even offer financial help in cases of distress was gradually easing its way into the general body of common-place ideas during the years between the wars' (ibid., pp. 231, 242).

These men and measures had a threefold significance for the present discussion. They show Labour as well as Conservative governments drawing upon a stock of organisational ideas about the public corpor-ation which excluded all such socialist notions as syndicalism, guild socialism, other more modest versions of 'workers control', or even effective 'participation'. Despite much subsequent debate within the Labour Party it was to be the independent public corporation that pro-vided the administrative form for Britain's nationalisation measures. Variations there were to be in plenty, yet all adhered to the essentially bureaucratic, hierarchical structure of authority, decision-making and status common to all previous large-scale organisation. This, along with the instruction laid upon them to operate by 'normal commercial prin-ciples', resulted in a work experience for their employees which differed little, if at all, from that in the private sector. For all practical purposes nothing changed for the unions, which brought to bear upon manage-ment in the public sector the same pattern of perceptions, dispositions and policies as they had developed in the private. The enlargement of the public sector brought no new principles or major initiatives to the industrial relations system.

The second significant feature is that Conservative industrialists are seen accepting posts in public corporations from a Labour government and thereby facilitating that process by which the upper levels of the Labour movement assimilated to the world of public and private capit-alism in what were the beginnings of the 'mixed economy'. And, finally, this group of powerful and influential industrialists included several who were among the more conspicuous exponents of so-called 'progressive management' between the wars. They were strong support-ers of rationalisation and other expressions of Scientific Management but, unlike F. W. Taylor, hoped to draw organised labour into that 'mental revolution' by which both sides would collaborate in maximis-ing the product and making possible larger shares for all. They were advanced in their introduction of personnel management and systematic labour relations policies; ICI, for example, working 'in close contact with union representatives to operate highly sophisticated consultative and judicial mechanisms in their factories, and to support industrial co-operation by means of a wide range of material benefits' (Child, 1969, p. 99). Although highly untypical in these respects, they made a concer-ted effort in the late 1920s, along with a few like-minded union leaders, to get Britain's industrial relations on to a positive-sum basis. Although, as we shall see, they failed, the initiative was not without its effect on the system.

Baldwin and Industrial Relations

Ideas of this sort were, of course, more than acceptable to Baldwin. Where he differed from some other Conservative politicians was not in wanting constructive collaboration between manager and workers – a fitting subject for any hack politician at any Rotary Club dinner – but in wanting to bring the unions into the process. Baldwin understood the British Labour movement better than any other Conservative politician before or since and his contribution to continuity was made possible by that very understanding. His reiterated plea for 'the beginning of a better feeling of unity between all classes of our people' could easily have been accompanied by the refusal or inability exhibited by so many politicians – and not only those of the Conservative Party – to attempt to understand the realities of workplace conflict and organisation as trade unionists see them. He could usually manage, however, to avoid this kind of humbug, so the unions were at least spared the frustrated irritation which so often afflicted them in their exchanges with the great and the good, from whom they tended, then as now, to receive self-righteous admonitions about individual freedom and elementary economics. Speaking to the House of Commons in 1925 about trade unions and employers' associations, Baldwin pointed out that

> the mere fact of organizing involves a certain amount of sacrifice of personal liberty. That cannot be helped ... To a certain extent both these organizations must on one side be uneconomic. A trade union is uneconomic ... when it restricts output, and when it levels down the work to a lower level. It is an association for the protection of the weaker man, which has often proved uneconomic. Exactly the same thing happens in the employers' organization ... in effect it is very often uneconomic, because it keeps in existence works which if left to the process of competition, would be squeezed out, and whose prolonged existence is really only a weakness to the country .. both these organizations are instinct with English traditions ... The whole tradition of our country has been to let Englishmen develop their own associations in their own way, and with that I agree. But there are limits to that – nothing must be done which injures the state (Milne-Bailey, 1929, pp. 457–8).

Baldwin spoke for substantial sections of his party whose intention was not simply to be the party of resistance to socialism but who wanted to find something to say which would save the party being branded as merely the instrument of the rich against the poor. This involved showing sensitivity to part of the atmosphere which Labour had created. 'This did not invariably mean making a point of accepting trade unionism as a necessary part of the scene, though it usually did mean that ... ' (Cowling, 1971, p. 407). The negative anti-labour stance persisted in some quarters – among some ex-Coalition ministers whom Baldwin felt constrained to take into his government, for example, and within the Liberty and Property Defence League, the Anti-Socialist Union and the British

Empire Union, which all survived the war, though the more rabid elements were drawn off by small fascist movements and what was left was no more potent politically than before.

This, then, was the structure of convictions and strategies, some of them shared with untypical industrialists, with which Baldwin moderated, as far as his own political security permitted, the hawkish anti-labour tendencies of fellow-ministers like Birkenhead, Churchill and Joynson-Hicks. It remains now to offer some practical instances of how Baldwin's stance crucially affected the condition of industrial relations. The first was the 1922 withdrawal from Coalition. 'Baldwin foresaw a supreme task for his party in ending the embattled confrontation with the working class; but first it had to be disengaged from Lloyd George' (Middlemas and Barnes, 1969, p. 99).

Baldwin's stance on class relations entered into the back-stage consultations as to whether he or Lord Curzon should succeed Bonar Law as Prime Minister in 1923. The issue was probably decided by Balfour's advice to the king that such was the growing importance of the House of Commons, especially given the rise of Labour, that from now on prime ministers must sit there and not in the Lords. It is worth noting, nevertheless, the famous memorandum sent by Davidson, Law's parliamentary private secretary, to Lord Stamfordham, the king's private secretary, who had requested a statement of the 'ordinary Conservative back-bencher's view'. It noted that Baldwin had 'the complete confidence of the City and the commercial world generally', while Curzon was 'regarded in the public eye as representing that section of privileged conservatism which has its value but which in this democratic age cannot be too assiduously exploited'. Worse, however, was the fact that Curzon's methods were 'inappropriate to harmony. The prospect of him receiving deputations as Prime Minister from the Miners' Federation or the Triple Alliance, for example, is capable of causing alarm for the future relations between the Government and labour – between moderate and less moderate opinion' (Rhodes James, 1969, pp. 154–5).

Once in office, Baldwin had a series of struggles with members of his own back bench as to what stance was to prevail. In 1925 a Scottish lawyer, Macquisten, tabled a Bill which obliged union members to contract into the political levy (the proceeds of which went to the Labour Party), if they wished to pay it, rather than, as at present, putting the onus on them to contract out if they did not. The issue, though adorned with much rhetoric about individual freedom, was really whether the Labour Party should or should not enjoy the benefit of human inertia. Some Conservative MPs had 'misgivings about such a blatant show of partiality' and a deputation urged caution. Baldwin, too, 'preferred to defeat his own extremists as a token of the Conservative party's will towards industrial peace'. Having managed to swing the Cabinet he told the House of Commons that 'we are not going to push our political advantage home at a moment like this'. The two great sets of organisations which for half a century had been largely free to develop in their own way, 'so similar in their strengths and . . . in their weaknesses', must learn to work in partnership, the key to future progress (Middlemas and Barnes, 1969, pp. 292–8).

Baldwin in this mood was capable of exceptional powers of class conciliation. Not that fellow-feeling between Conservative and Labour MPs was normally totally absent. Beneath the ritual abuse and shadow-boxing - and flashes of genuine class passion – there were, at a primitive level, many instincts in common between some Conservative and some Labour leaders. 'There was the same affectation of dislike for the million-aire press. There was the same distaste for the ostentation of wealth. There was the same concern with decency and virtue and a belief, derived from Disraeli, the Church of England and "gentry politics" in some cases and from Joseph Chamberlain, municipal socialism and the Penny Bank in the rest that the rich had a duty to be kind to the poor within the limits of existing inequality' (Cowling, 1971, p. 427). In order that some Conserva-tive leaders and activists should feel this unease about 'the poor' and be capable of wincing at Birkenhead's blatant meritocratic vulgarities there had to be a large and palpable problem of absolute poverty. This not only made it possible to see both the industrial and political wings of the Labour movement as on balance pursuing decent – even though, for Conserva-tives, wrong-headed – purposes, it also put some leverage in the hands of those Conservatives for whom it gave politics a moral basis.

Couched within this tradition, the speech 'took its place at once, by universal consent, among the uncommon masterpieces of parliamentary eloquence'. Many years later, David Kirkwood, in wartime the militant Clydeside Independent Labour Party shop steward and scourge of Lloyd George, revealed in his reactions to it just what a powerful instrument of assimilation the House of Commons is and how its effects can be deployed in the hands of a master. 'It seemed to me . . . ', he wrote to Baldwin, 'that in your speech you made flesh the feelings of us all, that the antagonism, the bitterness, the class rivalry, were unworthy, and that understanding and amity were possible' (Middlemas and Barnes, 1969, pp. 292–8).

If Baldwin could have this effect on a Scot his effect on the English was likely to be even more potent. Patriotism for Englishmen is anchored not in the state but in feelings about a shared unity of Englishness and Baldwin cultivated Englishness above everything. Having, as one biographer, G. M. Young, expressed it, become 'an Englishman not casually, by accident of birth, but deliberately and by election', he was fond of declaring that in being English 'we are all equals: there all of us are one'. The image of simple honesty of unpolitical Englishmen was a useful differentiating ploy not only against the unscrupulous brilliance of Bir-kenhead and Lloyd George but also against socialism and communism. 'It became the object of the "English party" to stimulate resistance to the corrupting cleverness with which alien and alienated minds had imposed themselves upon the great mass of good-hearted Englishmen' (Cowling, 1971, p. 243). The target now was not so much the trade unions as the 'intellectuals' who were misleading the working classes and destroying the natural unity of the English scene. Many Englishmen, including many workers, were receptive to such a message and the common mistrust of 'theory' at all social levels heightened that receptiveness.

On the face of it, such rallying cries might seem to be countered by the more sharply delineated class structure that was emerging. This had become palpable since the few years preceding the war. Until then English society was a complex hierarchy in which stratification by status overlay the basic three-tier structure. It then began to move towards a simpler form in which the differences that had graded manual workers as elaborately as the middle class became rather less distinct, while the basic social classes became rather more so (Waites, 1976, p. 45). Wage differentials between craftsmen and the less skilled, for example, narrowed during the war and although they widened again somewhat after 1921 were never to be of the same order as before. Technical and organisational changes, too, were reducing the relative role and status superiority of many, though certainly not all, apprenticed craftsmen, and the increasing interposition in the managerial hierarchy of specialist functionaries qualified by higher education was adding to the effect. Meanwhile many members of the lower working class were being upgraded by rising living standards, education and the effects of the wartime extension of trade unionism and collective bargaining. The old gulf between the labour aristocracy and the rest was closing. As the working class became more homogeneous the distinction from the middle class became more marked, helped by changes in religious belief and education. Because creeds had ceased to divide, class stood out the more sharply. And because the post-1918 extension of full-time education up to the age of 14 had been achieved by 'developing a different, and mainly inferior, education for those who had previously received none', class differences were made clearer and more effective. The dividing line between this system and the system of expensive boarding schools for the privileged 'was as hard as that between Hindu castes. No child ever crossed it' (A. J. P. Taylor, 1970, pp. 225, 233).

Yet there were a number of factors which, in Taylor's words, 'took the edge off the class war', quite apart from national health and unemployment benefit. The rich were consuming marginally less conspicuously; to be idle in one's wealth was not quite the boast it once was, and domestic service was no longer as large a mass occupation as it had been up to 1914. The working class continued refusing to translate class conflict at the workplace into class conflict at the political level. 'The majority of manual workers never voted Labour. Even the majority of trade union members rarely did so' (ibid., p. 233). When they did they were voting, in most cases, not for social transformation but for piecemeal reform. There was, in consequence, a good deal for Baldwin to appeal to and he made the most of it.

It is easy, in assessing Baldwin's style, to underplay two qualities. One was a capacity for steeliness when events seemed to him to require it. The other was the astuteness which came markedly into play in 1924 when, along with Asquith, he put the minority parliamentary Labour Party into office. Had they both believed, as apparently did Churchill, among others, that a Labour government composed of the existing leaders presented a genuine threat to the traditional order they would almost certainly have found some way, either through coalition or parliamentary support of one by the other, of keeping Labour out. That they did not arrive at any such belief may well have been due to some extent upon fortuitous circumstances. Had economic collapse come in 1918 instead of late 1920 the official Labour leaders might, given the 'need for a rhetoric, the readiness of their "extremists" and the example of the Russian revolution', have felt compelled seriously to attack the system if they were not to be pushed aside by those eager to do so. 'By the time the collapse came in late 1920, they had not only established a line of Labour policy which was ostentatiously unrevolutionary but had electoral success to "prove that Labour [was] no longer viewed as a freakish interference in national politics"' (Cowling, 1971, p. 40).

Now, in 1924, as Asquith observed, 'if a Labour government is ever to be tried in this country, as it will be sooner or later, it could hardly be tried under safer conditions' – at the first sign of real danger he and Baldwin could vote it down. Meanwhile, experience of the sweets of office would finally confirm Labour's assimilation into a safe constitutionalism by demonstrating that supreme power could apparently be won and by bonding Labour leaders to the system with a taste of honey. Davidson, now Baldwin's parliamentary private secretary, 'was probably echoing Baldwin's views exactly' when in a private letter he expressed himself hostile to any Conservative–Liberal alliance to keep Labour out – there had been much rank and file Conservative panic and anger against Baldwin for having gone to the country and exposed the 'nation' to such peril. 'I am a simple soul', wrote Davidson, 'but any dishonest combination of that sort – which means the sacrificing of principles by both Liberal and Tory to deprive Labour of their constitutional rights – is the first step down the road to revolution ... ' The king, also, not surprisingly a man of deeply right-wing convictions, 'expressed the view that a Socialist government would have an opportunity of learning their administrative duties and responsibilities under favourable conditions and that it was essential that their rights under the Constitution should in no way be impaired'. This was not a strategy of simple souls. Nor was the king's achievement in persuading 'the Labour party that he was entirely neutral. That must have required a very great deal of self-discipline ... he managed to keep his relations with Ramsay MacDonald and the rest of them so well that they became – and particularly some, like Jimmy Thomas – more royalist than the King' (Rhodes James, 1969, pp. 178, 189, 191).

These judgements and strategies were rewarded with the deep anxiety of every Labour government then and since to present itself as a national government, fit to govern, free from 'undue class bias', and as moralistic about strikes, restrictive practices and left-wing militancy as any Tory counterpart. Under the 1924 Labour administration Josiah Wedgwood was made Civil Commissioner in charge of preparations against stoppages in key industries, and in general 'the Cabinet conducted itself [towards strikes] as any Cabinet would have done, without partiality for one side or the other' (Cowling, 1971, pp. 378, 379). These characteristics were accompanied by an economic, financial and political orthodoxy that permitted continued high unemployment without reference to the TUC or its affiliated unions.

Just as Salisbury had wanted to keep Birkenhead out of the Conservative leadership because he stimulated class bitterness by provoking open conflict between the Haves and the Have-nots which the Have-nots, if driven to unified action, would win, so MacDonald . . . gave practical expression to the parallel belief that bare assertion of Have-not demands would deny the Labour party all hope of power for a generation. Have-not demands were made, but they were covered with moral merit and made on behalf of everyone except the rich. (ibid., p. 290)

The Beginnings of Mond–Turner

Back in office after the brief Labour tenure, Baldwin soon saw one of his favourite themes taken up. In a letter to *The Times* (2 November 1925), F. V. Willey, a Bradford wool merchant, brought into prominence again the old vision of a collaborative alliance between capital and labour. Criticising employers for a failure of leadership, he lamented the reputation suffered by Britain overseas that she is 'in a very bad economic state, that there is a bad spirit abroad among the workers, that our costs are too high, and that our unemployment is largely our own fault'. In combating this situation employers must strive to promote a spirit of co-operation, but would fail unless they freely conceded workers their full share of the increased returns that resulted. As the subsequent supportive letters showed, Willey was speaking for a mood that sought a revival of the Whitley spirit; a mood intensified by an awareness, voiced by Sir Harold Bowden in *The Times* (12 November 1925), that very different impulses were afoot. 'Both sides have their prophets who aver that the issue must be fought to a finish sooner or later, and therefore "the sooner it's over the better".' As against this there was, commented *The Times* editorially (10 November 1925) 'unquestionably an earnest desire for a new spirit, a searching for a better way and a happier relationship . . . a new spirit is abroad'. Bowden's letter urged a conference between a small group of union leaders and employers 'to lay down the main principles on the basis of which a state of perpetual distrust may be converted into mutual confidence and harmony'. On the day this letter was printed, Sir Alfred Mond appealed, at a meeting of the Society of British Gas Industries, for a 'round-table conference' which would seek, 'in place of a spirit of perpetual hostility, a spirit of co-operation'. Those 'who could not get on with their workmen would have to get out of industry' (*The Times*, 13 November 1925). When, early in the following year (11 January 1926), *The Times* reported Ben Turner, union leader in the woollen industry, appealing for 'forms of joint control' in industry, so that 'waste of effort, energy, and material could be avoided by a closer partnership', it became clear that the necessary dispositions were present in some quarters on both sides.

Mutual accommodation between management and unions was coming to be seen by some industrialists as the rational response to large-scale operations, intensive capitalisation and rapid technological change. Such circumstances heightened further the attractiveness of having labour as a partner rather than as an adversary, especially since large-scale resources could better accommodate to labour's needs. Another contributory factor was the growth of managerial specialisation and of some pretensions to professionalisation. Already there was talk of capital, labour and management being co-partners in the enterprise and of a 'professional' management's task as being that of holding the balance between the competing claims of shareholders, employees, consumers and some unspecified 'national interest'.

Along with the idea of seeking labour's co-operation went the belief that in the postwar world free market forces could not be relied on to produce the optimum state of affairs either for business organisation or for the economy as a whole. There was a need to control the economy rather than be controlled by it. Both ideas were manifest in the Liberal Industrial Inquiry of 1925–7 and the famous report that resulted in 1928, *Britain's Industrial Future*. Mond, a Liberal convert to Conservatism in 1926, fully shared these views. He 'was in the tradition of Mundella, Macara and Whitley in his belief in the possibility and desirability of an industrial system which met the needs of the unions while leaving the traditional structure of industry in essentials unchanged' (Charles, 1973, p. 273) – a tradition which hoped to gain in return the unions' commitment to a positively collaborative relationship.

Both ideas came to be acceptable to some top-level labour leaders, Bevin among them. Bevin welcomed the growth in scale, the emergence of the new type of industrialist, the growing emphasis on the need to organise economic life. But if large-scale industry and government were to make greater efforts to regulate economic forces, introduce rationalisation and promote concentration of ownership and control, the TUC itself must accept a 'new kind of responsibility'. Bevin 'now saw the economic function of the trade unions as a much wider one than that of raising working-class power to a position where it could successfully bargain with the power of industrial capital for a fair share of what was produced . . . He believed that it must make a positive contribution at the highest levels of economic policy . . . ', directing its energies 'not only to obtaining a fair division of existing production but to the establishment of conditions in which production could increase' (F. Williams, 1952, p. 150).

It was probably this kind of corporatist negotiation at top level that had most appeal for Bevin, who 'in many ways had a much more organized theory of the role of labour than Cripps on the left, and than his trade union colleagues on the right. At the core of that theory lay the notion of institutionalized co-operation between the trade unions, management and the state, supplemented by the parliamentary pressure of the Labour party' (Miliband, 1973, p. 206). Henderson and Arthur Pugh, chairman of the TUC General Council in 1926, likewise, had never given up hope of a National Industrial Council. Citrine's aspirations included this level but went beyond it to cover active management–worker collaboration at the workplace. Citrine was one of the few top union figures to support profit-sharing, ever favoured by those who sought shop-floor co-operation – Mond himself being among its keenest enthusiasts. Citrine later set out his wider views in an analysis of some interest. Trade unionism had so far pursued an unplanned development, but the next stage called for 'a general recognition . . . of the part which the workers' organizations are qualified to play in the promotion of efficiency, economy, and scientific development in the productive system'. This could be demonstrated by identifying the three alternative strategies confronting the unions. The first was to withhold all co-operation towards greater efficiency on the ground that this would merely postpone 'the inevitable breakdown of the existing system'; on the contrary the unions must work to hasten that collapse. The second was to 'keep up the defensive struggle for the maintenance of existing standards and to improve them as opportunity offers, but to accept no responsibility at all for any effort that can be made to improve the organization of industry on the present basis of private ownership'.

The second of these strategies described what had been the prevalent practice so far; the first described the aims of a tiny minority of class warriors. Citrine believed that the future lay with his third strategy, by which unions would 'actively participate in a concerted effort to raise industry to its highest efficiency by developing the most scientific methods of production, eliminating waste and harmful restrictions, removing causes of friction and avoidable conflict, and promoting the largest possible output so as to provide a rising standard of life and continuously improving conditions of employment'. But the employers would have to change as well if this strategy was to be possible. So far they had been 'only too prone to believe that efficiency and economy are synonymous with lower wages, longer hours, speeding-up, and such forms of "scientific management . . . "'. As long as workers were allowed to believe that they had little to gain either materially or in status by the introduction of measures designed to promote greater efficiency, and might even suffer by their adoption, 'progress is rendered difficult'. Citrine revived the idea of the TUC General Council, the FBI and the NCEO coming together in a National Industrial Council, with a separate Industrial Council for each industry 'with a much wider conception of their obligations than the adjustment of wage disputes only'. The latter was, of course, no more than a reassertion of the Whitley model, which had shown very little capacity so far to promote positive-sum collaboration in British industry. Citrine admitted that possibly 'no basis of confidence and goodwill exists upon which such a relationship can rest' (Milne-Bailey, 1929, pp. 432–7).

The General Strike

This analysis, however, lay in the future: for the time being any follow-up of the Mond–Turner initiatives was precluded by the General Strike and the events leading up to it. There is no need here to rehearse that long and complex sequence. For present purposes it is sufficient to note the widespread awareness in the trade union movement that for major groups of employers, especially those in the old declining staple industries, such as coal, textiles, heavy engineering and shipbuilding, attack on labour standards was the preferred method of coping with adverse market pressures. It is not to be inferred from this that the newer industries with better prospects necessarily exhibited 'progressive' and 'enlightened' practices – in car assembly, for example, the labour policies of Austin at Longbridge, Morris at Oxford and later Ford at Dagenham led to workplace cultures for which their successors paid a heavy price. It was, however, the old staples that were especially hard hit by the decline in exports and it was the old staples that exhibited to a well-developed degree the zero-sum adversary stance – which some of the newer industries were quick to acquire.

Already, in 1923, a TUC manifesto had shown how reports from affiliated unions 'clearly indicate that many employers of labour, having forced substantial reductions in wages, are attempting to follow up these successes by a further attack on the most vital condition of employment, namely, the normal working-day or week'. Most industries, immediately after the war, had adopted, under union pressure, a working week of 48 hours or thereabouts, and the historical trend towards hours reduction was deemed by the General Council 'the principal advantage secured by over 60 years of trade union effort and sacrifice'. Experience had also taught the unions the enormous importance to employers of being able to point to reductions of labour standards in other industries as a justification for following suit. 'As one group of employers secure success others follow, and the low standards obtained in one industry are quoted in other industries as a reason why the worker should submit to reductions without protest' (Milne-Bailey, 1929, pp. 415–17).

The fear of a major breach in the defences became greatly sharpened in 1925 when, under the chancellorship of Churchill, one of the most rabidly anti-labour of government ministers, Britain returned to the gold standard at the punishingly high prewar parity. It is relevant to later events and to the general cultural context of British politics that the operations of the gold standard and the balancing of the national budget were thought to provide 'an automatic guarantee against both public and private vices. It made impossible public profligacy; and it punished, by the scourge of unemployment, private extravagance.' Thus a strong moral element was injected into financial doctrine, which Labour as well as Conservative ministers were apt to present as being 'above politics'. The more candid, however, acknowledged the 'rules of sound finance' to be a defence not just against economic catastrophe but against state socialism (Skidelsky, 1981a, p. 169).

The return to gold at the prewar parity, though its long-term effects are now thought to have been exaggerated, was a further affliction for the export industries since it meant an immediate rise in prices if nothing was done to offset it. To avoid being priced out of their markets they must attempt to drive costs down by an equivalent amount and labour standards emerged as the obvious target. Industrialists could hardly be expected to be enthusiastic about the policy and Keynes, especially prominent among economists in his criticism of it, acknowledged that their interests had been subordinated 'to the preoccupation of the bankers with London's position as a centre of international banking and exchange'. Churchill, wrote Keynes, 'was committing himself to force down money-wages and all money values'. It would mean 'a struggle with each separate group in turn'. After one meeting between Baldwin and the TUC it was reported, though later denied, that he had said 'All the workers of this country have got to take reductions in wages to put industry on its feet.' Had industry's views 'been given as much weight as those of the City', comments Bullock, 'it is unlikely that the change would ever have been made' (Bullock, 1960, pp. 265–7). Samuel Courtauld, prominent leader in one of the new expanding industries, was to say later that 'most industrialists', like himself, were as mistrustful and 'suspicious of banking' as of the company promoter, the stock-jobber and all stock market speculation and financial manipulation – their interests not being 'identical with those of productive industry' (Courtauld, 1949, pp. 4, 17, 22, 83).

Given that an attack on hours and wage standards might soon be mounted who would bear the brunt of the first onslaught? Circumstances soon made clear that it would be the miners, who had been in intermittent conflict with the owners since the war. The return to gold no doubt heightened the owners' difficulties but it had certainly not caused them: coal had been recognised by the Treasury as a sick industry in 1921. The line-up was symbolic. Few industries exhibited more starkly the conflict posture; few groups of workers wore more convincingly the heroic mantle of the shock troops of labour. The latter point was important for the rest of organised labour. The rational self-interest case for supporting the miners in their struggle against owners' demands for lower wages and extended hours was apparent: the fear was that if the miners went down all would go down. Yet the self-interest case was powerfully reinforced – perhaps even swamped – by an emotional movement of sympathy and loyalty.

The issue in the General Strike of 1926, though to a limited extent infused with political intent by a minority on the left, was basically one of whether the government was to allow itself to be pressured by the TUC into enabling the coal industry – through a combination of direct subsidy and a government-stimulated programme of reorganisation – to maintain present standards of wages and working hours. For most trade unionists and most of their leaders, the General – or as the TUC preferred to call it, the National – Strike was 'political' only in the sense that it was directed against the government, a political agency. In terms of its substantive objectives it could still be presented as a 'trade dispute' and therefore covered by the 'golden formula' and legal immunities of the 1906 Act. The issue became one of keen contention between lawyers, Sir John Simon, a Liberal MP, arguing that 'a strike is a strike against employers to compel employers to do something, but a General Strike is a strike against the general public to make the public, parliament and the government do something' – and not a 'trade dispute' within the meaning of the Act (Simon, 1926, p. 16). This, he argued, rendered it unconstitutional and unlawful. Another lawyer, Professor Goodhart, 'convincingly argued that this particular dispute and strike remained a "furtherance of a trade dispute ..." The "political" element had not displaced the industrial content ...' Even if a non-violent General Strike *were* held to be techni-cally not the furtherance of a trade dispute, would it then of necessity be illegal? Goodhart thought not. It might be 'unquestionably contrary to the spirit of the English constitution but this does not necessarily render it criminal' (Wedderburn, 1971, p. 392; Kahn-Freund 1979, p. 93).

None knew better than Baldwin that most of the strike leaders and participants were simply pursuing a trade dispute and had no will to overthrow the government. He was also aware, however, that for a militant left-wing minority the strike's significance and the political hopes they vested in it transcended these considerations. This alone made it essential, so far as he was concerned, to win the strike. The immediate postwar events had left the issue of political strikes dangerously unresolved and the far left must be taught that there was no future for them along that road. For the purpose of establishing a definitive precedent, the strike must be designated unconstitutional. But there were two additional reasons for his pronouncing that 'the Constitution would not be safe until we had won the victory, and the victory depended on the surrender of the TUC' (Rhodes James, 1969, p. 232). First, as early as 1921, as President of the Board of Trade, he had accepted the Treasury case with respect to coal that the government could not carry the weight of an 'ailing and incompetent industry' (Middlemas and Barnes, 1969, p. 378). Secondly, Baldwin had to maintain his credentials with his own back-benchers and supporters, not to mention some fellow-ministers who were baying for blood.

When it eventually became clear that an agreement was nowhere within reach, he grasped an opportunity for precipitating the strike, made certain that the government would win it and, at the same time – because he wished to direct his fire mainly at the small far-left minority – sought to avoid alienating the broad mass of the trade union movement. His method of precipitation is fully described in the literature (for example, Clegg, forthcoming; Middlemas and Barnes, 1969, p. 409). He made certain of winning it by defining its nature in such a way as to make it impossible for him and the government to give way. 'Constitutional government is being attacked', he wrote in the government's news bulletin, the *British Gazette* (6 May 1926). 'Stand behind the government, who are doing their part, confident that you will co-operate in the measures they have undertaken to preserve the liberties and privileges of the people of these islands. The laws of England are the people's birthright. Those laws are in your keeping. You have made parliament their guardian. The General Strike is a challenge to parliament and is the road to anarchy and ruin.' Once he had defined the strike in these terms he had in effect committed himself and the government to stand fast until the TUC surrendered. Not that the government, the party and the press needed stiffening; Baldwin was simply identifying himself with the definition of the situation which had already been proclaimed by prominent politicians, newspapers and a judge (Astley) who had declared that 'no trade dispute does or can exist between the Trades Union Congress on the one hand and the Government and the nation on the other' (Simon, 1926, p. 68) – a declaration that the strike was therefore political and, *ipso facto*, unconstitutional.

The complaint by many members of his party, however, was that although he defined the strike as an attack on the constitution he did not treat it as one. This nonplussed even some of his opponents. J. H. Thomas, general secretary of the National Union of Railwaymen and member of the General Council, had been convinced that some council members would be shot, perhaps by fascist supporters of the government, while even the sober Citrine 'fully expected to be arrested' (Citrine, 1964, pp. 157–8). The Conservative Party Treasurer later wrote of party feeling in the constituencies: 'People can't understand why the strike was regarded as an industrial dispute and not as a revolutionary movement; why Cook was treated as if he had been an honest striker . . . ' (Middlemas and Barnes, 1969, p. 447). Baldwin sought in a number of ways to keep the temperature down. He appointed Churchill to run the *British Gazette* on the ground that it would 'keep him busy and stop him doing worse things'; he disowned inflammatory remarks that appeared in it; he decided against Churchill's bid to publicly commandeer the BBC; and he softened his statements of resolve in the House of Commons with such sweeteners as 'Before long the angel of peace . . . will be among us again, and when he comes let us be there to meet him'. When Churchill's assertion that 'the legal and constitutional aspects are entering upon a new phase' was taken by the TUC General Council to mean that the government was now viewing the situation in terms of civil war, Baldwin got private word to the council repudiating it (Miliband, 1973, p. 137). Churchill's whole handling of the *British Gazette* is indicative of the severe strains to which the industrial relations system would have been subjected had he occupied Baldwin's position. Described by one historian as 'an inflammatory, one-sided, highly provocative propaganda broadsheet', the *Gazette* referred to the strikers as 'the enemy'; printed allegations of a Bolshevik plot; carried leading articles by Churchill so wild that Davidson, Deputy Chief Commissioner in charge of publicity, appealed for support from Baldwin and the Cabinet in censoring them; and advanced propositions that the king and many others saw as highly provocative and irresponsible (Rhodes James, 1981, p. 220–2). It undoubtedly contributed to the increasing ugliness of mood as the strike progressed.

Baldwin and Davidson had not fought for restraint lone-handed. When Churchill tried to induce the governor of the Bank of England to sequestrate union funds he was refused. Churchill and Birkenhead were also, during the closing days of the stoppage, the driving spirits behind a Trade Union Bill, to be rushed into law in a single day, declaring general strikes illegal. Many powerful and influential voices were raised against such timing. Salisbury, Conservative leader in the Lords, and A. J. Balfour, Lord President of the Council, questioned whether such precipitate action could be defended during what was being presented as a defence of parliamentary government. The Conservative Chief Whip found that a majority of his MPs were 'strongly against provocative action against the trade unions at this moment'. Some of the most senior and influential civil servants in Whitehall expressed alarm. Thomas Jones, deputy secretary to the Cabinet, Welsh Liberal Nonconformist and life-long member of the Labour Party, had the ear of Baldwin and added his own entreaties. Men close to the crown organised a message from the king. The proposal was dropped (Jones, 1969, pp. 44–7).

There were other disappointments for the far right. The strike proved a traumatic experience for the British Fascists. 'Here was the great test they had been awaiting.' Rushing to offer their help, they were mortified to have it refused unless they renounced the title of Fascists and dismantled their military organisation (Griffiths, 1983, p. 88). The resulting disagreement split the movement.

With the return to work, Baldwin included in his statements to the House of Commons (13 May) an appeal in support of the TUC: 'I will not countenance any attack on the part of any employers to use this present occasion for trying in any way to get reductions in wages ... or any increase of hours ...' The occasion called neither 'for malice nor for recrimination, nor for triumph' and he would not countenance an 'attack on the trade unions as such ... There can be no greater disaster than that there should be anarchy in the trade union world. It would be impossible, in our highly organized and highly developed system of industry, to carry on unless you had organizations which could speak for and bind the parties on both sides' (Baldwin, 1926, cols 1045–51). The strategy of control through accommodation and at least partial assimilation emerges unmistakably from these words.

But Baldwin had few sanctions to wield on such an issue and it was not to be expected that his stance would be followed by all employers. Advantage was unquestionably taken. Nevertheless, in Parliament, 'his own extremists listened and backed down, and in the country, slowly and reluctantly, the employers were induced to followed suit, although some companies still took the chance of ridding themselves of "troublesome" shop stewards and union men' (Middlemas and Barnes, 1969, p. 419). There was little attempt outside the coal industry to reduce wages, which remained roughly stable for another three years – and given the fall in the cost of living those in work were by 1929 better off than ever before.

A similar verdict can be passed on other aspects of the strike. For all Baldwin's efforts and those of the many other influential figures who shared his views, the occasion could hardly be without its ugly features and the sentimentalism which later made so much of football matches between police and strikers hardly conveys the tensions that were generated. 'There were numerous instances of baton charges by mounted and foot police against strike pickets and gatherings of strikers; and there was also a fair amount of licensed brutality on the part of volunteer special constables' (Miliband, 1973, p. 137). Yet compared with a figure of between 2½ and 3 million strikers there were only 4,000 prosecutions for actual, or incitement to, violence and only about a quarter of these resulted in prison sentences (A. J. P. Taylor, 1970, pp. 312–13).

In his handling of the General Strike, therefore, Baldwin symbolised and led the containment of pressures from both the farther left and the farther right. This containment lay within limits which the prevailing forces within the state had been working out by trial and error for a century. On the left, those believed to offer a genuine threat to the social order had it indicated to them that they faced implacable resistance. On the right, those eager to bid up the stakes of conflict with a view to smashing or at least completely cowing labour's industrial or political organisations had to be restrained in the interests of the policy that had long proved its value for order and property – the policy of preserving the institutions and ideology of a relatively tolerant constitutionalism and making it sufficiently worthwhile for organised labour to assimilate to it.

Since the introduction of manhood suffrage in 1918 the inducement to pursue this policy had been greatly sharpened by electoral considerations. The Conservative trade unionist had to be considered and it had long been clear that there were many middle-class voters who, while anxious to see the unions contained, would not support their being smashed. Awareness of these considerations was manifest even in the policy and propaganda of the government's Organisation for the Maintenance of Supplies (OMS), which in 1925 mobilised 'citizens . . . prepared to volunteer to maintain supplies and services in the event of a general strike'. Manifestly concerned to avoid any blatant demonstration of class hostility, the OMS 'was at great pains to emphasize that it was non-political and non-party, that it had no aggressive or provocative aims, that it was not formed to oppose the legitimate efforts of trade unions to better the conditions of their members; indeed it was "in complete sympathy with any constitutional actions to bring about a more equitable adjustment of social and economic conditions"'. Its council was given an impressive appearance of neutrality, there being no representatives of industry and finance, and a careful distance was kept from the British Fascists (Miliband, 1973, pp. 124–5).

The General Strike had offered further evidence, however, if such were needed, that the differences between those who, like Baldwin and Davidson (Chairman of the Conservative Party 1927–30), favoured this kind of strategy, and those who, like Churchill and Birkenhead, pressed more openly aggressive and bellicose policies, were differences of means, not of ends. Both factions were determined to secure a TUC surrender, but whereas Churchill and Birkenhead wanted to pursue this by, among other things, openly commandeering the BBC and running it as a government propaganda agency, Baldwin and Davidson saw that this would defeat its own ends by inspiring strikers and their sympathisers with automatic mistrust of all broadcast news. Since Reith, managing director, 'never doubted that the BBC should back the constitutional government to the full', arrangements were soon reached by which Davidson vetted all news bulletins, declaring afterwards that 'my unofficial control was complete'. The BBC's much-vaunted 'independence' was therefore something a good deal less impressive, being conditional on a docility which enabled the government to dominate the communications battle far more subtly and effectively than Churchill's methods would have done, while at the same time appearing to preserve its liberal virtue – and that of the BBC (Rhodes James, 1969, pp. 246–50).

The Strike's Significance for Britain's Industrial Relations

The strike has usually been judged an unqualified failure, but it probably deterred employers in other industries from attacking wages and as an impressive display of labour solidarity and power it can hardly have failed to leave a mark on political as well as industrial thinking. Yet arguably the most significant aspect of the episode was the way in which it revealed the continued predominance on both sides of those forces and traditions that were anxious to contain rather than bid up class conflict. From this point of view it illustrates continuity rather than marking a turning-point. The received opinion hitherto, however, has usually been very different. The strike has most often been seen as a major turning-point in Britain's industrial relations. Bullock, quoting Beatrice Webb's comment during the strike that its failure 'will be one of the most significant landmarks in the history of the British working class', considers it 'fully justified'. 'Future historians', she had written, 'will . . . regard it as the death-gasp of that pernicious doctrine of "workers' control" of public affairs through the trade unions and by the method of direct action'. Bullock agrees that the strike was a 'watershed in the history of the trade union movement between 1910 and 1940' (Bullock, 1960, p. 345). In Taylor's estimate, the strike, 'apparently the clearest display of the class war in British history, marked the moment when class war ceased to shape the pattern of British industrial relations' (A. J. P. Taylor, 1970, p. 318). For Miliband, the manner of the strike's collapse 'is immensely important in the history of the labour movement'. Among the consequences was 'the fact that the surrender immeasurably advanced the transformation of the workers' movement into a tame disciplined trade union and electoral interest'. Not only would the unions and Labour Party never again 'seek to exercise political influence against the government of the day by the use of the political weapon'; they would also 'shun militancy over *industrial* issues' (Miliband, 1973, p. 148). Beatrice Webb's comments were made during the strike, Bullock's in 1960, Taylor's in 1965, Miliband's in 1961.

Many other observers made similar comments. Such interpretations would not have held the field so long had there not been a great deal of apparently supportive evidence. And among this evidence was the fact that there was indeed a long period of relative industrial peace after the strike. There were, too, conciliatory moves by the TUC and an important group of employers towards *rapproachement*. Yet most union leaders had always preferred to avoid strikes if they could. If they became even more wary about them now it was not the experience of the General Strike alone that influenced them. The wartime and postwar changes in the structure of bargaining towards national settlements had been followed by a new pattern of strikes and lockouts. Industry-wide stoppages had been the exception before 1911, but between 1919 and 1926 there were seventeen in a wide range of major industries.

Clegg was the first to challenge the received view that 1926 was a great turning-point (Clegg, 1954). With arguments developed at some length, he suggested that the strike 'was not solely, or mainly, responsible' for the long period of relative peace which followed it; that other and more convincing explanations can be adduced. He agreed, however, that as a weapon 'the General Strike, even if it had not been rendered entirely obsolete, was stored right at the back of the arsenal of trade union weapons'. It remained, however, available. The Webbs themselves had written in 1920: 'We can imagine occasions that might, in the eyes of the trade union world, fully justify a general strike of non-economic or political character' – for example, if legislation were passed depriving the unions 'of the rights and liberties now conceded to them' or if the courts were to attack them by methods of their own (Webb and Webb, 1920, p. 672). There could be no finality in any judgement that none of these things could ever happen again.

Judgements that the failure of the strike pushed union leaders towards conciliatory collective negotiation and away from aggressive class-war tactics are suspect on two counts. Not only do they overlook that other factors account as plausibly for the relative industrial peace that followed; they overlook also that, even before the strike, class-war belligerence had rarely been the preferred method of trade union leaders who, on the whole, had chosen to lead their members, when given the chance, into peaceful disciplined procedures. Thus while it is true that the strike was followed by an extended period of industrial peace, Clegg's query as to whether 'this can be shown to be much more than an accidental coincidence' has to be answered in the negative.

It might, however, be objected that the strike certainly had one major consequence in the 1927 Trade Disputes and Trade Unions Act, seen by the left as vindictive and savage. There might also seem to be contradiction here of the judgement that political predominance within the Conservative Party lay with those concerned to mitigate rather than intensify class conflict. Yet given the party mood the Act was probably the least that Baldwin and his fellow-moderates could have introduced. Violent emotions were displayed at the October 1926 party conference and it is probably safe to say that no party leadership seeking to stand pat could have long survived. Baldwin fought delaying actions until 1927 in order that the more extreme proposals might lose impetus, such as that pressed by majority opinion within the NCEO, for example, which 'sought a wholesale reconstruction of union law by the effective removal of the immunities regarding picketing and inducements to breaches of contract given to the unions under the 1906 Trade Disputes Act' (Garside, 1977, p. 258). There is no evidence, however, that Baldwin favoured doing nothing; a certain token baring of the teeth was required. Although there were influential voices within the party who urged that the Bill should not be wholly restrictive and repressive but should include a note of positive reconciliation, the Bill remained restrictive and 'it must be concluded that if Baldwin had wished otherwise he would have tried harder to amend it' (Middlemas and Barnes, 1969, p. 449).

Even so, the Act was more irritant than blood-bath. Most references get the Act wrong by describing two categories of strikes supposedly declared illegal: all sympathetic strikes and all those designed to coerce the government. In fact to be illegal a strike had to be both sympathetic and designed or calculated to coerce the government either directly or by inflicting hardship on the community. This was by its nature a very small category of stoppages. With reference to the political levy, contracting in was substituted for contracting out. Civil service unions were prohibited from affiliating to outside bodies – in practical terms the TUC. Additional restrictions were imposed on picketing. Public authorities were forbidden to require, as a condition of employment, either membership or non-membership of a trade union – a gesture in the direction of even-handed symmetry. The Act was intensely irksome to some labour leaders, especially Bevin, and its repeal, amid some fanfare, was among the first legislative acts of the postwar Labour government in 1946. The TUC and Labour Party mounted a massive campaign of opposition as the Bill went through Parliament, with 650 bookings of national speakers alone, covering a total of 1,150 meetings and demonstrations (Milne-Bailey, 1929, p. 404), but beyond the activist ranks the Act aroused little of the wrath predicted. Davidson, then chairman of the Conservative Party, attributed the 'complete fiasco' of the TUC's campaign to 'the very thorough educational propaganda we distributed throughout the country', 9 million pamphlets putting the government's case being issued by Conservative Central Office (Rhodes James, 1969, p. 297). The *Manchester Guardian*, no supporter of the government, considered this relatively quiet reception curious enough to warrant comment (Middlemas and Barnes, 1969, p. 450). Tom Jones, deputy secretary of the Cabinet and a Labour supporter, commenting in his diary on a repealing Bill prepared by the Labour government in 1931 but never carried through, reported 'no great enthusiasm among the rank and file . . . for the . . . Bill. Questions never asked about it' (Jones, 1969, p. 265). It is worth noting, as another indication of prevalent moods, a letter written to Baldwin only two years later by Harold Laski. 'I should like you to feel that outside the Conservative ranks, there are many socialists who, like myself, not only feel grateful for the quality of the human directness you bring to our political life, but also recognize gladly that the spirit you represent has made the peaceful evolution of English politics much more certain than it would otherwise have been' (Middlemas and Barnes, 1969, pp. 572–3).

The Mond–Turner Conferences

Many commentators have described the Mond–Turner conferences as a consequence of the General Strike and as a sign, despite their failure, that the strike was some sort of turning-point. We have already noted, however, that the initiative began in the preceding year, and was no more than yet another attempt to draw the unions into positive-sum collaboration. The 1927 Act did not long interrupt the initiative, which had been resumed soon after the strike. Some kind of attempt to re-knit the social fabric was probably to be expected in any case after the precedents of 1895, 1900, 1911 and 1919, with their gatherings of prominent figures from both sides either during or following a period of acute industrial conflict. In this case, renewed feelers were put out in December 1926 with Weir, privately prompted by Baldwin, making a plea in the House of Lords for an informal round-table meeting with a few union leaders. Though Bevin and Pugh considered the present mood not right, Baldwin continued his behind-the-scenes prodding and private conversations between leading TUC figures and a few industrialists began early in 1927. The exchanges ended for the time being in May when it was clear that the government was going ahead with its Trade Disputes Bill. Only a few months later, however, when the TUC met in September, George Hicks was put up by Citrine to propose in his presidential speech an exchange of views between the General Council and the employers.

This is usually taken as the beginning of what became known as the Mond–Turner conferences. Although they were to have little practical outcome they remain of considerable interest in the account of Britain's industrial relations system, in that they represent an attempt by some industrialists and some prominent union leaders to draw the conduct of industrial relations towards a new pattern which they saw as the progressive next step. They failed; had they succeeded many observers would no doubt have been tempted to see the new pattern as 'inevitable', for it was certainly not without plausibility and was undoubtedly viewed by its protagonists on both sides, as it had been by the Positivists and the Webbs, as the obvious next stage in a 'natural development'.

Citrine had early confirmation of his doubts as to whether a sufficient basis of mutual confidence and goodwill existed. While the informal soundings between Mond and Bevin proceeded during 1927, he had approached the NCEO and FBI but met only 'suspicion and pessimism, and even hostility'. Then came the Hicks proposal, inspired by Citrine, at the September Congress. The NCEO and the EEF returned the same frigid reception, but in November came an invitation from Mond and other influential industrialists to participate in joint talks covering the 'entire field of industrial reorganization and industrial relations'. Mond and Weir had mobilised, with Baldwin's private encouragement, as powerful and impressive a group as could be assembled. Between them, the twenty-four held directorships in 189 companies; the chairmanship in 98. They included two past presidents, six vice-presidents and three other members of the FBI executive council, as well as the chairman and past chairman of the NCEO. Eventually the number grew to thirty-six. The industries covered included chemicals, coal, gas, electricity, flour-milling, oil, engineering and shipbuilding, cars, steel, textiles, rayon and transport (Bullock, 1960, pp. 397–8), though the predominant influences appear to have been the large-scale, science-based industries and the newer domestically oriented and capital-intensive sectors (Garside, 1977, p. 259). The inner group which met the TUC's Industrial Committee – Mond, Weir, Ashfield, Courtauld, Willey, Milne-Watson, Hirst, Londonderry – were predominantly of the type of industrialist who had already made some effort to work with the unions and systematise personnel policies, though this must not necessarily be taken to imply a benign view of organised labour – Weir, for example, shared at least some of the attitudes of Sir Allan Smith, class warrior of the EEF. Public service and patronage of charities and the arts was also a marked characteristic. Most of them, along with some of the outer group, had held 'government posts or served on Royal and other Commissions and Committees, some of them many times over' (Charles, 1973, pp. 275–7).

On one level, the talks began promisingly enough for the participants. After the first full conference in January 1928 a joint sub-committee met ten times in the next few weeks and issued an interim report which, *inter alia*, declared the TUC's right to speak for the whole movement 'on any question of national policy affecting that movement'; approved the extension of collective bargaining to other matters of common interest; proposed a National Industrial Council comprising TUC, FBI and NCEO; criticised the gold standard as an inadequate basis for credit; and offered suggestions with respect to unemployment. But it was on the subject of rationalisation that the report ventured furthest into ground that for the NCEO and the EEF, in particular, was specially sensitive. Rationalisation 'was inevitable and beneficial but steps should be taken to counter the displacement of labour and deterioration of working standards it could involve. It was for employers and trade unions to co-operate in meeting the demands of the new situations and nothing which did not have the full agreement of both parties should be put into practice' (ibid., p. 288). It is safe to say that the closing sentiment must have chilled the blood of the die-hards who determined the predominant tone of the NCEO, such as Sir Allan Smith. They spoke for a tradition forged from fierce public struggles and many more covert guerrilla skirmishes with restrictionist craftsmen determined to defend jobs, status and earnings against technical and organisational innovation. Smith himself in 1922 had led another onslaught on the engineering craftsmen. Disputes about overtime and manning – which reveal little hard evidence of far-left influence – widened into a general conflict about the prerogatives of management and Smith had convinced the engineering employers that if managerial rights were ever to be placed on a firm footing the depression provided the opportunity. 'The issue was the traditional rights claimed by craftsmen to control their own jobs'. The lockout had ended in the unions' defeat and acceptance of the employers' terms, at least on paper. A little later, when further discussions on manning had been allowed by the employers to lapse, they 'may have begun to wonder whether their victory had been so complete as they had supposed' (Clegg, forthcoming). For employers with this background the idea of publicly declaring that change must be conditional on labour consent was itself guaranteed to confirm their hostility to the Mond–Turner explorations. But there were additional fears. 'In 1928 the Ministry of Labour noted that the reason for the NCEO's objection to the initiative taken by Mond . . . was the memory of the shock registered by the threat of legislation in 1919 on minimum wages and the standard week' (Charles, 1973, p. 253).

Mistrust was also manifest among the unions. The far left talked of class betrayal through collaboration with the class enemy and Citrine referred later to 'considerable opposition in the trade union world', commenting that 'many sincere trade unionists were puzzled'. Few in the higher ranks did not feel sceptical as to whether anything really constructive could result (Citrine, 1964, p. 247). Faced with these resistances and doubts on both sides, even well-wishers like Sir Horace Wilson, permanent secretary in the Ministry of Labour, expressed pessimism as to what would happen 'when things get lower down amongst the employers' organizations'. At the annual Trades Union Congress of 1928, which approved the report, Bevin pointed out that much union opposition was very similar to that of Sir Allan Smith of the EEF, 'an organization which had been formed to prevent progressives getting away from the old pattern'. Yet the report offered, in his view, an intelligent and rational way of exerting the maximum possible pressure towards their aims. Anyone, he argued, who believed that British trade unionists could be led in any other way than along constitutional negotiated lines was deceiving himself – they were most of them far less belligerent than even the assembled delegates.

Fully sanctioned by Congress to proceed, union leaders continued discussions. But in February 1929 the NCEO and FBI, in a joint letter, rejected the report and specifically the proposal for a National Industrial Council, insisting that 'labour' questions must be separated from 'trade' questions. This effectively killed the project, which had hinged on the explicit linking of pay and productivity. In December 1929 the Mond group formally disbanded. For the second time since the war the dominant voices among the organised employers had defeated an attempt by small minorities on both sides to reconstruct the industrial relations system. All that could be hoped for now was a decent tidying up of the wreckage. Too abrupt and violent a breakdown would weaken the union moderates and present the employers in a bad light. A clumsy procedure was devised for allocating issues for discussion between the TUC and one or other of the two employers' organisations, and for a while during 1930 these arrangements staggered along achieving nothing of consequence.

Meanwhile, the slump was deepening and increasing unemployment; by 1931 the TUC was in revolt against a National Government's economic policy that was openly supported by the organised employers and the City. The NCEO and FBI led the chorus of those who argued that the economic crisis called for a cut in social security expenditure, especially unemployment benefit, and who advocated renewed wage cutting as the best means to overcome world depression and restore national competitiveness. The attempt to reconstruct the pattern of Britain's industrial relations at both national and workplace levels had failed. Citrine salvaged something in the form of regular personal meetings with Forbes Watson, director of the NCEO, who at first was always 'metaphorically looking over his shoulder with a nervous dread that some of his members might spy him', an uneasiness which Citrine shared (Citrine, 1964, p. 251). The grand design, however, was dead.

It had been killed by the powerful groups of employers in the basic exporting industries who were still in control of the NCEO and who were more influenced by traditional relationships at the industry and workplace level than were the driving spirits among the Mond employers. The basic industries had their voices in the Mond group but they were far from representative. There was little love lost, in fact, between the general run of employers' associations and those emerging large enterprises whose leaders were seeking to develop personnel policies which they saw as more sophisticated and more appropriate to their own conditions. 'Employers are not by any means always well represented by their existing associations, many of which are quite out of date', wrote Samuel Courtauld in 1942. 'They were created long since to meet conditions now vanished, but they are very difficult to replace or reconstruct, and they still hold the field – especially in government eyes – by virtue of their official titles'

Courtauld, 1949, p. 8). Courtauld's proposition could, however, be turned on its head with the argument that the associations represented many of their members only too well in their lack of entrepreneurial dynamic. The ideas, concepts and activities of the 'new management movement con-tinued to remain alien to the great mass of practising managers and employers' and membership of the various management institutes remained minimal. J. A. Bowie in 1930 chastised 'the great bulk of British employers . . . for their conservative individualism, opposition to business education, ignorance of research findings, nepotism, and secretiveness' (Child, 1969, p. 103).

It will not do, however, to portray the failure of these attempts at reconstructing the industrial relations system as being due merely to employer stupidity. It was easier, for a variety of reasons, for industrialists in the newer, science-based, capital-intensive sectors to take a more hopeful view of management–worker relations. Many employers in the old staple industries had been reared in the history of a long experience shared with their trade union opposite numbers. It was an experience of keenly contested wage rates and restrictionist union or workplace strategies born of struggles to defend otherwise unprotected wage-earners against forces which they had no hand in determining. Now that they were being given the chance, some unions might well feel that they had nothing to lose and something to gain by securing a voice in the discussion of some, at least, of the relevant decisions. Many employers, on the other hand, saw in the proposed macro-level of discussion nothing for themselves but a series of rear-guard actions against union spokesmen seeking to enlarge the area of encroachment on employer prerogative. There was nothing in the employ-ers' experience – shaped by many generations of employers and workers before them – which encouraged any hope that union leaders would be free to bring a positive-sum game approach to joint deliberations, whatever enlightened sentiments might emanate from the TUC's general secretary. It still seemed to them that they would find themselves confronting, at best, defensive if constitutional restrictionism; at worst, pressure from left-wing subversives. The same considerations applied at the workplace level. Smith voiced the lowest-common-denominator sentiment of many employers in the older strongly unionised industries with his bellicose language and habit of referring to the workers as 'the enemy'. And one did not invite an enemy into one's inner sanctum to discuss matters that were believed to lie at the heart of organisational health and success. In other words, some trade union activists might be more than ready to accept a foothold at any level where employers made decisions – though others might be nervous of appearing to be drawn into accepting responsibility for them. But employers, looking around at the behaviour of most trade unionists as they knew them, might often decide that they themselves had little to gain and a great deal to lose.

MacDonald and the Economic Advisory Council

Concurrently with this petering out of the Mond initiative there had proceeded the rise and fall of another by Ramsay MacDonald. Galvanised, in all probability, by Lloyd George's promotion of that 'power-house of new ideas' which produced the *Liberal Industrial Report* of 1928, Mac-Donald set up during 1929–30 the Economic Advisory Council, a body of uncertain purpose whose discussions included industrial rationalisation and renewal. J. H. Thomas, railwaymen's leader and now Lord Privy Seal, described Britain's industrial problem as having its roots in the individualistic attitude of capital and labour. 'The difficulty is that both are selfish and refuse to look beyond their narrow interest.' The country was suffering from 'absurd trade union restrictions' which the unions had adopted in self-defence. Snowden, as Chancellor, echoed an employer's view that the unions 'had won enormous privileges through long years of fighting' but that it 'was now necessary that many of these should be surrendered. How could they be made to feel that what they were giving up would be for the good of the trade union and of the country? That was a very great difficulty.' Snowden urged upon Citrine that a 'new type of trade unionism was required which would bring a new message to the workmen and induce a different attitude to their work, and secure their active co-operation with the employers in their common interest. He would like to see workmen recognizing waste and inefficiency as no less harmful to the best interests of the workmen than to the employer.' Citrine replied: 'If I were to start to discuss getting rid of trade union restrictions I should have to ask for a *quid pro quo*. The trade unionist is weighed down with a sense of insecurity, and he is kept outside the business, and has not been allowed inside to see how far relaxations would really help him ...' A disposition towards co-operation 'did not now widely prevail among employers' (Jones, 1969, pp. 128, 221–2, 228). What this unsuccessful venture demonstrates is that the unions did not have to wait until after the Second World War to find Labour governments urging them to dismantle their workplace defences in the 'national interest', but offering them no changes of any consequence in the economic and social structures with which they had to conduct their bargaining.

'Corporate Bias'

Britain's pattern of industrial relations therefore proved resistant to attempts by powerful and influential figures on both sides of industry and by government to modify it in ways which would have significantly changed its nature. Yet although Bevin's design for fully fledged tripartite decision-making at top level had been frustrated, there continued the process by which the three interest groups took cautious soundings of each other when occasion required, often behind the scenes and independently of public political divergence. The unions and the organised employers each felt the other to be specially favoured by governments when it came to consultation: Forbes Watson of the NCEO complaining to Citrine that the government kept 'his organization too much at arm's length'; agreeable news to the TUC who had long supposed that employers had instant access (Citrine, 1964, p. 251). Nevertheless, government policy developed, on the whole, in some accord with both sets of institutions. Just as

Labour governments set out to convince big business and the City of their respectability, so Baldwin was careful not to make appointments to his second ministry which would antagonise union opinion (Middlemas, 1979, p. 193).

Both Conservative and Labour, therefore, were proceeding in terms of what has been called a 'corporate bias'; an expression which employs the word 'corporate' in its weakest sense. We have already registered that governments and government departments who sought to preserve the traditional style of British rule had long considered it judicious or helpful, when preparing legislation affecting a well-organised, articulate and powerful interest, to contemplate consulting its top-level spokesmen at some stage of the proceedings. Thereby they could ensure, if they chose, that their measure was being shaped in the light of full awareness as to the perceptions and policies of the interest in question. Though this might irritate parliamentary purists it could seem no more than commonsense to legislators on those occasions when they sought the highest common measure of agreement. This fell a long way short of that much stronger sense of corporatism by which the spokesmen of the interest conclude a deal or pact with government – or with top-level spokesmen of some other interest – and explicitly or implicitly include in the deal a guarantee that its terms will be accepted by, or imposed on, their members, followers, or affiliated organisations. In the British context the limits of corporatism in this strong sense were soon reached; neither the NCEO or the TUC felt confident of their ability to deliver.

Admittedly, the TUC had been strengthened in 1920 with some notion of establishing an authoritative union centre. The 1919 rail strike, with its vast implications for the economy and for the unions, was a key factor in an attempt to invest in the TUC the power to co-ordinate industrial actions. The newly formed General Council was authorised to hire full-time staff to handle an expanded range of functions which included helping to co-ordinate industrial action, promoting the settlement of inter-union disputes, speaking for the union movement in general, and conducting relations with international trade unionism. But the affiliated unions continued to deny the TUC sufficient authority to give coherence and force to its leadership. General Council members – general secretaries or presidents of affiliated unions – were only willing to authorise enlargements of TUC authority when convinced that collective action would either enhance or protect their personal or their union's interests. It was within these limits that Citrine sought to 'try to expand the activities of the TUC until we could establish an efficient system whereby the TUC would be regularly and naturally consulted by whatever government was in power on any subject of direct concern to the unions' (Citrine, 1964, p. 238).

Governments likewise were limited. It was one thing to recognise that powerful interests capable of disrupting the peaceful functioning of the established order – or simply of significantly affecting voting behaviour – must be contained within the bounds of the system by means of consultation and concession. But the possibilities of bold change and innovation were limited by the fact that if the leaders of the interests could not carry their membership there was not much the state could do to impose its preferences. It was therefore by means of a very gingerly and sensitive corporatism that the state supplemented its other processes of maintaining the status quo. Long experience had equipped the British state with considerable skill in preserving the delicate balances required for this preservation of inequality and privilege.

In conducting this process, neither the government nor the other major organised interests were likely to accept as given the present opinions or perceptions of their constituents. 'Opinion management' became increasingly important for them after the First World War and was greatly facilitated by mass readership of the press and by wireless, cinema newsreels and, later, television. 'Awareness of the need to take public opinion into consideration did not lead politicians and civil servants on to acceptance of popular democracy, but rather the reverse . . . ' The political élite superimposed, on general elections and party warfare, 'continuous contract' – by which is meant 'the fine measurement of opinion and its careful management by propaganda', together with a degree of mystification about the political process. The other two 'governing institutions' followed suit as far as they could. Thus, 'backward-looking in its aims, gradual in method, revisionistic in theory, the new system accommodated itself to change by moving at the least speed commensurate with the interests of each governing institution, while each vied with the rest to ostracise dissent and manage, or accommodate, mass opinion' (Middlemas, 1979, pp. 369, 377).

Modernisation and Scientific Management

The system continued, therefore, as in other periods of Britain's history, to purchase political and social stability at the price of diminished innovation and hyper-cautious attitudes to capital investment. Although entrepreneurial and innovatory zeal were far from absent from the British economy they were less in evidence than elsewhere, and this relieved the industrial relations system of pressures and strains which might well have left it modified in certain respects. Much of the wartime burst of technical and scientific innovation in Britain had dissipated with the peace. Government sponsorship was withdrawn; the 'central organizations were . . . swiftly dismantled; the supply of government funds was . . . cut off; few of the great advances made were . . . properly exploited. The old traditions of *laissez-faire* and free trade were to prove more durable than the new technology created by the war' (Rhodes James, 1978, p. 359).

Such government intervention as came later was facilitative and permissive rather than positively promotional. It was certainly far from authoritarian. 'The National Government might easily have been Britain's authoritarian response to the experience of the great depression. It was not so' (Middlemas and Barnes, 1969, p. 1077). This, too, spared the industrial relations system such disturbance as would have resulted. So much more firmly were the unions now integrated into the nation's institutional structure that any open attack by the state upon their restrictionist dispositions was even more unthinkable for most of the influential members of the Establishment than it had been several decades earlier. Moreover, as noted earlier, the relative weakness of the entrepreneurial drive throughout substantial sectors of British industry was another variable in the equation. The 'British management tradition and ethnocentrism complemented perfectly the worker conviction that only the restraint of output would prevent labour exploitation' (Merkle, 1980, p. 220). This conviction was receiving articulate and reasoned expression at the hands of trade union civil servants like W. Milne-Bailey, secretary of the TUC's Research and Economic Department. 'Trade union requirements do, in fact, lead to lower production than would otherwise be possible', but they were 'necessary safeguards against the various methods by which the workers' standard of life and of working conditions may be lowered, and they have been proved by much bitter experience to be absolutely essential . . . The worker cannot afford to take long views.' If security of employment and earnings was not guaranteed when innovation was introduced, 'it was idle to hope that restrictionism could be eliminated' (Milne-Bailey, 1924, p. 94).

Employers continued, on the whole, to show little inclination to grapple with these dispositions either by coercive frontal assault or by offering organised labour a high-consumption utopia based on a high-wage, high-output, mass-production technology. The philosophy underlying Scientific Management in its extended form offered just such a message. As already noted, however, it was not one to which the British situation lent itself. Success required either a situation where workers freely offered submission to management leadership, or one where management was prepared to run the risks of enforcing it. In the British scene neither alternative represented the prevalent mode. 'Technical retardation' continued to be noticeable. It was

> paralleled on the one side by the swift proliferation of an efficiency-inhibiting growth of closely-interwoven trade association and cartel controls, the effects of which upon production were generally of a restrictionist character, and on the other – in the face of chronic unemployment – by a wide-ranging and deeply rooted aversion to job-destroying technical change in trade union circles. Along with this, compared with either German or American practice, went little attention to industrial research, scientific management, standardization in the field of consumer goods, or technical rationalization on an industry-wide basis. (Merkle, 1980, p. 235)

Worker responses to such attempts as were made to introduce the Scientific Management style are exemplified in the reception given to the Bedaux efficiency system of work study, brought over from America in the late 1920s. The results showed that

> in the depths of the depression, British workers, both men and women, in a range of industries, in some instances poorly organized, were capable of putting up a spirited resistance to the introduction of methods of work and payment whose assumptions and methods of application

violated their traditions and neglected their interests; and that in many instances their resistance forced the withdrawal or substantial modification of the methods to which they objected. (Clegg, forthcoming)

Even those industrialists deemed 'progressive' who pursued with most vigour the 'modernization and adaptation of their modes of organization' – a process certainly evident in some specialised sectors – tended to emphasise the aspect of cost reductions rather than that of maximising output and sales. Mond was perhaps the leading advocate here, and his stress on the role of management in the reconciliation of labour and capital was in the context of cost cutting, not of maximisation of production. There was significance also in the fact that, in Britain, 'progressivism' among employers and managers tended to be linked, as in the case of the Quaker manufacturers, with the strain of thought that stressed managerial duties as well as rights – and duties included concern for the welfare of labour. All in all, therefore, the British economy was hardly a fruitful soil for Scientific Management. During the 'era of the accelerating campaign for Scientific Management' in Germany and America, the 'unique cultural and social conditions in Britain' prevented it from taking root. During the 1930s and after, one publication after another, remarking on Britain's decreasing ability to compete and the cultural attitudes that underlay it, pleaded for business education and 'increased status for management specialists'. Traditional class attitudes continued to prevail, however, over the *arriviste* bustle of a rising class of Taylorite efficiency engineers (Merkle, 1980, pp. 230, 234, 240). Reconciliation of labour and capital was certainly being achieved in Britain. It was being achieved, however, not through the technocratically based management solution offered by the full Scientific Management philosophy, but through the time-honoured British method of concession, manipulation and containment on the constitutional and political level. Taken together with the other constituent elements in the British technique of rule, it did little for modernisation. 'For all the talk of "managing the economy", the gap between the politicians' advocacy of expansion and the cartelization that actually went on grew rapidly: the price of avoidance of conflict turned out to be political compromise, industrial feather bedding, and low overall growth' (Middlemas, 1979, p. 230).

Challenges to the System

As the British economy moved into the 1930s, however, with their growing burdens of slump, mass unemployment and general mood of disorganisation, radical groups emerged on both the political left and right who made it clear that they did not view the traditional structures, conventions and values of the British strategy of rule with the same unquestioning reverence predominantly displayed by Conservative and still more by Labour governments. Skidelsky refers to the way in which, after 1931, 'under the impact of economic catastrophe, imaginative people of all political persuasions were starting to flee from the liberal centre of politics' (Skidelsky, 1981b, pp. 271–2). The challenges they offered had profound implications for the industrial relations system and for the trade unions in both their industrial and political operations.

The 1929 Labour ministry had pursued the same financial and fiscal orthodoxy as before and when, in August 1931, a European banking crisis had seemingly put the international financial structure in danger of collapse, MacDonald and Snowden prepared a plan for severe deflation 'in order to restore the country's fiscal integrity' and sought the TUC's support. Pressing instead an expansionist policy, the TUC refused and this strengthened the attitude of Henderson and others in the Cabinet who had doubts.

The unions emerged from the subsequent crisis in far better shape organisationally and psychologically than the parliamentary Labour Party. The extent to which certain party leaders now had some difficulty in remembering whose interests were supposed to head their priority list is illustrated by one of MacDonald's utterances on the subject of the proposed 10 per cent cut in unemployment benefit, the precipitating cause of the 1931 Cabinet crisis: '. . . if a scheme that imposed such grave sacrifices on other sections of the community left the unemployed in a privileged position', he told the Cabinet, referring to the public expenditure cuts demanded by American bankers before extending credits, 'the Labour party might lose moral prestige' (Miliband, 1973, p. 178). And Snowden's ideological *naïveté* can be gauged by the fact that, like many other Labour leaders, he supposed finance to be a neutral subject which had nothing to do with politics. Of Montagu Norman, governor of the Bank of England, he wrote: 'I know nothing at all about his politics. I do not know if he has any' (A. J. P. Taylor, 1970, p. 273).

Trade union leaders, by contrast, never forgot what they were in business to do and a few of them at least, especially Bevin after his experience on the Macmillan Committee on Finance and Industry (1929–31), were groping towards a Keynesian view of the relations between investment, employment and monetary policy. Despite a 10 per cent loss of membership between 1929 and 1933 and a weakening of bargaining position there was no panic among the union leadership, a situation to which several factors contributed. They were helped by the fact that in most industries the economic condition of workers in full-time employment 'improved as rapidly during this depression as in any other period of four years in British history for which figures are available' – an improvement due to rising productivity and falling prices of food and raw materials (Clegg, forthcoming). Even the weakness resulting from membership losses was more nominal than real – the proportion of the employed labour force that was unionised fell little. Union authority was less impaired than might have been expected and mass wage undercutting was inconceivable in most organised industries and towns. This owed something to the National Unemployed Workers' Movement under a Communist leadership which refused to sanction undercutting (Hannington, 1936), but also something to the unwillingness of employers to face another costly clash by trying to impose drastic wage cuts (Pollard, 1969, pp. 113–14).

The relative integrity of organisation and purpose with which the trade union movement emerged from the crisis and the worst of the slump proved to have two major consequences. First, it permitted the continuing predominance among TUC leadership of those who, while doffing the cap to a vague but persistent vision of a fairer and more humane society, directed their practical energies towards securing an economic environment within which the unions could exercise their independent bargaining and political functions more effectively and safely. Labour's parliamentary weakness gave them a unique opportunity to press their views on the party. Thus was renewed an alliance which had often been under considerable strain since the early 1920s.

Renewal was facilitated by the fact that the terms in which the TUC visualised the desirable future had much in common with the cautious constitutionalism favoured by predominant strains within the party. The General Council's resolution at the 1931 Congress expressing support for 'a planned and regulated economy' meant not detailed supervision and regimentation but 'the intelligent organization of production, distribution and finance in the interests of the whole community'. This was confirmed in a report submitted to Congress in 1932: *Trade Unionism and the Control of Industry*, which revived the Mond–Turner idea of a tripartite National Industrial Council with a policy-making role through which they might hope to pursue full employment and the control of investment. The report rejected the 'more ideal programme' of the complete socialisation of the economy and the elimination of private enterprise. Only certain industries and services (including the banks) were appropriate for socialisation. It rejected, too, the demand for 'workers' control'. Socialised industries were to be run by public corporations administered by professional expert managements free from 'political pressures', with governing boards appointed solely by merit and not on any basis of 'representation of interests'. Such proposals were much too conservative for many delegates and were attacked at several subsequent Congresses for failing to be sufficiently socialistic and for making no demands for workplace 'industrial democracy'. Yet there was little resistance from rank and file workers, who were 'far more interested in finding or keeping a job than in the control of decisions affecting their job by a workshop democracy' (Clegg and Chester, 1953, p. 12). It was the TUC's policies which were to prevail.

The second major consequence of the union movement's resilience was that the necessary power and confidence were forthcoming with which to fend off threats to union functions, serious or otherwise, from both left and right. The Communist Minority Movement had been brought under control, but there emerged in 1932 an Independent Labour Party declaration, borne of the widespread feeling throughout the Labour movement of having been tricked out of office by a 'bankers' ramp', that the strict constitutional niceties were no longer enough. The ILP had 'always recognized', declared a *Statement of Policy* in that year, 'that the approach to Socialism could not be made by parliamentary methods only ... the critical circumstances demand that socialists must be prepared to organize mass industrial action as an additional means to the attainment of their objectives and realize that the development of a capitalist dictatorship may compel the resort to extra-constitutional methods'. Disaffiliation from the Labour Party soon followed, for Labour Party leadership underwent no kind of ideological transformation under the impact of 1931 and remained totally and exclusively committed to parliamentary constitutionalism. This commitment remained in the form embodied in the 1928 statement, *Labour and the Nation*, which had asserted that 'the sole escape from the difficulties at present surrounding the nation is to be found in the accept-ance without reservations or qualifications of the full implications of democracy in their social and economic, no less than in their political significance', and that the party stood, 'it need hardly be said, for the unquestioned supremacy of the House of Commons'.

For the unions the ILP declaration was alarming. It raised the prospect that attempts might be made to mobilise industrial action in pursuit of political objectives which might not necessarily originate within, or be approved by, the unions themselves, thereby cutting across union lines of authority, disrupting established negotiating arrangements, and seriously prejudicing relations with employers. But worse was to come so far as the unions were concerned. After the break with the Labour Party in July 1932 many ILP members joined the Socialist League, which appealed to a wide spectrum of responses to the events of 1931, ranging from near-Communists to some barely left of centre who could not resist feelings of frustration and doubt about the Queensberry rules which appeared especi-ally to disadvantage Labour governments.

Formed in 1932, it attracted some prominent figures. R. H. Tawney and G. D. H. Cole, along with others, had come to believe 'that 1931 had destroyed the implicit contract on which a parliamentary constitution rested'; Stafford Cripps stated explicitly that it was 'no good pretending that Socialism can ever be accomplished by our existing parliamentary methods', and Harold Laski talked of the need to take vast powers, legislate by ordinance and decree, and 'suspend the classic formulae of normal opposition' (Middlemas and Barnes, 1969, pp. 693–4). The ruling class, argued Cripps, would go to almost any length to defeat parlia-mentary action 'if the issue is . . . the continuance of their financial and political control'. For the first time in the history of the Labour movement in the twentieth century, the notion that a parliamentary majority might not be enough gained a certain currency outside the ranks of Marxists and near-Marxists (Miliband, 1973, pp. 197–8). Such sentiments were strengthened by the Nazi overthrow of Weimar in 1933, which greatly increased doubts about a peaceful and parliamentary transition to social-ism. Fascism would be tempting even for Britain's ruling classes, it was thought, if they failed to defeat a challenge to their power and privilege within the framework of parliamentary government, so bitter resistance must be expected in the event of a serious attempt at socialist transformation.

For most trade union and Labour Party leaders, all this was so remote both from present political realities and from their own far more modest reformist hopes as to seem no more than a parlour game. Since they had no intention of attempting a socialist transformation the alleged uselessness of the parliamentary method for achieving it left them unmoved. The Socialist Leaguers did not, however, leave them unworried. What disturbed them was what had disturbed for nearly a century those labour leaders anxious to build up the organisational strength, status, security and functions of institutions which pursued incremental reforms within the broad framework of the status quo. It was the fear that to offer any overt threat to constitutional procedures and conventions might deliver them into the hands of their enemies on the farther right, who needed only just such an excuse to throw up their hands in holy horror as they proceeded to defend with violence the 'national heritage' against wicked subversions. 'If the line of argument implicit in what had been said by Sir Stafford Cripps had been in operation during the last century', Citrine told Socialist Leaguers during a private discussion, 'there would have been no Labour movement and no trade union movement'. Once the Labour movement subscribed to the principle that a government had the right to override all opposition by whatever means in its power, it was difficult to see how an independent trade union movement could continue. 'Such reasoning would justify the present National Government in overriding minority opinion completely, both in the House of Commons and out of it, including, presumably, trade union opinion.' References to Socialist League utterances 'were now all carefully annotated in the Speaker's Notes sent out from the Conservative Central Office'. If 'our opponents ... seriously believe that we have abandoned democratic methods and intend to establish what they regard as a dictatorship', the effect 'inevitably would be that they would establish a dictatorship of their own long before we had any opportunity to do so' (Citrine, 1964, pp. 296–300).

There need be no surprise that at Westminster Baldwin 'spent much of his time in the smoking room with the solid trade unionists whose worth he knew and whose opinions he valued' (Middlemas and Barnes, 1969, p. 694). What they told him no doubt confirmed his judgement that the revolutionary thrust within the British working class was very limited. He and the rest of the National government played the situation with no small skill. He went out of his way to give Labour the fullest opportunity for debate and opposition and was known to administer savage rebukes to those of his own party who insulted or showed contempt for the handful of Labour members. The Conservative Party did not indulge in the reactionary repression which some of their opponents predicted and made scarcely any attempts to exploit their enormous majority.

The Socialist League therefore made few dents in Labour Party aims and methods. There were much-diluted echoes of league utterances in a 1934 Labour Party publication, *For Socialism and Peace*, which declared that such traditional procedures of the House of Commons as facilitated obstruction must be reformed and that the House of Lords must go altogether. The Party Executive remained, however, 'increasingly worried and embarrassed' by the tone of league speeches and writings. Cripps had even breathed upon the sacred ark of the British covenant. 'We shall have to overcome opposition from Buckingham Palace as well.' Amid a flurry of party disclaimers, Cripps 'precipitately retreated' (Miliband, 1973, pp. 208–9). The end came in 1937 when the league invited its own destruction by participating in a 'United Front' with the Communists, now proscribed by the Labour Party. The party expelled the Socialist League, which thereupon dissolved, though minor reverberations rumbled on for several years.

The fear of some prominent figures within the union movement that league talk would give a handle to their enemies therefore came to nothing, for reasons which probably owe no small amount to the kind of leadership Baldwin gave the Conservative Party. Over the same period, however, and beyond, there was talk of a very different persuasion which likewise carried profound implications for union functions and the industrial relations system. Within some Conservative thinking, atomistic liberal individualism still seemed, as it had in an earlier period, irrelevant to twentieth-century politics and economy. A composite portrait of this freshly vocal radical Conservatism reveals a renewed public airing being given to ideas and sentiments that had accompanied the social imperialist movement in the late nineteenth and early twentieth centuries. The British style of minimum government, the absence of a strong concept of the state, and the squabbles and compromises of party-political democracy: all came under condemnation from some quarters as producing an inability to cope with the powerful economic forces currently sapping the country's strength and pride. Class conflict conducted by organised labour was seen as fatally dividing the nation. Private-enterprise capitalism itself did not always escape. Some of these right-wing voices were as prepared to savage the 'bankers' ramp' as the general strike. Anti-semitism provided a frequent scapegoat for the country's – indeed the world's – corruption, decadence, and moral and physical flabbiness.

Within this context of contempt for parliamentary democracy and liberal values and institutions, first Mussolini's Italy and, especially after the mid-1930s, Hitler's Germany offered alternatives which had strong appeal not only for members of small but vociferous fascist and pro-Nazi organisations, but also for other people at all social levels whose admiration for Hitler's achievements was little affected by his persecution of the Jews and the churches. He had unified a great nation with a noble vision of service, devotion and self-sacrifice which had transcended the petty self-seeking and class war of bourgeois liberalism. To spiritual regeneration he had added physical regeneration. Everywhere in Germany, health, character and order contrasted with the 'louts and hooligans and wastrels, sinister or feckless toughs or softies', who slouched and lounged at street corners in Britain (Griffiths, 1983, p. 227). Even more important for many was his value as a bulwark against communism. For these admirers, it all added up to a picture of fierce national pride, unification of the classes and, above all, forcefulness of rule which got to grips with unemployment, slackness and infirmity of national purpose.

Such sentiments were not necessarily accompanied by coherent ideas of a corporate structure which subdued – or in extreme versions totally extinguished – the strength and independence of organised labour within a rigorous tripartite regulation that included the state. Conversely, not all those favouring such a structure shared the composite array of sentiments sketched above. There was, however, a significant overlap. Some British fascists included, along with their detestation of liberal parliamentary democracy and dread of communism, a model of a corporate state that would control the economic interests so as to maintain social peace and serve the higher good of state and society. It seemed to some radical Conservatives that 'the old liberal values could only be made relevant' by moving towards 'large concentrations of economic power', if necessary through 'a willingness to use state power to bring them into existence in the interests of both efficient production and full employment' (O'Sullivan, 1976, p. 126). These, as semi-autonomous bodies, would in Keynes's words represent a return to 'medieval conceptions of separate autonomies'. This line of thought led on to various proposals for a corporatism which was far more structured and articulated than the cautious, backstage 'corporate bias' already developing. What these proposals had in common was the idea of setting up institutions of 'self-government' for the various industries and providing for overall unification and co-ordination through a national committee representing them and other interests, including the state. How they varied was in terms of whether self-government and overall co-ordination were tight or loose and whether the dominant role was vested in the state, in the co-ordinating machinery, or in the industries themselves. If the state was to be supreme, as in Continental fascism, there was little room for genuine corporatism.

Some versions of the 'higher good' stressed that it must include generous treatment of the lower classes; the state seeking to preserve 'a just balance between syndicate and corporation, so as to restrict the exploitation of any group or class by any other', and to promote a less unequal distribution of wealth. 'Admiration for Mussolini's Italy was ... fairly widespread in certain sections of British society when the Nazis came to power in 1933, but above all in those areas of Tory thought which were concerned with the failure of capitalism and the free society to give a fair deal to all' (Griffiths, 1983, pp. 19, 20, 25). Other versions were less accommodating.

The bulk of British corporatist thought, however, lay outside the fascist movement, though it, too, was often influenced by respect for Mussolini's ideas. The judgement has been offered that although most of the prominent proponents of corporatism were repelled by some aspects of fascist politics they were 'not so repelled that they would find fascism unthinkable' (Carpenter, 1976, p. 5). Those who offered more or less detailed proposals included Mond (by then Lord Melchett); Lord Eustace Percy, Conservative Minister of Education 1924–9; Sir Basil Blackett, a director of the Bank of England; Sir Arthur Salter, lately a high-ranking civil servant; Roy Glenday, economic adviser to the FBI; and two aspiring Conservative politicians, Hugh Sellon and Leo Amery, an ardent figure in prewar social imperialism with its 'national socialism' undertones.

Corporatism of this variety represented a drive towards regulation, order and national cohesion in a world where economic and social pressures and the pluralistic dispersiveness of organised sectional interests seemed to some to be threatening stability in ways which parliamentary democracy was unable to control. In some versions the emphasis was economic. Stability was to be sought through the restriction of

competition, the regulation of output, the elimination of industrial conflict. In others, the emphasis was also social – Amery praised Italy for being
'organic, totalitarian and patriotic'. From this view, defences were needed
against disorder, levelling and the breakdown of hierarchy. National unity
should be achieved 'through the voluntary subordination of all parts of life
to a politically defined order'.

Sometimes the practical realities broke through these visions. Percy
conceded that corporatism 'cannot be easily or directly copied in this
country', partly because British trade unions were not sufficiently docile.
But the implications for organised labour were threatening enough. For
the most part, workers were asked not for participation but for harmony,
patriotism, service and sacrifice. The elimination of conflict meant, explicitly, their 'accepting restraints on individual liberty'; implicitly it meant
ceasing to contest class prerogatives and power – there was considerable
interest in compulsory arbitration and the outlawing of strikes. Class
association was to prevail over class antagonism and 'national combination to supersede individual freedom'. There was some room for
Parliament in these ideas but not a great deal (ibid., pp. 5–8). Few explicit
repudiations of fascism were offered, other than in respect of civil liberties,
and even there they tended to be conditional. On the whole, however, it
was believed that corporatism could be separated from its fascist abuses.
Significantly, even within these schools of thought there were few signs of
any fascist theory of state supremacy. In the British context, order turned
out to mean tidiness more than an overriding national goal. The prevalent
tone was in the direction of restriction, price supports, quotas and tariffs.
Corporatists tended to be isolationists rather than militarists, with the
empire seen as an economic refuge rather than a market for vigorous
exploitation.

In another direction, Harold Macmillan headed an influential group
which sought a more growth-oriented corporatism through an active
partnership with the unions. He defended strikes and argued for expansion
in the scope of collective bargaining. His scheme for self-governing
industries, with compulsory union membership and statutory powers to
discipline members, which would apply rationalisation, eliminate surplus
capacity, regulate prices and use international cartels attracted the sympathy not only of men like Melchett but also of some Labour moderates.
Melchett even had a Bill drafted in 1934, but it met too many doubts – not
so much principled as practical. Even so, this was a scheme that some
TUC leaders could find attractive, for it revived the ideas cherished by
Bevin and Citrine, for example, in the late 1920s.

In the event, all these corporatist conceptions were, in effect, pre-
empted by much more limited developments. The conceptions themselves were but muted versions of what was developing elsewhere.
Though they often contained ideas and dispositions which embodied
concepts of national and class harmony and contempt for party politics,
they offered no concept of a powerful transcendental state with a national
purpose. And the actual developments which pre-empted them – variously termed 'corporate bias' or 'quasi-corporatism' – were in a highly
pragmatic category of trade associations and schemes to allot production

quotas; of cartels with not very effective powers; of consultation and negotiation – sometimes behind the scenes – between representative organisations which found it prudent to pay heed to rank and file opinion.

What appeared to be a version of corporatism which included an aggressively strong state was described in Oswald Mosley's *The Greater Britain*, though he later disclaimed any marked interest in corporatism as such. A National Council of Corporations would preside over corporations formed from the employers, unions and consumer interests of the various economic sectors. Within the guide-lines of the national plan, each corporation would work out its own policy for wages, prices, conditions of employment, investment and terms of competition. 'Government would intervene only to settle deadlocks between unions and employers. Strikes would be abolished' (Skidelsky, 1981, pp. 314–15). The government was to be completely free of any control by Parliament, which would be advisory only and elected on an occupational franchise – no longer able to obstruct swift, efficient, executive rule with old, out-dated oppositional procedures and traditions.

Mosley had earlier been able to attract 'a protectionist-imperialist cave within the Labour party'. Eight of the seventeen Mosleyite MPs in the parliamentary party came from the Birmingham area, where old traditions stirred afresh as severe depression descended in 1930. Protection, a 'self-supporting' empire, talk in the local press of the need for a 'national' government and of capital and labour facing the crisis shoulder to shoulder – these were echoes of early twentieth-century visions. 'Birmingham socialism looked very much like Chamberlain toryism, with certain variations' (Skidelsky, 1967, p. 274), and the Tory Amery was still MP for the Birmingham constituency he had represented since 1911. Mosley was now adding to this core conception all the earlier fringe features, and offering the British public what had only been incipient or latent in the early period – an attempt at a total and coherent national socialism package.

There were many reasons for his failure to mobilise a fascist movement of any proportions. On one level, the Public Order Act 1936 which banned political uniforms and gave police chiefs the power to ban processions was a severe blow. Long-standing dislikes among British citizens had asserted themselves vigorously; a passage in Cabinet minutes asserting that 'There is no doubt at all that the resentment against the wearing of uniforms by the Fascists is immense. The practice is felt to be repugnant to British ideas and to suggest the assumptions of authority by a private army. People are very much alive to the fact that in Germany the wearing of black or brown uniforms led to the overthrow of liberties' (Middlemas, 1979, p. 242). In Parliament, 'No one, except the odd right-wing eccentric ... was prepared to support Mosley's right to parade about in uniforms' (Skidelsky, 1981, p. 417). It revealed Mosley's poor judgement that he should apply this style within a culture so resistant at all social levels to the charm of strutting jack-boots.

He was also unlucky in his timing. Like Tariff Reform and some of its fringe movements, the British Union of Fascists was launched just as the economy began its upswing of recovery. Science-based and mass-production industries, in which Britain had fallen behind in the period 1900–30, experienced rapid advance during the 1930s and the country's overall growth rate in that period was one of the highest achieved by industrial nations. With prices of food and raw materials falling, real incomes rose. Those in work were better off than they had ever been, and wireless, the cinema, electrical appliances and a leap forward in holidays with pay made private life increasingly agreeable.

The despair engendered by mass long-term unemployment being heavily concentrated in the north-east, Scotland and south Wales, it remained remote from the rest of the British nation. Only hunger marches obtruded. Even here the Baldwin government exercised skilful restraint. In 1934 the government 'sought new and permanent police powers to combat the hunger marchers', but Baldwin and his colleagues were concerned 'to ensure that the Bill did not offend too greatly established conventions about civil liberties', and 'would not tolerate police demands for power to control all open-air meetings, judging that to be an intoler-able abrogation of traditional rights' (Middlemas, 1979, p. 242).

This illustrates another contributory factor to Mosley's failure; the political competence of a highly experienced governing class. From this competence flowed two further significant consequences. The British political system was not nearly so impervious to change and adaptation as Mosley made out, and as a result its institutions were more widely legitimated and approved than were those of Continental countries. The degree of crisis would have needed to be far greater in Britain to produce a political collapse of the sort that overtook Weimar.

Also among the basic structural reasons for Mosley's failure was the fact that the audience most eagerly receptive of the fascist message in Germany – the petty bourgeoisie – lacked organisation in Britain above the level of ratepayers' associations. 'Their voice penetrated only at one remove, via the Association of Municipal Corporations and the Chambers of Commerce, both significantly less important than they had been in the 1900s' (ibid., p. 237). These small shopkeepers, independent craftsmen and other small proprietors – roughly equivalent to the German *Mittelstand* – were 'the Britons who felt most neglected and unloved in the 1930s. They were typically the people who in previous ages had been protected by the guild system, but whose independence precluded effective trade union organi-zation' (Skidelsky, 1981b, p. 327). From 1935 on, the British Union of Fascists made a determined bid for the support of these groups who fell outside the capital-labour confrontation and who viewed both with sour moralising envy.

But with economic recovery many of these groups, too, made an acceptable living. In any case, at no socio-economic level did British culture and its thought structures and vocabularies lend themselves to the fascist cause. They offered little purchase for the transmutation of petty economic and social grievances into the blood-thrilling rhetoric of national destiny. Mosley did his best with the empire but this was too securely a Conservative Party monopoly to help him much. And here we are brought to another reason for the weak mobilisation of Britain's *Mittelstand*. As an aristocrat trying to capitalise the grievances of this stratum, Mosley was for all practical purposes on his own. He did, of course, derive support from a handful of upper-class, right-wing eccentrics and battling brigadiers. As Samuel Courtauld was to comment some years later: 'No doubt the Fascist leaders robbed a few wealthy fools and possibly a few industrialists (they tried to throw a fly over me once, but the attempt did not last five minutes) . . . ' (Courtauld, 1949, p. 71). But, for the most part, the really influential sections of Britain's traditional ruling class left him conspicuously alone, just as they had rejected the help of the British fascists in 1926.

The main reason is not far to seek. They did not need him. The Communist Party in Britain was negligible, and it became increasingly clear during the 1930s that the bulk of the Labour Party and the trade union movement, with their apparently unshakeable rejection of exotic revolutionary doctrines and their commitment to constitutionalism and moderate reformism, were still viewed by most of their members with that curious but 'safe' mixture of cynicism and underlying confidence which had long been a characteristic stance of the organised working class. Kahn-Freund, a committed Anglophile who lived through the dying days of the Weimar Republic and later developed close knowledge of the British trade union movement, wrote of the stabilising qualities of 'a union movement with which the members continue to identify, which is "we" to them and not "they"' (Kahn-Freund, 1979, p. 20). Membership of the political as well as the industrial wing of the movement was growing. The figure for the unions was rising again by 1934, and the shattering of the parliamentary Labour Party had not been paralleled in the country – the party had polled more votes in 1931 than in 1923, when it formed its first administration; party organisation remained intact and throughout the 1930s gained more votes.

Given this organisational security and support, both industrial and political leaders were able to contain and control certain expressions of militancy at local level which were considered threatening in that they extended horizontally to include Communists who contributed much to their energy and initiative. This was as true of the 'new industry' towns as of the old. In Oxford, for example, where the burgeoning car industry was attracting the organising attentions of the two great 'general' unions as well as others, an alliance between the Communist Party and the local Trades Council attempted to launch a militant trade unionism. The individuals involved appear at many points in the social and political as well as the industrial history of the Oxford working class. 'But by 1939 they had been contained by the institutions of the wider society.' Local activity in its various forms – by union branches themselves or in alliance with the Trades Council and the Communist Party, 'was limited by the power of central organizations'. The Trades Council was threatened with disaffiliation by the TUC for including Communist representatives, and the Oxford City Labour Party was likewise threatened by head office unless it disbanded its Co-ordinating Committee for Peace and Democracy, which also included Communist Party members. Thus 'the tension between . . . the local united front operating horizontally across various organizations, and the growth of trade union membership incorporated vertically into centralized institutions – was inevitably resolved at critical points in favour of the latter' (Whiting, 1978, pp. 338, 341, 404).

Given this successful integration of working-class industrial and political organisations into the established procedures of government, regulation and social control, the Conservative Party and ruling class generally had nothing to gain and much to lose by being seen to encourage or condone political behaviour within their own ranks which violated the canons of moderate constitutionalism – canons which working-class organisations had manifestly absorbed into their ideologies and traditions. The observance of constitutionalism and of the conventions and constraints of parliamentary democracy would, as the Socialist Leaguers had seen, limit Labour governments to incremental piecemeal reform, and nothing must be done which might weaken those observances and provide the far left with convincing arguments against maintaining them. So long as this structure of forces prevailed Mosley had nothing but danger to offer the ruling class. As so often, its more influential members adhered to this logic. By the late 1930s he was unable to break a national press boycott and was denied most of the big halls in the urban centres.

Continued Assimilation and Economic Revival

Meanwhile labour integration was being extended and consolidated. In 1935 Bevin was to 'help to bring back Labour as a parliamentary force; to a place which Baldwin had kept open for them'. Baldwin's dialogue with the union movement widened so far that 'of men like Bevin and Citrine he could ask advice about rearmament or the Abdication' (Middlemas and Barnes, 1969, pp. 695, 696). The abdication issue yielded another example of how the Establishment increasingly operated with the inclusion of Labour movement figures. For Davidson, Chancellor of the Duchy of Lancaster and closer to Baldwin than any other Conservative politician, it was the case, as it was for many others, that 'the really decisive influence was not the views of the Cabinet or even of the Dominion Premiers, but . . . that of the Labour movement'. Davidson wrote: 'We were close friends both of the Attlees and the Bevins, and I never had any doubt whatever where they stood . . . ' Much to his satisfaction, they asserted 'the strong Puritanism on such matters within the Labour party', especially among the trade unionists; it was 'impossible to conceive of any Labour or trade union leader' tolerating the twice-divorced Mrs Simpson 'as a consort of the King' (Rhodes James, 1969, p. 416). Cross-party sympathies could go even further. J. H. Thomas, damned by Beatrice Webb in 1929 as a foul-mouthed, drunken social climber and stock exchange gambler – 'our Birkenhead' – fell from office in disgrace in 1936 over the disclosure of Budget secrets but was rescued from financial embarrassment by discreet subventions from Conservative Party funds (Skidelsky, 1967, p. 138; Rhodes James, 1969, p. 411).

In the preceding year the Birthday Honours List had brought knighthoods for Citrine and Pugh and for Charles Edwards, Labour Whip, while Attlee, deputy leader, soon to become leader (and to be privately congratulated by Davidson), became Privy Councillor. Two years later Baldwin achieved an innovation he had first suggested to his colleagues in 1925. The Leader of the Opposition was to receive a salary. On him, said Baldwin, 'rests the responsibility for maintaining the traditions of this House', and he should enjoy independence and security. The concept of the loyal Opposition thus received its ultimate symbolic confirmation. Its leader was to be officially rewarded for mounting opposition to His Majesty's ministers within 'the traditions of this House'.

By the eve of the Second World War both the Labour movement and the traditional Establishment had passed through experiences from which they could learn important lessons about themselves and each other. Increasingly evident was the profoundly socialising effect of the country's institutions in moulding most working-class leaders towards constitutionalism as they ascended the hierarchies of their industrial and political organisations. Enjoying the protections as well as the constraints of this constitutionalism and rule of law, they had discovered that their organisations could survive the worst slump in world history and that they could continue to exercise the functions in which they had invested their convictions and their careers. Mass unemployment weakened the unions' bargaining power but it had not destroyed collective bargaining. Indeed, weakness at the workplace often drove men to fall back to the common defence line of the 'national standard rate', and top-level union leaders entered into a heyday of 'industry-wide' bargaining, widely assumed to be the ultimate development of 'mature' industrial relations systems. In general, employers' associations took little fundamental advantage of union weakness. Individual employers were often ready – at least until the beginnings of revival after the mid-1930s – to practice workplace encroachments upon standard terms and conditions, but there were no collective aspirations among them to overthrow union regulation altogether.

The unions had therefore amply proved to themselves and others that they were permanent institutions with a growing stake in their society. That society was at least as difficult as any other society to characterise. It is betrayed equally by uncritical panegyrics from hack journalists as by total denunciations from the far left. Orwell's picture of the social texture of Britain as he saw it in 1941 is one of the few to avoid both extremes. It was a society in which mistrust of militarism was 'mixed up with barbarities and anachronisms'. The fact of one law for the rich and another for the poor co-existed with an assumption that 'the law, such as it is, will be respected'. The attachment to justice, liberty and objective truth 'may be illusions, but they are very powerful illusions. The belief in them influences conduct, national life is different because of them. In proof of which, look about you. Where are the rubber truncheons, where is the castor oil? The sword is still in the scabbard, and while it is there corruption cannot go beyond a certain point.' In many ways the electoral system

is gerrymandered in the interest of the moneyed class. But until some deep change has occurred in the public mind, it cannot become *completely* corrupt. You do not arrive at the polling booth to find men with revolvers telling you which way to vote, nor are the votes miscounted, nor is there any direct bribery. Even hypocrisy is a powerful safe-guard. The hanging judge ... whom nothing short of dynamite will ever teach what century he is living in, but who will at any rate interpret the law according to the books and will in no circumstances take a money bribe, is one of the symbolic figures of England. He is a symbol of the strange mixture of reality and illusion, democracy and privilege, humbug and decency, the subtle network of compromises, by which the nation keeps itself in its familiar shape. (Orwell, 1982, pp. 41–6)

Baldwin and his associates did not create the society which lent itself to such appraisals. But by their choice of policy and utterance they, in effect, singled out for emphasis those strands of a complex social tapestry which helped to create this effect upon an acute and unsentimental observer.

It was fully compatible with such an appraisal that a society in which, for example, the restrictive practices of trade associations and the pro-fessions came under far less abuse than those of manual workers, and in which large-scale tax evasion was pursued far less punitively than petty social security fraud, should direct a steady stream of criticism at the unions and their policies. If Conservative politicians and hack journalists did not supply it there were always some ex-union officials who, having trodden an already familiar path from ardent supporter to censorious critic, were prepared, then as now, to make good the omission. J. H. Seddon, ex-President of the TUC, struck in 1932 an ever-familiar note in denouncing restrictive practices and the unions' growing political activi-ties. 'Originally established to secure the freedom of the individual, through combination based on moral suasion', trade unionism had 'now degenerated into mass picketing and compulsory membership under pressure of denial of employment unless a worker accepts the dictator-ship of officials ... ' (Seddon, 1932, pp. 40–2).

Such charges were the small change of Fleet Street journalism and the daily cut-and-thrust of class controversy. Yet the behaviour and utteran-ces of even right-wing politicians when more deeply considered judge-ments were required reveal also an awareness of the – from their point of view – profoundly 'stabilizing' qualities of the Labour movement (McKenzie and Silver, 1968, pp. 48–9). The 1929–31 crisis and long-term mass unemployment had neither crushed the unions nor inflamed them into insurgency. At a time when the problem of urban deprivation was less complicated by an assertive youth culture and by racial resentments, the unions had shown that 'social equilibrium' was possible at almost any level of unemployment. Unemployment as an issue, in fact, soon disappeared from frontal consciousness as soon as a peak had been reached and found to be bearable – and when demonstrations (mostly organised under Communist inspiration) tailed off after 1936 (Pollard, 1969, p. 115; Stevenson and Cook, 1979, p. 190). Apart from the Special Areas, the subject virtually disappeared from the agenda of TUC and union conferences. From the mid-1920s the unions had been demonstrating their 'acceptance of unemployment as the price to be paid for maintaining wages' and this 'made them less interested in increasing employment than in increasing unemployment benefit' (Skidelsky, 1967, p. 395).

Nominally the unions had, of course, committed themselves to the idea of a socialist planned economy. But on the practical level it was clear that what for them was a tolerable society which assured their rights to grow and maintain their negotiating functions could be achieved through appropriate forms of economic management without wholesale public ownership. So far as the majority of the union leadership was concerned the prophet was to be Keynes rather than Marx. Despite much appearance to the contrary something similar could be said of the political side of the Labour movement. This may seem improbable in the light of, for example, the New Left Book Club, with its 60,000 membership, its 1,200 local discussion groups, and its political literature much of which was inspired by Marxism, and in the light, too, of the fact that many more people than ever before came to think and speak of the Communist Party as 'The Party', to be influenced by it and to support its policies. Yet a remarkably small number actually joined it. The fact was that alongside this highly articulate presentation of Marxist analysis could be found the reaffirmation of a Fabian pragmatism and gradualism that expressed far more accurately the institutional and ideological temper of perhaps the bulk of the movement. It is 'as well to remember that it was in those years that a new generation of Fabian academics, like Evan Durbin, Hugh Gaitskell and Douglas Jay embraced Keynes and "practical socialism" with as much eagerness as their counterparts on the Left embraced Marxism, historical materialism, and the class struggle' (Miliband, 1973, p. 244).

The prevalent ideological temper of British socialism had in fact shifted little over the years. Admittedly, Ramsay MacDonald, in *Socialism and Government* (1909) had rejected the liberal individualist notion of society as an aggregate of 'separate and free individuals', and had sought instead 'a higher organic unity' directed by the 'superior will and intelligence' of the state, which he described as 'the embodiment of the general will' and the expression of 'the political personality of the whole'. He was even prepared to say that such a state would bring true 'liberty' and true 'realization' to the individual because it would be founded on his 'real will', the voice of his true 'moral self', and not upon his 'expressed will', which might indicate only 'short-sighted self interest'. But MacDonald went further here than any leading British politician before or since: so far indeed that he passed out of sight of most members of the movement. Most British socialists

saw the national will in strictly majoritarian terms as the will of 'the greater number' ... Moreover, the individuals that composed the social aggregate were deemed in British socialism, as in trade unionism and in liberal individualism, to be the best judge of their own interests: that is to say, their 'expressed will' *was* their 'real will'. Since individuals were the best judge of their own interest, the Labour party favoured individual or sectional self-help. In this respect it expressed the fundamental assumptions and attitudes of the trade unionists who financed and voted for it.

And although after 1931 there was much discussion of planning and nationalisation, 'both these were seen as measures for perfecting the "opportunity" of individuals to compete (by redistributing resources from the over- to the under-advantaged), rather than as meaningful attempts to replace competition by "co-operation"' (Currie, 1979, pp. 73–4, 146).

The Second World War

The war did nothing to change the direction of dominant trends in the development of industrial relations and Labour politics in Britain. Rather it confirmed and reinforced directions that had been evident for many decades. It did, of course, produce a whole set of special emergency arrangements, some of which persisted into peace, but these largely followed, though often improving on, precedents established in the first mass-participation war of 1914–18.

After some early false moves with respect to the control of employment, to which the TUC responded with considerable anger, the government was soon offering 'full and regular consultations'.

The wartime alliance between Conservative, Labour and Liberal parties, on terms far less unequal than in 1914–18, was a major stage in Labour's incorporation. The coalition embraced 'imperialists and social democrats, liberals and reformers. From the aristocrats of finance capital to the autodidacts of the trade unions, the war created a social and political amalgam which was not a fusion – each component retained its individuality – but which nonetheless transformed them all internally . . . ' Thus was formed the paradox of an alliance between Labour and one of its most ferocious arch-enemies in the fight against European fascism; an alliance with that strand of Toryism which 'in the last instance placed the Empire before the immediate interests of trade and industry' (A. Barnett, 1982, pp. 48, 49). Citrine informed Chamberlain in October 1939 that though the TUC strongly supported the government's efforts to intensify preparations for war the condition of its collaboration was the fullest recognition of the trade unions' right 'to function on the workers' behalf'. This conceded, the TUC's position within the movement was markedly enhanced, and it proceeded to make rapid decisions on crucial issues without reference to the polling of affiliated unions, these being perfunctorily put to Congress for ratification, often months later (Dorfman, 1973, p. 38).

The point at which the war began to be taken really seriously was marked by Labour's entry into Churchill's coalition government. The parliamentary Labour Party played an important part in Churchill's accession, just as it had done in Lloyd George's; it moved the decisive vote of censure on Chamberlain's government and refused to serve in any coalition under him. Labour's reward was a generous allocation of government posts; the most significant being Bevin's appointment as Minister of Labour and National Service.

Working through a tripartite Joint Consultative Committee (JCC), Bevin negotiated the consent of both sides of industry to a sequence of emergency legislation. Strikes and lockouts were prohibited, the existing collective bargaining machinery being supplemented by a National Arbitration Tribunal. Bevin was later to refer to this legislation as 'virtually a collective agreement, given the clothing of law'. Despite the growing extension of government control over so many aspects of the nation's economy the peacetime system of collective bargaining was never superseded. A brief hankering by Bevin for wage control was squelched by the JCC and the government went no further than to make occasional calls for pay restraint. It did not have to. Incomes stability was achieved by other means: by a mixture of skill and guile on the government's part and by the wholehearted commitment of the British people to winning the war. Given the government's anxiety to avoid the rapid increases in prices and wages which had caused so much discontent on the home front during the First World War, it was urged upon them by the TUC that the most favourable environment for pay restraint was price stability. Accordingly, the government undertook to stabilise the cost of living by means of subsidies, and an 'extremely old-fashioned cost of living index was carefully manipulated to hide the price increases which did occur' (Clegg, 1971, p. 1). Such relatively modest and infrequent claims and settlements as there were did little more than compensate wage rates for those increases, but actual earnings, including piece-work and overtime, rose rapidly and family incomes rose even faster given a spectacular increase in the employment of women. With wage incomes rising by 18 per cent between 1938 and 1947, salaries falling by 21 per cent, and property income falling by 15 per cent, there was a sharp shift towards economic equality. People's personal impressions of equality may well have been even greater than the reality and this greatly reinforced the readiness to accept the stresses and deprivations of total war. Corporate tripartitism at national level would have been worth little but for this popular backing.

Popular backing could not, of course, be total. The same need arose for 'dilution' as in 1914–18 and it was tackled by the same means – the suspension of workplace custom and practice. The Restoration of Pre-War Practices Act of 1942 made the guarantee implied in the title and this was duly honoured in 1950. But the wholesale upheaval wrought by war could not be without widespread minor frictions and once again the growing labour shortage and workplace bargaining power proved powerful stimulus to a brisk revival of the shop-steward system. Meanwhile the official union hierarchies were 'heavily committed to the Government's policy and involved in its administration at every level ... The annual reports of the TUC General Council began to read like the records of some special government department responsible for co-ordinating policy in the social and industrial spheres' (Pelling, 1963, p. 215). This created possibilities of the rank and file becoming exposed to unofficial grass-roots leadership by disaffected militants. This happened less than might have been expected, since the most obvious source of disaffection, the Communist Party, became, after the invasion of the Soviet Union in June 1941, the most enthusiastic supporter of higher productivity and the fiercest opponent of unofficial strikes.

That Communist influence could be overrated, however, was shown by the fact that despite its total commitment to the war effort the number of unofficial strikes rose considerably in the latter stages. These did not betoken anything approaching a significant crack in the unity with which the British people prosecuted the war; in 1945 the nation's social structure emerged from its prolonged strains relatively unmarked. National self-congratulation needed, of course, to take into account such material supports of this well-being as large-scale American aid and the massive sale of British capital assets abroad. Nevertheless, the social resilience displayed had been remarkable. Indeed it seemed as if it might now enjoy permanent reinforcement from the widespread generation of a popular radicalism that was anti-fascist, libertarian and egalitarian in nature. The old patriotic radicalism awakened again from its latency and publicists like George Orwell and J. B. Priestley found themselves equipped by tempera-ment and conviction to speak to the mood; the former through the written word alone, the latter also through the BBC spoken word, a method felt to be particularly threatening by some members of the Establishment, who took steps to ensure his removal from a regular weekly talk series.

Official Labour Party leadership was not so much inspiring and guiding this radicalism as trying to catch up with it. The social welfare and economic management schemes which came to the fore owed nothing to Labour or Conservative thinking. Admittedly, in so far as they envisaged a managed and humane capitalism they represented extrapolations of advanced 'new' Liberalism which were the peak aspirations of many within the Labour ranks at all levels. But the techniques were those of Beveridge and Keynes, both Liberals who were simply bringing their creed up to date. 'Both major parties absorbed the stimulus and re-acted, albeit slowly, in order to survive . . . ' (Middlemas, 1979, p. 334).

Continuities and the 1950s

It was soon apparent that popular radicalism had owed much, especially so far as its middle-class participants were concerned, to the mood and impetus of class unity induced by the war. Whether a bold and imaginative radical programme of social and economic transformation launched by the Labour government immediately after its entry into office in 1945 could have capitalised this mood and impetus into permanent institutional change can only be a matter for parlour-game debate. It is just conceivable that within such a transformed social context a state-led programme of modernisation, both industrial and political, might have been accom-panied by the acceptance of tripartite institutions which negotiated broad tolerances on profits, prices and all incomes. Even to state the possibility is to reveal its unlikelihood. The British social and political structure had survived the war intact; indeed, the 'historic compromise' had been consolidated and strengthened by two new factors. One was the full incorporation of Labour both as a major and highly successful ruling participant in the war effort and as the triumphant beneficiary of the postwar election. The other was the illusion – which leaders of all parties naturally encouraged – of having 'won' the war against the Axis powers – a victory achieved in fact predominantly by the Soviet forces and the immense productive capacity of the USA. Thus by contrast with Germany, Japan and France, which had experienced traumatic defeat and military occupation – experiences which have proved to be among the enabling conditions for modernisation – Britain suffered neither.

This has had profound consequences. Not only did it permit the continuance of traditional assumptions, values and institutions – not least those of Parliament and party – it also made it possible for leaders of both major parties to retain illusions of a world role for Britain; illusions which continued to emerge, despite the loss of empire, in the Falklands rhetoric (A. Barnett, 1982). Nothing had happened, either, to shift the essential stances of industry, finance and labour towards the state, themselves, and each other. Hence the paradox that a greatly weakened economy in need of state-promoted radical change, modernisation and reconstruction, coexisted with a polity and a set of national dispositions which had been confirmed and indeed reinforced in their traditional patterns. These included a range of archaic institutions and values relating to political procedures, education, class, status, industrialism, planning and the role of the state. The fact that the whole system had apparently successfully confronted two ruthless and powerful military regimes preserved it even more safely than before from radical reconstruction by either major party. Equally fundamental was the fact that Labour's seeming full incorporation into the system, with all the fruits of office, status and power, only confirmed its leaders' long-standing belief that the system was well worth playing.

The policies of successive Labour governments therefore seemed to vindicate the old strategy of rule, with its belief that while concession and incorporation would not be painless for the currently dominant interests they would probably conserve what those interests deemed essential. The cumulative inertia induced by this historical continuity, however, crowned by the self-congratulation of Britain's 'finest hour' and the fantasy of Labour's 'social revolution', resulted in a society too ossified in many of its features to be capable of adapting intelligently either to its second-rank status in international affairs or to the exposed position of its industry in an increasingly predatory world economy. This inertia is all the stronger from the fact of Labour, too, having built up such a massive investment in the system.

All this, however, was yet to emerge. Even so, certain familiar grooves and ruts soon began to reappear with the peace. Admittedly, the unions demonstrated, for a time, considerable loyalty towards 'their' government. But if there was ever a chance of drawing the British people into a high degree of peacetime collective unity and group restraint it was passing by 1947. By that time the overriding purposes of war had shredded out into the conflicting personal and private preoccupations of individuals and groups. Some of the editorials of the up-market press and, for example, *The Economist*, as one shortage-ridden year slipped into the next, provide vivid evidence of returning class labels and class venom. Constitutionally, the Labour government and the trade union movement were behaving strictly in the line of tradition. Labour leaders who 'looked outside the parliamentary field, especially Morrison, showed themselves keen, not just to brand the Conservative party as doctrinaire and reactionary, wedded to belief in a primitive, outmoded capitalism, but also to reassure employers and other forward-looking capitalists that a Labour government intended nothing untoward' (Middlemas, 1979, p. 292). 'During the Coalition', Morrison assured King George VI in November 1945, 'the Labour members had learnt a great deal from the Conservatives in how to govern.' Lord Woolton, postwar Conservative Party chairman, decreed, Lord Blake tells us, 'that henceforth in speech and writing Conservatives should never use the word "Labour", with its suggestions of honest British toil, but always substitute "Socialist" with its alien, doctrinaire, continental overtones'. The ploy misfired because some voters assumed that 'Socialist' must refer to some other party (Blake, 1972, p. 262).

The Labour document of April 1945, *Let Us Face the Future*, had indicated that the largest part by far of British industry and finance would remain in private hands indefinitely. The industries designated for public ownership, with the exception of steel, had long ceased to occupy a strategic place in the structure of capitalist power, a fact clearer to many Conservative than to many Labour supporters. Nationalisation was designed to improve the efficiency of predominantly capitalist economy, not to mark the beginning of its wholesale transformation. Its organisational vehicle was to be the independent public corporation, an ancient model whose modern form had been pioneered by a Conservative government of the 1920s. Management–worker relations were to remain of the conventional kind, though supplemented by 'joint consultation' which, it was hoped, would improve as well as humanise communications and raise efficiency. Neither the government nor most trade union leaders gave any sign that they wanted major changes in the pattern of industrial relations in the public sector. No creative initiative was forthcoming, either, from the Labour government with respect to the machinery of economic management. All the instruments they felt to need lay to hand already, fashioned under the imperatives of war – administrative controls, financial and currency management, regulatory fiscal policy – and no attempt was made to set up, for example, an adequate central directing authority equipped with a comprehensive statistical service.

In terms of medical care, housing, education and general welfare the achievement was greater than that of any previous government. Anything less, however, would have failed to meet the expectations of the war-generated radicalism. Yet perhaps it can be taken as a measure of how far this radicalism was simply an up-dated new Liberalism that it was mollified by reforms which in no sense added up to social transformation. 'It is clear that the Welfare State which developed between 1945 and 1951 was fully compatible with the traditions and customs of Western democracy . . . ' It did 'not conflict sharply with the interests of power groups in private industry, and for that reason alone . . . gained wide acceptance in Conservative political circles'. For Conservative political strategies the welfare state had 'the positive attraction of a society in which a large measure of class rule and general contentment can co-exist'. On certain issues where Labour government proposals met determined resistance from industry the government retreated. One such was the plan for a Development Council for each industry, which it was feared would undercut the position of the trade associations – 'by the end of World War Two cartelization and restrictionism had become leading characteristics of trade association policy' (Rogow and Shore, 1955, pp. 82, 85, 183, 184).

Such pressure as Labour leaders experienced to pursue a specifically 'socialist' programme came from a left wing with very limited representation in the House of Commons and a voice at the annual conference which was usually ignored. Although there was yet to come the open contempt for conference decisions displayed by some leading members of the parliamentary Labour Party, there was rigorous continuation of the long-accepted principle that Labour governments must insist on 'their prior constitutional responsibility to parliament'. Party leaders must be free from conference 'dictation'. Underlying this impressive language was, of course, anxiety to be free of radical pressures which might alarm the voters and threaten electoral success. Leaders remained convinced that 'the essential condition for that success was to present the Labour party as a moderate and respectable party, free from class bias, "national" in outlook . . . whose zeal for reform would always be tempered by its eager endorsement of the maxim that Rome was not built in a day – or even in a century' (Miliband, 1973, p. 339).

But if the 'mixed economy' was to be set up as the desirable condition, what must happen to old-style socialist convictions about the 'evils' inherent in capitalist property relations, with their gross inequalities of power, status and reward; and in competitive-market pressures, with their 'wastes' and 'heedless cruelties'? Labour leaders needed arguments to offer the party faithful as well as a wider public. The climate became sympathetic to a revisionism which dismissed 'ownership of the means of production' as an important issue for national efficiency or for pursuit of the good life, and which presented industrial managers as simply fellow-professionals doing their best in a difficult world. 'The Labour party recognizes', declared *Industry and Society* in 1957, 'that under increasingly professional managements, large firms are as a whole serving the nation well . . . We have therefore no intention of intervening in the management of any firm which is doing a good job.'

The severe limitations on Labour's political adventurousness stemmed ultimately from the lack of a sufficiently broad-based demand for fundamental structural change – a lack which the party leadership itself had over the years done little to remedy.

In the absence of any socialist ethic evocative of mass support, the Labour government was bound to operate the capitalist or middle-class hierarchy of values that is a characteristic of the acquisitive society. Full employment, for example, was regarded less as an end in itself than as an initial instalment of individual material advancement. Similarly, expanded opportunity tended to be interpreted as opportunity to emulate the standards and privileges associated with the middle and upper classes. Access to education, the opportunity to acquire decent housing, the right to improve one's economic and social status, the enjoyment of leisure – these attributes of a middle-class social ethic were in fact given fresh meaning and importance by the Labour government. The improvement in conditions, however, did not carry with it a transformation of ethics generated at lower social levels and borne upward through the whole society. Instead, there was a permeation downward of the middle-class value system, as, earlier in British history, certain standards of the aristocracy had been absorbed by the rising business class. (Rogow and Shore, 1955, p. 185)

This argument does not rest on over-simplified theories as to the 'embourgeoisement' of the working-class; theories which have been validly criticised. Rogow and Shore themselves indicated the limited dimensions which they deemed relevant.

The enlargement of opportunity was partly bestowed by state benefit but it was also an outcome of a shift in market power away from management towards organised labour, underpinned by sustained full employment. With union membership rising even higher than during the war, growing sections of the working class were able to participate in the individual and sectional struggle for advantage that was a predominant feature of the competitive acquisitive society. This was a world for which the unions were made and in which they thrived and prospered. There were, of course, many individual trade unionists who sought and campaigned, within the Labour Party and elsewhere, for a very different world. There can be no doubt, however, that any attempt by a Labour or any other government to introduce change which seriously encroached on the unions' independent bargaining functions or legal rights would have met implacable resistance, however 'socialist' its basis.

Circumstances nevertheless made possible from 1945 to 1951 a highly effective working partnership between Labour ministers and a small group of influential union leaders. The latter held political views which diverged little, if at all, from those of the former. They all commanded a strong following in their respective unions. Feelings of loyalty towards the first majority Labour government wasted only slowly. Some of the atmosphere of wartime emergency persisted. As a consequence, despite the return of competitive acquisitive preoccupations and of class feeling, these circumstances facilitated, between 1948 and 1950, certain 'self-imposed limitations on collective bargaining together with the acceptance of continuing [wartime] legal restrictions on that process and on the right to strike' (Barnes and Reid, 1980, p. 18). The restraint was on rates, however, not earnings, which continued to rise unevenly, and the unions retained the power to say yea or nay; a point on which the government had already offered complete assurance. An earlier attempt, in 1947, to discourage wage increases had produced only a sharp reaction by the TUC to the Prime Minister, who 'made it unmistakably plain that it is not his intention or that of the Government to interfere in any way with the normal procedure of wage negotiations through joint negotiating bodies in this country' (Fox, 1958, p. 605). Even so, the commitment of influential leaders to support of the government was sufficiently marked to create tensions and sometimes overt conflict with militant activists at lower levels, whose power base at the workplace was strengthening with continuing full employment.

As yet, however, these developments were not causing any major shift in the appraisal of Britain's industrial relations system and its place in the wider society. Given the many continuities apparent in British life it was understandable that some observers during the 1950s should evaluate the country's institutions in terms of 'progress' or 'development' along lines already laid down. Even those who fancied that there had been some sort of 'social revolution' could hardly deny that it had been introduced in the most decorous constitutional manner and with full observance of the traditional modes, restraints and conventions of parliamentary life. This seemed even more apparent to those who felt that what was happening was no more than the extension to the more fortunate working-class groups of some of the comforts, freedoms and security that the middle and upper classes had long taken for granted.

Politically and industrially, therefore, it could be supposed by those occupying the broad middle ground that, with postwar recovery under way, Britain's institutions were developing adequately to meet current needs. The period from 1945 to 1965 has been described as 'the apogee of political stability, industrial equilibrium and economic prosperity, fortified by prolonged absence of ideological or class cleavages in society or the political parties'. Observers seeking evidence of stability were disposed to decide that conflict had been fully institutionalised through a pluralist system of representation. Britain could be presented as a model of relatively harmonious relations between 'governing institutions', with corporate bias as a necessary and growing component of a political system in which economic management eliminated the need to defer gratification and social change could be achieved without undue strain on any group (Middlemas, 1979, pp. 428–9).

Among industrialists and executives the more currently influential voices, while ever alert to any threatening policy by the Labour Party, were able to find considerable common ground with its revisionist right wing. There had long been a basis for dialogue here, and even some of the same participants survived from the interwar period. Melchett and McGowan, for example, had been among those responsible for persuading the NCEO out of its earlier criticism of the Beveridge proposals – another influence being the managerial signatories of *A National Policy for Industry* which declared in favour of a welfare system including corporately provided employee housing, supplements to state pensions and subsidies against unemployment.

There were, of course, voices constantly uplifted that pressed a very different message. It was already clear by the 1950s that the unions were to be identified as the principal public scapegoat for the nation's economic ills. Restrictionism, unofficial strikes, upward pressure on rates and earnings and shop-steward interference with managerial prerogative were the chief economic targets. But unions were also condemned as destroying freedom through such practices as the closed shop and other forms of group tyranny over the individual. These evils were seen as springing from the fact that in Britain the unions had not been brought within an adequate framework of regulative law. The legislation of 1871, 1875 and 1906 had, in the words of *A Giant's Strength*, a study published in 1958 by the Inns of Court Conservative and Unionist Society, 'in many ways placed them beyond the rule of law'. The remedy was to bring them within it; a course constantly pressed on Conservative governments by impatient supporters. Within the Labour Movement, too, in both its political and industrial wings, could be found restlessness and impatience. There was nothing remarkable about this. What was new was that the gulf between those thinking in terms of socialist transformation, via wholesale nationalisation, and those for whom the Labour Party was simply a vehicle for bringing Liberalism up to date, now became explicitly defined and increasingly insistent. Until now the issue could be fudged with an agreement that the first priorities of a Labour government were a pro-gramme of social welfare and the public ownership of basic utilities and services. These having been achieved the question 'what next?' became unavoidable. It was being answered by the revisionists, especially after the third successive electoral failure in 1959, in terms which outraged the more radical sections of opinion within the party and the unions. National-isation, it was said, was not only an electoral liability; in a 'post-capitalist' society it was largely irrelevant.

The organisations of both the Conservative Party and the Labour movement, however, contained these stresses. Despite the weaknesses of the British economy, objectively viewed, the personal experience of most people was of relative prosperity. The radical thrusts from left and right could not yet mobilise enough support for a serious challenge to official policy. On the Conservative side, predominant power lay with those who, in the main, considered it still appropriate to apply the traditional techniques and styles of rule, supplemented as they had long been by a cautious and discriminating corporate bias. On the Labour side, too, survival into the 1950s of political and union leaders who had worked within the system helped to prolong the period of equilibrium. Not until a younger generation succeeded party leaders like Attlee and Morrison, and union leaders like Deakin, Williamson, Lawther and Carron, were there the beginnings of a break in transmission of the doctrine that it was 'the prior aim of government to prevent crisis and class confrontation', and of the governing institutions to assist (Middlemas, 1979, p. 22).

British Industrial Relations as the 'Mature Case'

It is understandable, therefore, that until the 1960s there seemed to be objective grounds on which to base a view that Britain's institutions were developing, and would continue to develop, along lines whose principal directions were largely extensions of those established long before. The same notion was applied to the industrial relations system. There was a disposition to see Britain as the 'mature case' of industrial capitalism. 'In Britain, and in all democratic countries with increasingly powerful trade unions, the trend in the evolution of collective bargaining has been towards a progressive enlargement of its scope' in terms both of content – the subjects with which it dealt – and of coverage – the numbers of employees covered by collective agreements (Flanders, 1954, p. 258). The history of British industrial relations showed a marked trend towards the centralisation of negotiation (H. A. Turner, 1957, p. 128).

Flanders noted that the growth of industry – wide bargaining had 'encouraged the neglect of subjects which can only be dealt with satisfactorily at works level'. However, there were signs that workplace bargaining on issues other than wages was receiving new emphasis 'and if the "rule of law" is extended at this level we may find that many local strikes would tend to disappear as national strikes have done' (Flanders, 1954, p. 321). He was referring here to what was believed in the 1950s to be an established feature of Britain's industrial relations – the virtual disappearance, since 1926, of the large-scale strike as an official instrument of union policy. The long-apparent movement towards industry-wide regulation and the acceptance of arbitration had produced, it was felt, a change in 'the social significance of strikes'. The long period of relatively low figures for working days lost through stoppages seemed to support the thesis that 'national regulation and . . . arbitration have tended to eliminate the strike as a bargaining weapon in union strategy, used on a national scale to advance their claims or to defend ground previously won'. Increasingly, it had become a form of local protest by a group of workers either against their own management or sometimes against a decision of their own union (Flanders, 1952, p. 120). No specialist observer of industrial relations supposed that the unions had abandoned the strike but there was an assumption that as an official instrument of policy it had been severely downgraded in the scale of priorities. This was often linked with the unions' increasing emergence as a powerful and respected estate.

> The reluctance of the unions to use the strike as a means of enforcing wage demands is a marked feature of the rise in their status . . . Whichever party is in power, the trade unions are consulted about every measure that affects them. They are represented on no fewer than sixty governmental committees and have access to Ministers at almost any time they desire . . . The British trade union leader of today considers himself to be a responsible industrial statesman: his status is assured and he is ready to accept responsibility with pride. (B. C. Roberts, 1957, pp. 109–10)

The notion of development towards maturity emerged explicitly in an evaluation by Kahn-Freund, doyen of labour law. In a paper published in 1954 he contrasted the 'static' forms of collective bargaining more characteristic of the Continent and North America with the 'dynamic' forms more widely found in Britain. Under the former the parties entered into 'contracts' from time to time in a process all too apt to be rigid and inflexible by comparison with the latter, under which permanent joint institutions adapted rules and mutual expectations flexibly in a constantly evolving accommodation to changing circumstances, a process more of continuous 'joint administration' than 'bargaining'. Thus was fostered a subtle and civilised web of mutual obligations betokening more 'highly-developed forms of labour–management relations'; a 'higher community' of intergroup relations than could be created by the crude blunt instruments of legal norms and sanctions, which signified the collapse of community rather than its promotion. 'It is the maturity of collective industrial relations in Britain which may explain the relative insignificance of legal sanctions ...' There was, consequently, 'a close connection between the largely "dynamic" character of collective bargaining in Britain and ... the insignificance of the law in the regulation of intergroup relations'. The same character could also account for the informality of intergroup standards, the lack of codification and the importance of custom and practice.

Kahn-Freund was 'strongly tempted to argue' a parallel between the British approach to law and the British approach to industrial relations, in their emphasis on procedural rather than substantive norms; their reliance on uncodified traditions; their aversion to schemes of systematic codification. He very much supported, too, the developmental conception of Britain's industrial relations. 'In the long run, the growing consistency and strength of the organizations on both sides and the emergence of established collective relations will make for industrial peace ... The strike and the lockout will become the sparingly used "ultima ratio" in the arsenal of the groups.' Spontaneity would appear at the rank and file level of the unofficial strike. This 'danger of a relapse into more primitive forms of conduct', however, was 'inherent in the rigidity of the social patterns of the labour dispute at the highest point of its development' (Kahn-Freund, 1954).

Although analysts both of the radical left and the radical right would have offered interpretations which diverged in every respect from the liberal-pluralist perspective of Kahn-Freund, the normative evaluation presented by his analysis was widely echoed throughout the British Labour movement and among many industrial relations specialists. By this somewhat Ptolemaic conception, Britain, as the mature case at the centre of the industrial relations universe, compared favourably with such countries as America, with its detailed and elaborate formal plant contracts striving to cover every contingency, and Germany, with its growing panoply of statutory Works Councils and co-determination machinery. These came in for some heavy patronising for their marked reliance on legal structuring, regulation and sanctions. Even some American observers were prepared to agree. It was argued that America was following in Britain's footsteps, 'with a couple of decades' lag, according to some assumed pattern of evolution in labour relations'. Even Lester, though sceptical of this notion, conceded that in some respects Britain's 'union–management relations are in a more mature stage of development than ours' (Lester, 1958, p. 73).

It was understandable, perhaps, that little attention should have been paid to the contingencies which underpinned the continuities in Britain's industrial relations system, for until the 1960s these contingencies did not change in ways that had much significance for that system. Between the wars Britain certainly had her economic problems and miseries, but she still possessed a nineteenth-century heritage of foreign assets which to some extent cushioned her economic weaknesses, thereby enabling the tradition to continue by which governments largely abstained from active economic management of the kind which has emerged since. Within this context, trade union leaders had been able to avoid major disputes between 1927 and 1939 – except in textiles. 'Prices were relatively stable compared with the years immediately after the [First World] war; in bad years reductions in official wage rates were, on the whole, not heavy; when prosperity returned wages rose but unemployment remained high' (Clegg, 1954, p. 8).

The substantial disposal of foreign assets to pay for the Second World War was offset by American aid until 1945, but then emerged starkly as a crucial factor in Britain's impoverishment. This, together with a significant shift of emphasis in social philosophy, made active economic management the major priority of postwar governments and the principal test of their political survival. Yet for twenty years or so the condition of Britain's economy in the world context, while it evoked great anxiety, was not such as to galvanise governments into the more radical forms of intervention in industrial relations that were to emerge later. While her economic performance hardly matched that of countries such as Germany, France and Japan, the rate of growth compared favourably with that in her earlier history. The crippling dilemmas that have boxed in the British economy did not then seem so permanently unyielding; and some palpable prosperity could reasonably support a belief that a 'solution' to 'the economic problem' could be found and that Britain would resume her place among the leading economies of the world. Equally it seemed reasonable to assume that Britain's industrial relations system would continue 'developing' along lines already laid down, with the future an extrapolation of past and present.

The wartime legislation imposing compulsory arbitration went in 1951, but provision remained whereby the terms of a collective agreement might be extended to cover a particular recalcitrant employer. Another of the many types of change defined as 'progress' had always been the amalgamation or merger movement towards fewer, bigger and more comprehensive unions, thought to make for rationalisation of collective bargaining and reduction of the 'disorder' produced by inter-union warfare. Successive statutes had progressively reduced the legal voting requirements and an Act of 1964 continued the trend. Minimum wage legislation was further extended and a new Fair Wages resolution shifted the emphasis even more firmly to the standards set by representative joint machinery of negotiation as the touchstone of 'fairness'. Compensation for injury had been caught up in the Beveridge rationalisation of welfare.

These few examples could be multiplied to give a detailed account which would reveal little, if anything, which might not be interpreted as contributing towards a continuity of tradition extending back for almost a century. It could, of course, be argued that a complete account would have to include successive attempts by Labour and Conservative governments to influence directly the course of wages and salaries – certainly unprecedented in peacetime. The wage restraint policy of 1948–50; the 'price freeze' of 1956–7; the 'pay pause' of 1961; the National Incomes Commission set up in 1962; the wages, prices and productivity agreements of 1964–5, with the National Board for Prices and Incomes of 1965 – are these not to be seen as a deeply significant parting of the ways from continuity and tradition? In retrospect they are, but two points need bearing in mind. First, as suggested before, the plight of the British economy did not, in the earlier postwar period, seem so chronic as it has appeared since; talk was still of an 'economic problem' which could be overcome in some once-for-all manner. Secondly, and more fundamentally, it was broadly true that until 1966 the government policies pursued and the special institutions set up were not accompanied by powers of legal intervention. In that sense the tradition, while strained, was not broken.

8

The System under Strain

The 1960s to the 1980s

When reference was made in the preceding chapter to Kahn-Freund's near-panegyric of 1954 on Britain's industrial relations system, no criticism was intended. His was a widespread assessment among specialists in the subject. Many agreed in viewing that system in terms of free and voluntary 'development' towards 'maturity', of 'progress' towards increasingly 'orderly' and sophisticated structures of bargaining and dispute settlement, with the large-scale national strike increasingly regarded by top-level union leaders as an outmoded weapon. This Whiggish perspective was not, of course, confined to industrial relations. 'Until the later nineteen sixties the generally accepted frame for the history of Britain over the previous century was that of a series of success stories: the bloodless establishment of democracy, the evolution of the welfare state, triumph in two world wars, and the enlightened relinquishment of empire' (Wiener, 1981, p. 3). The industrial relations systems of less 'mature' capitalisms such as the United States and Germany were thought to reveal their immaturity by their heavy dependence on legal definitions and sanctions and on their being more consciously and deliberately designed by the state. There was often an implication that further 'development' and experience would bring them ever closer to the British model.

It is now possible to see this conception of Britain as the centre of the industrial relations universe as the outcome of highly contingent circumstances which have already been analysed in earlier chapters. It was soon to suffer a long and agonising Copernican revolution. For help in clarification there may be value in setting up a simple model. Central to this body of contingent circumstances was the long persistence of the limited state, which allowed the pace of much, though not all, social and legislative change to be set by 'voluntary' (that is, non-state) associations, groups, or movements, either acting by themselves or bringing pressure to bear upon governments. Successive generations of the ruling class had judged that in the British context they could best conserve their power and privilege, and avoid falling out among themselves, by upholding this legacy of the limited state which moved largely in response to pressures and counter-pressures from interest groups and from organised impulses towards piecemeal empirical reform. There was room within this political nation for new participant groups provided they gave evidence of being prepared to work within a system which continued to bestow advantages upon the existing major beneficiaries. There was no room for those with long-term programmes of planned change which would require 'positive' government of a highly active and innovatory kind. The reasons were not far to seek, and went further than the fear of immediate threat to the status quo. The longer the system had persisted, the more extensive had become – given the traditions of free association, instrumental collectivism and lack of any state-imposed 'higher good' – a thicket of organised interests and voluntary associations, all pressing their own priorities and all armed with the habits and vocabulary of 'freedom' and a determination to advance their own institutional well-being. For politicians faced with the electoral test this was a set of vipers' nests between which they were anxious to steer with extreme care – provided the basic institutions, interests and expectations which they sought to conserve came under no serious and prolonged threat.

Given the strength of these deterrents it would require contingencies of crisis dimensions to push governments into risking collision with powerful organisations which might threaten them either electorally or by overt or covert extra-parliamentary resistance. This arrangement gave much scope for the rhetoric – and practice – of freedom, but it meant that problems and needs of less than totally compelling force were liable to fall between two stools. If it was not part of the state's duty to anticipate and meet needs which seemed likely to grow; and if the voluntary bodies had their own reasons for not taking them up, the failure to act might result in problems growing to major size before the state finally felt compelled to step in. Nevertheless, until the stage was reached when crisis brought the spotlight on a whole set of such neglected needs, there might well persist a misleading impression that the limited state and non-state sectors were between them managing to meet the situation – and deserving of the accolades of 'maturity' and 'freedom' into the bargain.

Were a government eventually to feel constrained to intervene and set itself against one or more of the larger organised interests, this might have implications beyond the creation of political difficulties for the government itself. All the parties would find themselves in a more violent political environment: a violence which could be latent or manifest, figurative or physical. Certain of these possibilities could have consequences for the state's coercive apparatus. Traditional dislike and mistrust among large sections of the ruling class of strong and obtrusive coercive state forces had been conditional upon their being able to conserve power and property without them. Their ability to do this had been underpinned by a broad consensus on basic institutions and political methods in which the organised Labour movement eventually came to participate – though in this case there were many for whom consensus meant little more than resigned acquiescence in the absence of any better available alternative. But what if the consensus gave signs of weakening in certain crucial ways? One implication would be a possible shift among powerful sections of opinion towards strengthening the coercive forces of the state.

Economic Strains and Political Consensus

Such a simple model as this can do no more than suggest lines of inquiry and prompt useful questions. One of them relates to the probable causes of breakdown in the broad consensus. It could be argued that what has ultimately supported the traditional strategy of rule over the past century has been the predominantly upward trend in economic growth. This has, of course, known recurrent periods of faltering and periods – such as the first decade of this century – when the working classes were denied their share in the improvement. Yet these do not characterise the general trend. Even the much-abused 1930s, still being described by some as 'the black and hopeless years' (Forman, 1979, p. 22), were a period of relative prosperity and rising standards for wage- and salary-earners in work, particularly those in the Midlands and the south-east.

Economic growth supported the consensus by, on the one hand, mitigating working-class discontents and, on the other, by enabling the ruling classes to feel that pressures from organised labour were not too dangerously threatening for profits, economic stability and the progress of the economy. They did not, therefore, feel impelled to change their style of rule and its relatively accommodating postures. The modesty of working-class expectations played its part in making this stance possible. Limited social perceptions as well as limited economic opportunities imposed restraints on aspirations.

When the threat to consensus began to build up, it originated not from organised labour but from alarm on the part of governments and state agencies that labour pressures were bearing over-hard on profits, earnings, prices, workplace order, managerial prerogative and individual freedoms. The workplace power conferred by full employment was enlarging the scope and strength of restrictive 'custom and practice' and the ability of work groups to impose sanctions on management with or without the support of the official union hierarchy. Concurrently the last barriers to 'consumerism' among some sections of the working classes were breaking down. Rising earnings, rehousing, the break-up of old and often inward-looking communities, television, mass advertising, the explosion of the mass-produced consumer goods and 'leisure' industries; all contributed towards an enlargement of perceptions and expectations.

Had the economy been able to cope with these pressures and, at the same time, yield satisfactory profits and a tax revenue adequate to meet rising government expenditure without inflation, the history of Britain over the past two decades would have been very different. The 1950s and early 1960s had not seemed too disastrous in these respects. Admittedly, by then the wartime mood of unity had long since worn off. Economic difficulties, dilemmas and conflicts racked successive governments, employers and unions alike. Yet Britain had shared in a massive growth of world trade and, given almost continuously expanding national production, nearly everyone's standards rose year by year. The Labour Party was continuing to pursue the socially integrative policy, manifest since its formation, of 'inculcating the working class in general and the trade union leadership in particular with national values consistent with consensus'

(Panitch, 1976, p. 236). Conservative commitment to full employment gave employers confidence that growth would continue and that they could concede wage claims without too much risk of pricing themselves out of markets (Crouch, 1979, p. 32). The currently predominant forces within Conservative governments, during the first half of their 1951–64 period of rule, appeared to accept not only full employment but also the welfare state, an active policy of conciliation in industrial disputes, and the practice of sympathetic consultation with the TUC. As late as 1959 the Conservative Party manifesto echoed the 'one nation' theme and included an undertaking that the government would invite representatives of employers and unions to 'consider afresh the human and industrial problems that the next five years will bring' (Barnes and Reid, 1980, p. 34). Macmillan plainly hoped to continue the conciliatory approach to the unions established in the earlier years of Tory rule from 1951.

Yet even during this relatively favoured period for the consensus, ideas likely to be disruptive of it were gathering vigour and were destined to triumph with the access of the Thatcher governments. These harked back to the economic liberalism that had long been a significant strand in Conservative thinking but which, contained by traditional Toryism, had not so far been allowed fully to have its head. Prominent in Treasury files even during the early 1950s was Operation Robot: a plan to 'abolish in one move all the restrictions and arrangements governing the permitted use of sterling abroad, and at the same time to make both the volume and direction of economic activity at home subject to the unimpeded play of world market forces'. There were to be only two instruments of public influence – bank rate and adjustments of the sterling exchange rate. 'Market forces would be relied upon to impose the necessary adjustments in domestic living standards or in the level of employment' – the general thrust being to recreate an approximation to the pre-1914 world and subject the economy to maximum international exposure. The plan received vigorous support from a number of powerful officials as well as from certain ministers. Though the Cabinet balked, the underlying notions retained much of their vigour (Shonfield, 1969, pp. 100–1). What was new here was not the thrust towards restoring as fully and as soon as possible a liberal world-wide trading and financial order in which Britain would be, as always, a committed participant. This renewal of commitment to the open economy had already been made in 1945, as it had been in 1918. Openness within a liberal world-wide trading order had long been assumed to be a structural necessity for Britain's economic health. It was a conception not seriously departed from even during Britain's mildly protectionist 1930s, and following the Second World War it was a major reason why Britain's leaders were prepared to submit to 'free world' leadership by the United States, now seen as the only power capable of upholding such an international capitalist trading system. What was new – or rather newly reasserted – was the argument that the domestic economy should be subjected without impediment or active state intervention to external economic pressures; that state attempts to maintain internal Keynesian demand management should be abandoned in favour of the upholding of a purely market order. Alongside this economic liberalism within the Conservative camp was a strengthening reassertion of hostility towards union and work-group encroachments on individual freedom – the closed shop and pressures on those displaying reluctance to strike or to support some other union or work-group tactic.

By 1956, and even more emphatically in 1957, the revived economic liberalism was beginning to show through in the form of orthodox restrictive measures applied to wage-price inflation, with protection of the exchange rate being given priority over growth, full employment and a conciliatory industrial relations policy (Crouch, 1979, p. 37). Already governments were being judged by their performance in handling a recurrent type of economic crisis. Even within a world context of growth and falling commodity prices, the inflationary combination of full employment and free sectional collective bargaining was regularly generating pressure on the balance of payments. Since this happened to be the most visible cause of government decisions to raise interest rates, restrict credit, raise taxation and cut public and private investment, the result was to isolate the trade unions and free collective bargaining as the prime sources of the nation's economic difficulties.

Yet the major causes of strain lay elsewhere. Organised labour – and for that matter organised employers – were being expected to adjust themselves, however painfully, within fixed points of domestic and foreign policies which they had no real opportunity of effectively influencing. These fixed points included the bipartisan resolve to accept the role of junior partner to the United States in world affairs and to continue to accept the dependence of the British economy on a still relatively open trading network. The first imposed quite exceptional burdens in terms of military spending at levels higher than in any member of the Western alliance other than the United States herself. The second helped to produce the paradox that a poorly performing economy was able, given Britain's international trading, financial and military connections, to develop a proliferation of multinational companies second only to America's. These contributed to a high rate of capital export which became massive after the Thatcher government abolished all exchange control. The forces determined to maintain Britain as a fully open economy were reinforced by the traditional resolve of the financial institutions, supported by the Treasury, to preserve London as a major financial centre, a role requiring freedom of international movement by both short- and long-term funds. 'The result of the renewal of Britain's traditional liberal orientation to the world economy was that a serious conflict began to develop between the international priorities of British policy and the needs of the domestic economy.' The clash 'was between the new and often combined international operations of British industry and British finance, and the requirements of domestic expansion' (Gamble, 1981, p. 114). The point was not that supposedly capital-hungry ventures at home were being denied funds that went abroad. It was that such dynamic impulses of expansionism and innovation as were generated in Britain were too disposed to seek expression overseas. Britain's most successful business sectors often found it easier to accumulate capital by expanding abroad than by investing at home. However valid the argument that this was for economically rational reasons, the process did nothing for domestic industrial renewal, innovation, expansion and job-creation.

Since levels of overseas spending were treated as the last to suffer cuts, the burden of adjustment in the event of sterling crisis was placed on the domestic economy. The price was paid in terms of, *inter alia*, domestic capital investment, which suffered regular bouts of deflation, and in terms of heightening tensions between governments, striving through a variety of means to restrain the inflationary growth of incomes, and unions, increasingly under pressure from a strengthening shop-floor movement determined to benefit from the tight labour market. Since all the other elements in the whole unstable economic equation were viewed by Establishment opinion as 'given' and beyond radical change, organised labour was expected to submit and adjust to the pay levels which the 'givens' of government policies were believed to dictate. Since there were no processes by which organised labour was either expected or able to influence these fixed points, the problem of consent became critical. In the absence of even the broadest agreement about allocation of the national product, competitive sectional bargaining thrived in conditions of labour shortage and inflation was the predictable result. Given its reluctance to submit to the implications of policies decided elsewhere, it was organised labour which was publicly identified as the 'cause' of the instability. The situation was beginning to demonstrate the difficulties of a society which has been politically reared on doctrines of individualism, the minimal state and consent; which contains strong organised corporate interests; and which cannot produce sufficient wealth to cover the costs of private corporate expectations and public policies. The corporate interests are in a position to frustrate public policies unless their consent to them is secured, yet the difficulties of winning that consent, and even more the consent of their rank and file constituents, are immense. The economy becomes overloaded and in an economy like Britain's the specially weak link is the value of the currency.

There were other features of the economy which led to the 1950s being described as 'a decade of decline and wasted opportunities' (Crouch, 1979, p. 32). The growth rate, though fully comparable with, and sometimes exceeding, Britain's past performance, looked feeble when set alongside that of other countries, and productivity improvements were unimpressive. 'The defensive strength and conservatism of the unions meshed with the conservatism and international orientation of large sections of British capital, and greatly reduced the scope of increasing productivity' (Gamble, 1981, p. 122). The failure of the growth rate to cover heavy overseas spending and investment and, at the same time, meet steadily rising expectations at home was all the more significant in that the consensual integration of the industrial relations system was coming increasingly to rest on economic prosperity. Conservative definitions of social justice, as manifested in government budgets, did not accord with those of the TUC, and in 1956 the General Council charged the government with 'deliberately dismantling the machinery of control and planning in order to return to a freer economy' (Dorfman, 1974, p. 88). Yet the period earned the journalistic tag of the Age of Affluence and economic weaknesses were not to emerge as salient until the 1960s, nor become major problems until the 1970s.

Rejected Strategies and Accepted Constraints

As the decades passed and Britain's economic failure became increasingly evident – and aggravated further by the oil-price revolution of the early 1970s – governments of both major parties threshed about within a limited spectrum of strategies. Though both veered from one style to another in their search for a solution – and often pursued contrasting styles at the same time – the methods of the older financial orthodoxy became more and more marked until, having been actively furthered by Labour ministers, they reached their apogee under the Thatcher government. The reasons for this triumph of orthodoxy must be sought in the persistence of those traditional postures which have emerged so often in the preceding analysis.

Governments of both parties expressed some of them through their readiness to work within tight constraints in their search for solutions. We have already noted, for example, the commitment, among Labour as well as Conservative leadership, to the open economy – to the principle that the economy should remain open to international economic forces and geared into international economic mechanisms and institutions. The reasons for the vehement Conservative attachment to this principle are clear enough, given the power of the City in their counsels, the weight of British industry heavily involved in international trade, and the continued ideological emphasis given to free markets. To explain its favour among many Labour leaders we need to examine briefly what the alternative strategy would involve. Any attempt significantly to reduce Britain's dependence upon outside economic forces and institutions would require rigorous controls over imports and over money movements in and out of London; withdrawal from the European Economic Community; transformation of relations with such institutions as the International Monetary Fund; the virtual certainty of punitive reactions from America, the oil states and elsewhere; and attempts through *dirigiste* planning to construct a more self-sufficient economy under state initiative, guidance and sanctions. Given this degree of control over the nation's economic variables, combined with an egalitarian programme which combined redistribution with freshly considered policies towards housing, education and health care, it might just be possible to offer the trade unions and their members a sufficiently attractive package to permit an effective incomes policy and the necessary centralisation of union bargaining authority. Technological innovation, growth and a high level of employment could then conceivably be combined with a manageable degree of inflation.

The reasons for the rejection of any such programme by the Labour centre and right are various. Among them are an appreciation of the magnitude of the political struggle required to implement it; a fear that the structure of Britain's political institutions and conventions might not survive such a struggle; the conviction that, in any case, a programme of that sort, along with its accompanying ideology, would be electorally disastrous, and probably a simple personal dislike of such radical departures. One Tory political journalist who displays a candour untypical of the British political scene attributes to the Labour right the beliefs that 'a middle class as strong as the one in Britain cannot be trifled with, even by a socialist government with a large majority; that any fundamental attempt to interfere with bourgeois hegemony, except by *force majeure* (and where could that force come from?) would put the socialist clock back rather than forward . . . that socialism only prospers in Britain when it serves middle-class interests, in practice, however little in theory' (Worsthorne, 1979–81). In addition, it was legitimate to have doubts about whether there were any circumstances, short of total social upheaval following violent revolution or war, in which the rank and file of British trade unions could be induced to accept a permanent incomes policy, or in which British managers could change the behavioural habits of centuries. The institutional and structural factors and habituated social relations and ideologies which have helped to sustain some of Britain's social and political decencies are also proving stubborn obstacles to economic modernisation.

These historical continuities are also displayed in persistent British attitudes towards active state co-ordination and planning. By comparison with what were deemed by other Western countries to be appropriate policies in pursuit of economic growth and modernisation, Britain continued to operate the minimal state.

> Britain's post-war experience provides another kind of illustration of the way in which a living tentacle reaches out of past history, loops itself round and holds fast to a solid block of the present. The striking thing in the British case is the extraordinary tenacity of older attitudes towards the role of public power. Anything which smacked of a restless or over-energetic state, with ideas of guiding the nation on the basis of a long view of its collective economic interest, was instinctively the object of suspicion.

Although in the few years following the Second World War 'the basic elements of modern planning were present in Britain as in no other major Western country', 'traditional ideology continued to assert itself' and the 'old instinctive suspicion of positive government, which purports to identify the needs of the community before the community itself has recognised them, remained as vigorous as ever' (Shonfield, 1969, pp. 88, 93, 94). Postwar Labour governments, which even in their approach to welfare manifested mainly 'new' Liberalism rather than socialism, directed such 'planning' as they undertook to strictly short-term objectives. They made no attempt to co-ordinate the policies of public utilities and services and soon accepted defeat, at the hands of industry's trade associations, of their ambiguously designed Development Councils which might have served as instruments of industrial modernisation (ibid., pp. 96–9; Rogow and Shore, 1955, chs 2 and 4). No attempt was made 'to tackle the uncompetitive, status-ridden institutions of British society, which assisted so much in ensuring the cohesion of the ruling class and in diverting energies into the service of the Empire and the state, but which generally encouraged conservative attitudes which impeded industrial rationalisation' (Gamble, 1981, p. 119).

'Instinctive suspicion' and 'traditional ideology' were kept vigorously alive by organisations and institutions which feared the encroachments of long-term planning upon their independence and functions; which could appeal to a rich potent vocabulary and emotive response attaching to the concept of 'freedom'; and which operated in a culture where the notion of a higher common good has historically possessed little power to move. Among these organisations were not only business and financial companies and their associations but also, of course, the unions. Although historical, institutional and personal ties helped Labour governments to maintain a 'special relationship' not available to Conservatives, union leaders would have been acutely embarrassed to be confronted by a long-term economic plan which included the planning of labour, its movement and its rewards. Increasingly, their embarrassment would have sprung not only from fears that their bargaining freedom might be threatened but also from doubts about their ability to guarantee their members' adherence to any national plan, whether imposed or negotiated. Shop-steward organisation at the workplace, growing spontaneously in highly favourable circumstances to serve growing rank and file aspirations towards the kind of protective job regulation of which Britain's craft groups had supplied the model for so long, now constituted a potentially independent power base over which national leaders had few effective sanctions.

Such were the pressures on governments, however, to master economic management and escape from 'stop–go' policies that administrations of both parties made gestures towards planning of a sort during the first half of the 1960s. A temporary and partial change in the balance of the Whitehall mood dispatched free markets briefly from favour and the Conservative government declared itself for more active long-term management and attempts at modernisation. Administrative structures making such management possible were established in 1962 but, according to Robert Neild, 'there was no fundamental change of method' and the Treasury remained unconverted. Two years later, under the Labour government, a fresh bid to use public power actively to reshape the private sector, speed growth and stimulate modernisation derived considerable impetus from the combination of 'an exceptionally powerful politician' (George Brown) and the recruitment to a new Department of Economic Affairs of 'a lot of outsiders, many of them academic economists with no attachment to the traditions of the permanent civil service, some of them businessmen'. Writing in 1965, Shonfield felt unable to predict the outcome of this power 'struggle between an old and a new civil service style' – the old being 'very powerful and very entrenched' (Shonfield, 1969, pp. 105, 175). We know the outcome now.

But the victory of Treasury old style was not the only factor in the ruination of this venture towards long-term management. Forecasts and objectives alike were rendered futile when yet another balance of payments crisis prompted the government to impose severe deflationary measures and the National Plan was officially abandoned in July 1966. The implications were clear. Long-term economic planning faces massive obstacles in a society densely thicketed with powerful and fiercely independent interest-group organisations which offer keen resistance to 'higher order' initiatives and admonitions from outside their ranks and even to moral leadership within them; a society in which governments commit the economy to a high degree of international exposure; and in which leading public servants are allowed to uphold traditions inimical to the positive state. So long as features like these persisted, expanding the economy meant predictable balance of payments and sterling crises followed by the familiar deflationary package to soothe foreign bankers and other sterling creditors. The Wilson governments showed neither ability nor apparent wish to escape these crippling structural dilemmas; the political risks of attempting it were still more daunting than those of not doing so.

For there was still the hope that short-term expedients would serve. Lacking the will and the political support to create conditions which might make long-term planning feasible, governments leaned on short-term expedients to meet their recurrent crises – expedients which sought to moderate the inflationary incomes-prices spiral either directly by acting in some way upon the unions or employers, or indirectly by acting upon the level of economic activity in a deflationary manner through fiscal and monetary means. They could, of course, combine both direct and indirect methods.

One much-used expedient has been propaganda. Prominent throughout the whole postwar period has been the use of direct exhortations and appeals to wage- and lower-salary-earners not only to restrain their pay claims, but also to abandon the restrictive spirit in their workplace practices and behaviour. Economic failure heightened the tendency, strongly supported by media journalism, to blame the adversary posture among large sections of Britain's workforce. Endlessly condemned was their disposition to play a zero-sum, win-lose game; to define management as the enemy and be excessively wary about accepting its leadership; to perceive situations in terms of 'them' and 'us'; to demand a financial price for their acceptance of every productive improvement whether it increased work strain or not; and to use the growing strength of their workplace organisation to apply restrictive demarcative protections and resist every innovation that appeared to threaten, even for a minority, earnings, status, job security, shop-steward rights, or union strength. The closed shop and the tendency for well-organized groups to squeeze out the remnants of non-unionism were often discussed as if they were postwar inventions, and the concept of individual liberty enjoyed as always the support of many highly placed champions. There was much nostalgia for a golden age when trade unions, instead of being the allegedly ruthless, selfish juggernauts they are now, played a noble role as protectors of the weak and poor. This conception owed much to the fact that in earlier times, when absolute poverty and hardship were far more palpable and widespread, it was a good deal easier to see trade unionism as being subsumed within a general struggle to alleviate the lot of the poor, though in fact even then it was a sectional phenomenon that was unlikely to benefit the worst-off.

Restrictionism and the National Culture

All this was par for the course. Much of it was descriptively valid. There was no attempt, of course, to understand such postures and policies in terms of organised labour's responses to the structures, values and ideologies imposed on them. It remains true, nevertheless, that there is no more reason now than in the past to deny the fact of workplace restrictionism – which must be seen as including not only continuing formal or informal regulation but also a considerable incidence of forms of 'industrial action' other than strikes. Pratten, in a study of labour productivity differences within multinational industrial companies, compared the performances, within each company, of plants located in a range of countries which included the United Kingdom and Germany. Twelve companies operating in both countries 'specifically referred to the greater ease of introducing changes in Germany ... In the UK, employees at many factories insisted on negotiating changes in pay when new machinery was introduced, and it was claimed that this was not the case in Germany'. By another judgement, 'a typical reaction' among workers in the UK 'is that improvements proposed by management are automatically going to be to the detriment of the employee either as an individual or as a group'. Discussions with trade union officers 'did not conflict with the evidence of difficult negotiations at many UK plants when new machinery is introduced'. Summing up, Pratten refers to the claim by 'many managers' that by comparison with other industrial countries 'employees in the UK were simply less willing to co-operate in achieving high productivity', and concludes that these differences 'probably reflect differences of history and tradition'. Like other careful appraisals of the adversary posture in Britain, Pratten's made clear that it is not universal and is but one factor among many causing economic weakness. He found that 'about half the firms operating in the two countries did not attribute any of the productivity differences to their labour force'. But although 'within international companies the lower performance of labour is not the sole cause of lower productivity in the UK, ... it is clear that it does play a part' (Pratten, 1976, pp. 55, 56, 58, 59, 66).

Another study carried out for the Anglo-German Foundation for the Study of Industrial Society was prepared to be bolder. 'It may well be' that what 'does much to account' for the contrasting economic performance of the two countries are the profound differences in their industrial relations systems. 'The dominant style' of the British system 'is its adversary nature', which extends not only to pay but is also 'the favoured means of addressing almost every kind of industrial problem that crops up. The great majority of issues are settled amicably enough but conflict potentially escalating into strike action is inherent in the adversary approach. It is a possibility that can never be remote from the mind of a management contemplating change or innovation' (Jacobs *et al.*, 1978, pp. 3, 131–2). The report employs a distinction drawn by Bergmann *et al.* between this adversary approach and the so-called co-operative policy. 'Co-operative trade unions try to protect the interests of their members by tailoring both wage demands and strategy to the state of the economy and the needs of growth. They take account of the marginal economic concessions available to the other side when formulating their wage policies, and, given the existence of institutionalised incomes policy, agree to abide by the targets and guidelines set by government economic policy' (Bergmann *et al.*, 1975, p. 28). Jacobs *et al.* were, in 1978, in 'no doubt that since the mid-1950s the majority of unions in the Federal Republic have predominantly followed a policy of co-operation' (Jacobs *et al.*, 1978, p. 48). Unions pursuing the adversary or conflictual strategy, on the other hand, 'attempt to realise the articulated interests of their members through immediate wage demands and strategies. They refuse to relate their wage demands according to the state of the national economy. Their demands take account of existing market conditions and of their own current strength. They refuse to take responsibility for the national economy as a whole' (Bergmann *et al.*, 1975, p. 28).

The simple 'conflictual–co-operative' framework is too crude as it stands. For the moment, however, our concern is with appraisals of the persistent restrictionist spirit within Britain's trade unions. Specially valuable here are Kahn-Freund's judgements. Speaking as one with experience of industrial relations in Germany as well as Britain, Kahn-Freund, himself of German origin, expressed the views of an Anglophile social democratic reformist and candid friend of the British unions. Adopting the definition of a restrictive practice as 'an arrangement under which labour is not used efficiently and which is not justifiable on social grounds', he supported the widespread view that 'many of these customs and regulations seriously restrict the optimal use of labour . . . ; that we are here confronted with a heritage of traditions, and that this heritage may be and is an obstacle to an urgently needed adjustment, that in other words to get rid of many of these regulations is without question a national necessity'. He acknowledged that such practices as output restriction, demarcation lines, the artificial creation of overtime, manning–scale rigidities and the employment of unproductive labour were products of the direct democracy of the work group rather than of the union *per se*, and that they could not exist without the consent or connivance of management.

These attempts to limit and control labour supply he saw, along with the greater incidence of direct democracy at the workplace, to be 'the most characteristically British feature of our industrial relations'. We noted earlier his observation that this tradition, 'which originated in craft rules and institutions, does not in Continental countries play the dominant role it does here'. It is a 'Bastille of customs, institutions, and rules whose spirit was and is as far away from that of capitalist market economics as from that of the Marxist class struggle'. This medieval survival, which had outlived the craft unions and spread into manufacturing industries, service industries and white-collar trades which never knew the old craft organisation, could only be understood as an element in the general history of Britain and not merely working-class or union history. Kahn-Freund here lifts the argument above commonplace scapegoating. It is a legacy in-herited not only by wage- and some salary-earners but by the entire nation – 'a society not separated from its medieval past by a social revolution'. The pre-eminence of demarcation lines and manning levels; restrictions of access to jobs and to the labour market; 'above all the insistence on a strictly protected status, is not just a characteristic of the British trade unions, it is a characteristic of British society. It is a pervasive element of the social structure of this country.' Anyone coming here from the Continent 'is puzzled beyond words by the careful and rigid division of professional and commercial activities in Britain. This, he feels, must be a nation riddled with demarcation lines, and with professional taboos and rituals'. The mode of evolving these regulations is as characteristic as the regulations themselves. 'The creation of norms of conduct through custom and practice, through experience manifested in precedents, is characteristic of the guild spirit . . . and therefore as characteristic of the English or Scottish common law as of the traditional regulation of labour relations in Britain.' So, too, is the strength of corporate identification. 'Where else in the world do you find this intensive "we" feeling towards organized and traditional social groups, schools and colleges, clubs and trade unions, that is regarded as a matter of course in this country?'

These survivals of a 'very deep-seated pre-capitalist guild spirit' engen-der 'what is in the strict sense an ideology; it is the ideology of conserva-tism – in the non-party political sense – an attitude which is shared by many adherents of all political parties, right and left. The spirit of "this is the way we have always done it, why change?" is the ideology corres-ponding to the structural division of labour . . . ' It has greater power and dangers here than in countries like Germany and France 'which have consciously and deliberately abandoned their medieval traditions' (Kahn-Freund, 1979, pp. 35–56).

Subsequent studies have enlarged on this theme that the restrictionist pre-industrial spirit among organised labour has its counterpart among other classes and sections of British society. Wiener has assembled a diversity of evidence which takes in, and elaborates, many points already noted in earlier chapters, showing that the very success of the landed aristocracy in maintaining social stability and continuity through the ready assimilation of rising industrialism often had the effect of muting such aggressive spirit of enterprise as that industrialism possessed. This muting, he argues, persists. He reminds us, too, that there also persists the distaste for industrialism, aggressive enterprise and single-minded profit-making which has long pervaded British culture and politics at all social levels.

The image of an essentially rural, traditional England, and the distrust of materialism and economic change that went along with it, had practical effects upon business . . . This myth of England both diverted talent and energies from industry and gave a particular 'gentry' cast to existing industry, discouraging commitment to a wholehearted pursuit of economic growth . . . As a rule, leaders of commerce and industry in England over the past century have accommodated themselves to an elite culture blended of pre-industrial aristocratic and religious values and more recent professional and bureaucratic values that inhibited their quest for expansion, productivity, and profit. (Wiener, 1981, p. 127)

This 'myth of England' and the values and dispositions it supports has its equivalents elsewhere. An impressive array of comparable evidence could be selected from the history not only of France (as already noted), but also of Germany. What Germany had, however, that Britain did not have, were a technocratic tradition that enjoyed high status, together with a strong, assertive nationalist state apparatus prepared actively to encourage economic growth as a buttress of state power and to promote the requisite structure of education. Since, in Britain, governments and state agencies were themselves deeply influenced by the anti-enterprise culture, business was supported in its 'gentry' posture rather than galvanised out of it and the system of education likewise was influenced accordingly.

It is not difficult to appreciate why, in the context of this social structure and culture, propaganda can hardly be said to have significantly affected mass work behaviour, especially when directed only at wage-earners. Little self-awareness has been manifested by the various groups within the Establishment of their own conservatism, protectionism and pre-industrial dispositions. The improbability, in such a culture, of one stratum only, and that the least favoured, responding to the summons urging a fundamental change of attitudes seems to have occurred to few.

Exhortatory propaganda has been directed 'principally to convincing the men on the workshop floor that . . . it is in their own interests to assist in making industry more efficient. The gospel that a larger cake means bigger shares all round has been indefatigably propagated to . . . get them to see that their real wages will not be improved by "fighting the bosses" but by a common effort to increase productivity' (Flanders, 1964, p. 240). The sentiments have age-long familiarity but nothing since 1964 prompts any revision of Flanders' judgement that to suppose workgroup co-operation towards raising productivity can be increased by exhortatory propaganda is a delusion. Flanders' own book was a descriptive analysis of an early example of 'productivity bargaining', which in its more comprehensive and rigorous forms sought to involve management, union and workgroup leaders in a joint negotiated recasting of work organisation and pay structures. In return for precisely specified and negotiated changes yielding greater efficiency, workers were granted precisely specified and negotiated improvements in their terms of employment. In these circumstances, shop stewards and their constituents felt able to relinquish or scale down some of their protective devices. The method had the virtue that it acknowledged, given the prevalence of adversary relations and shop-floor suspicion of managerial leadership, the more fruitful prospect offered by the bargaining method if a closer *rapprochement* was desired. But it made heavy demands upon management in terms of time, skill, patience, analytical ability and the constant vigilance and will required to maintain the changed patterns of relations and organisation. Productivity bargaining remained, for a while, on the agenda of thrusting companies where such qualities were to be found, but frequently degenerated into a device for evading incomes policy on the ground of being 'self-financing'. It can hardly be said to have established, as Flanders hoped, 'new norms of industrial conduct from which society will then permit no retreat' (ibid., p. 256). In other respects, also, 'few British industries adopted the kind of organizational practices which were developed by their competitors to overcome organizational practices on the shop floor and make investment pay. The failure was more a failure of management than of the work force' (Gamble, 1981, p. 122).

These and similar comments are usually directed at manufacturing industry, so it must be borne in mind that this employs a shrinking proportion – now well under half – of the total workforce. What must also be noted when assessing the present and future impact of the restrictionist spirit upon Britain's economic effort is that certain new growth industries may prove better able to establish a different pattern of relations. Examples are the activities connected with 'information technology', which seem more directly geared to international standards and moti- vations. As against this, however, it remains the case, as Kahn-Freund was concerned to emphasise, that labour in the non-manufacturing sectors now expanding have often shown at least as strong a disposition towards restrictionist strategies as elsewhere. Trade unionism and professional organisation in the public, professional and services sectors have often revealed no markedly different stance from those in manufacturing. There remains the possibility, nevertheless, that some leaders in these growing sectors may seek to promote more co-operative, positive-sum relations with management than have been prevalent in manual wage-earning. With the TUC General Council being remodelled to give these union sectors increased weight and influence, there could be a significant shift in temper and style. To have practical effect this shift would, of course, have to be accepted by those at the workplace, never a matter permitting confident predictions so far as British rank and file membership is con- cerned. Even if certain white-collar and professional sectors do pursue a somewhat different tack under the combined goads of technological change, Thatcher governments and what looks like being permanent massive unemployment, the manual sectors are unlikely to follow them. The possibility exists of a trade union movement more divided than for nearly a century.

Law and the Search for Solutions

Since exhortation by propaganda was easy, cheap and did not commit anybody to anything it continued to be popular. 'Above all', declared a White Paper, *The Regeneration of British Industry*, in 1975, 'we must get away from policies of confrontation and work together in the national interest towards agreed objectives' (Currie, 1979, pp. 242, 245). In the context of Britain's industrial relations, few admonitions can have a more hollow ring of futility. Propaganda had, nevertheless, the effect already noted of mobilising opinion against the unions and reinforcing the trad-itional view of them as the major economic handicap.

Increasingly, however, the attempt to change behaviour through propaganda was accompanied by attempts to change it through the mechanism of the law. By the mid-1960s little was left of the view that Britain's industrial relations system represented the mature case among advanced industrial countries, with maturity defined in terms of inform-ality and the relative absence of law. Kahn-Freund was by 1969 arguing that there must be 'more law and not less'; that the law must be 'called upon to play a much increased role in the moulding of industrial relations, and this in a manner which is contrary to a long established tradition, a tradition however which has already begun to fade' (Kahn-Freund, 1969, pp. 311, 315).

Under pressure from the political threat of continued economic failure, governments and their advisers pursued search processes of three kinds within the broad field of industrial and labour relations law. One of them grew out of the belief – supported by many specialists, including Kahn-Freund –

> that certain, at least, of labour's defensive and restrictionist tactics were a response to insecurities and fears to which voluntary collective bargaining had manifestly failed to offer a satisfactory creative response. Supplementary means must be sought for dealing with them. Along with this was now emerging the view that the very incompleteness and haphazardness of collective bargaining – especially in its relative neglect of workplace union organisation and workplace issues – was creating disorder on the shop floor. (Fox, 1979, p. 481)

There began a sequence of statutes seeking to make good some of the deficiencies of the voluntary system by enlarging the basic statutory floor of individual employment rights. This floor was already considerable, with its nineteenth-century accretion of statutory protections relating to truck, Factory Acts, and regulations on health, welfare and safety. There had never been any reason of principle why these protections could not be pursued by collective bargaining. It was expediency and historical acci-dent rather than theory which drew these boundaries and which estab-lished before the end of the nineteenth century the tradition that such issues should be dealt with across the board by legislation.

The persistence of this tradition had contributed to the slowness of union response towards problems not previously covered by bargaining but now seen as needing regulation. The hope was that the establishment of basic statutory obligations would provide both stimulus and support for an orderly joint regulation of issues that were manifestly becoming more contentious. Later measures of this kind, along with the statutory assistance they provided the unions in securing recognition and collective bargaining rights, can also be seen in the context of the Labour government's appeal for TUC support in its incomes policy.

The sequence began in 1963, with the Conservative government's Contracts of Employment Act, which gave employees rights to minimum periods of notice according to length of service, and followed with the Labour government's Redundancy Payments Act 1965, which compelled the employer to make a payment, likewise geared to service, to any employee declared redundant after two years' employment. The Conservative government's Industrial Relations Act 1971 gave the individual some protection against 'unfair' dismissal, and Labour statutes of 1974, 1975 and 1976 further extended this floor of rights to include guaranteed pay for workless days, paid maternity leave, increased minimum periods of notice, time off for trade union or public duties, protection of employees' financial position in cases of liquidation, and the right of union representatives to advance consultation, information and negotiation about impending redundancies. Industrial tribunals in London and provincial centres were to hear claims and complaints on these and other items in the enlarged floor of rights and there was a right of appeal on questions of law to an Employment Appeal Tribunal with High Court status. These were but some of the ways in which Britain's industrial relations system, instead of remaining the model towards which other countries were expected to move as they 'matured', itself moved to become more like them. Included in the later Labour measures were also provisions designed to strengthen collective bargaining. The independent Advisory Conciliation and Arbitration Service, put on a statutory basis in 1975, was given the general duty of promoting the improvement of industrial relations and the particular duty of encouraging the extension of collective bargaining and the reform of bargaining machinery.

Two further sequences of legislation relevant at this point are those asserting basic rights for two particular categories of persons liable to suffer discrimination by race or sex. The Race Relations Acts 1968 and 1976, the Equal Pay Act 1970, and the Sex Discrimination Act 1975 all bore witness to a belief that racial and sexual discrimination were becoming actual or potential sources of contention and disorder at the workplace and therefore in need of regulation. These and the foregoing measures wrought great changes in the institutional and regulative structure of Britain's industrial relations system, but in one sense the thrust underlying them was not new. It was the same longstanding strain towards 'order' that had made its appearance in the Labour Department of the Board of Trade in the 1880s. What was new was the conviction in currently influential quarters in governments and government departments that the voluntary regulative system was failing to get to grips with issues that were becoming increasingly urgent and that this failure was significantly impeding economic advance. This thrust embodied no animus towards labour collectivism provided it was deemed 'responsible'; indeed was designed to stimulate and strengthen it.

Very different were the impulses underlying many of the activities comprising the second search process. These too were far from new. They sprang from the age-long hostility always to be found among those of power and property towards organised labour, towards the collectivist strategies and values it espoused, and towards the actual or potential industrial and political threat it represented. The key notion at the heart of their counter-attack was individualism; both in the labour market and in social relations at the workplace. They had always enjoyed strong support from lawyers wedded to the individualist common-law tradition and continued to do so now. There was strong support, too, from the wider middle class. 'The traditional framework of British labour law really rested upon a middle-class acquiescence in the current balance of industrial power' (Wedderburn, 1972, p. 275). This acquiescence was cracking fast under the gathering strength and militancy of workplace organisation during the 1950s, led by the shop stewards and manifesting itself in the rising number of unofficial strikes, the spread of the closed shop, constant upward pressure on earnings, and a widening incidence of workplace job control manifesting itself as 'custom and practice'. In 1958 appeared *A Giant's Strength: Some Thoughts on the Constitutional and the Legal Position of Trade Unions in England*, prepared by a committee of the Inns of Court Conservative and Unionist Society. This expressed much previous Conservative thinking and reflected tensions between collectivist traditions and liberal individualism which existed within individual Conservatives as well as between them.

The document was not rabid in tone and even made suggestions anticipating the Contracts of Employment Act. There can be no doubt that much of it struck sympathetic chords with some members and leaders of the Labour Party who were not only publicly uneasy about the electoral implications of the unions' reputation, but also privately uneasy – given their liberal inheritance – about collectivist union pressures on the individual. It was a palpably Conservative movement, however, which began to develop a demand for a legal industrial relations code specifying union rights and obligations, curbing union power, and defining what was acceptable union behaviour and what was not. As always, the individualism with which it was suffused stemmed partly from fear of the strength which collectivism could mobilise in a tight labour market in daily relations with management, and partly from a professed concern for individual rights.

Given the gathering mood, the unions were in danger from the courts as well as from statute. Already some verdicts had been handed down which gave the unions anxiety, but these were overshadowed by the Lords' verdict in *Rookes v. Barnard* in 1964. This was described by Kahn-Freund as a 'frontal attack upon the right to strike', achieved by creating new liabilities which evaded the protections of the 1906 Act, long assumed to be comprehensive. 'What stands out in the speeches of the Law Lords', comments another leading legal authority, 'is their determination to reach this result' (Wedderburn, 1971, pp. 361, 364). Among the first statutes promoted by the incoming Labour government of 1964 was the Trade Disputes Act 1965 which, though it plugged the gap thus created, was described as 'a traditional "negative" protection', the 'very narrowest possible Act which could have been passed to deal with *Rookes v. Barnard*' (ibid., p. 372).

It was in this atmosphere that the government, in 1965, set up the Royal (Donovan) Commission on Trade Unions and Employers' Associations. Following its report in 1968 the Labour government's White Paper, *In Place of Strife*, 1969, adopted most of its recommendations – to set up a

Commission on Industrial Relations which was to foster, by voluntary means, the reform, extension and rationalisation of the collective bargaining system; to legislate for employee protection against 'unfair' dismissals; and to make various other innovations. But given Labour's self-imposed role as a 'national' party, taking a broad view of 'the national interest', and given, too, its acceptance of the mixed economy and all that was now deemed to go with it, government ministers felt bound to take heed of – and often gave signs of fully agreeing with – the standard condemnations of organised labour. The White Paper went further than the Donovan Report advised by proposing, among other things, compulsory strike ballots and a 'cooling-off' period ('conciliation pause') for serious strikes called in breach of, or in the absence of, an agreed disputes procedure, both to be enforced by financial penalties. After fierce union resistance and the TUC's declaration of a face-saving 'binding undertaking' the penal clauses were dropped.

This considerable struggle was symptomatic of the strains increasingly placed on the Labour Party by national economic failure. It was divided on the general principle of state intervention in industrial relations and divided on the particular issue of the penal clauses. More generally, economic pressure was heightening the tensions between, on the one hand, the objective of maintaining full employment, economic growth and a stable currency within a capitalist open-economy framework and, on the other hand, the objective of maintaining and even enlarging the unions' rights in their central activity of free sectional collective bargaining. It was heightening, too, the tensions between the strong liberal-individualist strain within Labour Party social democracy, and the collectivist ethic – instrumentally based though much of this was – that ran so pervasively through the trade union movement. One crucial fact was emerging more clearly than ever before. The dominant resolve of party leaders, evident since the 1920s, to repudiate the role of 'class party' and instead to represent the interests of the working class only within the framework of a broadly based national appeal based on class harmony and a presumed 'national interest', could only hope to escape effective grass-roots challenge given either satisfactory economic growth or organisational weakness in the position of the party's left. When neither condition was met, a basic fissure was bound to open up.

Less inhibited by such internal conflicts, the Conservative government's Industrial Relations Act 1971 combined all the diverse and, to some extent, contradictory impulses which postwar governments of both parties had directed with increasing desperation upon the problem. There was attention to the floor of individual rights, including, unprecedentedly in Britain, new if limited safeguards against unfair dismissal. There was some concern for the unions' institutional interests which even went beyond Donovan by providing unions, for the first time, with a statutory procedure for securing recognition and bargaining rights. These and similar provisions appeared to flow from the traditional official philosophy which sought the spread of orderly procedures and consistently applied standards, especially where these now seemed to matter most – at the place of work. But much of the Act was shaped by a very different philosophy which, to a muted extent, had also manifested itself intermittently in some quarters of the Labour Party ever since the first Labour government, but which now enjoyed far freer, more aggressive, and more punitive reign among Conservatives. Among some of Labour's liberal social democrats it took the form of an inability or refusal to understand the unions' needs, functions and values; a certain distaste for extra-parliamentary dealings with them; and a conviction that, in the interests of the national economy and Labour's electoral success, the inflationary earnings pressures, strikes, restrictionism and other activities which earned Labour a bad press must be subdued. Among Conservatives it took the form of asserting that organised labour had far too much power, more especially at the workplace, and that this seriously impeded not only managerial enterprise and initiative but also the individual rights of members and non-members alike. At the heart of their 1971 Act, therefore, lay the legal right to be a non-unionist, which along with other features expressed a philosophy of atomistic individualism designed to inhibit collective organisation. Ideas which had always found much favour among Conservatives, and which had surfaced increasingly since *A Giant's Strength*, were now brought to the forefront of government policy. The failure of other approaches had strengthened the position of those who argued that a new strategy was required and that the power, 'irresponsibility' and 'indiscipline' of workplace union organisation were the obvious targets.

Besides seeking legally to entrench the right to be a non-unionist, the Act attempted to put pressure upon official union hierarchies to quell their more recalcitrant workplace organisations. Hoping to overcome the manifest longstanding preference of both parties against legalism in their bargaining relations, the Act made collective agreements legally binding and enforceable unless they contained express provision otherwise, and sought to impose upon the unions a policing obligation whereby they were to keep members in line by all such steps as were 'reasonably practicable'. Yet, at the same time, the Act's designers could not resist provisions which weakened the unions' own security devices – particularly that *bête noire* of the Conservatives, the closed shop. Strikes deemed to create an 'emergency' situation could be acted upon directly by the Secretary of State, who could seek 'restraining orders' and call for secret strike ballots of the membership. And such benefits as the Act conferred upon the unions – including legal immunities which had previously been unconditionally available to them – were now conditional upon registration. The significance of this was that registration meant acceptance of the legislation and of the Registrar's considerable powers to oversee union rules, conduct and administration, and to require changes in them. Registration was, indeed, 'the cornerstone of the legislation'.

The Act has been described by one leading authority as 'spectacularly unsuccessful' (Davies, 1980, p. 267), and a detailed study has traced its failure to achieve any of the desired effects. Within a TUC posture of constitutionalism and rejection of industrial action, union opposition was widespread, immediate and thoroughgoing; most unions refused to register and thereby in effect destroyed the Act. Most employers, too, were hostile and abstained from using it (Weekes *et al.*, 1975). The Act soon became a political embarrassment ignored by all including the Heath government that produced it. None of this surprised those who had always predicted the failure of all legislation seeking to 'reform' industrial relations which worked against the grain of certain prominent character-istics that persisted, not simply through long habituation, but because they were consonant with other key features of British culture and tradition. Relief was expressed by some of these sceptics that legislation of the sort so long demanded had now given a practical demonstration of its futility, leaving the way clear for a more informed and rational debate. Their satisfaction was premature. Intensified economic difficulties and growing Conservative aversion to alternative strategies fostered a convic-tion that the Act failed only because it had been introduced when the unions were still strong; success required its imposition step by step when they were weak.

Evidence as to their supposed overweening power was strengthened for many by the outcome of Heath's clash with the miners in February 1974 over their current pay demand. This at once became firmly installed in national mythology as 'the destruction of the Heath government by the National Union of Mineworkers'. In reality, the Heath government was destroyed by Heath, who called an election under the mistaken conviction that he would sweep the country on the slogan 'Who governs?' Neverthe-less, the incident further consolidated the view of trade unions as the overmighty subject.

Meanwhile the incoming Labour government proceeded to reinforce the growing polarisation of the parties over the issue by passing, as noted earlier, a series of measures which, besides repealing the 1971 Act, extended union rights and benefits still further. The Trade Union and Labour Relations Act 1974, the Employment Protection Act 1975, and the Trade Union and Labour Relations Amendment Act 1976, carried a good deal further that supplementation and support of the industrial relations system which began in the mid-1960s. Between 1974 and 1979 at least ten major statutes were implemented dealing with trade unions and labour relations, health and safety, employment protection, occupational pen-sions, race and discrimination, equal pay and industrial strategy. As a result the system moved a good deal closer in its array of institutions and procedures to the Continental model than would have been thought conceivable in the 1950s. Nevertheless a central continuity remained.

> The recent spate of legislation provides a more extensive structure of positive trade union law than has existed in the past, but it does not change fundamentally the liberal base. The concept of the common law immunity, now considerably enlarged in its scope, remains at the heart of things. Unions prefer matters this way; the alternative would be law which prescribed under what conditions industrial action was legal and who had the right to take it, which would almost certainly be more restrictive than the present situation. It is, however, likely that conflicts with the courts will continue in future years. (Crouch, 1979, p. 136)

over, the new legal array could be made to look far more favourable
mployees than was the case in practice. Recognition procedures
d to have serious loopholes; unions have been shown not to have
unassailable privileges and workers not to have an inalienable right
to job and income security; by 1979 the success rate among 'unfair'
dismissal claims before industrial tribunals was less than one in three and
the median compensation payment awarded was £455; women's hourly
earnings remained on average only 72 per cent of men's; the weakness of
minimum wage legislation remained as chronic as ever; and career opportunities for women and blacks have not been enlarged. 'The new laws have
certainly changed the look of British industrial relations, but the extent to
which they are biased in favour of unions and employees is grossly
exaggerated' (McMullen, 1979, pp. 105–6).

Labour's readiness to extend legislative favours to the unions derived
generally from the special relationship but more specifically to the need for
union support of incomes policy. We come here to the third search process
– the search for ways of containing the inflationary incomes–prices spiral,
including, eventually, the use of statutory measures and legislative coercion. By the 1960s a variety of devices had been tried. In certain respects
the policies which sought direct restraint revealed in their changing
designations a growing modicum of awareness of the profound problems
of equity underlying them. During what now seem, in this respect, the
years of relative innocence, 1948–50, the appeal – surprisingly successful –
was for a 'wage restraint' which left privileged all higher salaries, prices
and incomes from profits, rents and interest. After this came the 'pay
pause' and later still 'income policies' which might aspire also to limit
prices and dividends. For those unable to see the existing distribution of
earned and unearned incomes as the last word in social justice, however,
the later devices were little more morally convincing than the earlier. This
provided a valid escape clause for trade unionists who, with the connivance of management, defied the policy or evaded it by booking unnecessary or even fictitious overtime, by securing a higher-paid job grading for
work which remained the same, or by simply pushing up piece-rates. It
also deprived the policy of moral legitimation for some onlookers who, as
a consequence, experienced difficulty in preaching to wage- and lower-
salary-earners the civic obligation of voluntary restraint and in supporting
proposals to apply statutory enforcement when persuasion failed. Given
the implications of opening up wide public debate about the ethical
validity of existing income distribution – and the distribution of wealth
that underlies it – it is not surprising that such issues were, for the most
part, studiously ignored – by trade union leaders as well as by politicians,
publicists and, needless to say, the media.

Press treatment usually took the form of references to pay demands as
greedy, arbitrary and irresponsible in their neglect of the 'national interest'. There was no acknowledgement of the fact that the same forces,
institutions and values which urged property owners towards capital
accumulation were also bound to urge wage- and lower-salary-earners
towards seeking higher pay. 'What has in fact happened in capitalist
societies since World War II, aided by the development of a massive

advertising industry' – its power greatly strengthened by television – 'has been a vast and continuing "expression of needs", which has in turn produced a necessary demand on the part of labour for increased wages.' Since employers generally seek to minimise labour costs in their own enterprise, conflict is inherent in the system. 'And while this conflict is inherent in capitalism itself, in a weak, inefficient and undercapitalized economy such as post-war Britain's, the wage demands which advertising and consumerism induce and which workers' alienation from the control of production reinforces, need not be very great to yield economic crisis' (Panitch, 1976, pp. 252–3).

With postwar governments of both colours struggling to resolve these instabilities mainly by demanding sacrifices of the working class, a turning-point in Britain's industrial relations system was reached in 1966 with the Labour government's Prices and Incomes Act, through which for the first time a government attempted statutory control over settlements and awards that were the outcome of collective bargaining. That this was a Labour government only gives emphasis to a point made earlier; that for all Labour's special relationship with the unions, governments of both major parties have worked their way through the same limited range of possibilities open to them within the constraints to which they had committed themselves. And given that the Wilson administration accepted the same definition of Britain's role in the world economy and the same imperatives of the American alliance as did the Conservatives, it proved fully as vulnerable to nudges from Washington. The move towards statutory powers began after the American Secretary of the Treasury intimated in 1965 that central bank aid for sterling might be difficult to organise so long as the British government did nothing to curb the voluntary system of collective bargaining. 'A Labour government was now involved in the business of preventing (or rather, postponing) pay increases by law – a development quite contrary to the understanding of the post-war consensus . . .' (Crouch, 1979, p. 55). In other words, a Labour government had launched itself on the path of attempting to discipline its own class base. Both in this and in their position on the Conservatives' Industrial Relations Act 1971, most Labour leaders showed that, despite the retreat after 1970 from state compulsion over the unions, their fundamental assumptions about the nature of industrial relations remained the same. A class interpretation was the minority view; predominantly the unions were seen as 'managers and mediators of conflict, seeking to achieve common aims with other interested parties, such as governments and employers', and in this endeavour the authority of unions over their members must be maintained (Moran, 1977, p. 106).

By late 1972 the Heath Conservative government, too, was introducing an entirely statutory pay and prices policy with far more rigorous sanctions. Though statutory enforcement was a measure of desperation which both party leaderships were anxious in public to regret – and often to suggest would never be used again – it was politically and industrially damaging to them. Many national union officers 'were . . . under increasing attack from activists and militants and aware of growing dissatisfaction amongst their members' and as a result 'were moving towards greater industrial militancy and politically towards the left' (Barnes and Reid, 1980, p. 97).

Reforming the System?

Along with these attempts, statutory and non-statutory, to secure pay restraint there had developed, as we have seen, a consciousness that Britain's system of industrial relations, hitherto widely admired for its informality, its flexibility and its minimal reliance on law for procedural support and substantive content, was failing to respond fast enough to new needs. Regulation was most failing precisely where it was most needed – at the workplace. From some critics had come emphasis on the need for rapid technical and organisational change and for efficient and orderly handling of the issues and disputes to which, in a period of rising shop-floor power, such changes gave rise. Far too little creative directorial and managerial attention was being directed, it was said, to matters which were generating forms of disorder that were bad for the economy as well as for the company – chaotic and irrational pay structures; inappropriate methods of payment; excessive overtime; clumsily handled redundancies; 'unfair' dismissals; and non-existent or inadequate procedures for hand-ling grievances on all these and other issues. Others had stressed the need for legislation to reduce disorder by guaranteeing a wide range of employee rights hitherto hardly figuring in union claims but giving rise to sporadic discontent. Champions of sexual and racial equality continued to press their own demands. From Conservative directions, especially, continued to come pressures for a more heavily regulative and punitive framework of industrial relations law which, it was hoped, could contain the unions and more expressly workplace behaviour. Senior management and boards of directors, too, must make a far more positive and considered contribution. Many observers noted that too many British boards were inclined to leave the tricky and distasteful arena of labour relations to lower levels of management. Instead of formulating a coherent long-term strategy and philosophy of industrial and personnel relations they waited on events, leaving managerial subordinates to meet a succession of exigencies with a hand-to-mouth, piecemeal opportunism, and taking an active role only when it was forced upon them by crisis.

What it all appeared to add up to was a need not only for more legislation but also for a far more structured system at plant and company levels. Representatives of management and employees needed to take the present loose and inadequate arrangements by the scruff of the neck and remould them into a pattern of collaborative negotiation and dispute settlement from which both sides, along with the economy, would derive greatly increased benefit. Top as well as middle managers would work with securely based shop stewards within properly constituted formal pro-cedures to handle their problems in the context of a carefully considered long-term company strategy.

If the Donovan Commission supplied the precept of this reconstruction it was the earlier examples of productivity bargaining in the 1960s that had appeared to supply the practice. In a few cases, managers, union officers and shop stewards had worked together in long and taxing negotiations to realise meticulously analysed plans whereby comprehensive changes in work organisation making for greater productivity were rewarded with generous increases in pay. Was this to be the long-sought cure for the British disease of workplace disorder and restrictionism? Was British management at last taking in hand that typical workplace situation where 'custom and practice' ruled and inefficiency thrived? Productivity bargaining at its comprehensive best seemed at least part of the broader reconstruction.

Certainly by all appearances, and in some respects more than appearances, the British system of industrial relations was transformed during the 1960s and 1970s. At the workplace, both sides greatly increased specialist provision for dealing with industrial relations. There are estimates that the number of shop stewards had increased by over 50 per cent since the mid-1960s and that the number of full-time shop stewards probably quadrupled during the 1970s, with shop steward organisation itself becoming more sophisticated through the wider emergence of senior steward structures and convenors. Parallel with this on the managerial side went a considerable increase in specialist employee relations and personnel management staffs, particularly after the mid-1970s. There was more responsibility shown towards industrial relations issues by boards of directors themselves.

The outcome was a notable spread of properly constituted formal grievance procedures, which now became part of the normal fabric of workplace industrial relations, at least in manufacturing industry. Union strength lent itself to pressures for increased union security. The (post-entry) closed shop spread rapidly, many managements finding it, at a time when they felt they needed all the regulative devices they could get, a method of increasing the representativeness and stability of collective bargaining. The check-off system by which union dues were deducted from pay by the company grew until by 1978 it covered 73 per cent of union members in manufacturing and 72 per cent in non-manufacturing – 'one of the most important advances in union security in the history of British trade unionism' (W. Brown, ed., 1981, p. 73).

Non-manual employees participated fully in these developments. In large manufacturing establishments, especially, the institutions and sanctions of collective bargaining that developed for these categories were increasingly like those of their manual counterparts. Here and in public services, white-collar resentment at their declining position relative to manual workers produced a major qualitative change towards greater militancy and an acceptance of what most of the other unions had long accepted already – that times and circumstances called for access to, and pressure on, governments. Large white-collar unions like the National Union of Teachers (NUT) and National and Local Government Officers (NALGO) began to affiliate to the TUC in order to secure a voice at this level – though not to indicate any mass conversion to the traditional link still existing between the predominantly manual unions and the Labour Party.

Finally, the increase in formalised workplace joint rule-making and managerial involvement in the shaping of workplace relations affected the importance and standing of 'national' or industry-wide bargaining, whose regulative significance had already, in many industries, been weakened by the postwar growth of informal, unsystematic dealings at shop-floor level. Most unions decentralised collective bargaining functions to some extent over the period.

Some of these changes were in directions strongly approved by those who hoped for more constructive relations between management and the managed. They appeared to provide the necessary joint institutional setting for that considered and coherent company strategy which would not only more successfully maintain order and minimise disruption, but more positively facilitate the negotiation of work systems from which all parties would gain. For this the earlier examples of successful comprehensive productivity bargaining seemed to provide the model. The study by Allan Flanders of the Fawley agreements, which he and others believed offered new standards of creative, positive-sum negotiation, was a source of hope. Fuller recognition and integration of shop stewards by unions; greater security assured them by management; improved co-ordination between the stewards themselves; a rational consistent company strategy on all manpower issues; the establishment of systematic joint procedures at the workplace – these seemed the necessary pre-conditions for that qualitative change in labour relations so widely seen as one of the required contributions towards a more adaptive' and efficient British economy.

Necessary conditions have to be distinguished, however, from sufficient conditions. Whether structural and institutional arrangements produce certain hoped-for results depends upon the will, motivation and habituated dispositions and perceptions of the participants. Certain kinds of arrangements may be necessary for making possible certain kinds of behaviour, but they do not in themselves guarantee that the behaviour will be forthcoming. The Conservative government's Industrial Relations Act 1971, for example, had attempted to provide a regulative framework of law and practice for the conduct of industrial relations at company and plant as well as industry-wide level. It became an embarrassing failure when both sides made evident that, for their own good reasons stemming from historic roots as well as present pressures, they had no intention of using most of it. Similarly, the indications in preceding pages of marked changes especially at company and plant level are susceptible of a different interpretation than that of a widespread will towards reform in the direction of jointly pursued collaboration benefiting both sides.

The increase in specialist employee-relations staffs, for example, has been attributed less to a widening company resolve to apply a rational, consistent and creative strategy in this field and more to a felt need to grapple with the mass of complex labour legislation appearing on the statute book. Marsh reports, in a survey of manufacturing industry, that companies 'have tended to develop cautiously, empirically, and with no intention of upsetting the traditional functions and authority of line management in dealing with employees' (Marsh, 1982, p. 62). In any case, the growth in specialist staffs was not conspicuous outside the larger establishments and was not over-bedecked with formal qualifications (Daniel and Willward, 1983, p. 286).

Although in larger and more complex multi-establishment companies there is now some tendency for boards to give more regular consideration to employee relations, it is hard to detect any major move towards planned forward strategies in this field. And if by 'policy' is meant an explicitly formulated system of principles by which all levels of management can decide what to do in any particular set of circumstances, it has to be said that company boards still concern themselves little with policy-making. The traditional British style persists by which boards fall back on *de facto* methods, commonly endorsing decisions taken elsewhere and involving themselves directly only when the situation is judged sufficiently serious to merit their attention.

It is hardly surprising, then, that Marsh found no more than 'a moderate movement in the "Donovan" direction of "comprehensive and authoritative agreements" at plant and/or company levels'. Informal and unsystematic shop-floor bargaining, unrelated to similar activities elsewhere in the plant or company, clearly continued in many factories. Even the trend towards formalisation was producing little codification of rules, practices and policy in the form of handbooks for managers. Industry-wide or national agreements (though in manufacturing very infrequently forming the sole basis for workplace settlements) were nevertheless found by Marsh to be still exercising 'considerable influence' in that improvements in terms and conditions negotiated nationally continued to be widely applied (Marsh, 1982, pp. 152–3, 158, 162, 188). On the whole, though, and especially when the non-manufacturing sectors are included, emphasis has to be on the diversity of systems of pay determination (Daniel and Willward, 1983, p. 290).

If the overall picture of change in all these respects is mixed and equivocal, it is equally so with respect to union organisation structure. Undy *et al.* found it not to be 'developing in any easily discernible direction according to a common pattern or trend. Indeed, if anything the government and structure of British unions appear to be more diverse, contradictory and conflicting at the end of our period of study than they were in 1960' (1981, p. 23).

Nevertheless, as already noted, many of the changes in the workplace situation have been in directions urged by reformists and represent a considerable transformation in the face of Britain's industrial relations. Surely these 'necessary' conditions have sometimes been completed by the 'sufficient' conditions? In some cases they undoubtedly have. But a recent verdict by an experienced empirical researcher is that from the reformists' point of view the achievement is small. Batstone's judgement is that these organisational changes reveal little association with greater efficiency and reduced conflict. The rate of productivity growth had declined after the beginnings of reform; the poorest productivity records in the 1970s were to be found in those industries where the reform package had been most fully implemented; and strikes increased and most dramatically after the late 1960s precisely in those sectors where grievance procedures and sophisticated shop steward structures had newly developed (Batstone,

1982, pp. 5–6). Detailed studies reveal that only a small minority of productivity bargaining agreements led to any substantial productivity improvements; and Clegg has noted that 'many of the companies which negotiated apparently successful productivity deals in the sixties were again faced with problems of low performance and substantial overmanning during the seventies' (Clegg, 1979, p. 143).

These findings suggest that habituated stances and dispositions on both sides, powerfully shaped by, and rooted in, past experience, are determining how the 'reformed' structures are used. On the employees' side, these include the wary zero-sum approach; the adversary posture; and the instinct to preserve and extend as much job-control through 'custom and practice' as can be squeezed out of management; all combined with an intense sectionalism which remains as little moved by wider sympathies or 'national-interest' arguments as are multinational companies and City speculators ranging world-wide for the fast buck. Management and ownership exhibit the reciprocal characteristics. Both sides are shaped by the particular nature of Britain's class structure and neither side takes any serious political steps to change it – ownership being constrained within a political system of immense inertia; the ranks of organised labour being disposed to preserve what they consider a tolerable accommodation and to reject the alternative visions offered them as being insufficiently convincing to be worth risking what they have already.

Both sets of dispositions also rendered abortive a different type of approach to reform. During the 1960s Britain witnessed a quickening interest in the idea of employee directors on company boards, stimulated by West German experience and further encouraged by the European Economic Commission, which was anxious to pre-empt more radical demands then highly vocal. The Wilson government that took office in 1974, hard pressed for union co-operation in incomes policy, considered it judicious to acknowledge this trend and in 1975 appointed the Committee of Inquiry on Industrial Democracy, chaired by Lord Bullock.

The vehemence of organised-employer resistance to its proposals for employee directorships ensured that the report sank without trace, especially since it was reinforced by opposition from some influential trade union leaders. Nevertheless, the debate is worth examining for what it reveals of persistent characteristics and dispositions. The committee's report accepted as axiomatic that any attempt to bypass the rapidly growing representative structure of unionism at the workplace would be seen as an attack, would be fiercely resisted and would doom any programme from the outset. The 'single channel of representation', a fiercely guarded principle of British unionism, was to remain sacrosanct and directorial appointment was to be vested in trade union machinery.

But the report's significance ranged wider than this. There is no mistaking, in some of its passages, the note of optimistic hope that here might be the mechanism which at long last would release the constructive and co-operative energies of British labour. Equally, however, there is no mistaking, in the TUC statement, *Industrial Democracy*, revised in 1977 to include its evidence to the Bullock Committee, a very different emphasis. An earlier version in 1974 had noted that the 'impact of closures, rationalisations and redundancies has become much more widespread, and the inability of trade unions to prevent or mitigate the effects of these in most cases has been a major deficiency'. Major decisions on company planning, allocation of investment resources, plant locations, closures, takeovers, mergers and top managerial appointments were generally taken at levels not reached by collective bargaining and were perhaps not readily covered by that method. 'New forms of control were needed.'

The phrasing indicated that the inspiration behind this resoluteness was not the vision of a joint pursuit of efficiency and growth, primed by a release of constructive energies from all ranks, but a resolve to strengthen the protective role of the unions by securing the formal responsibility of the directorial board to employees as well as to shareholders. It is not surprising that many employers and their associations feared that implementation of the Bullock proposals would too often facilitate the invasion of the board room, if not by the formal institutions of collective bargaining, then certainly by its adversary, zero-sum spirit. They preferred to pursue such closer dialogue as they wanted – and there were abundant issues on which they might wish to seek it – through the safer and more controllable method of 'joint consultation' (for an extended analysis see Fox, 1985).

Somewhat contrary to received opinion, joint consultation, long assumed to have little future in the British system, saw a notable growth during the 1970s. It had been supposed that where union organisation at the workplace was strong, workplace spokesmen would prefer overt negotiation to joint consultation, which left any managerial commitment diffuse and uncertain. Where workplace organisation was weak, joint consultation, like some earlier works councils, might simply provide management with an extra channel of influence. Its wider acceptance during the 1970s therefore probably expresses a confidence by workplace representatives that their position was now too strong to be undermined by such devices. Recent research confirms that joint consultation mainly grew not at the expense of, but as an adjunct to, union recognition and organisation (Daniel and Willward, 1983, pp. 278, 288–9).

Corporate Bargaining

Meanwhile, just as both party leaderships made use of statutory incomes policy and then set it aside, so also the practice of making policy dependent upon agreement with the TUC waxed and waned. Before turning to statutory enforcement the Heath government attempted to embody in explicit form what has been called 'bargained corporatism'. This was a limited and tentative move towards securing corporate consent for incomes policy by acknowledging that corporate interests, with their ability to frustrate government aims, had a direct or indirect interest in wide-ranging areas of government policy which they could not realistically expect to influence through parliamentary procedure. Unions 'sacrifice some of their entrenched but narrow and unambitious achievements in exchange for the possibility of greater political influence and more and broader power for their members in the workplace, but at the same time . . . accept more restraint, a more obvious role for the unions in restraining their members, more state interference and fuller acceptance of the industrial order and its priorities' (Crouch, 1979, p. 189).

In discussions with Heath in 1972, 'the unions were bargaining with government over issues which went beyond the traditional collective bargaining area . . . and extended to political objectives . . . It is true that these wider trade union interests had been pressed on governments after 1931 and by different means throughout the postwar period (and had been pursued through the established machinery of the labour movement).' Nevertheless 'the bargaining with the Heath government . . . can be regarded' as a significant feature 'in the change of union attitude towards government in general and to both political parties, a change which had been developing since 1961, partly in response to government pressures for wage restraint' (Barnes and Reid, 1980, p. 192). The union proposals, which included repeal of the Industrial Relations Act and the Housing Finance Act, were deemed to be too high a political price and the government backed off, subsequently introducing a unilaterally deter-mined statutory policy.

A Labour government took the method further in 1974–5. Under the so-called 'social contract' price controls were retained, food subsidies were introduced, council house rents were frozen, increases in various social benefits were announced, and legislation strengthening the unions' organisational position was promised. 'The idea behind the contract (at least in its early form) was that workers might be induced to moderate their claims for higher money wages if their "social wage" was improved. In return the TUC undertook to persuade affiliated unions not to push for increases in the *real* incomes of their members . . . ' (Hawkins, 1978, pp. 72–3).

This was a renewed attempt at securing consent by explicitly acknow-ledging the political relevance of organised labour and using that acknow-ledgement as a basis on which to construct an agreed compromise programme. Its limited coverage, however, is apparent. Major assump-tions and policies determining the context within which government calculated its incomes objectives played no part. The fact that there is no evidence of the unions pressing for their inclusion demonstrates a require-ment for adaptation on both sides if this method is to work. The pursuit of consent through corporate bargaining calls both for governments openly to acknowledge the practical limitations on their sovereignty, and for unions to acknowledge the relevance for their members of government policies not only on the social wage but also on domestic and overseas spending, fiscal and monetary policy, and other relevant variables. The deterrent they experience against acting on this relevance is expressed in Crouch's reference to 'a more obvious role for the unions in restraining their members'. A wide-ranging contract plays for high stakes and would involve the unions in far heavier commitments than they or their members show signs of being able to tolerate. The narrower conception itself foundered. During 1977–9 the Labour government felt impelled to proceed with a phase of its incomes policy which was manifestly without union backing. It sought to impose a 'norm' of 10 per cent and later, in the teeth of urgent advice from union leaders, of 5 per cent. The high level of industrial unrest during this final phase was widely regarded as a major factor in Labour's defeat in the 1979 general election.

Despite the difficulties attending it the method of corporate bargaining between two or all of the three major organised interests has been described as opening up 'a chink of light in what is otherwise a tight closed system'; developments along these lines indicating 'the most attractive opportunities presented to this country by the recent turmoil around industrial relations' and 'offering chances for the extension of real democracy in the management of economic affairs which has always eluded us' (Crouch, 1979, pp. 189, 195). The difficulties are frequently rehearsed and some of them overheavily laboured. It is said, for example, that in a political culture dominated by deals between the three giant powers – government, capital and organised labour – weak and minority interests would be neglected. Since they are usually neglected already the discussion is not much advanced. Humbug aside, the danger is nevertheless apparent. The central argument, however, is that corporate bargaining bypasses Parliament, bestows political power upon non-political organisations, and subverts what should be the true national decision-making body which takes all interests and opinions into account. The weaknesses of this argument will bear brief repetition. The myth of parliamentary sovereignty persists, yet every government is aware of measures it would like to take but from which it is deterred by awareness of powerful organised interests that would create acute political difficulties. Likewise, every government department puts before Parliament measures which have, to some extent, already been tailored and laundered to meet pressures previously exerted behind the scenes by the groups and organisations affected.

Often, of course, the myth of parliamentary sovereignty is invoked by those who are merely concerned to mobilise doubt and suspicion among the public against extra-parliamentary political pressures of which they happen to disapprove. Charges of constitutional impropriety are then deemed to be in order. Parliamentary Labour Party leaders themselves have sometimes made such charges, though more often against pressures from the far left than from, say, the City. But it is within the Conservative Party that such attitudinising is most often expressed in public, for it is the Conservative Party that is most conscious of threat from the largest potential source of extra-parliamentary pressure of them all, namely, organised labour. Since it remains an abiding fear of Conservatism that the mass industrial strength of the organised working class may be directed to overtly political ends, it is extra-parliamentary pressures from organised labour which are usually discovered to be constitutionally improper. Ideally, for Conservatives, union political activity should be tightly circumscribed. 'Conservative dealings with the unions have ... one over-riding aim: it is to separate unionism as a political and as an economic force, and to squeeze the life out of the former' (Gamble, 1974, p. 144).

Yet it becomes more and more difficult for them to do so. The disappearance of the conventional distinction between economics and politics draws the unions into the political arena whether they like it or not. In any case, the Conservative aim has long been surrounded with profound ambivalences and the intensifying economic problem has heightened them. The traditional strategy had been to admit to the political nation, after a suitable delaying action, such emergent organised interests as developed political aspirations. There seemed good evidence that the very process of accepting an emergent interest into the political nation played a significant part in its readiness to be assimilated; the succession of statutes enlarging the franchise being a case in point. But there had always been Conservatives for whom the argument faltered when the emergent interest was organised labour. What was the best policy? To accept and even perhaps facilitate the unions' participation in politics – needless to say through established constitutional channels – in the hope that this, while certainly strengthening them, would also tame them? Or to try to restrict their political role in the belief that only thus could property, privilege – civilisation – be preserved, meanwhile running the risk that a potentially crucial safety-valve was being sealed off? Given future uncertainties there was no way of proving either correct. Men had to make their own judgements and both policies had always had supporters among Conservatives. The gnawing doubt could never be banished and always became a political factor in specially disturbed times. Could organised labour be relied on to remain assimilated to the status quo?

From Disraeli to Baldwin and beyond, the predominant weight had, for most of the time, lain with those who judged that the safer course was to behave as if it would. And as long as the liberal separation of economics and politics could be presented as a plausible account of British society, the Baldwin doctrine was persuasive. By the perceptions of the majority of trade unionists and their leaders, the central preoccupations of the unions in industrial relations and collective bargaining were outside politics. It had, of course, long been commonplace for them to conduct lobbying, deputations and consultation on such matters as union legislation, factory health and safety, compensation for accidents and a host of detailed issues specific to particular industries. There was an awareness, too, which intensified between the wars, that governments could affect union members through policies on credit, exchange rates, public spending and the trade cycle. Yet so long as governments sought to minimise their direct economic involvement – and to present the issues as purely 'technical' matters which must be settled by 'experts' – they could hold the unions at arms-length and there was neither sufficient strength nor confidence among union leaders to support them in asserting an effective voice in decision-making.

The Politicising of Industrial Relations

As postwar economic problems drew governments into increasing direct involvement in the economy, however, with the incomes–prices spiral becoming a central preoccupation, industrial relations became 'politicised'. The term permitted of a strong and a weak sense. The strong sense would have meant wage- and lower-salary-earners at last breaking through the mystifications of the distinction between economics and politics; translating their workplace conflict into generalised political class conflict and behaving accordingly. The weak sense meant only that they saw government interfering in the processes of collective bargaining and attempting to regulate other workplace behaviour, and as a consequence were drawn into conducting industrial disputes with a political agency. The two senses were often confused. Some on the right feared, and some on the left hoped, that it was the first that was happening, but for most trade unionists it was the second. The longstanding disinclination of British labour to translate economic conflict at the workplace into political conflict outside it was far from disappearing. Nor was there disappearance of the tendency for much rank and file political opinion to differ from that of union leadership; a difference more likely to stem from the leadership being too strongly 'Labour' than too little. From the earliest days of trade unionism, leaders might be found uttering political sentiments and engaging in political behaviour that were in opposition to those favoured by large numbers of their members, and the tendency persists, even enlarges. Changes in the composition of the union movement towards a preponderance of white-collar members increase the likelihood, for example, that radical sentiments by leaders find no echo in the hearts of many followers. Sixty per cent of trade union members cast their votes against the Labour Party in the general election of 1983.

Under the new Conservatism there is a reassertion of those forces which seek to exploit this divergence of political direction between many union leaders and many of their members. The aim is, as far as possible, to sever the affiliation – and therefore financial – links that exist between many unions and the Labour Party. The second Thatcher administration promised legislation which in one way or another sought to weaken union political activity – perhaps take the newer white-collar unions, for example, out of politics altogether. Since the major manual worker unions are unlikely to follow them, the possibility becomes stronger, as we have already noted, that the trade union movement will become more divided than for some considerable time.

How far this will affect union responses with respect to politicisation remains to be seen. In the 1960s and 1970s, politicisation in its weak sense was a significant development. The living standards of union members and their families now seemed visibly and directly dependent upon government actions and policy, and this was bound to heighten the unions' role in politics. Governments were obtruding themselves into the central function of the unions: the function which touched the most sensitive nerves of the movement – collective bargaining. And even before Heath's 1971 Act a Labour government had proposed, in *In Place of Strife*, to regulate workplace behaviour. Politicisation meant not only the possibility of confrontation with governments but increased union embroilment in the affairs of the Labour Party. The unions' political interest was no longer relatively peripheral to their primary concerns, but was inextricably bound up with their very *raison d'être*. At the same time, these were also matters central to the political well-being and even survival of governments. Were the unions to be invited to participate in policy discussions, with the advantage that their consent might be won, but with the disadvantage that they might demand a *quid pro quo* that was politically unacceptable? The demand could, of course, always be refused, but for Tory activists the very sight of their leaders bargaining politically with the unions tends to arouse distaste if not outrage. Alternatively, were Conservative governments to proceed unilaterally and assert the freedom to decide policy 'unfettered' by 'sectional interests'? If so, they had to give consideration to ways of strengthening their own position in the enforcement of policy – and face whatever risks this alienation of the unions might seem to involve for the long-term stability of the system.

For obvious reasons the political hazards of pursuing negotiated understandings with the unions are less threatening for Labour than for Conservative governments. Yet the differences must not be exaggerated. Given that Labour governments had committed themselves to upholding mixed-economy capitalism; the status of London as an international private-enterprise financial centre; the exposure of the economy to international pressures; and the existing broad structure of rewards and status, there was not vastly greater scope for concessions available to Labour governments for distribution to the unions – at least not in the realm of economic and welfare policy. An indication of resulting tensions came when a left-wing member of the Labour Party National Executive, Ian Mikardo, publicly criticised Jack Jones, then general secretary of the Transport and General Workers Union (TGWU) and a leading figure in the fashioning of the social contract with the Labour government in 1974–5, for not pitching the union demands high enough. The incident may well have helped to confirm the opinion of many Conservatives that there was no future for them along that road. If corporate bargaining created a situation which brought home to unions the possibility of steadily raising the price of their co-operation it was a method full of dangers for Conservatives. Those for whom such considerations bulked large were likely to put a premium on economic strategies which did not rest on TUC acquiescence – and if such strategies also weakened the unions industrially then so much the better, since it made little sense to meet the unions at their strongest if policies were to be imposed on them.

Such considerations illustrate the major consequence of the politicising of industrial relations and of economic policy generally. The ideology of state 'even-handedness' between the classes had rested, for such plausibility as it had, upon the minimal state and the separation between economics and politics. So long as the state could manage to display some conviction in affecting to hold aloof from substantive policy intervention, it was possible to invoke as one of the legitimations of the system the myth of state impartiality. When, however, the state was manifestly no longer holding the ring but moving, however reluctantly, into it, each contestant was bound to become alive to the issue of whether state participation in the arena was on balance benefiting itself or its opponent. Since the policies of all governments have been predicated upon the strategy of upholding Britain's private-enterprise capitalism during decades of difficulty and crisis, state intervention has been perceived by the more politically alert sections of the Labour movement as being predominantly arrayed on the side of property and power.

Increasing involvement therefore heightens the state's political problem in that it forces more and more into the open, for public view, the state's attitude towards the existing social and economic system and towards policies of changing it. This drove a wedge between different sections within each of the two main parties. Labour governments became more and more sharply revealed in the most practical terms as predominantly composed of leaders with no aspirations towards fundamentally changing the system within any finite period of time, thereby intensifying the manifestations of a rift which had always been visible but never so starkly in its practical consequences. Less seriously for the Conservative Party, events aroused fears in some quarters that too overt and bellicose a government assertion and support of capitalist principles and capitalist 'needs' would be injudicious – the working classes, especially the organised working classes, must not be pushed too far.

The union involvement in politics was also bringing into sharp relief another problem of fundamental significance. This was the problem of consent and compliance. The claim of British governments to legitimacy rests on the electoral and parliamentary system, with its accepted conventions and fictions. In practice they have always been open as well to extra-parliamentary pressures from organised interests and opinion groups. Parliamentary representation, in other words, has been supplemented by corporate or 'functional' representation. There was always the potentiality here for difficulty and conflict. Corporate contacts with government might be too piecemeal, unsystematic and limited to convey the full extent of corporate concern about some specific government policy. And if that concern were not conveyed in its fullness, governments were hampered in their struggle to achieve the highest common level of consent. On the other hand, if corporate interests were asserted too strongly, the consent achieved by meeting them might clash with the consent engineered through the parliamentary and party system. Corporate and parliamentary methods of representation were different methods of pursuing consent and legitimation and in an increasingly complex society were all too likely to conflict (Moran, 1977).

The problem has become more palpable with the greatly increased extent to which governments are being brought into often abrasive contact with organised interests and opinion groups. The growing number, size and strength of such interests and groups constitute a considerable elaboration of corporate representation, and increased state intervention heightens the chances of collision. Particularly in the case of organised labour this has raised profound questions of compliance. The dilemma is genuine and acute. The disappearance of the distinction between economics and politics creates for the unions a need for a kind of political involvement which experience has long shown cannot be pursued through Parliament. Corporate representation seems the only alternative, yet the difficulties of securing harmonious coexistence with the parliamentary system are nowhere near solution, and given Conservative fears about union influence were bound to bulk even larger for them than for

Labour. The Thatcher rejection of genuine dialogue with the unions, in the teeth of the growing union need for such a dialogue, given the politicisation of industrial relations, met little challenge because both union strength and Labour sentiment among organised labour were on the decline. Reversal of these conditions would severely test this as well as other aspects of Thatcher policy.

The Impact on Party Structure

Circumstances were converging to make possible a breach within each of the major parties, though of greatly differing severity. In both cases, none of the policy impulses leading to the breach was new; what had changed were the relative degrees of influence which these policy impulses commanded within their party.

Within Labour ranks the power and influence of the liberal social democrats began to wane during the 1970s. Since the formation of the party their position had been paramount in shaping its actual behaviour and direction. Their stated ultimate aims might be couched in terms of some distant socialist goal, but inferences from their behaviour pointed to a preference for piecemeal reform within the existing broad structure of economic, social and political relations as being the limit of their aspirations. Policies and programmes were tightly constrained by electoral anxieties to present the party as 'national', 'responsible' and fully fit to govern. In practice this meant doing nothing which seriously violated the expectations of the middle and upper classes. 'The British system tends outwardly to display a sharp conflict between two evenly-matched adversaries, but inwardly it relies upon an informal consensus on policy, which depends upon the leaders of both parties, when they are in government, acting within limits of the politically practicable as these are perceived and defined by the state's permanent agencies' (Gamble, 1981, p. 34). Overriding importance was attached to preserving the traditional parliamentary procedures and the restraints they were deemed to require. These restraints extended to the analytical model of society to which one was assumed to work and to the vocabulary with which one conducted the political struggle. Certain types of analysis, certain types of argument and certain types of language must not be used. Analysis, argument and language thereby became adapted to the restraints and niceties deemed essential, in the British context, to the conduct of non-violent political institutions. The leaders of liberal social democracy gave little impression of straining against this leash of constraints.

Spokesmen of another group within the party did sometimes give the impression of feeling frustrated. These were the socialist social democrats. Though for the most part committed to traditional and constitutional procedures, some of them at least were more ready than the first group to accept the validity of extra-parliamentary political pressures. They chafed more restlessly against being a 'national' party and what it was deemed to require. A conception of socialism occupied a nearer and more compelling place within their political vision and vocabulary, and they often urged policies which, if put into effect, would have strained very severely the commitment of the British Establishment to the democratic and constitutional process. Their resolve was never put to the test. They remained subject to the dominance of the liberal social democrats, and in Parliament were always, in the last resort, contained by the electoral dangers to the party and their own seats of defying the official leadership.

Both these groups saw as a threat the growing strength within the party of the farther left. Always present in some form, this group has until recent years been regarded more as an embarrassing nuisance than as a serious contender for power. Asserting some form or forms of Marxist social analysis, its members alarm the liberal social democrats and many of the socialist social democrats with their class-war language and their alleged indifference to the code of tolerance and restraint defined by their critics as necessary ingredients of the British political system. Doubt has been expressed as to their commitment to the parliamentary process and to constitutionalism generally. In a political culture like Britain's this is a particularly strong card to play and the media have intensified the bidding. Along with all this, the far left dismiss the argument that Labour must always strive to hold large areas of the 'middle ground' and ridicule the time-hallowed struggle towards the concept of a national party preserving a 'fair balance' between 'all sections of the community'. This and the tight organisation and discipline through which their growing strength has enlarged their base within the party have fostered a charge that their influence is alien and somehow un-British. In a sense more fundamental than all this, however, is their assertion of the methods and slogans of direct democracy. Those who have hitherto had the running of the party have naturally been disposed to prefer the virtues and strengths of representative democracy, which left them with a wide discretion for which they were supposedly answerable, if at all, at some later stage. The new left have managed to assert the beginnings of a direct and more immediate answerability to the constituencies and to the annual party conference. In the process of fighting for this direct democracy the left have been perceived by their opponents and critics – especially given the harsher political vocabulary which they often employ – as being indifferent to the values implicit in the traditional liberal structures and styles of British politics. Needless to say, the media, ever eager to present all radical expressions of socialism as Eastern European totalitarianism, have fostered and enlarged these perceptions.

Although on many salient issues the members within each of these three groups were as one – liberal social democrats agreeing on Britain's continued membership of the EEC, for example, and the far left agreeing to oppose it – there were issues on which each group divided. These constituted, as it were, fault lines which, if put under severe strain, could open up into fissures. The one of immediate concern for our present purposes is determined by differing attitudes towards the trade unions and towards the idea of a unified industrial-political movement. Each group contained those who did not understand the unions and their *modus operandi* and those who did and felt the force of the idea that a political alliance with their mass industrial base must be preserved in the interests of an effective Labour movement.

This categorisation inevitably oversimplifies in that it implies sharp cut-off points within and between the groups, whereas the reality is more a spectrum within which each section shades into the next. Yet the model provides some help in understanding the polarising impact on British politics of economic decline and the measures adopted to grapple with it. The commitment of Labour's liberal, and even of many of its socialist, social democrats to preserve Britain's mixed economy and all that it implies had drawn them irresistibly into propping up Britain's ailing capitalism. From this followed a whole complex of policies which were perceived by a growing number of activists, including many trade unionists frustrated especially by incomes policies, as anti-working class. The mood was quickened by international radical impulses springing from disgust with the newly burgeoning international capitalism with its vast corporations, its smooth public relations, its high-pressure advertising, its sometimes manifestly cynical marketing strategies, its power to move governments, and its ability at top level where strategic decisions were made to operate beyond the reach of national trade union movements.

It seemed to many within the party that the Labour political machine was becoming more and more drawn into the practical support and service of such institutions and forces as these which were utterly antipathetic to the socialist cause. If this stance had produced rapid economic growth there might have been a different story to tell, but it reproduced only the old familiar scene of inflation, 'stop–go', incomes policies, cuts in investment and social spending, 'bondage' to either America or Europe and to international economic pressures, and more recently an increasing reliance on orthodox monetary policies and rising unemployment. While it would be unfair to judge the later postwar Labour governments solely by Wilsonian utterances, there is significance in the fact that the index to his book, *The Labour Government 1964–70* (1971), contains no references to 'capitalism' or 'socialism' but fifty-nine to 'sterling' (E. P. Thompson, 1980, p. 58). Economic decline seemed unstoppable by any of the stock of devices, expedients and policy combinations which both major parties had drawn upon over the preceding decades. For many of those who still looked beyond piecemeal reform and entertained the larger hope, the orthodox Labour stance of the liberal social democrats seemed played out and demonstrably bankrupt.

As we have seen, a major source of these strains were attempts by Labour governments 'to infuse the working class with national considerations at that level where economic class considerations had persisted most stubbornly – at the level of trade union wage bargaining'. With their conception of pursuing compromises between the sectional demands of various classes by means of policies 'in the national interest', the Labour leadership were prepared to assert, for example, that the 1964 tripartite agreement on productivity, prices and incomes 'heralded the end of the class war'. Yet it was wage militancy at the workplace which was currently the main expression of class conflict in British society. Given the Labour leadership's attempts to bring this under control, there was a sense in which the front line of class divisions lay within the Labour movement itself. With industrial relations thus politicised, 'the contradiction raised by an industrially militant working class tied to an ideologically integrative political party assumed an entirely new and critical dimension' (Panitch, 1976, pp. 5–6).

The strains ranged wider than this, however, for many socialists both inside and outside the unions.

> The story is largely told in the disappointment of trade union expectations of extensive influence in the framing of economic policy; in the operation of incomes policy as wage restraint in the context of the abandonment of even indicative planning; in the extreme reluctance of the Labour government to engage in price and profit controls; in the readiness with which the government dropped the voluntary principle upon which the incomes policy was founded and thus challenged the unions' view of themselves as free agents in collective bargaining. (ibid., p. 241)

These and all the other outcomes of the commitment to the mixed economy, together with the inevitably close proximity and susceptibility of Labour's leadership to the power pressures, values and traditions of the Establishment, had drawn the party in directions which for many socialists pointed to nothing hopeful. The answer, as they saw it, would have to lie in mobilising counter-pressures by which the rank and file could, if necessary, force their leaders into more acceptable paths. What seemed an inevitable tendency for Labour spokesmen to drift steadily to the right when in office – or, in some cases, simply after arrival in the House of Commons – would have to be organisationally countered by structured arrangements for keeping them vividly aware of rank and file policies and priorities, if necessary by painful sanctions.

This gathering mood brought strength to the struggle by the radical and ultra-left elements to capture the party machine for their own objectives. These were now a larger proportion of the party than ever before. It is in itself a significant indication of the shift to the left that in 1972 the party rules on proscribed organisations, for long extremely rigorous, were liberalised. Only members of organisations that ran rival candidates were to be excluded. Many among the ultra left now joined the party and set the face of the movement towards greater extra-parliamentary control over leadership elections and the parliamentary behaviour – and reselection – of MPs. This was not wholly a movement of the left – even a predominantly right-wing constituency might be ready to give some degree of support to ways of bringing to heel an indifferent, arrogant, or absentee MP. Moreover, after *In Place of Strife*, statutory incomes policies and the heavily asserted rigour of the 5 per cent norm in 1978–9, many 'moderate' union leaders were coming to see the advantages of having a hand in the election of party leaders. But there was no doubt about the direction from which the major emphasis came.

Among the liberal social democrats who felt themselves the prime targets of this attack the fault line increasingly revealed itself. Many stood their ground and declared their intention to fight – namely, those who understood the unions, and/or were committed to preserving the historic link which they saw as the only viable basis for an effective movement, and/or had simply made a personal calculation that only within such a movement could they pursue the career they sought. For those who had no particular feeling for the union link the apparently growing influence of the far left – many of whom, it is worth noting, themselves had no feeling for, or understanding of, the unions – brought only the prospect of a series of lost elections and much personal political harassment. For them, party ties weakened and the fault lines among the liberal social democrats began to open up into fissure.

This polarisation within the party was powerfully reinforced by the policies and utterances – and the social attitudes they revealed – of the Thatcher government which took office in 1979. These included the monetary policy which aggravated the unemployment induced by recession, the hostile stance towards all forms of social spending, disparagement of the public sector, the clear intention of redistributing income towards the better-off, emphatic assertions of support for the armed forces and police, and the constant tone of menace towards the unions. Those who acknowledged the class war perceived in these policies a considered resolve to prosecute it more openly and vigorously. The reciprocal responses which this evoked especially strongly within the left of the Labour movement had the effect of widening the breach with the liberal social democrats. Following the left's successes with the electoral college and MP reselection, those on one side of the fault line, the New Whigs, broke away as the Social Democratic Party. The rest remained to continue the internal struggle.

These events indicated that the institutional control wielded over the Labour Party by its parliamentary leaders was breaking down. More precisely, the 'old alliance between the parliamentary leadership, who controlled MPs through the Whips, and the major union leaders who controlled the NEC and the party conference through their block votes', was being eroded. This alliance, which had maintained the long dominance of the Labour right, was 'eroded by the steadily increasing support for the left in the constituency parties and in the trade unions which has been reflected on the NEC and at Labour Conferences' (Gamble, 1981, p. 227). Ever since the formation of the parliamentary party the strategies and style thought necessary and appropriate to parliamentary social democracy had prevailed over whatever policies were currently being emphasised as 'true socialism'. These parliamentary strategies and style were shaped and maintained by the immensely powerful conditioning forces exerted by the traditions and procedures of the House of Commons. From its earliest beginnings the parliamentary leadership had acted as 'one of the chief mechanisms for inculcating the organised working class with national values and symbols and of restraining and re-interpreting working class demands in this light'. By upholding the values of 'the nation', Parliament, and 'responsibility' against the values of direct action, revolution, or 'sectional interests', it has been 'performing a socialising role which both legitimates existing society and militates against the development of a revolutionary political consciousness on the part of the working class' (Panitch, 1976, pp. 235–6). For the first time this role was now being effectively challenged by substantial groups of rank and file members and their spokesmen among trade union, party and parliamentary leaders.

Meanwhile the Conservative Party, too, was undergoing its own ideological strains. Events had fostered a new blossoming of the policies of its right wing. For most of the postwar period the emphasis of the conservative social democrats had prevailed, with their somewhat more accommodating postures based on the belief, usually sanctified by the name of Disraeli but far more convincingly exemplified in Baldwin and later Butler, that preservation of the status quo required, in the name of the One Nation, mitigation rather than intensification of the class war. This called not only for the rhetoric and practice of compassion for society's casualties and losers. It called also for a readiness to deal with the spokesmen of organised labour, meet them some part of the way on occasion with gestures of respect and good will, and seek as far as was politically prudent to restrain belligerent colleagues from inflammatory verbiage or attacks on labour's organisations and activities.

Conservative governments, like the party, invariably contain spokesmen of a distinctly harsher stance. The question of which enjoy the ascendancy depends on the issue, the circumstances and the mood within the party and the wider public. We have noted the existence of the Operation Robot plan during the 1950s; a set of economic and financial orthodoxies and dispositions which, so far as the postwar world was concerned, had not then come back into their time. As government after government worked its way through the same set of policies and expedients, only to bequeath the same recurrent problems to its successor, the attractions of a strategy which had not yet been tried in the postwar context became as attractive to the farther right as to the farther left. Whatever the supposed appeal of 'middle ground' policies, they carried less and less conviction for significant elements within the Conservative and Labour parties. Indeed, there seemed reason to believe that it was as true of the wider public as of the parties that somewhat smaller members now occupied the middle ground, if by this was meant the range of expedients hitherto drawn upon by both parties. Those moving to the right, however, far outnumbered those moving to the left. Even within the working class, attitude surveys showed many prepared to agree that the unions – or at least other people's unions – had too much power and used it irresponsibly. Such responses had sharpened with the increased strength and militancy of, for example, public sector unionism, which took over the tactics of traditional unionism, with its closed shops, its strikes and its unblinking pursuit of sectional interest often unsoftened by any wider citizenship sympathies. However important it is, in trying to understand English social behaviour, to recall that early English philosophers were reflecting the realities of their society in fastening 'on social theory the presumption that individual self-interest is clear and compelling, while a public or a social interest is thin and unsubstantial' (Sabine, 1963, p. 529), it was unlikely to assuage the resentment of the harassed

citizen. The argument that public service strikers, like other trade unionists, were only applying the same principles of market behaviour as had
long been practised by their capitalist masters and mentors was unlikely to
occur to the wage- and salary-earning public when faced by refuse
collectors who left mountains of rubbish to rot in the streets, hospital
workers who appeared to threaten the health of patients, firemen who
severely qualified their responses to alarms, and social security staffs who
refused to distribute badly needed welfare benefits to recipients worse off
than themselves. There were other equally ominous signs. The many
wage-earners who had been carried by inflation and rising earnings into
the tax-paying category – and who might be buying their house on
mortgage – showed little receptiveness to the Labour programme, with its
levels of public expenditure that threatened high taxation and rates. And
among the wider electorate a diminishing number felt that Labour had
effective answers to the country's economic predicament. All the trends
pointed to a move to the right. The Thatcher government elected in 1979
supplied it.

Liberal-Conservatism and the Thatcher Strategy

The basic proposition of the ascendant liberal-conservatism was that
attempts by Conservatives to occupy the central ground through compromise measures of the middle-way variety must be rejected. 'In practice, it
is said, a middle way compromise will always be subject to irresistible
pressures for ever more government intervention in the interest of social
justice, and so will generate a constant movement towards the left'
(O'Sullivan, 1976, p. 140). The three ideas which characterise this liberal-
conservatism amount to a major programme of 'rolling back the frontiers
of the state', justified on the grounds that the preservation of political
liberty and constitutional government as well as the re-energising of
economic enterprise require the reassertion of a free market economy.
First, society should be based upon an acceptance in all the important
spheres of life of free market mechanisms rather than political control.
Secondly, government intervention in the economy, especially, must be
reduced. Finally, the growth of the welfare state must be, at the very least,
contained in order both to limit its cost and to retain to the individual some
degree of moral responsibility and initiative. These ideas were shared by
similarly ascendant movements widespread throughout the Western
world.

    In some respects the argument bearing upon social welfare benefits
closely resembles 'the argument before and after the Poor Law Amendment Act of 1834' (Halsey, 1983). Viewed more generally, the programme was akin to that pressed by the Liberty and Property Defence
League and similar organisations during the period when the Conservative Party was increasingly absorbing businessmen and others whose
views had been shaped by the older Liberalism. There was the overt
celebration of individualistic success in competitive struggles within
free markets, with market forces being elevated as the harmonising

determinants in economic and social development. There was the disposition towards moral disparagement of society's casualties and losers.
There was the open and unabashed importance attached to the preservation and even enlargement of proper, desirable and necessary inequalities of power, status and rewards. Birkenhead's 'glittering prizes' speech
of 1923, which sent shudders down the spines of the more prudent and
fastidious Conservative activists (see p. 311), would raise few eyebrows
among the Thatcher entourage. Along with this renewed glorification of
individual achievement went a publicly declared conviction that the
industrial strength of organised labour must be reduced, partly through a
shift of power at the workplace to favour the managers and partly through
legislation; similarly that its political strength must be reduced also. None
of these sentiments was new to the twentieth-century Conservative Party.
Their relative muting after 1922 had been due, not to a loss of their place in
Conservative hearts, but to the adoption of a different public political style
characterised by Baldwin and those who considered that his was a more
reliable strategy and tradition for conserving the status quo. Some
members of the Thatcher administration did not conceal their unease at its
supersession.

There were, however, significant differences between the Thatcher
conception and classical nineteenth-century *laissez-faire* doctrines. The
former included the notion of a 'social market economy' in which
significant concessions were made to the need for some government
intervention. Moreover, rolling back the frontiers of the state did not
extend to the police, or to the overall expenditure on arms, or to staffs
directed towards the detection of social security 'scrounging' and fraud.
Neither did it cover policies towards local government, which has become
subjected to authoritarian Whitehall control unprecedented in Britain's
history. Nevertheless, the Thatcher conception did represent a response to
the growing Conservative view that as a result of Britain's economic
decline the traditional strategy as it had now developed – as a consequence
of conceding 'middle-ground' compromises – was demanding too heavy a
price from its principal beneficiaries. But which way could the party go?
To break new ground by attempting a state-led modernisation of
economic, social and political institutions and processes was anathema
and, given a strong trade union movement, full of dangers. The only
acceptable direction led backwards. There was an attempt to return to the
Victorian state of affairs. The yearning for a narrowly limited state role,
for a Labour movement greatly reduced in industrial and political weight,
for a reduction in expectations of public spending, for a reassertion of
individualist values – these were signs of a belief that what had made
Britain great in the past could made her great again now. The events and
speeches of the Falklands War reveal this belief infused with nostalgia for
Britain's imperial and world role (A. Barnett, 1982). Government
economic policy took a corresponding shape, with a return to the old
emphasis by which exchange and the market took precedence over
manufacture – not that this emphasis had ever undergone much change.
To summarise: the Thatcher conception was literally 'reactionary' in one
of the dictionary senses, in that it sought to return to a previous condition.

In terms of specific content it saw the problems of the British economy as chronic inflation, high taxation and low productivity resulting from an excessive growth in government spending and from what was referred to as an 'imbalance' between the power of organised labour and management at the workplace. The prescriptions were to tighten control of the creation of money and credit to reduce inflation; to cut national and local government spending to reduce the tax burden; to ensure that public borrowing was reduced so that interest rates would not rise still higher; to return to private ownership such public assets as might be made to yield a profit; to stimulate energy and drive among the middle and top ranks of industry and commerce by tax concessions; and, finally, to weaken the power and influence of organised labour. The last objective on this list was to be pursued less precipitately than in the Industrial Relations Act 1971, which attempted comprehensive reconstruction in one major measure. The first move in a step-by-step approach was the Employment Act 1980, which included attempts to return some degree of individualism to the labour market (Wedderburn *et al.*, 1983, ch. 6). Some of these attempts operated directly, as, for example, through repeal of clauses in the Employment Protection Act 1975 under which 'black-sheep' employers could be required to apply terms and conditions of employment not less favourable than those established by relevant collective agreements. Others operated indirectly through restrictions upon employees' legal freedom to take industrial action. Underlying important sections dealing with picketing, 'secondary' tactics, and the civil liabilities of participants in industrial action lay judge-made common law liabilities. Developed largely from nineteenth-century notions, these were revived by the new Act's declaration that in certain circumstances the so-called 'immunities' do not apply. Other clauses were felt by the unions to put closed shops in jeopardy by enlarging the conscience grounds on which objectors could plead exemption to include 'deeply-held personal convictions'. The statutory union recognition procedure, too, was abolished. All these measures, which stress

> the rights of dissentient members or the values of the individual labour market will be perceived by trade unions, and correctly so, as containing threats to the effectiveness of their organizational arrangements at the workplace and to their ability to make gains for their members through collective bargaining. Indeed, in a thorough-going [economic] liberalist philosophy, it is difficult to see what role can be assigned to trade unions. (Davies, 1980, p. 267)

Other government steps in the same direction included more anti-union legislation in 1982, which, among other things, opened up union funds to massive claims by employers for financial compensation in certain cases. At the time of writing, still more is promised. Proposals include rendering every union open to civil actions for damages allegedly suffered by aggrieved parties during a strike unless the union has first held a secret strike ballot. How far employers would avail themselves of this option rests on the same uncertainties that have marked punitive union law from the Combination Acts to Taff Vale and the 1971 Act; a strike is not a isolated incident but an event within a continuing relationship which fo both sides has a future as well as a past. And it is the employer, not th state, who has to initiate the procedure. This and other proposed reforms, such as compulsory periodic ballots of union national executives and some general secretaries have, on poll evidence, the overwhelming support of the public and of a majority of trade unionists. It would not be easy for the Labour Party to go to the country declaring its intention to reverse them.

Meanwhile the misfortunes of the National Graphical Association (NGA), financially severely battered by the courts in their struggle to subdue one recalcitrant small-scale employer, have brought home to the unions the potential dangers that now await them at the hands of those employers prepared to exploit the new weapons available. Divisions are already evident among them as to how far and by what methods the new laws are to be fought. By strict constitutional legality or by open defiance? The issue threatens to join others that seem likely to aggravate disunity within the movement.

As was to be expected in the British scene, humbug was well in evidence in media and other public discussion of these events. Amid many holy protestations of horror at NGA illegality, the Thatcher government remained conspicuously unfussed by the constant criminality displayed by many employers who knowingly pay employees less than the statutory levels required by Wages Councils. The proposed solution is to abolish the Wages Councils. Another long-standing feature of the industrial relations scene has already succumbed to reforming zeal. The 1946 Fair Wages Resolution, which called upon all contractors for government work to pay wages and observe hours 'not less favourable' than those negotiated through the relevant joint procedures, has been swept away.

The attractions of this strategy for many Conservatives, including back-benchers, industrial managers and rank and file activists, were many. They had little to do with the techniques of monetarism. It is doubtful if more than a tiny handful of people throughout the country really understood the terms of that argument. Much of the strategy's appeal lay in its ability to mobilise deep economic and social resentments behind a class counter-attack which promised to throw back a postwar creeping encroachment of 'socialism', 'self-indulgent' welfare spending, 'arrogant' union power, and workplace restrictionism. Monetarism was only one element of a broadly based ideological and political attack upon government intervention and upon social democracy. And this had appeal for many besides committed Conservatives. The 'New Right' included a much wider populist movement which took up issues like immigration, state intervention, taxation, demonstrations, law and order, strikes, social security abuse, and permissiveness. What marked off the economic liberalism revival from the liberal thrust of the nineteenth century was its association with a whole set of illiberal perspectives on social and political issues.

It was also part of the appeal of the economic strategy that it was to be imposed and not made the subject of compromise through consultation with the TUC. By 1982 this exclusion of the unions had become a general policy. The *Guardian* (22 November) reported a 'confidential Cabinet Office document' which instructed the Office 'to freeze out the trade unions from membership of royal commissions and public bodies at national level'. The significance of this with respect to economic strategy was that there was to be no move in the direction of corporate bargaining. The strategy was to be self-sustaining in the sense that the resultant weakening of organised labour would ensure its acceptance. That dangerous development by which the unions were encouraged to lay down terms for their co-operation in government policy would not be necessary. Moreover, the weakening of the unions would make possible the reassertion of those statutory checks to their rights and activities which were unsuccessfully attempted when they were strong.

Much of this programme added up to a repudiation of the implicit postwar consensual settlement. In the eyes of the new Conservatives, the Baldwin–Butler–Attlee–Gaitskell consensus had manifestly failed to produce an economy sufficiently dynamic and efficient to sustain profits, growth and a stable place in the world economy, while, at the same time, meeting the pressures of a powerful trade union movement and rising expectations in health, education and welfare. The consensus must therefore go. Stirrings in the direction of this repudiation had come intermittently from earlier Conservative and Labour administrations: now it had become the systematic basis of government policy. Some observers considered this had implications for Tory policies towards the coercive forces of the state. If there was to be added to the convulsions of Northern Ireland and the violence of racial and inner-city resentments a wider unrest stemming from rigorous economic policies and changes in trade union law, the police and armed forces might well feel they had an enlarged role to play in future. They were the only elements in the public sector to receive the positive and benign approval of the Thatcher government.

The Thatcher programme also had implications for employers and managers. The shift in the balance of power produced by mass unemployment would make possible a reassertion of managerial authority at the workplace, so long felt to be in abeyance. High glee was expressed at what was presented as a turning of the tables – even vengeance (Torode, 1981). 'Management', proclaimed Sir Hector Laing, chairman of United Biscuits, 'are in the saddle' (G. Turner, 1981). Some, more public-relations conscious, simply expressed appreciation of the 'new spirit of realism' on the shop floor. 'Managers everywhere report that during the past two years they have achieved manning levels and shop floor flexibility of a standard previously thought unobtainable in this country. In many factories we have caught up with German levels of efficiency though not with the Japanese' (Smith, 1981). On a similar impressionistic level, other industrial journalists described how 'all over British manufacturing industry, managers are celebrating their return to life and power, like eunuchs miraculously restored to wholeness and to potency' (Turner, 1981). Everywhere, it was said, the bad old ways – overmanning, demarcations, restrictive practices generally – were being purged in a healthy cleansing process. Thus at last would be achieved that long-delayed and long-awaited break-through to the full modernisation of the British economy.

The contribution of the government's union legislation to this alleged transformation of the workplace scene appeared to be indirect rather than direct. The 1980 clauses and recommendations which attempt to regulate picketing, for example, have been shown to be commonly infringed, yet the law has been applied in only a tiny proportion of cases (Kahn *et al.*, 1983). The effects have been more to strengthen managerial confidence by demonstrating state support of 'the right to manage'.

But there was more behind this managerial resurgence than simply the impact of mass unemployment and direct encouragement by the Thatcher government. These were obviously facilitating factors behind the new mood. But what seemed to lend it, for many managers, a positive buoyancy and confidence was the release of a long-growing conviction that Labour policies had nothing to offer, not only in terms of efficiency (about which they had long had few doubts), but also in terms of social ethics (about which there had often been a lurking uneasiness). The latter consideration was not unimportant. Morally, British Conservatism has for some time included a defensive streak which expressed itself in a certain self-consciousness about profit, class and power. This derived from the awareness that there was a politically significant section of the middle class which, though not committed to the Labour camp, was not irrevocably bonded to every facet of the Tory cause either; which had no surpassing love and respect for large-scale business and the profit motive; and which could even be moved on occasion by considerations of 'fair play' between the classes. This social unease had recently been much allayed, however, by the sight of postwar shop-floor power pursuing shop-floor interests with apparently little or no concern for unorganised or weakly organised social groups or for the welfare of their fellow-citizens. Where lay the moral superiority in such a movement? Those who wished to free themselves from unease were happy to leave the appraisal there, less than half-explored. By the end of the winter of 1978–9, when the social contract had collapsed in a wave of bitter and socially damaging strikes, they felt free to argue that here was final proof that Labour and the unions had found neither a more efficient nor a more decent way of doing business than the free market provided (Torode, 1981). Even Labour supporters could feel their faith crumbling. Until the Second World War, sectional struggles could somehow be seen as serving the general struggle. Such arguments now seemed more like apologetics, and sectional struggles more like *sauve qui peut*. If managers returned to prewar styles, who could convincingly charge them with failure to respond to a new morality offered by Labour?

If anything it was the renewed emphasis on free markets that offered the moral language now. The whole strategy was often infused with a vocabulary which recalled a long-standing tendency for economic statements to embody highly normative assumptions and propositions. As in the 1920s and earlier, monetary and fiscal orthodoxy, along with the policies of promoting private enterprise and limiting state intervention and involvement, were presented as moral stiffeners against public and private profligacy. Economic debate in the popular arena saw a return of age-old and much-loved moralising analogies between the national and the family budget. Many economics graduates must have rubbed their eyes at seeing restored those pre-Keynesian images – which they had been taught to reject as absurdly fallacious in their first year – identifying the Chancellor with the prudent housewife.

It was, of course, recognised that in the new harsh but bracing climate some firms would fail to meet the challenge. There would be bankruptcies, closures of high-cost plants, a sloughing-off of economically flabby ventures. Yet the gains would be great. British industry would emerge from the ordeal leaner, fitter and well braced to meet world competition. 'Real unit labour costs are falling ... as productivity is raised by the massive once-for-all slimming operation by British industry', declared the *Quarterly Bulletin* of the Liverpool University Research Group in Macroeconomics (October 1981). The impetus must, it was thought, be maintained. Exhortations upon the government to this end sometimes contained not only the language of morals but also the language of war – for example, when they came from economists who believed they glimpsed on the horizon a golden vista of pure economic liberalism (Minford, 1981).

The Prime Minister sought to reinforce the general effect by appealing for the Falklands spirit to be applied to the economy. On the one hand, therefore, was the celebration of individualistic struggle, the proclamation that individual merit and success must be more highly rewarded, that collectivism was suspect, that trade unionism must be cut down to size, and that the interventionist and supportive functions of the state must be checked in favour of impersonal market forces. On the other hand, there was the appeal for a new national spirit of unity and purpose in which all would pull together for the common good. Little evidence emerged that sizeable numbers of the British people or their political commentators detected any incongruity between these positions. After Falklands, even the *sotto voce* unease expressed in some quarters of the Conservative camp about the whole strategy became stilled. It nevertheless calls for examination, since it spoke for a long-standing Conservative tradition.

Some 'Traditional' Conservative Resistance

As official unemployment figures moved towards the 3 million mark, as the nation's manufacturing base became more and more attenuated, and as the nation's health, welfare, education and other services became, along with the rest of the public sector, the objects of manifest government suspicion and even disparagement, some voices were up-raised among those sections of Conservative opinion, represented even in the Cabinet, which doubted if these were the best long-term methods of conserving hierarchy, social order and privilege. They spoke instead for the continuance of the traditional strategy in its modern development. Few of those subscribing to this strategy felt able to expound it fully in public, since it rested upon an analysis of the British political scene, past and present, which accorded ill with the shared pretences deemed necessary by both parties for the conduct of Britain's parliamentary system. One of the few to shed these inhibitions was the associate editor of the *Sunday Telegraph*. Over the years Worsthorne wrote a number of articles designed to warn his fellow Conservatives, and especially government ministers, that the British political system and the prevalent Conservative style within it have effectively conserved much of the old order and that they would be ill-advised to put it at hazard. On this point his analysis would be quite acceptable to a Marxist. 'Tory rhetoric in recent years tended to suggest that Socialism and egalitarianism had destroyed the old order beyond repair. According to these gloomy descriptions all the rich had been forced to flee by crippling taxation. The process of levelling down had turned Britain into a society of grey mediocrity . . . ' This, he commented in 1979, was not quite the impression conveyed by the new government. The Thatcher Cabinet was evidence 'of how little Socialist damage has been done, not how much'. It included 'almost as many aristocrats, property owners and millionaires as Disraeli's', and was 'a marvellous testimony to the success of the Conservative party during this last century in using democracy to safeguard privilege'. It has succeeded in 'what the Conservative party's main function has always been: to win mass support for the preservation of the traditional social hierarchy'. Certainly, Labour governments have done much to improve the material lives of working people, and according to British constitutional theory could have done far more. 'But this theory would not survive long if it was used in ways profoundly unacceptable to a majority of the middle class.' Short of a violent revolution which 'physically liquidates those at the top, it is extremely difficult to dislodge a ruling class which has not entirely lost its will to survive'. Even a left-wing government could not run the economy 'without the support of the bourgeoisie, which will only be forthcoming on its own terms.' Moreover, the army and the police 'have seldom been more deeply conservative'.

'What price', asked Worsthorne, 'the great social revolution that was meant to have got under way as far back as 1945?' – the pledges 'to remove great discrepancies of wealth, to do away with private education, to destroy the great estates, to break the Oxbridge hold, to prevent the inheritance of private fortunes?' He urged ministers to recognise the significance of the Conservative political skills through which 'a basically conservative order has survived and even prospered'. They have lain in moderating 'economic' realism with 'social' realism. Ministers must not go too far or too fast in their economic crusading zeal. Given the resulting social strains imposed by the new policies, there was 'bound to be a recrudescence of a far more virulent strain in Socialist sentiment than anything experienced in recent years'. These strains must be mitigated, therefore, by methods which may not always make economic sense but make a good deal of social sense in coping with 'the classical and pre-eminently Tory problem of reconciling the enfranchised working class – which is now both economically and politically powerful – to a social structure that is still deeply unequal'. If this 'splendidly Trollopian' Cabinet 'preserves the *status quo* half as successfully in the future as Labour governments have in the past, it will have proved miraculously successful' (Worsthorne, 1979–81). This was the authentic voice of the Cecilian and

Baldwinian Conservatism that had led the overthrow of the Coalition government and Lloyd George in 1922.

Such writings, in which references to Disraeli and One Nation emerged as code signals, were a response to the evidence that the Thatcher government was pressing hard in certain important respects against the traditional Tory technique of rule. The results were perceived by the 'traditionals' as policies 'which divide the nation, cripple industry (at any rate temporarily), provoke the working class, and run the risk of putting a Marxist-dominated Labour party, wedded to unilateral disarmament, back into power at the next election. If this is Conservatism, then the word must mean something very different to what one has always assumed' (ibid.). It was not so much a different Conservatism, however, as the releasing of long-standing Conservative impulses which had hitherto been largely contained and certainly rarely established as the systematic bases of a Conservative administration. The 1983 general election was to show, nevertheless, that they created little risk of returning a 'Marxist-dominated Labour party' to power. The unease, however, persisted, surfacing again in Francis Pym's first Commons speech (28 June 1983) after being displaced as Foreign Secretary. 'At its best, the Conservative party has always been broad in its views, national in its interests, tolerant in its outlook, constructive in its debate, and unifying in its aims.' Combined with his later observation that the party was currently apt to present, 'misleadingly', a somewhat hard face towards poverty and misfortune, this identified him as a leading critic of the Thatcher emphasis and style.

The stirrings of doubt in these explicitly Conservative circles had a certain parallel among the higher judiciary. This needs to be located within a wider focus on the law and its enforcement. Though the polarisation of opinion had also appeared in attitudes towards the police, whose behaviour and methods are now criticised or defended more emotionally than for a long time past, few would dispute that the rule of law, whatever its inadequacies and imperfections, remains a key feature of the British scene.

> The law rules in this sense: that governments and all who exercise power as part of established authority are themselves bound by the existing body of laws unless and until they repeal or reform any of those laws . . . The exercise of arbitrary power is contrary to the rule of law and the true mark of the despot is that he can, at his own wish and without restraint, set aside the existing laws in any case. Judges are similarly constrained in their law-making function by the doctrine of precedent. (Griffith, 1981, p. 233)

Both in the application of statute law, however, and (especially at the law lords level) the handling of precedent, the judicial function contains a discretionary and therefore creative possibility. A recent analysis sees judges as inevitably making what are, in effect, political decisions by exercising their discretion towards what they define as the public interest. 'And the public interest, so defined, is . . . the interest of others in authority, whether in government, in the City or in the church. It includes the maintenance of order, the protection of private property, the promotion of certain general economic aims, the containment of the trade union movement, and the continuance of governments which conduct their business largely in private and on the advice of other members of . . . the governing group.' In applying such criteria the bench combines incorruptibility and independence of government with a disposition nevertheless to uphold views 'normally associated with the Conservative party' (ibid., pp. 217, 240).

But just as the Conservative Party may contain differences about how best, in the broadest sense, to conserve, so may the bench. In a group of cases in 1978 and 1979 the Court of Appeal sought to limit the legal protection granted trade unionists from certain criminal and civil liabilities which they otherwise tend to incur when they act 'in contemplation or furtherance of a trade dispute'. Subsequently, in three cases decided between July 1979 and February 1980, the House of Lords reversed this development. This refusal to support the Court of Appeal in its determination to enlarge trade unionists' vulnerability to legal attack did not stem from a more benign stance. 'Both courts were agreed that trade union power should be curbed, and in this their political position was identical.' The difference was that the House of Lords defined the public interest, construed in its broadest possible sense, as calling at this particular juncture, for mitigation rather than aggravation of open and manifestly political conflict between the courts and the unions. 'Their Lordships may well have concluded that it would be wiser to leave such highly contentious political matters to the professional politicians', though some of them were assiduous in pushing the Conservative government in what they considered the right direction by criticising the protections presently enjoyed by trade unionists (ibid., pp. 80–3, 223–5). From the point of view of future British social and political relations, a good deal hangs on which of these two sets of tactics maintains the ascendancy.

A 'Temporary Deviation'?

Since the releasing of long-standing Conservative impulses by the Thatcher administration had its impact upon the industrial relations system and the political settlement within which it was contained, questions may usefully be posed as to the causes of the releasing. And what relation did the Thatcher administration's declared strategy bear to the traditional Conservative stance as sketched by Worsthorne? Was it a temporary deviation from a mainstream to which we may expect future Conservative governments to return? Or can we identify objective changes in the national economic and social context which may induce a permanent adjustment in the Conservative stance?

One obvious factor that has already emerged is national economic failure. Rising expenditures on defence, education, health and welfare call for steady economic growth if governments are to avoid the high taxation rates that can generate severe political tensions among taxpayers – who now include most trade unionists. But it is possible to identify another factor which both helps to explain the shift of emphasis within the party over the past two decades and indicates that it may remain easier in the foreseeable future for a Thatcher-type stance to secure the balance of Conservative favour. This factor is a fundamental shift in the moral basis of politics as perceived by many of those Conservatives for whom that moral basis had any relevance. Since the 1950s the objective structure of the Two Nations has appeared to undergo major transformation. Over the past half-century the extent of absolute 'destitution' poverty has diminished. The emphasis among those still ethically exercised about comparative living standards relates increasingly to 'inequality, exclusion, discrimination, injustice and "relative poverty"' (Donnison, 1982, p. 7). It is the former definition, however, that in the past stirred the conscience of the well-to-do if it was stirred at all. Now that the more glaring examples of absolute mass deprivation are less in evidence it is easier to believe that the problem is confined to limited pockets and special cases such as single-parent families, 'problem' families, the long-term unemployed, the chronic sick. For many this is so attractive a theory that it withstands much counter-evidence of widespread relative poverty and of indications that Britain is moving towards the American pattern of a polarised society with much more extreme inequality (Bosanquet, 1983). Where public order and property were threatened the Thatcher government took notice, though little action, as in the example of inner-city violence, but otherwise the assertion that poverty has been largely abolished proves a valuable anodyne. Moreover, the equal opportunities ostensibly offered by the educational system and the market place make inequalities of outcome appear to be the necessary result of individual talent and effort on the one hand, or of ineluctable economic forces on the other. In other words, the result of the widespread popular belief that our society has taken dramatic strides towards a 'meritocracy' is that large numbers of the British people, far from abandoning the attitudes of nineteenth-century Samuel Smiles poor law individualism, are comfortably confirmed in them. An EEC survey, *The Perception of Poverty in Europe* (1977), provided evidence of the 'distinctively harsh views of the British compared to people in other European countries'. Sixty-four per cent of UK respondents defined poverty in such a way that they believed none now remained. Of those who believed otherwise, 45 per cent considered the commonest cause to be laziness, compared with only 28 per cent in the Community as a whole, where the commonest causes were seen as outside individual control. Similarly, answers to a wider question: 'Why are there people who live in need?' revealed that in France and Italy the most common response was to blame society; in the UK it was to blame the individual – 43 per cent offering laziness and lack of will-power as the reasons. This was not simply a moralising by the rich. In all countries it was 'the poorer income groups, the less well educated and the non-leaders' who tended to blame the individual. The UK stood out, however, as having the largest 'hard core of social egoism and conservatism of the most reactionary type' (MacGregor, 1981, pp. 96–7). Another researcher has noted that 'there is evidence in some countries, most notably in the UK, that the growing numbers of unemployed receiving benefits is leading to pressures for more stringent policies and controls in this field' and that 'popular ideologies which identify the poor as "scroungers" are as likely to wax as to wane' (Dennett *et al.*, 1982, pp. 127, 163, 164, 173).

Totally displacing the older consciousness of poverty, for many Conservatives, is a newer consciousness of powerful militant sectional groups of organised labour fighting weaker groups, each other and their social betters, for material advantage. Trade unionism increasingly includes relatively well-placed groups of white-collar and even professional occupations. The Two Nations of 'rich' and 'poor' have, in many Conservative eyes, given way to One Nation composed of groups differentially placed on a scale of 'well-to-do' and 'less-well-to-do'. Since Conservatives are not egalitarians, the only moral element they detect in these struggles around the pork barrel is a negative one: namely, the envy exhibited by those lower down the scale. The great moral challenge once assumed to be posed by socialism has, for them, dwindled down, therefore, to the 'politics of envy'. Those adopting this view claim support from other evidence. Now that most of Britain's wage-earners have become taxpayers they show no greater willingness than other groups to finance ambitious programmes of public welfare and local authority spending. Private medicine and private education, on the other hand, are growth industries not wholly supported by the rich. Many wage-earners, moreover, manifestly share Conservative reservations about black and Asian ethnic minorities. These dispositions, more palpable now than at any time since the formation of the Labour Party, are taken, as we have seen, to demonstrate that the claim of the Labour movement that it can offer morally superior conceptions of social living has no validity outside election manifestos. As a consequence the position of those Conservatives who seek to uphold a more accommodating stance towards the Labour movement is therefore weakened – even open to ridicule.

In a very real sense, the current argument goes, the working classes have got in on the act. They are no longer a separate estate, contained ghetto-like within their old-fashioned communities, their own culture, their all-inclusive organisations, beliefs and institutions. They have become fully paid-up members of the competitive, acquisitive society, and a good thing too. Their trade unionism is no longer a total 'way of life', but merely an instrumentality that has got beyond itself and must be cut down to size. Since it is vested with no moral purpose there is no occasion to feel guilt at reducing its status and powers. Moreover, since it speaks only for a segmental aspect of the employed person's interests there is no occasion for it, or its central organisation, the TUC, to be accorded privileged treatment with respect to consultation, discussion and participation on public bodies generally.

Social perceptions and interpretations of this kind leave little room for that brand of traditional Toryism which acknowledged the terms 'rich' and 'poor', feared to alienate the latter lest their mass strength be mobilised behind a moral crusade of social transformation, and pursued policies of prudence and restraint infused to some extent with paternalist evangelical notions of duty towards the lower orders. Many modern Conservatives are likely to view this whole conception as old-fashioned and, in the modern context, sentimental. They see little in the behaviour of the postwar Labour movement that gives them any qualms of moral self-doubt, and as a consequence they see its organisations merely as self-interested pressure groups which must be defeated in open combat. For them the time for appeasement is past, if indeed it ever existed.

There is much in this picture which gives no ideological or moral offence to many trade unionists. There has always been a substantial working-class commitment to Conservatism and many, perhaps most, of those voting Labour do so not because they strain after a morally superior society but because they believe, with varying degrees of conviction, that Labour is the best bet for their interests. Given that Labour has often exasperated these as well as disappointing the idealists and taking into account, too, the appeal for many working-class voters of other aspects of the current Conservative stance, including those on defence, it is clear from the 1983 general election that the analysis of the Tory 'traditionals' overlooks some important variables. One of them springs from the fact that the Inland Revenue shovel of direct taxation now reaches far down the income scale, with the consequence that the line of resistance to generous levels of collective spending and collective citizenship has become more popularly based. Leo Amery might have scaled down his nightmare had he foreseen the enlargement of those sections of the working class that are relatively comfortably placed owner-occupiers and had he foreseen, too, other contentious issues that have led the Labour Party to lose touch with its class base. Yet such is the rate of change in the world scene that no projections can be relied on. The argument of the Tory traditionals that a tried and tested strategy of rule is being dangerously prejudiced will obviously suffer further eclipse for some considerable time, but to suppose that it has been submerged forever would be as rash as to assume that a liberal-spirited political radicalism will never again spark the emotions of the British people. Meanwhile, however, figures released to MPs by the Department of Social Security showing a dramatic rise in the numbers living on the margins of officially defined poverty created little stir. The total rose from 11·5 million in 1979 to 15 million in 1981. The DSS 'decided not to issue a public statement about the figures or release them to the press' (*Guardian*, 1 November 1983).

Observations and Extrapolations

Pressures, problems and events after the mid-1960s created an economic and political situation in which the industrial relations system underwent considerable and unforeseeable modifications of its 'traditional' shape, both in its internal regulative structuring and in its relations with governments and state agencies. The principal factor behind these changes has been a national economic failure conspicuous more in international comparisons than domestically. Average living standards have sometimes continued rising even during the most unlikely periods. The failure has been more evident to specialist observers and governments, which have felt driven to impose checks and create an atmosphere of crisis which brought people and their organisations a sense of frustration and deprivation even when their own standards were not falling.

No doubt even had a respectable rate of growth been maintained, the enlarged power of the Labour movement, industrially and politically, would still have led to changes, including attempts at containment from Conservative quarters. But a high technology, high productivity, high profits, high wage economy would have been better equipped to take the many diverse and conflicting strains.

As it was, the repeated failure – or in some cases the very nature – of the 'middle-ground' expediencies employed by both parties drove significant sections away from that middle ground. On the Labour side there can be little doubt that the policies pursued by the 1964–70 government, committed, as it chose to be, to accepting all the traditional constraints and thereby involved in continuing to expose a weak capitalism to penetration by a confident and aggressive international economic order, finally convinced many socialists, trade unionists among them, that the old models of Labour politics and ideology were bankrupt and played out. The struggle is still proceeding between them, on the one hand, and, on the other, the bulk of the parliamentary party and those union leaders who fear the loss of all political effectiveness if the far left captures parliamentary control, leaving them vulnerable for an indefinite period to the 'reforming' zeal of Conservative governments.

On the Conservative side, too, there was thought to be far more at stake than economic 'success' or 'failure', as those are defined. The politicising of industrial relations in the context of organised labour's industrial and political strength made an old recurrent dread seem, to some, on the brink of materialisation. As a consequence, whatever the manifest functions of extreme monetarist doctrines and governmental professions of reliance on market forces, they also had the latent function of trying to reduce the politicisation of industrial relations. Basically, they represented an aspiration to reassert the old liberal separation of economics and politics; a distinction now paper-thin and virtually moribund. The hope was that government would increasingly be able to disavow, and withdraw from responsibility for, involvement in certain strategic economic variables. Hence frequent government protestations that trade unionists were creating their own unemployment by pricing themselves out of markets; that unemployment so produced was not under government control.

In the most fundamental sense such a strategy could never succeed in 'de-politicising' industrial relations and wider economic policy. It was one thing for governments to declare their freedom from responsibility when no precedents existed for government involvement. But when precedents do exist, the assertion of aloofness or withdrawal itself becomes a positive political act which can excite positive political passions. Nevertheless, the reassertion of old liberal doctrines captured for the time being Conservatism both inside and outside Parliament. This resurgence of confidence undoubtedly owed much to the practical and moral bankruptcy of orthodox Labour and to a conviction that unorthodox Labour threatened immeasurably worse. It clearly aroused some unease among the ranks of traditional Tories, but they were in as defensive a position as was orthodox Labour in the extra-parliamentary Labour Party, and the chances of another Baldwin emerging in the near future seem remote for that reason alone.

This serves to emphasise that the significance of the Thatcher administration for the industrial relations system extended far beyond legal changes and the direct impact of monetary policy and unemployment upon firms' ability to moderate workplace union strength. A whole political atmosphere was created bearing some of the Coalition characteristics which rendered some Conservatives nervous in 1922 but which created no adverse political consequences in 1983 – the result, perhaps, of Labour failure as much as of Tory success. Such was the collapse of Labour support that the Conservatives were able to win their so-called 'landslide majority' on the basis of well under half the total vote. The new strategy represented what was, in the British context, a remarkable attempt to replace one national mood and set of trends and dispositions with another. This could not but have effects on the industrial relations system and its political expression. Along with policies designed to create an even more unequal society, and which celebrated and rewarded individualistic success even more emphatically, went the elimination of labour leaders from top-level political counsels and an unprecedented state encouragement of managers in public and private industry to challenge union restrictionism in the workplace.

One appraisal of the extent to which the Thatcher government could be seen as having departed from consensual and tripartite relationships was offered by Middlemas, who argued that this policy must be reversed. The imposition of policy must give way to a renewal of consultation: '... we have a weak central power much of whose directive force in the past rested on the tacit co-operation of capital and labour – whose constitutions consequently became themselves part of the "extended State". It is not much use now pretending that TUC and CBI are interlopers, or thinking that measures passed through parliament will find acceptance without practical daily renewal of consent.' Middlemas went on to suggest the bases for a process of corporate bargaining – 'it would be naive to imagine that industrial co-operation could be bought without a bargain'. Yet 'cynics could ask: why should CBI or TUC risk their members' hostility through a bargain with the State?' The answer was for the agenda to strengthen 'participants against the cry of selling out, by giving a little more to each side than it has to sacrifice' (Middlemas, 1981).

The hard-line Tory would plead that this had done little in the past for the British economy, for the stimulation of dynamic enterprise and for the restoration of managerial authority at the workplace – less than was now being achieved by the coercive but necessary brutalities of mass unemployment and fierce market pressures which have induced a new spirit of realism on the shop floor. But another body of criticism denied the achievement. One industrial correspondent of long and wide experience noted 'the new breed of management hawks' who spoke of vengeance and urged the need to 'grab back' authority now while they had the chance. But would they be capable of maintaining their new resolve when circumstances changed again? 'When ... the government runs out of steam, the unions get their act together, and ... the economy picks up again, it is a fairly safe, if depressing, bet that the unions will go in for vengeance and grabbing back, too. What we are seeing now is a short-term psychological shift in managerial will. Not a fundamental shift to "realism" on the shop floor' (Torode,1981). The chairman of the Advisory Conciliation and Arbitration Service (ACAS) reported that while 'some commentators feel that more constructive attitudes among the parties can already be discerned', others had found a tendency for managers to take advantage of 'the shift in the balance of power' by disregarding agreed procedures of negotiation and consultation (Lowry,1981, pp. 9–10). This, he argued in a lecture to the first ACAS national conference, marked an 'emerging school of "macho management"' which offered little in long-term solutions to industrial relations problems'. He offered a warning that some industrialists were clearly prepared to endorse. 'Industrial relations will certainly not thrive on the basis that "vengeance is mine" ... ' Commenting at a press conference that there had been references to 'the new sense of realism', he warned people not to assume that when the upturn came 'we shall not be returning to the bad habits and practices that have so contributed to our poor economic performance in the past'.

What kind of appraisal of these conflicting projections is suggested by the historical examination of Britain's industrial relations undertaken in preceding chapters? The most convincing is that the return of mass unemployment and the resolve among some managers to seize the advantage to impose policies and pay off old scores will confirm and reinforce the traditional pattern of adversary relations and institutional mistrust between capital and organised labour. It is probably futile to 'blame' managers for their response. To expect differently would be to underestimate the strength of the social forces which have shaped Britain's industrial relations over centuries. Managers are behaving as they are because organised workers behaved as they did when they held the margin of advantage – and these worker behaviours are, in turn, traceable to the ways in which their culture prompted them to react to the industrial system imposed upon them by the rich and powerful. Such are the circular interactions generated by history. The circles are never completely closed, but they present powerful resistances to being completely broken.

Given these persistent dispositions, certain possibilities of future outcomes present themselves. Other things being equal, we might suppose that when the upswing begins and the labour market starts to tighten, organised labour will be quick to exploit, in its turn, the marginal advantage in power. It will enjoy the benefit of a workplace union organisation that was granted a long period of full employment and opportunities for restrictive job control. Traditions and expectations thus created may have suffered some wasting from the ebbing of strength, but reviving business will renew them like the filling of dry waterways by spring floods. Work groups are hardly likely to be less disposed than before to restore protective devices, resume demarcations and raise manning levels. And if managers hungry for output and profits were to stand pat and fight tenacious and costly battles to defend their recently won gains, they would be behaving very differently from all previous generations of British management. Certain prominent industrialists have not concealed their fear that present managerial rigour will not survive the return of more active business (G. Turner, 1981). Similar scepticism could be extended to the attempts to reassert a measure of individualism in the labour market as well as in other spheres of life. Society is even more institutionally collectivist than when the Liberty and Property Defence League mounted its attacks, and many managers are conspicuously less enthusiastic about onslaughts on the closed shop than Conservative Party activists. They are likely to be still less so when the upswing arrives.

Here, however, we must acknowledge a heavily begged question. How widespread throughout the economy is any upswing likely to extend? Some industries will undoubtedly experience a brisk revival. Strong doubts have been expressed for some time, however, as to whether 'full employment' as previously understood will return in any foreseeable future. Expanding manufacturing industry in the eighteenth century and later provided employment for many who could not have been absorbed in agriculture, which was producing greater output per worker. But will the 'services' sector (including government), now the largest source of employment in all main Western countries, and itself making much use of labour-saving innovations, expand sufficiently or quickly enough to absorb the workers being rapidly 'freed' from manufacturing industry, which everywhere in the West is shrinking as a result of new technologies and other sources of rising productivity? There are opinions that 'it is highly unlikely that the labour shed by manufacturing can be fully absorbed in the expanding parts of the economy until the 1990s – if then' (Shanks, 1981).

The whole argument, however, itself begs questions. The proposition that new technology *per se* destroys jobs is contentious. Japan has both a high innovation rate and the lowest unemployment rate of all the developed market economies. There is no reason to assume that new technology permanently destroys more jobs than it creates unless institutional factors and government policies cause or allow it to. And here we return to our chronic domestic dilemma. Institutional and structural factors as they have historically developed in Britain render it likely that government policies to maintain 'high and stable' levels of employment will result in a considerable aggravation of inflation. To break these links would probably require fundamental shifts in the shape and objectives of British society and economy. Only then might governments be able to offer the necessary inducements to, in particular, the trade unions. The obstacles confronting such a radical social reconstruction have become apparent in the preceding pages. No popular political base exists for any movement towards overcoming these obstacles and there is none in sight. At the time of writing, no large-scale public revolt against mass unemployment seems probable. For two decades after the war it was customary to assume that 'public opinion' would never countenance the return of mass unemployment on the interwar scale. So far, events since the early 1970s have shown this assumption to be false. The relative docility with which unthinkable has been accepted must be assumed to have influenced government choices fundamentally, beginning with the monetarist policies of Healey as Chancellor, when unemployment under Labour was allowed to edge towards 'mass' dimensions. It seems probable now that no government, whatever its colour, is likely to engineer a move towards full employment of 1950s dimensions unless the political pains of forgoing it threaten to exceed those of embracing it, since it would add enormously to the problems of economic management. Even socialist commentators who press for a return to full employment, necessarily gradual, suggest that national union leaders could meanwhile take advantage of present shop-floor weakness to reconstruct the movement in the direction of more centralised bargaining authority, thereby facilitating the negotiation – and even more, the application – of a new and more ambitious social contract (Crouch, 1983, p. 132).

One of the many unpredictables, therefore, about Britain's future is whether public docility about mass unemployment, so far broken only by inner-city violence, remains a government bonus. On past form the unemployed themselves are more likely to lapse into apathy, broken no doubt among the young by undirected violence, than to pursue organised political action. Among those not afflicted there are few signs of a mass compassion which might affect political choices. As already noted, substantial numbers among the British public appear to retain, or to have reverted to, Samuel Smiles individualism. If we strive for a charitable interpretation here it might be derived from the supposition that the British people are baffled for an alternative acceptable solution. To see the poor and unemployed as the authors of their own misfortunes is one way of avoiding the thought that we are collectively imposing these miseries on our fellows because we refuse to face the difficulties presented by other ways out of our problems. Meanwhile a situation in which, for those in work, earnings are outstripping the rise in prices is likely to cause most of the tears for the unemployed to remain of the crocodile variety.

9

Summing Up and Conclusions

The preface to this book identified its purpose as that of attempting to answer the question: how did Britain's industrial relations system, and its place in the wider society, come to be what they are? The answer has revealed the importance both of historical continuities and of contingencies such as accidents of personality and the effects on the domestic economy of events and developments in the world outside. These continuities and contingencies have interacted within a social context itself marked by continuities of individualism and of a state seen in terms of instrumental convenience rather than intrinsic or transcendental value.

It has proved of central importance to the institutional shape and texture of British society in general, and of British labour organisation in particular, that both 'liberties' and 'liberty' have been key concepts for expressing, inspiring and legitimising group purposes. Those seventeenth- and eighteenth-century combinations of artisans whose values and methods echoed in important respects those of their social superiors, and whose successors were to put their imprint upon the trade union movement and its politics, took their stand on the 'liberties' originally conferred by pre-capitalist guild charters. Claims to the prescriptive and exclusive rights of the trade or 'mystery' – to its status, privileges, demarcations and restrictions – derived their peculiar force from the far more widespread phenomenon of freeholds and liberties that littered English life at all social levels and that, to recall Plumb's words, 'bred independence, (see p. 65 above) truculence, a willingness to fight and litigate that bordered on neurosis'. Along with this went an artisan preference, displayed in their trade clubs and in later radical movements, for 'direct democracy', overlaid since by union bureaucracy but never permanently buried.

But if 'liberties' in the form of the craft rights acquired in an earlier age were to be asserted against the repressive forces periodically presented by a growing industrial capitalism, organised labour had also to exploit that other concept developed by the gentry for their own use and for their own legitimation as a ruling order. This was the political 'liberty' which, along with the law, had been especially important for defence against encroachments by crown and executive. The gradual eighteenth-century fashioning of constitutionalism and a supposedly even-handed apparatus of law implied for the governing class a logic of rule which, in the early decades of the nineteenth, they came close to repudiating, but which in the end survived to yield a foothold of industrial and political rights to the artisan and later the wider working class.

The two principal institutions developed by the gentry for their own protection against royal absolutist tendencies had contradictory impacts upon organised labour. Parliament gave scope for the expression of all interests that could secure a voice there, but the common law, with its strong individualist bias, was a permanent threat to labour collectivism. Influence upon, or entry into, the first was necessary to combat the second. It is a struggle that has not ended. The separation of executive and judiciary has enduring consequences for Britain's trade union movement which must always seek, for this reason alone, to retain an effective political voice if it is not to be dependent for its safety upon the grace and favour of its most consistent and ingenious opponents, namely, those who speak from the courts.

The nineteenth-century links with middle-class groups which helped the unions to wage these political struggles carried echoes of seventeenth-century experience. Out of the economic, religious and political circumstances of that century there had developed, betwen the upper and lower strata of the 'middle sort of people', the possibility both of economic conflict and of religious and political alliance. It was these strata particularly for whom liberal individualism had been so important a creed for mobilising and articulating their attack on economic monopoly, religious authoritarianism and political exclusiveness. Two centuries later a whole liberal philosophy of political and civic freedoms had accreted round that individualism. Directed against a ruling class that had chosen for its own reasons to commit itself to law, constitutionality and political liberty, these powerful traditions won major legal victories for the unions. It was crucial for this success that the artisans, concerned as always to retain their economic and social status among the lower fringes of the middle strata and to avoid being pushed down to the despised labouring class, should have given evidence of their continued aspirations towards respectability, defined in terms not merely of superficial mannerisms or dress but in terms of a whole range of social and political behaviour.

The same liberal individualism applied in the economic sphere generated conflict. The early appearance of that individualism in agrarian, commercial and manufacturing capitalism drove out the paternalistic system of control and created conditions for the adversary arms-length relationships stressed by domestic and foreign observers alike. Within this adversary relationship the more successful groups of craftsmen might assert their workplace interests by unilateral enforcement of their own rules, but most of the non-craft groups that began to establish themselves after the mid-nineteenth century, lacking this tradition and leverage, had to try to bring the employers into bilateral negotiation. As the rate of change quickened and economic fluctuations became more marked, craft groups themselves – sometimes under pressure from the employers – moved more and more into collective bargaining, while often managing to retain also their workplace regulations and restrictions. Non-craft groups also sought leverage through workplace job regulation if they could manage it, since craft methods were both effective and a source of self-respect and status.

Employers began to organise themselves by trade or industry, sometimes for unilateral enforcement of terms, sometimes for their bilateral negotiation, sometimes in attempts to destroy the union confronting them. The social milieu was not, however, by comparison with the major Continental powers, encouraging to open onslaughts. Some sizeable groups of employers were already deciding that joint regulation with the unions might prove a useful technique of labour control. Those who felt otherwise soon discovered that no support, practical or moral, could be expected from government and state. Electoral considerations might or might not bulk large in this government stance after 1867; whatever their degree they reinforced the long-standing strategy of attempting to appear even-handed between the classes. The fact that the political ruling class was not wholly dependent upon the domestic economy helped it, in its handling of the working classes, to maintain its public commitment to constitutionalism, law and a not-too-heavy hand on the lower orders.

This commitment had already received expression in the circumstances of the Combination Acts, the aftermath of Tolpuddle, Chartism and the 1867 Reform Act. Their strategic investment in this system of control, so far successful in its orderly peaceful conservation of power and privilege, was now too great to squander on tactical support of particular groups of employers caught up in marginal squabbles over wages and profits. By the end of the century the relevant state agency was giving practical encouragement and stimulus to what was now becoming a system of union recognition, collective bargaining, conciliation and arbitration. Any likelihood that the employing classes might break out in a collective bid of their own to subdue the unions in a modernising drive towards the 'second industrial revolution' and greater efficiency had been rendered improbable. Their leading upper strata were fusing with a gentry and landed aristocracy which itself had long been extending its interests into finance, commerce and industry. The result was that much of the dominant culture of the old landed ruling class now became transmitted to the upper ranks of industrial ownership and management. It was in many respects an anti-enterprise culture which carried over a traditional style of giving priority to stability over innovation and to accommodation over confrontation. Public schools and the ancient universities reared generations of Establishment figures in this style. It was suffused with a spirit of service that both humanised some of the harshness of a competitive acquisitive society and idealised an imperialist consciousness which helped to renew the vertical cohesion of Britain's social structure. Among the many who were later to be moulded by this style were Baldwin and J. C. C. Davidson, who directly and indirectly were to be influential in applying it to the political atmosphere within which the industrial relations system operated between the two world wars. This widespread upper-class culture might not have been decisive had it not been combined with a conception of the state and a disposition of political forces which precluded active and creative state intervention in the economy. Talent, drive and idealism applied by state agencies might have hastened economic modernisation; they might also have rendered industrial relations more abrasive and would certainly have required the state to work to a different concept from that of 'holding the ring'.

The nineteenth century had therefore seen a pattern developing whereby a capacity for strong horizontal, though only sectional, cohesion among organised labour on industrial issues at the workplace coexisted with the possibility of strong vertical cohesion with sections of higher classes on political issues. Only a small and politically uninfluential minority were ever to want to see economic class conflict at the workplace translated into revolutionary political class conflict beyond it. The unions as well as the ruling class upheld the liberal separation of economics and politics. It was a separation which suited many trade unionists, who wanted to be able to challenge and negotiate with the employers in the workplace, yet support, or be supported by, the Liberal Party on free trade, the rights of Nonconformity, franchise extension, temperance reform, and other shared interests. The sizeable groups within the working classes who supported the Conservative cause made little impact on the organisational structure of trade union politics. When the unions formed their own party – and it was of the utmost significance that in Britain the party was the creature of the unions, not their creator – it was until 1918 no more than an appendage of the Liberals. After 1918 the situation was affected far less than might have been expected by the emergence of Labour as a mass party and the leading Opposition. Though the dominant influences within it regarded themselves as inheritors of the Liberal constitutionalist tradition which it was their destiny to bring up to date, they barely managed to follow the trajectory of the 'new' Liberalism. They were easily outbid by the radical expressions of it put forward by Lloyd George, Keynes and others in the late 1920s. Even within the socialist element there was a strong tradition which gave only qualified support to the international Marxist appeal – a strand of indigenous, as against exotic, socialism, characterised by such names as Morris, Blatchford, Tawney and later Orwell and Edward Thompson, which remained strongly libertarian and shared the old radical love of country.

Union leadership rarely wavered in its constitutionalism. While the unions were born out of labour's defensive responses to the British version of economic liberalism, their leaders exploited the British version of political liberalism to secure legal protections and a foothold in both industrial and political decision-making. Their commitment to the institutions and ideology of political liberalism therefore followed directly from their needs. They needed rights, freedoms and protections against some right-wing, and for that matter some left-wing, enemies which they have always been convinced they could secure and retain only within a stable structure of constitutionality, a measure of political freedom and the rule of law. They have for most of the time acknowledged that such a structure was indivisible and that they themselves had to observe its rules. The price they paid was the limitation those rules imposed on the use of industrial strength for political ends. It was the state who defined 'political' and when it exercised this definition against the unions a whole structure of rights and protections was in danger.

Yet what the unions, *qua* unions, surrendered was not the prospect of a fully planned socialist economy and the abolition of markets, wage labour and sectional manœuvring for economic advantage. This they did not have to surrender; they simply did not want it. They needed a measure of economic as well as political liberalism. What emerges here is that trade unionists, in creating machinery for a certain measure of their own emancipation, were also to some extent spinning a web for their own entrapment. Consciously or otherwise, leaders had to socialise their mass membership in the virtues of ordered procedure, the foolishness of overambitious aspirations, the necessary prudence of pursuing 'realistic' behaviour. And as the unions grew they developed institutional interests in their own survival and growth. Since they had survived and grown by adapting to a particular type of economic and social structure, any transformation in that structure would raise the possibility of a threat to the functions on which their existence presently rested. The recognition by the ruling class – or rather by the politically dominant forces within it – that this had become the union stance reinforced the ruling–class strategy. Practical state policy towards the unions had never been that of attempting to destroy them; by the late nineteenth century it was that of encouraging them, and by the early twentieth that of discouraging anything which might threaten their organisational integrity, whether the threat came from the far left or the far right.

The system to which the unions had adapted was one of competitive economic liberalism, and although they wanted this modified they still needed a loose-jointed economic system and space within which to exercise their negotiating functions and methods, just as they needed political space within which to extend their activities and interests. For all these reasons the trade union movement cannot be seen only in terms of its illiberal features, such as its demarcations, its restrictions, its closed shops and its assertions, sometimes with harsh and even violent sanctions, of majority against minority opinion and interest. These characteristics of an old, pre-industrial society were carried over into the new because they were found to be indispensable protections against the forces opposed to them. But survival in the new society called for additional protections as well, and in the pursuit and defence of these the union movement has become inextricably bound up with political and even some measure of economic liberalism. Britain's unions as they now exist cannot have their being within a totalitarian society whether of the left or right, and for that reason constitute one of the most powerful bulwarks against both. Any appraisal that focuses only on their illiberal features and sees them in terms of the faceless sinister mob bearing down upon civilisation and order lacks historical depth and may prove dangerous to the very order that is valued.

It is also significant in this context that they have offered abundant evidence over the past century and a half that they cannot be captured for social or political purposes which clash with, or come to diverge from, their self-defined functions and interests. A long succession of attempts to use them as a vehicle for such purposes includes those by Owenite co-operators, Christian Socialists, positivists, middle-class enthusiasts for 'positive-sum' conciliation, syndicalists, Communists, the Independent Labour Party and the Socialist League. All have failed. The unions have made use of them if, and to the extent that, they served union purposes, and beyond that point have insisted on going their own way. This has had its bitterness for those with broad and generous social visions as well as for the others.

Thereby arises a major consideration that the preceding account has sought to emphasise. As against a previous tendency to present the industrial relations system as having 'developed' towards some inevitable 'maturity', the account has directed attention to the suppressed alternatives of history; to the road forks that were not followed, to the contingencies by which the fortunes of the system were, so far as can be judged, significantly affected. Chance has played a considerable part at key points. Situations and events in the outside world contributed to conditions during that period from 1850 to 1875 when economic buoyancy and social optimism were sufficiently widespread to support an extension of industrial and political rights to the upper working class. During the late 1860s and 1870s the acceptability of a handful of middle-class Positivists to both the political Establishment and the relevant group of union leaders saved the latter from what might have proved for them some expensive mistakes. The death of Bonar Law and the sudden and unexpected accession to power in 1923 of Baldwin and a few close associates of similar disposition resulted in a political tone during the interwar period which profoundly affected the social context within which the industrial relations system operated.

The fact that these contingencies fell out in a certain way had the consequence that the logic of a preferred strategy of rule was in the main adhered to. The persistence of the strategy was cumulative, in that its success during each phase in maintaining order and privilege strengthened the motivation to follow its implications further. Perhaps the negative formulation of this proposition would better fit the case. Given that the ruling class wished, in its own interests, to maintain a regime of constitutionalism, the rule of law and a reputation of even-handedness, the cumulative discovery that the strategy could be extended to labour organisations without posing insuperable problems of control enabled the strategy to be continued. The fact that particular capitalists or groups of capitalists experienced harassment at the hands of the unions was far less important than that capitalism as a system was rendered more stable by admitting the unions as a committed partner in industrial regulation and as a growing influence in the political nation. Contributing to this virtuous circle, as the ruling order saw it, was of course the preferred strategy of working-class organisations themselves. However grudgingly conceded, even a minimal foothold in relevant decision-making seemed to most wage-earners, preoccupied as they were with the current week's rent and house-keeping bills, too important a bird in the hand to be lightly hazarded for two problematic birds in a distant bush. Evidence extending far beyond Britain's boundaries shows that when organised workers secure an established role in job regulation, are given official protection for

their organisations and are conceded expanding scope and rising status for
their activities, the appeal of the wider radical vision is weak. This
outcome reinforced the ruling class in its strategy. There were, of course,
at all times doubts and alarms enough, when some sections of all the
parties involved talked and even acted in ways that put the system at risk.
It survived, however, simply because they did not add up to a critical
mass, and the reason for this was that all parties, on balance, got enough
out of the system to make it worth preserving. On the whole, state and
employers felt they had more to lose than to gain by attempting to smash
the unions, while the unions felt they had more to lose than to gain by
throwing in their lot with any of the long series of groups who sought to
draw them away from their sober, prudent and essentially limited pursuit
of regulating market and managerial relations within the current social
context.

The longer the system continued to provide the higher classes with an
adequate approximation to social peace, stability and conservation of their
privileges, and the lower classes with both industrial and political organisations of their own and some measure of defence against power, the more
likely it became that for many participants the system, or their particular
part of it, would come to be valued for its own sake. Even by the
seventeenth century, for example, it was apparent that for many lawyers
the law and the principle of equality before the law had become sacred and
beyond mere political manipulation by others. Though the common law
often emerged as the unions' enemy there were limits to the extent to
which it could be exploited against them, and from the early nineteenth
century onwards the law officers of the crown could be remarkably
insistent that the reputational integrity of the law must not be weakened
by too blatant a partiality against labour movements. Not all of this can
convincingly be put down to conscious calculation, any more than can
Lord John Russell's Whiggish boasts about British liberty, still less
Baldwin's insistence on common decency and human feeling in relations
with labour. Men like these were successful in British politics for reasons
which included the fact that their personal convictions were congruent
with a strategy of rule that worked. Similarly, for many trade union
leaders and activists, the skills, traditions and values of a largely self-
serving sectional solidarity, though tempered only periodically and
uncertainly by gestures towards a wider vision, nevertheless became
invested with an intrinsic merit in a way that appeared impressive (though
to those hoping for social transformation, tragic). This strengthened the
system by raising the threshold at which disappointment, frustration, or
external pressures prompted thoughts of fundamental modification.
Major structural change, whether for ill or for good, came to seem less and
less thinkable.

This was to play its part in responses to the greatest background
contingency of them all: the economy. Until the Second World War, its
growth and adaptation were sufficient to cope adequately in peacetime
with both internal and external exigencies without governments feeling
forced to assume responsibility for active economic management. This
reinforced the process by which the industrial relations system became

shaped by 'voluntarism' – by sectional and competitive collective bargaining from which the state was only too ready during peacetime to exclude itself except at moments of severe disruption or in situations of exceptional labour weakness. This role of holding the ring had entered into the state ideology of the impartial ruler; it was an expression, too, of the conventional separation of politics and economics.

Both notions had become key ingredients of the system: both have now been eroded to vanishing point by the forces which compelled governments after the Second World War to attempt active economic management. They now had, to a degree unprecedented in peacetime, a direct and immediate interest in the conduct and outcomes of industrial relations, and the practical implementation of that interest proved fatal to the long-standing myth of state even-handedness between the classes. Since in the last resort it was the viability of a private-enterprise capitalist order that Labour as well as Conservative governments committed themselves to maintain, this alone rendered certain that organised labour must feel more than the employers the heavy hand of government involvement and objectives.

Given that state even-handedness was no longer available even as myth, what broad concept were British governments to work to now? In the British context the entry of the state into the ring brought it new problems of self-definition. Three possibilities presented themselves. All of them involved the state in projecting itself far more actively and substantively than ever before as embodying 'the national interest'. The first required the use of propaganda and exhortation in attempts to induce sectional interests to forgo or restrain their claims and voluntarily accept state leadership and policies. The second required the state to declare itself a participant bargainer with the other two major organised interests and seek to promote consensus on major economic policy by reaching tripartite agreements on the basis of corporate democracy. Finally, it could eschew such bargaining and simply attempt to enforce policies of economic management, however disagreeable, relying on virtual coercion by one means or another. Postwar governments drew at various times upon varying mixtures of all three options, the third only after the mid-1960s.

What can be said of these possibilities? The nature and history of Britain's institutions and culture give little reason for believing that the first has much to offer so long as her social structures and social relations survive in their present shape. The preceding account should help us decide whether there are elements of the industrial relations system and of the society containing it that must be judged very unlikely to change except as a result of social breakdown or of a popularly based social transformation of a sort that is not on the immediate political agenda. The judgement offered here is that among Britain's most persistent dispositions are individualism, both atomistic and collectivist, and the tradition of the minimal state. Historical chickens, in the form of those traditions which embody distaste for the active, manipulative, interventionist state, have come home to roost. Britain's institutions and values, suffused as they have long been with self-serving individualism, offer most of the population little consciousness of higher community needs which might restrain or at least muffle expressions of individual and group self-interest; which might invest the aim of, say, indicative planning with status and meaning; or which would promote the acceptance of leadership by those offering a programme for 'the national interest'. Whether such a consciousness would become accessible given radical social recasting is a debate in itself; what is certain is that, given British individualism – along with past and present inequalities – the limited style of politics which contributed to political freedom and tolerance extorts a heavy price when governments try to mobilise national consciousness of 'a common predicament'.

The second possibility, that of corporate bargaining, strikes a note far more congruous with the institutions and traditions involved. The notion of compromise has special prominence and significance in British political culture, and in industry, too, the language and culture of the unions is the language and culture of negotiated compromise. Bargaining is far from being the highest form of human relationship but it is also far from being the lowest. Arguments have been advanced that corporate bargaining would be at the expense of parliamentary procedure and local independence. Autocrats at the top levels of all three participant structures would concert deals among themselves, bypassing Parliament and overriding the preferences of their respective constituencies. That the parliamentary argument embodies no small amount of humbug has already been argued, and the notion that employers' associations in Britain are capable of tyrannising over their members can only evoke hollow laughter from their officers. There is no tradition of a strong central authority and attempts by the CBI in recent years to promote such changes as rationalisation of bargaining units and a mutual insurance fund against strikes have not been conspicuously successful. It would be a more persuasive argument against the corporate bargaining method to point to the uncertainties which the central authorities of both sides would experience in formulating, and even more in delivering, their part of the bargain. For the TUC is little better placed, if at all, with respect to its affiliated unions. These difficulties have been heightened in recent years by the tendency in large-scale manufacturing industries for employers' associations to become less significant in bargaining activities. Britain's collective bargaining structure, unlike that of some other advanced industrial countries, is now heavily decentralised. It is as true as it always was that for the wage- and lower-salary-earning rank and file the social circumstance most destructive of freedom is not domination by officials but long-term mass unemployment.

Fears have also been expressed that corporate bargaining might lead to a form of fascism, with the relevant organisations becoming agents of state dictation. The preceding account suggests this danger to be remote in Britain. For insight into the sort of official ideology that would be required to legitimise and support such a system we may turn to the Italian example, though it was more aspiration than reality. The Italian Charter of Labour of 1927 presented the nation as 'an organic whole having life, purposes, and means of action superior in power and duration to those of the individuals, single or associated, of which it is composed. It is a moral, political and economic unity.'

There are other sources of uneasiness about corporate bargaining that are far more relevant to Britain than these. Unless the unions enlarged their social as well as their industrial vision, corporate bargaining would do little to reassure those who believe that merely to strengthen and extend more widely the mechanisms for sectional defence and sectional improvement only consolidates a system that serves us badly in terms of both social justice and consciousness of community needs. Sectionalism is a slippery term and in some respects the past few decades have seen an increase in joint industrial action between organised groups and occupations. Nevertheless, the spread of trade unionism and collective bargaining to new groups and occupations (including many public sector, women and white-collar employees) has enlarged the area of competitive sectional bargaining. Given our kind of society this is a perfectly understandable aspiration on the part of the groups in question, but while so many women, blacks and others either remain excluded or wield little effective power within the system it does little to redeem the arrangements. If anything, the divisions grow deeper between skilled or well-established workers in secure and reasonably well-paid jobs and marginal members of the labour force in insecure and poorly paid jobs. Between 1961 and 1978 the number of jobs available to unskilled and semi-skilled manual workers shrank from 4·8 million to 2·8 million and the decline has continued since; one sign among several of a shift towards an American pattern (Bosanquet, 1983). And despite TUC condemnation, more and more skilled and white-collar workers are likely to negotiate private medical insurance for themselves. These trends were encouraged by the policies of the Thatcher administration and the *sauve qui peut* spirit they induced. They have 'given the game to the "money militants". There is no other game that anyone can play' (Donnison, 1980, p. 25).

Against these multiplying competitive sectionalisms and self-serving perspectives, where intra-class alliances usually depend for their existence upon their tactical usefulness to the participants, the wider vision struggles for the most part in vain. At the same time, however, this wider vision recognises the humbug implicit in the stance which condemns the pattern of sectional bargaining while approving the competitive, acquisitive, contractual society to which it is a necessary response. Many trade unionists themselves are only too aware of the many structural features of our society that serve even less adequately than sectional bargaining the twin requirements of social justice and due consciousness of community needs. If there were enough of them, and they enjoyed enough outside popular support, they could insist that their unions demand a radical recasting as the price of participation in corporate bargaining. Given the absence of a sufficient will or support, the hope, or danger, according to viewpoint, of this development is remote.

The Thatcher administration decided, in any case, not to run the risk. No government in recent British history has demonstrated so strong a determination to exclude the unions from any effective degree of political participation. Even more emphatically than most, this one rejected the argument that corporate bargaining offered a procedure by which the major interests in British society could hope to come to terms in a way that minimised political and social strains. The very notion, indeed, of 'coming to terms' begged the question. The new Conservatism clearly did not wish to come to terms with organised labour. The jargon of 'wets' and 'drys' brought out the hard-line view that it had been the long-term process of coming to terms with organised labour which had led directly or indirectly to the weakening of hierarchy, the impeding of modernisation, and the undermining of individual and family responsibility. The danger of corporate bargaining from the new Conservatism's point of view was that it admitted the unions into a widening realm of political compromise. Traditional Conservatism, it would be conceded, has preserved much, but the enlargement of a predatory left, consequent on economic failure, has now rendered dangerous the traditional strategies of accommodation. And whatever else Conservatism may be, it would be said, it is a stance which modifies its conserving strategies and ideologies according to changing circumstances. Given that the time has come to assert a new balance between the forces of organised labour, on the one hand, and the forces of political and industrial control on the other, corporate bargaining would lead away from such a new balance rather than towards it.

The Thatcher strategy therefore took up the third option, that of withdrawing from the tripartite tradition, abandoning even the idea of pursuing consent, and relying on being able to enforce policies on those interests that found them disagreeable. In imposing its rigorous deflation the Thatcher government exploited the political loyalty of organised capital and relied on mass unemployment for reducing the forces of organised labour. This policy of indirect coercion can hardly escape certain consequences. Whatever, in the eyes of the government, might have been its short-term successes, there seems no way by which such a strategy can fail in the longer run to produce industrial or political strains of a considerable order, though quite possibly not on a mass scale. If unemployment is ever encouraged or allowed to fall to a level at which significant sections of organised labour recover their strength, there will be a release of much pent-up frustration and the traditional practice of paying off old scores and seeking to reassert restrictionism will be resumed. There seems no reason why returning strength should not bring just as violent an explosion of suppressed claims as have followed incomes policies of the direct kind in the past; explosions which the Thatcher administration gave as the reason for not seeking such a policy. If, on the other hand, unemployment retains mass proportions it would be surprising should this not further harden sentiment and organisation on the farther left. On present showing this hardening does not seem of a kind that can mobilise a popular base for radical social change. Even so, the result of keeping the unions industrially weak and politically at arm's length would seem to be an aggravation of the political polarisation that began to open up with the chronic world-wide economic difficulties after the late 1960s.

The underlying process at work here is that when the state engages in active economic management in ways experienced as fundamentally hostile by major organised interests it presses hard against its own legitimacy. It becomes a palpably positive force within the ring and can no longer pose as the referee. This strengthens those forces inside and outside the trade union movement who assert that if the referee joins in the contest he can no longer plead immunity from being hit.

The conventional counter-argument would be that the blows must take political forms and be exerted through specified constitutional procedures which exclude the use of industrial strength. For most of the time these conventions have been observed. The TUC has shown throughout its life that it sees the best future for preserving the freedoms and functions of the movement in maintaining a liberal constitutional order. Its leaders have believed that to violate the conventions of that order would invite severe injury by releasing the state from its own restraints.

Yet these conventions have never been susceptible of precise definition or of total observance. The channelling of political aspirations and griev- ances through party and parliamentary procedure and constitutional protocol has always been a matter of degree. An important part has been played by extra-parliamentary pressure and power, even since the widen- ing of the franchise. People take to the streets, demonstrate and show their anger. Businessmen and bankers discreetly indicate that they may review their annual contribution to the Conservative Party, or, less discreetly, that if Labour governments proceed with certain policies they will 'lose the confidence' of the financial community with adverse results on the exchange rate. Union leaders air doubts about the link with Labour. Pressure groups seek to popularise their cause, hoping that mass feeling will force governments to make concessions for fear of electoral penalty. These are examples of how governments may feel constrained to behave in certain ways by actual or threatened sanctions of a painful kind which operate outside the conventional channels.

Since the Second World War there has been an increase in social issues which have aroused much local or national popular feeling that could not be expressed through, or contained within, parliamentary or local government procedure. They include the Campaign for Nuclear Dis- armament, the anti-Vietnam War movement, the Industrial Relations Act 1971, Upper Clyde Shipbuilders, Grunwick and scores of factory 'occupa- tions'. Trades councils and shop stewards committees can sometimes be found co-operating with local interest groups on issues such as nuclear policy, the women's movement, race relations, unemployment and the interests of social security claimants. These express the frustration of people who, keenly concerned to press a particular political opinion, find national or local procedure inaccessible to them, or that non-parliamen- tary forces of bureaucracy or wealth cannot, in any case, be effectively reached by conventional political means. This bursting of formal bounds has been furthered by the paradox that, despite the failure of the left to create a popular radical base, radical analyses which de-mystify the pretences and humbug surrounding power and its highly unequal dis- tribution have never been more accessible. The 'radicalisation' of many students, intellectuals and activists during the 1960s and 1970s, besides arousing deep distrust among the Establishment towards universities and polytechnics, has produced strains upon a political system that was designed for participation only by representative spokesmen who accepted the mystifications as a necessary feature of the system. There seems good reason to believe that more will be seen of this blurring of substantive and procedural boundaries, with industrial relations issues to some extent penetrating, and being penetrated by, political and social issues.

Even for the formal top-level participants, the democratic logic of reciprocal restraints has limits, as major sections of Britain's ruling order showed in 1912–14 when they indicated that they would not consent to see Irish Home rule imposed on Ulster even by a constitutionally elected British Parliament. The issue of the political general strike can never be definitively resolved. If either party to the democratic conventions believes that severe injury is to be imposed on it whatever it does then the incentive to uphold the conventions is that much weakened. British governments of both colours have pressed dangerously close to these limits on several occasions since the war. Apart from the one limited venture by a Labour government towards corporate bargaining, not repeated, there has been no real search for practical ways of securing full corporate consent to comprehensive economic strategies. Governments followed the practice of unilaterally determining, more or less independently of organised labour, certain fixed points of policy relating to, for example, overseas spending and defence expenditure as well as key features of domestic strategy, and then expecting organised labour to adjust itself to the economic consequences of these fixed points.

The Thatcher government went further by totally excluding the forces of labour from its counsels. The trade union movement was defined as needing to be weakened by legislation and by a shift of power towards management, precisely in order that its ability to challenge necessary policies be undermined and the problem of consent be eliminated. If this strategy proves to be more than a temporary deviation, and future Conservative governments aspire to maintain a permanent subduing of organised labour in the national economic and political life, the nation's social cohesion will need to be strong indeed to contain the resultant strains. The collapse of the conventional separation between politics and economics brings few problems if it takes place in circumstances when the economy is able to meet all the demands made on it. When it takes place in circumstances of economic failure, with the Conservative Party apparently resolved permanently to reverse the power and status of organised labour, there is not merely destruction of the postwar settlement but a threat to a process that extends back for well over a century. We are seeing partial materialisation of Leo Amery's nightmare when he contemplated the dangers of a stationary or regressive economy in a society where welfare commitments and public needs were under constant pressure to expand. There would be attempts to make good the shortfall by increasing encroachment, through taxation, on the standards and property of the higher classes, who would mobilise aggressively in defence. Amery's fear, however, that the working classes would then be driven into a struggle for socialism which they would win by sheer weight of numbers remains as yet unreal in the British context. Political alignments are complicated by, among many other things, the fact that as inflation and rising earnings carry many wage- and lower-salary-earners into the tax-paying category, the line of resistance to collective spending and collective citizenship cuts across class and becomes more popularly based.

Defenders of the status quo and of Thatcherian strategies need to hesitate, however, before cheering too resoundingly. Industrially, organised labour may be somewhat subdued, but a balanced appraisal has to be a complex one. On some fronts the prospect facing it is ominous. As the National Graphical Association (NGA) dispute of 1983 revealed, a legal net is being drawn round the unions. Influential judges, consulted, with doubtful constitutionality, by government ministers, have indicated that they hope to see the law move even more searchingly into the industrial relations field. It is far from certain, however, that many employers will welcome such trends any more than the unions do. At the workplace level the weakening effects of unemployment and other government policies are highly uneven; the poorest and weakest are getting poorer and weaker, but the better-placed groups are not noticeably suffering. Total union membership has fallen from its late-1970s peak, but the proportion of trade unionists to the employed workforce has, at the time of writing, declined little. Strikes and working days lost have fallen dramatically, but currently a larger proportion are about manning, work allocation and redundancies. The evidence hardly suggests a conspicuously crushed Labour movement; neither does it, taken together with the outcomes so far of the 'reforming' impulses, suggest much change in the traditional workplace stances of British labour and management.

Politically, too, the appraisal has to be no less complex. Even in the absence of a popular base for radical social change and a comprehensive alternative programme, the effects of the Thatcher strategy threaten to be unconstructively divisive, socially embittering and politically fragmenting. It is not certain that the longer-term consequences, as Britain's economic predicament becomes even more acute with the decline in oil revenues, will be agreeable even to many Conservative voters. Political fragmentation and disarray among the anti-Conservative forces may result in Conservative parliamentary majorities, but they are likely to rest on minority votes that, from the point of view of consent and legitimation, are dangerously small even for the British system.

The fact remains, however, that we are bound to ask whether we are witnessing the beginnings of a movement among Britain's middle and upper classes to bring to an end that long slow process of accommodation and concession on which her peaceful democratic development has rested. Even if intended to be less than that, the strategy will probably prove an expensive one. If, in other words, the attempt to subdue organised labour industrially and politically was intended only as a temporary expedient to reduce inflation and promote modernisation, it seems unlikely, given the strength of restrictionist labour traditions, to achieve any fundamental readjustment of attitudes. If, however, it is indeed intended as a long-term programme for readjusting economic and political forces, it takes on profound significance. The permanent subduing of labour could only be maintained by policies which perpetuate massive unemployment, exact enormous economic loss, possibly goad even its own industrial supporters into revolt and, most significant of all, promote a growing realisation within the Labour movement that the conventions of the political game have been changed in fundamental ways.

Any attempt to appraise these political possibilities, however, is complicated by three major considerations. First, the stance of the new Conservatism covers more than economic policy and includes attractions for many working-class voters. Among them are not only its preferences with respect to taxation and rates, but also its attitudes towards immigration and race relations, social security abuse and welfare state 'scroungers', the women's movement, sexual permissiveness and homosexuality, and nationalist assertiveness in foreign policy and defence, exemplified in the Falklands episode. The Conservative Party gains support from the widespread belief that Labour attitudes are more liberal, indulgent, flabby, or open-handed on these issues. On some of them, Labour governments have sought to mend their fences. It is not only the Conservative Party that has been dragged in directions unwelcome to rank and file membership by the electoral appeal of its political opponents. The Labour leadership has often dismayed supporters with its concern for what seemed to them a fictitious 'national interest', with its censorious postures towards strikes and other union practices, and in recent decades, with its manifest anxiety that it must not be seen to fall too far behind Tory rigour with respect to, for example, immigration policies. Attitude surveys among a union membership of which nearly half the total are now white-collar employees show declining support for the political levy, and rising support for such propositions as that unions have too much power and that strikes should be subject to secret ballot. Militant attitudes in pay struggles – often intensified by the urge to seek compensation for rising direct taxation – appear, if anything, to be increasingly divorced from socialist values, a fact causing dismay among some of the farther left, where it has been assumed, against all past British experience, that by some inevitable process the two would strengthen together. The practical significance of attitude-survey evidence must always be suspect, but taken along with other pointers it appears to reduce further the likelihood – never as yet even approached in Britain – of a clear-cut electoral class confrontation.

Secondly, despite the increase in harsher political dispositions on both left and right, it is probably correct to regard as still considerable the forces of social cohesion and resilience in Britain. Its political and social system has been uninterruptedly in the making for three centuries, and the probability is that while minorities on both sides may be prepared in the last resort to test class relations to destruction, majorities will not. Admittedly there may seem to be some weakening, given the fact that certain sources of vertical bonding have disappeared. With the loss of empire went the loss of a principal prop of the ruling-class mystique. One result was a greater bruising of working-class sentiment than many on the left care to admit. Another was the disappearance of that notion of the gentleman ruler and leader which imperialist consciousness helped to sustain. The British public have now, as it were, gone through that myth and come out on the other side. Burgess, Maclean, Philby and Blunt, names bearing public labels of treachery, drunkenness and buggery, all hatched in those symbols of innate upper-class superiority, the public school and ancient university, finally extinguished such flickering gleams as might still have survived of the gentleman mystique. In its place, however, a new populist Conservative nationalism leaning heavily on the Cold War seems to be in the making, and the socially cohesive symbols of a skilfully developed television popular monarchy show no signs of weakening.

Thirdly, resistance to the new Conservatism's economic policies has so far lacked mass conviction, no satisfactory alternative strategy having yet been put forward that commands widespread political confidence. The postwar sequence of inflation, pressure on the balance of payments, and varying measures to restrain incomes and investment became so wearily familiar that probably decisive numbers believe no really satisfactory solution can be found except at a price in political and economic transformation which they seem at present unprepared to pay.

This alone demonstrates the weaknesses of the Labour movement. Politically, its forces have been fatally divided between a parliamentary party which in pursuit of electoral success has often been dismissive of grass-roots sensibilities and convictions; a far left whose adherents have failed to strike sympathetic resonance with most of their fellow-countrymen; and a trade union movement that has, not wholly but for the most part, adapted apparently irreversibly to the competitive self-seeking to which it was a necessary response and is now a powerful reinforcement. The growing weight and influence within the movement of white-collar and professional unionism seems likely to weaken further the attachment to political Labour. Meanwhile, the very appearance of the new Conservatism points up the failure of its opponents to offer with any conviction an economically effective and morally decent alternative way of arranging things. This is not a situation which inspires much support for confident challenges to the prevailing range of economic orthodoxies.

Our concluding view therefore locates the industrial relations system within a political scene of great uncertainty. It is a measure of how Britain's, and indeed the world's, circumstances have changed that here, as to varying extents elsewhere, the issues of industrial relations have become, more palpably than ever before, issues for the state, and vice versa. Given that this strains to breaking point the distinction between the spheres of economics and politics – each of which, under parliamentary democratic conventions, had its own, largely separate, decision-making institutions – the question arises whether the pressures causing this breakdown are to receive new institutional procedures for their resolution and if so how. The new Conservatism, alarmed at the fuller implications for itself of pursuing accommodation to such threatening lengths, has demonstrated a very different type of response. This displays the paradox, however, that if the strategy is not intended to be permanent the old familiar problems seem likely to re-emerge multi-fold as soon as it begins to relax, while if the attempt is made to retain it the political price is likely to be considerable.

It could reinforce trends already visible. George Orwell, offering in 1941 his impressionistic picture of the essential England, a picture which Crick sets above 'the celebratory offerings of Sir Arthur Bryant and Dr. A. L. Rowse' because of its critical edge, noted the 'gentleness of the English civilization' as 'perhaps its most marked characteristic' (Orwell, 1982, pp. 17–18, 41). He could hardly write that today. In other ways, too, Orwell's picture has changed for the worse. One characteristic of modern states is that they are increasingly authoritarian and the United Kingdom is no exception. Techniques of opinion management by public and private bureaucracies have been greatly strengthened by scientific developments and professional specialisation in communication and persuasion. Exploitation of the Official Secrets Act and manipulation of the press in the manufacture of opinion by ministerial and departmental 'leaks' have probably reached new heights (E. P. Thompson, 1980, pp. 113–33). And whereas in some countries the state has been forced to give ground in terms of 'open government' and freedom of information, in Britain the various elements of the Establishment continue the tradition of supporting each other in a perpetual and mostly successful struggle to preserve secrecy. The Watergate revelations; the official Israeli report on the Beirut massacre which dislodged a defence minister and service chiefs; the French decision to touch one of the most sensitive nerves in French society by bringing to trial a Nazi who might publicly incriminate well-known figures as wartime collaborators – all these would as yet be impossible in Britain. In so far as this fact is perceived, by groups with strong feelings about an issue, as a denial of democratic rights, they may be driven by sheer frustration and desperation towards increasingly assertive direct action.

This is the context in which the Thatcher administration singled out for financial favour in the public services the police and armed forces and sought to give the former increased powers. Some chief constables appeared to be disinclined to wait to be given them and simply assumed them. The principle that they are in any real sense 'servants of the community' has, on occasion, been flatly repudiated. We appear to have moved far from the situation in which a Home Secretary, as in 1889, would be prepared to sack the Chief Commissioner of the London Metropolitan Police for his attempts to close Trafalgar Square to labour demonstrations and to enforce his policy with military and police violence. The fierce liberal vigilance towards the danger of overmighty police and security officers has become distinctly blunted since then. Orwell would have been disgusted but probably not surprised to discover that postwar Labour Home Secretaries have been apparently no less eager than their Conservative counterparts to concede such services increased powers and to condone, for example, much fudging of answers to parliamentary questions about telephone-tapping. The growing impotence of Parliament in the face of increased state powers, official secrecy, opinion management and party discipline has become evident also in even greater matters. Massive issues in defence and other realms of policy have been decided during Labour and Conservative administrations without reference to Parliament or indeed the full Cabinet.

Even some aspects of Britain's rule of law have suffered erosion. In 1977, for example, a Labour ministry enacted legislation which transferred whole categories of offences from the crown courts to summary jurisdiction, thereby extinguishing the right of the accused to opt for trial by jury. It has been suggested that a leading and favoured member of the Thatcher administration itched to dispense with the jury system altogether in the interests of 'efficiency'.

Finally, the debasement of press standards has probably reached new postwar depths. The 1983 electoral campaign for the Bermondsey parliamentary seat was notable for semi-criminal harassment of one of the candidates, Peter Tatchell, by sections of the national press, using methods that were exceptionally dingy even for Fleet Street and which repay study by those confident that British freedoms are still secure.

All these features of the modern British state have potential relevance as elements in the total social context within which industrial relations are conducted. Admittedly, the justifications offered in the defence of some of them can often be made to sound reasonable enough – the need for modern governments to communicate complex problems and policies clearly to the public; the requirements of 'national security' in a world of nuclear tensions, espionage, 'terrorism' and 'subversion'; the ever-rising crime rate and the importance of maximising police efficiency and streamlining the procedures of justice in order to 'protect the freedoms of the ordinary citizen'. The significance of these features of the modern state for industrial relations derive, however, from the use that could be made of them by governments and a state apparatus which succeeded in convincing themselves and large sections of the public that industrial stoppages and restrictionism were a threat to 'the nation's' economic security which 'in the interests of all' could no longer be tolerated; that militant industrial leadership must have subversive political intent; and that the 'national interest' requires the inclusion in police computer records of industrial 'troublemakers'.

Such possibilities must be viewed in the context of the new Conservatism, which promoted an industrial relations situation more threateningly open than at any time since 1945; threatening in that there was no political settlement between organised labour and the state. Instead there was only a deeply hostile set of policies imposed on the Labour movement under duress. The difference in 1945 lay in the existence of a mood of national unity and popular radicalism which guaranteed a settlement incorporating the unions. The mood was only to a limited extent capitalised by the Labour government – and this may yet be seen by historians as Labour's great missed opportunity – yet the outcome was a politically stable context. The policies of the new Conservatism represented an attempt, given acute economic difficulties and a determination to subdue the influence of the Labour movement, to break out of the long-standing, ruling-class readiness to put accommodation before confrontation and stability before innovation. These policies may yet be reversed, possibly after severe strains, by an equally long-standing British political instinct to renew social cohesion. But this does not mean there can be a return to the system as it operated before the 1970s. The Labour Party is not the same

Labour Party and the trade union movement will emerge from the present experience deeply marked, almost certainly in conflicting and contradictory ways. Given these fracturings the future is even more than usually formless. We must add to these uncertainties those of the world outside, stemming from an aggressive international capitalism, the imponderables of oil price, massive structures of debt among the developing countries and a consequently unstable world banking system.

Given all these uncertainties and their potential influences upon the system of industrial relations we can do no more than survey a range of possible outcomes. It remains to be seen, for example, whether the organisations of the Labour movement can yet mobilise sufficient resilience, flexibility and courage for an alternative strategy which combines a programme of economic and social reconstruction with retention of what is best in the British heritage. It would be the ultimate irony if the organisations slowly and painfully fashioned as defences against power proved so to have shaped men's perceptions and behaviour as to render those organisations incapable of any radical departure from the social structures and values to which they were a response.

We face here the issue whose outcome will shape the nature of future British society. There is, perhaps, a sense in which a whole political and industrial tradition has been played out. This does not mean that British society is incapable, on some level, of continuing, perhaps for some considerable time, relatively comfortably. It does mean that it may be incapable of the sort of renewal necessary to sustain long-term adaptation at a high level of economic and social welfare. A plausible case can be argued that such a renewal would require, along with preservation of the good things in the British scene – particularly the still deeply rooted legal and constitutional defences against political power – a reconstruction towards greater equality that might just make it possible for the concept of community needs to have some practical behavioural significance for everyday life. A new radicalism, seeking such renewal, would have to concert with the trade union movement on the basis that the industrial relations system could not be exempted from the reconstruction. At the moment few outcomes seem less likely. The new Conservatism, assuming it proves to be more than a temporary mode, rejects its older predominant tradition more emphatically and overtly than any previous administration of recent times, yet the oppositional forces remain deeply divided. There seems little prospect of them being able to mobilise a popular base for a programme of radical social change that might conceivably draw the unions into a positive-sum game and an incomes policy that permitted growth with minimal inflation. There are a number of small growth-points which may give radicals hope, but they are as yet mainly local and there seems little prospect of mobilising the big battalions behind a unified campaign at the necessary national level. Given present conditions, only the most extreme of optimists would deny that any such vision faces a very long haul.

One thing seems certain. It would have to be a very different programme from the one assumed by traditional-style socialists. An ever-growing white-collar sector and a shrinking body of wage-earners, many of whom, besides being tax payers, reach eagerly for that house-ownership that the middle classes have long taken for granted – these hardly provide fruitful soil for the old-style vision, especially when there is added a widespread indifference to nationalisation, suspicions about 'socialist' attitudes on 'patriotism' and defence, and a quickening interest in private health care. There is some reason for believing that latent impulses towards egalitarian reconstruction may be more widespread within the British people than these observations suggest, but if they are they are not being unlocked by any political vision currently on offer.

Even if they were, could they make decisive headway against the great power and inertia of the status quo and its Establishment? Could a programme of radical reconstruction be carried through without severe damage to the political and social tolerances, decencies and myths of moderation which mark the British style and which are manifestly valued by large numbers of the British people? The inability of many on the radical left to reassure their fellow-countrymen on this score is among the reasons for their failure. It may be, too, that the bulk of the British people, most of them still far better off materially than were their parents, will remain unmoved by predictions that long slow decline is inevitable unless great changes are made in British economy and society, including their own behaviour. They and their forebears have been hearing such talk for a century and the show is still on the road, bringing substantial sections of the working class a better living than they have ever had. One possible future for Britain is that enough of its citizens will prefer to retain as much of the characteristic structures and textures of British society as is compatible with the necessary minimum of adjustment to a rapidly changing world. The result might be neither economic miracles nor total disaster. The structures and textures of industrial relations would continue to be shaped within limits significantly narrower than are currently hoped for or feared by either left or right. Most of Britain's organised labour would continue to disappoint the right by maintaining, as would most of their managers, their wary, zero–sum, adversary postures, but would continue also to disappoint the left by stubbornly declining to translate their workplace frustrations into radical political terms. This scene would bring little significant reduction in the inequalities and humbug that mark British life, but it might turn out to be what a majority of its people continue to want. As the Tory Disraeli observed to the Marxist Hyndman in 1881: 'It is a very difficult country to move, Mr. Hyndman, a very difficult country indeed.'

But will this latter option remain available? The circumstances bearing upon the nation now may prove too severe a test on its ability to preserve its familiar shape. It may fail either to break through to dynamic growth or to resume its halting liberal movement towards a less divided society. It may become embedded instead in a texture of politics and industrial relations more harsh, vengeful and embittered than any it has known before, with a 'moderate' middle – that would include, as always, a substantial section of the working class – increasingly under siege by opposed 'extremes' each convinced that the old patterns of mutual accommodation are played out.

The possibility that seems least likely, given Britain's historical development and deeply ingrained continuities, is the one most prominent in Thatcher rhetoric – that organised wage- and salary-earners will from now on display a 'new realism' and, with due concern for the 'national interest', freely accept managerial 'leadership' towards a more dynamic, innovative economy.

None of this offers much cheer for millenarians, but there are consolations. Life in Britain retains many decencies, and most of them are connected with painfully constructed defences against the arrogances, impertinences and corruptions of power. These decencies are under threat from different directions. An independent-spirited, independently organised working class can sometimes bring its own minor threats, but as a bulwark against the major threats its record in Britain gives hope. In other ways, too, Britain will continue to be marked by its history and its heritage, and contained in that heritage are traditions that are creative, radical and reveal a love of country that stops short of bellicose assertiveness against others. They may surface again. It is too soon to declare 'the end of an old song' and consign Britain to the category of failed enterprises.

REFERENCES

Adderley, Sir C. (1860), *Hansard*, 3rd ser., vol. 157.

Adderley, Sir C. (1871), *Hansard*, 3rd ser., vol. 204.

Allen, E., Clarke, J. F., McCord, N., and Rowe, D. J. (1971), *The North-East Engineers' Strikes of 1871: The Nine Hours League* (Newcastle upon Tyne: Frank Graham).

Amery, L. S. (1953), *My Political Life: Vol. 1, England before the Storm 1896–1914* (London: Hutchinson).

Amulree, Lord (1929), *Industrial Arbitration in Great Britain* (London: Oxford University Press).

Anderson, P. (1965), 'Origins of the present crisis', in P. Anderson and R. Blackburn (eds), *Towards Socialism* (London: Fontana), pp. 11–52.

Arnold, M. (1971), *Culture and Anarchy*, with introduction by J. Dover Wilson (Cambridge: Cambridge University Press). First published 1869.

Askwith, Lord (1920), *Industrial Problems and Disputes* (London: John Murray).

Aspinall, A. (ed.) (1949), *The Early English Trade Unions: Documents from the Home Office Papers in the Public Record Office* (London: Batchworth Press).

Bagehot, W. (1867), *The Economist*, vol. 25, 27 April.

Bagehot, W. (1869), *The Economist*, vol. 27, 10 July.

Bagehot, W. (1963), *The English Constitution*, with introduction by R. H. S. Crossman (London: Fontana). First published 1867.

Bagwell, P. S. (1971), 'The Triple Industrial Alliance 1913–1922', in A. Briggs and J. Saville (eds), *Essays in Labour History 1886–1923* (London: Macmillan), pp. 96–128.

Bain, G. S., and Price, R. (1980), *Profiles of Union Growth: A Comparative Statistical Portrait of Eight Countries* (Oxford: Blackwell).

Baldwin, S. (1926), *Hansard*, Commons, 5th ser., vol. 195.

Bamford, S. (1841), *Passages in the Life of a Radical*, Vol. 1, (London: Simpkin, Marshall).

Barnes, D., and Reid, E. (1980), *Governments and Trade Unions: The British Experience, 1964–79* (London: Heinemann).

Barnett, A. (1982), *Iron Britannia* (London: Allison & Busby).

Barnett, C. (1967), 'The education of military elites', *Journal of Contemporary History*, vol. 2, no. 3 (July), pp. 15–35.

Batstone, E. (1982), 'Reform of industrial relations in a changing society', Seventh Countess Markievicz Memorial Lecture, Irish Association for Industrial Relations, Dublin.

Bendix, R. (1956), *Work and Authority in Industry: Ideologies of Management in the Course of Industrialization* (New York: Wiley).

Bergmann, J., Jacobi, O., and Müller-Jentsch, W. (1975), *Gewerkschaften in der Bundesrepublik*, (Frankfurt am Main: Aspekte Verlag).

Berlin, I. (1980), *Personal Impressions*, ed. Henry Hardy (London: Hogarth Press).

Best, G. F. A. (1975), *Shaftesbury* (London: New English Library).

Blake, R. (1969), *Disraeli* (London: Methuen).

Blake, R. (1972), *The Conservative Party from Peel to Churchill* (London: Fontana).

Blanch, M. (1979)], 'Imperialism, nationalism, and organized youth', in J. Clarke, C. Critcher and R. Johnson (eds), *Working Class Culture: Studies in History and Theory* (London: Hutchinson, in association with the Centre for Contemporary Cultural Studies, University of Birmingham), pp. 103–20.

Blaug, M. (1974), 'The myth of the old Poor Law and the making of the new', in M. W. Flinn and T. C. Smout (eds), *Essays in Social History* (Oxford: Clarendon Press), pp. 123–53.

Bosanquet, N. (1983), *After the New Right* (London: Heinemann).

Bowle, J. (1963), *Politics and Opinion in the Nineteenth Century* (London: Cape).

Brailsford, H. N. (1976), *The Levellers and the English Revolution*, ed. C. Hill (London: Spokesman Books).

Briggs, A. (1959), *The Age of Improvement* (London: Longmans, Green).

Briggs, A. (1961), 'The welfare state in historical perspective', *European Journal of Sociology*, vol. 2, no. 2, pp. 221–58.

Briggs, A. (1965), *Victorian People: A Reassessment of Persons and Themes 1851–67.* (Harmondsworth, Middx: Penguin).

Briggs, A. (1967), 'The language of "class" in early nineteenth-century England', in A. Briggs and J. Saville (eds), *Essays in Labour History 1886–1923* (London: Macmillan), pp. 43–73.

Briggs, A. (1968), *Victorian Cities* (Harmondsworth, Middx: Penguin).

Bristow, E. (1974), 'Profit-sharing, socialism and labour unrest', in K. D. Brown (ed.), *Essays in Anti-Labour History: Responses to the Rise of Labour in Britain* (London: Macmillan), pp. 262–89.

Brock, W. R. (1941), *Lord Liverpool and Liberal Toryism: 1820 to 1827* (Cambridge: Cambridge University Press).

Brown, K. D. (1974), 'The Anti-Socialist Union, 1908–49', in K. D. Brown (ed.), *Essays in Anti-Labour History: Responses to the Rise of Labour in Britain* (London: Macmillan), pp. 234–51.

Brown, K. D. (1982), 'Trade unions and the law', in C. Wrigley (ed.), *A History of British Industrial Relations 1875–1914* (Brighton, Sussex: Harvester Press), pp. 116–34.

Brown, W. (ed.) (1981), *The Changing Contours of British Industrial Relations: A Survey of Manufacturing Industry* (Oxford: Blackwell).

Bruce, H. A. (1869), *Hansard*, 3rd ser., vol. 197.

Bruce, H. A. (1871), *Hansard*, 3rd ser., vol. 204.

Bullock, A. (1960), *The Life and Times of Ernest Bevin: Vol. 1, Trade Union Leader 1881–1940* (London: Heinemann).

Butler, R. A. B. (1980), Introduction to Benjamin Disraeli's *Sybil* (Harmondsworth, Middx: Penguin).

Cababé, M. (1894), Introduction to W. S. Jevons's *The State in Relation to Labour*, 3rd edn (London: Macmillan).

Caldwell, J. A. M. (1959), 'The genesis of the Ministry of Labour', *Public Administration*, vol. 37 (Winter), pp. 367–91.

Carlyle, T. (1971), *Selected Writings* (Harmondsworth, Middx: Penguin).

Carpenter, L. P. (1976), 'Corporatism in Britain 1930–45', *Journal of Contemporary History*, vol. 11, no. 1 (January), pp. 3–25.

Castles, F. G., Murray, D. J., and Potter, D. C. (eds) (1971), *Decisions, Organizations and Society* (Harmondsworth, Middx: Penguin).

Catherwood, H. F. R. (1966), 'The curious attitude of the educated Englishman to industry', *Britain with the Brakes Off* (London: Hodder & Stoughton).

Chamberlain, C. (1973), 'The growth of support for the Labour Party in Britain', *British Journal of Sociology*, vol. 24, no. 4 (December), pp. 474–89.

Chapman, S. D. (1972), *The Cotton Industry in the Industrial Revolution* (London: Macmillan).

Charles, R. (1973), *The Development of Industrial Relations in Britain 1911–1939* (London: Hutchinson).

Child, J. (1969), *British Management Thought: A Critical Analysis* (London: Allen & Unwin).

Christie, I. R. (1970), *Myth and Reality in Late-Eighteenth-Century British Politics, and other Papers* (London: Macmillan).

Citrine, W. M. (1934), 'The Martyrs of Tolpuddle', in W. M. Citrine (ed.), *The Martyrs of Tolpuddle 1834–1934* (London: Trades Union Congress General Council), pp. 1–101.

Citrine, W. M. (ed.) (1934), *The Martyrs of Tolpuddle 1834–1934* (London: Trades Union Congress General Council).

Citrine, Lord (1964), *Men and Work* (London: Hutchinson).

Clay, H. (1929), *The Problem of Industrial Relations* (London: Macmillan).

Clegg, H. A. (1951), *Industrial Democracy and Nationalization* (Oxford: Blackwell).

Clegg, H. A. (1954), *Some Consequences of the General Strike* (Manchester: Manchester Statistical Society).

Clegg, H. A. (1960), *A New Approach to Industrial Democracy* (Oxford: Blackwell).

Clegg, H. A. (1971), *How to Run an Incomes Policy* (London: Heinemann).

Clegg, H. A. (1975), 'Pluralism in industrial relations', *British Journal of Industrial Relations*, vol. 13, no. 3 (November), pp. 309–16.

Clegg, H. A. (1979), *The Changing System of Industrial Relations in Great Britain* (Oxford: Blackwell).

Clegg, H. A. (1983), 'Otto Kahn-Freund and British industrial relations', in Lord Wedderburn, R. Lewis and J. Clark (eds), *Labour Law and Industrial Relations: Building on Kahn-Freund* (Oxford: Clarendon Press), pp. 14–28.

Clegg, H. A. (forthcoming), *A History of British Trade Unions: Vol. 2, 1910–1933* (Oxford: Clarendon Press).

Clegg, H. A., and Chester, T. E. (1953), *The Future of Nationalization* (Oxford: Blackwell).

Clegg, H. A., Fox, A., and Thompson, A. F. (1964), *A History of British Trade Unions since 1889: Vol. 1, 1889–1910* (Oxford: Clarendon Press).

Clynes, J. R. (1934), 'Melbourne fears the unions', in W. M. Citrine, (ed.), *The Martyrs of Tolpuddle 1834–1934* (London: Trades Union Congress General Council), pp. 159–70.

Cole, G. D. H. (1919), *The World of Labour* (London: Bell). First published 1913.

Cole, G. D. H. (1927), *A Short History of the British Working Class Movement 1789–1927*, Vol. 3 (London: Allen & Unwin).

Cole, G. D. H. (1954), *Socialist Thought: Marxism and Anarchism 1850–1890*, Vol. 2 of *A History of Socialist Thought* (London: Macmillan).

Cole, G. D. H. (1956), *The Second International 1889–1914*, Vol. 3, Pt 1 of *A History of Socialist Thought* (London: Macmillan).

Cole, G. D. H. (1972), *Self-Government in Industry* (London: Hutchinson). First published 1917.

Cole, G. D. H. (1973), *Workshop Organisation* (London: Hutchinson). First published 1923.

Coleman, D. C. (1975), *Industry in Tudor and Stuart England* (London: Macmillan).

Coleman, D. C. (1977), *The Economy of England 1450–1750* (Oxford: Oxford University Press).

Commons, J. R. (1957), *Legal Foundations of Capitalism* (Madison, Wis: University of Wisconsin Press). First published 1924.

Corrigan, P. (1977), 'Feudal relics or capitalist monuments?', *Sociology*, vol. 11, no. 3 (September), pp. 435–63.

Courtauld, S. (1949), *Ideals and Industry* (Cambridge: Cambridge University Press).

Cowling, M. (1971), *The Impact of Labour 1920–1924* (Cambridge: Cambridge University Press).

Crompton, H. (1876), *Industrial Conciliation* (London: Henry S. King).

Cronin, J. E. (1982), 'Strikes 1870–1914', in C. Wrigley (ed.), *A History of British Industrial Relations 1875–1914*, (Brighton, Sussex: Harvester Press), pp. 74–98.

Crouch, C. (1979), *The Politics of Industrial Relations* (London: Fontana).

Crouch, C. (1983), 'Industrial relations', in T. Atkinson *et al.* (eds), *Socialism in a Cold Climate* (London: Unwin Paperbacks), pp. 124–43.

Currie, R. (1979), *Industrial Politics* (Oxford: Clarendon Press).

Currie, R., and Hartwell, R. M. (1965), 'The making of the English working class', *Economic History Review*, 2nd ser., vol. 18, no. 3 (December), pp. 635–43.

Dangerfield, G. (1936), *The Strange Death of Liberal England* (London: Constable).

Daniel, W. W., and Willward, N. (1983), *Workplace Industrial Relations in Britain* (London: Heinemann).

David, E. (ed.) (1977), *Inside Asquith's Cabinet: From the Diaries of Charles Hobhouse* (London: John Murray).

Davidson, R. (1972), 'Llewellyn Smith, the Labour Department and government growth 1886–1909', in G. Sutherland (ed.), *Studies in the Growth of Nineteenth-Century Government* (London: Routledge & Kegan Paul), pp. 227–62.

Davidson, R. (1978), 'The Board of Trade and industrial relations 1896–1914', *Historical Journal*, vol. 21, no. 3, pp. 571–91.

Davidson, R. (1982), 'Government administration', in C. Wrigley (ed.), *A History of British Industrial Relations 1875–1914* (Brighton, Sussex: Harvester Press), pp. 159–83.

Davidson, R., and Lowe, R. (1981), 'Bureaucracy and innovation in British welfare policy 1870–1945', in W. J. Mommsen (ed.), *The Emergence of the Welfare State in Britain and Germany 1850–1950* (London: Croom Helm), pp. 263–95.

Davies, P. (1980), 'How to make the unions feel insecure', *New Society*, 7 August, pp. 267–8.

Dennett, J., James, E., Room, G., and Watson, P. (1982), *Europe against Poverty: The European Poverty Programme 1975–80* (London: Bedford Square Press).

Derby, Earl of (1867), *Hansard*, 3rd ser., vol. 185.

Dibblee, G. B. (1902), 'The printing trades and the crisis in British Industry', *Economic Journal*, vol. 12, (March), pp. 1–14.

Digby, A. (1975), 'The labour market and the continuity of social policy after 1834: the case of the eastern counties', *Economic History Review*, 2nd ser., vol. 28, no. 1 (February), pp. 69–83.

Disraeli, B. (1980), *Sybil: Or the Two Nations* (Harmondsworth, Middx: Penguin). First published 1845.

Dobson, C. R. (1980), *Masters and Journeymen: A Prehistory of Industrial Relations 1717–1800* (London: Croom Helm).

Donnison, D. (1980), 'New times, new politics', *New Society*, 2 October, pp. 25–6.

Donnison, D. (1982), *The Politics of Poverty* (Oxford: Martin Robertson).

Dore, R. (1973), *British Factory – Japanese Factory: The Origins of National Diversity in Industrial Relations* (London: Allen & Unwin).

Dorfman, G. A. (1973), *Wage Politics in Britain 1945–1967* (London: Charles Knight).

Douglas, R. (1974), 'Labour in decline, 1910–14' in K. D. Brown (ed.), *Essays in Anti-Labour History: Responses to the Rise of Labour in Britain* (London: Macmillan), pp. 105–25.

Driver, C. (1946), *Tory Radical: The Life of Richard Oastler* (London: Oxford University Press).

Dudley, Earl of (1867), *Hansard*, 3rd ser., vol. 185.

Emden, C. S. (ed.) (1939), *Selected Speeches on the Constitution* (London: Oxford University Press).

Engels, F. (1967), *Engels: Selected Writings*, ed. W. O. Henderson (Harmondsworth, Middx: Penguin).

Engels, F. (1969a), 'Ludwig Feuerbach and the end of classical German philosophy' [1888], *Marx and Engels: Basic Writings on Politics and Philosophy*, ed. L. S. Feuer (London: Fontana), pp. 236–82.

Engels, F. (1969b), *The Condition of the Working Class in England* (London: Panther). First published, in German, 1845; in Britain, 1892.

Faber, G. (1957), *Jowett: A Portrait with Background* (London: Faber).

Field, C. D. (1977), 'The social structure of English Methodism: eighteenth-twentieth centuries', *British Journal of Sociology*, vol. 28, no. 2 (June), pp. 199–225.

Flanders, A. (1952), 'Industrial relations', in G. D. N. Worswick and P. H. Ady (eds), *The British Economy 1945–1950*, (Oxford: Clarendon Press), pp. 101–24.

Flanders, A. (1954), 'Collective bargaining', in A. Flanders and H. A. Clegg (eds), *The System of Industrial Relations in Great Britain: Its History, Law and Institutions* (Oxford: Blackwell), pp. 252–322.

Flanders, A. (1964), *The Fawley Productivity Agreements* (London: Faber).

Flanders, A. (1967), *Collective Bargaining: Prescription for Change* (London: Faber).

Fogarty, M. P. (1965), *Company and Corporation – One Law?* (London: Chapman).

Ford, D. J. (1974), 'W. H. Mallock and socialism in England, 1880–1918', in K. D. Brown (ed.) *Essays in Anti-Labour History: Responses to the Rise of Labour in Britain* (London: Macmillan), pp. 317–42.

Forman, C. (1979), *Industrial Town* (London: Paladin).

Fox, A. (1958), *A History of the National Union of Boot and Shoe Operatives* (Oxford: Blackwell).

Fox, A. (1974), *Beyond Contract: Work, Power and Trust Relations* (London: Faber).

Fox, A. (1978), 'Corporatism and industrial democracy: the social origins of present forms and methods in Britain and Germany', *Industrial Democracy: International Views* (SSRC International Conference on Industrial Democracy, Cambridge 1977).

Fox, A. (1979). 'Labour in a new era of law', *New Society*, 1 March, pp. 480–3.

Fox, A. (1985), *Man Mismanagement*, 2nd edn (London: Hutchinson).

Fraser, D. (1981), 'The English Poor Law and the origins of the British Welfare State', in W. J. Mommsen (ed.), *The Emergence of the Welfare State in Britain and Germany 1850–1950* (London: Croom Helm), pp. 9–29.

Frow, E., and Katanka, M. (eds) (1968), *1868: Year of the Unions: A Documentary Survey* (London: Michael Katanka).

Gamble, A. (1974), *The Conservative Nation* (London: Routledge & Kegan Paul).

Gamble, A. (1981), *Britain in Decline: Economic Policy, Political Strategy and the British State* (London: Macmillan).

Garside, W. R. (1977), 'Management and men: aspects of British industrial relations in the inter-war period', in B. Supple (ed.), *Essays in British Business History* (Oxford: Clarendon Press), pp. 244–67.

Gaskell, E. (1970), *North and South* (Harmondsworth, Middx: Penguin). First published 1854–5.

George, D. (1953), *England in Transition* (Harmondsworth, Middx: Penguin).

Gilbert, A. D. (1976), *Religion and Society in Industrial England: Church, Chapel and Social Change 1740–1914* (London: Longman).

Goodman, E. (1951), *Forms of Public Control and Ownership* (London: Christophers).

Goodrich, C. L. (1975), *The Frontier of Control: A Study in British Workshop Politics*, foreword by R. Hyman (London: Pluto Press). First published 1920.

Gore, V. (1982), 'Rank and file dissent', in C. Wrigley (ed.), *A History of British Industrial Relations 1875–1914* (Brighton, Sussex: Harvester Press), pp. 47–73.

Goschen, G. J. (1897), *Hansard*, 4th ser., vol. 6.

Gray, R. Q. (1974), 'The labour aristocracy in the Victorian class structure', in F. Parkin (ed.), *The Social Analysis of Class Structure* (London: Tavistock), pp. 19–38.

Griffith, J. A. G. (1981), *The Politics of the Judiciary* (London: Fontana).

Griffiths, R. (1983), *Fellow Travellers of the Right: British Enthusiasts for Nazi Germany 1933–9* (Oxford: Oxford University Press).

Grigg, J. (1973), *The Young Lloyd George* (London: Eyre Methuen).

Grigg, J. (1978), *Lloyd George: The People's Champion 1902–1911* (London: Eyre Methuen).

Guttsman, W. L. (ed.) (1969), *The English Ruling Class* (London: Weidenfeld & Nicolson).

Halévy, E. (1961a), *England in 1815* (London: Benn). First published in English 1927.

Halévy, E. (1961b). *The Liberal Awakening 1815–1830* (London: Benn). First published in English 1926.

Halévy, E. (1961c), *The Triumph of Reform 1830–1841* (London: Benn). First published in English 1927.

Halévy, E. (1961d), *Imperialism and the Rise of Labour 1895–1905* (London: Benn). First published in English 1929.

Halévy, E. (1961e), *The Rule of Democracy 1905–1914* (London: Benn). First published in English 1934.

Hall, J. A. (1977), 'The roles and influence of political intellectuals: Tawney versus Sidney Webb', *British Journal of Sociology*, vol. 28, no. 3 (September), pp. 351–62.

Halsbury, Lord (1906), *Hansard*, 4th ser., vol. 166.

Halsey, A. H. (1983), 'The social services in adversity – a review', Sidney Ball Lecture, Oxford University, unpublished.

Halsey, A. H. (1984), 'T. H. Marshall: past and present', *Sociology*, vol. 18, no. 1 (February), pp. 1–18.

Hammond, J. L., and Hammond, B. (1919), *The Town Labourer 1760–1832: The New Civilization* (London: Longmans, Green).

Hammond, J. L., and Hammond, B. (1945), *The Village Labourer*, Vol. 2, (London: Guild Books). First published 1911.

Hammond, J. L., and Hammond, B. (1979), *The Skilled Labourer* (London: Longman). First published 1919.

Hannington, W. (1936), *Unemployed Struggles 1919–1936: My Life and Struggles among the Unemployed* (London: Lawrence & Wishart).

Hanson, C. G. (1975), 'Craft unions, welfare benefits, and the case for trade union law reform 1867–75', *Economic History Review*, 2nd ser., vol. 28, no. 2 (May), pp. 243–58.

Harris, J. (1977), *William Beveridge* (Oxford: Clarendon Press).

Harris, J. (1981), 'Some aspects of social policy in Britain during the Second World War', in W. J. Mommsen (ed.), *The Emergence of the Welfare State in Britain and Germany 1850–1950* (London: Croom Helm), pp. 247–62

Harris, R. W. (1969), *Romanticism and the Social Order 1780–1830* (London: Blandford Press).

Harrison, B. (1971), *Drink and the Victorians: The Temperance Question in England 1815–1872* (Pittsburgh, Pa: University of Pittsburgh Press).

Harrison, F. (1975), *Order and Progress* (East Brunswick, NJ: Fairleigh Dickinson University Press). First published 1875.

Harrison, R. (1965), *Before the Socialists: Studies in Labour and Politics 1861–1881* (London: Routledge & Kegan Paul).

Harrison, R. (1967), 'Professor Beesly and the working-class movement', in A. Briggs and J. Saville (eds), *Essays in Labour History* (London: Macmillan), pp. 205–41.

Hart, J. (1974), 'Nineteenth-century social reform: a Tory interpretation of history', in M. W. Flinn and T. C. Smout (eds), *Essays in Social History* (Oxford: Clarendon Press), pp. 197–217.

Hawkins, K. (1978), *The Management of Industrial Relations* (Harmondsworth, Middx: Penguin).

Hay, D. (1977), 'Property, authority and the criminal law', in D. Hay, P. Line-baugh, J. G. Rule, E. P. Thompson and C. Winslow, *Albion's Fatal Tree: Crime and Society in Eighteenth-Century England* (Harmondsworth, Middx: Penguin), pp. 17–63.

Hay, R. (1977), 'Employers and social policy in Britain: the evolution of welfare legislation 1905–1914', *Social History*, vol. 1, no. 4 (January), pp. 435–55.

Hay, R. (1981), 'The British business community, social insurance and the German example', in W. J. Mommsen (ed.), *The Emergence of the Welfare State in Britain and Germany 1850–1950* (London: Croom Helm), pp. 107–32

Hayes, P. (1973), *Fascism* (London: Allen & Unwin).

Hayter, T. (1978), *The Army and the Crowd in Mid-Georgian England* (London: Macmillan).

Herbert, A. (1871), *Hansard*, 3rd ser., vol. 205.

Henderson, A. (1934), 'The parliamentary scene', in W. M. Citrine (ed.), *The Martyrs of Tolpuddle 1834–1934* (London: Trades Union Congress General Council), pp. 187–97.

Hill, B. W. (1975), Introduction to *Edmund Burke on Government, Politics and Society* (London: Fontana/The Harvester Press).

Hill, C. (1968), *Puritanism and Revolution* (London: Panther).

Hill, C. (1969a), *Society and Puritanism in Pre-Revolutionary England* (London: Panther).

Hill, C. (1969b), *Reformation to Industrial Revolution* (Harmondsworth, Middx: Penguin).

Hill, C. (1975), *The World Turned Upside Down: Radical Ideas during the English Revolution* (Harmondsworth, Middx: Penguin).

Hill, R. L. (1929), *Toryism and the People: 1832–1846* (London: Constable).

Hinton, J. (1971), 'The Clyde Workers' Committee and the dilution struggle', in A. Briggs and J. Saville, (eds), *Essays in Labour History 1886–1923* (London: Macmillan), pp. 152–84.

Hinton, J. (1982), 'The rise of a mass labour movement: growth and limits', in C. Wrigley (ed.), *A History of British Industrial Relations 1875–1914* (Brighton, Sussex: Harvester Press), pp. 20–46.

Hinton, J., and Hyman, R. (1975), *Trade Unions and Revolution: The Industrial Politics of the Early Communist Party* (London: Pluto Press).

Hobhouse, L. T. (1911), *Liberalism* (London: Oxford University Press).

Hobsbawm, E. J. (1964), *The Age of Revolution 1789–1848*, (New York: Mentor Books).

Hobsbawm, E. J. (1968), *Labouring Men: Studies in the History of Labour* (London: Weidenfeld & Nicolson).

Hobsbawm, E. J. (1977), *The Age of Capital 1848–1875* (London: Abacus).

Hobson, J. A. (1926), *The Evolution of Modern Capitalism*, rev. edn (London: Walter Scott). First published 1894.

Holms, W. (1875), *Hansard*, 3rd ser., vol. 225.

Holyoake, G. J. (1906), *Sixty Years of an Agitator's Life* (London: T. Fisher Unwin).

Hughes, H. S. (1974), *Consciousness and Society: The Reorientation of European Social Thought 1890–1930* (London: Paladin).

Hughes, T. (1860), *Trades' Societies and Strikes* in National Association for the Promotion of Social Science (London: J. W. Parker).

Hughes, T. (1869), *Hansard*, 3rd ser., vol. 197.

Hume, J. (1824a), *Hansard*, 2nd ser., vol. 10.

Hume, J. (1824b), *Hansard*, 2nd ser., vol. 11.

Hunt, E. H. (1981), *British Labour History 1815–1914* (London: Weidenfeld & Nicolson).

Huskisson, W. (1825a), *Hansard*, 2nd ser., vol. 12.

Huskisson, W. (1825b), *Hansard*, 2nd ser., vol. 13.

Hyman, R. (1978), 'Pluralism, procedural consensus and collective bargaining', *British Journal of Industrial Relations*, vol. 16, no. 1 (March), pp. 16–40.

Hyndman, H. M. (1911), *The Record of an Adventurous Life* (London: Macmillan), quoted in V. I. Lenin (1969), *British Labour and British Imperialism* (London: Lawrence & Wishart), p. 86.

Jacobs, E., Orwell, S., Paterson, P., and Weltz, F. (1978), *The Approach to Industrial Change in Britain and Germany* (London: Anglo-German Foundation for the Study of Industrial Society).

Jefferys, J. B. (1945), *The Story of the Engineers 1800–1945* (London: Lawrence & Wishart).

Jenks, C. (1977), 'T. H. Green, the Oxford philosophy of duty and the English middle class', *British Journal of Sociology*, vol. 28, no. 4 (December), pp. 481–97.

Jessop, B. (1974), *Traditionalism, Conservatism and British Political Culture* (London: Allen & Unwin).

Jevons, W. S. (1894), *The State in Relation to Labour* (London: Macmillan). First published 1882.

Joll, J. (1976), *Europe since 1870: An International History* (Harmondsworth, Middx: Penguin).

Jones, T. (1969), *Whitehall Diary: Vol. 2, 1926–1930*, ed. K. Middlemas (London: Oxford University Press).

Joyce, P. (1980), *Work, Society and Politics: The Culture of the Factory in Later Victorian England* (Brighton, Sussex: Harvester Press).

Kahn, P. *et al.* (1983), *Picketing: Industrial Disputes, Tactics and the Law* (London: Routledge & Kegan Paul).

Kahn-Freund, O. (1954), 'Intergroup conflicts and their settlement', *British Journal of Sociology*, vol. 5, no. 3 (September), pp. 193–227.

Kahn-Freund, O. (ed.) (1965), *Labour Relations and the Law: A Comparative Study* (London: Steven).

Kahn-Freund, O. (1969), 'Industrial relations and the law – retrospect and prospect', *British Journal of Industrial Relations*, vol. 7, no. 3 (November), pp. 301–16.

Kahn-Freund, Sir O. (1979), *Labour Relations: Heritage and Adjustment* (Oxford: Oxford University Press, for the British Academy).

Kauffman, C. J. (1974), 'Lord Elcho, trade unionism and democracy', in K. D. Brown (ed.), *Essays in Anti-Labour History: Responses to the Rise of Labour in Britain* (London: Macmillan), pp. 183–207.

Kellett, J. R. (1958), 'The Breakdown of Guild and Corporation Control over the handicraft and retail trade in London', *Economic History Review*, 2nd ser. vol. 10, no. 3 (April), pp. 381–94.

Kelsall, R. K. (1972), 'Wage regulation under the Statute of Artificers', in W. E.

Minchinton (ed.), *Wage Regulation in Pre-Industrial England* (Newton Abbot, Devon: David & Charles), pp. 94–197. First published 1938.

Labouchère, H. (1858), *Hansard*, 3rd ser., vol. 105.

Lane, T. (1974), *The Union Makes Us Strong* (London: Arrow).

Laski, H. J. (1934), 'Actors in the drama', in W. M. Citrine (ed.), *The Martyrs of Tolpuddle 1834–1934* (London: Trades Union Congress General Council), pp. 145–56.

Laski, H. J. (1936), *The Rise of European Liberalism: An Essay in Interpretation* (London: Allen & Unwin).

Law, B. A. (1912), *Hansard*, Commons, 5th ser., vol. 41.

Lee, J. (1924), *The Principles of Industrial Welfare* (London: Pitman).

Lenin, V. I. (1969), *British Labour and British Imperialism* (London: Lawrence & Wishart).

Lester, R. A. (1958), *As Unions Mature: An Analysis of the Evolution of American Unionism* (Princeton, NJ: Princeton University Press).

Levine, A. L. (1967), *Industrial Retardation in Britain 1880–1914* (London: Weidenfeld & Nicolson).

Lewis, R. (1979), 'Kahn-Freund and labour law: an outline critique', *Industrial Law Journal*, vol. 8, no. 4 (December), 202–21.

Lewis, W. A. (1949), *Economic Survey 1919–1939* (London: Allen & Unwin).

Lloyd, D. (1979), *The Idea of Law* (Harmondsworth, Middx: Penguin).

Loades, D. M. (1974), *Politics and the Nation 1450–1660: Obedience, Resistance and Public Order* (London: Fontana).

Lowe, R. (1875), *Hansard*, 3rd ser., vol. 225.

Lowry, J. P. (1981), *Annual Report 1980* (London: Advisory Conciliation and Arbitration Service).

Lukes, S. (1973), *Individualism* (Oxford: Blackwell).

Macaulay, T. B. (1967), *Critical and Historical Essays*, Vol. 2 (London: Dent).

Macoby, S. (1935), *English Radicalism 1832–1852* (London: Allen & Unwin).

McBriar, A. M., *Fabian Socialism and English Politics 1884–1918* (Cambridge: Cambridge University Press).

Macfarlane, A. (1978), *The Origins of English Individualism: The Family, Property and Social Transition* (Oxford: Blackwell).

MacGregor, S. (1981), *The Politics of Poverty* (London: Longman).

MacKenzie, N., and Mackenzie, J. (1979), *The First Fabians* (London: Quartet).

McKenzie, R., and Silver, A. (1968), *Angels in Marble: Working Class Conservatives in Urban England* (London: Heinemann).

Mackinnon, H. (1859), *Hansard*, 3rd ser., vol. 155.

McMullen, J. (1979), 'Workers need unions', *New Statesman*, 26 January.

Macpherson, C. B. (1962), *The Political Theory of Possessive Individualism: Hobbes to Locke* (London: Oxford University Press).

Macpherson, C. B. (1980), *Burke* (Oxford: Oxford University Press).

Magnus, P. (1954), *Gladstone* (London: John Murray).

Magnus, P. (1967), *King Edward the Seventh* (Harmondsworth, Middx: Penguin).

Malcolmson, R. W. (1981), *Life and Labour in England 1700–1780* (London: Hutchinson).

Manchester, W. (1970), *The Arms of Krupp 1587–1968* (New York: Bantam).

Mann, M. (1973), *Consciousness and Action among the Western Working Class* (London: Macmillan).

Manning, B. (1978), *The English People and the English Revolution* (Harmondsworth, Middx: Penguin).

Mantoux, P. (1928), *The Industrial Revolution in the Eighteenth Century* (London: Cape).

Marsh, A. (1982), *Employee Relations Policy and Decision Making* (London: Gower).

Marshall, J. D. (1968), *The Old Poor Law 1795–1834* (London: Macmillan).

Marshall, T. H. (1950), *Citizenship and Social Class* (Cambridge: Cambridge University Press).

Martin, R. (1969), *Communism and the British Trade Unions 1924–1933: A Study of the National Minority Movement* (Oxford: Clarendon Press).

Martin, R., and Fryer, R. H. (1973), *Redundancy and Paternalist Capitalism* (London: Allen & Unwin).

Marx, K. (1969), 'The Eighteenth Brumaire of Louis Bonaparte' [1869], *Marx and Engels: Basic Writings on Politics and Philosophy*, ed. L. S. Feuer (London: Fontana).

Marx, K. (1976), *Capital*, Vol. 1 (Harmondsworth, Middx: Penguin). First published 1867.

Marx, K., and Engels, F. (1967), *The Communist Manifesto* (Harmondsworth, Middx: Penguin). First published 1848.

Marx, K., and Engels, F. (1975), *Articles on Britain* (Moscow: Progress Publishers).

Mason, J. W. (1974), 'Thomas Mackay: The Anti-Socialist Philosophy of the Charity Organization Society', in K. D. Brown (ed.), *Essays in Anti-Labour History: Responses to the Rise of Labour in Britain* (London: Macmillan), pp. 290–316.

Mather, F. C. (1959), 'The government and the Chartists', in A. Briggs (ed.), *Chartist Studies* (London: Macmillan), pp. 372–405.

Mathias, P. (1983), 'Entrepreneurship and economic history', in M. J. Earl (ed.), *Perspectives on Management: A Multidisciplinary Analysis* (Oxford: Oxford University Press), pp. 40–54.

Merkle, J. A. (1980), *Management and Ideology: The Legacy of the International Scientific Management Movement* (Berkeley, Calif.: University of California Press).

Middlemas, K. (1979), *Politics in Industrial Society: The Experience of the British System since 1911* (London: Deutsch).

Middlemas, K. (1981), *Daily Telegraph*, 17 March.

Middlemas, K., and Barnes, J. (1969), *Baldwin* (London: Weidenfeld & Nicolson).

Miliband, R. (1973), *Parliamentary Socialism: A Study in the Politics of Labour* (London: Merlin Press).

Mill, J. S. (1878), *Principles of Political Economy*, 8th edn (London: Longmans, Green, Reader & Dyer). First published 1848.

Milne-Bailey, W. (1924), *The Waste of Capitalism* (London: Trades Union Congress and Labour Party).

Milne-Bailey, W. (1929), *Trade Union Documents* (London: Bell). '

Minchinton, W. E. (1972) 'Wage regulation in pre-industrial England', in W. E. Minchinton (ed.), *Wage Regulation in Pre-Industrial England* (Newton Abbot, Devon: David & Charles), pp. 16–36.

Minchinton, W. E. (ed.) (1972), *Wage Regulation in Pre-Industrial England* (Newton Abbot, Devon: David & Charles).

Minford, P. (1981), *Daily Telegraph*, 26 October.

Mommsen, W. J. (ed.) (1981), *The Emergence of the Welfare State in Britain and Germany 1850–1950* (London: Croom Helm).

Moran, M. (1977), *The Politics of Industrial Relations: The Origins, Life and Death of the 1971 Industrial Relations Act* (London: Macmillan).

More, T. (1965), *Utopia* (Harmondsworth, Middx: Penguin). First published 1516.

Morgan, K. O. (1974), 'The new liberalism and the challenge of Labour: the Welsh experience 1885–1929', in K. D. Brown (ed.), *Essays in Anti-Labour History: Responses to the Rise of Labour in Britain* (London: Macmillan), pp. 159–82.

Morgan, K. O. (1978), *The Age of Lloyd George: The Liberal Party and British Politics 1890–1929* (London: Allen & Unwin).

Morley, J. (1908), *The Life of William Ewart Gladstone*, Vol. 1 (London: Edward Lloyd).

Morley, Earl of (1871), *Hansard*, 3rd ser., vol. 205.

Mundella, A. J. (1869), *Hansard*, 3rd ser., vol. 197.

Mundella, A. J. (1871), *Hansard*, 3rd ser., vol. 204.

Mundella, A. J. (1875), *Hansard*, 3rd ser., vol. 225.

Musson, A. E. (1972), *British Trade Unions 1800–1875* (London: Macmillan).

Nairn, T. (1977), *The Break-up of Britain: Crisis and Neo-Nationalism* (London: New Left Books).

Namier, L. B. (1957), *The Structure of Politics at the Accession of George III* (London: Macmillan).

Neale, R. S. (1975), *Feudalism, Capitalism and Beyond*, ed. E. Kamenka and R. S. Neale (London: Arnold).

Nicolson, J. S. (1896), *Strikes and Social Problems* (London: Adam & Charles Black).

Nossiter, T. J. (1975), *Influence, Opinion and Political Idioms in Reformed England: Case Studies from the North-East 1832–1874* (Brighton, Sussex: Harvester Press).

O'Brien, T. H. (1979), *Milner: Viscount Milner of St. James's and Cape Town* (London: Constable).

Orwell, G. (1962), 'Boys' Weeklies', *Inside the Whale and Other Essays* (Harmondsworth, Middx: Penguin).

Orwell, G. (1982), *The Lion and the Unicorn: Socialism and the English Genius*, with introduction by B. Crick (Harmondsworth, Middx: Penguin).

O'Sullivan, N. (1976), *Conservatism* (London: Dent).

Owen, R. (1927), *A New View of Society and Other Writings* (London: Dent). First published 1813–21.

Packe, M. St John (1970), *The Life of John Stuart Mill* (New York: Capricorn).

Pakenham, T. (1982), *The Boer War* (London: Macdonald).

Panitch, L. (1976), *Social Democracy and Industrial Militancy: The Labour Party, the Trade Unions and Incomes Policy 1945–1974* (Cambridge: Cambridge University Press).

Parker, T. M. (1967), 'Religion and politics in Britain', *Journal of Contemporary History*, vol. 2, no. 4 (October), pp. 123–35.

Payne, P. L. (1974), *British Entrepreneurship in the Nineteenth Century* (London: Macmillan).

Pelling, H. (1963), *A History of British Trade Unionism* (Harmondsworth, Middx: Penguin).

Pelling, H. (1979), *Popular Politics and Society in Late Victorian Britain*, 2nd edn (London: Macmillan).

Perkin, H. (1972), *The Origins of Modern English Society 1780–1880* (London: Routledge & Kegan Paul).

Phelps Brown, E. H. (1959), *The Growth of British Industrial Relations* (London: Macmillan).

Plamenatz, J. (1949), *The English Utilitarians* (Oxford: Blackwell).

Plamenatz, J. (1963), *Man and Society*, Vol. 2 (London: Longman).

Plumb, J. H. (1979), *The Growth of Political Stability in England 1675–1725* (London: Macmillan). First published in 1967.

Pollard, S. (1968), *The Genesis of Modern Management: A Study of the Industrial Revolution in Great Britain* (Harmondsworth, Middx: Penguin).

Pollard, S. (1969), 'Trade union reactions to the economic crisis', *Journal of Contemporary History*, vol. 4, no. 4 (October), pp. 101–15.

Pollard, S. (1971), *The Idea of Progress: History and Society* (Harmondsworth, Middx: Penguin).

Postgate, R. W. (1923), *The Builders' History* (London: National Federation of Building Trade Operatives).

Postgate, R. (1951), *The Life of George Lansbury* (London: Longmans, Green).

Pratt, E. A. (1904)], *Trade Unionism and British Industry* (London: Methuen).

Pratten, C. F. (1976), *Labour Productivity Differentials within International Companies* (Cambridge: Cambridge University Press).

Pribićević, B. (1959), *The Shop Stewards' Movement and Workers' Control 1910–1922* (Oxford: Blackwell).

Price, R. (1972), *An Imperial War and the British Working Class* (London: Routledge & Kegan Paul).

Reader, W. J. (1977), 'Imperial Chemical Industries and the state 1926–1945', in B. Supple (ed.), *Essays in British Business History* (Oxford: Clarendon Press), pp. 227–43.

Reid, A. (1978), 'Politics and economics in the formation of the British working class: a response to H. F. Moorhouse', *Social History*, vol. 3, no. 3 (October), pp. 347–61.

Reisman, D. A. (1976), *Adam Smith's Sociological Economics* (London: Croom Helm).

Rhodes James, R. (1969), *Memoirs of a Conservative: J. C. C. Davidson's Memoirs and Papers, 1910–1937* (London: Weidenfeld & Nicolson).

Rhodes James, R. (1978), *The British Revolution: British Politics 1880–1939* (London: Methuen).

Rhodes, James, R. (1981), *Churchill: A Study in Failure 1900–1939* (Harmondsworth, Middx: Penguin).

Richter, M. (1966), 'Intellectuals and class alienation: Oxford idealist diagnoses and prescriptions', *European Journal of Sociology*, vol. 7, no. 1, pp. 1–26.

Roberts, B. C. (1957), 'Trade union behaviour and wage determination in Great Britain', in J. T. Dunlop (ed.), *The Theory of Wage Determination* (London: Macmillan), pp. 107–22.

Roberts, D. (1979), *Paternalism in Early Victorian England* (London: Croom Helm).

Roberts, R. (1973), *The Classic Slum* (Harmondsworth, Middx: Penguin).

Roderick, G. W., and Stephens, M. D. (1978), *Education and Industry in the Nineteenth Century: The English Disease?* (London: Longmans, Green).

Rogow, A. A., and Shore, P. (1955), *The Labour Government and British Industry 1945–1951* (Oxford: Blackwell).

Roll, E. (1973), *A History of Economic Thought*, 4th edn (London: Faber).

Rose, M. E. (1972), *The Relief of Poverty 1834–1914* (London: Macmillan).

Royle, E. (1974), *Victorian Infidels: The Origins of the British Secularist Movement 1791–1866* (Manchester: University of Manchester Press).

Royle, E. (1976), *The Infidel Tradition from Paine to Bradlaugh* (London: Macmillan).

Rudé, G. (1980), *Ideology and Popular Protest* (London: Lawrence & Wishart).

Rudé, G. (1981), *The Crowd in History: A Study of Popular Disturbances in France and England, 1730–1848*, rev. edn (London: Lawrence & Wishart).

Rule, J. (1979), Introduction to J. L. Hammond and B. Hammond, *The Skilled Labourer* (London: Longman).

Rule, J. (1981), *The Experience of Labour in Eighteenth-Century Industry* (London: Croom Helm).

Russell, Lord J. (1860), *Hansard*, 3rd ser., vol. 156.

Sabine, G. H. (1937), *A History of Political Theory*, 1st edn (London: Harrap).

Sabine, G. H. (1963) *A History of Political Theory*, 3rd edn (London: Harrap).

Sanders, W. S. (1916), *Trade Unionism in Germany*, with Preface by Sidney Webb (London: Fabian Research Department).

Schumpeter, J. A. (1954), *Capitalism, Socialism, and Democracy*, 4th edn (London: Allen & Unwin).

Seddon, J. H. (1932), in *Towards the Light* ed. J. A. Bibby (Liverpool: Bibby Firm).

Selznick, P. (1969), *Law, Society and Industrial Justice* (New York: Russell Sage Foundation).

Semmel, B. (1960), *Imperialism and Social Reform: English Social-Imperial Thought 1895–1914* (London: Allen & Unwin).

Shadwell, A. (1909), *Industrial Efficiency* (London: Longmans, Green). First published 1906.

Shanks, M. (1981), *Guardian*, 13 May.

Shelton, G. (1981), *Dean Tucker and Eighteenth-Century Economic and Political Thought* (London: Macmillan).

Shonfield, A. (1969), *Modern Capitalism: The Changing Balance of Public and Private Power* (London: Oxford University Press).

Shuttleworth, J. P. Kay (1860), *Trades' Societies and Strikes* in National Association for the Promotion of Social Science, (London: J. W. Parker).

Simon, Sir J. (1926), *Three Speeches on the General Strike* (London: Macmillan).

Skidelsky, R. (1967), *Politicians and the Slump: The Labour Government of 1929–1931* (London: Macmillan).

Skidelsky, R. (1981a), 'Keynes and the Treasury view: the case for and against an active unemployment policy 1920–1939', in W. J. Mommsen (ed.), *The Emergence of the Welfare State in Britain and Germany 1850–1950* (London: Croom Helm), pp. 167–87.

Skidelsky, R. (1981b), *Oswald Mosley* (London: Macmillan).

Smith, A. W. (1981), *Daily Telegraph*, 13 June.

Snaith, J. (1981), *Guardian*, 10 June.

Soldon, N. (1974), 'Laissez-faire as dogma: the Liberty and Property Defence League', in K. D. Brown (ed.), *Essays in Anti-Labour History: Responses to the Rise of Labour in Britain* (London: Macmillan), pp. 208–33.

Stanworth, P., and Giddens, A. (1974), 'An economic élite: a demographic profile of company chairmen', in P. Stanworth and A. Giddens (eds), *Elites and Power in British Society* (Cambridge: Cambridge University Press), pp. 81–101.

Stevas, N. St John (ed.) (1974), *The Collected Works of Walter Bagehot*, Vol. 8 (London: The Economist).

Stevenson, J., and Cook, C. (1979), *The Slump* (London: Quartet).

Stone, L. (1972), *The Causes of the English Revolution 1529–1642* (London: Routledge & Kegan Paul).

Summers, A. (1976), 'Militarism in Britain before the Great War', *History Workshop*, issue 2 (Autumn), pp. 104–23.

Supple, B. (1973), 'The state and the Industrial Revolution 1700–1914', *Fontana Economic History of Europe: The Industrial Revolution*, ed. Carlo M. Cippola (London: Fontana), pp. 9–28.

Supple, B. (1977), 'A framework for British business history', in B. Supple (ed.), *Essays in British Business History* (Oxford: Clarendon Press).

Tawney, R. H. (1938), *Religion and the Rise of Capitalism* (Harmondsworth, Middx: Penguin). First published 1926.

Tawney, R. H. (1961), *The Acquisitive Society* (London: Collins). First published 1921.

Tawney, R. H. (1972), 'The assessment of wages in England by the justices of the peace', in W. E. Minchinton (ed.), *Wage Regulation in Pre-Industrial England* (Newton Abbot, Devon: David & Charles), pp. 38–85. First published in 1913.

Taylor, A. J. P. (1970), *English History 1914–1945* (Harmondsworth, Middx: Penguin).

Taylor, A. J. P. (1976), *Essays in English History* (Harmondsworth, Middx: Penguin).

Taylor, A. J. (1972), *Laissez-faire and State Intervention in Nineteenth-century Britain* (London: Macmillan).

Tholfsen, T. R. (1976), *Working Class Radicalism in Mid-Victorian England* (London: Croom Helm).

Thomas, K. (1965), 'The social origins of Hobbes' political thought', in K. C. Brown (ed.), *Hobbes Studies* (Oxford: Blackwell), pp. 185–236.

Thomas, W. (1979), *The Philosophic Radicals* (Oxford: Clarendon Press).

Thompson, E. P. (1968), *The Making of the English Working Class* (Harmondsworth, Middx: Penguin).

Thompson, E. P. (1974a), 'Patrician society, plebeian culture', *Journal of Social History*, vol. 7, no. 4 (Summer), pp. 382–405.

Thompson, E. P. (1974b), 'Time, work–discipline, and industrial capitalism', in M. W. Flinn and T. C. Smout (eds), *Essays in Social History* (Oxford: Clarendon Press), pp. 39–77.

Thompson, E. P. (1976), 'On history, sociology and historical relevance', *British Journal of Sociology*, vol. 27, no. 3 (September), pp. 387–402.

Thompson, E. P. (1977), *Whigs and Hunters: The Origin of the Black Act* (Harmondsworth, Middx: Penguin).

Thompson, E. P. (1978a), 'Eighteenth-century English society: class struggle without class?' *Social History*, vol. 3, no. 2 (May), pp. 133–65.

Thompson, E. P. (1978b), *The Poverty of Theory, and Other Essays* (London: Merlin).

Thompson, E. P. (1980), *Writing by Candlelight* (London: Merlin).

Thompson, L.(1951), *Robert Blatchford: Portrait of an Englishman* (London: Gollancz).

Thomson, D. (1966), *Europe since Napoleon* (Harmondsworth, Middx: Penguin).

Tobias, J. J. (1972), 'Police and public in the United Kingdom', *Journal of Contemporary History*, vol. 7, nos 1–2 (January–April), pp. 201–19.

Torode, J. (1981), *Guardian*, 8 January.

Tuchman, B. W. (1980), *The Proud Tower: A Portrait of the World before the War 1890–1914* (London: Macmillan).

Turner, G. (1981), *Daily Telegraph*, 13 and 16 February.

Turner, H. A. (1957), 'Inflation and wage differentials in Great Britain', in J. T. Dunlop (ed.), *The Theory of Wage Determination*, (London: Macmillan), pp. 123–35.

Turner, H. A. (1962), *Trade Union Growth, Structure and Policy: A Comparative Study of the Cotton Unions* (London: Allen & Unwin).

Undy, R., Ellis, V., McCarthy, W. E. J., and Halmos, A. M. (1981), *Change in Trade Unions: The Development of U.K. Unions since the 1960s* (London: Hutchinson).

Veblen, T. (1954), *Imperial Germany and the Industrial Revolution* (New York: Viking). First published 1915.

Waites, B. A. (1976), 'The effect of the First World War on class and status', *Journal of Contemporary History*, vol. 11, no. 1 (January), pp. 201–19.

Wallas, G. (1918), *The Life of Francis Place 1771–1854* (London: Allen & Unwin).

Ward, D. (1967), 'The public schools and industry in Britain after 1870', *Journal of Contemporary History*, vol. 2, no. 3 (July), pp.37–52.

Ward, J. T. (1973), *Chartism* (London: Batsford).

Webb, B. (1938), *My Apprenticeship*, Vol. 1 (Harmondsworth, Middx: Penguin).

Webb, B. (1948), *Our Partnership*, ed. B. Drake and M. I. Cole (London: Longmans, Green).

Webb, S. (1916), Preface to W. Stephen Sanders, *Trade Unionism in Germany* (London: Fabian Research Department).

Webb, S., and Webb, B. (1894), *The History of Trade Unionism* (London: Longmans, Green).

Webb, S., and Webb, B. (1902), *Industrial Democracy* (London: Longmans, Green). First published 1897.

Webb, S., and Webb, B. (1920), *The History of Trade Unionism*, new edn (London: Longmans, Green).

Webb, S., and Webb, B. (1963), *Statutory Authorities for Special Purposes* (London: Frank Cass). First published 1922.

Wedderburn, K. W. (1971), *The Worker and the Law*, 2nd edn (Harmondsworth, Middx: Penguin).

Wedderburn, K. W. (1972), 'Labour law and labour relations in Britain', *British Journal of Industrial Relations*, vol. 10, no. 2 (July), pp. 270–90.

Wedderburn, Lord, Lewis, R., and Clark, J. (1983), *Labour Law and Industrial Relations: Building on Kahn-Freund* (Oxford: Clarendon Press).

Weekes, B., Mellish, M., Dickens, L., and Lloyd, J. (1975), *Industrial Relations and the Limits of Law: The Industrial Effects of the Industrial Relations Act 1971* (Oxford: Blackwell).

Wells, H. G. (1946), *The New Machiavelli* (Harmondsworth, Middx: Penguin). First published 1911.

White, R. J. (1953), *Political Tracts of Wordsworth, Coleridge and Shelley* (Cambridge: Cambridge University Press).

Whiting, R. C. (1978), 'The working class in the "new industry" towns between the wars: the case of Oxford', D. Phil. thesis, University of Oxford.

Wiener, M. J. (1981), *English Culture and the Decline of the Industrial Spirit 1850–1980* (Cambridge: Cambridge University Press).

Wilkinson, R. (1964), *The Prefects: British Leadership and the Public School Tradition* (London: Oxford University Press).

Williams, E. N. (1972), *The Ancien Régime in Europe: Government and Society in the Major States 1648–1789* (Harmondsworth, Middx: Penguin).

Williams, F. (1952), *Ernest Bevin: Portrait of a Great Englishman* (London: Hutchinson).

Williams, G. L. (1976), *John Stuart Mill on Politics and Society* (London: Fontana).

Williams, R. (1958), *Culture and Society: 1780–1950* (London: Chatto & Windus).

Woolf, L. (1937), *After the Deluge: A Study of Communal Psychology* (Harmondsworth, Middx: Penguin).

Worsthorne, P. (1979–81), *Sunday Telegraph*, 13 May 1979, 3 February 1980, 2 November 1980, 21 December 1980, 15 March 1981.

Wrigley, C. (1982), 'The government and industrial relations', in C. Wrigley (ed.) *A History of British Industrial Relations 1875–1914* (Brighton, Sussex: Harvester Press), pp. 135–58.

Ziegler, P. (1978), *Melbourne* (London: Fontana).

Index